CLASSIC READINGS IN ORGANIZATIONAL BEHAVIOR

Fourth Edition

J. Steven Ott
University of Utah

Sandra J. Parkes
University of Utah

Richard B. Simpson
Colorado State University

WADSWORTH
CENGAGE Learning·

Australia • Brazil • Japan • Korea • Mexico • Singapore • Spain • United Kingdom • United States

WADSWORTH
CENGAGE Learning

**Classic Readings in Organizational Behavior,
Fourth Edition**
**J. Steven Ott, Sandra J. Parkes, and
Richard B. Simpson**

Acquisitions Editor: Michael Rosenberg

Editorial Assistant: Megan Garvey

Marketing Manager: Karin Sandberg

Marketing Assistant: Teressa Jessen

Marketing Communications Manager: Heather Baxley

Senior Project Manager, Editorial Production:
  Kim Adams

Creative Director: Rob Hugel

Executive Art Director: Maria Epes

Print Buyer: Nora Massuda

Permissions Editor: Bob Kauser

Production Service: ICC Macmillan Inc.

Copy Editor: Debbie Stone

Illustrator: ICC Macmillan Inc.

Cover Designer: StarText

Cover Printer: Thomson West

Compositor: ICC Macmillan Inc.

Printer: Thomson West

For product information and technology assistance, contact us at
Cengage Learning Customer & Sales Support, 1-800-354-9706

For permission to use material from this text or product,
submit all requests online at **cengage.com/permissions**
Further permissions questions can be e-mailed to
permissionrequest@cengage.com

Library of Congress Control Number: 2006937607

ISBN-13: 978-0-495-09474-6

ISBN-10: 0-495-09474-9

Wadsworth
10 Davis Drive
Belmont, CA 94002-3098
USA

Cengage Learning is a leading provider of customized learning solutions with office locations around the globe, including Singapore, the United Kingdom, Australia, Mexico, Brazil, and Japan. Locate your local office at: **international.cengage.com/region**

Cengage Learning products are represented in Canada by Nelson Education, Ltd.

For your course and learning solutions, visit **academic.cengage.com**

Purchase any of our products at your local college store or at our preferred online store **www.ichapters.com**

Printed in the United States of America
2 3 4 5 6 7 11 10 09 08

Brief Contents

CONTENTS

CHAPTER 2   **Motivation** 130

CHAPTER 5 **Power and Influence**   336

CHAPTER 6 **Organizational Change**   402

Foreword to the Foreword

Apparently, the innovative lives side by side with the classic, because I have been given the unusual task of writing a foreword to the foreword written by Fred Fiedler for the second edition of *Classic Readings in Organizational Behavior*. It might be said that Fred's foreword has become a classic, and well it should be—and I would say so, even if Fred weren't my mentor, colleague, co-author, and old friend.

Fred's foreword makes very clear the influences of the early theorists in our field. What they may have lacked in sophisticated methodological and analytic techniques, they made up for with broad perspectives and deep insights. Many of today's research programs have sprung from the seeds offered in the classic articles, whether acknowledged or not.

The contributions of the classics are both timeless and timely. The field of organizational behavior is as healthy as it has been in a long time. When I first became a student of organizational behavior (almost 40 years ago) and in the decade that followed, our field was characterized by controversy and contradiction. More recently, we have seen many indicators of a more vibrant and self-confident scholarship and practice. For this reason, I applaud the authors' decision to include a few contemporary (potentially impactful) works along with the acknowledged classic articles. I, personally, am flattered to have one of my recent chapters in that category. The inclusion of recent works recognizes the positive developments in our field.

The signs of the current renaissance in the study of organizational behavior can be seen in the development of integrative theories seeking a broader, more general understanding of organizational principles. Sophisticated analytic tools (structural equation modeling, hierarchical linear modeling, and others) point researchers toward more comprehensive models and enable us to test their predictions more easily.

The draw of organizational behavior for researchers and theorists from allied disciplines is another sign—as well as a source—of vitality. Social identity theory has brought new insights about how the relationships between groups affect the internal dynamics within a group. Procedural justice research, which began with studies of distributive justice in work organizations, has returned bearing the fruits of social psychological perspectives about the nature of interpersonal relationships surrounding authority in organizations. Gender and feminist perspectives provide new bases for understanding status accrual and dominance negotiations in groups. A rich literature in social cognition is bringing greater awareness of the role of subjective forces and social construction in organizational processes. These and other new research areas, many of which certainly were suggested in the classic writings, now hold potential for the consistent revitalization on which any scientific discipline thrives.

Being asked to write a foreword awakens the sort of egotistical posture that might tempt one to make predictions about the future, so let me try. Recent developments in organizational theory and research and ideas prevalent in the broader scope of the social sciences suggest some likely direction for our field in the new century. I believe that general, integrative theory will emerge, some of it attempting to link macro (strategic) and micro (behavioral) levels of analysis. Our recognition that our planet includes more than North America will accelerate comparative work that both assesses the contribution of cultural differences to organizational processes and investigates the effects of globalization on the sustainability or modification of those differences. Exciting work on emotions, temperament, and even psychophysiology might become a source of new ideas about motivation, satisfaction, and related processes in organizations. Finally, as our society attempts to come to grips with the implications of amazing new technologies, we must turn to the examination of ethical considerations. From the past to the future, these are interesting and exciting prospects.

Martin M. Chemers
University of California, Santa Cruz

FOREWORD

Who has not come across master's theses, dissertations, or journal articles that start by telling us that nobody in the whole world has ever thought of the brilliant new hypothesis, much less seen the earth-shaking results, to be unfolded to our amazed and unbelieving eyes? All too often, as it turns out, this happens to be hyperbole. In fact, if the truth be told, the history of psychology begins for many budding organizational psychologists on the day they enroll in their first psychology course. They are amazed that Nicole Machiavelli's treatise, *The Prince,* was only one early version of the "How to Lead" books, and few graduate students in industrial and organizational (I/O) psychology know that they owe anything to people with such strange names as Chester Barnard, Elton Mayo, or Hugo Münsterberg, who gave I/O psychology its start.

And why, one might ask, should students be concerned with these names, which they are no longer required to know on tests? Most of us feel that we don't have the time to dig up "old," outdated, and, in some cases, superseded articles. Going into the stacks to rummage among old journals is not everyone's favorite occupation, especially when passing exams, preparing for the next class, or preparing another article for publication is more pressing.

Nevertheless, we do need to remember that we are building on the work of others. To think otherwise is not only a mark of arrogance but also of folly. Moreover, there is a lot of scientific pay-dirt in "them thar hills": One good example is the sudden reemergence of Max Weber's articles on the topic of charisma. This old chestnut has suddenly sprouted into one of the most active current topics in the organizational literature. It is almost embarrassing to note how many points old Max Weber made that we are now rediscovering.

Another concept that has recently come to life again is the work on leader intelligence. The problem of how the leader's intelligence contributes to leadership status or effectiveness, interestingly enough, was the topic of the very first empirical paper in leadership. In "A Preliminary Study of the Psychology and Pedagogy of Leadership," Lewis Terman (1904) anticipated current contingency theories of leadership by pointing out that the selection of a leader depends not only on the leader's own attributes but on the needs of the group. Quite apart from the scholarly tradition of citing one's predecessors when it comes to theory building, many of the great insights about how organizations work are to be found in papers that today are considered classics. I am reminded of Mark Twain's little story about how dumb his father was when Mark Twain was growing up, how much dumber the old man got year after year, and, even more surprising, how much the old man learned in the few years of his son's absence.

This thoughtfully assembled collection of classic papers makes a major contribution to our thinking. It is not only a welcome reminder that the field of organizational behavior did not begin the first year we entered college, but that these early papers became classics because their insights are still valid today. They contain wisdom that has not gone out of style, and they represent a rich source of hypotheses that are yet to be tested. This selection will undoubtedly find a useful place in the graduate school curriculum, as well as provide the researcher with a valuable and convenient collection of papers, spanning the field of organizational behavior, which is not always easily obtained from the nearest library.

Fred E. Fiedler
University of Washington

PREFACE

Classic Readings in Organizational Behavior has been designed to meet several purposes: (1) to be a stand-alone collection of the most important writings in the field of organizational behavior from across the decades, (2) to supplement any of several excellent college and graduate-level texts in organizational behavior and administrative practice, and (3) to mesh with and to supplement the sixth edition of *Classics of Organization Theory* (2005) by Jay Shafritz, Steven Ott, and Jong Suk Jang. Only one chapter in *Classics of Organization Theory* is devoted to organizational behavior and, as Shafritz, Ott, and Jang explain in their Introduction, "Organizational behavior is a very large field of study unto itself with an enormous body of literature. . . . It is impossible to do much more than provide a 'flavor' of this body of theory and research in a single chapter."

As the title *Classic Readings in Organizational Behavior* implies, this book is a collection of previously published classics. Although several important recent works are included, no attempt has been made to incorporate selections that reflect all of the recent trends and developments in the field. Current trends are not the purpose of this book. Rather, this collection presents the most enduring themes and works of organizational behavior, organized in a way that is conceptually sound, useful in practice, and enables the reader to track the historical development of the most important topics.

The older works have not been included simply because they are interesting relics, reminders of quaint but outdated thinking. Although organizational behavior has experienced marked growth and maturation over the decades, many of the basics remain the same. In fact, this is a field in which it sometimes feels as though the more we learn about the important things, the less we truly know. The laws of physics and gravity do not change with intellectual fashions or technological advances, nor do the basic psychological, cultural, or social characteristics of people. Just as those who would build spaceships have to start by studying Newton, those who would work with people in organizations must start with writers of the 1920s and 1930s, such as Fritz Roethlisberger, Mary Parker Follett, and Chester I. Barnard.

The future will always build on what is enduring from the past. That is the rationale for this book—to provide those who seek to understand or to advance organizational behavior with a convenient place to find the essentials, indeed the classics, of organizational behavior's past. Once-dominant ideas and perspectives on organizations may lose the center stage, but they do not die. Their thinking influences subsequent writers, even those who may reject their basic assumptions and tenets. However old some of the articles may be, they are not dated. A classic is a classic because it continues to be of value to each new generation of students and practitioners.

Inherently, organizations are part of the society and the culture in which they are situated and operate. Human behavior—and thus organizational behavior—is heavily influenced by culturally rooted beliefs, values, assumptions, and behavioral norms affecting all aspects of organizational life. For this reason, a society's ways of thinking about how people behave in organizations do not develop in a vacuum. They reflect what is going on in the contemporary world of the time. Thus, contributions to organizational behavior vary by what was happening when and where, and in different cultures and subcultures. The advent of World War II, the American POWs who defected following the Korean War, the "flower child"/antiestablishment/self-development era of the 1960s, the computer/information society of the 1970s, the competitive scare from Japanese industry in the 1980s, and the advent of the Internet, e-mail, Web-cam video-conferencing, and virtual organizations, all have substantially influenced the evolution of our thinking and research about people in organizations.

To truly understand organizational behavior as it exists today, one must appreciate the historical contexts in which it developed and the cultural milieu during and in which important contributions were made to its body of knowledge. To help readers place writings in their historical contexts, "A Chronology of Organizational Behavior," which reviews the most important events and publications in the field, follows the Introduction.

CRITERIA FOR SELECTION

Several criteria were used to select these particular classics of organizational behavior for inclusion. The first was the answer to this question: "Should the serious student of organizational behavior be expected to be able to identify this author and his or her basic themes?" If the answer was "yes," then it was so because such a contribution has been, or is increasingly being, recognized as an important theme by a significant writer. We expect to be criticized for excluding other articles and writers, but it will be more difficult to honestly criticize our inclusions. The writers and classic pieces chosen are among the most widely quoted and reprinted by students and theorists in the field of organizational behavior. We felt it was important to include a sprinkling of potentially important current articles as well, however, and these newer articles have not been cited as extensively as those written 20 or 30 years earlier. Thus, more subjective judgments were required about their inclusion.

The second criterion is related to the first: Each article or chapter from a book had to make a basic statement that has been consistently echoed or attacked over the years. The selection had to be acknowledged as important—significant—in the sense that it must have been (or will become) an integral part of the foundation for the subsequent building of the field of organizational behavior.

The third criterion was that articles had to be readable. Fortunately, this was a relatively easy criterion to meet. Much of the literature on organizational behavior is easily understandable and interesting. However, many of the truly great works are of a length, which, in our judgment, detracts from their major themes. Consequently, articles have been shortened for this book, but the only editing has been "editing out." No sentences have been changed or added to the original.

ORGANIZATION OF THE BOOK

This book is structured around the most important topics in the field of organizational behavior. The readings within each topical chapter are organized chronologically. An author's choice of major topics and the sequence of their presentation reflect his or her conceptual framework of a field. Thus, the structure of this book in-and-of-itself communicates the editors' implicit perspective of the field.

The readings are grouped in six chapters that reflect the most pervasive themes in the literature of organizational behavior:

- Leadership
- Motivation
- Individuals in Teams and Groups
- Effects of the Work Environment
- Power and Influence
- Organizational Change

The development of behavioral science theory tends to be cumulative, but almost never in a straight line. Sometimes the cumulative building of theory is accomplished through adoption of prior theorists' logic and research findings; in other instances, it is by trying unsuccessfully to use prior theorists' works, rejecting them, and veering off in a new exploratory direction. The chronological sequencing of readings within topics should enable the reader to track some of the important ebbs and flows of theory development over the decades.

CHANGES FROM THE THIRD EDITION

This fourth edition attempts to retain the essence of the earlier editions. It has not changed in level of presentation, point of view, purpose, or emphasis. Its scope has been expanded to incorporate important developments in the field, including the ever-more-sophisticated integrative models of behavior that incorporate learning theory, virtual teams and networked organizations, and psychological contracts.

A number of people who have used the earlier editions asked that we "update" the book's coverage to include readings that "bring the book into the new millennium." Other reviewers have disagreed, urging us to resist the temptation to venture into new writing that has not yet withstood the test of time. This fourth edition attempts to walk the line, retaining its classics focus and identity while presenting a sprinkling of newer important works. For example, Chapter 3, "Individuals in Teams and Groups," includes readings on self-directed work teams and empowerment, and on work teams that do not meet face-to-face because the members are geographically separated from each other—two themes that are influencing the field of organizational behavior.

Chapter-by-chapter, the following selections have been added and deleted from the third to the fourth edition:

CHAPTER 1: LEADERSHIP

Deletions from the Third Edition

Paul Hersey and Kenneth H. Blanchard, "Life Cycle Theory of Leadership" (1969)

Karl E. Weick, "Leadership as the Legitimization of Doubt" (2001)

Additions to the Fourth Edition

Lee G. Bolman and Terrence D. Deal, "The Power of Reframing: Reframing Leadership" (2003)

CHAPTER 2: MOTIVATION

Deletions from the Third Edition

Nancy H. Leonard, Laura L. Beauvais, and Richard W. Scholl, "Work Motivation: The Incorporation of Self-Concept-Based Processes" (1999)

Edwin A. Locke, "Self-Set Goals and Self-Efficacy as Mediators of Incentives and Personality" (2001)

Additions to the Fourth Edition

Bradley E. Wright, "The Role of Work Context in Work Motivation" (2004)

Edwin A. Locke and Gary P. Latham, "What Should We Do About Motivation Theory? Six Recommendations for the Twenty-First Century" (2004)

CHAPTER 3: TEAMS AND GROUPS

Deletions from the Third Edition

Taylor Cox, Jr., "Cultural Diversity in Organizations: Intergroup Conflict" (1993)

Ruth Wageman, "Critical Success Factors for Creating Superb Self-Managing Teams" (1997)

Jessica Lipnack and Jeffrey Stamps, "Virtual Teams: The New Way to Work" (1999)

Additions to the Fourth Edition

Roosevelt Thomas, "A Diversity Framework" (1995)

Jack D. Orsburn and Linda Moran, "The New Self-Directed Work Teams: Mastering the Challenge" (2000)

Ann Majchrzak, Arvind Malhotra, Jeffrey Stamps, and Jessica Lipnack, "Can Absence Make a Team Grow Stronger?" (2004)

CHAPTER 4: EFFECTS OF THE WORK ENVIRONMENT

Deletions from the Third Edition

Eric L. Trist and K. W. Bamforth, "Some Social and Psychological Consequences of the Longwall Method of Coal-Getting" (1951)

Jeffrey Pfeffer, "Organization Theory and Structural Perspectives on Management" (1991)

Denise M. Rousseau, "Psychological Contracts in Organizations: Violating the Contract" (1995)

Additions to the Fourth Edition

Jerry B. Harvey, "The Abilene Paradox: The Management of Agreement" (1974)

Edgar H. Schein, "The Psychological Contract and Motivation in Perspective" (1980)

CHAPTER 5: POWER AND INFLUENCE

Deletions from the Third Edition

Dorwin Cartwright, "Power: A Neglected Variable in Social Psychology" (1959)

Jeffrey Pfeffer, "Managing with Power" (1992)

Additions to the Fourth Edition

Amitai Etzioni, "Three Kinds of Power: A Comparative Dimension" (1975)

Rosabeth Moss Kanter, "Power Failure in Management Circuits" (1979)

Janet O. Hagberg, "Women and Power" (2003)

CHAPTER 6: ORGANIZATIONAL CHANGE

Deletions from the Third Edition

Herbert C. Kelman and Donald P. Warwick, "The Ethics of Social Intervention: Goals, Means, and Consequences" (1978)

Richard T. Pascale, "Laws of the Jungle and the New Laws of Business" (2001)

Lillas M. Brown and Barry Z. Posner, "Exploring the Relationship between Learning and Leadership" (2001)

Additions to the Fourth Edition

John Kotter, "Transforming Organizations: Why Firms Fail" (1996)

Larry E. Greiner, "Evolution and Revolution as Organizations Grow" (1998)

David L. Cooperrider and Diana Whitney, "Appreciative Inquiry" (1999)

ACKNOWLEDGMENTS

Many people have contributed invaluable insights and assistance that have allowed us to assemble, edit, and write this fourth edition. We are reluctant to list names, for any listing is certain to overlook some people who should be recognized. Also, a mere listing of names is entirely inadequate thanks. Nevertheless, some individuals simply must be acknowledged. First and foremost is Jay Shafritz, at the University of Pittsburgh, who is a part of this book in so many ways.

We are very pleased that Martin Chemers, University of California, Santa Cruz, agreed to write the "Foreword to the Foreword" for this edition and that he urged us to retain the "Foreword" that Fred Fiedler wrote for the second edition. Together, these two forewords provide a wonderful opening for the book and an insightful introduction to the field of organizational behavior. We thank the scholars who reviewed the third edition and provided highly useful suggestions for strengthening the contents and the structuring of this fourth edition: Jeff Bumgarner, Minnesota State University; Dr. Russ

Cheatham, Cumberland University; Enamul Choudhury, Miami University, Ohio; Alan B. Eisner, Lubin School of Business, Pace University; Gerald Andrews Emison, Ph.D., Mississippi State University; Daniel F. Fahey, California State University San Bernardino; Larry T. Hoover, Ph.D., Sam Houston State University; Douglas M. Ihrke, University of Wisconsin–Milwaukee; Kato B. Keeton, Walden University; Samuel M. McCreary, Florida State University; Reginald Shareef, Ph.D., Radford University; Christopher Stream, University of Nevada Las Vegas. We'd also like to thank April Heiselt, who provided thorough, accurate, and persistent assistance with the permissions and wrote many of the new entries in the Chronology.

Finally, we want to put readers on notice that changed standards of language are evident in some of the readings. Many terms and phrases that are sexist and racist by today's standards were in common use 20 or 30 years ago. When it was possible to do so, offensive language was removed from articles by editing out sentences or paragraphs. A few words and phrases, however, are essential to the text and could not be deleted.

J. Steven Ott
University of Utah
Sandra J. Parkes
University of Utah
Richard B. Simpson
Colorado State University

INTRODUCTION

DEFINING ORGANIZATIONAL BEHAVIOR

Organizational behavior seeks to understand human behavior in organizational contexts. It examines the ways people cope with the problems and opportunities of organizational life. It asks questions such as these:

- Why do people behave the way they do when they are in organizations?
- Under what circumstances will people's behavior in organizations change?
- What impacts do organizations have on the behavior of individuals, formal groups (such as departments), and informal groups (such as people from several departments who meet regularly in the company lunchroom)?
- Why do different groups in the same organization develop different behavioral norms?

Organizational behavior results from the many complex interactions that occur daily between humans, groups of humans, and the organizational environment in which they spend their workday. To understand these interactions, it is first necessary to know something about the behavior of people and groups in general, organizations and organizational environments, and the behavior of people and groups when they are in organizations.

Organizational behavior has at least two very different meanings, and these differences are important. First, organizational behavior (OB) is the actual behavior of individuals and groups in and around purposeful organizations. It is the application of the theories, methods, and research findings of the behavioral sciences—particularly those of psychology, social psychology, sociology, cultural anthropology, and to a lesser degree economics and political science—to promote understanding of the behavior of humans in organizations. However, understanding is not the sole goal of organizational behavior. OB practitioners apply knowledge, understanding, and techniques from the behavioral sciences in attempts to improve the functioning of organizations and to improve the fit between the needs and wants of organizations and those of their members.

Although behavioral scientists are interested in human behavior in any organizational setting, their primary focus always has been on behavior in the workplace—on employment-related organizational behavior. Organizational behavior is mostly about behavior in settings where there tend to be constraints on people and where there is an economic relationship between individuals and their organizations. People are not as free to establish and terminate employment relationships as they are other types of relationships with organizations. Usually there is a structured set of roles, a hierarchy of relations, and ongoing goal-related activities (although the goals may or may not be organizationally sanctioned).

Second, organizational behavior is one of several frameworks or perspectives on what makes an organization work. A *perspective* defines the organizational variables that are important enough to warrant the attention of managers and students of organizations. It identifies what a person sees when looking at an organization and, therefore, almost prescribes what *levers* to use when trying to change or stabilize an organization. But a perspective is more than a way of seeing and approaching an organization. It is also a set of bedrock beliefs and values about, for example, the basic purposes for organizations, their fundamental right to exist, the nature of their links to the surrounding environment, and—most important for organizational behavior—the whole of their relationships with the people who work in them.

Students and practitioners of management have always been interested in and concerned with the behavior of people in organizations. But fundamental assumptions about the behavior of people at work did not change dramatically from the beginnings of humankind's attempts to organize until the middle decades of the 20th century. Using the traditional "the boss knows best" mindset (set of assumptions), Hugo Münsterberg (1863–1916), the German-born psychologist whose later work at Harvard would earn him the title of "father" of industrial or applied psychology, pioneered the application of psychological findings from laboratory experiments to practical matters. He sought to match the abilities of new hires with a company's work demands, to positively influence employee attitudes toward their work and their company, and to understand the impact of psychological conditions on employee productivity (H. Münsterberg, 1913; M. Münsterberg, 1922). Münsterberg's approach characterized how the behavioral sciences tended to be applied in organizations well into the 1950s. During and following World War II, the armed services were particularly active in conducting and sponsoring research into how the military could best "find and shape people to fit its needs." This theme or quest became known as *industrial psychology* and more recently as *industrial/organizational psychology* or *I/O psychology.*

In contrast to the Hugo Münsterberg–type perspective on organizational behavior, the "modern breed" of applied behavioral scientists try to answer questions such as how organizations can and should allow and encourage their people to grow and develop. From this perspective, it is assumed that organizational creativity, flexibility, and prosperity will flow naturally from employee growth and development. The essence of the relationship between organization and people has been redefined from dependence to codependence. People are considered to be as important as or more important than the organization itself. The organizational behavior methods and techniques of this current decade could not have been used in Münsterberg's days, because we didn't believe or assume that codependence was the "right" relationship between an organization and its employees. All of this is what is meant by a *perspective.*

Although practitioners and researchers have been interested in the behavior of people inside organizations for a very long time, it has been only since about 1957—when our basic assumptions about the relationship between organizations and people truly began to change—that the *organizational behavior perspective* came into being. Those who see organizations through the lens of the organizational behavior perspective focus on people and groups and on the relationships among them and the organizational environment (Cohen & Fink, 2003). For example, when organizational behaviorists contemplate the introduction of a new technology, they will immediately start thinking about planning ahead:

- How to minimize fear of change by involving people at all levels in designing the introduction of the changes
- How to minimize the negative impacts of the change on groups of workers (such as older, less-skilled, or younger)
- How to co-opt informal leaders, especially those who might become antagonistic
- Alternatives for employees who do not see the changes as being consistent with their personal goals

Because the organizational behavior perspective places a very high value on humans as individuals, things typically are done openly and honestly, providing employees with maximum amounts of accurate information, so they can make informed decisions with free will about their future (Argyris, 1970).

But there are other perspectives as well, each with its own assumptions, values, and levers—ways of approaching issues such as organizational change and stabilization (Shafritz, Ott, & Jang, 2005). The systems perspective focuses on things such as an organization's information systems and its decision processes (Kast & Rosenzweig, 1970; Thompson, 1967); the structural perspective emphasizes things like the structural arrangement of the organization, the organization of work within the structure, and the procedures and rules that maintain order (Blau & Scott, 1962; Burns & Stalker, 1961; Mintzberg, 1979);

and the power perspective looks mostly at managing conflict, building, maintaining, and using coalitions, and the nature of real and perceived power relationships (Kotter, 1985; Pfeffer, 1981, 1992; Salancik & Pfeffer, 1977).

Thus, as a perspective of organization theory, organizational behavior is one of several ways of looking at and thinking about organizations (and people). It is defined by a set of basic assumptions about people, organizations, and the relationships, dynamics, and tensions between and among them. It is common to refer to this second use of the phrase *organizational behavior* as the *human relations* or *human resources school, perspective,* or *frame* of organization theory. To distinguish clearly between the two meanings and thus to avoid confusion, the phrase *organizational behavior* is used throughout this book to mean "the behavior of individuals and groups in and around purposeful organizations." To differentiate, the phrase *organizational behavior perspective,* or *human relations perspective,* refers to the school or perspective of organization theory that reflects basic managerial assumptions about employees similar to those of Theory X and Theory Y, as articulated by Douglas McGregor. (See the reading by McGregor in Chapter 2, "Motivation.")

Organizational behavior is solidly grounded in theory and in empirical research. It uses applications of theory, methods, and findings about the behavior of people and groups in general, about social organizations, and about people in purposeful social organizations, adapted from long-established behavioral science disciplines. No other perspective of organizations has ever had such a wealth of research findings and methods at its disposal.

It is difficult to draw a clear distinction between what behavior is and is not *organizational,* because out-of-organizational behavior affects behavior in organizations and vice versa. In general, however, behavior is considered organizational if something associated with the organization causes or enhances the behavior, the behavior results from an organizational activity or function, or organizational meaning is attached to the behavior.

Assumptions about human behavior are crucial for understanding how managers and workers interact in organizations. Each perspective on organizations has its own fundamental tenets or assumptions, which are very different. The assumptions of the structural perspective and the organizational behavior perspective, as articulated by Bolman and Deal (2003), who use the labels "human resources frame" and "structural frame," are presented side by side in Table 1 to emphasize the differences and to highlight how the differences cause these two perspectives to differ with respect to almost everything!

Assumptions are more than beliefs or values: they are givens or truths that are held so strongly that they are no longer questioned nor even consciously thought about. They are the foundation and the justification (Sathe, 1985) for the perspective's beliefs, truths, values, and ways of doing things.

For example, the assumptions of the Münsterberg–early I/O psychology perspective continued well into the 1950s. It was simply assumed that people should be fit to the organization: the organization had set needs to be filled. Thus, during the "classical era" of organization theory—from the late 1800s through the 1940s—the organizational role of the applied behavioral sciences

TABLE I	ASSUMPTIONS OF THE STRUCTURAL PERSPECTIVE AND THE ORGANIZATIONAL BEHAVIOR PERSPECTIVE

Structural Perspective	Organizational Behavior Perspective
1. Organizations are rational institutions whose primary purpose is to accomplish established objectives; rational organizational behavior is achieved best through systems of defined rules and formal authority. Organizational control and coordination are key for maintaining organizational rationality.	1. Organizations exist to serve human needs. Humans do not exist to serve organizational needs.
2. There is a "best" structure for any organization in light of its given objectives, the environmental conditions surrounding it, the nature of its products and/or services, and the technology of the production process.	2. Organizations and people need each other. Organizations need the ideas, energy, and talent that people provide; and people need the careers, salaries, and work opportunities that organizations provide.
3. Specialization and the division of labor increase the quality and quantity of production—particularly in highly skilled operations and professions.	3. When the fit between the individual and the organization is poor, one or both will suffer. The individual will be exploited or will seek to exploit the organization or both.
4. Most problems in an organization result from structural flaws and can be solved by changing the structure.	4. When the fit is good between the individual and the organization, both benefit. Humans are able to do meaningful and satisfying work while providing the resources the organization needs to accomplish its mission.

Source: Adapted from Bolman, L. G., and Deal, T. E. (2003). *Reframing Organizations*. 3rd ed., mostly from pp. 45 and 115. San Francisco: Jossey-Bass/Wiley.

largely consisted of helping organizations find and shape people to serve as *replacement parts* for *organizational machines.* The dominant theorists of organizations during these years were people such as Frederick Winslow Taylor (1911) and his disciples in *scientific management,* and Max Weber (1922), the brilliant theorist of *bureaucracy* (Shafritz, Ott, & Jang, 2005).

Although the Münsterberg–I/O psychology theme provided important early background for organizational behavior, its more important direct genealogy lies in social psychology. The one most significant set of events that led to a conscious field of organizational behavior was the multilayer work done by the Elton Mayo team at the Hawthorne plant of the Western Electric Company beginning in 1927 (Mayo, 1933; Roethlisberger & Dixon, 1939). Three other significant threads or forces also accounted for a great deal of the direction of industrial social psychology research and practice into the 1950s (Haire, 1954):

1. The late 1930s contributions by Kurt Lewin in group dynamics, with important contributions by Lippett and White (group climate and leadership) and Bavelas (leadership as a group problem)
2. Jacob Moreno's work on sociometry (the network of relations among people in a group) and sociodrama (role playing)

3. The rapid rise of industry and government willingness to ask social psychologists for help during World War II, a trend that began establishing a role for social scientist (*process*) consultants that differed substantially from *content consultants*

During these early years, industrial social psychology differed quite markedly from I/O psychology in its interests and premises. Whereas I/O psychology was busily engaged in trying to solve organizational problems (for example, selecting people to fit into positions), industrial social psychology developed an early concern for creating a psychological (rather than an institutional or technical) definition of the work setting. In this arena, the Hawthorne studies of Mayo and his collaborators were extraordinary contributions.

Once again, the difference between the I/O psychology approach and the work of Mayo, Roethlisberger, and their associates at the Hawthorne plant lay in their *assumptions*. The I/O psychologists adopted these assumptions of classical organization theory and shaped their field to fits its tenets:

1. Organizations exist to accomplish production-related and economic goals.
2. There is one best way to organize for production, and that way can be found through systematic, scientific inquiry (in this instance, systematic, scientific, *psychological inquiry*).
3. Production is maximized through specialization and division of labor.
4. People and organizations act in accordance with rational economic principles.

It is important to note that the Mayo team, like the I/O psychology groups, began its work trying to fit into the mold of classical organization theory thinking. The team phrased its questions in the language and concepts in use by industry to see and explain problems such as productivity in relation to factors such as the amount of light, the rate of flow of materials, and alternative wage payment plans. The Mayo team succeeded in making significant breakthroughs in understanding only after it redefined the Hawthorne problems as social psychological problems—problems conceptualized in terms such as *interpersonal relations in groups, group norms, control over one's own environment,* and *personal recognition*. It was only after the Mayo team achieved this breakthrough that it became the "grandfather"—the direct precursor—of the field of organizational behavior and of the human relations perspective of organization theory. The Hawthorne studies laid the foundation for a set of assumptions that would be fully articulated and would displace the assumptions of classical organization theory 20 years later.

Despite their later start, the industrial social psychologists were years ahead of the industrial psychologists in understanding that behavior in organizations could neither be understood nor controlled by viewing behavior solely as an organizational phenomenon or solely from an organizational vantage point. The organization is not the independent variable to be manipulated in order to change behavior (as a dependent variable)—even though organizations pay employees to help them achieve organizational goals.

Instead, the organization must be seen as the context in which behavior occurs. It is both an independent and a dependent variable. The organization influences human behavior just as behavior shapes the organization. The interactions shape conceptualizations of jobs, human communication, and interaction in work groups, the impacts of participation in decisions about one's own work, roles (in general), and the roles of leaders.

Between 1957 and 1960, the organizational behavior perspective literally exploded onto the organization scene. On April 9, 1957, Douglas M. McGregor delivered the Fifth Anniversary Convocation address to the School of Industrial Management at the Massachusetts Institute of Technology. He titled his address "The Human Side of Enterprise." Three years later, McGregor expanded his talk into what has become one of the most influential books on organizational behavior and organization theory. In *The Human Side of Enterprise* (1960), McGregor articulated how managerial assumptions about employees become self-fulfilling prophesies. He labeled his two sets of contrasting assumptions *Theory X* and *Theory Y*, but they are more than just theories. McGregor had articulated the basic assumptions of the organizational behavior perspective.

The organizational behavior perspective is the most optimistic of all perspectives of organization. Building from Douglas McGregor's Theory X and Theory Y assumptions, organizational behavior has assumed that under the right circumstances people and organizations will grow and prosper together. The ultimate worth of people is an overarching value of the human relations movement—a worthy end in and of itself—not simply a means or process for achieving a higher-order organizational end. Individuals and organizations are not necessarily antagonists. Managers can learn to unleash previously stifled energies and creativities. The beliefs, values, and tenets of organizational behavior are noble, uplifting, and exciting. They hold a promise for humankind, especially those who will spend their lifetime working in organizations.

As one would expect of a field that is based on a very optimistic and humanistic set of assumptions and values, the strategies of organizational behavior became strongly normative (prescriptive). For many organizational behavior practitioners since the 1960s, the perspective's assumptions and methods have become a cause. This volume communicates these optimistic tenets and values and articulates the logical and emotional reasons the organizational behavior perspective developed into a virtual movement. In our view, this is the true essence of "organizational behavior."

As we have progressed through the 1990s and into the 21st century, organizational behavior has maintained its relevance, vibrancy, and optimistic perspective. The new century will be an exciting time for those of us who follow organizational behavior research, writing, and practice. Organizational behavior will continue to include interdisciplinary contributions from an array of social and behavioral sciences, the health and biological sciences, and professional schools including business, social work, engineering, and computer sciences. Significant work will emerge as organizational behavior feels the impact of the electronic information age, new employment relationships, positive and negative consequences of innovation, and the internationalization, or globalization, of organizations.

In this first decade of the 21st century, we are confronted daily with the realities of terrorism, global instability, rapid swings in economic and market cycles, rapidly shifting demographics, and the impacts of major natural disasters during which there have been inadequate preparedness, instability, and ambiguity. The realities of organizational life continue to include rapidly changing technologies in our work and personal contexts as well as outsourcing, domestically and internationally. Our interpersonal communication systems are incorporating more and more "virtual" interactions with cell phones, e-mail, text messaging, video phones, smart phones, video cameras, and computing devices. We cannot ignore our collective interconnectedness and mutual interdependencies—locally, regionally, nationally, and internationally. Our most important collective challenge as teams, organizations, and networks of organizations is to develop an increasingly sophisticated ability to creatively use leadership, learning, and adaptive change to achieve organizational excellence.

Interdisciplinary approaches to theory building, applications, and interventions will continue to become more pronounced in organizational behavior in the years ahead. For example, "Darwinism" has been proposed as a "new paradigm" for organizational behavior. A series of articles in the *Journal of Organizational Behavior* (March 2006) addresses a variety of topics in the field using Darwinian notions. In one of the articles, Nicholson and White apply Darwinian theory to human emotions and motivation; individual differences and human universals; cognition, metacognition, judgment, and decision-making; interpersonal dealing, negotiation, trust and deception; communal aspects of organizations, networking; and ethical behaviors and leadership (pp. 141–149).

AN ORCHESTRA AS METAPHOR

We have chosen to use a metaphor—an orchestra—at the beginning of each chapter to illustrate and to bring to life the vibrant nature of the theories and concepts reprinted in this book. These brief vignettes highlight the richness, beauty, and complexity of the emerging field of organizational behavior. As you progress from the first through the last chapter, we hope that the "orchestra" will help you to feel the artistry uniquely complementing these classic readings and bringing to life this ongoing story. You might want to consider creating your own metaphors as you move through the chapters; it can be an enjoyable learning experience.

REFERENCES

Alderfer, C. P. (1972). *Existence, relatedness, and growth: Human needs in organizational settings.* New York: Free Press.

Allport, G. W. (1954). The historical background of modern social psychology. In G. Lindzey (Ed.), *Handbook of social psychology: Volume II: Special fields and applications* (pp. 3–56). Reading, MA: Addison-Wesley.

Argyris, C. (1970). *Intervention theory and method*. Reading, MA: Addison-Wesley.

Blau, P. M., and Scott, W. R. (1962). *Formal organizations: A comparative approach*. San Francisco: Chandler.

Bolman, L. G., and Deal, T. E. (2003). *Reframing organizations: Artistry, choice, and leadership* (3rd ed.). San Francisco: Jossey-Bass/Wiley.

Bowditch, J. L., and Buono, A. F. (2004). *A primer on organizational behavior* (6th ed.). New York: John Wiley.

Burns, T., and Stalker, G. M. (1961). *The management of innovation*. London: Tavistock.

Cohen, A. R., and Fink, S. L. (2003). *Effective behaviour in organizations* (7th ed.). New York: McGraw-Hill/Irwin.

Gantt, H. L. (1908). Training workmen in habits of industry and cooperation. Paper presented to the American Society of Mechanical Engineers.

Haire, M. (1954). Industrial social psychology. In G. Lindzey (Ed.), *Handbook of social psychology: Volume II: Special fields and applications* (pp. 1104–1123). Reading, MA: Addison-Wesley.

Kast, F. E., and Rosenzweig, J. E. (1970). *Organization and management: A systems approach*. New York: McGraw-Hill.

Kotter, J. P. (1985). *Power and influence: Beyond formal authority*. New York: Free Press.

Kuhn, T. S. (1970). *The structure of scientific revolutions* (2nd ed., enlarged). Chicago: University of Chicago Press.

Lewin, K. (1947). Frontiers in group dynamics: Concept, method and reality in social science: Social equilibrium and social change. *Human Relations, 1*, 5–41.

Lewin, K. (1948). *Resolving social conflicts*. New York: Harper.

Mayo, G. E. (1933). *The human problems of an industrial civilization*. Boston: Harvard Business School, Division of Research.

McClelland, D. C. (1962). Business drive and national achievement. *Harvard Business Review,* July–August, 99–112.

McGregor, D. M. (1957, April). The human side of enterprise. Address to the Fifth Anniversary Convocation of the School of Industrial Management, Massachusetts Institute of Technology. In *Adventure in thought and action*. Cambridge, MA: M.I.T. School of Industrial Management, 1957. Reprinted in W. G. Bennis, E. H. Schein, and C. McGregor (Eds.), (1966), *Leadership and motivation: Essays of Douglas McGregor* (pp. 3–20). Cambridge, MA: MIT Press.

McGregor, D. M. (1960). *The human side of enterprise*. New York: McGraw-Hill.

Mintzberg, H. (1979). *The structuring of organizations*. Englewood Cliffs, NJ: Prentice-Hall.

Münsterberg, H. (1913). *Psychology and industrial efficiency*. Boston: Houghton Mifflin.

Münsterberg, M. (1922). *Hugo Münsterberg, his life and work*. New York: D. Appleton and Company.

Nicholson, N., and White, R. (2006, March). Darwinism—A new paradigm for organizational behavior? *Journal of Organizational Behavior, 27*(2), 111–119.

Organ, D. W., and Bateman, T. (1986). *Organizational behavior: An applied psychological approach* (3rd ed.). Plano, TX: Business Publications.

Pfeffer, J. (1981). *Power in organizations*. Boston: Pitman.

Pfeffer, J. (1992). *Managing with power: Politics and influence in organizations*. Boston: Harvard Business School Press.

Roethlisberger, F. J., and Dixon, W. J. (1939). *Management and the worker*. Cambridge, MA: Harvard University Press.

Salancik, G. R., and Pfeffer, J. (1977). Who gets power—and how they hold on to it: A strategic-contingency model of power. *Organizational Dynamics, 5*, 2–21.

Sathe, V. (1985). *Culture and related corporate realities*. Homewood, IL: Richard D. Irwin.

Schermerhorn, J. R., Hunt, J. G., and Osborn, R. N. (2005). *Organizational behavior* (9th ed.). New York: John Wiley.

Shafritz, J. M., Ott, J. S., and Jang, Y. S. (2005). *Classics of organization theory* (6th ed.). Belmont, CA: Thomson-Wadsworth.

Taylor, F. W. (1911). *The principles of scientific management.* New York: W. W. Norton.

Thompson, J. D. (1967). *Organizations in action.* New York: McGraw-Hill.

Weber, M. (1922). Bureaucracy. In H. Gerth and C. W. Mills (Eds.), *Max Weber: Essays in sociology.* Oxford, UK: Oxford University Press.

Wilson, J. A. (1951). *The culture of ancient Egypt.* Chicago: University of Chicago Press.

Wren, D. A. (1972). *The evolution of management thought.* New York: Ronald Press.

A CHRONOLOGY OF ORGANIZATIONAL BEHAVIOR

2100 B.C. Hammurabi, King of Babylon, establishes a written code of 282 laws that control every aspect of Babylonian life, including individual behavior, interpersonal relations, and other societal matters. This may have been the first employee policy handbook.

1750 B.C. Ancient Egyptians assign 10 workers to each supervisor while building the pyramids. This may have been the earliest recorded use of the span-of-control concept.

1491 B.C. During the exodus from Egypt, Jethro, the father-in-law of Moses, urges Moses to delegate authority over the tribes of Israel along hierarchical lines.

525 B.C. Confucius writes that obedience to the organization (government) is the most "respectable goal of citizenship." This becomes the basic justification for authority systems.

1200 Medieval European guilds function as quality circles to ensure fine craftsmanship.

1490 John Calvin, Protestant religious reformer, promotes the merit system by promising a reward "of eternal life in His (God's) kingdom to the faithful who do God's work." The Puritan movement champions the concepts of time management, duty to work, and motivation theories; wasting time is considered the "deadliest of sins."

1527 Machiavelli's *The Prince* offers managers practical advice for developing authoritarian structures within organizations. His justification is that "all men are bad and ever ready to display their vicious nature."

1651 In his essay, "Leviathan," Thomas Hobbes advocates strong centralized leadership as a means of bringing "order to the chaos created by man." He provides a justification for autocratic rule, thereby establishing the pattern for organizations throughout the 19th century.

1690 In his *Two Treatises of Government,* John Locke provides the philosophical framework for the justification of the U.S. Declaration of Independence. In effect, Locke advocates participatory management when he argues that leadership is granted by the governed.

1762 Jean Jacques Rousseau, in *The Social Contract,* postulates that governments work best when they are chosen and controlled by the governed. This concept furthers the idea of participatory management.

1776 Adam Smith, in *The Wealth of Nations,* revolutionizes economic and organizational thought by suggesting the use of centralization of labor and equipment in factories, division of specialized labor, and management of specialization in factories.

1800   In Britain, the Roebuck and Garrett Company seeks to maintain organizational harmony by putting factories only in locations where workers are perceived to be "reliable, loyal, and controllable."

1811   The Luddites, workers in English textile mills, seek to destroy new textile machinery that is displacing them. This is an early example of management's need to plan for organizational change.

1813   In his "Address to the Superintendents of Manufactures," Robert Owens encourages managers to provide their *vital machines* (employees) with as much attention as they do their *inanimate machines.*

1832   In the first managerial textbooks, *The Carding and Spinning of Masters' Assistant* and *The Cotton Spinners' Manual,* James Montgomery promotes the control function of management: Managers must be "just and impartial, firm and decisive, and always alert to prevent rather than check employee faults."

1883   Frederick W. Taylor begins experiments in Midvale and Bethlehem Steel plants that eventually lead to his concepts of *scientific management.*

1902   Vilfredo Pareto becomes the "father" of the concept of *social systems;* his societal notions would later be applied by Elton Mayo and the human relationists in an organizational context.

1903   Frederick W. Taylor's book, *Shop Management,* explains the role of management in motivating workers to avoid "natural soldiering," the natural tendency of people to "take it easy."

1909   Hugo Münsterberg, considered the "father of organizational psychology," writes "The Market and Psychology," in which he cautions managers to be concerned with "all the questions of the mind . . . like fatigue, monotony, interest, learning, work satisfaction, and rewards." He is the first to encourage government-funded research in the area of industrial psychology.

1911   Frederick W. Taylor's book, *The Principles of Scientific Management,* investigates the influence of salary, mechanical design, and work layout on individual job performance to discover the "one best way" of accomplishing a given task.

Walter D. Scott's series of articles, "The Psychology of Business," published in *System Magazine,* are some of the first to apply principles of psychology to motivation and productivity in the workplace.

1912   Edward Cadbury, using his chocolate factories as a laboratory, pioneers the field of industrial psychology with his book, *Experiments in Industrial Organization.*

1913   Hugo Münsterberg's book, *Psychology and Industrial Efficiency,* addresses personnel selection, equipment design, product packaging, and other concerns in an attempt to match the "best man" with the "best work" in order to get the "best possible effect."

Lillian M. Gilbreth's "The Psychology of Management," published in *Industrial Engineering Magazine,* becomes one of the earliest contributions to the understanding of human behavior in the industrial setting.

1924   As a joint project, the National Research Council, Massachusetts Institute of Technology, and Harvard University begin their investigations of group behavior and worker sentiments at the Hawthorne works of the Western Electric Company in Chicago.

Elton Mayo explains in "The Basis of Industrial Psychology," published in the *Bulletin of the Taylor Society,* that short work breaks improve worker motivation and decrease employee turnover rates; this notion supports the importance of the social environment in the workplace.

1926   Mary Parker Follett's chapter, "The Giving of Orders," is one of the very first calls for the use of a participatory leadership style, in which employees and employers cooperate to assess the situation and collaboratively decide what should be done.

1933   Elton Mayo makes the first significant call for the human relations movement in his Hawthorne studies interim report titled "The Human Problems of an Industrial Civilization."

1937   The American Association for Applied Psychology is organized to study industrial and organizational psychology.

Walter C. Langer publishes *Psychology and Human Living,* in which he provides the first significant discussion of human needs, repression, and integration of personality, and their application to the workplace.

1938   *Functions of the Executive,* by Chester I. Barnard, suggests that the purpose of a manager is to balance organizational and workers' needs. This encourages and foreshadows the postwar revolution in thinking about organizational behavior.

1939   Kurt Lewin, Ronald Lippett, and Ralph K. White's article, "Patterns of Aggressive Behavior in Experimentally Created Social Climates," published in the *Journal of Social Psychology,* is the first empirical study of the effects of the various leadership styles. Their work becomes the basis of the popularity of participative management techniques.

F. J. Roethlisberger and W. J. Dickson publish *Management and the Worker,* the definitive account of the Hawthorne studies.

1940   Robert K. Merton's Social Forces article, "Bureaucratic Structure and Personality," explains how bureaucratic structures exert pressures on people to conform to patterns of obligations, and eventually cause people to adhere to rules as a matter of blind conformance.

1942   Carl Rogers's *Counseling and Psychotherapy* offers human relations training as a method to overcome communication barriers and enhance interpersonal skills. These techniques lead to "control through leadership rather than force."

1943   Abraham Maslow's *needs hierarchy* first appears in his *Psychological Review* article, "A Theory of Human Motivation."

1945   Kurt Lewin forms the Research Center for Group Dynamics at MIT to perform experiments in group behavior. In 1948, Lewin's research center moves to the University of Michigan and becomes a branch of the Institute for Social Research.

1946   Rensis Likert develops the Institute for Social Research at the University of Michigan to conduct studies in the social sciences.

1947   The National Training Laboratory for Group Development, the predecessor to the National Training Laboratory Institute for Applied Behavioral Science, is established in Bethel, Maine, to conduct experimentation and training in group behavior.

1948   In their *Human Relations* article, "Overcoming Resistance to Change," Lester Coch and John R. P. French, Jr., note that employees resist change less when the need for it is effectively communicated to them and when the workers are involved in planning the changes.

Kenneth D. Benne and Paul Sheats's article, "Functional Role of Group Members," published in the *Journal of Social Issues,* identifies three group role categories: *group task, group building and maintenance,* and *nonparticipatory.* These become the basis for future leadership research and training programs.

1949   In his *Public Administration Review* article, "Power and Administration," Norton E. Long finds that power is the lifeblood of administration, and that managers have to do more than simply apply the scientific method to problems—they have to attain, maintain, and increase their power, or risk failing in their mission.

The term *behavioral sciences* is first put into use by the Ford Foundation to describe its funding for interdisciplinary research in the social sciences; the term is later adopted by a group of University of Chicago scientists seeking such funding.

1950   Ralph M. Stogdill, in his *Psychological Bulletin* article, "Leadership, Membership, and Organization," identifies the importance of the leader's role in influencing group efforts toward goal setting and goal achievement. His ideas become the basis for modern leadership research.

1951   Alex Bavelas and Dermot Barrett's article, "An Experimental Approach to Organizational Communication," appearing in *Personnel,* recognizes that the effectiveness of an organization is based on the availability of information and that communication is "the basic process out of which all other functions derive."

Eric L. Trist and K. W. Bamforth's pioneering sociotechnical systems study of British miners, "Some Social and Psychological Consequences of the Long-wall Method of Coal-Getting," demonstrates that the introduction of new structural and technological systems can destroy important social systems.

"Effects of Group Pressure Upon the Modification and Distortion of Judgments," by Solomon Asch, describes his experiments showing that a sizable minority of subjects alter their judgment to match that of the majority, even when the facts clearly demonstrate the majority is wrong.

1952 In "Group Decision and Social Change," Kurt Lewin explores the social aspects of group decision making and resistance to change. He proposes a general model of change consisting of three phases, *unfreezing, change,* and *refreezing,* which becomes the conceptual frame for organization development.

1953 Dorwin Cartwright's address to the Society for the Psychological Study of Social Issues, titled "Power: A Neglected Variable in Social Psychology," identifies leadership and social roles, public opinion, rumor, propaganda, prejudice, attitude change, morale, communications, race relations, and conflicts of value, as leading social issues that cannot be understood except through the concept of power.

1954 *The Practice of Management,* by Peter F. Drucker, outlines his famous *management by objectives* (MBO) approach: a way that management might give "full scope to individual strength and responsibility, and at the same time give direction of vision and effort, establish teamwork, and harmonize the goals of the individual."

Bernard M. Bass's *Psychological Bulletin* article, "The Leadership Group Discussion," identifies a leadership training program in which a leader is not selected but rather emerges from the group's task.

In their *American Sociological Review* article, "Some Findings Relevant to the Great Man Theory of Leadership," Edgar F. Boigatta, Robert F. Bales, and Arthur S. Couch promote the concept of leader assessment centers as a way to recognize individual leadership ability.

1955 Arthur H. Brayfield and Walter H. Crockett's *Psychological Bulletin* article, "Employee Attitudes and Employee Performance," claims that there is no direct influence of job satisfaction on worker performance; in other words, a happy worker is not necessarily a better worker.

The Organization Man, by William H. Whyte Jr., describes empirical findings about individuals who accept organizational values and find harmony in conforming to all policies.

1957 Robert Merton proclaims that the "ideal-type" bureaucracy espoused by Max Weber has characteristics that prevent it from being optimally efficient and also do psychological harm to its members, in "Bureaucratic Structure and Personality."

Chris Argyris asserts in his first major book, *Personality and Organization,* that there is an inherent conflict between the personality of a mature adult and the needs of modern organizations.

Philip Selznick, in *Leadership in Administration,* anticipates many of the 1980s notions of *transformational leadership* when he asserts that the function of an institutional leader is to help shape the environment in which the institution operates and to define new institutional directions through recruitment, training, and bargaining.

The first organization development (OD) program is designed by Herbert Shepard and Robert Blake and is implemented at Standard Oil Company (Esso).

On April 9, Douglas M. McGregor delivers the Fifth Anniversary Convocation address to the School of Industrial Management at the Massachusetts Institute of Technology. His address, "The Human Side of Enterprise," was expanded into a book with the same title in 1960.

Leon Festinger's *A Theory of Cognitive Dissonance* suggests that dissonance is a motivator of human behavior.

Alvin W. Gouldner's *Administrative Science Quarterly* study, "Cosmopolitans and Locals: Toward an Analysis of Latent Social Roles," finds that people with different role orientations differ in their degree of influenceability, level of participation in the organization, willingness to accept organizational rules, and informal relations at work.

1958 Robert Tannenbaum and Warren H. Schmidt's *Harvard Business Review* article, "How to Choose a Leadership Pattern," describes "democratic management" and devises a leadership continuum ranging from authoritarian to democratic.

Organizations, by James G. March and Herbert Simon, provides an overview of the behavioral sciences' influence in organization theory.

Leon Festinger, the father of cognitive dissonance theory, writes "The Motivating Effect of Cognitive Dissonance," which becomes the theoretical foundation for the "inequity theories of motivation."

1959 John R. P. French and Bertram Raven identify five bases of power (expert, referent, reward, legitimate, and coercive) in their article "The Bases of Social Power." They argue that managers should not rely on coercive and expert power bases because they are least effective.

Frederick Herzberg, Bernard Mausner, and Barbara Snyderman's *The Motivation to Work* puts forth the motivation–hygiene theory of worker motivation.

In *Modern Organizational Theory*, Richard Cyert and James March's chapter, "A Behavioral Theory of Organizational Objectives," postulates that power and politics have an impact on the formation of organizational goals. Their work is an early precursor of the power and politics school.

1960 Herbert Kaufman's *The Forest Ranger* describes how employee conformity can be increased through organizational and professional socialization efforts.

Donald F. Roy's *Human Organization* study, "Banana Time: Job Satisfaction and Informal Interaction," finds that workers in monotonous jobs survive psychologically through informal interaction; they keep from "going nuts" by talking and fooling around in a nonstop, highly stylized, and ritualistic manner.

Douglas M. McGregor's book, *The Human Side of Enterprise*, articulates the basic assumptions of the organizational behavior perspective and becomes perhaps the single most influential work in organizational behavior and organizational theory.

1961 Tom Burns and Graham Stalker's *The Management of Innovation* advocates a contingency model of leadership when it articulates the need for different types of management systems (organic and mechanistic) under differing circumstances.

Rensis Likert's *New Patterns of Management* offers an empirically based defense of participatory management and organization development techniques.

1962   In his *Administrative Science Quarterly* article, "Control in Organizations: Individual Adjustment and Organizational Performance," Arnold S. Tannenbaum explains that distributing control more broadly within the organization helps to encourage involvement and adherence to the group norms by its members.

David Mechanic's *Administrative Science Quarterly* article, "Sources of Power of Lower Participants in Complex Organizations," explores factors that account for the power in organizations of lower-level participants over those above them.

Robert L. Kahn and Daniel Katz report their findings on the supervisor's role, the closeness of supervision, the quality of supportiveness, and the amount of group cohesiveness on the productivity and level of morale of organizational groups, in "Leadership Practices in Relation to Productivity and Morale."

In "The Concept of Power and the Concept of Man," Mason Haire traces the change in the ultimate sources of organizational authority from the state to organizational ownership and forecasts an eventual shift to the authority of the work group.

Robert Prethus's work, *The Organizational Society,* presents his threefold classification of patterns of organizational accommodations: *upward-mobiles,* those who accept goals and values of the organization as their own; *indifferents,* those who reject organizational values and seek personal satisfaction off the job; and *ambivalents,* those unable to cope with organizational demands but who still desire its rewards.

Peter Blau and Richard Scott write *Formal Organizations: A Comparative Approach,* in which they argue that all organizations have both an informal and formal structure and that one cannot understand formal structure without first understanding the informal workings of an organization.

In his article "Business Drive and National Achievement," David McClelland develops the learned needs theory, which says that motivation is closely associated with learning concepts that are culturally and socially acquired. These needs include the need for achievement, the need for affiliation, and the need for power. When a need is strong, it will motivate an individual to behave in a way that will satisfy the need.

1964   Considered the father of Transactional Analysis (TA), Eric Berne in his book, *Games People Play: The Psychology of Human Relationships,* identifies three ego states: the *parent,* the *adult,* and the *child;* he suggests that successful managers should strive for adult–adult relationships.

In "Foundations and Dynamics of Intergroup Behavior," which is reprinted in this book, Robert R. Blake, Herbert A. Shepard, and Jane S. Mouton identify the roles, responsibilities, forces, and assumptions associated with understanding conflict between individuals and groups in organizations.

The Management Grid: Key Orientations for Achieving Production through People, by Robert Blake and Jane Mouton, is a diagnostic device for leadership development programs that provides a grid of leadership style possibilities based on managerial assumptions about people and production.

In "Work and Motivation," Victor Vroom proposes a process approach to individual motivation, known as expectancy theory. He explains motivation as a process in which individuals choose among alternative voluntary activities. Vroom argues that people have preferred outcomes, and *expectancy* is the belief in the likelihood that outcomes will occur as a result of particular behaviors.

1965   Robert L. Kahn's *Organizational Stress* is the first major study of the mental health consequences of organizational role conflict and ambiguity.

James G. March prepares *Handbook of Organizations,* a series of essays that attempt to consolidate all scientific knowledge about organizations and organizational behavior.

1966   *Think Magazine* publishes David C. McClelland's article, "That Urge to Achieve," in which he identifies two groups of people: the majority group, who are not concerned about achieving, and the minority group, who are challenged by the opportunity to achieve. This notion becomes a premise for future motivation studies.

The Social Psychology of Organizations, by Daniel Katz and Robert L. Kahn, seeks to unify the findings of behavioral science on organizational behavior through open systems theory.

Fred Fiedler, in "The Contingency Model: A Theory of Leadership Effectiveness," argues that organizations should not try to change leaders to fit them but instead should change their situations to mesh with the style of their leaders.

In "Applying Behavioral Sciences to Planned Organizational Change," a chapter from his book, *Changing Organizations,* Warren Bennis describes planned change as a link between theory and practice and as a deliberate and collaborative process involving change agents and client-systems brought together to solve a problem.

1967   *The Personnel Administration* article, "Organizations of the Future," by Warren Bennis states that bureaucracy will disappear because of rapid and unexpected change, unprecedented growth in organizational size, increasing complexity in modern technology, and philosophical changes in managerial controls and behaviors.

In their *Personnel Administration* article, "Grid Organization Development," Robert A. Blake and Jane S. Mouton explain that organizational goals determine managers' actions; they offer an innovative, systematic approach to "organizational development."

Fred E. Fiedler publishes his work, *A Theory of Leadership Effectiveness,* which proposes that leadership style must fit the circumstances; there is no one best way to perform leadership tasks.

Norman Maier, in his *Psychological Review* article, "Assets and Liabilities in Group Problem-Solving," explains that the benefits of group versus individual problem solving depend on the "nature of the problem, the goals to be achieved, and the skill of the discussion leader."

Anthony Downs's *Inside Bureaucracy* seeks to develop laws and propositions that would aid in predicting the behavior of bureaus and bureaucrats.

William G. Scott's *Organization Theory: A Behavioral Analysis for Management* suggests that an "individual's opportunity for self-realization at work" can be actualized by applying "industrial humanism" concepts such as reducing authoritarian tendencies in organizations, encouraging participatory decision making on all levels, and integrating individual and corporate goals.

Anthony Jay's *Management and Machiavelli* applies Machiavelli's political principles (from *The Prince*) to modern organizational management.

1968   Dorwin Cartwright and Alvin Zander, in "Origins of Group Dynamics" (reprinted in this book), define group dynamics as a unique field of inquiry that is theoretically significant, dynamic, applicable, and broadly relevant across multiple disciplines.

John Po Campbell and M. D. Dunnette's "Effectiveness of T-Group Experiences in Managerial Training and Development," appearing in *Psychological Bulletin,* provides a critical review of T-Group literature. They conclude that "an individual's positive feelings about his T-Group experiences" cannot be scientifically measured, nor should they be based entirely on "existential grounds."

Frederick Herzberg's *Harvard Business Review* article, "One More Time, How Do You Motivate Employees?" catapults motivators or satisfiers and hygiene factors into the forefront of organizational motivation theory.

1969   In Fred E. Fiedler's *Psychology Today* article, "Style or Circumstance: The Leadership Enigma," three elements of effective leadership are identified: power of the leader, the task at hand, and the leader–member relationships. He determines that jobs should be designed to fit individual leadership styles rather than the reverse.

Paul Hersey and Kenneth R. Blanchard's "Life Cycle Theory of Leadership," appearing in *Training and Development Journal,* asserts that the appropriate leadership style for a given situation depends on the employee's education and experience levels, achievement motivation, and willingness to accept responsibility by subordinates. Hersey and Blanchard have revised their views on "Situational Leadership" quite substantially, most recently in 2001 with D. E. Johnson, which is included in this volume.

Wendell French, in his *California Management Review* article, "Organization Development: Objectives, Assumptions, and Strategies," defines organization development as a total system of planned change.

Harold M. F. Rush's *Behavioral Science: Concepts and Management Application* challenges managers to better understand the behavioral sciences so they can more effectively motivate the "new breed of employee," who is better educated, more politically, socially, and economically astute, and more difficult to control.

Richard E. Walton and John M. Dutton's *Administrative Science Quarterly* article, "The Management of Interdepartmental Conflict: A Model and Review," provides a diagnostic model for managers to determine what needs changing to prevent or terminate interdepartmental conflicts.

1970   In his book, *Organizational Psychology*, Edgar H. Schein distinguishes between formal and informal groups within organizations and indicates that effective group work is a result of considering the "characteristics of the members and assessing the likelihood of their being able to work with one another and serve one another's needs."

In "Expectancy Theory," John P. Campbell, Marvin D. Dunnette, Edward E. Lawler III, and Karl E. Weick, Jr., articulate the *expectancy theories of motivation*. People are motivated by calculating how much they want something, how much of it they think they will get, how likely it is their actions will cause them to get it, and how much others in similar circumstances have received.

Chris Argyris writes *Intervention Theory and Methods*, which becomes one of the most widely cited and enduring works on organizational consulting for change that is written from the organizational behavior/organization development perspective.

1971   Rensis Likert's *Michigan Business Review* article, "Human Organizational Measurements: Key to Financial Success," emphasizes that assessing human elements of an organization can identify organizational problems before they occur; he argues that implementing human organizational measurements can help ensure an organization's long-term success.

B. F. Skinner, in *Beyond Freedom and Dignity*, demands a change in the contemporary views of people and how they are motivated in an organization; his alternative includes using *behavior modification* strategies by applying operant conditioning principles to improve employee motivation.

In their *Journal of Applied Psychology* article, "Employee Reactions to Job Characteristics," J. Richard Hackman and Edward E. Lawler III identify four core job dimensions—variety, autonomy, task identity, and feedback—which they claim relate to job satisfaction, motivation, quality of work, and decreased absenteeism.

Irving Janis's "Groupthink," first published in *Psychology Today*, proposes that group cohesion can lead to the deterioration of effective group decision-making efforts.

1972   Clayton Alderfer, in *Existence, Relatedness, and Growth: Human Needs in Organizational Settings,* agrees with Maslow that needs are hierarchically arranged, but presents a hierarchy that includes existence, relatedness, and growth as needs.

In the classic article "Evolution and Revolution as Organizations Grow," originally written in 1972, Larry E. Greiner explores the phases of development that are often faced by growing organizations. Greiner explains that each phase often begins with a period of evolution, and ends with a period of revolutionary change. Managers must be proactive in creating practices and solutions that will prepare their organizations to cope with each period effectively. This article, which was revised and republished in 1998, is included in this volume.

1974   In "The Abilene Paradox: The Management of Agreement," reprinted in this book, Jerry B. Harvey demonstrates that when organization members agree with a decision simply to placate others or when agreement masks disagreement, the problems can be potentially serious.

Robert J. House and Terrence R. Mitchell's *Journal of Contemporary Business* article, "Path–Goal Theory of Leadership," offers path–goal theory as a useful tool for explaining the effectiveness of certain leadership styles in given situations.

Victor H. Vroom's *Organizational Dynamics* article, "A New Look at Managerial Decision-Making," develops a useful model whereby leaders can perform a diagnosis of a situation to determine which leadership style is most appropriate.

Steven Kerr's *Academy of Management Journal* article, "On the Folly of Rewarding A, While Hoping for B," substantiates that many organizational reward systems are "fouled up"—they pay off for behaviors other than those they are seeking.

1975   Amitai Etzioni claims that the "power means" an actor uses to induce or influence another to carry out directives fall into three categories: *coercive power,* the application or threat of application of physical sanctions; *remunerative power,* the allocation of material resources and rewards; and *normative power,* or *persuasive power* or *manipulative power,* which rests on the use of symbolic manipulations, rewards, and deprivations.

Behavior in Organizations, by Lyman Porter, Edward Lawler III, and Richard Hackman, focuses on the interaction between individuals and work organizations. It examines how individual–organizational relationships emerge and grow, including how groups can exert influence on individuals in organizations and how such social influences relate to work effectiveness.

1976   Douglas W. Bray's "The Assessment Center Method," part of the *Training and Development Handbook,* promotes the idea of observing individual behaviors in simulated job-related situations (assessment centers) for evaluative purposes.

Michael Maccoby psychoanalytically interviews 250 corporate managers and discovers *The Gamesman,* a manager whose main interest lies in "competitive activity where he can prove himself a winner."

In "Moral Stakes: Where Have All the Leaders Gone?" Warren Bennis coins the phrase *social architects* to describe what he considers to be the most important roles of organizational leaders: understanding the organizational culture, having a sense of vision, and encouraging people to be innovative.

1977   *The American Psychologist* article "Job Satisfaction Reconsidered," by Walter R. Nord, explains that a revision of accepted economic and political ideologies is necessary if distribution of power in organizations is to be altered.

Gerald Salancik and Jeffrey Pfeffer's *Organizational Dynamics* article, "Who Gets Power—And How They Hold on to It: A Strategic-Contingency Model of Power," views power by subunits as an important means by which organizations align themselves with their critical needs; thus, suppression of the use of power reduces organizational adaptability.

John P. Kotter's *Harvard Business Review* article, "Power, Dependence, and Effective Management," describes how successful managers build their power by creating a sense of obligation in others, creating images, fostering unconscious identification with these images, and feeding people's beliefs that they are dependent on these images.

1978   Daniel Katz and Robert L. Kahn publish *The Social Psychology of Organizations,* in which they coin the term *open system approach.* They advocate creating organizations that are open to change.

Edwin A. Locke's article, "The Ubiquity of the Technique of Goal Setting in Theories of and Approaches to Employee Motivation," argues that goals motivate. His review of the Hawthorne study data, for example, demonstrates that workers are more responsive to goal-based financial incentives than to the widely reported social influences.

William G. Ouchi and Alfred M. Jaeger popularize a third ideal type organization in their *Academy of Management Review* article, "Type Z Organization: Stability in the Midst of Mobility." The three types include: Type A (American); Type J (Japanese); and Type Z (one that combines the best of both types). This article becomes the first of many dealing with Japanese management strategies.

Thomas J. Peters's *Organizational Dynamics* article, "Symbols, Patterns, and Settings: An Optimistic Case for Getting Things Done," is the first major analysis of symbolic management in organizations to gain significant attention in the mainstream literature of organization theory.

1979   Rosabeth Moss Kanter's "Power Failure in Management Circuits" identifies organizational positions that tend to have power problems and argues that powerlessness is often more of a problem for organizations than is power. Kanter also analyzes the special power failures that female managers experience.

1980   Edgar H. Schein's "The Psychological Contract and Motivation in Perspective" hypothesizes that whether people work effectively with commitment, loyalty, and enthusiasm for an organization depends largely on their often not-voiced expectations about what the organization will provide to them and what they owe to the organization, and the degree to which these expectations are met.

J. Richard Hackman and Greg R. Oldham attempt to answer the oft-asked question, "Which is better, individuals or groups?" Some tasks should be done by individuals and some by groups. In the latter case, though, tasks should be redesigned for groups and groups for the nature of the tasks; in *Work Redesign.*

1981   *Power in Organizations,* by Jeffrey Pfeffer, proposes that intergroup conflicts are inevitable in organizations because of inherent differences between perspectives and ongoing competition for scarce organizational resources; coalitions are the means through which people muster power for political contests.

In "'Democracy' as Hierarchy and Alienation," Frederick Thayer proposes that employee alienation can be ended by eradicating hierarchy and that alienation cannot be eradicated so long as hierarchy remains.

1982   Barry Staw's chapter, "Motivation in Organizations: Toward Synthesis and Redirection," echoes wide disenchantment with the usefulness of existing theories of motivation and attempts to broaden the conceptualization of motivation by viewing individuals as actors who change the "rules" of traditional motivation theories.

1983   Henry Mintzberg, in *Power in and Around Organizations,* proposes that "everyone exhibits a lust for power" and the dynamic of the organization is based on the struggle between various *influencers* to control the organization. As a result, he molds the power and politics school of organizational theory into an integrative theory of management policy.

In "Equity Theory Predictions of Behavior in Organizations," Richard T. Mowday argues that the presence of inequity motivates individuals to change the situation through behavioral or cognitive means to return to a condition of equity.

Daniel C. Feldman and Hugh J. Arnold's *Managing Individual and Group Behavior in Organizations* concludes that individual motivation is based on the sum of intrinsic and extrinsic motivation sources and not merely on a manager's ability to motivate.

In *The Change Masters,* Rosabeth Moss Kanter defines *change masters* as architects of organizational change; they are the right people in the right places at the right time.

1984   Thomas J. Sergiovanni's "Leadership as Cultural Expression" proposes that organizational leadership is a cultural artifact: The shape and style of leadership results from the unique mixture of organizational culture and the density of leadership competence.

Noel Tichy and David Ulrich's *Sloan Management Review* article, "The Leadership Challenge—A Call for the Transformational Leader," describes the functions of a transformational leader as those of a cheerleader and a belief model during radical organizational change.

Caren Siehl and Joanne Martin report the findings of the first major quantitative and qualitative empirical study of organizational culture in their "The Role of Symbolic Management: How Can Managers Effectively Transmit Organizational Culture?"

In *Goal Setting: A Motivational Technique That Works,* Edwin A. Locke and Gary P. Latham encourage managers to set goals based on their findings that an individual worker's performance increases as goal difficulty increases (assuming the person is willing and has the ability to do the work).

1985 Edgar Schein writes his comprehensive and integrative statement of the organizational culture school in *Organizational Culture and Leadership*.

In *The Politics of Management*, Douglas Yates, Jr., describes the management of political conflict as the process of managing strategic conflict between actors who possess different forms of resources, and reminds managers that using power is costly: It depletes one's reservoir of credible power.

Warren Bennis and Burt Nanus reemphasize the importance of vision, power, and context for establishing leadership in organizations, in *Leaders: The Strategies for Taking Charge*.

1986 S. G. Harris and R. I. Sutton's *Academy of Management Journal* article, "Functions of Parting Ceremonies in Dying Organizations," focuses on the particular importance of symbolic leadership during periods of organizational decline.

In *The Transformational Leader*, Noel Tichy and Mary Anne Devanna propose a Lewin-type "three-act framework" for transformational leadership—the "leadership of change, innovation, and entrepreneurship."

1987 Research findings by Edward Lawler and Susan Morhman suggest, in the *Organizational Dynamics* piece, "Quality Circles: After the Honeymoon," that in the long term, quality circles have difficulty coexisting with traditional management approaches. Quality circles require basic management changes or they will not be effective, and alternative strategies should be used.

Clayton P. Alderfer's analysis, "An Intergroup Perspective on Group Dynamics," explores the influence on intergroup analysis of the persistently problematic relationship between individuals and collective social processes. He asserts that intergroup theory provides interpretations for individual, interpersonal, group, intergroup, and organizational relations.

1988 Ralph Kilmann and Teresa Joyce Covin publish the first comprehensive collection of research studies and practitioner papers targeting the implementation of transformational change, in *Corporate Transformation*.

In *The Leadership Factor*, John Kotter expands on his prior studies of power and leadership in organizations to explain why organizations often do not have adequate leadership capacity, and proposes steps to rectify the problems.

1989 In "People as Sculptors versus Sculpture: The Roles of Personality and Personal Control in Organizations," Nancy E. Bell and Barry M. Staw provide evidence that people may not be as malleable or open to organizational influence as they have been depicted, particularly in the literature on organizational socialization. People may shape their work environments as much as or more than they are shaped by their environments.

1990 Warren Bennis concludes that we have never needed leaders more but held them in lower regard. Circumstances and the American people conspire against them without meaning to. *Why Leaders Can't Lead: The*

Unconscious Conspiracy Continues predicts that change for the better is possible, but the outlook for leadership is not optimistic.

In "Psychological Conditions of Personal Engagement and Disengagement at Work," William Kahn concludes that the three most important psychological conditions that influence the willingness of employees to engage and disengage with work organizations are psychological meaningfulness, psychological safety, and psychological availability.

Jack Orsburn, Linda Moran, Ed Musselwhite, and John Zenger write their extensive analysis of self-directed work teams, highly trained groups of employees that are fully responsible for turning out a well-defined segment of finished work—in *Self-Directed Work Teams: The New American Challenge.*

Peter Senge's book, *The Fifth Discipline: The Art and Practice of the Learning Organization,* argues that we should—and can—build organizations where people continually expand their capacity to create, in which collective aspiration is set free, and in which people are continually learning how to learn together.

1991   Lee G. Bolman and Terrence E. Deal produce their first edition of *Reframing Organizations: Artistry, Choice, and Leadership,* in which they first present their "framing model," which includes four organizational perspectives: structural, human resource, political, and symbolic.

Marvin R. Weisbord's book, *Productive Workplaces,* examines the importance of effective teamwork in a fast-changing world. Teams get much "lip service," but the term rivals "quality" as a business cliché. Managers must consciously strive to transform individuals and groups into effective teams.

Jeffrey Pfeffer's article, "Organization Theory and Structural Perspectives on Management," builds a persuasive argument that an individual's structural position in an organization affects organizational behavior. "Structural position" includes network location, physical location, and demographic relationship to others.

1992   In *Changing the Essence,* Richard Beckhard and Wendy Pritchard identify the leadership behaviors necessary for initiating and managing fundamental change in organizations. They also attempt to find ways to manage the tension between dealing with short-term pressures and addressing the long-term strategic management of organizations' identities and destinies.

In "The Empowerment of Service Workers: What, Why, How, and When," David Bowen and Edward Lawler III assess the key business characteristics that determine whether empowerment of service workers is beneficial. Managers need to be certain that there is a good fit between organizational needs and their approach before deciding to empower front-line service employees.

In the second edition of *Leadership and Organizational Culture,* Edgar H. Schein shows how leaders create, embed, develop, and sometimes deliberately attempt to change cultural assumptions during different phases of an organization's development and maturation.

Margaret J. Wheatley's book, *Leadership and the New Science*, proposes that managers need to look to the "new sciences" of quantum physics, self-ordering systems, and chaos theory to find clues about how to improve their leadership behavior in organizations.

Jeffrey Pfeffer discusses the relationship between power and influence and decision making and implementation in *Managing with Power*. Effective organizations need leaders who are not afraid to exercise power and influence. The more that managers recognize and understand the importance of power, the more likely they are to be effective in implementing decisions and achieving organizational success.

1993   In "Why Teams?" Jon R. Katzenbach and Douglas K. Smith assert that teamwork is an effective means for enhancing organizational performance and predict that high-performing organizations of the future will nurture environments in which teams can flourish.

"Intergroup Conflict," a chapter in *Cultural Diversity in Organizations,* by Taylor Cox, Jr., examines the potential benefits and the difficulties that may accrue to an organization from cultural diversity. Cox identifies various sources of conflict among culture identity groups and how intergroup conflict is manifested in organizations. He suggests ways in which intergroup conflict can be minimized.

1995   Roosevelt Thomas, in "A Diversity Framework," which is reprinted in this book, introduces a strategic diversity management framework for decision making, in which he argues that diversity is not simply a workplace issue, but is something that should be incorporated into all aspects of our lives.

Diana Pounder, Rodney Ogawa, and Ann Adams argue that leadership affects school performance by shaping the way that work is organized, developing solidarity among the members of the organization, managing schools' relationships with their external environments, and building organizational members' commitment to their schools, in "Leadership as an Organization-Wide Phenomena: Its Impact on School Performance."

Denise Rousseau, in "Psychological Contract in Organizations," argues that although people in organizations often fail to live up to the terms of psychological contracts, the more important issue is whether people interpret an unkept psychological contract as a "violation." When an individual perceives that a contract violation has occurred, the aftermath may include declining loyalty to the organization and increased litigation.

1996   In "Transforming Organizations: Why Firms Fail," a chapter reprinted in this volume from John Kotter's book *Leading Change,* the author highlights some common errors made during processes of change: complacency, lack of support and vision, poor communication, and poor incorporation of changes into the culture of an organization. Kotter uses these errors to create a multistage process for leading change efforts.

1997   Ruth Wageman explains why self-managing work teams often fail to meet performance expectations, in "Critical Success Factors for Creating

Superb Self-Managing Teams." Her study of self-managing work teams at Xerox Corporation concluded that how teams are set up and supported is more important for team success than the behavior of team leaders or coaches.

1998   In "The Secrets of Great Groups," Warren Bennis asserts that the important problems we face are too complex to be solved by individuals. "Great Groups" of strong individual achievers provide multiple perspectives, psychic support, and personal fellowship, and help generate courage. Thus, they can get things done that individuals cannot.

"Two Faces of the Powerless: Coping with Tyranny in Organizations," by Robert J. Bies and Thomas M. Tripp, reports on an empirical study of tyranny as inflicted by abusive bosses and how people cope with such tyranny in the workplace.

Daniel Goleman's article, "What Makes a Leader?" emphasizes that IQ and technical skills are important but that emotional intelligence is an absolute prerequisite of leadership. This article elaborates on his 1995 best-selling book, *Emotional Intelligence*. Goleman points out that emotional intelligence plays a critical role in a leader's overall effectiveness and identifies five components of emotional intelligence at work: self-awareness, self-regulation, motivation, empathy, and social skills.

1999   David L. Cooperrider and Diana Whitney, in *Appreciative Inquiry*, offer a new approach for dealing with organizational change that includes discovery, intelligent involvement, vision, systematic thinking, and sustainability. *Appreciative Inquiry* recognizes that positive change is something that is owned by all involved, and that individuals will grow toward desired ends if they stay focused on them. An excerpt from this book is included in this volume.

Nancy Leonard, Laura Beauvais, and Richard Scholl seek to unify theories of work motivation into a "meta-theory" which includes an understanding of how the self-concept also influences behavior within organizations, in "Work Motivation: The Incorporation of Self-Concept–Based Processes."

2000   In *The New Self-Directed Work Teams: Mastering the Challenge*, portions of which are reprinted in this book, Jack Orsburn and Linda Moran describe a process for creating and using self-directed work teams, and argue that such teams enhance individual commitment, responsibility, and performance, thus increasing the overall success of today's organizations.

Bowling Alone, by Robert Putnam, presents an extensive analysis of causes and consequences of the 30-year decline in social capital in the United States. Using data from several major databases, Putnam describes how we have become increasingly disconnected from others in our personal and work lives, and thus how our access to social capital is shrinking.

Karl Weick discusses "Leadership and the Legitimation of Doubt." Weick suggests that the hallmarks of the 21st century will include unknowability and unpredictability. He develops the value of uncertainty and a path through it that uses animation, improvisation, lightness, authenticism, and learning.

Warren Bennis publishes *Managing the Dream: Reflections on Leadership and Change.* In the chapter titled "The New Metaphysics," Bennis discusses avenues of change, comments on innovators and leaders, and discusses how to avoid disaster during change.

2001   In "Self-Set Goals and Self-Efficacy as Mediators of Incentives and Personality," Edwin Locke proposes that "self-set or personal goals and self-efficacy are the most immediate, motivational determinants of action and that they mediate or link the effects of other motivators."

In "Exploring the Relationship between Learning and Leadership," Lillas Brown and Barry Posner argue that active and versatile learners are more frequently involved in leadership. More successful leaders are necessarily lifelong learners. Thus, research about leadership and learning must be integrated.

By the time Paul Hersey, Kenneth Blanchard, and Dewey Johnson had published the eighth edition of their text, *Management of Organizational Behavior,* that included a chapter on "Situational Leadership," their model had become a true classic in the literature on leadership.

In "Laws of the Jungle and the New Laws of Business," Richard Pascale identifies two imperatives that govern organizational survival and contribute to organizational excellence: agility in the face of ambiguity and a rapidly changing external environment, and a change in culture to one in which there is lively, organic competitive essence. In this type of culture, ongoing learning and change support entrepreneurial initiatives that can exploit opportunities.

2002   Martin Chemers argues that intelligence is a set of skills and knowledge that changes and develops in interaction with the environment, not a fixed and unchanging capacity, in "Efficacy and Effectiveness: Integrating Models of Leadership and Intelligence."

2003   Janet Hagberg continues her examination of a wide array of gender-based power issues, which she initiated in the 1980s, in "Women and Power" (reprinted in this book). Because relationships between women and organizations are still going through major transitions, it is necessary to understand the six stages of personal power and how each influences leadership.

Lee G. Bolman and Terrence E. Deal produced the third edition of their popular work, "The Power of Reframing: Reframing Leadership" (excerpts are included this volume). In it the authors explain how this "framing" approach can be a powerful tool for leading and managing organizations.

2004   In their article "Can Absence Make a Team Grow Stronger?" (reprinted in this book), Ann Majchrzak, Arvind Malhotra, Jeffrey Stamps, and Jessica Lipnack assert that high productivity and high-quality work can be achieved *virtually* through careful management of processes and team dynamics, and through effective use of technology.

Edwin A. Locke and Gary P. Latham continue their contributions to the field of organizational behavior in "What Should We Do about Motivation Theory? Six Recommendations for the Twenty-First Century," which is included in this volume. In it, they present recommendations for building theories of work motivation that are more valid, more complete, broader in scope, and more useful to practitioners.

Bradley E. Wright, in his article entitled "The Role of Work Context in Work Motivation: A Public Sector Application of Goal and Social Cognitive Theories," explores how an organization's work context interacting with job characteristics and job attitudes influences work motivation and, consequently, productivity in the public sector.

2005   Barbara C. Crosby and John M. Bryson argue that because powerful groups strongly influence what is held to be "rational," altering power distributions and relationships undermines the legitimacy of perceived rationalities about the world as it is, in *Leadership for the Common Good*.

Carlo Borzaga and Ermanno Tortia's large-scale study of the relationship between incentive mixes and attitudes, and job satisfaction and loyalty in public and nonprofit social services organizations in Italy showed that intrinsic and relational attitudes are most important for job satisfaction, whereas employee loyalty is influenced more by satisfaction with the economic and process-related aspects of their jobs, in the *Nonprofit and Voluntary Sector Quarterly* article, "Worker Motivations, Job Satisfaction, and Loyalty in Public and Nonprofit Social Services."

Paul H. Ephross and Thomas V. Vassil explore the critical functions of task-focused groups in organizations: the development and allocation of resources, quality control, outcome evaluation, and creative problem solving, in *Groups That Work: Structure and Process*. They argue that individuals must learn to perform these functions in order to be effective participants in work groups.

In *Eating the Menu Rather than the Dinner: Tao and Leadership*, Lesley Prince reflects on how conceptions of leadership are rooted in cultural frameworks and how language shapes leadership models and approaches. Multiculturalism and globalism will continue to strongly influence emerging concepts and frameworks for understanding and describing organizational leadership.

Steve Kelman directly experienced the need for positive change in the federal government as the procurement czar during the Clinton Administration. In *Unleashing Change: A Study of Organizational Renewal in Government*, Kelman provides advice on introducing change, gathering relevant data, and implementing practical and positive change.

2006   In "Abu Ghraib, Administrative Evil, and Moral Inversion," Guy B. Adams, Danny L. Balfour, and George E. Reed analyze why U.S. military personnel could casually engage in torture "and perhaps even believe that it was part of their job to do so." This *Public Administration Review* article concludes that "group and organizational roles and social structures play a far more powerful part in everyday human behavior than most of us would consider. . . . Individual morality and ethics can be swallowed and effectively erased by social roles and structures."

Stewart R. Clegg, David Courpasson, and Nelson Phillips address the power dynamics that are at the heart of all organizational arenas, and thereby shed light on the dark side of organizational life as well as its creative potentialities, in *Power and Organizations*.

In a *Leader to Leader* article, "Know Thy Times," Frances Hesselbein explains that although it is important to look to our history to understand the present, it is equally important to know the ambiguities of our current times. In doing so, we can develop the insight and awareness to look past the horizon to what the future may hold.

Nigel Nicholson and Rod White's *Journal of Organizational Behavior* article, "Darwinism—A New Paradigm for Organizational Behavior?" reflects a growing interest in Darwinian ideas and their increasing applicability in the study of organizational behavior, processes, and outcomes.

Gary Johns argues that the impact of context is not sufficiently recognized and incorporated into models and theories of organizational behavior. He proposes two levels of analysis for theories relating to context in his *Academy of Management Review* article, "The Essential Impact of Context on Organizational Behavior." One level of analysis is derived from journalistic practice; the second is embedded in classical social psychology.

Christopher G. Worley and Edward E. Lawler III explain that many change efforts fail to meet expectations because of poor organizational design, cultural barriers, and/or poor management. Talented management, person-based pay, structural redesign, front-line decision making, and collaborative leadership are key elements in an organization that supports and encourages change, in "Designing Organizations That Are Built to Change," an article in *Leadership and Organizational Studies*.

Leigh Buchanan and Andrew O'Connell artfully trace the history of intellectual contributions to decision-making models and ideas from Chester Barnard up to the 21st century, in their *Harvard Business Review* article, "A Brief History of Decision Making."

2007   Jagdeep S. Chhokar, Robert J. House, and Felix C. Brodbeck's book, *Culture and Leadership Across the World*, documents a large-scale examination of relevant leadership approaches in more than 1000 organizations in 62 countries. The study identifies new ideas, models, and conceptual frameworks for leadership models in a wide variety of cultural milieus.

LEADERSHIP

Heading off for an exciting evening at the symphony is an experience common to many of us. As audience members, we expect to be able to "sit back and enjoy the show." Before the performance begins, we relax and talk idly with family or friends as we watch an interesting array of activities. Orchestra members mill about, talk, sit and play, or tune their instruments. These seemingly random, uncoordinated, individualistic, preparatory activities are signposts that the orchestra is "getting ready" for the performance.

As the performance nears, things change. We notice a "hush" or a "quiet" moment and a sense of impending "focus" just before the conductor enters the stage. Then the "leader" walks to his or her appointed position, and all eyes converge on that place. The conductor will soon enlist the aid and support of the orchestra members to create magic for the audience.

Orchestra members know the pieces to play and have a collective agenda for the performance. In a more diffuse way, they also have a sense of the symphony's role and purpose in the community, the region, the state, and the nation. They may also have a sense of their place within the international community of orchestras.

Sometimes the magic does occur, and the audience is swept away in the ecstasy of the performance. Other times, the audience leaves with a less enthusiastic response. Members of the orchestra also experience these different types of feelings about the performance.

What are the leadership dynamics? Clearly, the way the conductor relates to each orchestra member is an important variable. The rigor and organizational skill—command and control—of the leader affects the process. The developmental stage of the orchestra also matters. For example, how long has the conductor played his or her role? The same could be asked of the orchestra members and members of the instrument sections. The fit between the orchestra members as a group and the leader's style is important. Characteristics of the group, including critical cultural issues within the orchestra such as norms, expectations, climate, and status, also must be considered. Traits of the leader, such as emotional intelligence (or other intelligences), may be important factors.

In music, as in all artistic endeavors, a certain element of uncertainty or chaos can make the difference between a superb performance and an average one. Strange or unique events may enter the equation of the performance, and "something" just happens—and magic results. Finally, incremental and transformational events combine leadership with learning and cause the orchestra to evolve into something new and different. The collective cognitive capacity, talent, and potential for change give the orchestra the competitive edge to grow and thrive.

WHAT IS LEADERSHIP?

Over the years, the significance attributed to the position of leader has led innumerable practitioners and theorists to ask a seemingly unanswerable question—"What does it take to be an effective leader?"—and almost as many behavioral scientists have offered answers. This chapter discusses some of the more important approaches proposed to answer this most basic but elusive question of leadership.

Although we need to have an understanding of what leadership is in order to discuss it, we should realize that there are no clear-cut, universally accepted definitions. Lombardo and McCall (1978, p. 3) describe the situation well: "'Leadership' is one of the most magnetic words in the English language. Mention it, and a perceptible aura of excitement, almost mystical in nature appears.... [Yet] if leadership is bright orange, leadership research is slate gray." Complicating this is the fact that we also need to distinguish between *leadership* (or *leader*) and *management* (or *manager*). Although the two functions and roles overlap substantially, *manager* implies that authority has been formally granted to an individual by an organization. Management involves power (usually formal authority) bestowed on the occupant of a position by a higher organizational authority. With the power of management comes responsibility and accountability for the use of organizational resources. In contrast, *leader* implies effective use of influence that is rather independent of the authority granted to one because of position. Leadership cannot be bestowed upon a person by a higher authority. Effective managers also must be leaders, and many leaders become managers, but the sets of rules and functions differ for the two.

One group of authors began defining a *successful leader* as one who is able to transform an organization when situations call for such action (Bennis, 1984; Bennis & Nanus, 1985; Tichy, 1983; Tichy & Devanna, 1986). The most widely accepted current definitions view leadership as an interpersonal process through which one individual influences the attitudes, beliefs, and especially the behavior of one or more other people.

The subject of leadership raises many complex issues that have plagued behavioral scientists for generations. For example, what gives a manager or a leader legitimacy? Shafritz (1988, p. 324) described *legitimacy* as "a characteristic of a social institution, such as a government or a family [or an organization], whereby it has both a legal and a perceived right to make binding decisions." Thus, managers presumably have legitimacy because of the legal and perceived rights that accompany their organizational positions. In contrast, the legitimacy of a leader—separate and distinct from the legitimacy of a manager—cannot be addressed without introducing the concept of *charisma*. *Charisma* is "leadership based on the compelling personality of the leader rather than on formal position" (Shafritz, 1988, p. 89). The concept was first articulated by the German sociologist Max Weber (1922), who distinguished charismatic authority from the traditional authority of a monarch and the legal authority one receives by virtue of law—such as the authority that legitimizes organizational executives.

Despite the differences and the unresolved questions, two important definitional givens are evident: First, leadership involves a relationship between people in which influence and power are unevenly distributed on a legitimate basis; and second, a leader cannot function in isolation. In order for there to be a leader, someone must follow (Fiedler & Chemers, 1974). In his enduring chapter, "The Functions of the Executive" (1938, reprinted in this chapter), Chester Barnard defines three essential functions of leaders of executives: to provide a system of communication, to promote the securing of essential efforts, and to formulate and define the purposes and goals of an organization. He was decades ahead of his time in arguing that the most critical function of a chief executive is to establish and communicate a system of organizational values among organizational members. If the value system is clear and strong, the day-to-day concerns will take care of themselves.

TRAIT THEORIES

Over the years, studies of leadership have taken different approaches based on divergent perspectives. The trait approach to leadership dominated into the 1950s. The trait theories assume that leaders possess traits that are fundamentally different from the traits of followers. A *trait* is a "personality attribute or a way of interacting with others which is independent of the situation, that is, a characteristic of the person rather than of the situation" (Fiedler & Chemers, 1974, p. 22). Advocates of trait theory believe that some individuals have characteristics and qualities that enable them to "rise above the population," to assume responsibilities not everyone can execute, and therefore to become leaders (Hampton, Summer, & Webber, 1982, p. 566). Under trait theory, the task of the behavioral sciences is to identify those traits and learn how to identify people who possess them.

It is no longer fashionable to contend that people will be effective leaders because they possess certain traits without also considering other variables that influence leadership effectiveness. The arguments against trait theory are persuasive and come from a number of points of view. First, trait theory has largely fallen out of favor because reality never matched the theory. Instead, starting in the late 1950s, it became standard practice to view leadership as a relationship, an interaction between individuals. The interaction was called a *transaction*, so the term *transactional leadership* became the umbrella label encompassing many theories of leadership of the 1950s, 1960s, and 1970s. Second, the situation strongly influences leadership. As Stogdill (1948) stated, the situation has an active influence in determining the qualities, characteristics, and skills needed in a leader.

Probably the most damaging criticism of trait theory, however, has been its lack of ability to identify which traits make an effective leader. Even among the traits that have been most commonly cited—intelligence, energy, achievement, dependability, and socioeconomic status—there is a lack of consensus across studies. Leadership involves more than possessing certain traits. A leader may be effective in one setting and ineffective in another—it depends on the situation (Fiedler, 1967).

TRANSACTIONAL APPROACHES TO LEADERSHIP

The transactional approaches to leadership had beginnings in the 1930s but did not emerge as the dominant view of leadership until the 1950s. Two primary forces were behind the ascendancy: frustration and disappointment with trait theories, and dramatic post–World War II advances in the applied behavioral sciences.

Whereas the trait approaches view leadership as something (or some things) inherent in a leader, the transactional approaches see leadership as a set of functions and roles that develop from an interaction between two or more people. The interaction between a person who leads and those who follow is labeled a *transaction*—much the same as in transactional analysis (Berne, 1964; Harris, 1969; James & Jongeward, 1971). Although there are vast differences in emphasis among groupings of transactional leadership theories, all of them focus on the transaction—what happens and why, and what directly and indirectly influences or shapes it. Thus, for example, the transactional theorist Fiedler (1966) emphasizes the leader—but in the context of the match between leaders and followers. In contrast, Hersey and Blanchard (1969) focus on subordinates—but in a leader–follower context.

LEADERSHIP STYLE THEORIES

The early transactional leadership theories tended to assume that people have relatively fixed styles; thus, these were often labeled *leadership style theories*. Many of the more recent theories also involve leadership styles, but because the earlier assumption of style inflexibility has been abandoned, they usually are called *situational* or *contingency approaches*. In both cases, however, leadership is seen as a transaction. Whereas the central question for the trait approach is "Who exerts leadership?" the quest of the transactional approaches is to determine how leadership is established and exerted.

Leadership style–oriented transactional approaches all follow in the tradition of the famous Lewin, Lippitt, and White (1939) studies of the effectiveness of leadership styles on group productivity. These researchers studied groups of 10-year-old children engaged in hobby activities. The leader in each group was classified as authoritarian, democratic, or laissez-faire. Authoritarian leaders determined all policies, set all work assignments, and were personal in their criticisms. They were product (or task)-oriented and practiced initiating structure. Democratic-oriented leaders shared decision-making powers with subordinates, left decisions about assignments to the group, and participated in group activities but tried not to monopolize. They used high levels of consideration. Laissez-faire–oriented leaders allowed freedom for individual and group decision making, provided information (or supplies) only when requested, and did not participate in the group except when called upon. They functioned more as facilitators.

Groups with democratic-oriented leaders were the most satisfied and productive. The authoritarian-led groups showed the most aggressive behavior and were the least satisfied, but they were highly productive (possibly because of fear of the leader). The groups with laissez-faire–oriented leaders showed low satisfaction and low production and were behaviorally aggressive toward group members and other groups.

The leadership style–oriented transactional approaches attempt to identify styles of leader behavior that result in effective group performance. Probably the best-known groups of studies using this approach were conducted at the University of Michigan and at Ohio State University. They were widely known as the Michigan studies and the Ohio State studies.

Most of the Michigan studies analyzed two extreme leadership styles, product-oriented and employee-oriented. A *product-oriented leadership style* focuses on accomplishing the task of the organization producing the product. This style is exhibited in activities such as setting organizational or group goals, assigning work to subordinates, and constantly evaluating performance. The *employee-oriented leadership style* pays more attention to how well subordinates are doing and to their feelings and attitudes.

Typically, the Michigan studies had subordinates rate their supervisors on the degree to which "he treats people under him without considering their feelings," or "he does personal favors for the people under him" (Fleishman & Harris, 1962, p. 10). Findings from the Michigan studies have shown that high productivity may be associated with either style of leadership, but product-oriented leaders tend to be confronted more often and their employees to have more job dissatisfaction, higher turnover rates, and higher absenteeism rates (Fleishman & Harris, 1962). Finally, other studies have shown that work output is correlated with the freedom supervisors give to workers, and that employees produce more under loose supervision than under close supervision.

Like the Michigan studies, the Ohio State studies classified leader behavior as either product-oriented or employee-oriented, but they used different terminology: initiation of structure and consideration. The Ohio State studies treated the two behaviors as independent dimensions rather than as scalar opposites. In other words, a leader can rank high on consideration and either high or low on initiation of structure. Thus, leaders can be grouped into four quadrants.

Initiation of structure is "the leader's behavior in delineating the relationship between himself and members of the work group and in endeavoring to establish well-defined patterns of organization, channels of command, and methods of procedure" (Bozeman, 1979, p. 208). It is a variety of leader actions used "to get the work out." The leader plans, directs, sets standards, and controls the work of subordinates.

Consideration is "any action which the leader takes to perceive the human needs of his subordinates and to support the subordinates in their own attempts to satisfy their needs" (Hampton et al., 1982, p. 569). Or as stated by Stogdill, consideration is "any behavior indicative of friendship, mutual trust, respect, and warmth in the relationship between the leader and a member of his staff" (as cited in Bozeman, 1979, p. 208).

The Ohio State studies found that the productivity of individuals and groups is higher when leaders initiate structure than when they do not. Some studies have found consideration positively related to productivity, whereas others show a negative effect or no effect at all. As for satisfaction, studies have shown that the initiation of structure is received differently by different people in different situations. For example, House's (1971) work illustrated that the larger the organization, the more employees need some stability, order, and direction. At the other extreme, considerate behavior has almost always been shown to increase employee satisfaction (Fleishman & Harris, 1962).

In their 1969 article, "Life Cycle Theory of Leadership," and later in their text, *Management of Organizational Behavior,* Hersey and Blanchard emphasize that leadership should be appropriate for a given situation. "Situational Leadership is based on an interplay among (1) the amount of guidance and direction (task behavior) a leader provides; (2) the amount of socio-emotional support (relationship behavior) a leader provides; and (3) the readiness level that followers exhibit in performing a specific task ..." (Hersey & Blanchard, 2001, p. 172). Using *initiation* of structure and *consideration* as dimensions, they develop a two-by-two matrix of leadership styles that are most useful for the followers' needs: telling, selling, participating, and delegating. When a work group is not mature enough to assume a task, the leader should be high in initiation (task) and low in consideration behavior (relationship) to help the group understand what is required of them. On the other hand, when a group is mature, the leader should be high in consideration (relationship) and low in initiation behavior (task), because the group is able to complete its task without much guidance. "The more leaders can adapt their behaviors to the situation, the more effective their attempts to influence will be" (Hersey & Blanchard, 2001, p. 175). Although the model is conceptually intriguing, a major weakness is its lack of a "systematic measurement device to measure maturity" (Schein, 1980).

SITUATIONAL OR CONTINGENCY APPROACHES

Probably, the earliest situationist was the classical organizational philosopher, Mary Parker Follett. In her 1926 article, "The Giving of Orders" (reprinted in this chapter), Follett discusses how orders should be given in any organization: They should be depersonalized "to unite all concerned in a study of the situation, to discover the law of the situation and obey that." Follett thus argues for a *participatory leadership style,* in which employees and employers cooperate to assess the situation and decide what should be done at that moment—in that situation. Once the *law of the situation* is discovered, "the employee can issue [an order] to the employer as well as employer to employee." This manner of giving orders facilitates better attitudes within an organization because nobody is necessarily under another person; rather, all take their cues from the situation.

The early approach to transactional leadership assumed that leaders should be trained to act in the appropriate way, as called for by their organization. This has proven to be a major weakness. When leaders return to their organizations after leadership training sessions, they seldom exhibit behavior changes. Despite training, department heads will not necessarily act considerately toward subordinates if their own supervisors do not act supportively toward them. One obvious implication is that changes must be introduced into an organization as a whole—not just to certain employees.

In practice, leaders apply different styles in different situations. Thus, the "pure" leadership style emphasis has given way to the contingency approaches. Unlike the trait theory and leadership style approaches, the contingency approaches take into consideration many factors that may influence a leader's style. They recognize that a successful leader in one type of organization may not be successful in another simply because the new organization differs from the previous one. Its situation (or context) is different, and the choice of a style needs to be contingent upon the situation. As Stogdill (1974) notes, the contingency theories stress these factors:

1. The type, structure, size, and purpose of the organization
2. The external environment in which the organization functions
3. The orientation, values, goals, and expectations of the leader, his superiors, and subordinates
4. The expert or professional knowledge required of the position

The contingency approaches assert that different leadership styles will differ in their effects in different situations. The situation (not traits or styles themselves) determines whether a leadership style or a particular leader will be effective. Thus, contingency theorists maintain that there is no "one best way" of effective leadership.

Tannenbaum and Schmidt (1958, 1973) conducted one of the first studies that actually indicated a need for leaders to evaluate the situational factors prior to the implementation of a particular leadership style (Blunt, 1981). Tannenbaum and Schmidt grouped leader decision-making behavior into seven categories along a continuum from *boss-centered* to *subordinate-centered*. Each category is based on a single variable: the degree of participation in making decisions that is allowed to subordinates. For example:

- Category 1 assumes that the leader makes all decisions and announces them to subordinates.
- Category 7 assumes that the leader defines limits but allows the group to define the problem and to make the final decision.

Tannenbaum and Schmidt (1973) also specify three factors that influence where along their continuum a decision will be made. These factors are forces in the leader, forces of the subordinates, and forces in the situation:

> The successful manager of men can be primarily characterized neither as a strong leader nor as a permissive one. Rather, he is one who maintains a high batting average in accurately assessing the forces that determine what his most appropriate behavior at any given time should be and in actually being able to behave accordingly. (p. 180)

Whereas Tannenbaum and Schmidt focused mostly on variables involving followers, Fred Fiedler has emphasized the leader (but still from a transactional perspective). In "The Contingency Model: A Theory of Leadership Effectiveness" (included in this chapter), Fiedler (1966) discusses a study done with the Belgian Naval Forces. Some earlier leadership theorists had believed that leaders could be trained to adopt styles that are suitable for situations, but Fiedler found the opposite to be true. It is easier to change the work environment, the situation, to fit a leader's style. A person's underlying leadership style depends upon his or her personality. According to Fiedler, a leader's personality is not likely to change because of a few lectures or a few weeks of intensive training. Therefore, an organization should not choose a leader who fits a situation but should change the situation to mesh with the style of its leader (see also Cooper & Robertson, 1988).

CULTURAL AND TRANSFORMATIVE THEORIES

A growing number of leadership theorists have moved past the transactional approaches to write about leadership from an organizational culture perspective or, as it is sometimes called, a symbolic management perspective (Ott,

1989; Shafritz, Ott, & Jang, 2005). Edgar Schein probably is the best-known writer about organizational culture, and his book, *Organizational Culture and Leadership,* has been the most widely cited source on the topic since publication of the first edition in 1985. "The Learning Leader as Culture Manager," a chapter from the second edition (1992), is reprinted here. In it, Schein argues "that leadership and culture are closely connected.... Leaders create, embed, develop, and sometimes deliberately attempt to change cultural assumptions." Different kinds of culture management are needed at different stages in an organization's development and maturation: culture creation, at organizational midlife, and in mature and potentially declining organizations. Schein examines how these stages of culture management affect organizational strategy formation and discusses the implications for the selection and development of leaders.

Like Senge (reprinted in Chapter 6), Schein concludes that leaders of the future will have to be perpetual learners. "If the leaders of today want to create organizational cultures that will themselves be more amenable to learning, they will have to set the example by becoming learners themselves and involving others in the learning process.... In the end, cultural understanding and cultural learning start with self-insight."

Transformational leadership or *transformative leadership* is a somewhat recent slant on leadership that is theoretically consistent with the organizational culture perspective. Whereas the transactional theories of leadership apply primarily to leadership roles, functions, and behavior *within* an existing organizational culture, transformative leadership is about leadership to *change* a culture. Transactional leadership focuses on incremental change; transformative leadership is about radical change. It is interesting to note that transformational leadership theories have many similarities with the trait theories of leadership. Transformational leadership borders on "great man" theory: Leaders are born, not made. In many ways, leadership theory is once again involved in seeking to find the basis of leadership in traits rather than in relational and cultural factors.

Noel Tichy and David Ulrich's 1984 *Sloan Management Review* article, "The Leadership Challenge—A Call for the Transformational Leader" (reprinted in this chapter), describes a transformational leader as "one who must develop and communicate a new vision and get others not only to see the vision but also to commit themselves to it." They describe transformational leaders as those rare individuals who can lead employees through their fears and uncertainties to the realization of the vision. This requires transformational leadership—leadership that successfully changes people's perceptions of the organization. Transformational change is more than a rational, technical, incremental approach to change. The leader's primary function is to lead and support through carefully conceived change stages, acting as a *cheerleader* and as a *belief model*—verbally and nonverbally communicating belief in the benefits to all that will accrue from the changes.

LEADERSHIP: WHERE FROM HERE?

During the past 50 years, leadership theory has wound its way tortuously over twisting and often seemingly fruitless paths. For every gain in understanding, there have been more new questions to answer. The search for a comprehensive theory of leadership is a seemingly never-ending quest. Since the 1940s, the search has led us through trait theories, myriad transactional approaches, and transformative/ cultural theories. Now we are seeing a return to "trait" thinking, with the concepts of emotional intelligence (Goleman, 1998, reprinted in this chapter) and multiple intelligences (Gardner, 2000) combined with integrative theories (Chemers, 2002) creatively blending components of trait, transactional, and transformative/cultural theories. Martin Chemers has written a chapter (reprinted in this chapter) titled "Efficacy and Effectiveness: Integrating Models of Leadership and Intelligence" (in Riggio, Murphy, & Pirozzolo, 2002). Chemers points out (p. 140):

> contemporary approaches . . . are moving in the direction of the conceptualization of a more fluid interaction between the person and the environment with an acknowledgement of the individual's actions in construction and shaping of the environment rather than just reacting to it. Thus, rather than a fixed and unchanging capacity, intelligence (or leadership) becomes a set of skills and knowledge that change and develop in interaction with an environment that can, in turn, be shaped and modified to facilitate a good (i.e., effective) fit.

Without question, we are in an age when leadership is a multidimensional process in a world of uncertainty, chaos, and change. Leadership requires all organizational members to develop and enhance their skills, knowledge, and talents to contribute effectively to organizational excellence. Organizational learning in response to continuous and ever-increasing levels of change will continue to be a top priority (see the reading by Senge in Chapter 6).

No one truly believes that the answers to the most basic questions about leadership have been found. However, it looks as though we are moving in the direction of "things coming together." When confronted with the practical realities of leading, many of us share Warren Bennis's (1990) frustration: Why can't leaders lead? Where have all the leaders gone? Further, as pointed out by Karl Weick (2001), leadership is in reality a "Legitimation of Doubt." Weick proposes that excellence in leadership for the 21st century will necessarily be crafted and developed from creative energy drawn from both science and art in a sea of continuous uncertainty, chaos, and change.

Since the first edition of their book, *Reframing Organizations: Artistry, Choice, and Leadership,* was published in 1991, Bolman and Deal have been developing and refining a useful and popular model for enhancing skills of leaders and for improving the efficiency and effectiveness of the leadership process. In their third edition (a reading is reprinted in this chapter), Bolman and Deal explain how the leadership tactic of "reframing" can provide a powerful tool for improving organizational outcomes and finding new opportunities and options in complex organizational situations.

We will return to these leadership concepts in the concluding chapter in this book, "Organizational Change," and link them with the writings of Senge, Kotter, Griener, Cooperrider, Whitney, and Bennis, who have been at the forefront in addressing issues of organizational change, learning, transformation, and excellence in a world filled with uncertainty, ambiguity, and at times, complete chaos.

REFERENCES

Barnard, C. I. (1968). *The functions of the executive*. Cambridge, MA: Harvard University Press. (Originally published in 1938).

Bennis, W. G. (1984). Transformative power and leadership. In T. J. Sergiovanni and J. E. Corbally (Eds.), *Leadership and organizational culture* (pp. 64–71). Urbana: University of Illinois Press.

Bennis, W. G. (1990). *Why leaders can't lead: The unconscious conspiracy continues*. San Francisco: Jossey-Bass.

Bennis, W. G., & Nanus, B. (1985). *Leaders: The strategies for taking charge*. New York: Harper & Row.

Berne, E. (1964). *Games people play*. New York: Grove Press.

Blunt, B. E. (1981). *Organizational leadership*. Ann Arbor, MI: University Microfilm International.

Bolman, L. G., & Deal, T. E. (2003). *Reframing organizations: Artistry, choice, and leadership*. San Francisco: Jossey-Bass/Wiley.

Bozeman, B. (1979). *Public management and policy analysis*. New York: St. Martin's Press.

Chemers, M. M. (2002). Efficacy and effectiveness: Integrating models of leadership and intelligence. In R. E. Riggio, S. E. Murphy, & F. J. Pirozzolo (Eds.), *Multiple intelligences and leadership* (pp. 139–159). Mahwah, NJ: Lawrence Erlbaum.

Cooper, C. L., and Robertson, I. (Eds.). (1988). *International review of industrial and organizational psychology*. New York: John Wiley.

Deal, T. E. (1985). Cultural change: Opportunity, silent killer, or metamorphosis? In R. H. Kilmann, M. J. Saxton, and R. Serpa (Eds.), *Gaining control of the corporate culture* (pp. 292–331). San Francisco: Jossey-Bass.

Fiedler, F. E. (1966). The contingency model: A theory of leadership effectiveness. In C. W. Backman and P. F. Secord (Eds.), *Problems in social psychology* (pp. 278–289). New York: McGraw-Hill.

Fiedler, F. E. (1967). *A theory of leadership effectiveness*. New York: McGraw-Hill.

Fiedler, F. E. (1969). Style or circumstance: The leadership enigma. *Psychology Today* 2(10), 38–43.

Fiedler, F. E., and Chemers, M. M. (1974). *Leadership style and effective management*. Glenview, IL: Scott, Foresman.

Fiedler, F. E., Chemers, M. M., & Mahar, L. (1976). *Improving leadership effectiveness: The leader match concept*. New York: John Wiley.

Fleishman, E. A., & Harris, E. F. (1962). Patterns of leadership behavior related to employee grievances and turnover. *Personnel Psychology, 15*, 43–56.

Fleishman, E. A., & Hunt, J. G. (1973). *Current developments in the study of leadership*. Carbondale: Southern Illinois University Press.

Follett, M. P. (1926). The giving of orders. In H. C. Metcalf (Ed.), *Scientific foundations of business administration*. Baltimore: Williams & Wilkins.

Gardner, H. E. (2000). *Intelligence reframed: Multiple intelligences for the 21st century*. New York: Basic Books.

Goleman, D. P. (1998, Nov.–Dec.). What makes a leader? *Harvard Business Review*, 73–102.

Hampton, D. R., Summer, C. E., & Webber, R. A. (1982). *Organizational behavior and the practice of management*. Glenview, IL: Scott, Foresman.

Harris, T. A. (1969). *I'm OK—You're OK*. New York: Harper & Row.

Hersey, P., & Blanchard, K. H. (1969, May). Life cycle theory of leadership. *Training and Development Journal*, 26–34.

Hersey, P., & Blanchard, K. H. (2001). *Management of organizational behavior* (8th ed.). Upper Saddle River, NJ: Prentice-Hall.

House, R. J. (1971). Path-goal theory of leadership effectiveness. *Administrative Sciences Quarterly, 16*, 321–338.

House, R. J., & Mitchell, T. M. (1974, Autumn). Path-goal theory of leadership. *Journal of Contemporary Business, 3*(4), 81–97.

James, M., & Jongeward, D. (1971). *Born to win*. Reading, MA: Addison-Wesley.

Lewin, K., Lippitt, R., & White, R. K. (1939). Patterns of aggressive behavior in experimentally created social climates. *Journal of Social Psychology, 10*, 271–299.

Likert, R. (1961). *New patterns of management*. New York: McGraw-Hill.

Lombardo, M. M., & McCall, M. W., Jr. (1978). Leadership. In M. W. McCall Jr. and M. M. Lombardo (Eds.), *Leadership: Where else can we go?* (pp. 3–34). Durham, NC: Duke University Press.

Ott, J. S. (1989). *The organizational culture perspective*. Chicago: The Dorsey Press.

Riggio, R. E., Murphy, S. E., & Pirozzolo, F. J. (Eds.). (2002). *Multiple intelligences and leadership*. Mahwah, NJ: Lawrence Erlbaum.

Schein, E. H. (1980). *Organizational psychology* (3rd ed.). Englewood Cliffs, NJ: Prentice-Hall.

Schein, E. H. (1992). *Organizational culture and leadership* (2nd ed.). San Francisco: Jossey-Bass.

Schein, E. H. (1999). *The corporate culture survival guide*. San Francisco: Jossey-Bass/Wiley.

Shafritz, J. M. (1988). *The Dorsey dictionary of politics and government*. Chicago: The Dorsey Press.

Shafritz, J. M., Ott, J. S., & Jang, Y. S. (Eds.). (2005). *Classics of organization theory* (6th ed.). Belmont, CA: Wadsworth-Thomson.

Stogdill, R. M. (1948). Personal factors associated with leadership: A survey of the literature. *Journal of Psychology, 25*, 35–71.

Stogdill, R. M. (1974). *Handbook of leadership: A study of theory and research*. New York: Free Press.

Stogdill, R. M., & Coons, A. E. (Eds.). (1957). *Leader behavior: Its description and measurement*. Columbus: Ohio State University Press.

Tannenbaum, R. J., & Schmidt, W. H. (1958, March–April). How to choose a leadership pattern. *Harvard Business Review, 36*(2), 95–101.

Tannenbaum, R. J., & Schmidt, W. H. (1973, May–June). How to choose a leadership pattern. *Harvard Business Review, 51*(3), 1–10.

Tannenbaum, R. J., Weschler, I. R., & Massarik, F. (1961). *Leadership and organization*. New York: McGraw-Hill.

Tichy, N. M. (1983). *Managing strategic change: Technical, political and cultural dynamics*. New York: John Wiley.

Tichy, N. M., & Devanna, M. A. (1986). *The transformational leader*. New York: John Wiley.

Tichy, N. M., & Ulrich, D. O. (1984). The leadership challenge—a call for the transformational leader. *Sloan Management Review, 26*, 59–68.

Weber, M. (1922). Bureaucracy. In H. Gerth & C.W. Mills (Eds.), *Max Weber: Essays in sociology*. Oxford, UK: Oxford University Press.

Weick, K. E. (2001). Leadership and the legitimation of doubt. In W. Bennis, G. M. Spreitzer, & T. G. Cummings (Eds.), *The future of leadership* (pp. 91–103). San Francisco: Jossey-Bass.

Wheatley, M. J. (2000). *Leadership and the new science*. San Francisco: Berrett-Koehler.

The Giving of Orders

Mary Parker Follett

To some men the matter of giving orders seems a very simple affair; they expect to issue their own orders and have them obeyed without question. Yet, on the other hand, the shrewd common sense of many a business executive has shown him that the issuing of orders is surrounded by many difficulties; that to demand an unquestioning obedience to orders not approved, not perhaps even understood, is bad business policy. Moreover, psychology, as well as our own observation, shows us not only that you cannot get people to do things most satisfactorily by ordering them or exhorting them; but also that even reasoning with them, even convincing them intellectually, may not be enough. Even the "consent of the governed" will not do all the work it is supposed to do, an important consideration for those who are advocating employee representation. For all our past life, our early training, our later experience, all our emotions, beliefs, prejudices, every desire that we have, have formed certain habits of mind that the psychologists call habit-patterns, action-patterns, motor-sets.

Therefore it will do little good merely to get intellectual agreement; unless you change the habit-patterns of people, you have not really changed your people....

If we analyse this matter a little further we shall see that we have to do three things. I am now going to use psychological language [to]: (1) build up certain attitudes; (2) provide for the release of these attitudes; (3) augment the released response as it is being carried out. What does this mean in the language of business? A psychologist has given us the example of the salesman. The salesman first creates in you the attitude that you want his article; then, at just the "psychological" moment, he produces his contract blank which you may sign and thus release that attitude; then

if, as you are preparing to sign, someone comes in and tells you how pleased he has been with his purchase of this article, that augments the response which is being released.

If we apply this to the subject of orders and obedience, we see that people can obey an order only if previous habit-patterns are appealed to or new ones created....

This is an important consideration for us, for from one point of view business success depends largely on this—namely, whether our business is so organized and administered that it tends to form certain habits, certain mental attitudes. It has been hard for many old-fashioned employers to understand that *orders will not take the place of training*. I want to italicize that. Many a time an employer has been angry because, as he expressed it, a workman "wouldn't" do so and so, when the truth of the matter was that the workman couldn't, actually couldn't, do as ordered because he could not go contrary to life-long habits. This whole subject might be taken up under the heading of education, for there we could give many instances of the attempt to make arbitrary authority take the place of training. In history, the aftermath of all revolutions shows us the results of the lack of training.

... A boy may respond differently to the same suggestion when made by his teacher and when made by his schoolmate. Moreover, he may respond differently to the same suggestion made by the teacher in the schoolroom and made by the teacher when they are taking a walk together. Applying this to the giving of orders, we see that the place in which orders are given, the circumstances under which they are given, may make all the difference in the world as to the response which we get. Hand them down a long way from President or Works Manager and the effect is

Source: "The Giving Orders" by Mary Parker Follett, 1926.

weakened. One might say that the strength of favourable response to an order is in inverse ratio to the distance the order travels. Production efficiency is always in danger of being affected whenever the long-distance order is substituted for the face-to-face suggestion. There is, however, another reason for that which I shall consider in a moment.

... I should say that the giving of orders and the receiving of orders ought to be a matter of integration through circular behavior, and that we should seek methods to bring this about.

Psychology has another important contribution to make on this subject of issuing orders or giving directions: before the integration can be made between order-giver and order-receiver, there is often an integration to be made within one or both of the individuals concerned. There are often two dissociated paths in the individual; if you are clever enough to recognize these, you can sometimes forestall a Freudian conflict, make the integration appear before there is an acute stage....

Business administration has often to consider how to deal with the dissociated paths in individuals or groups, but the methods of doing this successfully have been developed much further in some departments than in others. We have as yet hardly recognized this as part of the technique of dealing with employees, yet the clever salesman knows that it is the chief part of his job. The prospective buyer wants the article and does not want it. The able salesman does not suppress the arguments in the mind of the purchaser against buying, for then the purchaser might be sorry afterwards for his purchase, and that would not be good salesmanship. Unless he can unite, integrate, in the purchaser's mind, the reasons for buying and the reasons for not buying, his future sales will be imperilled, he will not be the highest grade salesman.

Please note that this goes beyond what the psychologist whom I quoted at the beginning of this section told us. He said, "the salesman must create in you the attitude that you want his article." Yes, but only if he creates this attitude by integration, not by suppression.

Apply all this to orders. An order often leaves the individual to whom it is given with two dissociated paths; an order should seek to unite, to integrate, dissociated paths. Court decisions often settle arbitrarily which of two ways is to be followed without showing a possible integration of the two, that is, the individual is often left with an internal conflict on his hands. This is what both courts and business administration should try to prevent, the internal conflicts of individuals or groups....

... Probably more industrial trouble has been caused by the manner in which orders are given than in any other way. In the *Report on Strikes and Lockouts*, a British government publication, the cause of a number of strikes is given as "alleged harassing conduct of the foreman," "alleged tyrannical conduct of an under-foreman," "alleged overbearing conduct of officials." The explicit statement, however, of the tyranny of superior officers as the direct cause of strikes is I should say, unusual, yet resentment smoulders and breaks out in other issues. And the demand for better treatment is often explicit enough. We find it made by the metal and woodworking trades in an aircraft factory, who declared that any treatment of men without regard to their feelings of self-respect would be answered by a stoppage of work. We find it put in certain agreements with employers that "the men must be treated with proper respect, and threats and abusive language must not be used."

What happens to man, *in* a man, when an order is given in a disagreeable manner by foreman, head of department, his immediate superior in store, bank or factory? The man addressed feels that his self-respect is attacked, that one of his most inner sanctuaries is invaded. He loses his temper or becomes sullen or is on the defensive; he begins thinking of his "rights"—a fatal attitude for any of us. In the language we have been using, the wrong behaviour pattern is aroused, the wrong motor-set; that is, he is now "set" to act in a way which is not going to benefit the enterprise in which he is engaged.

There is a more subtle psychological point here, too; the more you are "bossed" the more your activity of thought will take place within the bossing-pattern, and your part in that pattern seems usually to be opposition to the bossing.

This complaint of the abusive language and the tyrannical treatment of the one just above the worker is an old story to us all, but there is an opposite extreme which is far too little considered. The immediate superior officer is often so close to the worker that he does not exercise the proper duties of his position. Far from taking on himself an aggressive authority, he has often evaded one of the chief problems of his job: how to do what is implied in the fact that he has been put in a position over others....

Now what is our problem here? How can we avoid the two extremes: too great bossism in giving orders, and practically no orders given? I am going to ask how *you* are avoiding these extremes. My solution is to depersonalize the giving of orders, to unite all concerned in a study of the situation, to discover the law of the situation and obey that. Until we do this I do not think we shall have the most successful business administration. This is what does take place, what has to take place, when there is a question between two men in positions of equal authority. The head of the sales departments does not give orders to the head of the production department, or vice versa. Each studies the market and the final decision is made as the market demands. This is, ideally, what should take place between foreman and rank and file, between any head and his subordinates. One *person* should not give orders to another *person,* but both should agree to take their orders from the situation. If orders are simply part of the situation, the question of someone giving and someone receiving does not come up. Both accept the orders given by the situation. Employers accept the orders given by the situation; employees accept the orders given by the situation. This gives, does it not, a slightly different aspect to the whole of business administration through the entire plant?

We have here, I think, one of the largest contributions of scientific management: it tends to depersonalize orders. From one point of view, one might call the essence of scientific management the attempt to find the law of the situation. With scientific management the managers are as much under orders as the workers, for both obey the law of the situation. Our job is not how to get people to obey orders, but how to devise methods by which we can best *discover* the order integral to a particular situation. When that is found, the employee can issue it to the employer, as well as employer to employee. This often happens easily and naturally. My cook or my stenographer points out the law of the situation, and I, if I recognize it as such, accept it, even although it may reverse some "order" I have given.

If those in supervisory positions should depersonalize orders, then there would be no overbearing authority on the one hand, nor on the other that dangerous *laissez-aller* which comes from the fear of exercising authority. Of course we should exercise authority, but always the authority of the situation. I do not say that we have found the way to a frictionless existence, far from it, but we now understand the place which we mean to give to friction....

I call it depersonalizing because there is not time to go any further into the matter. I think it really is a matter of *repersonalizing*. We, persons, have relations with each other, but we should find them in and through the whole situation. We cannot have any sound relations with each other as long as we take them out of that setting which gives them their meaning and value. This divorcing of persons and the situation does a great deal of harm. I have just said that scientific management depersonalizes; the deeper philosophy of scientific management show us personal relations within the whole setting of that thing of which they are a part....

I said above that we should substitute for the long-distance order the face-to-face suggestion. I think we can now see a more cogent reason for this than the one then given. It is not the face-to-face suggestion that we want so much as the joint study of the problem, and such joint study can be made best by the employee and his immediate superior or employee and special expert on that question.

I began this talk by emphasizing the advisability of preparing in advance the attitude necessary for the carrying out of orders . . . ; but we have now, in our consideration of the joint study of situations, in our emphasis on obeying the law of the situation, perhaps got a little beyond that, or rather we have now to consider in what sense we wish to take the psychologist's doctrine of prepared-in-advance attitudes. . . .

We should not try to create the attitude we *want*, although that is the usual phrase, but the attitude required for cooperative study and decision. This holds good even for the salesman. We said above that when the salesman is told that he should create in the prospective buyer the attitude that he wants the article, he ought also to be told that he should do this by integration rather than by suppression. We have now a hint of *how* he is to attain this integration.

I have spoken of the importance of changing some of the language of business personnel relations. We considered whether the words "grievances," "complaints," or Ford's "trouble specialists" did not arouse the wrong behaviour-patterns. I think "order" certainly does. If that word is not to mean any longer external authority, arbitrary authority, but the law of the situation, then we need a new word for it. It is often the order that people resent as much as the thing ordered. People do not like to be ordered even to take a holiday. I have often seen instances of this. The wish to govern one's own life is, of course, one of the most fundamental feelings in every human being. To call this "the instinct of self-assertion," "the instinct of initiative," does not express it wholly. . . .

We have here something far more profound than "the egoistic impulse" or "the instinct of self-assertion." We have the very essence of the human being.

This subject of orders has led us into the heart of the whole question of authority and consent. When we conceive of authority and consent as parts of an inclusive situation, does that not throw a flood of light on this question? The point of view here presented gets rid of several dilemmas which have

seemed to puzzle people in dealing with consent. The feeling of being "under" someone, of "subordination," of "servility," of being "at the will of another," comes out again and again in the shop stewards movement and in the testimony before the Coal Commission. One man said before the Coal Commission, "It is all right to work *with* anyone; what is disagreeable is to feel too distinctly that you are working *under* anyone." *With* is a pretty good preposition, not because it connotes democracy, but because it connotes functional unity, a much more profound conception than that of democracy as usually held. The study of the situation involves the *with* preposition. . . .

Twice I have had a servant applying for a place ask me if she would be treated as a menial. When the first woman asked me that, I had no idea what she meant, I thought perhaps she did not want to do the roughest work, but later I came to the conclusion that to be treated as a menial meant to be obliged to be under someone, to follow orders without using one's own judgment. If we believe that what heightens self-respect increases efficiency, we shall be on our guard here.

Very closely connected with this is the matter of pride in one's work. If an order goes against what the craftsman or the clerk thinks is the way of doing his work which will bring the best results, he is justified in not wishing to obey that order. Could not that difficulty be met by a joint study of the situation? It is said that it is characteristic of the British workman to feel, "I know my job and won't be told how." The peculiarities of the British workman might be met by a joint study of the situation, it being understood that he probably has more to contribute to that study than anyone else. . . .

There is another dilemma which has to be met by everyone who is in what is called a position of authority: how can you expect people merely to obey orders and at the same time to take that degree of responsibility which they should take? Indeed, in my experience, the people who enjoy following orders blindly, without any thought on their own part, are those who like thus to get rid of responsibility. But the taking of responsibility, each according to his capacity, each according to his function in the whole..., this taking of responsibility is usually the most vital matter in the life of every human being, just as the allotting of responsibility is the most important part of business administration.

A young trade unionist said to me, "How much dignity can I have as a mere employee?" He can have all the dignity in the world if he is allowed to make his fullest contribution to the plant *and to assume definitely the responsibility therefor.*

I think one of the gravest problems before us is how to make the reconciliation between receiving orders and taking responsibility. And I think the reconciliation can be made through our conception of the law of the situation....

We have considered the subject of symbols. It is often very apparent that an order is a symbol. The referee in the game stands, watch in hand, and says "Go." It is an order, but order only as symbol. I may say to an employee, "Do so and so," but I should say it only because we have both agreed, openly or tacitly, that that which I am ordering done is the best thing to be done. The order is then a symbol. And if it is a philosophical and psychological truth that we owe obedience only to a functional unity to which we are contributing, we should remember that a more accurate way of stating that would be to say that our obligation is to a unifying, to a process.

This brings us now to one of our most serious problems in this matter of orders. It is important, but we can touch on it only briefly; it is what we spoke of ... as the evolving situation. I am trying to show here that the order must be integral to the situation and must be recognized as such. But we saw that the situation was always developing. If the situation is never stationary, then the order should never be stationary, so to speak; how to prevent it from being so is our problem. The situation is changing while orders are being carried out, because, by and through orders being carried out. How is the order to keep up with the situation? External orders never can, only those drawn fresh from the situation.

Moreover, if taking a *responsible* attitude toward experience involves recognizing the evolving situation, a *conscious* attitude toward experience means that we note the change which the developing situation makes in ourselves; the situation does not change without changing us....

... When I asked a very intelligent girl what she thought would be the result of profit sharing and employee representation in the factory where she worked, she replied joyfully, "We shan't need foremen any more." While her entire ignoring of the fact that the foreman has other duties than keeping workers on their jobs was amusing, one wants to go beyond one's amusement and find out what this objection to being watched really means....

I have seen similar instances cited. Many workmen feel that being watched is unbearable. What can we do about it? How can we get proper supervision without this watching which a worker resents? Supervision is necessary; supervision is resented—how are we going to make the integration there? Some say "Let the workers elect the supervisors." I do not believe in that.

There are ... other points closely connected with the subject of this paper which I should like merely to point out. First, when and how do you point out mistakes, misconduct? One principle can surely guide us here: don't blame for the sake of blaming, make what you have to say accomplish something; say it in that form, at that time, under those circumstances, which will make it a real education to your subordinate. Secondly, since it is recognized that the one who gives the orders is not as a rule a very popular person, the management sometimes tries to offset this by allowing the person who has this onus upon him to give any pleasant news to the workers, to have the credit of any innovation which the workers very much desire. One manager told me that he always tried to do this. I suppose that this is good behaviouristic psychology, and yet I am not sure that it is a method I wholly like. It is quite different, however, in the case of a mistaken order having been given; then I think the one who made the mistake should certainly be the one to rectify it, not as a matter of strategy, but because it is better for him too....

Reading 2	**The Functions of the Executive**
	Chester I. Barnard

The coördination of efforts essential to a system of coöperation requires, as we have seen, an organization system of communication. Such a system of communication implies centers or points of interconnection and can only operate as these centers are occupied by persons who are called executives. It might be said, then, that the function of executives is to serve as channels of communication so far as communications must pass through central positions. But since the object of the communication system is coördination of all aspect of organization, it follows that the functions of executives relate to all the work essential to the vitality and endurance of an organization, so far, at least, as it must be accomplished through formal coördination. The executive functions serve to maintain a system of cooperative effort. They are impersonal. The functions are not, as so frequently stated, to manage a group of persons. I do not think a correct understanding of executive work can be had if this narrower, convenient, but strictly speaking erroneous, conception obtains. It is not even quite correct to say that the executive functions are to manage the system of coöperative efforts. As a whole it is managed by itself, not by the executive organization, which is a part of it. The functions with which we are concerned are like those of the nervous system, including the brain, in relation to the rest of the body. It exists to maintain the bodily system by directing those actions which are necessary more effectively to adjust to the environment, but it can hardly be said to manage the body, a large part of whose functions are independent of it and upon which it in turn depends.

The essential executive functions, as I shall present them, correspond to the elements of organization....

They are, first, to provide the system of communication; second, to promote the securing of essential efforts; and, third, to formulate and define purpose. Since the elements of organization are interrelated and interdependent, the executive functions are so likewise; nevertheless they are subject to considerable specialization and as functions are to a substantial degree separable in practice. We shall deal with them only as found in complex, though not necessarily large, organizations.

I. The Maintenance of Organization Communication

We have noticed ... that, when a complex of more than one unit is in question, centers of communication and corresponding executives are necessary. The need of a definite system of communication creates the first task of the organizer and is the immediate origin of executive organization. If the purpose of an organization is conceived initially in the mind of one person, he is likely very early to find necessary the selection of lieutenants; and if the organization is spontaneous its very first task is likely to be the selection of a leader. Since communication will be accomplished only through the agency of persons, the selection of persons for executive functions is the concrete method of establishing the *means* of communication, though it must be immediately followed by the creation of positions, that is, a *system* of communication; and, especially in established organizations, the positions will exist to be filled in the event of vacancies....

Therefore, the problem of the establishment and maintenance of the system of communication, that is, the primary task of the executive organization, is perpetually that of obtaining the

Source: Reprinted by permission of the publisher from "The Executive Functions," in THE FUNCTIONS OF THE EXECUTIVE by Chester I. Barnard, pp. 215–234, Cambridge, Mass.: Harvard University Press, Copyright ©1938, 1968 by the President and Fellows of Harvard College.

coalescence of the two phases, executive personnel and executive positions. Each phase in turn is the strategic factor of the executive problem—first one, then the other phase, must be adjusted. This is the central problem of the executive functions. Its solution is not in itself sufficient to accomplish the work of all these functions; but no others can be accomplished without it, and none well unless it is well done. . . .

The Scheme of Organization

Let us call the first phase of the function—the definition of organization positions—the "scheme of organization." This is the aspect of organization which receives relatively excessive formal attention because it can apparently be reduced to organization charts, specifications of duties, and descriptions of divisions of labor, etc. It rests upon or represents a coördination chiefly of the work to be done by the organization, that is, its purposes broken up into subsidiary purposes, specializations, tasks, etc., which will be discussed in [the third section] of this chapter; the kind and quantity of *services* of personnel that can be obtained; the kind and quantity of *persons* that must be included in the coöperative system for this purpose; the inducements that are required; and the places at which and the times when these factors can be combined, which will not be specifically discussed here.

It is evident that these are mutually dependent factors, and that they all involve other executive functions which we shall discuss later. So far as the *scheme* of organization is separately attacked, it is always on the assumption that it is then the strategic factor, the other factors of organization remaining fixed for the time being; but since the underlying purpose of any change in a scheme of organization is to affect these other factors as a whole favorably, any scheme of organization at any given time represents necessarily a result of previous successive approximations through a period of time. It has always necessarily to be attacked on the basis of the present situation.

Personnel

The scheme of organization is dependent not only upon the general factors of the organizations as a whole, but likewise, as we have indicated, on the availability of various kinds of services for the executive positions. This becomes in its turn the strategic factor. In general, the principles of the economy of incentives apply here as well as to other more general personnel problems. The balance of factors and the technical problems of this special class, however, are not only different from those generally to be found in other spheres of organization economy but are highly special in different types of organizations. The most important single contribution required of the executive, certainly the most universal qualification, is loyalty, domination by the organization personality. This is the first necessity because the lines of communication cannot function at all unless the personal contributions of executives will be present at the required positions, at the times necessary, without default or ordinary personal reasons. This, as a personal qualification, is known in secular organizations as the quality of "responsibility"; in political organizations as "regularity"; in governmental organizations as fealty or loyalty; in religious organizations as "complete submission" to the faith and to the hierarchy of objective religious authority.

The contribution of personal loyalty and submission is least susceptible to tangible inducements. It cannot be bought either by material inducements or by other positive incentives, except all other things be equal. This is as true of industrial organizations, I believe, as of any others. It is rather generally understood that although money or other material inducements must usually be paid to responsible persons, responsibility itself does not arise from such inducements.

However, love of prestige is, in general, a much more important inducement in the case of executives than with the rest of the personnel. Interest in work and pride in organization are other incentives that usually must be present. These facts are much obscured as respects commercial organizations, where material inducements appear to be the effective factors partly because such inducements are more readily offered in such organizations and partly because, since the other incentives are often equal as between such organizations, material inducements are the only available differential factor. It also becomes an important secondary factor to individuals in many cases, because prestige and official responsibilities impose heavy material burdens on them. Hence neither churches nor socialistic states have been able to escape the necessity of direct or indirect material inducements for high dignitaries or officials. But this is probably incidental and superficial in all organizations. It appears to be true that in all of them adequate incentives to executive services are difficult to offer. Those most available in the present age are tangible, materialistic; but on the whole they are both insufficient and often abortive.[1]

Following loyalty, responsibility, and capacity to be dominated by organization personality, come the more specific personal abilities. They are roughly divided into two classes: relatively general abilities, involving general alertness, comprehensiveness of interest, flexibility, faculty of adjustment, poise, courage, etc; and specialized abilities based on particular aptitudes and acquired techniques. The first kind is relatively difficult to appraise because it depends upon innate characteristics developed through general experience. It is not greatly susceptible of immediate inculcation. The second kind may be less rare because the division of labor, that is, organization itself, fosters it automatically, and because it is susceptible to development (at a cost) by training and education. We deliberately and more and more turn out specialists; but we do not develop general executives well by specific efforts, and we know very little about how to do it.

The higher the positions in the line of authority, the more general the abilities required. The scarcity of such abilities, together with the necessity for keeping the lines of authority as short as feasible, controls the organization of executive work.

It leads to the reduction of the number of formally executive positions to the minimum, a measure made possible by creating about the executives in many cases staffs of specialists who supplement them in time, energy, and technical capacities. This is made feasible by elaborate and often delicate arrangements to correct errors resulting from the faults of over-specialization and the paucity of line executives....

Thus, jointly with the development of the scheme of organization, the selection, promotion, demotion, and dismissal of men becomes the essence of maintaining the system of communication without which no organization can exist. The selection in part, but especially the promotion, demotion, and dismissal of men, depend upon the exercise of supervision or what is often called "control."

Control relates directly, and in conscious application chiefly, to the work of the organization as a whole rather than to the work of executives as such. But so heavily dependent is the success of coöperation upon the functioning of the executive organization that practically the control is over executives for the most part. If the work of an organization is not successful, if it is inefficient, if it cannot maintain the services of its personnel, the conclusion is that its "management" is wrong; that is, that the scheme of communication or the associated personnel or both, that is, the executive department directly related, are at fault. This is, sometimes at least, not true, but often it is. Moreover, for the correction of such faults the first reliance is upon executive organization. The methods by which control is exercised are, of course, numerous and largely technical to each organization, and need not be further discussed here.

Informal Executive Organizations

The general method of maintaining an informal executive organization is so to operate and to select and promote executives that a general condition of compatibility of personnel is maintained. Perhaps often and certainly occasionally men cannot be promoted or selected, or even must be relieved, because they cannot function, because they "do not fit," where there is no question of formal competence. This question of "fitness" involves such matters as education, experience, age, sex, personal distinctions, prestige, race, nationality, faith, politics, sectional antecedents; and such very special personal traits as manners, speech, personal appearance, etc. It goes by few if any rules, except those based at least nominally on other, formal, considerations. It represents in its best sense the political aspects of personal relationship in formal organization. I suspect it to be most highly developed in political, labor, church, and university organizations, for the very reason that the intangible types of personal services are relatively more important in them than in most other, especially industrial, organizations. But it is certainly of major importance in all organizations.

This compatibility is promoted by educational requirements (armies, navies, churches, schools); by requirement of certain background (European armies, navies, labor unions, Soviet and Fascist governments, political parties); by conferences and conventions; by specifically social activities; by class distinctions connected with privileges and "authority" (in armies, navies, churches, universities). A certain conformity is required by unwritten understanding that can sometimes be formally enforced, expressed for its negative aspect by the phrase "conduct unbecoming a gentleman and an officer." There are, however, innumerable other processes, many of which are not consciously employed for this purpose.

It must not be understood that the desired degree of compatibility is always the same or is the maximum possible. On the contrary it seems to me to be often the case that excessive compatibility or harmony is deleterious, resulting in "single track minds" and excessively crystallized attitudes and in the destruction of personal responsibility; but I know from experience in operating with new emergency organizations, in which there was no time and little immediate basis for the growth of an informal organization

properly coördinated with formal organization that it is almost impossible to secure effective and efficient coöperation without it.

The functions of informal executive organizations are the communication of intangible facts, opinions, suggestions, suspicions, that cannot pass through formal channels without raising issues calling for decisions, without dissipating dignity and objective authority, and without overloading executive positions; also to minimize excessive cliques of political types arising from too great divergence of interests and views; to promote self-discipline of the group; and to make possible the development of important personal influences in the organization. There are probably other functions.

I shall comment on only two functions of informal executive organization. The necessity for avoiding formal issues, that is, for avoiding the issuance of numerous formal orders except on routine matters and except in emergencies, is important.[2] I know of major executives who issue an order or judgement settling an important issue rather seldom, although they are functioning all the time. The obvious desire of politicians to avoid important issues (and to impose them on their opponents) is based upon a thorough sense of organization. Neither authority nor coöperative disposition (largely the same things) will stand much overt division on formal issues in the present stage of human development. Hence most laws, executive orders, decisions, etc., are in effect formal notice that all is well—there is agreement, authority is not questioned.

The question of personal influence is very subtle. Probably most good organizations have somewhere a Colonel House; and many men not only exercise beneficent influence far beyond that implied by their formal status, but most of them, at the time, would lose their influence if they had corresponding formal status. The reason may be that many men have personal qualifications of high order that will not operate under the stress of commensurate official responsibility. By analogy I may mention the golfers of first class skill who cannot "stand up" in public tournaments....

II. The Securing of Essential Services from Individuals

The second function of the executive organization is to promote the securing of the personal services that constitute the material of organizations.

The work divides into two main divisions: (I) the bringing of persons into coöperative relationship with the organization; (II) the eliciting of the services after such persons have been brought into that relationship.

1.

The characteristic fact of the first division is that the organization is acting upon persons who are in every sense outside it. Such action is necessary not merely to secure the personnel of new organizations, or to supply the material for the growth of existing organizations, but also to replace the losses that continually take place by reason of death, resignation, "backsliding," emigration, discharge, excommunication, ostracism. These factors of growth or replacement of contributors require bringing persons by organization effort within range of the consideration of the incentives available in order to induce some of these persons to attach themselves to the organization. Accordingly the task involves two parts: (a) bringing persons within reach of specific effort to secure services, and (b) the application of that effort when they have been brought near enough. Often both parts of the task occupy the efforts of the same persons or parts of an organization; but they are clearly distinct elements and considerable specialization is found with respect to them.

(a) Bringing persons within reach of recruiting or proselyting influence is a task which differs in practical emphasis among organizations in respect both to scope and to method. Some religious organizations—especially the Catholic Church, several Protestant Churches, the Mormon Church, for example—have as ideal goals the attachment of all persons to their organizations, and the wide world is the field of proselyting propaganda. During many decades the United States of America invited all who could reach its shores to become American citizens. Other organizations, having limits on the volume of their activities, restrict the field of propaganda. Thus many nations in effect now restrict substantial growth to those who acquire a national status by birth; the American Legion restricts its membership to those who have acquired a status by certain type of previous service, etc. Others restrict their fields practically on the basis of proportions. Thus universities "in principle" are open to all or to all with educational and character qualifications but may restrict their appeals to geographical, racial, and class proportions so as to preserve the cosmopolitan character of their bodies, or to preserve predominance of nationals, etc. Industrial and commercial organizations are theoretically limited usually by considerations of social compatibility and additionally by the costs of propaganda. They usually attempt no appeal when the geographic remoteness makes it ineffective....

(b) The effort to induce specific persons who by the general appeal are brought into contact with an organization actually to become identified with it constitutes the more regular and routine work of securing contributors. This involves in its general aspects the method of persuasion which has already been described, the establishment of inducements and incentives, and direct negotiation. The methods required are indefinitely large in number and of very wide variety....[3]

2.

Although the work of recruiting is important in most organizations, and especially so in those which are new or rapidly expanding or which have high "turnover," nevertheless in established and enduring organizations the eliciting of the quantity and quality of efforts from their adherents is usually more important and occupies the greater part of personnel effort. Because of the more tangible character of "membership," being an "employee," etc., recruiting is apt to receive more attention as a field of personnel work than the business of promoting the actual output of efforts and influences, which are the real material of organization.[4] Membership, nominal adherence, is merely the starting point; and the minimum contributions which can be conceived as enabling retention of such connection would generally be insufficient for the survival of active or productive organization.... In short, every organization to survive must deliberately attend to the maintenance and growth of its authority to do the things necessary for coördination, effectiveness, and efficiency. This, as we have seen, depends upon its appeal to persons who are already related to the organization....

III. The Formulation of Purpose and Objectives

The third executive function is to formulate and define the purposes, objectives, ends, of the organization. It has already been made clear that, strictly speaking, purpose is defined more nearly by the aggregate of action taken than by any formulation in words; but that the aggregate of action is a residuum of the decisions relative to purpose and the environment, resulting in closer and closer approximations to the concrete acts. It has also been emphasized that purpose is something that must be accepted by all the contributors to the system of efforts. Again, it has been stated that purpose must be broken into fragments, specific objectives, not only ordered in time so that detailed purpose and detailed action follow in the series of progressive coöperation, but also ordered contemporaneously into the specializations—geographical, social, and functional—that each unit organization implies. It is more apparent here than with other executive functions that it is an entire executive organization that formulates, redefines, breaks into details, and decides on the innumerable simultaneous and progressive actions that are the stream of syntheses constituting purpose or action. No single executive can under any conditions accomplish this function alone, but only that part of it which relates to his position in the executive organization.

Hence the critical aspect of this function is the assignment of responsibility—the delegation of objective authority. Thus in one sense this function is that of the scheme of positions, the system of communication, already discussed. That is its potential aspect. Its other aspect is the actual decisions and conduct which make the scheme a working system. Accordingly, the general executive states that "this is the purpose, this the objective, this the direction, in general terms, in which we wish to move, before next year." His department heads, or the heads of his main territorial divisions, say to their departments or suborganizations: "This means for us these things now, then others next month, then others later, to be better defined after experience." Their subdepartment or division heads say: "This means for us such and such operations now at these places, such others at those places, something today here, others tomorrow there." Then district or bureau chiefs in turn become more and more specific, their sub-chiefs still more so....

The formulation and definition of purpose is then a widely distributed function only the more general part of which is executive. In this fact lies the most important inherent difficulty in the operation of coöperative systems—the necessity for indoctrinating those at the lower levels with general purposes, the major decisions, so that they remain cohesive and able to make the ultimate detailed decisions coherent; and the necessity, for those at the higher levels, of constantly understanding the concrete conditions and the specific decisions of the "ultimate" contributors from which and from whom executives are often insulated. Without that up-and-down-the-line coördination of purposeful decisions, general decisions and general purposes are mere intellectual processes in an organization vacuum, insulated from realities by layers of misunderstanding. The function of formulating grand purposes and providing for their redefinition is one which needs sensitive systems of communication, experience in interpretation, imagination, and delegation of responsibility.

Perhaps there are none who could consider even so extremely condensed and general a description of the executive functions as has here been presented without perceiving that these functions are merely elements in an organic whole. It is their combination in a working system that makes an organization.

This combination involves two opposite incitements to action. First, the concrete interaction and mutual adjustment of the executive functions are partly to be determined by the factors of the environment of the organization—the specific coöperative system as a whole and its environment. This involves fundamentally the logical processes of analysis and the discrimination of the strategic factors....

NOTES

1. After much experience, I am convinced that the most ineffective services in a continuing effort are in one sense those of volunteers, or of semi-volunteers; for example, half-pay workers. What appears to be inexpensive is in fact very expensive, because non-material incentives—such as prestige, toleration of too great personal interest in the work with its accompanying fads and "pet" projects, the yielding to exaggerated conceptions of individual importance—are causes of internal friction and many other undesirable consequences. Yet in many emergency situations, and in a large part of political, charitable, civic, educational, and religious organization work, often indispensable services cannot be obtained by material incentives.

2. When writing these lines I tried to recall an important general decision made by me on my initiative as a telephone executive within two years. I could recall none, although on reviewing the record I found several. On the other hand, I can still recall without any record many major decisions made by me "out of hand" when I was a Relief Administrator. I probably averaged at least five a day for eighteen months. In the latter case I worked with a very noble group but a very poor informal organization under emergency conditions.

3. I must repeat that although the emphasis is on the employee group of contributors, so far as industrial organizations are concerned, nevertheless "customers" are equally included. The principles broadly discussed here relate to salesmanship as well as employing persons.

4. As an instance, note the great attention in civil service regulations, and also in political appointments, to obtaining and retaining employment, and the relatively small attention to services.

Reading 3 | # The Contingency Model: A Theory of Leadership Effectiveness[1]
Fred E. Fiedler

Leadership, as a problem in social psychology, has dealt primarily with two questions, namely, how one becomes a leader, and how one can become a *good* leader, that is, how one develops effective group performance. Since a number of excellent reviews (e.g., Stogdill, 1948; Gibb, 1954; Mann, 1959; Bass, 1960) have already dealt with the first question we shall not be concerned with it in the present paper.

The second question, whether a given leader will be more or less effective than others in similar situations, has been a more difficult problem of research and has received correspondingly less attention in the psychological literature. The theoretical status of the problem is well reflected by Browne and Cohn's (1958) statement that "leadership literature is a mass of content without coagulating substances to bring it together or to produce coordination...." McGrath (1962), in making a similar point, ascribed this situation to the tendency of investigators to select different variables and to work with idiosyncratic measures and definitions of leadership. He also pointed out, however, that most researchers in this area have gravitated toward two presumably crucial clusters of leadership attitudes and behaviors. These are the critical, directive, autocratic, task-oriented versus the democratic, permissive, considerate, person-oriented type of leadership. While this categorization is admittedly oversimplified, the major controversy in this area has been between the more orthodox viewpoint, reflected in traditional supervisory training and military doctrine that the leader should be decisive and forceful, that he should do the planning and thinking for the groups, and that he should coordinate, direct, and evaluate his men's actions. The other viewpoint, reflected in the newer human relations oriented training and in the philosophy behind non-directive and brain-storming technique stresses the need for democratic, permissive, group-oriented leadership techniques. Both schools of thought have strong adherents, and there is evidence supporting both points of view (Gibb, 1954; Hare, 1962).

While one can always rationalize that contradictory findings by other investigators are due to poor research design, or different tests and criteria, such problems present difficulties if they appear in one's own research. We have, during the past thirteen years, conducted a large number of studies on leadership and group performance, using the same operational definitions and essentially similar leader attitude measures. The inconsistencies which we obtained in our own research program demanded an integrative theoretical formulation which would adequately account for the seemingly confusing results.

The studies which we conducted used as the major predictor of group performance an interpersonal perception or attitude score which is derived from the leader's description of his most and of his least preferred co-workers. He is asked to think of all others with whom he has ever worked, and then to describe first the person with whom he worked best (his most preferred co-worker) and then the person with whom he could work least well (his least preferred co-worker, or *LPC*). These descriptions are obtained, wherever possible, before the leader is assigned to his team. However, even when we deal with already existing groups, these descriptions tend to be of individuals whom the subject has known in the past rather than of persons with whom he works at the time of testing.

The descriptions are typically made on 20 eight-point bi-polar adjective scales, similar to Osgood's Semantic Differential (Osgood et al., 1957), e.g.,

Pleasant _:_:_:_:_:_:_:_ Unpleasant

Friendly _:_:_:_:_:_:_:_ Unfriendly

Source: "The Contingency Model," Fred E. Fiedler, 190. Used by permission.

These items are scaled on an evaluative dimension, giving a score of 8 to the most favorable pole (i.e., Friendly, Pleasant) and a score of 1 to the least favorable pole. Two main scores have been derived from these descriptions. The first one, which was used in our earlier studies, is based on the profile similarity measure D (Cronbach and Gleser, 1953) between the descriptions of the most and of the least preferred co-worker. This score, called the Assumed Similarity between Opposites, or ASo, indicates the degree to which the individual perceives the two opposites on his co-worker continuum as similar or different. The second score is simply based on the individual's description of his least preferred co-worker, LPC, and indicates the degree to which the subject evaluates his LPC in a relatively favorable or unfavorable manner. The two measures are highly correlated (.80 to .95) and will here be treated as interchangeable.

We have had considerable difficulty in interpreting these scores since they appear to be uncorrelated with the usual personality and attitude measures. They are, however, related to the Ohio State University studies' "Initiation of structure" and "Consideration" dimensions (Stogdill and Coons, 1957). Extensive content analysis (Meuwese and Oonk, 1960; Julian and McGrath, 1963; Morris and Fiedler, 1964) and a series of studies by Hawkins (1962) as well as research by Bass, Fiedler, and Krueger (1964) have given consistent results. These indicate that the person with high LPC or ASo, who perceives his least preferred co-worker in a relatively favorable, accepting manner, tends to be more accepting, permissive, considerate, and person-oriented in his relations with group members. The person who perceives his most and least preferred co-workers as quite different, and who sees his least preferred coworker in a very unfavorable, rejecting manner tends to be directive, task-oriented and controlling on task relevant group behaviors in his interactions. . . .

The results of these investigations clearly showed that the direction and magnitude of the correlations were contingent upon the nature of the group-task situation with which the leader had to deal. Our problem resolved itself then into (a) developing a meaningful system for categorizing group-task situations; (b) inducing the underlying theoretical model which would integrate the seemingly inconsistent results obtained in our studies, and (c) testing the validity of the model by adequate research.

Development of the Model

Key Definitions. We shall here be concerned solely with "interacting" rather than "co-acting" task groups. By an interacting task group we mean a face-to-face team situation (such as a basketball team) in which the members work *interdependently* on a common goal. In groups of this type, the individual's contributions cannot readily be separated from total group performance. In a co-acting group, however, such as a bowling or a rifle team, the group performance is generally determined by summing the members' individual performance scores. . . .

The leader's effectiveness is here defined in terms of the group's performance on the assigned primary task. . . .

The Categorization of Group-Task Situations. Leadership is essentially a problem of wielding influence and power. When we say that different types of groups require different types of leadership we imply that they require a different relationship by which the leader wields power and influence. Since it is easier to wield power in some groups than in others, an attempt to categorize groups might well begin by asking what conditions in the group-task situation will facilitate or inhibit the leader's exercise of power. On the basis of our previous work we postulated three important aspects in the total situation which influence the leader's role.

1. *Leader-member relations.* The leader who is personally attractive to his group members, and who is respected by his group, enjoys considerable power (French, 1956). In fact, if he has the confidence and loyalty of his men he has less need of official rank. This dimension can generally be measured by means of sociometric indices or by group atmosphere scales (Cf. Fiedler, 1962) which indicate the degree to which the leader experiences the groups as pleasant and well disposed toward him.

2. *Task structure.* The task generally implies an order "from above" which incorporates the authority of the superior organization. The group member who refuses to comply must be prepared to face disciplinary action by the higher authority. For example, a squad member who fails to perform a lawful command of his sergeant may have to answer to his regimental commander. However, compliance with a task order can be enforced only if the task is relatively well structured, i.e., if it is capable of being programmed, or spelled out step by step. One cannot effectively force a group to perform well on an unstructured task such as developing a new product or writing a good play.

Thus, the leader who has a structured task can depend on the backing of his superior organizations, but if he has an unstructured task the leader must rely on his own resources to inspire and motivate his men. The unstructured task thus provides the leader with much less effective power than does the highly structured task.

We operationalized this dimension by utilizing four of the aspects which Shaw (1962) recently proposed for the classification of group task. These are, (*a*) decision *verifiability,* the degree to which the correctness of the solution can be demonstrated objectively; (*b*) *good clarity,* the degree to which the task requirements are clearly stated or known to the group; (*c*) *goal path multiplicity,* the degree to which there are many or few procedures available for performing the task (reverse scoring); and (*d*) *solution specificity,* the degree to which there is one rather than an infinite number of correct solutions (e.g., writing a story vs. solving an equation). Ratings based on these four dimensions have yielded interrater reliabilities of .80 to .90.

3. *Position power.* The third dimension is defined by the power inherent in the position of leadership irrespective of the occupant's personal relations with his members. This includes the rewards and punishments which are officially or traditionally at the leader's disposal, his authority as defined by the group's rules and by-laws, and the organizational support given to him in dealing with his men....

A Three-Dimensional Group Classification. Group-task situations can now be rated on the basis of the three dimensions of leader-member relations, task structure, and position power. This locates each group in a three dimensional space. A rough categorization can be accomplished by halving each of the dimensions so that we obtain an eight celled cube (Fig. 1). We can now determine

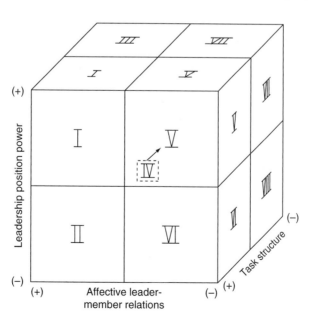

FIGURE 1
A MODEL FOR THE CLASSIFICATION OF GROUP-TASK SITUATIONS

Leadership position power

Affective leader-member relations

Task structure

TABLE I | MEDIAN CORRELATION BETWEEN LEADER LPC AND GROUP PERFORMANCE IN VARIOUS OCTANTS

	Leader-Member Relations	Task Structure	Position Power	Median Correlation	Number of Relations Included in Median
Octant I	Good	Structured	Strong	−.52	2
Octant II	Good	Structured	Weak	−.58	3
Octant III	Good	Unstructured	Strong	−.41	4
Octant IV	Good	Unstructured	Weak	.47	10
Octant V	Mod. poor	Structured	Strong	.42	6
Octant VI	Mod. poor	Structured	Weak		0
Octant VII	Mod. poor	Unstructured	Strong	.05	10
Octant VIII	Mod. poor	Unstructured	Weak	−.43	12

whether the correlations between leader attitudes and group performance within each of these eight cells, or octants, are relatively similar in magnitude and direction. If they are, we can infer that the group classification has been successfully accomplished since it shows that groups falling within the same octant require similar leader attitudes.

An earlier paper has summarized 52 group-task situations which are based on our previous studies (Fiedler, 1964). These 52 group-task situations have been ordered into the eight octants. As can be seen from Table 1, groups falling within the same octant show correlations between the leader's *ASo* or *LPC* score and the group performance criterion which are relatively similar in magnitude and direction. We can thus infer that the group classification has been accomplished with at least reasonable success.

Consideration of Figure 1 suggests a further classification of the cells in term of the effective power which the group-task situation places at the leader's disposal, or more precisely, the favorableness of the situation for the leader's exercise of his power and influence.

Such an ordering can be accomplished without difficulty at the extreme poles of the continuum. A liked and trusted leader with high rank and a structured task is in a more favorable position than is a disliked and powerless leader with an ambiguous task.... In the present instance we have postulated that the most important dimension in the system is the leader-member relationship since the highly liked and respected leader is less in need of position power or the power of the higher authority incorporated in the task structure. The second-most important dimension in most group-task situations is the task structure since a leader with a highly structured task does not require a powerful leader position.... This leads us here to order the group-task situations first on leader-member relations, then on task structure, and finally on position power. While admittedly not a unique solution, the resulting ordering constitutes a reasonable continuum which indicates the degree of the leader's effective power in the group.[2]

As was already apparent from Table 1, the relationship between leader attitudes and group performance is contingent upon the accurate classification of the group-task situation. A more meaningful model of this contingency relationship emerges when we now plot the correlation between *LPC* or *ASo* and group performance on the one hand, against the octants ordered on the effective power, or favorableness-for-the-leader dimension on the other. This is shown on Figure 2. Note that each point in the plot is a *correlation*

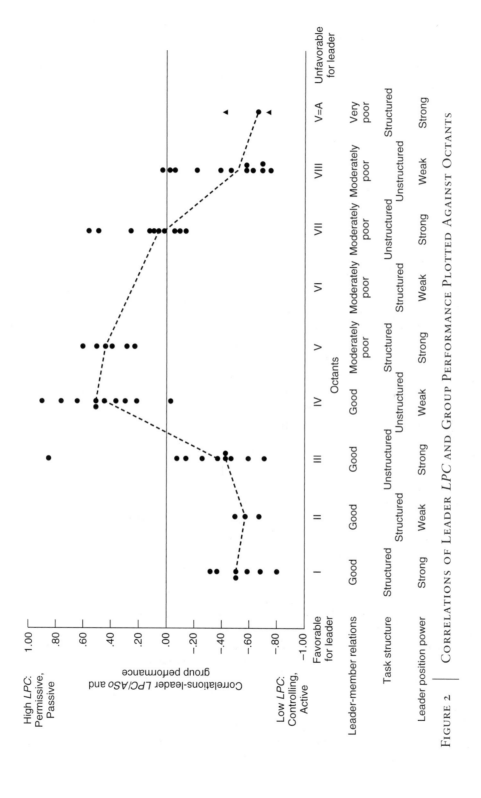

FIGURE 2 | CORRELATIONS OF LEADER *LPC* AND GROUP PERFORMANCE PLOTTED AGAINST OCTANTS

predicting leadership performance or group effectiveness. The plot therefore represents 53 *sets of groups* totalling over 800 separate groups.

As Figure 2 shows, managing, controlling, directive (low *LPC*) leaders perform most effectively either under very favorable or under very unfavorable situations. Hence we obtain negative correlations between *LPC* and group performance scores. Considerate, permissive accepting leaders obtain optimal group performance under situations intermediate in favorableness. These are situations in which (*a*) the task is structured, but the leader is disliked and must, therefore, be diplomatic; (*b*) the liked leader has an ambiguous, unstructured task and must, therefore, draw upon the creativity and cooperation of his members. Here we obtain positive correlations between *LPC* and group performance scores. Where the task is highly structured and the leader is well-liked, non-directive behavior or permissive attitudes (such as asking how the group ought to proceed with a missile count-down) is neither appropriate nor beneficial. Where the situation is quite unfavorable, e.g., where the disliked chairman of a volunteer group faces an ambiguous task, the leader might as well be autocratic and directive since a positive, non-directive leadership style under these conditions might result in complete inactivity on the part of the group. This model, thus, tends to shed some light on the apparent inconsistencies in our own data as well as in data obtained by other investigators.

Empirical Tests Extension of the Model

The basic hypothesis of the model suggests that the directive, controlling, task oriented (low *LPC*) leader will be most successful in group-task situations which are either very favorable or else very unfavorable for the leader. The permissive, considerate, human relations oriented (high *LPC*) leader will perform best under conditions which are intermediate in favorableness....

Experimental Test of the Contingency Model

In cooperation with the Belgian Naval Forces we recently conducted a major study which served in part as a specific test of the model. Only aspects immediately relevant to the test are here described. The investigation was conducted in Belgium where the French and Dutch speaking (or Flemish) sectors of the country have been involved in a long standing and frequently acrimonious dispute. This conflict centers about the use of language, but it also involves a host of other cultural factors which differentiate the 60 per cent Flemish and 40 per cent French speaking population groups in Wallonie and Brussels. This "linguistic problem" which is rooted in the beginning of Belgium's national history, has in recent years been the cause of continuous public controversy, frequent protest meetings, and occasional riots.

The linguistic problem is of particular interest here since a group, consisting of members whose mother tongue, culture, and attitudes differ, will clearly present a more difficult problem in leadership than a group whose members share the same language and culture. We were thus able to test the major hypothesis of the model as well as to extend the research by investigating the type of leadership which linguistically and culturally heterogeneous groups require.

Design.   The experiment was conducted at the naval training center at Ste. Croix-Bruges.[3] It utilized 48 career petty officers and 240 recruits who had been selected from a pool of 546 men on the basis of a pre-test in which we obtained *LPC*, intelligence, attitude, and language comprehension scores.

The experiment was specifically designed to incorporate the three major group classification dimensions shown on Figure 1, namely, leader-member relations, position power, and task structure. It also added the additional dimension of group homogeneity vs. heterogeneity. Specifically, 48 groups had leaders with high position power (petty officers) while 48 had leaders with low position power (recruits); 48 groups began with the unstructured task, while the other 48 groups began with two structured tasks; 48 groups were homogeneous, consisting of three French or three Dutch speaking men, while the other 48 groups were heterogeneous, consisting of a French speaking leader and two Flemish members, or a Dutch speaking,

Flemish leader and two French speaking members. The quality of the leader-member relations was measured as in our previous studies by means of a group atmosphere scale which the leader completed after each task session.

Group Performance Criteria. Two essentially identical structured tasks were administered. Each lasted 25 minutes and required the groups to find the shortest route for a ship which, given certain fuel capacity and required ports of call, had to make a round trip calling at respectively ten or twelve ports. The tasks were objectively scored on the basis of sea miles required for the trip. Appropriate corrections and penalties were assigned for errors.

The unstructured task required the groups to compose a letter to young men of 16 and 17 years, urging them to choose the Belgian Navy as a career. The letter was to be approximately 200 words in length and had to be completed in 35 minutes. Each of the letters, depending upon the language in which it was written, was then rated by Dutch or by French speaking judges on style and use of language, as well as interest value, originality, and persuasiveness. Estimated reliability was .92 and .86 for Dutch and French speaking judges, respectively.

It should be noted in this connection that the task of writing a letter is not as unstructured as might have been desirable for this experiment.... High and low task-structure is, therefore, less well differentiated in this study than it has been in previous investigations.

Results. The contingency model specifies that the controlling, managing, low *LPC* leaders will be most effective either in very favorable or else in relatively unfavorable group-task situations, while the permissive, considerate, high *LPC* leaders will be more effective in situations intermediate in difficulty....

The hypothesis can be tested most readily with correlations of leader *LPC* and group performance in homogeneous groups on the more reliably scorable second structured task.... We have here made the fairly obvious assumption that the

powerful leader or the leader who feels liked and accepted faces an easier group-task situation than low ranking leaders and those who see the groups as unpleasant and tense. Each situation is represented by two cells of six groups, each. Since there were two orders of presentation—half the groups worked first on the structured task, the other half on the unstructured task—arranging the group-task situations in order of favorableness for the leader then gives us the following results:

	Order 1	Order 2
High group atmosphere and high position power	−.77	−.77
High group atmosphere and low position power	+.60	+.50
Low group atmosphere and high position power	+.16	+.01
Low group atmosphere and low position power	−.16	−.43

These are, of course, the trends in size and magnitude of correlations which the model predicts. Low *LPC* leaders are again most effective in favorable and unfavorable group-task situations: the more permissive, considerate high *LPC* leaders were more effective in the intermediate situations....

The resulting weighting system leads to a scale from 12 to 0 points, with 12 as the most favorable pole. If we now plot the median correlation coefficients of the 48 group-task situations against the scale indicating the favorableness of the situation for the leader, we obtain the curve presented on Figure 3.

As can be seen, we again obtain a curvilinear relationship which resembles that shown on Figure 2. Heterogeneous groups with low position power and/or poor leader-member relations fall below point 6 on the scale, and thus tend to perform better with controlling, directive, low *LPC* leaders. Only under otherwise very favorable conditions do heterogeneous groups perform better with permissive, considerate high *LPC* leaders, that is, in group-task situations characterized by

Code for two-digit numbers. Figure indicating the type of group involved.

Composition	Position Power	High Group Atmos.	Low Group Atmos.	Task	1st Pres.	2nd Pres.
Homogeneous	High	1	5	Structured I	1	2
Homogeneous	Low	2	6	Structured II	3	4
Heterogeneous	High	3	7	Unstructured	5	6
Heterogeneous	Low	4	8			

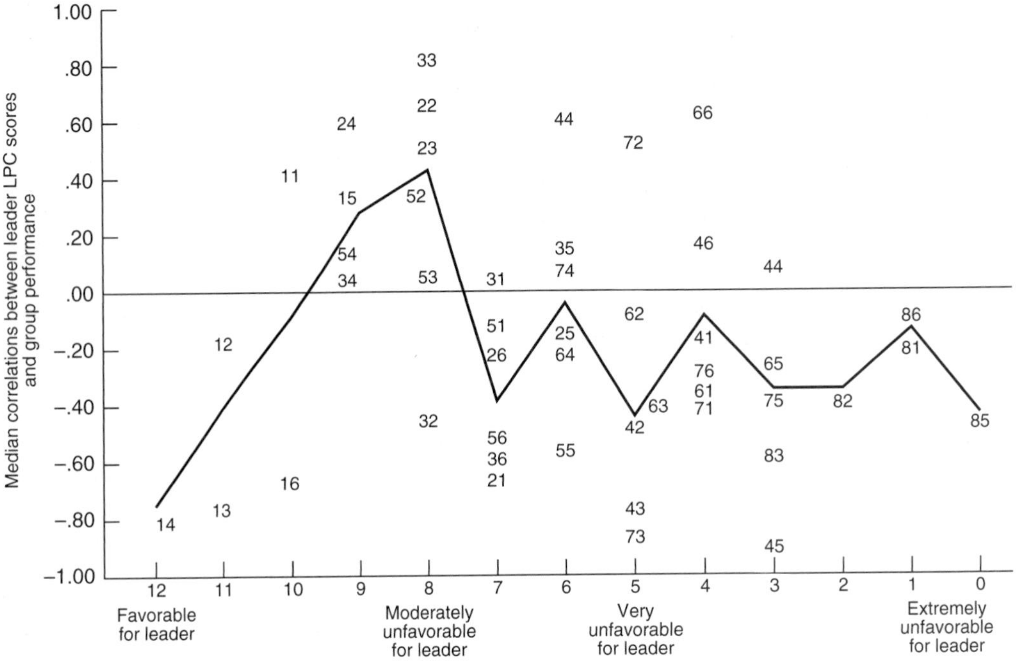

FIGURE 3 | MEDIAN CORRELATIONS BETWEEN LEADER *LCP* AND GROUP PERFORMANCE SCORES PLOTTED AGAINST FAVORABLENESS-FOR-LEADER SCALE IN THE BELGIAN NAVY STUDY

high group atmosphere as well as high position power, four of the six correlations (66%) are positive, while only five of eighteen (28%) are positive in the less favorable group-task situations.

It is interesting to note that the curve is rather flat and characterized by relatively low negative correlations as we go toward the very unfavorable end of the scale. This result supports Meuwese's (1964) recent study which showed that correlations between leader *LPC* as well as between leader intelligence and group performance tend to become attenuated under conditions of relative stress. These findings suggest that the leader's ability to influence and control the group decreases

beyond a certain point of stress and difficulty in the group-task situation.

Discussion

The contingency model seeks to reconcile results which up to now had to be considered inconsistent and difficult to understand....

The model has a number of important implications for selection and training, as well as for the placement of leaders and organizational strategy. Our research suggests, first of all, that we can utilize a very broad spectrum of individuals for positions of leadership. The problem becomes one of placement and training rather than of selection since both the permissive, democratic, human-relations oriented, and the managing, autocratic, task-oriented leader can be effectively utilized. Leaders can be trained to recognize their own style of leadership as well as the conditions which are most compatible with their style.

The model also points to a variety of administrative and supervisory strategies which the organization can adopt to fit the group-task situation to the needs of the leader. Tasks can, after all, be structured to a greater or lesser extent by giving very specific and detailed, or vague and general instructions; the position power of the group leader can be increased or decreased and even the congeniality of a group, and its acceptance of the leader can be affected by appropriate administration action, such as for instance increasing or decreasing the group's homogeneity.

The model also throws new light on phenomena which were rather difficult to fit into our usual ideas about measurement in social psychology. Why, for example, should groups differ so markedly in their performance on nearly parallel tasks? The model—and our data—shows that the situation becomes easier for the leader as the group moves from the novel to the already known group-task situations. The leaders who excel under relatively novel and therefore more difficult conditions are not necessarily those who excel under those which are more routine, or better known and therefore more favorable. Likewise, we find that different types of task structure require different types of leader behavior. Thus, in a research project's early phases the project director tends to be democratic and permissive; everyone is urged to contribute to the plan and to criticize all aspects of the design. This situation changes radically in the more structured phase when the research design is frozen and the experiment is underway. Here the research director tends to become managing, controlling, and highly autocratic and woe betide the assistant who attempts to be creative in giving instructions to subjects, or in his timing of tests. A similar situation is often found in business organizations where the routine operation tends to be well structured and calls for a managing, directive leadership. The situation becomes suddenly unstructured when a crisis occurs. Under these conditions the number of discussions, meetings, and conferences increases sharply so as to give everyone an opportunity to express his views.

At best, this model is of course only a partial theory of leadership. The leader's intellectual and task-relevant abilities, and the members' skills and motivation, all play a role in affecting the group's performance. It is to be hoped that these other important aspects of group interaction can be incorporated into the model in the not too distant future.

REFERENCES

Bass, A. R., Fiedler, F. E., and Krueger, S. Personality correlates of assumed similarity (ASo) and related scores. Urbana, Ill.: Group Effectiveness Research Laboratory, University of Illinois, 1964.

Bass, B. M. *Leadership psychology and organizational behavior.* New York: Harper Brothers, 1960.

Browne, C. G., and Cohn, T. S. (Eds.) *The study of leadership.* Danville, Illinois. The Interstate Printers and Publishers, 1958.

Cleven, W. A., and Fiedler, F. E. Interpersonal perceptions of open hearth foremen and steel production. *J. Appl. Psychol.* 1956, 40, 312–314.

Cronbach, J. J., and Gleser, Goldene C. Assessing similarity between profiles. *Psychol. Bull.,* 1953, 50, 456–473.

Fiedler, F. E. Assumed similarity measures as predictors of team effectiveness. *J. Abnorm. Soc. Psychol.* 1954, 49, 381–388.

Fiedler, F. E. Leader attitudes, group climate, and group creativity. *J. Abnorm. Soc. Psychol.,* 1962, 64, 308–318.

Fiedler, F. E. A contingency model of leadership effectiveness. In L. Berkowtiz (Ed.) *Advances in experimental social psychology.* New York: Academic Press, 1964. Vol. I.

Fiedler, F. E., and Meuwese, W. A. T. The leader's contribution to performance in cohesive and uncohesive groups. *J. Abnorm. Soc. Psychol.* 1963, 67, 83–87.

Fiedler, F. E., Meuwese, W. A. T., and Oonk, Sophie. Performance of laboratory tasks requiring group creativity. *Acta Psychologica,* 1961, 18, 100–119.

French, J. R. P., Jr. A formal theory of social power. *Psychol. Rev.,* 1956, 63, 181–194.

Gibb, C. A. "Leadership" in G. Lindzey (Ed.) *Handbook of Social Psychology,* Vol. II, Cambridge, Mass.: Addison-Wesley, 1954.

Godfrey, Eleanor P., Fiedler, F. E., and Hall, D. M. *Boards, management, and company success.* Danville, Illinois: Interstate Printers and Publishers, 1959.

Hare, A. P. *Handbook of small group research.* New York: Free Press, 1962.

Hawkins, C. A study of factors mediating a relationship between leader rating behavior and group productivity. Unpublished Ph. D. dissertation, University of Minnesota, 1962.

Hutchins, E. B., and Fiedler, F. E. Task-oriented and quasi-therapeutic role functions of the leader in small military groups. *Sociometry,* 1960, 23, 293–406.

Julian, J. W., and McGrath, J. E. The influence of leader and member behavior on the adjustment and task effectiveness of negotiation groups. Urbana, Ill.: Group Effectiveness Research Laboratory, University of Illinois, 1963.

McGrath, J. E. A summary of small group research studies. Arlington Va.: Human Sciences Research Inc., 1962 (Litho.).

Mann, R. D. A review of the relationship between personality and performance in small groups. *Psychol. Bull.,* 1959, 56, 241–270.

Meuwese, W., and Oonk, S. *Performance on laboratory tasks requiring group creativity: An exploratory study.* Center for Research in Social Psychology. University of Illinois, 1960.

Meuwese, W. A. T. The effect of the leader's ability and interpersonal attitudes on group creativity under varying conditions of stress. Unpublished doctoral dissertation, University of Amsterdam, 1964.

Morris, C. G., and Fiedler, F. E. Application of a new system of interaction analysis to be relationships between leader attitudes and behavior in problem solving groups. Urbana, Ill.: Group Effectiveness Research Laboratory, University of Illinois, 1964.

Osgood C. A., Suci, G. A., and Tannenbaum, P. H. *The measurement of meaning.* Urbana, Ill.: University of Illinois Press, 1957.

Shaw, M. E. Annual Technical Report, 1962. Gainesville, Florida: University of Florida, 1962 (Mimeo.).

Stogdill, R. Personal factors associated with leadership: a survey of the literature. *J. of Psychol.* 1948, 25, 35–71.

Stogdill, R. M., and Coons, A. E. Leader behavior: its description and measurement. Columbus, Ohio: Ohio State University, *Research Monograph,* No. 88, 1957.

NOTES

1. The present paper is mainly based on research conducted under Office of Naval Research Contracts 170–106, N6-ori-07135 (Fred E. Fiedler, Principal Investigator) and RN 177–472, Noor 1834(36) (Fred E. Fiedler, C. E. Osgood, L. M. Stolurow, and H. C. Triandis, Principal Investigators). The writer is especially indebted to his colleagues, A. R. Bass, L. J. Cronbach, M. Fishbein, J. E. McGrath, W. A. T. Meuwese, C. E. Osgood, H. C. Triandis, and L. R. Tucker, who offered invaluable suggestions and criticisms at various stages of the work.

2. Another cell should be added which contains real-life groups which reject their leader. Exercise of power would be very difficult in this situation, and such a cell should be placed at the extreme negative end of the continuum. Such cases are treated in the section on validation.

3. This investigation was conducted in collaboration with Dr. J. M. Nuttin (Jr.) and his students while the author was Ford Faculty Research Fellow at the University of Louvain, 1963–1964. The experiment, undertaken with permission of Commodore L. Petitjean, then Chief of Staff of the Belgian Naval Forces, was carried out at the Centre de Formation Navale, Ste. Croix-Bruges. The writer wishes to express his especial gratitude and appreciation to the commandant of the center, Captain V. Van Laethem, who not only made the personnel and the facilities of the center available to us, but whose active participation in the planning and the execution of the project made this study possible. We are most grateful to Dr. U. Bouvier, Director of the Center for Social Studies, Ministry of Defense, to Capt. W. Cafferata, USN, the senior U.S. Naval representative of the Military Assistance and Advisory Group, Brussels, and to Cmdr. J. Robison, U.S. Naval Attache in Brussels, who provided liaison and guidance.

The Leadership Challenge—A Call for the Transformational Leader

Noel M. Tichy & David O. Ulrich

Some optimists are heralding in the age of higher productivity, a transition to a service economy, and a brighter competitive picture for U.S. corporations in world markets. We certainly would like to believe that the future will be brighter, but our temperament is more cautious. We feel that the years it took for most U.S. companies to get "fat and flabby" are not going to be reversed by a crash diet for one or two years. Whether we continue to gradually decline as a world competitive economy will largely be determined by the quality of leadership in the top echelons of our business and government organizations. Thus, it is our belief that now is the time for organizations to *change* their corporate lifestyles.

To revitalize organizations such as General Motors, American Telephone and Telegraph, General Electric, Honeywell, Ford, Burroughs, Chase Manhattan Bank, Citibank, U.S. Steel, Union Carbide, Texas Instruments, and Control Data—just to mention a few companies currently undergoing major transformations—a new brand of leadership is necessary. Instead of managers who continue to move organizations along historical tracks, the new leaders must *transform* the organizations and head them down new tracks. What is required of this kind of leader is an ability to help the organization develop a vision of what it can be, to mobilize the organization to accept and work toward achieving the new vision, and to institutionalize the changes that must last over time. Unless the creation of this breed of leaders becomes a national agenda, we are not very optimistic about the revitalization of the U.S. economy.

We call these new leaders transformational leaders, for they must create something new out of something old: out of an old vision, they must develop and communicate a new vision and get others not only to see the vision but also to commit themselves to it. Where transactional managers make only minor adjustments in the organization's mission, structure, and human resource management, transformational leaders not only make major changes in these three areas but they also evoke fundamental changes in the basic political and cultural systems of the organization. The revamping of the political and cultural systems is what most distinguishes the transformational leader from the transactional one.

Lee Iacocca: A Transformational Leader

One of the most dramatic examples of transformational leadership and organizational revitalization in the early 1980s has been the leadership of Lee Iacocca, the chairman of Chrysler Corporation. He provided the leadership to transform a company from the brink of bankruptcy to profitability. He created a vision of success and mobilized large factions of key employees toward enacting that vision while simultaneously downsizing the workforce by 60,000 employees. As a result of Iacocca's leadership, by 1984 Chrysler had earned record profits, had attained high levels of employee morale, and had helped employees generate a sense of meaning in their work.

Until Lee Iacocca took over at Chrysler, the basic internal political structure had been unchanged for decades. It was clear who reaped what benefits from the organization, how the pie was to be divided, and who could exercise what power. Nonetheless, Mr. Iacocca knew that he needed to alter these political traditions, starting with a new definition of Chrysler's link to external stakeholders. Therefore, the government was given a great deal of control over Chrysler in return for the guaranteed loan that staved off

Source: "The Leadership Challenge," by Noel M. Tichy and David O. Ulrich (1984), MIT Sloan Management Review. Reprinted by permission of the publisher.

bankruptcy. Modification of the political system required other adjustments, including the "trimming of fat" in the management ranks, limiting financial rewards for all employees, and receiving major concessions from the UAW. An indicator of a significant political shift was the inclusion of Douglas Frazer on the Chrysler Board of Directors as part of UAW concessions.

Equally dramatic was the change in the organization's cultural system. First, the company had to recognize its unique status as a recipient of a federal bailout. This bailout came with a stigma, thus Mr. Iacocca's job was to change the company's cultural values from a loser's to a winner's feeling. Still, he realized that employees were not going to be winners unless they could, in cultural norms, be more efficient and innovative than their competitors. The molding and shaping of the new culture was clearly and visibly led by Mr. Iacocca, who not only used internal communication as a vehicle to signal change but also used his own personal appearance in Chrysler ads to reinforce these changes. Quickly, the internal culture was transformed to that of a lean and hungry team looking for victory. Whether Chrysler will be able to sustain this organizational phenomenon over time remains to be seen. If it does, it will provide a solid corporate example of what Burns referred to as a transforming leader.[1]

Lee Iacocca's high visibility and notoriety may be the *important* missing elements in management today: there seems to be a paucity of transformational leader role models at all levels of the organization.

Organizational Dynamics of Change

Assumption One: Trigger Events Indicate Change Is Needed

Organizations do not change unless there is a trigger which indicates change is needed. This trigger can be as extreme as the Chrysler impending bankruptcy or as moderate as an abstract future-oriented fear that an organization may lose its competitiveness. For example, General Electric's trigger for change is a view that by 1990 the company will not be world competitive unless major changes occur in productivity, innovation, and marketing.... For General Motors, economic factors of world competition, shifting consumer preferences, and technological change have driven it to change.

In a decade of increased information, international competition, and technological advances, triggers for change have become commonplace and very pressing. However, not all potential trigger events lead to organizational responses, and not all triggers lead to change. Nonetheless, the trigger must create a *felt need* in organizational leaders. Without this felt need, the "boiled frog phenomenon" is likely to occur.

The Boiled Frog.   This phenomenon is based on a classic experiment in biology. A frog which is placed in a pan of cold water but which still has the freedom to jump out can be boiled if the temperature change is gradual, for it is not aware of the barely detectable changing heat threshold. In contrast, a frog dropped in a pot of boiling water will immediately jump out: it has a felt need to survive. In a similar vein, many organizations that are insensitive to gradually changing organizational thresholds are likely to become "boiled frogs"; they act in ignorant bliss of environmental triggers and eventually are doomed to failure. This failure, in part, is a result of the organization having no felt need to change.

Assumption Two: A Change Unleashes Mixed Feelings

A felt need for change unleashes a mix of forces, both a positive impetus for change as well as a strong negative individual and organizational resistance. These forces of resistance are generated in each of three interrelated systems—technical, political, cultural—which must be managed in the process of organizational transitions (see Table 1).[2] Individual and organizational resistance to change in these three systems must be overcome if an organization is to be revitalized.[3]

TABLE I | A LIST OF TECHNICAL, POLITICAL, AND CULTURAL SYSTEM RESISTANCES

Technical System Resistances Include:

Habit and inertia. Habit and inertia cause task-related resistance to change. Individuals who have always done things one way may not be politically or culturally resistant to change, but may have trouble, for technical reasons, changing behavior patterns. Example: some office workers may have difficulty shifting from electric typewriters to word processors.

Fear of the unknown or loss of organizational predictability. Not knowing or having difficulty predicting the future creates anxiety and hence resistance in many individuals. Example: the introduction of automated office equipment has often been accompanied by such resistances.

Sunk costs. Organizations, even when realizing that there are potential payoffs from a change, are often unable to enact a change because of the sunk costs of the organizations' resources in the old way of doing things.

Political System Resistances Include:

Powerful coalitions. A common threat is found in the conflict between the old guard and the new guard. One interpretation of the exit of Archie McGill, former president of the newly formed AT&T American Bell, is that the backlash of the old-guard coalition exacted its price on the leader of the new-guard coalition.

Resource limitations. In the days when the economic pie was steadily expanding and resources were much less limited, change was easier to enact as every part could gain—such was the nature of labor management agreements in the auto industry for decades. Now that the pie is shrinking decisions need to be made as to who shares a smaller set of resources. These zero-sum decisions are much more politically difficult. As more and more U.S. companies deal with productivity, downsizing, and divestiture, political resistance will be triggered.

Indictment quality of change. Perhaps the most significant resistance to change comes from leaders having to indict their own past decisions and behaviors to bring about a change. Example: Roger Smith, chairman and CEO of GM, must implicitly indict his own past behavior as a member of senior management when he suggests changes in GM's operations. Psychologically, it is very difficult for people to change when they were party to creating the problems they are trying to change. It is much easier for a leader from the outside, such as Lee Iacocca, who does not have to indict himself every time he says something is wrong with the organization.

Cultural System Resistances Include:

Selective perception (cultural filters). An organization's culture may highlight certain elements of the organization, making it difficult for members to conceive of other ways of doing things. An organization's culture channels that which people perceive as possible; thus, innovation may come from outsiders or deviants who are not as channeled in their perceptions.

Security based on the past. Transition requires people to give up the old ways of doing things. There is security in the past, and one of the problems is getting people to overcome the tendency to want to return to the "good old days." Example: today, there are still significant members of the white-collar workforce at GM who are waiting for the "good old days" to return.

Lack of climate for change. Organizations often vary in their conduciveness to change. Cultures that require a great deal of conformity often lack much receptivity to change. Example: GM with its years of internally developed managers must overcome a limited climate for change.

Managing technical systems refers to managing the coordination of technology, capital information, and people in order to produce products or services desired and used in the external marketplace. Managing political systems refers to managing the allocation of organizational reward such as money, status, power, and career opportunities and to exercising power so employees and departments perceive equity and justice. Managing cultural systems refers to managing the set of shared values and norms which guides the behavior of members of the organization.

When a needed change is perceived by the organizational leaders, the dominant group in the organization must experience a dissatisfaction with the status quo. . . .

The technical, political, and cultural resistances are most evident during early stages of an organizational transformation. At GM the early 1980s were marked by tremendous uncertainty concerning many technical issues such as marketing strategy, production strategy, organization design, factory automation, and development of international management. Politically, many powerful coalitions were threatened. The UAW was forced to make wage concessions and accept staffing reductions. The white-collar workers saw their benefits being cut and witnessed major layoffs within the managerial ranks. Culturally, the once dominant managerial style no longer fit the environmental pressures for change: the "GM way" was no longer the right way.

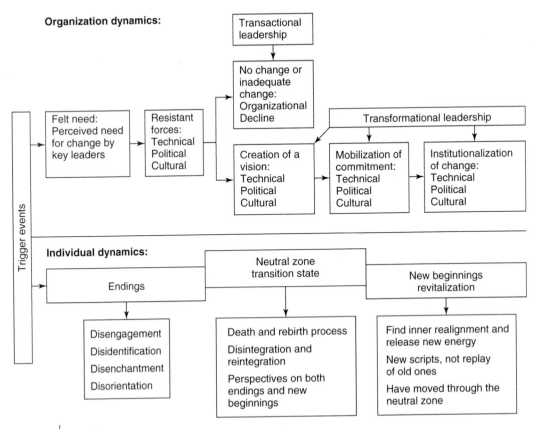

FIGURE I | TRANSFORMATIONAL LEADERSHIP

One must be wary of these resistances to change as they can lead to organizational stagnation rather than revitalization. In fact, some managers at GM in late 1983 were waiting for "the good old days" to return. Such resistance exemplifies a dysfunctional reaction to the felt need. As indicated in Figure 1, a key to whether resistant forces will lead to little or inadequate change and hence organizational decline or revitalization lies in an organization's leadership. Defensive, transactional leadership will not rechannel the resistant forces....

Assumption Three: Quick-Fix Leadership Leads to Decline

Overcoming resistance to change requires transformational leadership, not defensive, transactional managers who are in search of the one minute quick fix. The transformational leader needs to avoid the trap of simple, quick-fix solutions to major organizational problems. Today, many versions of this quick-fix mentality abound: the book, *The One Minute Manager,* has become a best seller in companies in need of basic transformation.[4] Likewise, *In Search of Excellence* has become a cookbook for change.[5] In fact, a number of CEOs have taken the eight characteristics of the "excellent" companies and are trying to blindly impose them on their organizations without first examining their appropriateness. For example, many faltering organizations try to copy such company practices as Hewlett-Packard's (HP) statement of company values. Because they read that HP has a clearly articulated statement of company values—the HP equivalent of the ten commandments—they want to create their [own] list of ten commandments....

The problem with the ten-commandments quick fix is that the CEOs tend to overlook the lesson Moses learned several thousand years ago—namely, getting the ten commandments written down and communicated is the easy part; getting them implemented is the challenge. How many thousands of years has it been since Moses received the ten commandments, and yet today there still

seems to be an implementation challenge. Transformational leadership is different from defensive, transactional leadership. Lee Iacocca did not have to read about what others did to find a recipe for his company's success.

Assumption Four: Revitalization Requires Transformational Leadership

There are three identifiable programs of activity associated with transformational leadership.

1. *Creation of a Vision.* The transformational leader must provide the organization with a vision of a desired future state. While this task may be shared with other key members of the organization, the vision remains the core responsibility of the transformational leader. The leader needs to integrate analytic, creative, intuitive, and deductive thinking. Each leader must create a vision which gives direction to the organization while being congruent with the leader's and the organization's philosophy and style.

For example, in the early 1980s at GM, after several years of committee work and staff analysis, a vision of the future was drafted which included a mission statement and eight objectives for the company. The statement was the first articulation of a strategic vision for General Motors since Alfred Sloan's leadership. This new vision was developed consistently with the leadership philosophy and style of Roger Smith. Many people were involved in carefully assessing opportunities and constraints for General Motors. Meticulous staff work culminated in committee discussions to evoke agreement and commitment to the mission statement. Through this process a vision was created which paved the way for the next phases of the transformation at GM.

At Chrysler, Lee Iacocca developed a vision without committee work or heavy staff involvement. Instead, he relied more on his intuitive and directive leadership, philosophy, and style. Both GM and Chrysler ended up with a new vision because of transformational leader proactively shaping a new organization mission and vision....

2. *Mobilization of Commitment.* Here, the organization, or at least a critical mass of it, accepts the new mission and vision and makes it happen. At General Motors, Roger Smith took his top 900 executives on a five-day retreat to share and discuss the vision. The event lasted five days not because it takes that long to share a one-paragraph mission statement and eight objectives, but because the process of evolving commitment and mobilizing support requires a great deal of dialogue and exchange. It should be noted that mobilization of commitment must go well beyond five-day retreats; nevertheless, it is in this phase that transformational leaders get deeper understanding of their *followers....* After transformational leaders create a vision and mobilize commitment, they must determine how to institutionalize the new mission and vision.

3. *Institutionalization of Change.* Organizations will not be revitalized unless new patterns of behavior within the organization are adopted. Transformational leaders need to transmit their vision into reality, their mission into action, their philosophy into practice. New realities, action, and practices must be shared throughout the organization. Alterations in communication, decision making, and problem-solving systems are tools through which transitions are shared so that visions become a reality. At a deeper level, institutionalization of change requires shaping and reinforcement of a new culture that fits with the revitalized organization. The human resource systems of selection, development, appraisal, and reward are major levers for institutionalizing change.

Individual Dynamics of Change

The previous section outlined requisite processes for organizational revitalization. Although organizational steps are necessary, they are not sufficient in creating and implementing change. In managing transitions, a more problematic set of forces which focuses on individual psychodynamics of change must be understood and managed. Major transitions unleash powerful

conflicting forces in people. The change invokes simultaneous positive and negative personal feelings of fear and hope, anxiety and relief, pressure and stimulation, leaving the old and accepting a new direction, loss of meaning and new meaning, threat to self-esteem and new sense of value. The challenge for transformational leaders is to recognize these mixed emotions, act to help people move from negative to positive emotions, and mobilize and focus energy that is necessary for individual renewal and organizational revitalization.

Figure 1 provides a set of concepts for understanding the individual dynamics of transitions. The concepts, drawn from the work by Bridges, propose a three-phase process of individual change: first come endings, followed by neutral zones, and then new beginnings.[6] During each of these phases, an identifiable set of psychological tasks can be identified which individuals need to successfully complete in order to accept change.

The Three-Phase Process

Endings.   All individual transitions start with endings. Endings must be accepted and understood before transitions can begin. Employees who refuse to accept the fact that traditional behaviors have ended will be unable to adopt new behaviors. The first task is to disengage, which often accompanies a physical transaction. For example, when transferring from one job to another, individuals must learn to accept the new physical setting and disengage from the old position: when transferred employees continually return to visit former colleagues, this is a sign that they have inadequately disengaged. The second task is to disidentify. Individual self-identity is often tied to a job position in such a way that when a plant manager is transferred to corporate staff to work in the marketing department, he or she must disidentify with the plant and its people and with the self-esteem felt as a plant manager. At a deeper personal level, individual transactions require disenchantment. Disenchantment entails recognizing that the enchantment or positive feelings associated with past situations will not be possible to replicate in the future.... Finally, individuals need to experience and work through disorientation which reflects the loss of familiar trappings. As mature organizations become revitalized, individuals must disengage, disidentify, disenchant, and disorient with past practices and discover in new organizations a new sense of worth or value.

To help individuals cope with endings, transformational leaders need to replace past glories with future opportunities. However, leaders must also acknowledge individual resistances and senses of loss in a transitional period while encouraging employees to face and accept failures as learning opportunities. Holding on to past accomplishments and memories without coming to grips with failure and the need to change may be why companies such as W. T. Grant, International Harvester, and Braniff were unsuccessful at revitalization. There is a sense of dying in all endings, and it does not help to treat transactions as if the past can be buried without effort. Yet, one should see the past as providing new directions.

Neutral Zone.   The key to individuals being able to fully change may be in the second phase which Bridges terms the neutral zone.[7] This phase can be interpreted as a seemingly unproductive "time out" when individuals feel disconnected from people and things of the past and emotionally unconnected with the present. In reality, this phase is a time of reorientation where individuals complete endings and begin new patterns of behavior. Often Western culture, especially in the U.S., avoids this experience and treats the neutral zone like a busy street, to be crossed as fast as possible and certainly not a place to contemplate and experience. However, running across the neutral zone too hurriedly does not allow the ending to occur nor the new beginning to properly start. A death and rebirth process is necessary so that organizational members can work through the disintegration and reintegration. To pass through the neutral zone requires taking the time and thought to gain perspective on both the endings— what went wrong, why it needs to be changed, and

what must be overcome in both attitude and behavioral change—and the new beginning— what the new priorities are, why they are needed, and what new attitudes and behaviors will be required. It is in this phase that the most skillful transformational leadership is called upon....

Failure to lead individuals through the neutral zone may result in aborted new beginnings. In 1983, International Harvester appeared to be stuck in the neutral zone. In order for International Harvester to make a new beginning, it must enable people to find a new identification with the future organization while accepting the end of the old organization. Such a transformation has successfully occurred at Chrysler Corporation where morale and esprit de corps grew with the new vision implanted by Lee Iacocca. In the end, organizational revitalization can only occur if individuals accept past failures and engage in new behaviors and attitudes.

New Beginnings.   After individuals accept endings by working through neutral zones, they are able to work with new enthusiasm and commitment. New beginnings are characterized by employees learning from the past rather than reveling in it, looking for new scripts rather than acting out old ones, and being positive and excited about current and future work opportunities rather than dwelling on past successes or failures. When Mr. Iacocca implemented his vision at Chrysler, many long-term employees discovered new beginnings. They saw the new Chrysler as an opportunity to succeed, and they worked with a renewed vigor.

What Qualities Do Transformational Leaders Possess?

So what does it take to transform an organization's technical, political, and cultural systems? The transformational leader must possess a deep understanding, whether it be intuitive or learned, of organizations and their place both in society at large and in the lives of individuals. The ability to build a new institution requires the kind of political dialogue our founding fathers had when

Jefferson, Hamilton, Adams, and others debated issues of justice, equity, separation of powers, checks and balances, and freedom. This language may sound foreign to corporate settings but when major organization revitalization is being undertaken, all of these concepts merit some level of examination. At Chrysler, issues of equity, justice, power, and freedom underlay many of Mr. Iacocca's decisions. Thus, as a start, transformational leaders need to understand concepts of equity, power, freedom, and the dynamics of decision making. In addition to modifying systems, transformational leaders must understand and realign cultural systems.

In addition to managing political and cultural systems, transformational leaders must make difficult decisions quickly. Leaders need to know when to push and when to back off. Finally, transformational leaders are often seen as creators of their own luck. These leaders seize opportunities and know when to act so that casual observers may perceive luck as a plausible explanation for their success; whereas, in reality it is a transformational leader who knows when to jump and when not to jump. Again, Mr. Iacocca can be viewed either as a very lucky person or as the possessor of a great ability to judge when to act and when not to act.

The Significance of Corporate Cultures

Much has been written about organizational cultures in recent years.[8] ...

Culture plays two central roles in organizations. First, it provides organizational members with a way of understanding and making sense of events and symbols. Thus, when employees are confronted with certain complex problems, they "know" how to approach them the "right" way. Like the Eskimos who have a vocabulary that differentiates the five types of snow, organizations create vocabularies to describe how things are done in the organization. At IBM, it is very clear to all insiders how to form a task force and to solve problems since task forces and problem solving are a way of life in IBM's culture.

Second, culture provides meaning. It embodies a set of values which helps justify why certain behaviors are encouraged at the exclusion of other behaviors. Companies with strong cultures have been able to commit people to the organization and have them identify very personally and closely with the organization's success. Superficially, this is seen in the "hoopla" activities associated with an IBM sales meeting, a Tupperware party, or an Amway distributor meeting. Outsiders often ridicule such activities, yet they are part of the process by which some successful companies manage cultural meaning. On one level, corporate culture is analogous to rituals carried out in religious groups. The key point in assessing culture is to realize that in order to transform an organization the culture that provides meaning must be assessed and revamped. The transformational leader needs to articulate new values and norms and then to use multiple change levers ranging from role modeling, symbolic acts, creation of rituals, and revamping of human resource systems and management processes to support new cultural messages.

CONCLUSION

Based on the premise that the pressure for basic organizational change will intensify and not diminish, we strongly believe that transformational leadership, not transactional management, is required for revitalizing our organizations. Ultimately, it is up to our leaders to choose the right kind of leadership and corporate lifestyle.

NOTES

1. See J. M. Burns, *Leadership* (New York: Harper & Row, 1978).
2. See N. M. Tichy, *Managing strategic change: technical, political and cultural dynamics* (New York: John Wiley & Sons, 1983).
3. Ibid.
4. See K. H. Blanchard and S. Johnson, *The one minute manager* (New York: Berkeley Books, 1982).
5. See T. J. Peters and R. J. Waterman, Jr., *In search of excellence* (New York: Harper & Row, 1982).
6. See W. Bridges, *Making sense of life's transitions* (New York: Addison-Wesley, 1980).
7. Ibid.
8. See: T. E. Deal and A. A. Kennedy, *Corporate cultures* (Reading, MA: Addison-Wesley, 1982); "Corporate culture: the hard-to-change values that spell success or failure," *Business Week*, 27 October 1980, pp. 148–160; W. Ulrich, "HRM and culture: history, rituals, and myths," *Human Resource Management* *(23/2)* Summer 1984.

The Learning Leader as Culture Manager
Edgar H. Schein

Leadership can occur anywhere in the organization. Leadership is the attitude and motivation to examine and manage culture. Accomplishing this goal is more difficult lower down in the organization but by no means impossible in that subcultures can be managed just as can overall organizational cultures.

The issues that make the most difference to the kind of leadership required are twofold. First, different stages of organizational development require different kinds of culture management. Second, different strategic issues require a focus on different kinds of cultural dimensions. Each of these points is briefly examined below.

Leadership in Culture Creation

In a growing organization leaders externalize their own assumptions and embed them gradually and consistently in the mission, goals, structures, and working procedures of the group. Whether we call these basic assumptions the guiding beliefs, the theories-in-use, the mental models, the basic principles, or the guiding visions on which founders operate, there is little question that they become major elements of the organization's emerging culture (for example, Argyris, 1976; Bennis, 1989; Davis, 1984; Donaldson and Lorsch, 1983; Dyer, 1986; Kotter and Heskett, 1992; Pettigrew, 1979; Schein, 1983).

In a rapidly changing world, the learning leader/founder must not only have vision but must be able to impose it and to develop it further as external circumstances change. Inasmuch as the new members of an organization arrive with prior organizational and cultural experiences, a common set of assumptions can only be forged by clear and consistent messages as the group encounters and survives its own crises. The culture creation leader therefore needs persistence and patience, yet as a learner must be flexible and ready to change.

As groups and organizations develop, certain key emotional issues arise. These have to do with dependence on the leader, with peer relationships, and with how to work effectively. Leadership is needed to help the group identify the issues and deal with them. During this process leaders must often absorb and contain the anxiety that is unleashed when things do not work as they should (Hirschhorn, 1988; Schein, 1983). Leaders may not have the answer, but they must provide temporary stability and emotional reassurance while the answer is being worked out. This anxiety-containing function is especially relevant during periods of learning, when old habits must be given up before new ones are learned. Moreover, if the world is increasingly changing, such anxiety may be perpetual, requiring learning leaders to assume a perpetual supportive role. The traumas of growth appear to be so constant and so powerful that unless a strong leader takes the role of anxiety and risk absorber, the group cannot get through its early stages of growth and fails. Being in an ownership position helps because everyone then realizes that the founder is in fact taking a greater personal financial risk; however, ownership does not automatically create the ability to absorb anxiety. For many leaders this is one of the most important things they have to learn.

When leaders launch new enterprises, they must be mindful of the power they have to impose on those enterprises their own assumptions about what is right and proper, how the world works, and how things should be done. Leaders should not apologize for or be cautious about their assumptions. Rather, it is intrinsic to the leadership role to create order out of chaos, and leaders are expected to provide their own assumptions as an initial road map into the uncertain future. The more aware leaders are of this process, the more consistent and effective they can be in implementing it.

The process of culture creation, embedding, and reinforcement brings with it problems as well as solutions. Many organizations survive and grow but at the same time operate inconsistently or do things that seem contradictory. One explanation of this phenomenon that has been pointed out repeatedly is that leaders not only embed in their organizations what they intend consciously to get across, but they also convey their own inner conflicts and the inconsistencies in their own personal makeup (Schein, 1983; Kets de Vries and Miller, 1984; Miller, 1990). The most powerful signal to which subordinates respond is what catches leaders' attention consistently, particularly what arouses them emotionally. But many of the things to which leaders respond emotionally reflect not so much their conscious intentions as their unconscious conflicts. The organization then either develops assumptions around these inconsistencies and conflicts and they become part of the culture, or the leader gradually loses a position of influence if the behavior begins to be seen as too disruptive or actually destructive. In extreme cases the organization isolates or ejects the founder. In doing so, however, it is not rejecting all of the founder's assumptions but only those that are inconsistent with the core assumptions on which the organization was built.

The period of culture creation, therefore, puts an additional burden on founders—to obtain enough self-insight to avoid unwittingly undermining their own creations. Founding leaders often find it difficult to recognize that the very qualities that made them successful initially, their strong convictions, can become sources of difficulty later on and that they also must learn and grow as their organizations grow. Such insights become especially important when organizations face issues of leadership succession because succession discussions force into the open aspects of the culture that may not have been previously recognized.

What all of this means for leaders of developing organizations is that they must have tremendous self-insight and recognize their own role not only in creating the culture but also their responsibility in embedding and developing culture. Inasmuch as the culture is the primary source of identity for young organizations, the culture creation and development process must be handled sensitively with full understanding of the anxieties that are unleashed when identity is challenged.

Leadership at Organizational Midlife

As the organization develops a substantial history of its own, its culture becomes more of a cause than an effect. As subgroups develop their own subcultures, the opportunities for constructive use of cultural diversity and the problems of integration both become greater. The leader must be able to pay attention to diversity and assess clearly how much of it is useful for further organizational development and how much of it is potentially dysfunctional. The culture is now much less tied to the leader's own personality, which makes it easier to assess objectively, though there are likely to be sacred cows, holdovers from the founding period, that have to be delicately handled.

The leader at this stage must be able to detect how the culture influences the strategy, structure, procedures, and ways in which the group members relate to one another. Culture is a powerful influence on members' perceptions, thinking, and feeling, and these predispositions, along with situational factors, influence members' behavior. Because culture serves an important anxiety-reducing function, members cling to it even if it becomes dysfunctional in relationship to environmental opportunities and constraints.

Leaders at this stage need diagnostic skill to figure out not only what the cultural influences are, but also what their impact is on the organization's ability to change and learn. Whereas founding leaders most need self-insight, midlife leaders most need the ability to decipher the surrounding culture and subcultures. To help the organization evolve into whatever will make it most effective in the future, leaders must also have culture management skills. In some instances this may mean increasing cultural diversity, allowing some of the uniformity that may have been built up in the growth stage to erode. In other instances it may mean pulling together a culturally diverse set of organizational units and attempting to impose new common assumptions on them. In either case the leader needs (1) to be able to analyze the culture in sufficient detail to know which cultural assumptions can aid and which ones will hinder the fulfillment of the organizational mission and (2) to possess the intervention skills to make desired changes happen.

Most of the prescriptive analyses of how to maintain the organization's effectiveness through this period emphasize that the leader must have certain insights, clear vision, and the skills to articulate, communicate, and implement the vision, but these analyses say nothing about how a given organization can find and install such a leader. In U.S. organizations in particular, the outside board members probably play a critical role in this process. If the organization has had a strong founding culture, however, its board may be composed exclusively of people who share the founder's vision. Consequently, real changes in direction may not become possible until the organization experiences serious survival difficulties and begins to search for a person with different assumptions to lead it.

One area to explore further here is the CEO's own role in succession. Can the leader of a midlife organization perceive the potential dysfunctions of some aspects of the culture to a sufficient extent to ensure that his or her successor will be able to move the culture in an appropriate new direction? CEOs have a great deal of power to influence the choice of their successor. Do they use that power wisely in terms of cultural issues? For example, it is alleged that one of the main reasons why Reginald Jones as CEO of General Electric "chose" Jack Welch to be his successor was because he recognized in Welch a person who

would create the kinds of changes that were necessary for GE to remain viable. Similarly, Steve Jobs "chose" John Sculley to head Apple even though at some level he must have sensed that this choice might eventually lead to the kind of conflict that in the end forced Jobs to leave. The ultimate paradox here is that truly learning leaders may have to face the conclusion that they must replace themselves, that they do not have the vision needed to bring the midlife organization into alignment with a rapidly changing world.

Leadership in Mature and Potentially Declining Organizations

In the mature stage if the organization has developed a strong unifying culture, that culture now defines even what is to be thought of as leadership, what is heroic or sinful behavior, and how authority and power are to be allocated and managed. Thus, what leadership has created now either blindly perpetuates itself or creates new definitions of leadership, which may not even include the kinds of entrepreneurial assumptions that launched the organization in the first place. The first problem of the mature and possibly declining organization, then, is to find a process to empower a potential leader who may have enough insight to overcome some of the constraining cultural assumptions.

What the leader must do at this point in the organization's history depends on the degree to which the culture of the organization has, in fact, enabled the group to adapt to its environmental realities. If the culture has not facilitated adaptation, the organization either will not survive or will find a way to change its culture. If it is to change its culture, it must be led by someone who can, in effect, break the tyranny of the old culture. This requires not only the insight and diagnostic skill to determine what the old culture is, but to realize what alternative assumptions are available and how to start a change process toward their acceptance.

Leaders of mature organizations must, as has been argued repeatedly, make themselves sufficiently marginal in their own organization to be able to perceive its assumptions objectively and nondefensively. They must, therefore, find many ways to be exposed to their external environment and, thereby facilitate their own learning. If they cannot learn new assumptions themselves, they will not be able to perceive what is possible in their organizations. Even worse, they may destroy innovative efforts that arise within their organizations if those innovative efforts involve countercultural assumptions.

Leaders capable of such managed culture change can come from inside the organization if they have acquired objectivity and insight into elements of the culture. Such culture objectivity appears to be related to having had a nonconventional career or exposure to many subcultures within the organization (Kotter and Heskett, 1992). However, the formally designated senior managers of a given organization may not be willing or able to provide such culture change leadership. Leadership then may have to come from other boundary spanners in the organization or from outsiders. It may even come from a number of people in the organization, in which case it makes sense to talk of turnaround teams or multiple leadership.

If a leader is imposed from the outside, she or he must have the skill to diagnose accurately what the culture of the organization is, what elements are well adapted and what elements are problematic for future adaptation, and how to change that which needs changing. In other words the leader must be a skilled change manager who first learns what the present state of the culture is, unfreezes it, redefines and changes it, and then refreezes the new assumptions. Talented turnaround managers seem to be able to manage all phases of such changes, but sometimes different leaders will be involved in the different steps over a considerable period of time. They will use all the mechanisms previously discussed in the appropriate combinations to get the job done provided that they have the authority and power to use extreme measures, such as replacing the people who perpetuate the old cultural assumptions.

In summary, leaders play a critical role at each developmental stage of an organization, but that role differs as a function of the stage. Much of what leaders do is to perpetually diagnose the particular assumptions of the culture and figure out how to use those assumptions constructively or to change them if they are constraints.

Leadership and Culture in Strategy Formulation

Many companies have found that they or their consultants can think of new strategies that make sense from a financial, product, or marketing point of view, yet they cannot implement those strategies because such implementation requires assumptions, values, and ways of working that are too far out of line with the organization's existing assumptions. In some cases, the organization cannot even conceive of certain strategic options because they are too out of line with shared assumptions about the mission of the organization and its way of working, what Lorsch (1985) has aptly called "strategic myopia."

...We must remember that cultural assumptions are the product of past successes. As a result they are increasingly taken for granted and operate as silent filters on what is perceived and thought about. If the organization's environment changes and new responses are required, the danger is that the changes will not be noticed or, even if noticed, that the organization will not be able to adapt because of embedded routines based on past success. Culture constrains strategy by limiting what the CEO and other senior managers are able to think about and what they perceive in the first place.

One of the critical roles of learning leadership, then, is first of all to notice changes in the environment and then to figure out what needs to be done to remain adaptive. I am defining leadership in this context in terms of the role, not the position. The CEO or other senior managers may or may not be able to fulfill the leadership role, and leadership in the sense that I am defining it can occur anywhere in the organization. However, if real change and learning are to take place, it is probably necessary that the CEO or other very senior managers be able to be leaders in this sense.

Leaders must be somewhat marginal and must be somewhat embedded in the organization's external environment to fulfill this role adequately. At the same time, leaders must be well connected to those parts of the organization that are themselves well connected to the environment—sales, purchasing, marketing, public relations and legal, finance, and R & D. Leaders must be able to listen to disconfirming information coming from these sources and to assess the implications for the future of the organization. Only when they truly understand what is happening and what will be required in the way of organizational change can they begin to take action in initiating a learning process.

Much has been said about the need for vision in leaders, but too little has been said about their need to listen, to absorb, to search the environment for trends, and to build the organization's capacity to learn. Especially at the strategic level, the ability to see and acknowledge the full complexity of problems becomes critical. The ability to acknowledge complexity may also imply the willingness and emotional strength to admit uncertainty and to embrace experimentation and possible errors as the only way to learn. In our obsession with leadership vision, we may have made it possible for learning leaders to admit that their vision is not clear and that the whole organization will have to learn together. Moreover, as I have repeatedly argued, vision in a mature organization only helps when the organization has already been disconfirmed and members feel anxious and in need of a solution. Much of what learning leaders must do occurs before vision even becomes relevant.

To summarize, the critical roles of leadership in strategy formulation and implementation are (1) to perceive accurately and in depth what is happening in the environment, (2) to create enough disconfirming information to motivate the organization to change without creating too much anxiety, (3) to provide psychological safety by either providing a vision of how to change and in what direction or by creating a process of visioning that allows the organization itself to find a path, (4) to acknowledge uncertainty, (5) to embrace errors in the learning process as inevitable and desirable, and (6) to manage all phases of the change process, including especially the management of anxiety as some cultural assumptions are given up and new learning begins. . . .

Implications for the Selection and Development of Leaders

A dynamic analysis of organizational culture makes it clear that leadership is intertwined with culture formation, evolution, transformation, and destruction. Culture is created in the first instance by the actions of leaders; culture is embedded and strengthened by leaders. When culture becomes dysfunctional, leadership is needed to help the group unlearn some of its cultural assumptions and learn new assumptions. Such transformations sometimes require what amounts to conscious and deliberate destruction of cultural elements. This in turn requires the ability to surmount one's own taken-for-granted assumptions, seeing what is needed to ensure the health and survival of the group, and orchestrating events and processes that enable the group to evolve toward new cultural assumptions. Without leadership in this sense, groups will not be able to adapt to changing environmental conditions. Let us summarize what is really needed to be a leader in this sense.

Perception and Insight

First, the leader must be able to perceive the problem, to have insight into himself or herself and into the culture and its dysfunctional elements. Such boundary-spanning perception can be difficult because it requires one to see one's own weaknesses, to perceive that one's own defenses not only help in managing anxiety but can also hinder one's efforts to be effective. Successful architects of change must have a high degree of objectivity about themselves and their own organizations, and such objectivity results from spending portions of their careers in diverse settings that permit them to compare and contrast different cultures. International experience is therefore one of the most powerful ways of learning.

Individuals often are aided in becoming objective about themselves through counseling and psychotherapy. One might conjecture that leaders can benefit from comparable processes such as training and development programs that emphasize experiential learning and self-assessment. From this perspective one of the most important functions of outside consultants or board members is to provide the kind of counseling that produces cultural insight. It is therefore far more important for the consultant to help the leader figure out for himself or herself what is going on and what to do than to provide recommendations on what the organization should do. The consultant also can serve as a "cultural therapist," helping the leader figure out what the culture is and what parts of it are more or less adaptive.

Motivation

Leadership requires not only insight into the dynamics of the culture but the motivation and skill to intervene in one's own cultural process. To change any elements of the culture, leaders must be willing to unfreeze their own organization. Unfreezing requires disconfirmation, a process that is inevitably painful for many. The leader must find a way to say to his or her own organization that things are not all right and, if necessary, must enlist the aid of outsiders in getting this message across. Such willingness requires a great ability to be concerned for the organization above and beyond the self, to communicate dedication or commitment to the group above and beyond self-interest.

If the boundaries of organization become looser, a further motivational issue arises in that it is less and less clear where a leader's ultimate loyalty should lie—with the organization, with industry, with country, or with some broader professional community whose ultimate responsibility is to the globe and to all of humanity.

Emotional Strength

Unfreezing an organization requires the creation of psychological safety, which means that the leader must have the emotional strength to absorb much of the anxiety that change brings with it and the ability to remain supportive to the organization through the transition phase even if group members become angry and obstructive. The leader is likely to be the target of anger and criticism because, by definition, he or she must challenge some of what the group has taken for granted. This may involve closing down the company division that was the original source of the company's growth and the basis of many employees' sense of pride and identity. It may involve laying off or retiring loyal, dedicated employees and old friends. Worst of all, it may involve the message that some of the founder's most cherished assumptions are wrong in the contemporary context. It is here that dedication and commitment are especially needed to demonstrate to the organization that the leader genuinely cares about the welfare of the total organization even as parts of it come under challenge. The leader must remember that giving up a cultural element requires one to take some risk, the risk that one will be very anxious and in the end worse off, and yet the leader must have the strength to forge the way into this unknown territory.

Ability to Change the Cultural Assumptions

If an assumption is to be given up, it must be replaced or redefined in another form, and it is the burden of leadership to make that happen. In other words, the leader must have the ability to induce cognitive redefinition by articulating and selling new visions and concepts. The leader must be able to bring to the surface, review, and change some of the group's basic assumptions....

Ability to Create Involvement and Participation

A paradox of culture change leadership is that the leader must be able not only to lead but also to listen, to emotionally involve the group in achieving its own insights into its cultural dilemmas, and to be genuinely participative in his or her approach to learning and change. The leaders of social, religious, or political movements can rely on personal charisma and let the followers do what they will. In an organization, however, the leader has to work with the group that exists at the moment, because he or she is dependent on the group members to carry out the organization's mission. The leader must recognize that, in the end, cognitive redefinition must occur inside the heads of many members, and that will happen only if they are actively involved in the process. The whole organization must achieve some degree of insight and develop motivation to change before any real change will occur, and the leader must create this involvement.

The ability to involve others and to listen to them also protects leaders from attempting to change things that should not be changed. When leaders are brought in from the outside this becomes especially important because some of the assumptions operating in the organization may not fit the leader's own assumptions yet be critical to the organization's success. To illustrate the kinds of mistakes that are possible, we need remember only the period in the Atari Company's history when Warner Communications, the parent company, decided to improve Atari's marketing by bringing in as president an experienced marketing executive from the food industry. This executive brought with him the assumption that the key to success is high motivation and high rewards based on individual performance. He created and imposed an incentive system designed to select the engineers who were doing the best job in inventing and designing new computer games and gave them large monetary rewards. Soon some of the best engineers were leaving, and the company was getting into technical difficulty. What was wrong?

The new executive had created and articulated clear symbols, and everyone had rallied around them. Apparently, what was wrong was the assumption that the incentives and rewards should be based on individual effort. What the president failed to understand, coming from the food industry with its individualistic product management orientation, was that the computer games were designed by groups and teams and that the engineers considered the assignment of individual responsibility to be neither possible nor necessary.

They were happy being group members and would have responded to group incentives, but unfortunately, the symbol chosen was the wrong symbol from this point of view. The engineers also noted that the president, with his nontechnical background, was not adept at choosing the best engineers, because their key assumption was that "best" was the product of group effort, not individual brilliance. Given the incompatible assumptions, it is no surprise that the president did not last long. Unfortunately, damage in terms of the loss of employees and in esprit had been done.

Ability to Learn a New Culture

Culture change leaders often have to take over a company in which they did not previously have any experience. If they are to diagnose and possibly change the culture they have entered, it is, of course, mandatory that they first learn what the essence of that culture is. This point raises the question of how much an individual can learn that is totally new. My hypothesis, based on various streams of research on leadership and management, is that leaders can cross boundaries and enter new organizational cultures fairly easily if they stay within a given industry, as defined by a core technology. A manager growing up in one chemical company can probably become the successful CEO of another chemical company and can learn the culture of that company. What appears to be much more difficult is to cross industry or national boundaries, because cognitive frames that are built up early in the manager's career are fundamentally more embedded. The ability of a John Sculley to become a successful leader of Apple is unusual. . . .

In any case, the leader coming into a new organization must be very sensitive to his or her own need to truly understand the culture before assessing it and possibly changing it. A period of learning lasting a year or more, if the situation allows that much time, is probably necessary. If the situation is more critical, the leader could speed up his or her own learning by systematically involving the layers of the organization below him or her in culture deciphering exercises. . . .

SUMMARY AND CONCLUSIONS

It seems clear that the leaders of the future will have to be perpetual learners. This will require (1) new levels of perception and insight into the realities of the world and also into themselves; (2) extraordinary levels of motivation to go through the inevitable pain of learning and change, especially in a world with looser boundaries in which one's own loyalties become more and more difficult to define; (3) the emotional strength to manage their own and others; anxiety as learning and change become more and more a way of life; (4) new skills in analyzing and changing cultural assumptions; (5) the willingness and ability to involve others and elicit their participation; and (6) the ability to learn the assumptions of a whole new organizational culture.

Learning and change cannot be imposed on people. Their involvement and participation are needed diagnosing what is going on, figuring out what to do, and actually doing it. The more turbulent, ambiguous, and out of control the world becomes, the more the learning process will have to be shared by all the members of the social unit doing the learning. If the leaders of today want to create organizational cultures that will themselves be more amenable to learning they will have to set the example by becoming learners themselves and involving others in the learning process.

The essence of that learning process will be to give organizational culture its due. Can we as individual members of organizations and occupations, as managers, teachers, researchers, and, sometimes, leaders recognize how deeply our own perceptions, thoughts, and feelings are culturally determined? Ultimately, we cannot achieve the cultural humility required to live in a turbulent culturally diverse world unless we can see cultural assumptions within ourselves. In the end, cultural understanding and cultural learning start with self-insight.

REFERENCES

Argyris, C. *Increasing leadership effectiveness.* New York: Wiley-Interscience, 1976.

Bennis, W. *On becoming a leader.* Reading, Mass.: Addison-Wesley, 1989.

Davis, S. M. *Managing corporate culture.* New York: Ballinger, 1984.

Donaldson, G., and Lorsch, J. W. *Decision making at the top.* New York: Basic Books, 1983.

Dyer, W. G., Jr. *Culture change in family firms.* San Francisco: Jossey-Bass, 1986.

Hirschhorn, L. *The workplace within: psychodynamics of organizational life.* Cambridge, Mass.: MIT Press, 1988.

Kets de Vries, M. F. R., and Miller, D. *The neurotic organization: diagnosing and changing counterproductive styles of management.* San Francisco: Jossey-Bass, 1984.

Kotter, J. P., and Heskett, J. L. *Corporate culture and performance.* New York: Free Press, 1992.

Lorsch, J. W. "Strategic myopia: culture as an invisible barrier to change." In R. H. Kilmann, M. J. Saxton, R. Serpa, and others, *Gaining Control of the Corporate Culture.* San Francisco: Jossey-Bass, 1985.

Miller, D. *The Icarus paradox.* New York: Harper & Row, 1990.

Pettigrew, A. M. "On studying organizational cultures." *Administrative Science Quarterly,* 1979, 24, 570–581.

Schein, E. H. "The role of the founder in creating organizational culture." *Organizational Dynamics,* Summer 1983, pp. 13–28.

What Makes a Leader?

Daniel Goleman

Every businessperson knows a story about a highly intelligent, highly skilled executive who was promoted into a leadership position only to fail at the job. And they also know a story about someone with solid—but not extraordinary—intellectual abilities and technical skills who was promoted into a similar position and then soared.

Such anecdotes support the widespread belief that identifying individuals with the "right stuff" to be leaders is more art than science. After all, the personal styles of superb leaders vary: some leaders are subdued and analytical; others shout their manifestos from the mountaintops. And just as important, different situations call for different types of leadership. Most mergers need a sensitive negotiator at the helm, whereas many turnarounds require a more forceful authority.

I have found, however, that the most effective leaders are alike in one crucial way: they all have a high degree of what has come to be known as *emotional intelligence*. It's not that IQ and technical skills are irrelevant. They do matter, but mainly as "threshold capabilities"; that is, they are the entry-level requirements for executive positions. But my research, along with other recent studies, clearly shows that emotional intelligence is the sine qua non of leadership. Without it, a person can have the best training in the world, an incisive, analytical mind, and an endless supply of smart ideas, but he still won't make a great leader.

In the course of the past year, my colleagues and I have focused on how emotional intelligence operates at work. We have examined the relationship between emotional intelligence and effective performance, especially in leaders. And we have observed how emotional intelligence shows itself on the job. How can you tell if someone has high emotional intelligence, for example, and how can you recognize it in yourself? In the following pages, we'll explore these questions, taking each of the components of emotional intelligence—self-awareness, self-regulation, motivation, empathy, and social skill—in turn.

Evaluating Emotional Intelligence

Most large companies today have employed trained psychologists to develop what are known as "competency models" to aid them in identifying, training, and promoting likely stars in the leadership firmament. The psychologists have also developed such models for lower-level positions. And in recent years, I have analyzed competency models from 188 companies, most of which were large and global and included the likes of Lucent Technologies, British Airways, and Credit Suisse.

In carrying out this work, my objective was to determine which personal capabilities drove outstanding performance within these organizations, and to what degree they did so. I grouped capabilities into three categories: purely technical skills like accounting and business planning; cognitive abilities like analytical reasoning; and competencies demonstrating emotional intelligence such as the ability to work with others and effectiveness in leading change.

To create some of the competency models, psychologists asked senior managers at the companies to identify the capabilities that typified the organization's most outstanding leaders. To create other models, the psychologists used objective criteria such as a division's profitability to differentiate the star performers at senior levels within their organizations from the average ones. Those individuals were then extensively interviewed and tested, and their capabilities were compared. This process resulted in the creation of lists of ingredients for highly effective leaders. The lists ranged in length from 7 to 15 items and included such ingredients as initiative and strategic vision.

When I analyzed all this data, I found dramatic results. To be sure, intellect was a driver of

Source: What Makes a Leader? by Daniel Goleman. Nov–Dec 1998, pp. 93–102. ©1999 by Harvard Business School Publishing. Reprinted by permission of the publisher.

THE FIVE COMPONENTS OF EMOTIONAL INTELLIGENCE AT WORK

	Definition	Hallmarks
Self-Awareness	the ability to recognize and understand your moods, emotions, and drives, as well as their effect on others	self-confidence realistic self-assessment self-deprecating sense of humor
Self-Regulation	the ability to control or redirect disruptive impulses and moods the propensity to suspend judgment— to think before acting	trustworthiness and integrity comfort with ambiguity openness to change
Motivation	a passion to work for reasons that go beyond money or status a propensity to pursue goals with energy and persistence	strong drive to achieve optimism, even in the face of failure organizational commitment
Empathy	the ability to understand the emotional makeup of other people skill in treating people according to their emotional reactions	expertise in building and retaining talent cross-cultural sensitivity service to clients and customers
Social Skill	proficiency in managing relationships and building networks an ability to find common ground and build rapport	effectiveness in leading change persuasiveness expertise in building and leading teams

outstanding performance. Cognitive skills such as big-picture thinking and long-term vision were particularly important. But when I calculated the ratio of technical skills, IQ, and emotional intelligence as ingredients of excellent performance, emotional intelligence proved to be twice as important as the others for jobs at all levels.

Moreover, my analysis showed that emotional intelligence played an increasingly important role at the highest levels of the company, where differences in technical skills are of negligible importance. In other words, the higher the rank of a person considered to be a star performer, the more emotional intelligence capabilities showed up as the reason for his or her effectiveness. When I compared star performers with average ones in senior leadership positions, nearly 90% of the difference in their profiles was attributable to emotional intelligence factors rather than cognitive abilities.

Other researchers have confirmed that emotional intelligence not only distinguishes outstanding leaders but can also be linked to strong performance. The findings of the late David McClelland, the renowned researcher in human and organizational behavior, are a good example. In a 1996 study of a global food and beverage company, McClelland found that when senior managers had a critical mass of emotional intelligence capabilities, their divisions outperformed yearly earnings goals by 20%. Meanwhile, division leaders without that critical mass underperformed by almost the same amount. McClelland's findings, interestingly, held as true in the company's U.S. divisions as in its divisions in Asia and Europe.

In short, the numbers are beginning to tell us a persuasive story about the link between a company's success and the emotional intelligence of its leaders. And just as important, research is also demonstrating that people can, if they take the right approach, develop their emotional intelligence. [See the insert "Can Emotional Intelligence Be Learned?"]

Self-Awareness

Self-awareness is the first component of emotional intelligence—which makes sense when one considers that the Delphic oracle gave the advice to "know thyself" thousands of years ago. Self-awareness means having a deep understanding of one's emotions, strengths, weaknesses, needs, and drives. People with strong self-awareness are neither overly critical nor unrealistically hopeful. Rather, they are honest—with themselves and with others.

People who have a high degree of self-awareness recognize how their feelings affect them, other people, and their job performance. Thus a self-aware person who knows that tight deadlines bring out the worst in him plans his time carefully and gets his work done well in advance. Another person with high self-awareness will be able to work with a demanding client. She will understand the client's impact on her moods and the deeper reasons for her frustration. "Their trivial demands take us away from the real work that needs to be done," she might explain. And she will go one step further and turn her anger into something constructive.

Self-awareness extends to a person's understanding of his or her values and goals. Someone who is highly self-aware knows where he is headed and why; so, for example, he will be able to be firm in turning down a job offer that is tempting financially but does not fit with his principles or long-term goals. A person who lacks self-awareness is apt to make decisions that bring on inner turmoil by treading on buried values. "The money looked good so I signed on," someone might say two years into a job, "but the work means so little to me that I'm constantly bored." The decisions of self-aware people mesh with their values; consequently, they often find work to be energizing.

How can one recognize self-awareness? First and foremost, it shows itself as candor and an ability to assess oneself realistically. People with high self-awareness are able to speak accurately and openly—although not necessarily effusively or confessionally—about their emotions and the impact they have on their work. For instance, one manager I know of was skeptical about a new personal-shopper service that her company, a major department-store chain, was about to introduce. Without prompting from her team or her boss, she offered them an explanation: "It's hard for me to get behind the rollout of this service," she admitted, "because I really wanted to run the project, but I wasn't selected. Bear with me while I deal with that." The manager did indeed examine her feelings; a week later, she was supporting the project fully.

Such self-knowledge often shows itself in the hiring process. Ask a candidate to describe a time he got carried away by his feelings and did something he later regretted. Self-aware candidates will be frank in admitting to failure—and will often tell their tales with a smile. One of the hallmarks of self-awareness is a self-deprecating sense of humor.

Self-awareness can also be identified during performance reviews. Self-aware people know—and are comfortable talking about—their limitations and strengths, and they often demonstrate a thirst for constructive criticism. By contrast, people with low self-awareness interpret the message that they need to improve as a threat or a sign of failure.

Self-aware people can also be recognized by their self-confidence. They have a firm grasp of their capabilities and are less likely to set themselves up to fail by, for example, overstretching on assignments. They know, too, when to ask for help. And the risks they take on the job are calculated. They won't ask for a challenge that they know they can't handle alone. They'll play to their strengths.

Consider the actions of a mid-level employee who was invited to sit in on a strategy meeting with her company's top executives. Although she was the most junior person in the room, she did not sit there quietly, listening in awestruck or fearful silence. She knew she had a head for clear logic and the skill to present ideas persuasively, and she offered cogent suggestions about the company's strategy. At the same time, her self-awareness stopped her from wandering into territory where she knew she was weak.

Despite the value of having self-aware people in the workplace, my research indicates that senior executives don't often give self-awareness the credit it deserves when they look for potential leaders. Many executives mistake candor about feelings for "wimpiness" and fail to give due respect to employees who openly acknowledge their short-comings. Such people are too readily dismissed as "not tough enough" to lead others.

In fact, the opposite is true. In the first place, people generally admire and respect candor. Further, leaders are constantly required to make judgment calls that require a candid assessment of capabilities—their own and those of others. Do we have the management expertise to acquire a competitor? Can we launch a new product within six months? People who assess themselves honestly—that is, self-aware people—are well suited to do the same for the organizations they run.

Can Emotional Intelligence Be Learned?

For ages, people have debated if leaders are born or made. So too goes the debate about emotional intelligence. Are people born with certain levels of empathy, for example, or do they acquire empathy as a result of life's experiences? The answer is both. Scientific inquiry strongly suggests that there is a genetic component to emotional intelligence. Psychological and developmental research indicates that nurture plays a role as well. How much of each perhaps will never be known, but research and practice clearly demonstrate that emotional intelligence can be learned.

One thing is certain: emotional intelligence increases with age. There is an old-fashioned word for the phenomenon: maturity. Yet even with maturity, some people still need training to enhance their emotional intelligence. Unfortunately, far too many training programs that intend to build leadership skills including emotional intelligence—are a waste of time and money. The problem is simple: they focus on the wrong part of the brain.

Emotional intelligence is born largely in the neurotransmitters of the brain's limbic system, which governs feelings, impulses, and drives. Research indicates that the limbic system learns best through motivation, extended practice, and feedback. Compare this with the kind of learning that goes on in the neocortex, which governs analytical and technical ability. The neocortex grasps concepts and logic. It is the part of the brain that figures out how to use a computer or make a sales call by reading a book. Not surprisingly—but mistakenly—it is also the part of the brain targeted by most training programs aimed at enhancing emotional intelligence. When such programs take, in effect, a neocortical approach, my research with the Consortium for Research on Emotional Intelligence in Organizations has shown they can even have a *negative* impact on people's job performance.

To enhance emotional intelligence, organizations must refocus their training to include the limbic system. They must help people break old behavioral habits and establish new ones. That not only takes much more time than conventional training programs, it also requires an individualized approach.

Imagine an executive who is thought to be low on empathy by her colleagues. Part of that deficit shows itself as an inability to listen; she interrupts people and doesn't pay close attention to what they're saying. To fix the problem, the executive needs to be motivated to change, and then she needs practice and feedback from others in the company. A colleague or coach could be tapped to let the executive know when she has been observed failing to listen. She would then have to replay the incident and give a better response; that is, demonstrate her ability to absorb what others are saying. And the executive could be directed to observe certain executives who listen well and to mimic their behavior.

With persistence and practice, such a process can lead to lasting results. I know one Wall Street executive who sought to improve his empathy—specifically his ability to read people's reactions and see their perspectives. Before beginning his quest, the executive's subordinates were terrified of working with him. People even went so far as to hide bad news from him. Naturally, he was shocked when finally confronted with these facts. He went home and told his family—but they only confirmed what he had heard at work. When their opinions on any given subject did not mesh with his, they, too, were frightened of him.

Enlisting the help of a coach, the executive went to work to heighten his empathy through practice and feedback. His first step was to take a vacation to a foreign country where he did not speak the language. While there, he monitored his reactions to the unfamiliar and his openness to people who were different from him. When he returned home, humbled by his week abroad, the executive asked his coach to shadow him for parts of the day, several times a week, in order to critique how he treated people with new or different perspectives. At the same time, he consciously used on-the-job interactions as opportunities to practice "hearing" ideas that differed from his. Finally, the executive had himself videotaped in meetings and asked those who worked for and with him to critique his ability to acknowledge and understand the feelings of others. It took several months, but the executive's emotional intelligence did ultimately rise, and the improvement was reflected in his overall performance on the job.

It's important to emphasize that building one's emotional intelligence cannot—will not—happen without sincere desire and concerted effort. A brief seminar won't help; nor can one buy a how-to manual. It is much harder to learn to empathize—to internalize empathy as a natural response to people—than it is to become adept at regression analysis. But it can be done. "Nothing great was ever achieved without enthusiasm," wrote Ralph Waldo Emerson. If your goal is to become a real leader, these words can serve as a guidepost in your efforts to develop high emotional intelligence.

Self-Regulation

Biological impulses drive our emotions. We cannot do away with them—but we can do much to manage them. Self-regulation, which is like an ongoing inner conversation, is the component of emotional intelligence that frees us from being prisoners of our feelings. People engaged in such a conversation feel bad moods and emotional impulses just as everyone else does, but they find ways to control them and even to channel them in useful ways.

Imagine an executive who has just watched a team of his employees present a botched analysis to the company's board of directors. In the gloom that follows, the executive might find himself tempted to pound on the table in anger or kick over a chair. He could leap up and scream at the group. Or he might maintain a grim silence, glaring at everyone before stalking off.

But if he had a gift for self-regulation, he would choose a different approach. He would pick his words carefully, acknowledging the team's poor performance without rushing to any hasty judgment. He would then step back to consider the reasons for the failure. Are they personal—a lack of effort? Are there any mitigating factors? What was his role in the debacle? After considering these questions, he would call the team together, lay out the incident's consequences, and offer his feelings about it. He would then present his analysis of the problem and a well-considered solution.

Why does self-regulation matter so much for leaders? First of all, people who are in control of their feelings and impulses—that is, people who are reasonable—are able to create an environment of trust and fairness. In such an environment, politics and infighting are sharply reduced and productivity is high. Talented people flock to the organization and aren't tempted to leave. And self-regulation has a trickle-down effect. No one wants to be known as a hothead when the boss is known for her calm approach. Fewer bad moods at the top mean fewer throughout the organization.

Second, self-regulation is important for competitive reasons. Everyone knows that business today is rife with ambiguity and change. Companies merge and break apart regularly. Technology transforms work at a dizzying pace.

People who have mastered their emotions are able to roll with the changes. When a new change program is announced, they don't panic; instead, they are able to suspend judgment, seek out information, and listen to executives explain the new program. As the initiative moves forward, they are able to move with it.

Sometimes they even lead the way. Consider the case of a manager at a large manufacturing company. Like her colleagues, she had used a certain software program for five years. The program drove how she collected and reported data and how she thought about the company's strategy. One day, senior executives announced that a new program was to be installed that would radically change how information was gathered and assessed within the organization. While many people in the company complained bitterly about how disruptive the change would be, the manager mulled over the reasons for the new program and was convinced of its potential to improve performance. She eagerly attended training sessions—some of her colleagues refused to do so—and was eventually promoted to run several divisions, in part because she used the new technology so effectively.

I want to push the importance of self-regulation to leadership even further and make the case that it enhances integrity, which is not only a personal virtue but also an organizational strength. Many of the bad things that happen in companies are a function of impulsive behavior. People rarely plan to exaggerate profits, pad expense accounts, dip into the till, or abuse power for selfish ends. Instead, an opportunity presents itself, and people with low impulse control just say yes.

By contrast, consider the behavior of the senior executive at a large food company. The executive was scrupulously honest in his negotiations with local distributors. He would routinely lay out his cost structure in detail, thereby giving the distributors a realistic understanding of the company's pricing. This approach meant the executive couldn't always drive a hard bargain. Now, on occasion, he felt the urge to increase profits by withholding information about the company's costs. But he challenged that impulse because he saw that it made more sense in the long run to counteract it. His emotional self-regulation paid off in strong, lasting relationships with distributors that benefited the company more than any short-term financial gains would have.

The signs of emotional self-regulation, therefore, are not hard to miss: a propensity for reflection and thoughtfulness; comfort with ambiguity and change; and integrity—an ability to say no to impulsive urges.

Like self-awareness, self-regulation often does not get its due. People who can master their emotions are sometimes seen as cold fish—their considered responses are taken as a lack of passion. People with fiery temperaments are frequently thought of as "classic" leaders—their outbursts are considered hallmarks of charisma and power. But when such people make it to the top, their impulsiveness often works against them. In my research, extreme displays of negative emotion have never emerged as a driver of good leadership.

Motivation

If there is one trait that virtually all effective leaders have, it is motivation. They are driven to achieve beyond expectations—their own and everyone else's. The key word here is *achieve*. Plenty of people are motivated by external factors such as a big salary or the status that comes from having an impressive title or being part of a prestigious company. By contrast, those with leadership potential are motivated by a deeply embedded desire to achieve for the sake of achievement.

If you are looking for leaders, how can you identify people who are motivated by the drive to achieve rather than by external rewards? The first sign is a passion for the work itself—such people seek out creative challenges, love to learn, and take great pride in a job well done. They also display an unflagging energy to do things better. People with such energy often seem restless with the status quo. They are persistent with their questions about why things are done one way rather than another; they are eager to explore new approaches to their work.

A cosmetics company manager, for example, was frustrated that he had to wait two weeks to get sales results from people in the field. He finally tracked down an automated phone system that would beep each of his salespeople at 5 P.M. every day. An automated message then prompted them to punch in their numbers—how many calls and sales they had made that day. The system shortened the feedback time on sales results from weeks to hours.

That story illustrates two other common traits of people who are driven to achieve. They are forever raising the performance bar, and they like to keep score. Take the performance bar first. During performance reviews, people with high levels of motivation might ask to be "stretched" by their superiors. Of course, an employee who combines self-awareness with internal motivation will recognize her limits but she won't settle for objectives that seem too easy to fulfill.

And it follows naturally that people who are driven to do better also want a way of tracking progress—their own, their team's, and their company's. Whereas people with low achievement motivation are often fuzzy about results, those with high achievement motivation often keep score by tracking such hard measures as profitability or market share. I know of a money manager who starts and ends his day on the Internet, gauging the performance of his stock fund against four industry-set benchmarks.

Interestingly, people with high motivation remain optimistic even when the score is against them. In such cases, self-regulation combines with achievement motivation to overcome the frustration and depression that come after a setback or failure. Take the case of another portfolio manager at a large investment company. After several successful years, her fund tumbled for three consecutive quarters, leading three large institutional clients to shift their business elsewhere.

Some executives would have blamed the nose-dive on circumstances outside their control; others might have seen the setback as evidence of personal failure. This portfolio manager, however, saw an opportunity to prove she could lead a turnaround.

Two years later, when she was promoted to a very senior level in the company, she described the experience as "the best thing that ever happened to me; I learned so much from it."

Executives trying to recognize high levels of achievement motivation in their people can look for one last piece of evidence: commitment to the organization. When people love their job for the work itself, they often feel committed to the organizations that make that work possible. Committed employees are likely to stay with an organization even when they are pursued by headhunters waving money.

It's not difficult to understand how and why a motivation to achieve translates into strong leadership. If you set the performance bar high for yourself, you will do the same for the organization when you are in a position to do so. Likewise, a drive to surpass goals and an interest in keeping score can be contagious. Leaders with these traits can often build a team of managers around them with the same traits. And of course, optimism and organizational commitment are fundamental to leadership—just try to imagine running a company without them.

Empathy

Of all the dimensions of emotional intelligence, empathy is the most easily recognized. We have all felt the empathy of a sensitive teacher or friend; we have all been struck by its absence in an unfeeling coach or boss. But when it comes to business, we rarely hear people praised, let alone rewarded, for their empathy. The very word seems unbusinesslike, out of place amid the tough realities of the marketplace.

But empathy doesn't mean a kind of "I'm okay, you're okay" mushiness. For a leader, that is, it doesn't mean adopting other people's emotions as one's own and trying to please everybody. That would be a nightmare—it would make action impossible. Rather, empathy means thoughtfully considering employees' feelings—along with other factors—in the process of making intelligent decisions.

For an example of empathy in action, consider what happened when two giant brokerage companies merged, creating redundant jobs in all their divisions. One division manager called his people together and gave a gloomy speech that emphasized the number of people who would soon be fired. The manager of another division gave his people a different kind of speech. He was upfront about his own worry and confusion, and he promised to keep people informed and to treat everyone fairly.

The difference between these two managers was empathy. The first manager was too worried about his own fate to consider the feelings of his anxiety-stricken colleagues. The second knew intuitively what his people were feeling, and he acknowledged their fears with his words. Is it any surprise that the first manager saw his division sink as many demoralized people, especially the most talented, departed? By contrast, the second manager continued to be a strong leader, his best people stayed, and his division remained as productive as ever.

Empathy is particularly important today as a component of leadership for at least three reasons: the increasing use of teams; the rapid pace of globalization; and the growing need to retain talent.

Consider the challenge of leading a team. As anyone who has ever been a part of one can attest, teams are cauldrons of bubbling emotions. They are often charged with reaching a consensus—hard enough with two people and much more difficult as the numbers increase. Even in groups with as few as four or five members, alliances form and clashing agendas get set. A team's leader must be able to sense and understand the viewpoints of everyone around the table.

That's exactly what a marketing manager at a large information technology company was able to do when she was appointed to lead a troubled team. The group was in turmoil, overloaded by work and missing deadlines. Tensions were high among the members. Tinkering with procedures was not enough to bring the group together and make it an effective part of the company.

So the manager took several steps. In a series of one-on-one sessions, she took the time to listen to everyone in the group—what was frustrating them, how they rated their colleagues, whether they felt they had been ignored. And then she directed the team in a way that brought it together: she encouraged people to speak more openly about their frustrations, and she helped people raise constructive complaints during meetings. In short, her empathy allowed her to understand her team's emotional makeup. The result was not just heightened collaboration among members but also added business, as the team was called on for help by a wider range of internal clients.

Globalization is another reason for the rising importance of empathy for business leaders. Cross-cultural dialogue can easily lead to miscues and misunderstandings. Empathy is an antidote. People who have it are attuned to subtleties in body language; they can hear the message beneath the words being spoken. Beyond that, they have a deep understanding of the existence and importance of cultural and ethnic differences.

Consider the case of an American consultant whose team had just pitched a project to a potential Japanese client. In its dealings with Americans, the team was accustomed to being bombarded with questions after such a proposal, but this time it was greeted with a long silence. Other members of the team, taking the silence as disapproval, were ready to pack and leave. The lead consultant gestured them to stop. Although he was not particularly familiar with Japanese culture, he read the client's face and posture and sensed not rejection but interest—even deep consideration. He was right: when the client finally spoke, it was to give the consulting firm the job.

Finally, empathy plays a key role in the retention of talent, particularly in today's information economy. Leaders have always needed empathy to develop and keep good people, but today the stakes are higher. When good people leave, they take the company's knowledge with them.

That's where coaching and mentoring come in. It has repeatedly been shown that coaching and mentoring pay off not just in better performance but also in increased job satisfaction and decreased turnover. But what makes coaching and mentoring work best is the nature of the relationship. Outstanding coaches and mentors get inside the heads of the people they are helping. They sense how to give effective feedback. They know when to push for better performance and when to hold back. In the way they motivate their protégés, they demonstrate empathy in action.

In what is probably sounding like a refrain, let me repeat that empathy doesn't get much respect in business. People wonder how leaders can make hard decisions if they are "feeling" for all the people who will be affected. But leaders with empathy do more than sympathize with people around them: they use their knowledge to improve their companies in subtle but important ways.

Social Skill

The first three components of emotional intelligence are all self-management skills. The last two, empathy and social skill, concern a person's ability to manage relationships with others. As a component of emotional intelligence, social skill is not as simple as it sounds. It's not just a matter of friendliness, although people with high levels of social skill are rarely mean-spirited. Social skill, rather, is friendliness with a purpose: moving people in the direction you desire, whether that's agreement on a new marketing strategy or enthusiasm about a new product.

Socially skilled people tend to have a wide circle of acquaintances, and they have a knack for finding common ground with people of all kinds—a knack for building rapport. That doesn't mean they socialize continually; it means they work according to the assumption that nothing important gets done alone. Such people have a network in place when the time for action comes.

Social skill is the culmination of the other dimensions of emotional intelligence. People tend to be very effective at managing relationships when they can understand and control their own emotions and can empathize with the feelings of others. Even motivation contributes to social skill.

Remember that people who are driven to achieve tend to be optimistic, even in the face of setbacks or failure. When people are upbeat, their "glow" is cast upon conversations and other social encounters. They are popular, and for good reason.

Because it is the outcome of the other dimensions of emotional intelligence, social skill is recognizable on the job in many ways that will by now sound familiar. Socially skilled people, for instance, are adept at managing teams—that's their empathy at work. Likewise, they are expert persuaders—a manifestation of self-awareness, self-regulation, and empathy combined. Given those skills, good persuaders know when to make an emotional plea, for instance, and when an appeal to reason will work better. And motivation, when publicly visible, makes such people excellent collaborators; their passion for the work spreads to others, and they are driven to find solutions.

But sometimes social skill shows itself in ways the other emotional intelligence components do not. For instance, socially skilled people may at times appear not to be working while at work. They seem to be idly schmoozing—chatting in the hallways with colleagues or joking around with people who are not even connected to their "real" jobs. Socially skilled people, however, don't think it makes sense to arbitrarily limit the scope of their relationships. They build bonds widely because they know that in these fluid times, they may need help someday from people they are just getting to know today.

For example, consider the case of an executive in the strategy department of a global computer manufacturer. By 1993, he was convinced that the company's future lay with the Internet. Over the course of the next year, he found kindred spirits and used his social skill to stitch together a virtual community that cut across levels, divisions, and nations. He then used this de facto team to put up a corporate Web site, among the first by a major company. And, on his own initiative, with no budget or formal status, he signed up the company to participate in an annual Internet industry convention. Calling on his allies and persuading various divisions to donate funds, he recruited more than 50 people from a dozen different units to represent the company at the convention.

Management took notice: within a year of the conference, the executive's team formed the basis for the company's first Internet division, and he was formally put in charge of it. To get there, the executive had ignored conventional boundaries, forging and maintaining connections with people in every corner of the organization.

Is social skill considered a key leadership capability in most companies? The answer is yes, especially when compared with the other components of emotional intelligence. People seem to know intuitively that leaders need to manage relationships effectively; no leader is an island. After all, the leader's task is to get work done through other people, and social skill makes that possible. A leader who cannot express her empathy may as well not have it at all. And a leader's motivation will be useless if he cannot communicate his passion to the organization. Social skill allows leaders to put their emotional intelligence to work.

It would be foolish to assert that good-old-fashioned IQ and technical ability are not important ingredients in strong leadership. But the recipe would not be complete without emotional intelligence. It was once thought that the components of emotional intelligence were "nice to have" in business leaders. But now we know that, for the sake of performance, these are ingredients that leaders "need to have."

It is fortunate, then, that emotional intelligence can be learned. The process is not easy. It takes time and, most of all, commitment. But the benefits that come from having a well-developed emotional intelligence, both for the individual and for the organization, make it worth the effort.

Efficacy and Effectiveness: Integrating Models of Leadership and Intelligence

Martin M. Chemers

The Role of Intelligence in Leadership Effectiveness

Except for one very notable exception, contemporary leadership researchers and theorists have largely ignored the role of intelligence in leadership effectiveness. Among leadership theories of the last thirty or forty years, only Cognitive Resources Theory (Fiedler & Garcia, 1987) regards intelligence as an important variable. This was not always true. Early approaches to the study of leadership were strongly influenced by the apparent success of intelligence tests in the prediction of important outcomes, e.g., performance during military training. Stogdill's (1948) review of leadership traits, which showed that traits alone were not sufficient to predict either leadership emergence or effectiveness, also acknowledged that intelligence was one of the traits with the strongest association with leadership. (About 35% of the studies involving measures of intelligence and leadership revealed a significant relationship between the two variables.)

I will develop the premise that not only is intelligence a useful variable for understanding the processes that underlie effective leadership, but even more, that contemporary intelligence theories can serve as useful models for similar approaches in leadership research. Indeed, there are intriguing parallels in the research histories of the two constructs. Leadership ability, like intellectual ability, was first regarded as a trait that people either had or didn't have, and little attention was paid to situational or environmental factors that might mitigate the utility of particular capabilities.

Later models began to emphasize an interaction between the characteristics of the individual and the nature of the environment with this interaction being the somewhat mechanical fit between stable traits and a relatively static environment. In leadership, this approach might manifest as a hypothesis that one type of leadership behavior (e.g., giving directions versus being emotionally supportive) would be more effective in some situations than in others (e.g., in situations of high versus low clarity and structure).

Finally, contemporary approaches (Sternberg, 1988; Cantor & Kihlstrom, 1987; Chemers, 1997) are moving in the direction of the conceptualization of a more fluid interaction between person and environment with an acknowledgement of the individual's actions in construction and shaping of the environment rather than just reacting to it. Thus, rather than a fixed and unchanging capacity, intelligence (or leadership) becomes a set of skills and knowledge that change and develop in interaction with an environment that can, in turn, be shaped and modified to facilitate a good (i.e., effective) fit.

A Functional Model of Leadership Effectiveness

Before turning to the application of contemporary intelligence models to leadership theory, it is useful to develop a model of leadership effectiveness that integrates what is currently known about what makes some leaders more effective than others. I will define leadership as "a process of social influence in which one person is able to enlist the aid and support of others in the accomplishment of a common task" (Chemers, 1997, page 1). The important points of this definition are that leadership is social, involves influence, and is centered on a task. The definition is quite simple, but the reality of leadership is very complex.

Part of that complexity is rooted in the nature of organizational functioning. To be effective, an organization must attend two critical demands. First, it must develop a system of rules, norms, and standards that provide the internal order, reliability, and predictability necessary to address recurrent and routine events. Organizations

Source: "Efficacy and Effectiveness: Integrating Models of Leadership and Intelligence," by Martin Chemers, 2002. Used by permission of Lawrence Erlbaum Associates.

must assign jobs, titles, and offices, meet payrolls, pay suppliers, file governmental reports, etc. However, because organizations also exist within a dynamic environment, they must develop the systems and strategies that foster the sensitivity and flexibility that make it possible to respond to novel challenges. Organizational prosperity (even survival) depends on the appropriate balance between these two somewhat incompatible functions—stability and change.

Organizational effectiveness depends on leadership effectiveness. Leaders must help groups and individuals accomplish the tasks on which the organization's internal stability and external adaptability depend. To do this, leaders must enlist the aid and support of followers, guide and encourage the efforts of those followers, and direct the collective efforts of the team toward task accomplishment. Leadership effectiveness depends on the leader behaving in a manner that (1) elicits the trust and loyalty of followers (image management); (2) motivates followers toward enthusiastic effort (relationship development); and (3) applies the efforts, knowledge, and material resources of the group to mission accomplishment (resource deployment). Although the leadership literature is large, extensive, and somewhat fragmentary, it is the case that considerable agreement exists on the factors that determine these three key elements.

Image Management

It is important to recognize that the decision to act as a follower (i.e., to give up some of one's autonomy and independence of action) represents a social cost that must be balanced by some benefit. The benefit that makes the exchange equitable and attractive occurs when the leader appears able to increase the likelihood that the follower will be able to satisfy personal needs and achieve personal goals.

Hollander's (1958; 1964; Hollander & Julian, 1970) "idiosyncrasy credit" model of status accrual in groups directly addressed this exchange. Hollander showed, both through laboratory and field studies, that when a leader is seen as competent in task-related domains and committed to the

group's core values, followers are willing to give the leader greater latitude of action and authority. The task-related competency provides the basis for the leader moving the group toward goal accomplishment, and the loyalty to group values fosters the assurance that the goal pursued by the leader will be one that serves the collective interests of the group. How are such judgments normally made by followers?

Although many researchers have written about leadership attributions, the most integrated and comprehensive treatment of the subject is in the writings of Robert Lord and his associates (Lord, 1985; Lord, Foti, & De Vader, 1984). Lord and Maher's (1991) information processing model posits that leadership is assessed through both recognition and inferential processes. Recognition-based processes are dependent on the implicit theories that each person holds about the traits and characteristics that comprise leadership. The implicit models of "good" leadership result in prototypes (Rosch, 1978; Cantor & Mischel, 1979), sets of characteristics that we consciously or unconsciously associate with the leadership role. When an individual seems (through appearance or behavior) to possess a sufficient number of these characteristics, observers make a generalized attribution (i.e., reach a conclusion) that the individual has leadership capacity. Once a decision is made that an individual is "leaderly," subsequent attention, interpretation, and memory are likely to be consistent with and reinforce the initial judgment.

Inferential attributional processes occur when we ascribe the causes for a group's success to the leader's actions or abilities. The tendency to assign causality as internal to the actor (in this case, the leader) is so pervasive that social psychologists have dubbed it the "fundamental attribution error" (Jones & Nisbett, 1971). Leaders who are associated with successful outcomes are seen as effective, based on the assumption that the leader caused the outcome. Meindl (1990) argues that tendency to credit leaders for anything—good or bad—that happens within an organization is so strong in our culture that it constitutes a "romance of leadership."

Several studies have been done on the particular characteristics that make up the leadership prototype (Lord, Foti, & De Vader, 1984). Although there are some differences between the prototypes for different classes of leaders (i.e., business, military, sports, etc.), there are common elements across these categories. In a simple study reported by Kouzes and Posner (1987), 1,500 managers and workers were asked to describe the characteristics of an outstanding leader they had known. Honesty and competence led the list, with over 80% of the respondents mentioning honesty, reaffirming Hollander's (1964) early results along the same lines.

A consistent theme in the literature on perceptions and attributions of leadership is that such judgments are fraught with biases. Assumptions, implicit theories, and romantic notions may induce observers to see what they are expecting to see and to remember what is consistent with their expectations. Nonetheless, creating the impression of competence and trustworthiness is an essential element of effective leadership, and little influence is possible until a leadership image is established.

Relationship Development

The establishment of a leader's legitimacy through competence and trustworthiness provides the basis for a relationship between leader and follower. The features of a successful leader–follower relationship are threefold. First, the leader must provide the follower with a supervisory context that is motivating and allows the follower to perform effectively. Second, the ability to provide such positive guidance and support depends on accurate judgments of the followers, needs, goals, and capabilities. Finally, the relationship must be equitable and fair.

Research on intrinsic motivation (Deci & Ryan, 1985; Hackman & Oldham, 1976) reveals that tasks are motivating to the extent that they provide one with autonomy, feedback, and an opportunity to engage one's skills and abilities toward meaningful goals. Feedback about performance makes possible a positive self-evaluation for a job well done. Autonomy (i.e., control over one's work) enhances the personal significance of positive feedback. The opportunity to use a variety of skills is interesting, and the entire endeavor is made more meaningful if the goal of the task is important. These characteristics of intrinsic motivation provide the bases for effective supervision.

A leader must provide the follower with direction and guidance that is sufficient to allow the subordinate to perform well and reap the benefits of positive feedback. However, the level of supervisory directiveness is a critical and subtle element. Too little direction might make the task overly ambiguous and difficult, reducing the likelihood of positive feedback. On the other hand, too much direction robs the follower of the autonomy necessary to make the feedback personally meaningful.

Path-goal theory (House, 1971; House and Dessler, 1974) prescribes that two general classes of behavior available to the leader are structuring (i.e., providing direction and task-related feedback) and consideration (i.e., providing emotional support). According to the theory, leader-structuring behavior will have the most positive effects on subordinate morale and performance when the ambiguity or difficulty of the subordinate's task makes direction valuable for goal attainment. Conversely, when the task is well understood by the subordinate, structuring behavior will be seen as overly close monitoring, pushing for performance, and robbing the subordinate of autonomy. Consideration and morale-boosting leader behavior should have their most positive effects when the subordinate's task is aversive by being boring or unpleasant. If the subordinate's task, however, is interesting and engaging, leader consideration will be regarded as unnecessary and distracting. The leader must be familiar with both the demands of the task and the capabilities of the follower to judge how much structuring and consideration would be useful. However, it is more complex than that.

The research findings on path-goal theory are quite mixed. One reason for the lack of consistent findings may be revealed in a study by Griffin

(1981). In addition to measuring the nature of the subordinates' tasks, Griffin also measured a subordinate's personality characteristics—"growth need strength," Hackman and Oldham's (1976) measure of an individual's desire for growth and challenge in the workplace. Griffin found that growth need strength (GNS) moderated the predicted relationship between leader behavior and follower motivation and performance. High GNS subordinates, who were energized by difficult and unstructured tasks, responded negatively to leader structuring regardless of task condition, but responded quite positively to leader consideration when the task was highly structured and boring. Low GNS subordinates showed the opposite pattern. Boring tasks did not create as strong a positive reaction to supportive, considerate behavior by the leader, and structuring was well appreciated even when tasks were already fairly structured. Griffin's findings indicate that leaders must be sensitive not only to task features and follower skill levels, but also to followers' personality, needs, and expectations. Accurate judgment becomes a critical part of effective leadership.

The leader–follower relationship is a dynamic one. Subordinates are assigned tasks that they perform well or poorly. Follow-up actions are taken by the leader, and new tasks are assigned. Subordinates are rewarded or chastised; sent for training or given enhanced responsibilities; promoted or not. Thus, another important feature of leadership judgments centers on how the leader interprets this flow of actions and performance. Research by Mitchell and his associates (Green & Mitchell, 1979; Mitchell, Larson, & Green, 1977; Mitchell & Wood, 1980) indicates that attributions about followers by leaders obey many of the principles of classic attribution theory (Jones & Davis, 1965; Kelley, 1967). That is, leaders integrate information about how well the subordinate has performed on other tasks, and at other times, and how well other workers perform at similar tasks. Consistent and distinctive performance outcomes (i.e., success or failure that is consistent over time, but different from other workers) are likely to lead to strong attributions about the subordinate's ability, which lead to actions consistent with those judgments.

However, attributional processes in the leadership relationship have some additional features not usually addressed in social psychological studies of person perception. These additional processes are related to the fact that the leader and follower are engaged in a relationship with reciprocal causality and connected outcomes. By this I mean that follower performance may be caused by the leader. Poor leadership is a potential explanation for poor follower performance. Furthermore, poor performance by a follower has important implications for the leader's success and evaluation by superiors.

This mutual dependence makes the subordinate's behavior and performance and subsequent explanations surrounding that performance very important to the leader. This increases the tendency for judgments by the leader to be ego-defensive, self-protective, and occasionally extreme. Because the leader is taking action with respect to the subordinate based on these judgments, biased processes can have serious negative outcomes. Followers who are blamed for failures outside their control are likely to become resentful and problematic employees. The leader–follower relationship can become a descending spiral. This possibility leads to a discussion of the third element of relationship development—equity and fairness.

At base, the leader–follower relationship is a transaction in which the follower provides effort and loyalty to the group and leader in exchange for help in attaining personal goals. Graen (1976; Graen & Cashman, 1975; Graen, Cashman, Ginsburgh, & Schiemann, 1978; Graen & Scandura, 1987) has presented a model of leader–follower exchange that acknowledges the qualitative range of such transactions. Because a leader needs the help of followers to accomplish the leader's and the group's goals, the leader and follower will undergo a perhaps unspoken but important negotiation of the nature of their relationship. The leader may regard a subordinate as a valued partner who is given interesting tasks, made privy to inside information, provided training and development opportunities, and rewarded well, or may be regarded as a "hired hand" who is afforded far less attractive options. Research indicates better leader–follower exchanges are associated with better job-related communication (Graen & Schiemann, 1978) and greater satisfaction (Graen & Ginsburgh, 1977).

Resource Deployment

The successful negotiation of image management and relationship development provides the leader with a legitimate basis for authority that can be used to develop a team of motivated subordinates ready to direct their knowledge, skills, and energy toward mission accomplishment. The actual effectiveness of the team is determined by how successfully the intellectual, motivational, and material resources of the team are utilized to achieve the goal. Like a military commander who must deploy troops, weapons, and materials based on an informed estimate of the enemy's strengths and strategies, an effective leader must deploy the team's resources based on an informed judgment of the critical demands created by the task and mission environment.

Resource deployment is achieved on two levels. First, each member of the group must make the most effective use of his or her personal resources, i.e., intelligence, knowledge, skills, etc. Second, the individual efforts of team members must be coordinated and applied to the task environment in a manner that makes the most efficient use of those resources. Both self-deployment and team deployment are strongly influenced by the match between situational variables and team and personal characteristics.

Self-deployment addresses the ability to make the best use of personal resources. The basic premise of the Contingency Model of leadership effectiveness (Fiedler, 1967; Fiedler & Chemers, 1974, 1984) is that leaders function most effectively when their personal orientation or motivational pattern (i.e., toward task versus interpersonal accomplishment) is appropriate to (i.e., "matched" with) the situation. Extensive

research (see meta-analyses by Peters, Hartke, & Pohlmann, 1983; Strube & Garcia, 1981) indicates that task-motivated leaders are most effective when the leadership situation (i.e., task, authority, and relationship with subordinates) provides the leader with a stable and predictable leadership environment. Relationship-motivated leaders perform most effectively—i.e., lead groups with high performance and satisfied subordinates—when situational contingencies create an environment of some complexity, ambiguity, and unpredictability.

Applying the Contingency Model to job stress, Chemers, Hays, Rhodewalt, and Wysocki (1985) found that "in-match" leaders reported lower levels of job stress and stress-related illness than did "out-of-match" leaders. Chemers, Ayman, Sorod, and Akimoto (1991) reported that in-match leaders evidenced more positive moods, greater confidence, and greater satisfaction than out-of-match leaders in both laboratory and field studies.

Fiedler and Garcia (1987) extended the logic of the Contingency Model to explain the effective deployment of leaders' cognitive resources (i.e., intelligence and experience) to effective group performance. Studies with the Cognitive Resources Model have indicated that the most effective use of intelligence and experience depends on two factors—the level of stress the leader is experiencing, and the willingness of the leader to provide clear direction to subordinates. Leaders under stress are less able to use their intelligence to solve problems, ostensibly because of the interference of anxiety on thought process, but are able to make good use of highly learned information provided by previous experience in similar situations. We see here the effect of positive and negative emotional states on the ability to make use of personal resources.

Fiedler and Leister (1977) have also shown that unless the leader is active in directing the activities of subordinates, intelligence and experience do not have much impact on the group's success. Fiedler (1993) suggests that match between leadership style and situation is related to the leader's level of directiveness. This notion is consistent with Eagly and Johnson's (1990) conclusions based on a meta-analysis of gender effects in leadership. They found that when a leadership situation was judged to be "congenial" (i.e., a situation in which a leader would be most comfortable) leaders were found to be more directive and judged to be more effective by observers.

Staw and Barsade (1992), who observed M.B.A. students in an assessment center simulation, found leaders with more positive affect to be more effective in the in-basket decision-making task, using more information and making more complex decisions, and were also more likely to be judged as an emergent leader in a leaderless discussion group. Individuals with positive affect are also more likely to take risks (Isen, Nygren, & Ashby, 1988), solve problems creatively (Isen, Daubman, & Nanicki, 1987), and make better decisions (Carnevale & Isen, 1986)—all of which are characteristics that are related to effective leadership.

It appears, then, that confidence plays an important role in the ability of individuals to make the most effective use of personal resources. One contributor to confidence is the degree of fit between the leader's personality, leadership style, gender, or other personal characteristics with features of the task, group, or organizational environment. I will develop this idea a bit more fully in a later section.

Team deployment refers to the effective coordination and application of the individual and collective resources of the team to the accomplishment of the group or organization's mission. The contingency theories (e.g., Fiedler, 1967; Vroom & Yetton, 1973) provide the most relevant explanatory premises for understanding team deployment.

All of the leadership functions discussed in earlier sections are dependent on subjective perceptions. The extent to which the leader looks like a leader (i.e., matches the leadership prototype) or the degree to which the leader's structuring and considerate behavior are seen by the subordinate as appropriate and motivating are influenced primarily by perceptions and judgments that are endogenous to the leader–follower relationship.

However, the strategies and actions that are used to affect the coordination of team resources for task accomplishment have their interface with the more concrete constraints of the external environment. Generally speaking, situations of high predictability make the use of directive, highly structured strategies more likely to yield positive results, while more complex and unpredictable circumstances benefit from the information sharing and creative problem solving made possible by more participative and flexible strategies. For example, Vroom and Yetton (1973) maintain that the wrong decision-making strategy (e.g., the use of autocratic [low follower input], decision making when the leader lacks relevant information and structure) is likely to lead to less efficient use of resources and lower effectiveness. A voluminous literature on the Contingency Model (Fiedler, 1978; Strube & Garcia, 1981) supports the notion that team effectiveness is dependent on the proper match between leadership style and situational factors.

Effective coordination of team resources requires the use of communication and decision-making structures that are compatible with the environment. Successful leaders must make accurate judgments about the nature of the environment and implement strategies that fit.

Transformational Leadership

Leadership researchers have always been interested in that class of exceptionally effective leaders that political historian James McGregor Burns (1978) referred to as "transformational" leaders—i.e., leaders who transcend the "transactional," quid pro quo bases of leadership authority to transform their followers into dedicated agents of collective achievement (Bass, 1985; 1998; Conger, 1989; Conger & Kanungo, 1987; House, 1977; House & Shamir, 1993). Like Weber's (1947) "charismatic" leaders, this class of exceptional leaders is seen as qualitatively different from their more mundane counterparts. I don't find this to be a defensible or useful distinction. Rather, I would argue that so-called transformational leaders are those who exhibit the highest levels of the three elements of image management, relationship development, and resource deployment.

The transformational theories all stress the important role of impression management in eliciting the high levels of follower commitment that define charismatic or transformational leadership. House's (1977) analysis of historical figures with charismatic effects on followers emphasizes the use of image management, such as bold gestures and risk-taking, to establish an image of commitment and trust-evoking dedication to the mission. Conger and Kanungo (1987) place great importance on the leader's technical expertise and "depth of knowledge" for achieving desired objectives. Bass (1985) uses the term "idealized influence" to refer to the leader's image as supremely competent, and "inspirational motivation" to underscore the necessity of stating the group's goal in terms that inspire trust and dedication to the leader and to the mission. House (1977) and House and Shamir (1993) stress that transformational leaders evince extremely high levels of confidence in themselves and their followers. This confidence leads to followers' self-perceptions of competence and subsequently to high expectations and high goals.

Relationship development with its components of judgment and guidance is an important feature of the transformational theories. Bass (1985) argues that transformational leaders employ "individualized consideration" (i.e., a highly personalized understanding of and reaction to follower needs and abilities) to create "intellectual stimulation" (i.e., providing guidance that stretches subordinates to think independently and creatively). This is very similar to the basic elements of relationship development, which are the sensitive understanding of follower needs and abilities in order to provide coaching, and guidance that stretch the follower's capacities and promote growth of knowledge and skills.

Finally, the notion that leaders must coordinate group activities through judgment and

process for effective resource deployment is most clearly expressed by Conger and Kanungo (1987), who maintain that an important component of outstanding leadership is the ability to accurately assess the strategic factors affecting the attainment of the leader's vision.

Effective leadership can be conceived of as a continuum from very poor to very excellent. The successful fulfillment of the three elements of image management, relationship development, and resource deployment provides the basis for movement towards the positive pole of that dimension.

The Role of Intelligence in Leadership Effectiveness

Leadership research has never been strongly focused on specific skills or knowledge bases that leaders might possess. Since Stogdill's (1948) critical examination of leadership traits, only minimal interest had been shown in intelligence—either as a trait or skill—until Fiedler and Garcia's (1987) presentation of Cognitive Resources Theory. However, in recent years, the conceptualization of intelligence has moved from a trait to a process. These modern approaches to intelligence hold great promise for illuminating the bases of successful leadership. I will address three of the most prominent of the modern conceptualizations of intelligence and examine how they might contribute to the functional, integrative view of leadership presented previously. The three intelligence models are Sternberg's (1988) Triarchic Theory of Intelligence, Cantor and Kihlstrom's (1987) Social Intelligence Theory, and Salovey and Mayer's (1990; Mayer & Salovey, 1993) Theory of Emotional Intelligence.

Contemporary Models of Intelligence

What sets apart the newer conceptualizations of intelligence from the older "intelligence as stable trait" approaches is the view of intelligence as a process of adaptation. Cognitive skills and knowledge interact with environmental demands in a mutual shaping and development that enhances the adaptive fit of the individual to the environment. Robert Sternberg's Triarchic Theory of Intelligence (1988), which led the way in this approach, regards the individual as possessing internal resources in the form of cognitive abilities, such as specific knowledge and learning strategies that are applied to the solution of problems in the life environment. The relative utility of these internal resources are defined by the degree to which they are appropriate to the environmental demands. By interacting with the environment, the individual develops and refines the resources necessary to be effective, and in the process selects, shapes, and adapts elements of the environment for better fit with existing and developing internal resources. A central process in effective adaptation is turning the novel and unfamiliar into the predictable and routine, which can then be managed for attaining desired goals. The intelligent person, then, is one who can muster current knowledge and ability to relate to the problem environment in a flexible way that allows for the acquisition of new skills and knowledge that help the individual to develop the solutions necessary for goal attainment.

Cantor and Kihlstrom's (1987) Theory of Social Intelligence proceeds from a similar position of intelligence as "problem solving in a context." The socially intelligent person is one who possesses a sophisticated "perceptual readiness" to interpret social life accurately and respond to social situations effectively, i.e., managing interpersonal interactions to attain personal goals. Like Sternberg's "metacomponents," individuals possess internal resources or expertise in the social domain, consisting of concepts, interpretive rules, scripts, etc. These internal resources are applied to "life-task contexts" that afford the opportunity for the individual to accomplish his or her central life tasks. Intelligence becomes the ability to act wisely in human relations and involves the selection and shaping of contexts to provide the best fit with knowledge and abilities. The intelligent person understands the cultural expectations and normative processes governing social interaction and can recognize when and how social rules are applied.

Salovey and Mayer (1990; Mayer & Salovey, 1993) have directed attention to the extent to which emotional as well as cognitive knowledge is an important component of effective mastery of the personal environment. They discuss four types of emotional intelligence: (1) the accurate perception of one's own and others' emotions, (2) the use of emotions to facilitate thinking (i.e., the ability to create task-congruent emotions that help one focus on task demands), (3) emotional knowledge and understanding, including empathy and judgment, and (4) regulation of one's emotions to promote personal growth (i.e., self-control, coping with stressful situations). Emotional intelligence contributes to an individual's ability to control oneself and to understand and influence others.

Intelligences as Contributors to Leadership Effectiveness

A reexamination of the key elements of effective leadership affords an opportunity to recognize the role of the various types and aspects of intelligence.

Image management involved the establishment of the credibility and legitimacy of authority by matching subordinate prototype-based expectations for leadership. The strongest components of the leadership prototype across all types of leaders are competence and honesty. A potential leader's ability to match observer expectations depends on two factors; the understanding of what the content of the prototype is, and the capability for presenting the expected behaviors and attitudes. Social intelligence is clearly the basis for the first requirement, and emotional intelligence is a significant contributor to the latter.

Social intelligence includes the knowledge of prototypical characteristics and situational scripts. The socially intelligent person is adept at reading the characteristics of the situation for cues and clues that define the nature of the interpersonal context and the appropriate behaviors for the context. The effective leader knows when a situation requires a formal authority and presentation or a more informal and intimate interactional style. A CEO who attends the corporation's shareholders meeting dressed in jeans and a sweatshirt and gives the annual report while leaning against a table would be as out of place and unconvincing as one who attends the company picnic in a three-piece suit. Social knowledge is a requisite for appearing as a credible leadership figure.

It is also the case that leadership prototypes involve more than appropriate clothing. The projection of competence includes proper attitude, emotions, and demeanor. "Cool under pressure," "calm and self-assured," and "possessing a fire in the belly" have all become common phrases used to describe valued leaders in our culture. Social intelligence contributes to the ability to discern when one should be calm or fiery, but emotional intelligence plays a critical role in the would-be leader's ability to regulate self-control and emotional state to meet situational demands.

If the foregoing descriptions of the uses of intelligence in image management give the impression of a manipulation or insincerity, it would be misleading. Understanding where others "are coming from" and being able to harness and control one's emotions in order to meet the challenges of demanding situations need not imply any insincerity. In the long run, it is the person who is really "calm under pressure" but can "rise to the challenge" that will be recognized and afforded the status to lead.

Relationship development has, as its most central feature, the ability to accurately judge the needs and expectations of followers so that coaching and guidance can be given in a manner that encourages motivation and promotes growth. Again, both social and emotional intelligence are the bases for that ability. Coaching, with its sometimes oppositional components of correction and encouragement, is one of the most subtle and potentially volatile of social interactions. An understanding of the norms surrounding such interactions and a knowledge of the impact of feedback and of how to phrase both praise and criticism is essential for acting effectively in the coaching situation. This ability to understand others and act in ways that are in tune with the feelings of followers is what we mean by the term "consideration."

However, transformational leadership theory (Bass, 1985) makes clear that outstanding leadership goes beyond a generalized knowledge of what considerate behavior is to achieve an "individualized consideration" that is sensitive to the unique personality and situation of a particular follower. We have also discussed the impediments to sensitive understanding of subordinates that are inherent in the leader's own vulnerability to criticism and need to defend self-esteem. It is at this deeper level of understanding that emotional intelligence becomes critical. The leader needs first to control his or her own emotional reactions to the coaching situation, both in terms of anxiety about delivering feedback, as well as in terms of threats to one's own sense of competence. Second, the ability to read and understand the emotions of others, i.e., empathy, forms the basis for truly individualized consideration.

Resource deployment is the facet of leadership that mobilizes and applies the group's collective resources to accomplish the task or mission. At this level, intelligence theories may provide both strikingly apt metaphors as well as useful models for understanding effective leadership. Sternberg's (1988) triarchic model presents intelligence as the employment (or read "deployment") of the individual's internal resources to attain desired goals. To do this, the individual engages the environment in order to both bring to bear existing knowledge and to sample environmental demands to determine what new knowledge or skills must be developed. This interface with the environment is shaped to fit the individual's capabilities just as capabilities are expanded and developed to fit the environment. The hallmark of this process is the turning of the novel and unpredictable aspects of the environment into the well understood and routinely manageable—thus freeing the individual's capabilities to access new novel problems.

If we make a few substitutions in words, we have a very good description of effective leadership. For a group to attain its goals and accomplish its mission, it must bring to bear the individual capabilities, knowledge, skills, and energy of its members to address the demands of the task environment. It begins by selecting and shaping the problem to fit existing knowledge, as well as by activating the learning processes of each individual member. Just as with individual intelligence, the group's immediate goal is to process information and make decisions that turn novel and unpredictable environmental features into routine events that can be reliably and predictably managed to effect solutions.

Although aspects of this metaphor are obvious, some less obvious ideas are brought into relief. The notion of the group as a learning organism reorganizing and expanding knowledge and skills to meet challenges may be more or less explicit in some approaches to organization (Senge, 1990), but those ideas have not been as clearly integrated into leadership theory. Likewise, the idea that effective problem solving is the conversion of novelty into order is not a new concept, but it is relatively new to contemporary leadership theory.

Social and emotional intelligence may also affect the resource deployment process. Clearly, emotional intelligence, i.e., the regulation of one's own emotion and others' emotions, is central to self-deployment—the effective release of personal resources. By managing anxiety, maintaining a positive attitude, and successfully coping with stress, leaders and followers are more able to make use of the resources of knowledge and skill that they possess. In addition, as House and Shamir (1993) point out, the arousal of motives that are appropriate to task performance (e.g., achievement motivation for difficult tasks or "aggression" for competitive situations) enhance ability. Emotional intelligence provides a basis for understanding how a leader's behavior might arouse appropriate moods or motivations in oneself or in one's followers.

Leadership Efficacy and Leadership Performance

Personal Dispositions and Leadership Capabilities

Except for some work on self-esteem (Korman, 1968), the empirical literature on leadership has not reflected a great deal of interest in constructs related to positive affect or self-perception. Comprehensive reviews of leadership trait research (Bass, 1990; Yukl, 1994) reveal just a few studies of confidence, with mixed results. And in most of the studies of leadership confidence (e.g., Kipnis & Lane, 1962), constructs of self-esteem, self-confidence, and self-efficacy were not clearly differentiated from one another.

More qualitative approaches to leadership have touched on these issues. For example, after a loosely structured interview study of 90 outstanding leaders in the public and private sectors, Bennis and Nanus (1985) concluded that all of these individuals shared high levels of self-confidence about their own capabilities and optimism about the outcomes of their actions. Corporate CEOs, political leaders, professional sports coaches, symphony conductors, and others shared the beliefs that (a) they were capable of doing what had to be done (self-efficacy), and (b) if they did what they should do, the environment would respond positively (optimism). In a similar vein, Boyatzis (1982) conducted critical incident interviews with 253 managers preselected on the basis of high effectiveness ratings. Content analyses of the interviews revealed that effective managers demonstrated a strong belief in their own capabilities (self-efficacy) and an internal locus of control.

In purely theoretical analyses, House and Shamir (House, 1977; House & Shamir, 1993; Shamir, House, & Arthur, 1992) have included self-confidence and high expectations for self and followers among the list of traits that have distinguished charismatic leaders throughout history. In other words, traits like confidence and optimism crop up when analysts think about very effective leaders, but these constructs are less prevalent in the empirical work that addresses the more mundane aspects of organizational leadership.

In some empirical studies, positive affect has been found to be associated with better relations between soldiers and their superiors (Solomon, Mikulincer, & Hobfall, 1986). High levels of self-esteem have been related to a greater sense of personal locus of control (Deci & Ryan, 1985), and a greater willingness to assume positions of leadership (Linimon, Barron, & Falbo, 1984). Self-efficacy has been related to work motivation (Gist & Mitchell, 1992) and to better leadership performance under stress (Murphy, 1992).

An extensive literature on self-efficacy (Bandura, 1982; 1997) reveals that perceptions of efficacy can enhance or impair motivation and performance in a variety of ways, e.g., by influencing the kinds of activities in which people choose to engage (Bandura, 1982), the level of the goals they set (Locke, Frederick, Lee, & Bobko, 1984), and their effort and persistence at achieving those goals (Bandura & Cervone, 1983). Self-efficacy judgments are important because they influence not only what skills people perceive themselves to have, but also what they believe they can do with the skills they possess. Self-efficacy beliefs can affect attentional and thinking processes, eliciting either confidence, with positive concomitants, or debilitating self-doubt (Bandura & Wood, 1989), with a resultant tendency to withdraw or give up (Carver, Peterson, Follansbee, & Scheier, 1983). Bandura and Jourdan (1991) found that M.B.A. students given efficacy-enhancing feedback showed improved performance in a management simulation, decision-making task.

Although these various personal dispositions do not describe a single, unidimensional construct, they do share a focus on the positive effects of confidence in one's ability and positive expectancies about the outcomes of one's actions. In summary, feelings of enhanced self-efficacy should be related to high levels of motivation, which could affect levels of aspiration, goal setting, perseverance in the face of difficulty, and enthusiasm, causing a leader to work harder and longer to achieve group goals. Such feelings might also be contagious to followers, affecting their confidence and related perceptions.

Leadership Efficacy and Effectiveness

Bandura (1982; 1997) has maintained that self-efficacy is quite domain-specific. Therefore, only leadership efficacy, not generalized self-esteem or positive affect, should lead specifically to leadership effectiveness. In a series of recent studies, my colleagues and I (Chemers, Watson, & May, 2000; Watson, Chemers, and Preiser, 1996; Murphy, this volume), have found strong support for the predictive utility of leadership self-efficacy in group and organizational performance.

Chemers, Watson, and May (2000) measured the leadership self-efficacy of approximately 100 cadets enrolled in the Reserve Officer Training Corps (ROTC) at five colleges and universities in southern California and Arizona. Third-year cadets (i.e., juniors) responded to a measure of self-esteem, the Revised Janis-Field Scale (Brockner, 1988); to a measure which asked for their self-evaluation of a number of leadership skills (e.g., decision making, delegation, oral communication) and general leadership capabilities (e.g., "I know how to get a group to work well together"); and to a measure of generalized optimism, the Life Orientations Test (LOT; Scheier & Carver, 1985). The cadets were rated on leadership potential by their military science class instructors (career military officers). Results indicated that leadership efficacy and optimism, but not general self-esteem, were strongly related to the leadership potential ratings.

Follow-up data on these same cadets were collected during their attendance at a U.S. Army six-week summer leadership training camp. Companies of approximately 40 cadets lived in common barracks and rotated through leadership duties. Cadets also underwent extensive training in leadership, as well as in nonleadership skills (e.g., marksmanship, navigation), and participated in highly realistic and demanding leadership simulation exercises. Leadership ratings were obtained from cadet peers, superior officers (regular army), and from simulation observers

(Pentagon-trained evaluators). In all analyses, leadership efficacy (but not self-esteem or optimism) was strongly related to leadership ratings by all parties, but not to nonleadership measures. The authors conclude that the leadership efficacy measure provided evidence of strong concurrent (instructor ratings), predictive (summer camp ratings and score), and discriminant (nonleadership measures) validity.

Watson, Chemers, and Preiser (1996) examined the effects of leadership efficacy on collective efficacy and team performance among men's and women's college basketball teams. Small college basketball team members responded to measures of leadership efficacy, individual basketball efficacy, and team collective efficacy prior to the beginning of the basketball season and also identified the player regarded as the team leader. Results indicated that the leadership efficacy of the identified leader (usually the team captain) was strongly predictive of the team's collective efficacy, which, in turn, was strongly predictive of the team's win-loss record during the season. Leaders with high leadership efficacy led more confident and more successful teams. Efficacy was, in fact, a better predictor of performance than more frequently used "objective" measures of talent, such as previous year's win-loss record, number of returning lettered players, or players out for the team.

CONCLUSION

This chapter has presented an integrated theory of leadership that regards effective leadership as grounded in three critical functions. Image management is essential to the development of credibility of the leader and the acceptance of influence by followers and is dependent on follower perceptions of the leader as competent and trustworthy. Relationship development is the basis for the development of a motivated and competent group of followers and is dependent on a leader's ability to recognize follower capabilities and needs, and to provide intrinsically motivating coaching and direction. Finally, resource deployment encompasses a leader's ability to get the most out of individual and collective effort by the appropriate matching of strategy to environment.

An additional thesis of this chapter is that all of these leadership capabilities are dramatically enhanced by a leader's sense of personal efficacy in the leadership role, and in fact, outstanding levels of leadership are not possible without high levels of confidence. Empirical evidence from three major studies support the value of leadership efficacy as a predictor of leadership, group, and organizational performance as measured in a variety of ways.

The chapter also presents an intriguing hypothesis to guide future research—i.e., that situational self-efficacy (leadership efficacy in this case) is rooted in intelligence, which provides the actor with a sense of personal agency. In particular, social and emotional intelligence may be very highly related to a leader's success at image management and relationship development, and general intelligence to a leader's ability to read and respond to task environments. An exciting direction for future research would be to probe the effects of social and emotional intelligence on leadership efficacy and leadership performance.

REFERENCES

Bandura, A. (1982). Self-efficacy mechanism in human agency. *American Psychologist, 37,* 122–147.

Bandura, A. (1997). *Self-efficacy: The exercise of the self.* New York: W. H. Freeman & Company.

Bandura, A., & Cervone, D. (1983). Self-evaluative and self-efficacy mechanisms governing the motivational effects of goal systems. *Journal of Personality and Social Psychology, 45,* 1017–1028.

Bandura, A., & Jourdan, F. J. (1991). Self-regulatory mechanisms governing the impact of social comparison on complex decision making. *Journal of Personality and Social Psychology, 60,* 941–951.

Bandura, A., & Wood, R. (1989). Effect of perceived controllability and performance standards on self-regulation of complex decision making. *Journal of Personality and Social Psychology, 56,* 805–814.

Bass, B. M. (1985). *Leadership and performance beyond expectations.* New York: Free Press.

Bass, B. M. (1990). *Bass & Stogdill's handbook of leadership: Theory, research, and managerial applications.* (3rd ed.). New York: Free Press.

Bass, B. M. (1998). *Transformational leadership: Industry, military, and educational impact.* Mahwah, NJ: Lawrence Erlbaum Associates.

Bennis, W. G., & Nanus, B. (1985). *Leaders: The strategies for taking charge.* New York: Harper & Row.

Boyatzis, R. E. (1982). *The competent manager.* New York: John Wiley.

Brockner, J. (1988). *Self-esteem at work: Research, theory, and practice.* Lexington, MA: D. C. Heath and Company.

Burns, J. M. (1978). *Leadership.* New York: Harper & Row.

Cantor, N., & Kihlstrom, J. F. (1987). *Personality and social intelligence.* Englewood Cliffs, NJ: Prentice-Hall, Inc.

Cantor, N., & Mischel, W. (1979). Prototypes in person perception. In L. Berkowitz (Ed.), *Advances in experimental social psychology (Vol. 12).* New York: Academic Press.

Carnevale, P. J. D., & Isen, A. M. (1986). The influence of positive affect and visual access on the discovery of integrative solutions in bilateral negotiation. *Organizational Behavior and Human Decision Processes, 37,* 1–13.

Carver, C. S., Peterson, L. M., Follansbee, D. J., & Scheier, M. F. (1983). Effects of self-directed attention on performance and persistence among persons high and low in test anxiety. *Cognitive Therapy and Research, 7,* 333–354.

Chemers, M. M. (1997). *An integrative theory of leadership.* Mahwah, NJ: Lawrence Erlbaum Associates.

Chemers, M. M. & Ayman, R. (1985). Leadership orientation as a moderator of the relationship between performance and satisfaction of Mexican managers. *Personality and Social Psychology Bulletin, 11,* 359–367.

Chemers, M. M., Ayman, R., Sorod, B., & Akimoto, S. (1991). Self-monitoring as a moderator of leader-follower relationships. Presented at the International Congress of Psychology, Brussels.

Chemers, M. M., Hays, R., Rhodewalt, F., & Wysocki, J. (1985). A person-environment analysis of job stress: A contingency model explanation. *Journal of Personality and Social Psychology, 49,* 628–635.

Chemers, M. M., Watson, C. B., & May, S. (2000). Dispositional affect and leadership effectiveness: A comparison of self-esteem, optimism, and efficacy. *Personality and Social Psychology, Bulletin, 26,* 267–277.

Conger, J. A. (1989). The dark side of the charismatic leader. In J. A. Conger (Ed.), *The charismatic leader.* San Francisco: Jossey-Bass.

Conger, J. A., & Kanungo, R. A. (1987). Towards a behavioral theory of charismatic leadership in organizational settings. *Academy of Management Review, 12,* 637–647.

Deci, E. L., & Ryan, R. M. (1985). *Intrinsic motivation and self-determination in human behavior.* New York: Plenum Press.

Eagly, A. H., & Johnson, B. T. (1990). Gender and leadership style: A meta-analysis. *Psychological Bulletin, 108,* 233–256.

Fiedler, F. E. (1967). *A theory of leadership effectiveness.* New York: McGraw-Hill.

Fiedler, F. E. (1978). The contingency model and the dynamics of the leadership process. In L. Berkowitz (Ed.), *Advances in experimental social psychology.* Vol. 11. New York: Academic Press.

Fiedler, F. E. (1993). The leadership situation and the black box in contingency theories. In M. M. Chemers & R. Ayman (Eds.), *Leadership theory and research: Perspectives and directions.* San Diego: Academic Press.

Fiedler, F. E., & Chemers, M. M. (1974). *Leadership and effective management.* Glenview, IL: Scott, Foresman & Company.

Fiedler, F. E., & Chemers, M. M. (1984). *Improving leadership effectiveness: The Leader Match concept* (2nd ed.). New York: Wiley.

Fiedler, F. E., & Garcia, J. E. (1987). *New approaches to effective leadership: Cognitive resources and organizational performance.* New York: Wiley.

Fiedler, F. E. & Leister, A. F. (1977). Leader intelligence and task performance: A test of the multiple screen model. *Organizational Behavior and Human Performance, 20,* 1–14.

Gist, M. E. & Mitchell, T. R. (1992). Self-efficacy: A theoretical analysis of its determinants and malleability. *Academy of Management Review, 17,* 183–211.

Graen, G. (1976). Role-making processes within complex organizations. In M. D. Dunnette (Ed.), *Handbook of industrial and organizational psychology.* Chicago, IL: Rand McNally.

Graen, G., & Cashman, J. (1975). A role-making model of leadership in formal organizations: A developmental approach. In J. G. Hunt and L. L. Larson (Eds.), *Leadership frontiers.* Kent, OH: Kent State University Press.

Graen, G., Cashman, J. F., Ginsburgh, S., & Schiemann, W. (1978). Effects of linking-pin quality on the quality of working life of lower participants: A longitudinal investigation of the managerial understructure. *Administrative Science Quarterly, 22,* 491–504.

Graen, G., & Ginsburgh, S. (1977). Job resignation as a function of role orientation and leader acceptance: A longitudinal investigation of organizational assimilation. *Organizational Behavior and Human Performance, 19,* 1–17.

Graen, G., & Scandura, T. A. (1987). Toward a psychology of dyadic organizing. *Research in Organizational Behavior, 9,* 175–208.

Graen, G. & Schiemann, W. (1978). Leader-member agreement: A vertical dyad linkage approach. *Journal of Applied Psychology, 63*(2), 206–212.

Green, S. G., & Mitchell, T. R. (1979). Attributional processes of leaders in leader-member interactions. *Organizational Behavior and Human Performance, 23,* 429–458.

Griffin, R. N. (1981). Relationships among individual, task design, and leader behavior variables. *Academy of Management Journal, 23,* 665–683.

Hackman, J. R., & Oldham, G. R. (1976). Motivation through the design of work: Test of a theory. *Organizational Behavior and Human Performance, 16,* 250–279.

Hollander, E. P. (1958). Conformity, status, and idiosyncrasy credit. *Psychological Review, 65,* 117–127.

Hollander, E. P. (1964). *Leaders, groups, and influence.* New York: Oxford Press.

Hollander, E. P., & Julian, J. W. (1970). Studies in leader legitimacy, influence, and innovation. In L. Berkowitz (Ed.), *Advances in experimental social psychology,* Vol. 5. New York: Academic Press.

House, R. J. (1971). A path-goal theory of leadership. *Administrative Science Quarterly, 16,* 321–338.

House, R. J. (1977). A 1976 theory of charismatic leadership. In J. G. Hunt & L. L.Larson (Eds.), *Leadership: The cutting edge.* Carbondale, IL: Southern Illinois University Press.

House, R. J. & Dessler, G. (1974). The path-goal theory of leadership: Some post-hoc and a priori tests. In J. G. Hunt & L. L. Larson (Eds.), *Contingency approaches to leadership.* Carbondale, IL: Southern Illinois University Press.

House, R. J., & Shamir, B. (1993). In M. M. Chemers & R. Ayman (Eds.), *Leadership theory and research: Perspective and directions.* San Diego: Academic Press.

Isen, A. M., Daubman, K. A., & Nanicki, G. P. (1987). Positive affect facilitates creative problem solving. *Journal of Personality and Social Psychology, 51,* 1122–1131.

Isen, A. M., Nygren, J. E., & Ashby, G. F. (1988). The influence of positive affect on the subjective utility of gains and losses: It's not worth the risk. *Journal of Personality and Social Psychology, 55,* 710–717.

Jones, E. E., & Davis, K. E. (1965). From acts to dispositions: The attribution process in person perception. In L. Berkowitz (Ed.), *Advances in experimental social psychology,* Vol. 2. New York: Academic Press.

Jones, E. E. & Nisbett, R. E. (1971). *The actor and the observer: Divergent perceptions of the causes of behavior.* Morristown, NJ: General Learning Press.

Kelley, H. H. (1967). Attribution theory in social psychology. In D. Levine (Ed.), *Nebraska symposium on motivation.* Lincoln: University of Nebraska Press.

Kipnis, D. & Lane, W. P. (1962). Self-confidence and leadership. *Journal of Applied Psychology, 46,* 291–295.

Korman, A. K. (1968). The prediction of managerial performance: A review. *Personnel Psychology, 21,* 295–322.

Kouzes, J. M. & Posner, B. Z. (1987). *The leadership challenge: How to get extraordinary things done in organizations.* San Francisco: Jossey-Bass.

Linimon, D., Barron, W. L., & Falbo, T. (1984). Gender differences in perceptions of leadership. *Sex Roles, 11,* 1075–1089.

Locke, E. A., Frederick, E., Lee, C., & Bobko, P. (1984). Effect of self-efficacy, goals, and task strategies on task performance. *Journal of Applied Psychology, 69,* 241–251.

Lord, R. G. (1985). An information-processing approach to social perceptions, leadership, and behavioral measurement in organizations. In B. M. Staw & L. L. Cummings (Eds.), *Research in organizational behavior,* Vol. 7. Greenwich, CT: JAI Press.

Lord, R. G., Foti, R. J., & De Vader, C. (1984). A test of leadership categorization theory: Internal structure, information processing, and leadership perceptions. *Organizational Behavior and Human Performance, 34,* 343–378.

Lord, R. G. & Maher, K. J. (1991). *Leadership and information processing: Linking perceptions and performance.* Boston: Unwin Hyman.

Mayer, J. D. & Salovey, P. (1993). The intelligence of emotional intelligence. *Intelligence, 17,* 433–442.

Meindl, J. R. (1990). On leadership: An alternative to the conventional wisdom. In B. A. Staw (Ed.),

Research in organizational behavior (Vol. 12, pp. 159–203). New York: JAI Press.

Mitchell, T. R., Larson, J. R., & Green, S. G. (1977). Leader behavior situational moderators in group performance: An attributional analysis. *Organizational Behavior and Human Performance, 18,* 254–268.

Mitchell, T. R. & Wood, R. E. (1980). Supervisor's responses to subordinate poor performance: A test of an attribution model. *Organizational Behavior and Human Performance, 25,* 123–138.

Murphy, S. E. (1992). The contribution of leadership experience and self-efficacy to group performance under evaluation apprehension. Unpublished doctoral dissertation, University of Washington, Seattle.

Peters, L. H., Hartke, D. D., & Pohlmann, J. T. (1983). Fiedler's contingency theory of leadership: An application of the meta-analysis procedure of Schmidt and Hunter. *Psychological Bulletin, 97,* 274–285.

Riggio, R. E., Murphy, S. E., & Pirozzolo, F. J. (2001). *Multiple intelligences and leadership.* Mahwah, NJ: Lawrence Erlbaum Associates.

Rosch, E. (1978). Principles of categorization. In E. Rosch & B. B. Lloyd (Eds.), *Cognition and categorization.* Hillsdale, NJ: Lawrence Erlbaum Associates.

Salovey, P. & Mayer, J. D. (1990). Emotional intelligence. *Imagination, Cognition, and Personality, 9,* 185–211.

Scheier, M. F. & Carver, C. S. (1985). Optimism, coping, and health: Assessment and implications of generalized outcome expectancies. *Health Psychology, 4,* 219–247.

Senge, P. M. (1990). *The fifth discipline: The art and practice of the learning organization.* New York: Doubleday.

Shamir, B., House, R. J., & Arthur, M. B. (1992). The motivational effects of charismatic leadership: A self-concept-based theory. *Organizational Science, 4,* 577–594.

Snyder, C. R., Harris, C., Anderson, J. R., Holleran, S. A., Irving, L. M., Sigmon, S. T., Yoshinobu, L., Gibb, J., Langelle, C., & Harney, P. (1991). The will and the ways: Development and validation of an individual-differences measure of hope. *Journal of Personality and Social Psychology, 60,* 570–585.

Solomon, Z., Mikulincer, M., & Hobfall, S. E. (1986). Effects of social support and battle intensity on loneliness and breakdown during combat. *Journal of Personality and Social Psychology, 51,* 1269–1276.

Staw, B. M. & Barsade, S. G. (1992). Affect and managerial performance: A test of the sadder-but-wiser vs. happier-and-smarter hypothesis. *Administrative Science Quarterly, 38,* 304–331.

Sternberg, R. J. (1988). *The triarchic mind: A new theory of human intelligence.* New York: Viking.

Stogdill, R. M. (1948). Personal factors associated with leadership: A survey of the literature. *Journal of Psychology, 25,* 35–71.

Strube, M. J., & Garcia, J. E. (1981). A meta-analytical investigation of Fiedler's Contingency Model of leadership effectiveness. *Psychological Bulletin, 90,* 307–321.

Vroom, V. H., & Yetton, P. W. (1973). *Leadership and decision-making.* Pittsburgh: University of Pittsburgh Press.

Watson, C. B., Chemers, M. M., & Preiser, N. (1996, June). *Collective efficacy: A multi-level analysis.* Presented at the annual meetings of the American Psychological Society, San Francisco, CA.

Weber, M. (1947). *The theory of social and economic organization.* (A. M. Henderson & T. Parsons, Transls.: T. Parsons, Ed.). New York: Free Press. (Originally published in 1924.)

Yukl, G. (1994). *Leadership in organizations* (3rd ed.) Englewood Cliffs, NJ: Prentice-Hall.

Reading 8	The Power of Reframing: Reframing Leadership

Lee G. Bolman and Terrence E. Deal

Virtues and Drawbacks of Organized Activity

The first humanlike primates appeared on earth about twelve million years ago. During most of human evolution, our ancestors were hunters and gatherers. Only the last ten or fifteen thousand years have seen the emergence of institutions more complex than small, simple, nomadic communities. Large organizations emerged to dominate the social landscape even more recently.

There was little need for professional managers when individuals managed their own affairs. Today, things are very different. The challenge of finding the right way to frame our world has become overwhelming in the twenty-first century's turbulent and roiling times. Forms of management and organization effective a few years ago are obsolete today. Sérieyx (1993) calls it the organizational big bang: "The information revolution, the globalization of economies, the proliferation of events that undermine all our certainties, the collapse of the grand ideologies, the arrival of the CNN society which transforms us into an immense, planetary village—all these shocks have overturned the rules of the game and suddenly turned yesterday's organizations into antiques" (pp. 14–15).

The proliferation of complex organizations has made most human activities collective endeavors. We grow up in and start families. We work in and rely on organizations for goods and services. We learn in schools and universities. We play sports in teams. We join clubs and associations. Many of us will grow old and die in hospitals or nursing homes. We build these human enterprises because of what they can do for us. They produce consumer goods, offer entertainment, provide social services and health care, and deliver the mail.

All too often, however, we experience the darker side. Organizations can frustrate and exploit people. Too often, products are flawed, families are dysfunctional, students fail to learn, patients stay sick, and policies make things worse instead of better. Many organizations infuse work with so little meaning that jobs have hardly any value beyond a paycheck. It's hard to find a company these days that doesn't aim officially to delight its customers, but a national survey found that customer satisfaction across industries mostly went downhill between 1995 and 2001 (American Customer Satisfaction Index, 2002). NASA, the same organization that put a man on the moon, launched America's ill-fated space shuttles *Challenger* and *Columbia*. Around the world, schools are blamed for social ills, universities are said to close more minds than they open, and government agencies are criticized for red tape and rigidity. The sarcastic phrase "good enough for government work" reflects widespread cynicism about the performance of public agencies. The private sector has its own problems. Automakers recall faulty cars, baby food producers apologize for adulterated fruit juice, and software companies deliver bugs and "vaporware." Industrial accidents dump chemicals, oil, toxic gas, and radioactive materials into the air and water. Too often, corporate greed and insensitivity create havoc for lives and communities. The bottom line: we are hard pressed to manage organizations so that benefits regularly exceed costs. The big question: Why should this be?

The Curse of Cluelessness

Year after year, the best and brightest managers maneuver or meander their way to the apex of great enterprises. Then they do really dumb things. How do bright people turn out so dim? One theory is that they're too smart for their own good. Feinberg and Tarrant (1995) label it the "self-destructive intelligence syndrome." They argue smart people act stupid because of personality flaws—things like pride, arrogance, and unconscious needs to fail. Lundin and Lundin

Source: From Reframing Organizations 3/e. Reprinted by permission of John Wiley & Sons, Inc.

(1998) came to a similar conclusion: "[Bosses'] dumb behavior is motivated by self-love and ego, which block the capacity for empathy."

It's true that psychic flaws have been apparent in such brilliantly self-destructive individuals as Adolph Hitler, Richard Nixon, and Bill Clinton. But on the whole, intellectually challenged people have as many psychological problems as the best and brightest. The real source of cluelessness is not personality or IQ. It's in *how we think and make sense of the world around us.* Regardless of intellectual wattage, we're out to lunch if we use the wrong ideas for the situation at hand. When you see a distorted picture, you react the wrong way. But you'll probably stick with erroneous ideas if they're all you have. The problem is they lead you into trouble and mask their flaws at the same time. You may be confident that everything is humming along. If not, at least it's not your fault.

Vaughan (1995), in trying to explain the *Challenger* space shuttle disaster, underscored how hard it is for people to surrender their ingrained mental models: "They puzzle over contradictory evidence, but usually succeed in pushing it aside—until they come across a piece of evidence too fascinating to ignore, too clear to misperceive, too painful to deny, which makes vivid still other signals they do not want to see, forcing them to alter and surrender the world-view they have so meticulously constructed" (p. 235).

Charan and Useem (2002) found that this tendency to see no evil is a common problem in organizational disasters. Cisco Systems, for example, had one of the most sophisticated forecasting systems in the business. The system worked superbly during ten years of phenomenal growth in the 1990s but misfired once demand started going downhill. Cisco's leadership had trouble believing that the bottom was really falling out.

Floyd Norris wrote about Enron's former CEO: "There were no problems at Enron while Jeffrey K. Skilling was running the company. Or at least, none that he noticed: [in his testimony to Congress] Mr. Skilling may not have persuaded many listeners. But he did make it clear to those who are investigating Enron at the Justice Department and the S.E.C. that they will have to work to prove he was aware of anything at all during the period he was running one of America's largest companies." (Norris, 2002, p. C-l).

Too often, psychic prisons prevent managers and leaders from seeing old problems in a new light or finding more promising ways to work on perennial challenges. When they don't know what to do, they do more of what they know. This helps explain a number of unsettling reports from the managerial front lines:

- In 2000, the United States was again the world's strongest economy, yet corporate America set a new record for failure: 176 public companies with $95 billion in assets went bankrupt. Aided by a business downturn, it got worse the following year, as 257 companies with $258 billion in assets went under (Charan and Useem, 2002). Charan and Useem traced all that failure back to a single source: "Most companies founder for one reason: managerial error" (p. 52).

- The annual value of corporate mergers grew a hundredfold between 1980 and 2000 (Renner, 2000), even though a recent study found that "83 percent of mergers were unsuccessful in producing any business benefit as regards shareholder value" (KPMG, 2000). Mergers typically benefit shareholders of the acquired firm but harm almost every one else—customers, employees, and the acquiring firm (Tichy, forthcoming). Despite this dismal record, the vast majority of the managers who engineered mergers believed they were successful (KPMG, 2000).

- Hogan, Curphy, and Hogan (1994) estimate that one-half to three-quarters of all American managers are incompetent. The authors didn't study managers in other countries, but, given America's comparative economic success, the results are probably no better elsewhere.

- A study by CSC Index (cited in Gertz and Baptista, 1995) found that fewer than one-third of reengineering initiatives met or exceeded their goals. The same could be said for almost any other popular business improvement scheme, including total quality management and strategic planning.

Small wonder that so many corporate veterans nod assent to Scott Adams's admittedly unscientific "Dilbert principle" "the most ineffective workers are systematically moved the place where they can do the least damage—management" (1996, p. 14).

Strategies for Improving Organizations: The Track Record

We have certainly tried to improve organizations. Legions of managers go to work every day with that hope in mind. Authors and consultants spin out a steady flow of new answers and promising solutions. Policy makers develop laws and regulations to guide organizations on a more correct path.

The most common strategy aims at improving management. Modern mythology promises organizations will work splendidly if well managed. Managers are supposed to have the big picture and look out for their organization's overall health and productivity. Unfortunately, they have not always been equal to the task, even when armed with computers, information systems, flowcharts, quality programs, and a panoply of other tools and techniques. They go forth with this rational arsenal to try to tame our wild and primitive workplace. Yet in the end, irrational forces most often prevail.

When managers cannot solve problems, they hire consultants. Today, the number and variety of advice givers is overwhelming. Most have a specialty: reengineering, quality, mergers and acquisitions, strategy, human resource management, information technology, executive search, outplacement, training, organization development, and many more. For every managerial question or issue, there is a consultant willing to offer assistance—at a premium price.

For all their sage advice and remarkable fees, consultants have yet to make a significant dent in pressing problems plaguing businesses, public agencies, military services, hospitals, or schools. Sometimes the consultants are more hindrance than help. More than a few managers wish that

consultants, like physicians, were bound by the oath "Above all else, do no harm." Meanwhile, consultants grouse about clients' failure to implement their insights. McKinsey & Co., "the high priest of high-level consulting" (Byrne, 2002a, p. 66) worked so closely with Enron that managing partner Rajat Gupta sent his chief lawyer down to Houston after Enron's collapse to see if the consulting company might be in legal trouble. The lawyer reported that McKinsey was safe, and Gupta insisted bravely, "We stand by all the work we did. Beyond that, we can only empathize with the trouble they are going through. It's a sad thing to see" (Byrne, 2002a, p. 68). Clients can be confident that, no matter how bad the results, they are responsible if anything goes wrong. But at least they'll get empathy.

When managers and consultants fail, government frequently jumps in with legislation, policies, and regulations. Constituents badger elected officials to "do something" about a variety of ills: pollution, dangerous products, hazardous working conditions, and chaotic schools, to name a few. Governing bodies respond by making "policy." But policies regularly go awry while meandering from the legislative floor to the targeted problems. A sizable body of research records a continuing saga of perverse ways in which policy implementation distorts policy makers' intentions (Bardach, 1977; Elmore, 1978; Freudenberg and Gramling, 1994; Peters, 1999; Pressman and Wildavsky, 1973).

Difficulties surrounding each strategy for improving organizations are well documented. Exemplary intentions produce more costs than benefits. Problems outlast solutions. It is as if tens of thousands of hard-working, highly motivated pioneers keep hacking away at a swamp that continues to produce new growth faster than the old can be cleared.

There are reasons for optimism. Organizations have changed about as much in the past decade or two as in the previous century. To survive, they had to. Revolutionary changes in technology, the rise of the global economy, and shortened product life cycles have spawned a flurry of activity to design more fluid and more flexible organizational forms. These efforts have engendered a bewildering variety of labels: networks (Chaize, 1992), virtual organizations, adhocracies (Mintzberg, 1979), atomized organizations (Deal and Kennedy, 1982), spider plants (Morgan, 1993), PALs (Kanter, 1989), and many others. These new forms can be seen in network organizations such as the French packaging giant Carnaud et Metal Box. CEO Jean-Marie Descarpentries said his approach to management was simple: "You catalyze toward the future, you trust people, and they discover things you never would have thought of" (Aubrey and Tilliette, 1990, p. 142).

New organization models also flourish in companies such as Pret à Manger (the U.K.'s socially conscious sandwich shops), Saturn (the automobile producer with a soul), and Novo-Nordisk (the Danish pharmaceutical company that includes environmental and social metrics in its bottom line). All three are passionate about core values and create familylike bonds among employees and customers. The information technology revolution has bred an array of innovative forms visible in such firms as eBay, the phenomenally successful Internet auction company, and software innovator SAS Institute. Despite such successes, there are still too many failures. How can leaders and managers improve the odds for themselves as well as their organizations?

Theory Base

Managers, consultants, and policy makers draw, formally or otherwise, on a variety of theories in an effort to change or improve organizations. Yet only in the past few decades have social scientists devoted much time or attention to developing ideas about how organizations work (or why they often fail). In the social sciences, several major schools of thought have evolved. Each has its own concepts and assumptions and espouses a view of how to bring social collectives under control.

Each tradition claims a scientific foundation. But theories easily become theologies, preaching a single, parochial scripture. Competing gospels present limited versions of reality but expanded prophetic visions of what the future holds, along with a definite set of strategies for reaching the Promised Land. Modern managers trying to get on top of things encounter a cacophony of voices and visions.

Consider an executive browsing in the management section of her local bookstore on a brisk winter day early in 2003. She is worried about her company's flagging performance and about the chance that her job might soon disappear. She spots the black-on-white spine of *The Six Sigma Way: How GE, Motorola, and Other Top Companies Are Honing Their Performance* (Pande, Neuman, and Cavanagh, 2000). She's not exactly sure what six sigma is, but she knows a lot of her peers are talking about it. Scanning the book, she is drawn to phrases such as "a flexible system for improved business leadership and performance," and "a new formula for 21st-century business success." Jumping to chapter 2, she encounters, "In Figure 2.2 you see a model of a company as seen from a process-flow perspective. On the far left are the inputs to the process (or system); in the middle is the organization or process itself (depicted as a process map or flowchart). Finally, on the far right, are the all-important customer, end products and (let's hope) profits."

"This stuff may be terrific," the executive tells herself, "but it seems a little dry."

Then she spots *Primal Leadership: Realizing the Power of Emotional Intelligence* (Goleman, McKee, and Boyatzis, 2002). The authors talk about how leaders can cultivate good feelings by developing the "four domains of emotional intelligence": self-awareness, self-management, social awareness, and relationship management.

"Nice," she mumbles, "but a little squishy. Let's look for something a little more down to earth."

She finds *What Would Machiavelli Do? The Ends Justify the Meanness* (Bing, 2000). She ponders the book's basic premise: those who get ahead in business aren't necessarily smarter, just meaner. She reads, "A simple, detailed plan for those with the courage to leave kindness and decency behind, to seize the future by the throat and make it cough up money, power, and superior office space."

"He can't be serious, can he?" she wonders. "Anyway, it's too cynical. Isn't there something more uplifting?"

She spots *From Worst to First: Behind the Scenes of Continental's Remarkable Comeback* (Bethune and Huler, 1999). She glances at some of the chapter titles: "The Last Suppers, or Whose Problem Is It?" "Fly to Win, or You Can Make Pizza So Cheap No One Wants to Eat It," and "Crop Duster's Son." She reads that Gordon Bethune's first official act when he took charge of Continental was to unlock the executive suite doors to show employees he wasn't trying to shut them out. He also gathered a group of employees in the company's parking lot to burn the old restrictive policy manuals.

"Bonfires in my company?" she muses. "I don't think so."

Frames and Reframing

Had the executive visited another store in another year, she might have encountered other works but a similar range of opinions. Our purpose is to sort through multiple voices competing for managers' attention. In doing so, we consolidate major schools of organizational thought into four perspectives.[1] There are many ways to label such outlooks—mental models, maps, mind-sets, schema, and cognitive lenses, to name a few. We have chosen the label *frames*. In describing frames, we deliberately mix metaphors, referring to them as windows, maps, tools, lenses, orientations, and perspectives because all of those images capture part of the ecumenical idea we want to convey.

As a mental map, a frame is a set of ideas or assumptions you carry in your head. It helps you understand and negotiate a particular "territory." The territory isn't necessarily defined by geography. It could be a sport, an art form, an academic subject, or anything else you care about. Suppose you like to cook and particularly enjoy Chinese food. You might develop an extensive stock of knowledge and concepts about Chinese cuisine. Eventually your understanding of subtle regional differences in spicing and ingredients might enable you to pinpoint which part of China a dish came from. Someone else trying to identify the same dish might not be sure whether it came from Beijing or Bombay. As the example indicates, the better your map, the easier it is to negotiate a terrain. But every map is bounded. A map of New York won't be of much help trying to navigate San Francisco. Modern automobiles often come with computerized navigation systems that tell you where you are and guide you turn-by-turn to your destination. It would be a big help if organizations could provide the same thing to managers. Unfortunately, to avoid getting lost, managers still need to develop and carry accurate maps in their heads.

Frames are windows on the world of leadership and management. A good frame makes it easier to know what you are up against and what you can do about it. Goran Carstedt, the talented executive who led the turnaround of Volvo's French division in the 1980s, put it this way: "The world simply can't be made sense of, facts can't be organized, unless you have a mental model to begin with. That theory does not have to be the right one, because you can alter it along the way as information comes in. But you can't begin to learn without some concept that gives you expectations or hypotheses" (Hampden-Turner, 1992, p. 167).

Artistic managers such as Carstedt learn fluidly because they are able to frame and reframe experience, sorting through the tangled underbrush to find solutions to problems. A critic once commented to Cézanne, "That doesn't look anything like a sunset." Pondering his painting, Cézanne responded, "Then you don't see sunsets the way I do." Like Cézanne, leaders have to find new ways to see things. They must also articulate and communicate their vision so others can learn to shift perspectives when needed.

Like maps, frames are both windows on a territory and tools for navigation. Every tool has distinctive strengths and limitations. The right tool makes a job easier, but the wrong one just gets in the way. One or two tools may suffice for simple jobs, but not for more complex undertakings. Managers who master the hammer and expect all problems to behave like nails find organizational life confusing and frustrating. The wise manager, like a skilled carpenter or a professional chef, wants at hand a diverse collection of high-quality implements. Experienced managers also understand the difference between possessing a tool and knowing how to use it. Only experience and practice bring the skill and wisdom to size up a situation and use tools well.

Our goal is usable knowledge. We have sought ideas powerful enough to capture the subtlety and complexity of life in organizations yet simple enough to be useful. Our distillation has drawn much from the social sciences—particularly from sociology, psychology, political science, and anthropology. Thousands of managers and scores of organizations have also been our mentors. They helped us sift through social science research to identify ideas that work in practice. We have sorted insights drawn from both research and practice into four major frames, used by academics and practitioners alike to make sense of organizations. The four frames that we first described in the early 1980s—structural, human resource, political, and symbolic (Bolman and Deal, 1984)—have since been explored and adapted by other organizational scholars (including Bergquist, 1992; Birnbaum, 1988, 1992; and Dunford, 1992). The worried executive earlier in the chapter, seeking revelation in a bookstore, rediscovered the same four perspectives.

The first book she stumble on, *The Six Sigma Way*, extends a long tradition that treats an organization as a factory. Drawing from sociology and management science, the *structural frame* emphasizes goals, specialized roles, and formal relationships. Structures—commonly depicted by organization charts—are designed to fit an organization's environment and technology.

Organizations allocate responsibilities to participants ("division of labor"). They then create rules, policies, procedures, and hierarchies to coordinate diverse activities into a unified strategy. Problems arise when structure is poorly aligned with current circumstances. At that point, some form of reorganization or redesign is needed to remedy the mismatch.

A simple but fateful example: Riebling (2002) documents the long history of conflict and head butting between America's two intelligence agencies, the Federal Bureau of Investigation and the Central Intelligence Agency. Both are charged to combat espionage and terrorism, but the FBI's writ runs within the United States, while the CIA's mandate is everywhere else. Structurally, the FBI is housed in the Department of Justice and reports to the Attorney General, while the CIA reports through the Director of Central Intelligence to the president. At a number of major junctures in American history (including the assassination of President John F. Kennedy, the Iran-Contra scandal, and the September 11 terrorist attack), each agency held pieces of a larger puzzle, but coordination snafus made it hard for anyone to identify the individual pieces, much less to put them together.

Our executive next encountered *Primal Leadership,* with its focus on an organization's human side. The *human resource frame,* based particularly on ideas from psychology, sees an organization as much like an extended family, made up of individuals with needs, feelings, prejudices, skills, and limitations. People have a great capacity to learn and often an even greater capacity to defend old attitudes and beliefs. From a human resource perspective, the key challenge is to tailor organizations to individuals—to find a way for people to get the job done while feeling good about what they are doing. The conflict between the FBI and the CIA, for example, was fueled in part by a long-running feud between the agencies' two patron saints, J. Edgar Hoover and "Wild Bill" Donovan. When he first became FBI director in the 1920s, Hoover reported to Donovan, who tried to get him fired. When

World War II broke out, Hoover wanted the FBI to become the nation's worldwide intelligence agency. He fumed when President Franklin D. Roosevelt instead created a new agency and made Donovan its director.

What Would Machiavelli Do? is a contemporary application of the *political frame*, rooted in the work of political scientists. It sees organizations as arenas, contests, or jungles. Parochial interests compete for power and scarce resources. Conflict is rampant because of enduring differences in needs, perspectives, and lifestyles among competing individuals and groups. Bargaining, negotiation, coercion, and compromise are a normal part of everyday life. Coalitions form around specific interests and change as issues come and go. Problems arise when power is concentrated in the wrong places or is so broadly dispersed that nothing gets done. Solutions arise from political skill and acumen—as Machiavelli suggested centuries ago in *The Prince* ([1514] 1961). Conflict between the FBI and the CIA was exacerbated by competition for support and funding from Congress and the White House.

Finally, our executive encountered *From Worst to First,* with its emphasis on cultural change as the key to organizational transformation. The *symbolic frame,* drawing on social and cultural anthropology, treats organizations as tribes, theaters, or carnivals. It abandons assumptions of rationality more prominent in other frames. It sees organizations as cultures, propelled more by rituals, ceremonies, stories, heroes, and myths than by rules, policies, and managerial authority. Organization is also theater: actors play their roles in the organizational drama while audiences form impressions from what is seen onstage. Problems arise when actors blow their parts, when symbols lose their meaning, or when ceremonies and rituals lose their potency. We rebuild the expressive or spiritual side of organizations through the use of symbol, myth, and magic. The FBI, which built its image with the dramatic capture or killing of notorious gang leaders, bank robbers, and foreign agents, liked to pounce quickly and publicly on suspects.

The CIA preferred to work in the shadows, believing that patience and secrecy were a better route to its long-term goal of collecting intelligence and rooting out foreign spies.

The overview of the four-frame model in Table 1a shows that each of the frames has its own image of reality. You may be drawn to one or two frames and repelled by others. Some frames may seem clear and straightforward, while others seem puzzling. But learning to apply all four deepens your appreciation and understanding of organizations. Galileo discovered this when he devised the first telescope. Each lens he added contributed to a more accurate image of the heavens. Successful managers take advantage of the same truth. They reframe until they understand the situation at hand. They do this by using more than one frame, or perspective, to develop both a diagnosis of what they are up against and strategies for moving forward.

This claim has stimulated a growing body of research. Dunford and Palmer (1995) found that management courses teaching multiple frames had significant positive effects over both the short run and the long—in fact, 98 percent of their respondents rated reframing as helpful or very helpful, and about 90 percent felt it gave them a competitive advantage. Another series of studies has shown that the ability to use multiple frames is associated with greater effectiveness for managers and leaders (Bensimon, 1989, 1990; Birnbaum, 1992; Bolman and Deal, 1991, 1992a, 1992b; Heimovics, Herman, and Jurkiewicz Coughlin, 1993, 1995; Wimpelberg, 1987).

Multiframe thinking requires elastic movement beyond narrow and mechanical approaches for understanding organizations. Table 2 presents two distinctive ways of approaching management and leadership. One is a rational-technical approach emphasizing certainty and control. The other is a more expressive, artistic conception encouraging flexibility, creativity, and interpretation. The first sees managers as technicians; the second sees them as leaders and artists.

We cannot count the number of times managers have told us that they handled some

TABLE 1A │ OVERVIEW OF THE FOUR-FRAME MODEL

	Frame			
	Structural	Human Resource	Political	Symbolic
Metaphor for organization	Factory or machine	Family	Jungle	Carnival, temple, theatre
Central concepts	Rules, roles, goals, policies, technology, environment	Needs, skills, relationships	Power, conflict, competition, organizational politics	Culture, meaning, metaphor, ritual, ceremony, stories, heroes
Image of leadership	Social architecture	Empowerment	Advocacy	Inspiration
Basic leadership challenge	Attune structure to task, technology, environment	Align organizational and human needs	Develop agenda and power base	Create faith, beauty, meaning

TABLE 2 │ EXPANDING MANAGERIAL THINKING

How Managers Think	How Managers Might Think
They often have a limited view of organizations (for example, attributing almost all problems to individuals' flaws and errors).	They need a holistic framework that encourages inquiry into a range of significant issues: people, power, structure, and symbols.
Regardless of a problem's source, managers often choose rational and structural solutions: facts, logic, restructuring.	They need a palette that offers an array of options: bargaining as well as training, celebration as well as reorganization.
Managers often value certainty, rationality, and control while fearing ambiguity, paradox, and "going with the flow."	They need to develop creativity, risk taking, and playfulness in responses to life's dilemmas and paradoxes, focusing as much on finding the right question as the right answer, on finding meaning and faith amid clutter and confusion.
Leaders often rely on the "one right answer" and the "one best way"; they are stunned at the turmoil and resistance they generate.	Leaders need passionate, unwavering commitment to principle, combined with flexibility in understanding and responding to events.

problem the "only way" it could be done. Such statements betray a failure of both imagination and courage. It may be comforting to think that failure was unavoidable and we did all we could. But it can be enormously liberating to realize there is *always* more than one way to respond to any problem or dilemma. Those who master the ability

to reframe report a liberating sense of choice and power. Managers are imprisoned only to the extent that their palette of ideas is impoverished.

This lack of imagination—Langer (1989) calls it "mindlessness"—is a major cause of the shortfall between the reach and the grasp of so many organizations—the empty chasm between dreams and reality, between noble aspirations and disappointing results. The gap is painfully acute in a world in which organizations dominate so much of our lives.

Akira Kurosawa's film *Rashomon* recounts the same event through the eyes of several witnesses. Each tells a very different story. Organizations are filled with people who have their own interpretations of what is and should be happening. Each version contains a glimmer of truth, but each is a product of the prejudices and blind spots of its maker. No single story is comprehensive enough to make an organization truly understandable or manageable. Effective managers need multiple tools, the skill to use each of them, and the wisdom to match frames to situations.[2]

Artistry is neither exact nor precise. Artists interpret experience and express it in forms that can be felt, understood, and appreciated by others. Art embraces emotion, subtlety, ambiguity. An artist reframes the world so others can see new possibilities. Modern organizations often rely too much on engineering and too little on art in searching for attributes such as quality, commitment, and creativity. Art is not a replacement for engineering but an enhancement. Artistic leaders and managers help us see beyond today's reality to new forms that release untapped individual energies and improve collective performance. The leader as artist relies on images as well as memos, poetry as well as policy, reflection as well as command, and reframing as well as refitting.

As organizations have become pervasive and dominant, they have also become formidably difficult to understand and manage. The result is that managers are often nearly as clueless as the Dilberts of the world think they are. The consequences of myopic management and leadership show up every day, sometimes in small and subtle ways, sometimes in catastrophes like the collapse of Enron or WorldCom. Our basic premise is that a primary cause of managerial failure is faulty thinking rooted in inadequate ideas. Managers and those who try to help them too often rely on narrow models that capture only part of the realities of organizational life.

Learning multiple perspectives, or frames, is a defense against cluelessness. Frames serve multiple functions. They are maps that aid navigation, and tools for solving problems and getting things done. This book is organized around four frames that are rooted in both managerial practice and social science research. The *structural frame* focuses on the architecture of organization—the design of units and subunits, rules and roles, goals and policies—that shape and channel decisions and activities. The *human resource frame* emphasizes an understanding of people, with their strengths and foibles, reason and emotion, desires and fears. The *political frame* sees organizations as competitive arenas characterized by scarce resources, competing interests, and struggles for power and advantage. Finally, the *symbolic frame* focuses on issues of meaning and faith. It puts ritual, ceremony, story, play, and culture at the heart of organizational life.

Each of the frames is both powerful and coherent. Collectively, they make it possible to reframe, viewing the same thing from multiple perspectives. When the world seems hopelessly confusing and nothing is working, reframing is a powerful tool for gaining clarity, generating new options, and finding strategies that work.

The Idea of Leadership

Leadership is universally offered as a panacea for almost any social problem. Around the world, middle managers say their enterprise would thrive if only senior management showed "real leadership." A widely accepted canon holds that leadership is a very good thing that we need more of—at least, more of the right kind. "For many—perhaps for most—Americans, leadership is a word that has risen above normal workaday usage as a conveyer of meaning and has become a kind of incantation. We feel that if we repeat it often enough with sufficient ardor, we shall ease our sense of having lost our way, our sense of things unaccomplished, of duties unfulfilled" (Gardner, 1986, p. l). Yet there is confusion and disagreement about what leadership means and how much difference it can make.

Sennett (1980, p. 197) writes, "Authority is not a thing; it is a search for solidity and security in the strength of others which will seem to be like a thing." The same is true of leadership. It is not a tangible thing. It exists only in relationships and in the imagination and perception of the engaged parties. Most images of leadership suggest that leaders get things done and get people to do things; leaders are powerful. Yet many examples of the exercise of power fall outside our image of leadership: armed robbers, extortionists, bullies, traffic cops. Implicitly, we expect leaders to persuade or inspire rather than to coerce or give orders. We also expect leaders to produce cooperative effort and to pursue goals that transcend narrow self-interest.

Leadership is also distinct from authority, though authorities may be leaders. Weber (1947) linked authority to legitimacy. People choose to obey authority so long as they believe the authority is legitimate. Authority and leadership are both built on voluntary obedience. If leaders lose legitimacy, they lose the capacity to lead. But many examples of obeying authority fall outside the domain of leadership. As Gardner (1989, p. 7) put it, "The meter maid has authority, but not necessarily leadership."

Heifetz (1994) argues that authority can be an impediment to leadership: "Authority constrains leadership because in times of distress, people expect too much. They form inappropriate dependencies that isolate their authorities behind a mask of knowing. [The leadership role] is played badly if authorities reinforce dependency and delude themselves into thinking that they have the answers when they do not. Feeling pressured to know, they will surely come up with an answer, even if poorly tested, misleading, and wrong" (p. 180).

Leadership is also different from management, though the two are easily confused. One may be a leader without being a manager, and many managers could not "lead a squad of seven-year-olds to the ice-cream counter" (Gardner, 1989, p. 2). Bennis and Nanus (1985) offer the distinction that "managers do things right, and leaders do the right thing" (p. 21). Kotter (1988) echoes many writers in seeing management as primarily about structural nuts and bolts: planning, organizing, and controlling. He views leadership as a change-oriented process of visioning, networking, and building relationships. But Gardner (1989) argues against contrasting leadership and management too sharply because leaders may "end up looking like a cross between Napoleon and the Pied Piper, and managers like unimaginative clods" (p. 3). He suggests several dimensions for distinguishing leadership from management. Leaders think long-term, look outside as well as inside, and influence constituents beyond their immediate formal jurisdiction. They emphasize vision and renewal and have the political skills to cope with the challenging requirements of multiple constituencies.

The Context of Leadership

In story and myth, leaders are often lonely heroes and itinerant warriors, wed only to their honor and their cause. Think of Joan of Arc, Sir Lancelot, the Lone Ranger, or Rambo. But traditional notions of solitary, heroic leaders can lead us to focus too much on individuals and too little on the stage where they play their parts. Leaders make things happen, but things also make leaders happen. We need only look at the transformation in Giuliani's image after September 11 to see that situation influences what leaders must do and what they can do. Giuliani found himself on-stage in an unplanned theater of horror, and he delivered the performance of his life. Another stage would have required, and permitted, different leadership. No single formula is possible or advisable for the great range of situations potential leaders encounter.

Heroic images of leadership convey the notion of a one-way process: leaders lead and followers follow. This view blinds us to the reality of the relationship between leader and follower. Leaders are not independent actors; they both shape and are shaped by their constituents (Gardner, 1989; Simmel, 1950). Leaders often promote a new idea or initiative only *after* a large number of their constituents already favor it (Cleveland, 1985). Leadership, then, is not simply a matter of what a leader does but of what occurs in a relationship. Leaders' actions generate responses from others that in turn affect the leaders' capacity for taking further initiatives (Murphy, 1985). As Briand (1993, p. 39) puts it, "A 'leader' who makes a decision and then attempts to 'sell' it to the public is not a wise leader and will likely not prove an effective one. The point is not that those who are already leaders should do less, but that everyone else can and should do more. Everyone must accept responsibility for the people's well-being, and everyone has a role to play in sustaining it."

It is common to equate leadership with position, but this relegates all those in the low hierarchy to the passive role of follower. It also reinforces the widespread tendency of senior executives to take on more responsibility than they can adequately discharge (Oshry, 1995). Administrators are leaders only to the extent that others grant them cooperation and follow their lead. Conversely, one can be a leader without a position of formal authority. Good organizations encourage leadership from many quarters (Kanter, 1983; Barnes and Kriger, 1986).

Leadership is thus a subtle process of mutual influence fusing thought, feeling, and action to produce cooperative effort in the service of purposes and values embraced by *both* the leader and the led. Single-frame managers are unlikely to understand and attend to the intricacies of a holistic process.

Reframing Leadership

Reframing offers a way to get beyond narrow and oversimplified views of leadership. Each of the frames offers a distinctive image of the leadership process. Depending on leader and circumstance, each view can lead to compelling and constructive leadership images, but none is right for all times and seasons. In this section, we discuss four images of leadership summarized in Table 1b. For each, we examine skills and processes and propose rules of thumb for successful leadership practice.

Architect or Tyrant? Structural Leadership

Structural leadership often evokes images of petty tyrants and rigid bureaucrats who never met a rule they didn't like. Little literature exists on structural leadership in comparison to other frames. Some structural theorists have argued

TABLE 1B | REFRAMING LEADERSHIP

| Frame | Leadership Is Effective When | | Leadership Is Ineffective When | |
| | Leadership | | Leadership | |
	Leader Is	Process Is	Leader Is	Process Is
Structural	Analyst, architect	Analysis, design	Petty tyrant	Management by detail and fiat
Human resource	Catalyst, servant	Support, empowerment	Weakling, pushover	Abdication
Political	Advocate, negotiator	Advocacy, coalition building	Con artist, thug	Manipulation, fraud
Symbolic	Prophet, poet	Inspiration, framing experience	Fanatic, fool	Mirage, smoke and mirrors

that leadership is neither important nor basic (Hall, 1987). But the effects of structural leadership can be powerful and enduring, even if the style is subtler and less obviously heroic than other forms. Collins and Porras (1994) reported that the founders of many highly successful companies, such as Hewlett-Packard and Sony, had neither a clear vision for their organization nor even a particular product in mind. They were "clock builders": social architects who focused on designing and building an effective organization.

One of the great architects in business history was Alfred P. Sloan, Jr., who became president of General Motors in 1923 and remained a dominant force in the company until his retirement in 1956. The structure and strategy he established made GM the world's largest corporation. He has been described as "the George Washington of the GM culture" (Lee, 1988, p. 42), even though his "genius was not in inspirational leadership, but in organizational structures" (p. 43).

At the turn of the twentieth century, some thirty manufacturers produced automobiles in the United States. In 1899, they produced a grand total of about six hundred cars. Most of these small carmakers stumbled out of the starting gate, leaving two late entries, the Ford Motor Company (founded by Henry Ford in 1903) and GM (founded by William Durant in 1908) as front-runners in the race to dominate the American automobile industry. Henry Ford's single-minded determination to build an affordable car pushed Ford into a commanding lead when Sloan took over General Motors.

Under GM's founder, Billy Durant, the company's divisions operated as independent fiefdoms. Durant had built GM by buying everything in sight, thus forming a loose combination of previously independent firms. "GM did not have adequate knowledge or control of the individual operating divisions. It was management by crony, with the divisions operating on a horse-trading basis. The main thing to note here is that no one had the needed information or the needed control over the divisions. The divisions continued to spend lavishly, and their requests

for additional funds were met" (Sloan, 1965, pp. 27–28).

Uncontrolled costs and a business slump in 1920 created a financial crisis. Chevrolet lost $5 million in 1921, and only Du Pont money and Buick's profitability kept GM afloat (Sloan, 1965). In Sloan's first year, 1923, matters got worse. GM's market share dropped from 20 percent to 17 percent, while Ford's increased to 55 percent. But change was afoot. Henry Ford had a disdain for organization and clung to his original vision of a single, low-priced, mass-market car. The Model T was cheap and reliable, but Ford stuck with the same design for almost twenty years. The "Tin Lizzie" was a marketing miracle when customers would buy anything with four wheels and a motor. Ford saw no great need for creature comforts in the Model T, but Sloan surmised that consumers would pay more for amenities (like windows to keep out rain and snow). His strategy worked, and Chevrolet soon began to gnaw off large chunks of Ford's market share. By 1928, Model T sales had dropped so precipitously that Henry Ford was forced to close his massive River Rouge plant for a year to retool. General Motors took the lead in the great auto race for the first time in twenty years. For the rest of the twentieth century, no company ever sold more cars than General Motors.

Sloan recognized that GM needed a better structural form. The dominant model of the time was a centralized, functional organization, but Sloan felt that such a structure would not work for GM. Instead, he created one of the world's first decentralized organizations. His basic principle was simple: centralize planning and resource allocation; decentralize operating decisions. Under Sloan's model, divisions focused on making and selling cars, while top management focused on long-range strategy and major funding decisions. The central staff made sure that top management had the information and control systems it needed to make strategic decisions.

The structure worked. By the late 1920s, GM had a more versatile organization with a broader product line than Ford. With Henry Ford still dominating his highly centralized company, Ford was poorly positioned to compete with GM's multiple divisions, each producing its own cars at different prices. GM's pioneering structural form eventually set the standard for others: "Although they developed many variations and although in very recent years they have been occasionally mixed into a matrix form, only two basic organizational structures have been used for the management of large industrial enterprises. One is the centralized, functional departmentalized type perfected by General Electric and Du Pont before World War I. The other is the multidivisional, decentralized structure initially developed at General Motors and also at Du Pont in the 1920s" (Chandler, 1977, p. 463).

In the 1980s, GM found itself with another structural leader, Roger Smith, at the helm. The results were less satisfying. Like Sloan, Smith ascended to the top job at a difficult time. In 1980, his first year as GM's chief executive, all American automakers lost money. It was GM's first loss since 1921. Recognizing that the company had serious competitive problems, Smith relied on structure and technology to make it "the world's first 21st century corporation" (Lee, 1988, p. 16). He restructured vehicle operations and spent billions of dollars in a quest for paperless offices and robotized assembly plants. The changes were dramatic, but the results were dismal.

Why did Smith stumble where Sloan had succeeded? They were equally uncharismatic. Sloan was a somber, quiet engineer who habitually looked as if he were sucking a lemon. Smith's leadership aura was not helped by his blotchy complexion and squeaky voice. Neither had great sensitivity to human resource or symbolic issues. Why, then, was Sloan's structural contribution so durable and Smith's so problematic? The answer comes down to how well each implemented the right structural form. Structural leaders succeed not because of inspiration but because they have the right design for the times and are able to get their structural changes implemented.

Effective structural leaders share several characteristics.

Structural Leaders Do Their Homework. Sloan was a brilliant engineer who had grown up in the auto industry. Before coming to GM, he was chief executive of an auto accessories company where he implemented a divisional structure. When GM bought his firm in 1916, Sloan became a vice president and board member. Working under Durant, he devoted much of his energy to studying GM's structural problems. He pioneered the development of more sophisticated internal information systems and better market research. He was an early convert to group decision making and created a committee structure to make major decisions.

Roger Smith had spent his entire career with General Motors, but most of his jobs were in finance. Much of his vision for General Motors involved changes in production technology, an area where he had little experience or expertise.

Structural Leaders Rethink the Relationship of Structure, Strategy, and Environment. Sloan's new structure was intimately tied to a strategy for reaching the automotive market. He foresaw a growing market, improvements in automobiles, and more discriminating consumers. In the face of Henry Ford's stubborn attachment to the Model T, Sloan introduced the "price pyramid" (cars for every pocketbook) and the annual model change. Automotive technology in the 1920s was evolving almost as fast as electronics in the 1990s, and the annual model change soon became the industry norm.

For a variety of reasons, GM in the 1960s began to move away from Sloan's concepts. Fearing a government effort to break up the corporation, GM reduced the independence of the car divisions and centralized design and engineering. Increasingly, the divisions became marketing groups required to build and sell cars the corporation designed. In the early 1980s, "look-alike cars" became the standard across divisions. Many consumers became confused and angry when they found it hard to see the subtle differences between a Chevrolet and a Cadillac.

Smith's vision was truncated, focused more on reducing costs than on selling cars. As he saw it, GM's primary competitive problem was high costs driven by high wages. He hoped to solve that by replacing workers with machines. He gave little support to efforts already under way at GM to improve working conditions on the shop floor. Ironically, his two best investments—NUMMI and Saturn—succeeded precisely because of innovative approaches to managing people: "With only a fraction of the money invested in GM's heavily robotized plants, [the NUMMI plant at] Fremont is more efficient and produces better-quality cars than any plant in the GM system" (Hampton & Norman, 1987, p. 102).

Structural Leaders Focus on Implementation.

Structural leaders often miscalculate difficulties of putting their design in place. They underestimate resistance, skimp on training, fail to build a political base, and misread cultural cues. As a result, they are often thwarted by neglected human resource, political, and symbolic barriers. Sloan was no human resource specialist, but he intuitively saw the need to get understanding and acceptance of major decisions. He did that by continually asking for advice and by establishing committees and task forces to address major issues.

Effective Structural Leaders Experiment, Evaluate, and Adapt.

Sloan tinkered constantly with GM's structure and strategy and encouraged others to do likewise. The Great Depression produced a drop of 72 percent in sales at GM between 1929 and 1932, but the company adapted very adroitly to hard times. It increased its market share and made money every year. Sloan briefly centralized operations to survive the depression but decentralized again once business began to recover. In the 1980s, Smith spent billions on his campaign to modernize the corporation and cut costs, yet GM lost market share every year and continued to be the industry's highest-cost producer: "Much of the advanced technology that GM acquired at such high cost hindered rather than improved productivity. Runaway robots started welding doors shut

at the new Detroit-Hamtramck Cadillac plant. Luckily for Ford and Chrysler, poverty prevented them from indulging in the same orgy of spending on robots" ("On a Clear Day . . . ," 1989, p. 77).

Catalyst or Wimp? Human Resource Leadership

The tiny trickle of writing about structural leadership is swamped by a torrent of human resource literature (among the best: Argyris, 1962; Bennis and Nanus, 1985; Blanchard and Johnson, 1982; Bradford and Cohen, 1984; Fiedler, 1967; Fiedler and Chemers, 1974; Hersey, 1984; Hollander, 1978; House, 1971; Levinson, 1968; Likert, 1961, 1967; Vroom and Yetton, 1973; and Waterman, 1994). Human resource theorists typically advocate openness, mutuality, listening, coaching, participation, and empowerment. They view the leader as a facilitator and catalyst who motivates and empowers subordinates. The leader's power comes from talent, sensitivity, and service rather than position or force. Greenleaf (1973) argues that followers "will freely respond only to individuals who are chosen as leaders because they are proven and trusted as servants" (p. 4). He adds, "The servant-leader makes sure that other people's highest priority needs are being served. The best test [of leadership] is: do those served grow as persons; do they, *while being served,* become healthier, wiser, freer, more autonomous, more likely themselves to become servants?" (p. 7).

Will managers who adhere to such images be respected leaders who make a difference? Or will they be seen as naïve and weak, carried along on the current of other people's energy?

Human Resource Leaders Believe in People and Communicate Their Belief.

Human resource leaders are passionate about "productivity through people" (Peters and Waterman, 1982). They demonstrate this faith in their words and actions and often build it into a core philosophy or credo. Fred Smith, founder and CEO of Federal Express, sees "putting people first" as the cornerstone of his company's success: "We discovered a long time ago that customer satisfaction really begins with employee satisfaction. That belief is incorporated in our corporate philosophy statement: People—Service—Profit" (Waterman, 1994, p. 89).

William Hewlett, cofounder of the electronics giant Hewlett-Packard, put it this way:

> The dignity and worth of the individual is a very important part of the HP Way. With this in mind, many years ago we did away with time clocks, and more recently we introduced the flexible work hours program. This is meant to be an expression of trust and confidence in people, as well as providing them with an opportunity to adjust their work schedules to their personal lives. Many new HP people as well as visitors often note and comment to us about another HP way—that is, our informality and our being on a first-name basis. I could cite other examples, but the problem is that none by [itself] really catches the essence of what the HP Way is all about. You can't describe it in numbers and statistics. In the last analysis, it is a spirit, a point of view. There is a feeling that everyone is part of a team, and that team is HP. It is an idea that is based on the individual. (Peters and Waterman, 1982, p. 244)

Human Resource Leaders Are Visible and Accessible. Peters and Waterman (1982) popularized the notion of "management by wandering around"—the idea that managers need to get out of their offices and spend time with workers and customers. Patricia Carrigan, the first woman to be a plant manager at General Motors, modeled this technique in the course of turning around two GM plants, each with a long history of union-management conflict (Kouzes and Posner, 1987). In both situations, she began by going to the plant floor to introduce herself to workers and ask how they thought the plant could be improved. One worker commented that before Carrigan came, "I didn't know who the plant manager was. I wouldn't have recognized him if I saw him." When she left her first assignment after three years, the local union gave her a plaque. It concluded, "Be it resolved that Pat M. Carrigan, through the exhibiting of these qualities as a people person, has played a vital role in the creation of a new way of life at the Lakewood plant. Therefore, be it

resolved that the members of Local 34 will always warmly remember Pat M. Carrigan as one of us" (Kouzes and Posner, 1987, p. 36).

Effective Human Resource Leaders Empower Others. Human resource leaders often refer to their employees as "partners," "owners," or "associates." They make it clear that employees have a stake in the organization's success and a right to be involved in making decisions.

Advocate or Hustler? Political Leadership

Sometimes, even in the private sector leaders find that they have to plunge into a political arena to move their company where it needs to go. Consider two chief executives from quite dissimilar eras: Lee Iacocca, who became chief executive of Chrysler when the company was near death in the late 1970s, and Carleton "Carly" Fiorina, who became CEO of Silicon Valley giant Hewlett-Packard in July 1999.

Even though Iacocca had done his homework before accepting Chrysler's offer, things were even worse than he expected. Chrysler was losing money so fast that bankruptcy seemed almost inevitable. He concluded that the only way out was to persuade the U.S. government to guarantee massive loans. It was a tough sell; much of Congress, the media, and the American public were against the idea. Iacocca had to convince all of them that government intervention was in their best interest as well as Chrysler's.

Like Iacocca, Fiorina came in to head a troubled giant. HP's problems were not as bad as Chrysler's; it was still a profitable company with more than $40 billion in annual revenue. But customer service was deteriorating, bureaucracy was stifling innovation, and HP seemed to be falling behind the technology curve. *Business Week* described HP as part of "the clueless establishment" (Burrows and Elstrom, 1999, p. 76). Fiorina's arrival was big news for more than one reason. She was only the fifth CEO in HP's sixty-year history, and she was the first to come from outside since Bill (Hewlett) and Dave

(Packard) founded the company in a Palo Alto garage in 1938. She was also the first woman to head a company of HP's size in any industry. She brought many strengths, including "a silver tongue and an iron will" (Burrows and Elstrom, 1999, p. 76). But she faced daunting challenges, especially after she set her sights on a merger with another, floundering, $40 billion company, Compaq. Her board supported her initiative, but Bill and Dave's heirs, who controlled more than 15 percent of HP's stock, didn't. Fiorina had to win a massive gunfight at HP corral or lose her job.

Ultimately, Iacocca got his guarantees and Fiorina got her merger. Both won their battles by artfully employing a set of principles for political leaders.

Political Leaders Clarify What They Want and What They Can Get.   Political leaders are realists. They avoid letting what they want cloud their judgment about what is possible. Iacocca translated Chrysler's survival into the realistic goal of getting enough help to make it through a couple of difficult years without going under. He was always careful to ask not for money but for loan guarantees, insisting that the guarantees would cost the taxpayers nothing because Chrysler would pay back its loans. Fiorina, too, was realistic. Once she knew she was in a nasty, public squabble, she zeroed in on one goal: getting enough votes to put the merger through.

Political Leaders Assess the Distribution of Power and Interests.   Political leaders map the political terrain by thinking carefully about the key players, their interests, and their power, asking: Whose support do I need? How do I go about getting it? Who are my opponents? How much power do they have? What can I do to reduce or overcome their opposition? Is this battle winnable?

Political Leaders Build Linkage to Key Stakeholders. Political leaders focus their attention on building relationships and networks. They recognize the value of personal contact and face-to-face conversations. Iacocca worked hard to build linkages with Congress, the media, and the public. He spent hours meeting with members of Congress and testifying before congressional committees. After he met with thirty-one Italian American members of Congress, all but one voted for the loan guarantees. Said Iacocca, "Some were Republicans, some were Democrats, but in this case they voted the straight Italian ticket. We were desperate, and we had to play every angle" (Iacocca and Novak, 1984, p. 221).

Fiorina's primary target was institutional shareholders, who held about 57 percent of the company's stock, and the analysts whose opinions mattered. Armed with a fifty-page document that laid out the strategic and financial rationale for the merger, Fiorina and Compaq CEO Michael Capellas hit the road, speaking to every analyst they could find. Fiorina focused on big picture, strategic issues, while Capellas backed her up on the nitty-gritty details of integrating the two firms.

Political Leaders Persuade First, Negotiate Second, and Coerce Only if Necessary.   Wise political leaders recognize that power is essential to their effectiveness; they also know to use it judiciously. William P. Kelly, an experienced public administrator, put it well: "Power is like the old Esso ad—a tiger in your tank. But you can't let the tiger out, you just let people hear him roar. You use power terribly sparingly because it has a short half-life. You let people know you have it and hope that you don't have to use it" (Ridout and Fenn, 1974, p. 10).

Sophisticated political leaders know that influence begins with an understanding of others' concerns and interests. What is important to them? How can I help them get what they want?

Iacocca and Fiorina both won their battles. Chrysler pulled out of its tailspin, repaid its loans, ignited the minivan craze, and had many profitable years before it was acquired by German automaker Daimler Benz in 1998. HP fell short of analysts' expectations with a loss of $2 billion in its first postmerger quarterly financial report, but it is still too soon to know if the merger will go down in management history as an example of inspired leadership or simply as Fiorina's Folly.

Prophet or Zealot? Symbolic Leadership

The symbolic frame represents a fourth turn of the leadership kaleidoscope. This lens sees an organization as both theater and temple. As theater, an organization creates a stage on which actors play their roles and hope to communicate the right impression to the right audience. As temple, an organization is a community of faith, bonded by shared beliefs, traditions, myths, rituals, and ceremonies.

Symbolically, leaders lead through both their actions and their words as they *interpret and reinterpret experience*. What are the real lessons of history? What is really happening in the world? What will the future bring? What mission is worthy of our loyalty and investment? Data and analysis offer few adequate answers to such questions. Symbolic leaders interpret experience so as to impart meaning and purpose through phrases of beauty and passion. Franklin D. Roosevelt reassured a nation in the midst of its deepest economic depression that "the only thing we have to fear is fear itself." At almost the same time, Adolph Hitler assured Germans that their severe economic and social problems were the result of betrayal by Jews and communists. Germans, he said, were a superior people who could still fulfill their nation's destiny of world mastery. Though many saw the destructive paranoia in Hitler's message, millions of fearful citizens were swept up in Hitler's bold vision of German ascendancy.

Burns (1978) was mindful of leaders such as Franklin Roosevelt; Mohandas Gandhi; and Martin Luther King, Jr., when he drew a distinction between "transforming" and "transactional" leaders. According to Burns, transactional leaders "approach their followers with an eye to trading one thing for another: jobs for votes, subsidies for campaign contributions" (p. 4). Transforming

leaders are rarer. As Burns describes them, they evoke their constituents' better nature and move them toward higher and more universal needs and purposes. They are visionary leaders whose leadership is inherently symbolic. Symbolic leaders follow a consistent set of practices and rules.

They Lead by Example. Symbolic leaders demonstrate their commitment and courage by plunging into the fray. In taking risks and holding nothing back, they reassure and inspire others. New York Mayor Rudy Giuliani's leadership in the aftermath of the September 11 terrorist attacks is again a dramatic case in point. Risking his own life, he moved immediately to the scene. When the first tower collapsed, he was caught for fifteen minutes in the rubble.

They Use Symbols to Capture Attention. When Diana Lam became principal of the Mackey Middle School in Boston in 1985, she faced a substantial challenge. Mackey had the usual problems of an urban school: decaying physical plant, poor discipline, racial tension, disgruntled teachers, and limited resources (Kaufer and Leader, 1987a). In such a situation, a symbolic leader does something visible and dramatic to signal that change is coming. During the summer before assuming her duties, Lam wrote a personal letter to every teacher requesting an individual meeting. She met teachers wherever they wanted (in one case driving two hours). She asked teachers how they felt about the school and what changes they wanted. Then she recruited members of her family as a crew to repaint the school's front door and some of the most decrepit classrooms. "When school opened, students and staff members immediately saw that things were going to be different, if only symbolically. Perhaps even more important, staff members received a subtle challenge to make a contribution themselves" (Kaufer and Leader, 1987b, p. 3).

When Iacocca became president of Chrysler, one of his first steps was to announce that he was reducing his salary from $360,000 to $1 a year. "I did it for good, cold pragmatic reasons. I wanted our employees and our suppliers to be thinking: 'I can follow a guy who sets that kind of example,'" Iacocca explained in his autobiography (Iacocca and Novak, 1984, pp. 229–230).

Symbolic Leaders Frame Experience. In a world of uncertainty and ambiguity, a key function of symbolic leadership is to offer plausible interpretations of experience. Jan Carlzon mobilized front-line staff at SAS around the idea that each short encounter with a customer was a "moment of truth" (Carlzon, 1987). When Martin Luther King, Jr., spoke at the March on Washington in 1963 and gave his extraordinary "I Have a Dream" speech, his opening line was, "I am happy to join with you today in what will go down in history as the greatest demonstration for freedom in the history of our nation." He could have interpreted the event in a number of other ways: "We are here because progress has been slow, but we are not ready to quit yet"; "We are here because nothing else has worked"; "We are here because it's summer and it's a good day to be outside." Each version is about as accurate as the next, but accuracy is not the real issue. King's assertion was bold and inspiring; it told members of the audience that they were making history by their presence at a momentous event.

Symbolic Leaders Communicate a Vision. One powerful way in which a leader can interpret experience is by distilling and disseminating a vision—a persuasive and hopeful image of the future. A vision needs to address both the challenges of the present and the hopes and values of followers. Vision is particularly important in a time of crisis and uncertainty. When people are in pain, when they are confused and uncertain, or when they feel despair and hopelessness, they desperately seek meaning and hope.

Where does such vision come from? One view is that leaders create a vision and then persuade others to accept it (Bass, 1985; Bennis and Nanus, 1985). An alternative view is that leaders discover and articulate a vision that is already there, even if in an inchoate and unexpressed

form (Cleveland, 1985). Kouzes and Posner (1987) put it well: "Corporate leaders know very well that what seeds the vision are those imperfectly formed images in the marketing department about what the customers really wanted and those inarticulate mumblings from the manufacturing folks about the poor product quality, not crystal ball gazing in upper levels of the corporate stratosphere. The best leaders are the best followers. They pay attention to those weak signals and quickly respond to changes in the corporate course" (p. 114).

Early in his career, Jan Carlzon had learned this lesson the hard way when he and a group of young executives designed a set of tour packages offering Swedish senior citizens what Carlzon knew they wanted: safe, risk-free travel to familiar places. The product bombed because the seniors really wanted variety and adventure. For Carlzon it was a memorable lesson: listen to your customers and to the front-line staff who know their real desire (Carlzon, 1987).

Leadership is a two-way street. No amount of charisma or rhetorical skill can sell a vision that reflects only the leader's values and needs; Carlzon's team had spent a fortune on beautiful color brochures to promote the doomed tour packages. Effective symbolic leadership is possible only for those who understand the deepest values and most pressing concerns of their constituents. But leaders still play a critical role. They can bring a unique, personal blend of poetry, passion, conviction, and courage to articulating a vision. They can play a key role in distilling and shaping the direction to be pursued. Most important, they can choose which stories to tell as a means of communicating the vision.

Symbolic Leaders Tell Stories. Symbolic leaders often embed their vision in a story—a story about "us" and about "our" past, present, and future. *Us* could be the Sorbonne, Chrysler, the people of Thailand, or any other audience a leader hopes to reach. The past is usually a golden one, a time of noble purposes, of great deeds, of heroes and heroines. The present is a time of trouble, challenge, or crisis—a critical moment when we have to make fateful choices. The future is the dream: a vision of hope and greatness often linked directly to greatness in the past.

This is just the kind of story that helped Ronald Reagan, a master storyteller, become president of the United States. Reagan's golden past was the frontier, a place of rugged, sturdy, self-reliant men and women who built a great nation and took care of themselves and their neighbors without the intervention of a monstrous national government. It was an America of small towns and volunteer fire departments. America had fallen into crisis, said Reagan, because "the liberals" had created a federal government that was levying oppressive taxes and eroding freedom through regulation and bureaucracy. Reagan offered a vision: a return to American greatness by "getting government off the backs of the American people" and restoring traditional American values of freedom and self-reliance. It worked for Reagan and worked again twenty years later for a Reagan acolyte, George W. Bush.

The success of such stories is only partly related to their historical validity or empirical support. The central question is whether they are credible and persuasive to their audiences. A story, even a flawed story, will work if it taps persuasively into the experience, values, and aspirations of listeners.

Mohammed Said Sahaf, Iraq's information minister during the war in 2003, was mostly dismissed by Westerners as a source of lies and misinformation. He repeatedly predicted Iraqi victories that never materialized. Two days before Baghdad fell, he brazenly told reporters that there were no American forces in the city, despite the conspicuous presence of an American armored battalion at a presidential palace less than half a mile away. But Sahaf became a media star in much of the Arab world, where many viewers saw him as more interesting and credible than the boring briefers for the U.S. military. His military uniform, pistol on hip, and rakish beret conveyed spirit and élan. Arabs admired his creativity in generating pungent insults for the Americans ("bloodsucking worms," "sick dogs," "donkeys"). They particularly liked the story Sahaf told with flair and conviction: the infidel invaders were plunging ever deeper into a trap in which they would soon be destroyed by heroic Iraqi fighters. Sahaf's star turn ended abruptly with the collapse of the government he served, but for a time millions of Arabs who felt enraged and humiliated by the invasion of Iraq could take delight in a man who told the story as they wanted it to be (Lamb, 2003).

Good stories are truer than true: this reflects both the power and the danger of symbolic leadership. In the hands of a Gandhi or a King, the constructive power of stories is immense. Told by a Hitler, their destructive power is almost incalculable. In the wake of World War I and the Great Depression, Germany in the 1930s was hungry for hope. Other stories might have caught the imagination of the German people, but Hitler's passion and single-mindedness brought his story to center stage and carried Europe to a catastrophe of war and holocaust.

Symbolic Leaders Respect and Use History. When leaders make the mistake of assuming that history started when they walked in the door, they usually misread their circumstances and alienate their constituents. Wise leaders attend to history, and link their initiatives to the values, stories, and heroes of the past. Even as she unleashed massive changes at HP, Carly Fiorina told Bill and Dave stories and insisted on her fidelity to the HP Way.

Sometimes the use of history is deliberately selective. When Hu Jintao became chief of the Chinese Communist Party in the fall of 2002, many wondered whether he would ever escape the long shadow of his predecessor, Jiang Zemin, who had bequeathed a party leadership stacked with his loyalists. Hu was unstinting in his praise of Jiang's legacy but began to differentiate himself symbolically (Eckholm, 2003). Hu enlisted a symbolic ally, Mao Zedong, the supreme hero of the Chinese Communist revolution. In December 2002, only a month after coming to power, Hu traveled to Xibaipo, a town where Mao had given a famous speech in 1949. In contrast to Jiang, who consistently talked up the economic successes of his reign, Hu emphasized the need to help the poor and dispossessed deal with the changes sweeping over China. He referred often to Mao and rarely to Jiang. He repeated Mao's call to the faithful to practice "plain living and arduous struggle" more than sixty times. As the editor of a party paper commented, "He showed that his legitimacy comes ultimately from Mao, not Jiang" (Eckholm, 2003, p. A6).

CONCLUSION

Though leadership is universally accepted as a cure for all organizational ills, it is also widely misunderstood. Many views of leadership fail to recognize its relational and contextual nature and its distinction from power and position. Inadequate ideas about leadership often produce oversimplified advice to managers. We need to reframe leadership to move beyond the impasse created by oversimplified models.

Each of the frames highlights significant possibilities for leadership, but each is incomplete in capturing a holistic picture. Early in the twentieth century, implicit models of managerial leadership were narrowly rational. In the 1960s and 1970s, human resource leadership became fashionable.

In recent years, symbolic leadership has moved to center stage, and the literature abounds with advice on how to become a visionary leader capable of transforming cultural patterns. Organizations need vision, but it is not their only need and not always their most important one. Ideally, managers combine multiple frames into a comprehensive approach to leadership. Still, it is unrealistic to expect everyone to be a leader for all times and seasons. Wise leaders understand their own strengths, work to expand them, and build teams that can offer an organization leadership in all four modes: structural, political, human resource, and symbolic.

REFERENCES

Adams, S. *The Dilbert principle.* New York: Harper Business, 1996.

Allison, G. *Essence of decision: Explaining the Cuban Missile Crisis.* New York: Little, Brown, 1971.

American Customer Satisfaction Index, 2002 (www.theacsi.org/third_quarter.htm#app).

Argyris, C. *Interpersonal competence and organizational effectiveness.* Homewood, Ill.: Irwin, 1962.

Argyris, C. *Integrating the individual and the organization.* New York: Wiley, 1964.

Aubrey, B., and Tilliette, B. *Savoir faire savoir: L'apprentissage de l'action en entreprise* [Knowing and teaching: Action learning in the enterprise]. Paris: Inter Éditions, 1990.

Bardach, E. *The implementation game: what happens after a bill becomes law.* Cambridge, Mass.: MIT Press, 1977.

Barnes, L. B., and Kriger, M. P. "The hidden side of organizational leadership." *Sloan Management Review,* Fall 1986, pp. 15–25.

Bass, B. M. *Leadership and performance beyond expectations.* New York: Free Press, 1985.

Bennis, W. G., and Nanus, B. *Leaders: Strategies for taking charge.* New York: HarperCollins, 1985.

Bensimon, E. M. "The meaning of 'good presidential leadership': a frame analysis." *Review of Higher Education,* 1989, *12,* 107–123.

Bensimon, E. M. "Viewing the presidency: perceptual congruence between presidents and leaders on their campuses." *Leadership Quarterly,* 1990, *1,* 71–90.

Bergquist, W. H. *The Four cultures of the academy: insights and strategies for improving leadership in collegiate organizations.* San Francisco: Jossey-Bass, 1992.

Bernstein, A. "Why ESOP deals have slowed to a crawl." *Business Week,* Mar. 18, 1996, pp. 101–102.

"The Best Places to Work in America." *Fortune,* 2002. (www.fortune.com/fortune/bestcompanies)

Bethune, G., and Huler, S. *From worst to first: Behind the scenes of Continental's remarkable comeback.* New York: Wiley, 1999.

Bing, S. *What would Machiavelli do? The ends justify the meanness.* New York: HarperBusiness, 2000.

Bion, W. R. *Experience in groups.* London: Tavistock, 1961.

Birnbaum, R. *How colleges work: The cybernetics of academic organization and leadership.* San Francisco: Jossey-Bass, 1988.

Birnbaum, R. *How academic leadership works: understanding success and failure in the college presidency.* San Francisco: Jossey-Bass, 1992.

Blake, R., and Mouton, J. S. *Managerial grid III.* Houston, Tex.: Gulf, 1985.

Blanchard, K., and Johnson, S. *The one-minute manager.* New York: Morrow, 1982.

Bolman, L. G., and Deal, T. E. "leadership and management effectiveness: a multi-frame, multi-sector analysis." *Human Resource Management,* 1991, *30,* 509–534.

Bolman, L. G., and Deal, T. E. "Leading and managing: effects of context, culture, and gender." *Education Administration Quarterly,* 1992(a), *28,* 314–329.

Bolman, L. G., and Deal, T. E. "Reframing leadership: the effects of leaders' images of leadership." In K. E. Clark, M. B. Clark, and D. Campbell (eds.), *Impact of leadership.* Greensboro, N.C.: Center for Creative Leadership, 1992(b).

Bolman, L. G., and Deal, T. E. *Leading with soul: an uncommon journey of spirit* (2nd ed.) San Francisco: Jossey-Bass, 2001.

Bradford, D. L., and Cohen, A. R. *Managing for excellence.* New York: Wiley, 1984.

Briand, M. "People, lead thyself." *Kettering Review,* Summer 1993, pp. 38–46.

Brief, A. P., and Downey, H. K. (1983). "Cognitive and organizational structure: A conceptual analysis of implicit organizing theories." *Human Relations,* 1983, *36*(12), 1065–1090.

Burns, J. M. *Leadership.* New York: HarperCollins, 1978.

Burrows, P., and Elstrom, P. "HP's Carly Fiorina: The boss." *Business Week,* Aug. 2, 1999, pp. 76–84.

Byrne, J. A. "The Shredder: Did CEO Dunlap save Scott Paper—or just pretty it up?" *Business Week,* Jan. 15, 1996, pp. 56–61.

Byrne, J. A. "Inside McKinsey." *Business Week,* July 8, 2002(a), pp. 66–76.

Carlzon, J. *Moments of truth.* New York: Ballinger, 1987.

Chaize, J. *La porte du changement s'ouvre de l'interieur: Les trois mutations de l'entreprise* [The door to change opens from the inside: The three transformations of the corporation]. Paris: Calmann-Lévy, 1992.

Chandler, A. D., Jr. *The visible hand: the managerial revolution in American business.* Cambridge, Mass.: Harvard University Press, 1977.

Charan, R., and Useem, J. "Why companies fail." *Fortune,* May 27, 2002, pp. 50–62.

Cleveland, H. *The knowledge executive: leadership in an information society.* New York: Dutton, 1985.

Collins, J. C., and Porras, J. I. *Built to last: successful habits of visionary companies.* New York: HarperBusiness, 1994.

Cronshaw, S. F. "Effects of categorization, attribution, and encoding processes on leadership perspectives." *Journal of Applied Psychology,* 1987, *72*(1), 91–106.

Deal, T. E., and Kennedy, A. A. *Corporate cultures.* Reading, Mass.: Addison-Wesley, 1982.

Dunford, R. W. *Organizational behavior: An organizational analysis perspective.* Sydney: Addison-Wesley, 1992.

Dunford, R. W., and Palmer, I. C. "Claims about frames: practitioners' assessment of the utility of reframing." *Journal of Management Education,* 1995, *19,* 96–105.

Eckholm, E. "China's new leader works to set himself apart." *New York Times,* Jan. 12, 2003, p. A6.

Elmore, R. F. "Organizational models of social program implementation." *Public Policy,* 1978, *26,* 185–228.

Feinberg, M., and Tarrant, J. J. *Why smart people do dumb things.* New York: Simon & Schuster, 1995.

Fiedler, F. E. *A theory of leadership effectiveness.* New York: McGraw-Hill, 1967.

Fiedler, F. E., and Chemers, M. *Leadership and effective management.* Glenview, Ill.: Scott, Foresman, 1974.

Fiedler, K. "Causal schemata: Review and criticism of research on a popular construct." *Journal of Personality and Social Psychology,* 1982, *42,* 1001–1013.

Fisk, S. T. & Dyer, L. M. "Structure and development of social schemata: Evidence from positive and negative transfer effects." *Journal of Personality and Social Psychology,* 1985, *48*(4), 839–852.

Frensch, P. A. & Sternberg, R. J. "Skill related differences in chess playing." In R J. Sternberg and P. A. Frensch (eds.), *Complex problem solving.* Hillsdale, NJ: Erlbaum, 1991.

Freudenberg, W. R., & Gramling, R. Bureaucratic slippage and failures of agency vigilance. *Social Problems,* 1994, *4*(1), 214–239.

Gardner, J. W. *Handbook of strategic planning.* New York: Wiley, 1986.

Gardner, J. W. *The moral aspects of leadership.* Washington, D.C.: Independent Sector, 1987.

Gardner, J. W. *On leadership.* New York: Free Press, 1989.

Gertz, D., and Baptista, J.P.A. *Grow to be great: breaking the downsizing cycle.* New York: Free Press, 1995.

Goffman, E. *Frame analysis*. Cambridge, Mass.: Harvard University Press, 1974.

Goleman, D., McKee, A., and Boyatzis, R. E. *Primal leadership: Realizing the power of emotional intelligence*. Boston, MA: Harvard Business School Publishing, 2002.

Greenleaf, R. K. *The servant as leader*. Newton Center, Mass.: Robert K. Greenleaf Center, 1973.

Gregory, K. L. "Native view paradigms: Multiple cultures and cultural conflict in organizations." *Administrative Science Quarterly*, 1983, 28, 359–376.

Hall, R. H. "The concept of bureaucracy: an empirical assessment." *American Journal of Sociology*, 1963, 49, 32–40.

Hall, R. H. *Organizations: Structures, processes, and outcomes* (4th ed.) Upper Saddle River, N.J.: Prentice Hall, 1987.

Hampden-Turner, C. *Creating corporate culture: From discord to harmony*. Reading, Mass.: Addison-Wesley, 1992.

Hamper, B. *Rivethead: Tales from the assembly line*. New York: Warner Books, 1992.

Hampton, W. J., and Norman, J. R. "General Motors: What went wrong—eight years and billions of dollars haven't made its strategy succeed." *Business Week*, Mar. 16, 1987, p. 102.

Heifetz, R. A. *Leadership without easy answers*. Cambridge, Mass.: Belknap Press, 1994.

Heimovics, R. D., Herman, R. D., and Jurkiewicz Coughlin, C. L. "Executive leadership and resource dependence in nonprofit organizations: a frame analysis." *Public Administration Review*, 1993, 53, 419–427.

Heimovics, R. D., Herman, R. D., and Jurkiewicz Coughlin, C. L. "The political dimension of effective nonprofit executive leadership." *Nonprofit Management and Leadership*, 1995, 5, 233–248.

Hersey, P. *The situational leader*. New York: Warner Books, 1984.

Hersey, P., and Blanchard, K. H. *The management of organizational behavior* (3rd ed.) Upper Saddle River, N.J.: Prentice Hall, 1977.

Hogan, R., Curphy, G. J., and Hogan, J. "What we know about leadership." *American Psychologist*, 1994, 49, 493–504.

Hollander, E. P. *Leadership dynamics*. New York: Free Press, 1978.

House, R. J. "The path-goal theory of effectiveness." *Administrative Science Quarterly*, 1971, 16, 321–338.

Iacocca, L., and Novak, W. *Iacocca*. New York: Bantam Books, 1984.

Kanter, R. M. *The change masters: Innovations for productivity in the American corporation*. New York: Simon & Schuster, 1983.

Kanter, R. M. *When giants learn to dance*. New York: Simon & Schuster, 1989.

Kaufer, N., and Leader, G. C. "Diana Lam (A)." Case. Boston University, 1987(a).

Kaufer, N., and Leader, G. C "Diana Lam (B)." Case. Boston University, 1987(b).

Kotter, J. P. *The leadership factor*. New York: Free Press, 1988.

Kotter, J. P., and Cohen, D. S. *The heart of change: Real life stories of how people change their organizations*. Boston: Harvard Business School Press, 2002.

Kouzes, J. M., and Posner, B. Z. *The leadership challenge: how to get extraordinary things done in organizations*. San Francisco: Jossey-Bass, 1987.

KPMG. "Mergers and acquisitions: a global research report." KPMG, 2000. (www.kpmg.co.uk/kpmg/uky/image/m&a_99.pdf).

Kuhn, T. S. *The structure of scientific revolutions* (2nd ed.). Chicago: University of Chicago Press, 1970.

Lamb, D. "He wages war—on reality." *Los Angeles Times*, Apr. 8, 2003. (www.latimes.com/news/printedition/la-war-sahaf8apr08010418,l,1881104.story).

Langer, E. *Mindfulness*. Reading, Mass.: Addison-Wesley, 1989.

Lee, A. *Call me Roger*. Chicago: Contemporary Books, 1988.

Lesgold, A., and Lajoie, S. "Complex problem solving in electronics." In R. J. Sternberg and P. A. Frensch (eds.), *Complex problem solving*. Hillsdale, N. J.: Erlbaum 1991.

Levinson, H. *The exceptional executive*. Cambridge, Mass.: Harvard University Press, 1968.

Levinson, H., and Rosenthal, S. *CEO: Corporate leadership in action*. New York: Basic Books, 1984.

Likert, R. *New patterns of management*. New York: McGraw-Hill, 1961.

Likert, R. *The human organization*. New York: McGraw-Hill, 1967.

Lord., R. G. and Foti, R. J. "Schema theories, information processing, and organizational behavior." In H. P. Sims, Jr., D. A. Gioia, and Associates (eds.). *The thinking organization*. San Francisco: Jossey-Bass, 1986.

Lundin, W., and Lundin, K. *When smart people work for dumb bosses*. New York: McGraw-Hill, 1998.

Machiavelli, N. *The Prince*. New York: Penguin Books, 1961. (Originally published 1514)

Mintzberg, H. *The structuring of organizations*. Upper Saddle River, N.J.: Prentice Hall, 1979.

Morgan, G. *Images of organization*. Thousand Oaks, Calif.: Sage, 1986.

Morgan, G. *Imaginization: The art of creative management*. Thousand Oaks, Calif.: Sage, 1993.

Murphy, J. T. *Managing matters: reflections from practice.* (Monograph.). Cambridge, Mass.: Graduate School of Education, Harvard University, 1985.

Norris, F. K. "A tale told to congress, full of sound, but blurry." *New York Times,* Feb. 8, 2002, p. C-l.

"On a clear day you can still see General Motors." *Economist,* Dec. 2, 1989, pp. 77–78, 80.

Oshry, B. *Seeing systems: unlocking the mysteries of organizational life.* San Francisco: Berrett-Koehler, 1995.

O'Toole, P. *Corporate Messiah: The hiring and firing of million-dollar managers.* New York: Morrow, 1984.

Pande, P. S., Neuman, R. P., and Cavanagh, R. R. *The six sigma way: How GE, Motorola and other top companies are honing their performance.* New York: McGraw-Hill, 2000.

Perrow, C. *Complex organizations: A critical essay* (3rd ed.). New York: Random House, 1986.

Peters, B. G. *American public policy: Promise and performance.* New York: Chatham House, 1999.

Peters, T. J., and Waterman, R. H. *In Search of Excellence.* New York: HarperCollins, 1982.

Pressman, J. L., and Wildavsky, A. B. *Implementation.* Berkeley: University of California Press, 1973.

Quinn, R. E. *Beyond rational management: Mastering the paradoxes and competing demands of high performance.* San Francisco, Calif.: Jossey-Bass, 1988.

Quinn, R. E., Faerman, S. R., Thompson, M. P., and McGrath, M. R. *Becoming a master manager: A competency framework.* New York: Wiley, 1996.

Renner, M. "Corporate mergers skyrocket." Worldwatch Institute, 2000. (www.globalpolicy.org/socecon/tncs/mergers/renner.htm).

Ridout, C. F., and Fenn, D. H. "Job corps." Boston: Harvard Business School Case Services, 1974.

Riebling, M. *Wedge: From Pearl Harbor to 9/11—How the secret war between the FBI and CIA has endangered national security.* New York: Touchstone, 2002.

Scott, W. R. *Organizations: Rational, natural, and open systems.* Upper Saddle River, N. J.: Prentice Hall, 1981.

Senge, P. M. *The fifth discipline: The art and practice of the learning organization.* New York: Knopf, 1990.

Sennett, R. *Authority.* New York: Knopf, 1980.

Sérieyx, H. *Le big bang des organisations* [The organizational big bang]. Paris: Calmann-Lévy, 1993.

Simmel, G. *The sociology of Georg Simmel.* New York: Free Press, 1950.

Sloan, A. P., Jr. *My years with General Motors.* New York: Macfadden, 1965.

Tichy, G. "What do we know about success and failure of mergers." *Journal of Industry, Competition and Trade.* New York: Springer, 2001.

Vaughan, D. *The Challenger launch decision: Risky technology, culture, and deviance at NASA.* Chicago: University of Chicago, 1995.

Voss, J. F., Wolfe, C. R., Lawrence, J. A., and Engle, R. A. From representation to decision: An analysis of problem solving in international relations. In R. J. Sternberg and P. A. Frensch (eds.), *Complex problem solving.* Hillsdale, N.J.: Erlbaum, 1991.

Vroom, V. H., and Yetton, P. W. *Leadership and decision making.* Pittsburgh: University of Pittsburgh Press, 1973.

Waterman, R. H., Jr. *What America does right: learning from companies that put people first.* New York: Norton, 1994.

Weber, M. *The theory of social and economic organization.* (T. Parsons, trans.) New York: Free Press, 1947.

Weick, K. E., and Bougon, M. G. "Organization as cognitive maps." In H. P. Sims Jr., D. A. Gioia and Associates (eds.), *The thinking organization.* San Francisco, Calif.: Jossey-Bass, 1986.

Wimpelberg, R. K. "Managerial images and school effectiveness." *Administrators' Notebook,* 1987, *32,* 1–4.

NOTES

1. Among the possible ways of talking about frames are schemata or schema theory (Fiedler, 1982; Fiske and Dyer, 1985; Lord and Foti, 1986), representations (Frensch and Sternberg, 1991; Lesgold and Lajoie, 1991; Voss, Wolfe, Lawrence, and Engle, 1991), cognitive maps (Weick and Bougon, 1986), paradigms (Gregory, 1983; Kuhn, 1970), social categorizations (Cronshaw, 1987), implicit theories (Brief and Downey, 1983), mental models (Senge, 1990), and root metaphors. We follow Goffman (1974) in using the term *frame.*

2. A number of management scholars (including Allison, 1971; Bergquist, 1992; Birnbaum, 1988; Elmore, 1978; Morgan, 1986; Perrow, 1986; Quinn, 1988; Quinn, Faerman, Thompson, and McGrath, 1996; and Scott, 1981) have made similar arguments for a multiframe approach to organizations.

2 CHAPTER | MOTIVATION

Many factors may—or may not—motivate individual members of our metaphoric orchestra to do their jobs with high enthusiasm and energy. Thundering applause, the sound of the music, relationships with other members of the orchestra, a personal goal, a commitment to parents who paid for an education, the honored first-chair position, a drive to succeed, a monetary reward, public recognition, or even the grateful smile of the conductor—all are possibilities from a potentially limitless number of choices. These motivating factors cause individual musicians to come together to produce, entertain, create, and, potentially, to excel collectively as an orchestra.

How does the conductor keep the musicians motivated, show after show, and season after season? Is the conductor responsible for motivating members of the orchestra, or are the individual musicians responsible because of their personal self-concepts and goals as professionals? What other needs must be met for the musicians to become or remain motivated members of the orchestra? To what extent are the board of directors, the musicians' union, the orchestra's benefactors, and the audience's perception of the orchestra motivating factors? What opportunities for self-development are available within the structure of the orchestra—opportunities that can motivate individuals to grow and improve? For many decades, questions such as these have concerned researchers dealing with motivation theories.

For hundreds of years, the motivation of workers has been the proverbial "pot of gold at the end of the rainbow" for management practitioners and students of organizational behavior. If employees could be motivated to produce just slightly more, the economic rewards to individual organizations and to societies would be immense. Although there always has been consensus about the need for motivated employees, the same cannot be said for beliefs about how to induce higher levels of motivation. Not only have prevailing views (or theories) of motivation changed radically over the course of organizational history, but incompatible theories usually have competed with each other at the same time. Some theories of motivation have developed from empirical research, but most have not. Some theories assume that employees act logically, and that managers simply need to manipulate rewards and punishments rationally, fairly, and consistently. Other theories start from the position that managerial assumptions about employees—which undergird such systems of rewards and punishments—actually stifle employee motivation.

Even today, widely divergent views remain about the essence of motivation in organizations. This chapter attempts to sort, organize, and summarize some of the more important theories proposed over the years. As in all chapters of this book, the readings are organized chronologically. For purposes of perspective, we start our analysis in the 1760s, at the beginning of the Industrial Revolution.

MOTIVATION THEORY PRIOR TO THE HAWTHORNE STUDIES

Even in the early years of the Industrial Revolution (beginning about 1760), *employee discipline* was one of the most vexing problems confronting managers in the factory system of mass production. Motivation of employees and strategic use of negative sanctions were integral tactics for maintaining production and discipline. Prior to the Industrial Revolution, most workers worked under craft traditions or were agrarians and had some degree of independence (Wren, 1972). But the new-style factories needed workers who fit into the factory systems' production concept, which was driven by the principle of the *division of labor* (Smith, 1776). Workers had to produce on a schedule not of their own choosing. Expensive machines had to be kept busy. Production shifted from labor-intensive to capital-intensive; and society's basic concept of humans at work changed with this shifting economic base (Haire, 1962). Although some early industrialists reportedly threw periodic feasts in attempts to build company loyalty, reduce absenteeism, and thereby keep production high, the backbone of motivational strategy was the incentive piece-rate system of compensation. Workers were paid for production output rather than for hours at work.

The 20th century scientific management movement led by Frederick Winslow Taylor, Lillian and Frank Gilbreth, Henry Gantt, and others followed naturally from the piece-rate payment system ethic of the Industrial Revolution factory system of production (see Shafritz, Ott, & Jang, 2005). Under scientific management principles, motivational methods were rooted in the concept of workers as *rational economic men*. People work for money: Tie compensation to production, and employees produce more (Gantt, 1910). Deal only with individual employees, and try to prevent the formation of groups, which may lead to unions, because they restrict output. Beyond restricting output, Taylor saw productivity limited primarily by workers' ignorance of how to maximize production. To Taylor, scientific study of production process (what he called *scientific management*) was the answer. It would provide for standardization, for the improvement of practices, and for techniques that would reduce worker fatigue. With better procedures and less fatigue, employee income and company profits would increase (Taylor, 1911).

THE HAWTHORNE STUDIES

In 1924 a team of researchers, under the aegis of the National Academy of Sciences' National Research Council, went to the Hawthorne plant of the Western Electric Company near Chicago to study ways to improve productivity. The research team began its work from the perspective—the assumptions, precepts, and principles—of scientific management. Scientific investigative procedures (including control groups) were used to find and identify environmental changes that would increase worker productivity. Their investigations focused on room temperature, humidity, and illumination levels (Pennock, 1930). Interestingly, illumination was included as an experimental variable because scientific management studies by Frederick Winslow Taylor (1911) years earlier had identified illumination as an easily controlled variable for influencing productivity. But the early Hawthorne studies caused confusion. Worker output continued to increase even as illumination decreased.

By 1927 the results were so snarled that Western Electric and the National Research Council were ready to abandon the entire endeavor. In that year, George Pennock, Western Electric's superintendent of inspection, heard Harvard professor Elton Mayo speak at a meeting and invited him to take a team to Hawthorne. Team members eventually included Fritz Roethlisberger, George Homans, and T. N. Whitehead. The results are legendary. However, it was not until the Mayo-led Hawthorne team discarded its rational economic man/scientific management assumptions about people at work that the groundwork was laid for the field of *organizational behavior*—a perspective with its own very different set of assumptions. (See the Introduction to this book.) The long-held assumptions of industrial/organizational psychology, that people could and should be fit to organizations, had been challenged. The process had begun that would render obsolete scientific management's assumptions about people and how to motivate them.

The Hawthorne experiments were the emotional and intellectual wellspring of the organizational behavior perspective and of modern theories of motivation. The Hawthorne experiments showed that complex, interactional variables make the difference in motivating people—things like attention paid to workers as individuals, workers' control over their own work, differences between individuals' needs, the willingness of managers to listen, group norms, and direct feedback.

Fritz J. Roethlisberger, of the Harvard Business School, is the best-known chronicler of the Hawthorne studies. Roethlisberger, with William J. Dickson of the Western Electric Company, wrote the most comprehensive account of the Hawthorne studies, *Management and the Worker* (1939). Roethlisberger's chapter "The Hawthorne Experiments" (which is reprinted in this book) is from his shorter 1941 book, *Management and Morale*.

NEED THEORIES OF MOTIVATION

All discussions of need theories of motivation start with Abraham Maslow. His hierarchy of needs stands alongside the Hawthorne experiments and Douglas McGregor's Theory X and Theory Y as *the* departure points for studying motivation in organizations. An overview of Maslow's basic theory of needs is presented here from his 1943 *Psychological Review* article, "A Theory of Human Motivation." Maslow's theoretical premises can be summarized in a few phrases:

- All humans have needs that underlie their motivational structure.
- As lower levels of needs are satisfied, they no longer "drive" behavior.
- Satisfied needs are not motivators.
- As lower-level needs of workers become satisfied, higher-order needs take over as the motivating forces.

Maslow's theory has been attacked frequently. Few empirical studies have supported it, and it oversimplifies the complex structure of human needs and motivations (e.g., see Wahba & Bridwell, 1973). Several modified hierarchies of needs have been proposed over the years that reportedly are better able to withstand empirical testing (e.g., Alderfer, 1969). But despite the criticisms and the continuing advances across the spectrum of applied behavioral sciences, Abraham Maslow's theory continues to occupy a most honored and prominent place in organizational behavior and management textbooks.

THEORY X AND THEORY Y

Douglas McGregor's *The Human Side of Enterprise* (1960) is about much more than the motivation of people at work. In its totality, it is a cogent articulation of the basic assumptions of the organizational behavior perspective. Theory X and Theory Y are contrasting basic managerial assumptions about employees, which, in McGregor's words, become self-fulfilling prophesies— managerial assumptions *cause* employee behavior. Theory X and Theory Y are ways of seeing and thinking about people that in turn affect their behavior. Thus, "The Human Side of Enterprise" (1957b, reprinted in this chapter) is a landmark theory of motivation.

Theory X assumptions represent a restatement of the tenets of the scientific management movement. For example, human beings inherently dislike work and will avoid it if possible. Most people must be coerced, controlled, directed, or threatened with punishment to get them to work toward the achievement of organizational objectives; humans prefer to be directed, to avoid responsibility, and will seek security above all else. These assumptions serve as polar opposites to McGregor's Theory Y.

Theory Y assumptions postulate, for example, that people do not inherently dislike work; work can be a source of satisfaction. People will exercise self-direction and self-control if they are committed to organizational objectives. People are willing to seek and to accept responsibility; avoidance of responsibility is not natural, it is a consequence of experiences. The intellectual potential of most humans is only partially used at work.

COGNITIVE DISSONANCE AND INEQUITY THEORIES OF MOTIVATION

When two or more people or things around a person are in a state of disharmony, imbalance, or incongruity, that imbalance causes *dissonance* (or discomfort). According to cognitive dissonance theory, people will act—will do something—to reduce or eliminate dissonance. For example, I like two people, "A" and "B," but "A" does not like "B." An imbalance exists that causes dissonance, and I will act to eliminate it. The theory of cognitive dissonance cannot predict what I will do, but it says that I will be motivated to do something. I might try to change "A's" feelings toward "B"; or I might change my feelings about either "A" or "B" and then sever my relationship with the out-of-favor person. Similarly, if I believe that wearing a seat belt will not save my life in the event of a car accident, but I fasten my seat belt anyway because state law says I must, dissonance is created by the incongruity between my belief and my behavior. Cognitive dissonance theory predicts that I will be motivated to reduce or eliminate the dissonance. I might stop wearing a seat belt (e.g., by convincing myself that the probability of getting caught violating the law is low or the legal penalty is too small to worry about), or, as the authors of the state law hope, I could allow my belief to be altered. If my belief does change, I probably will continue to "buckle up" even if the seat belt law is repealed some day.

Cognitive dissonance theory has many practical managerial applications for motivating employees. For example, management can require workers to do certain things in the hope that attitudes or beliefs will follow—just as in the seat belt example. On the other hand, management can attempt to change people's attitudes or beliefs (Zimbardo & Ebbesen, 1970) in the hope that the resulting cognitive dissonance will motivate a behavior change. In contrast, under cognitive dissonance theories, motivation is *engineered* by intentionally creating dissonance and then not allowing the desired state to change (in the examples used here, beliefs or behavior).

Cognitive dissonance provides the theoretical basis for what are known as equity theories of motivation. Equity theories postulate that workers are motivated to act (e.g., to produce more or less) by their perceptions of inequities in the environment, such as between *their* levels of work and compensation and *others'* levels of work and compensation (Mowday, 1983). The theory of cognitive dissonance assumes that a worker performing the same work as another but being paid significantly less will do something to relieve this dissonance. Among the worker's options are asking for a raise, restricting output, or seeking another job. The 1958 article "The Motivating Effect of Cognitive Dissonance" by Leon Festinger, the "father" of cognitive dissonance theory, is reprinted in this chapter.

EXPECTANCY THEORY OF MOTIVATION

Expectancy theory holds that people are motivated by two dynamics: how much they want certain rewards (or to avoid negative sanctions) and the expectancy (probability) that their actions will garner the rewards. Victor Vroom (1964, 1969), the most respected expectancy theorist, identifies four classes of variables that comprise expectancy theory:

1. The amounts of particular classes of outcomes, such as pay, status, acceptance, and influence, attained by the person.
2. The strength of the person's desire or aversion for outcomes.
3. The amounts of these outcomes believed by the person to be received by comparable others.
4. The amounts of these outcomes the person expected to receive or has received at earlier points in time. (1969, p. 207)

Very simply, expectancy theory claims that people are motivated by calculating how much they want something, how much of it they think they will get, how likely it is that their actions will cause them to get it, and how much others in similar circumstances have received.

ANOTHER NEED THEORY

Frederick Herzberg is one of the most widely cited of the numerous students and theorists who studied and wrote about motivation in organizations during the 1960s. Herzberg began construction of his motivation theory with Abraham Maslow's needs theory and was also influenced substantially by the Theory X and Theory Y assumptions of Douglas McGregor.

Herzberg's theory of motivation evolved from extensive empirical research. Herzberg and his collaborating researchers would ask people to identify situations in which they felt particularly satisfied and dissatisfied with their job (Herzberg, Mausner, & Snyderman, 1959). From thousands of responses, Herzberg developed the motivation-hygiene theory, which can be stated in this way:

- *Motivators* or *satisfiers* are variables centered in the work (or work content) that satisfy self-actualization-type needs (Maslow, 1943) and lead to higher motivation. Examples of Herzberg's motivators include achievement, recognition for achievement, and opportunities for self-development.

- In contrast, *hygiene factors* are maintainers—preventers of dissatisfaction. A few examples of hygiene factors are supervision, administrative practices, and (in most respects) pay.

According to Herzberg's theory, which is described here in his 1968 article, "One More Time: How Do You Motivate Employees?" motivators and hygiene factors are on different dimensions or planes. They are not extreme points on a single scalar continuum. The presence of hygiene factors does not motivate, it only prevents dissatisfaction; and the absence of motivators does not cause employees to be dissatisfied, it only yields nonmotivated employees. If managers want satisfied employees, they should pay attention to hygiene factors, such as pay and working conditions. However, hygiene factors do not "turn employees on"; they only neutralize negative sentiments. To increase motivation, managers must work with motivators.

Herzberg's work has been attacked with great vigor on two fronts. First, numerous behavioral researchers have tried unsuccessfully to replicate his findings, raising serious questions about the validity of his research methods (Vroom, 1964). The second line of criticism directed at Herzberg has essentially been an argument against any and all simplistic, static, one- or two-dimensional theories of motivation, and for more complex, contingency-type theories (Behling, Labovitz, & Kosmo, 1968; Schein, 1980). Despite the sometimes bitter criticisms of motivation-hygiene theory, its popularity continues among management practitioners and trainers. Its greatest weakness—simplicity—also gives it credibility.

SELF-ORIENTED THEORIES TO MEGA-THEORIES OF WORK MOTIVATION

Theories of motivation have evolved throughout the 20th century and are continuing to develop as we move through the first decade of the 21st. The quest to understand the dynamics of motivation in organizations, however, still centers on three key questions. What raises the level of energy, positive emotions, and appropriate attitudes, beliefs, and values of organizational members? What provides the essential directional headings for organizational members in doing important work well? Finally, what sustains energy, focus, commitment, and productivity over time for organizational members?

Many long-standing motivation theories provide answers to some of these core questions. Leonard, Beauvais, and Scholl (1999) remind us that "there is a growing realization that traditional models of motivation do not explain the diversity of behavior found in organizational settings." Their theory integrates individual traits, competencies, and values and suggests that there are five primary sources of motivation: intrinsic processes, extrinsic/instrumental rewards, external and internal self-concept, and goal internalization. Edwin Locke (2001) notes that self-set or personal goals and self-efficacy are the most immediate, motivational determinants of action, and they mediate or link the effects of other motivators. Locke (1978) had earlier identified needs and values—not goals—as the most important factors in motivation because they determine goals. By 2001, he was arguing that personal goals and intentions, along with task-specific self-confidence, are the most direct motivational determinants of action, and that other factors—including needs, values, motives, personality, and incentives—need to be considered as situations require.

The notion of work context having a significant impact on work motivation has a long history in organizational behavior. Bradley E. Wright's article (included in this chapter) develops a conceptual model building on goal setting and social cognitive theories. He demonstrates how work context (goal conflict, procedural constraints, and goal ambiguity) factors interacting with job characteristics (job goal specificity and job difficulty) and job attitudes (particularly one's sense of self-efficacy) provide leveraging options capable of increasing work motivation and potentially productivity in the public sector.

Finally, Edwin A. Locke and Gary P. Latham, long-time contributors to the field of organizational behavior, in their 2004 article "What Should We Do About Motivation Theory?" (included in this volume), present six recommendations for building theories of work motivation. They argue that we now must integrate existing theories and models into coherent mega-theories of work motivation. For example, we need ways to merge trait and situational approaches. We need to recognize both conscious and unconscious processes. We need to find ways to use introspective processes in theory building. We need to recognize the key factor of human volition. Finally, many different disciplines can contribute to our understanding and research in this domain.

CONCLUSION

In this chapter we present a balanced sampling of the more important theories of motivation. If the result is inconclusive, we apologize. In many ways, motivation is that "pot of gold." We may never totally unlock its mysteries. Humans are complicated, ever-changing, and diverse beings. Organizations are complex social systems in which these beings must live and work. Understanding and predicting either is extremely difficult (Schein, 1980). Discovering universal truths about what motivates people in the context of organizations may be an unrealistic goal. On the other hand, much has been learned about what does and does not cause people to "turn on" or "tune out" at work.

REFERENCES

Alderfer, J. S. (1969). An empirical test of a new theory of human needs. *Organizational Behavior and Human Performance, 4,* 142–175.

Behling, O., Labovitz, G., & Kosmo, R. (1968). The Herzberg controversy: A critical reappraisal. *Academy of Management Journal, 11*(1), 99–108.

Festinger, L. (1954). Motivations leading to social behavior. In M. R. Jones (Ed.), *Nebraska symposium on motivation*. Lincoln, NE: University of Nebraska Press.

Festinger, L. (1957). *A theory of cognitive dissonance*. Stanford, CA: Stanford University Press.

Festinger, L. (1958). The motivating effect of cognitive dissonance. In G. Lindzey (Ed.), *Assessment of human motives* (pp. 69–86). New York: Holt, Rinehart.

Gantt, H. L. (1910). *Work, wages, and profit*. New York: Engineering Magazine.

Gilbreth, F., & Gilbreth, L. (1917). *Applied motion study*. New York: Sturgis & Walton.

Haire, M. (1962). The concept of power and the concept of man. In G. B. Strother (Ed.), *Social science approaches to business behavior* (pp. 163–183). Homewood, IL: Irwin.

Herzberg, F. (1968, January/February). One more time: How do you motivate employees? *Harvard Business Review, 46*(1).

Herzberg, F., Mausner, B., & Snyderman, B. B. (1959). *The motivation to work*. New York: John Wiley & Sons.

Leonard, N. H., Beauvais, L. L., & Scholl, R. W. (1999, August). Work motivation: The incorporation of self-concept-based processes. *Human Relations, 52*(8), 969–998.

Locke, E. A. (1978, July). The ubiquity of the technique of goal setting in theories of and approaches to employee motivation. *Academy of Management Review*, 594–601.

Locke, E. A. (2001). Self-set goals and self-efficacy as mediators of incentives and personality. In M. Erez, U. Kleinbeck, & H. Thierry (Eds.), *Work motivation in the context of a globalizing economy*. Mahwah, NJ: Lawrence Erlbaum.

Locke, E. A., & Latham, Gary P. (2004). What should we do about motivation theory? Six recommendations for the twenty-first century. *Academy of Management Review, 29*(3), 388–403.

Maslow, A. H. (1943). A theory of human motivation. *Psychological Review, 50*.

Mayo, E. (1933). *The human problems of an industrial civilization*. New York: Macmillan.

McClelland, D. C. (1961). *The achieving society*. Princeton, NJ: Van Nostrand.

McClelland, D. C. (1966). That urge to achieve. *Think* (published by International Business Machines Corporation), 82–89.

McGregor, D. M. (April 1957a). The human side of enterprise. Address to the Fifth Anniversary Convocation of the School of Industrial Management, Massachusetts Institute of Technology. In *Adventure in thought and action*. Cambridge, MA: MIT School of Industrial Management, 1957. Reprinted in W. G. Bennis, E. H. Schein, & C. McGregor (Eds.), *Leadership and motivation: Essays of Douglas McGregor* (pp. 3–20). Cambridge, MA: The MIT Press, 1966.

McGregor, D. M. (November 1957b). The human side of enterprise. *Management Review*, 22–28, 88–92.

McGregor, D. M. (1960). *The human side of enterprise*. New York: McGraw-Hill.

Mowday, R. T. (1983). Equity theory predictions of behavior in organizations. In R. W. Steers & L. W. Porter (Eds.), *Motivation and work behavior* (3rd ed., pp. 91–113). New York: McGraw-Hill.

Pennock, G. (1930). Industrial research at Hawthorne. *The Personnel Journal, 8*, 296.

Roethlisberger, F. I. (1941). *Management and morale*. Cambridge, MA: Harvard University Press.

Roethlisberger, F. J., & Dickson, W. J. (1939). *Management and the worker*. Cambridge, MA: Harvard University Press.

Schein, E. H. (1980). *Organizational psychology* (3rd ed.). Englewood Cliffs, NJ: Prentice-Hall.

Shafritz, J. M., Ott, J. S., & Jang, Y. S. (2005). *Classics of organization theory* (6th ed.). Belmont, CA: Wadsworth-Thomson.

Smith, A. (1776). Of the division of labor. In A. Smith, *The wealth of nations* (chapter 1). New York: Random House.

Taylor, F. W. (1903). *Shop management.* New York: Harper & Row.

Taylor, F. W. (1911). *The principles of scientific management.* New York: Harper & Row.

Vroom, V. H. (1964). *Work and motivation.* New York: John Wiley.

Vroom, V. H. (1969). Industrial social psychology. In G. Lindzey & E. Aronson (Eds.), *The handbook of social psychology* (vol. 5, 2nd ed., pp. 200–208). Reading, MA: Addison-Wesley.

Vroom, V. H., & Deci, E. L. (Eds.) (1970). *Management and motivation.* Harmondsworth, UK: Penguin Books.

Wahba, M. A., & Bridwell, L. G. (1973). Maslow reconsidered: A review of research on the need hierarchy theory. Boston: *Proceedings of the 1973 meetings of the Academy of Management.*

Wren, D. A. (1972). *The evolution of management thought.* New York: The Ronald Press.

Wright, B. E. (2004). The role of work context in work motivation: A public sector application of goal and social cognitive theories. *Journal of Public Administration Research and Theory, 14,*(1), 59–78.

Zimbardo, P., & Ebbesen, E. B. (1970). *Influencing attitudes and changing behavior* (rev. printing). Reading, MA: Addison-Wesley.

Reading 9	The Hawthorne Experiments

Frederick J. Roethlisberger

There seems to be an assumption today that we need a complex set of ideas to handle the complex problems of this complex world in which we live. We assume that a big problem needs a big idea; a complex problem needs a complex idea for its solution. As a result, our thinking tends to become more and more tortuous and muddled. Nowhere is this more true than in matters of human behavior. It seems to me that the road back to sanity—and here is where my title comes in—lies

1. In having a few simple and clear ideas about the world in which we live.

2. In complicating our ideas, not in a vacuum, but only in reference to things we can observe, see, feel, hear, and touch. Let us not generalize from verbal definitions; let us know in fact what we are talking about.

3. In having a very simple method by means of which we can explore our complex world. We need a tool which will allow us to get the idea from which our generalizations are to be drawn. We need a simple skill to keep us in touch with what is sometimes referred to as "reality."

4. In being "tough-minded," i.e., in not letting ourselves be too disappointed because the complex world never quite fulfills our most cherished expectations of it. Let us remember that the concrete phenomena will always elude any set of abstractions that we can make of them.

5. In knowing very clearly the class of phenomena to which our ideas and methods relate. Now, this is merely a way of saying, "Do not use a saw as a hammer." A saw is a useful tool precisely because it is limited and designed for a certain purpose. Do not criticize the usefulness of a saw because it does not make a good hammer. . . .

It is my simple thesis that a human problem requires a human solution. First, we have to learn to recognize a human problem when we see one; and, second, upon recognizing it, we have to learn to deal with it as such and not as if it were something else. Too often at the verbal level we talk glibly about the importance of the human factor; and too seldom at the concrete level of behavior do we recognize a human problem for what it is and deal with it as such. A *human problem to be brought to a human solution requires human data and human tools.* It is my purpose to use the Western Electric researchers as an illustration of what I mean by this statement, because, if they deserve the publicity and acclaim which they have received, it is because, in my opinion, they have so conclusively demonstrated this point. In this sense they are the road back to sanity in management-employee relations.

Experiments in Illumination

The Western Electric researches started about sixteen years ago, in the Hawthorne plant, with a series of experiments on illumination. The purpose was to find out the relation of the quality and quantity of illumination to the efficiency of industrial workers. These studies lasted several years, and I shall not describe them in detail. It will suffice to point out that the results were quite different from what had been expected.

In one experiment the workers were divided into two groups. One group, called the "test group," was to work under different illumination intensities. The other group, called the "control group," was to work under an intensity of illumination as nearly constant as possible. During the first experiment, the test group was submitted to three different intensities of illumination of increasing

Source: Reprinted by permission of the publisher from "The Hawthorne Experiments," in MANAGEMENT AND MORALE by F. J. Roethlisberger pp. 7–26, Cambridge, Mass.: Harvard University Press, Copyright ©1941 by the President and Fellows of Harvard College, © renewed 1969 by F. J. Roethlisberger.

magnitude, 24, 46, and 70 foot candles. What were the results of this early experiment? Production increased in both rooms—in both the test group and the control group—and the rise in output was roughly of the same magnitude in both cases.

In another experiment, the light under which the test group worked was decreased from 10 to 3 foot candles, while the control group worked, as before, under a constant level of illumination intensity. In this case the output rate in the test group went up instead of down. It also went up in the control group.

In still another experiment, the workers were allowed to believe that the illumination was being increased, although, in fact, no change in intensity was made. The workers commented favorably on the improved lighting condition, but there was no appreciable change in output. At another time, the workers were allowed to believe that the intensity of illumination was being decreased, although again, in fact, no actual change was made. The workers complained somewhat about the poorer lighting, but again there was no appreciable effect on output.

And finally, in another experiment, the intensity of illumination was decreased to .06 of a foot candle, which is the intensity of illumination approximately equivalent to that of ordinary moonlight. Not until this point was reached was there any appreciable decline in the output rate.

What did the experimenters learn? Obviously, as Stuart Chase said, there was something "screwy," but the experimenters were not quite sure who or what was screwy—they themselves, the subjects, or the results. One thing was clear: the results were negative. Nothing of a positive nature had been learned about the relation of illumination to industrial efficiency. If the results were to be taken at their face value, it would appear that there was no relation between illumination and industrial efficiency. However, the investigators were not yet quite willing to draw this conclusion. They realized the difficulty of testing for the effect of a single variable in a situation where there were many uncontrolled variables. It was thought therefore that another experiment should be devised in which other variables affecting the output of workers could be better controlled.

A few of the tough-minded experimenters already were beginning to suspect their basic ideas and assumptions with regard to human motivation. It occurred to them that the trouble was not so much with the results or with the subjects as it was with their notion regarding the way their subjects were supposed to behave—the notion of a simple cause-and-effect, direct relationship between certain physical changes in the workers' environment and the responses of the workers to these changes. Such a notion completely ignored the human meaning of these changes to the people who were subjected to them.

In the illumination experiments, therefore, we have a classic example of trying to deal with a human situation in nonhuman terms. The experimenters had obtained no human data; they had been handling electric-light bulbs and plotting average output curves. Hence their results had no human significance. That is why they seemed screwy. Let me suggest here, however, that the results were not screwy, but the experimenters were—a "screwy" person being by definition one who is not acting in accordance with the customary human values of the situation in which he finds himself.

The Relay Assembly Test Room

Another experiment was framed, in which it was planned to submit a segregated group of workers to different kinds of working conditions. The idea was very simple: A group of five girls were placed in a separate room where their conditions of work could be carefully controlled, where their output could be measured, and where they could be closely observed. It was decided to introduce at specified intervals different changes in working conditions and to see what effect these innovations had on output. . . . Under these conditions of close observation the girls were studied for a period of five years. Literally tons of material were collected. Probably nowhere in the world has so much material been collected about a small group of workers for such a long period of time. But what about the results? They can be stated very briefly. When all is said and done, they amount roughly to this: A skillful statistician spent several years trying to relate variations to output with variations in the physical circumstances of these five operators. . . . The attempt to relate changes in physical circumstances to variations in output resulted in not a single correlation of enough statistical significance to be recognized by any competent statistician as having any meaning.

Now, of course, it would be misleading to say that this negative result was the only conclusion reached. There were positive conclusions, and it did not take the experimenters more than two years to find out that they had missed the boat. After two years of work, certain things happened which made them sit up and take notice. Different experimental conditions of work, in the nature of changes in the number and duration of rest pauses and differences in the length of the working day and week, had been introduced in this Relay Assembly Test Room. For example, the investigators first introduced two five-minute rests, one in the morning and one in the afternoon. Then they increased the length of these rests, and after that they introduced the rests at different times of the day. During one experimental period they served the operators a specially prepared lunch during the rest. In the later periods, they decreased the length of the working day by one-half hour and then by one hour. They gave the operators Saturday morning off for a while. Altogether, thirteen such periods of different working conditions were introduced in the first two years.

During the first year and a half of the experiment, everybody was happy, both the investigators and the operators. The investigators were happy because as conditions of work improved the output rate rose steadily. Here, it appeared, was strong evidence in favor of their preconceived hypothesis that fatigue was the major factor limiting output. The operators were happy because their conditions of work were being improved, they were earning more money, and they were objects of considerable attention from top management. But

then one investigator—one of those tough-minded fellows—suggested that they restore the original conditions of work, that is, go back to a full forty-eight-hour week without rests, lunches, and what not. This was Period XII. Then the happy state of affairs, when everything was going along as it theoretically should, went sour. Output, instead of taking the expected nose dive, maintained its high level.

Again the investigators were forcibly reminded that human situations are likely to be complex. In any human situation, whenever a simple change is introduced—a rest pause, for example—other changes, unwanted and unanticipated, may also be brought about. What I am saying here is very simple. If one experiments on a stone, the stone does not know it is being experimented upon—all of which makes it simple for people experimenting on stones. But if a human being is being experimented upon, he is likely to know it. Therefore, his attitudes toward the experiment and toward the experimenters become very important factors in determining his responses to the situation.

Now that is what happened in the Relay Assembly Test Room. To the investigators, it was essential that the workers give their full and wholehearted coöperation to the experiment. They did not want the operators to work harder or easier depending upon their attitude toward the conditions that were imposed. They wanted them to work as they felt, so that they could be sure that the different physical conditions of work were solely responsible for the variations in output. For each of the experimental changes, they wanted subjects whose responses would be uninfluenced by so-called "psychological factors."

In order to bring this about, the investigators did everything in their power to secure the complete coöperation of their subjects, with the result that almost all the practices common to the shop were altered. The operators were consulted about the changes to be made, and, indeed, several plans were abandoned because they met with the disapproval of the girls. They were questioned sympathetically about their reactions to the conditions imposed, and many of these conferences took place in the office of the superintendent. The girls were allowed to talk at work; their "bogey" was eliminated. Their physical health and well-being became matters of great concern. Their opinions, hopes, and fears were eagerly sought. What happened was that in the very process of setting the conditions for the test—a so-called "controlled" experiment—the experimenters had completely altered the social situation of the room. Inadvertently a change had been introduced which was far more important than the planned experimental innovations: the customary supervision in the room had been revolutionized. This accounted for the better attitudes of the girls and their improved rate of work.

The Development of a New and More Fruitful Point of View

After Period XII in the Relay Assembly Test Room, the investigators decided to change their ideas radically. What all their experiments had dramatically and conclusively demonstrated was the importance of employee attitudes and sentiments. It was clear that the responses of workers to what was happening about them were dependent upon the significance these events had for them. In most work situations the meaning of a change is likely to be as important, if not more so, than the change itself. This was the great *éclaircissement,* the new illumination, that came from the research. It was an illumination quite different from what they had expected from the illumination studies. Curiously enough, this discovery is nothing very new or startling. It is something which anyone who has had some concrete experience in handling other people intuitively recognizes and practices.

Whether or not a person is going to give his services whole-heartedly to a group depends, in good part, on the way he feels about his job, his fellow workers, and supervisors—the meaning for him of what is happening about him.

However, when the experimenters began to tackle the problem of employee attitudes and the factors determining such attitudes—when they began to tackle the problem of "meaning"—they entered a sort of twilight zone where things are never quite what they seem. Moreover, overnight, as it were, they were robbed of all the tools they had so carefully forged; for all their previous tools were nonhuman tools concerned with the measurement of output, temperature, humidity, etc., and these were no longer useful for the human data that they now wanted to obtain. What the experimenters now wanted to know was how a person felt, what his intimate thinking, reflections, and preoccupations were, and what he liked and disliked about his work environment. In short, what did the whole blooming business—his job, his supervision, his working conditions— mean to him? Now this was human stuff, and there were no tools, or at least the experimenters knew of none, for obtaining and evaluating this kind of material.

Fortunately, there were a few courageous souls among the experimenters. These men were not metaphysicians, psychologists, academicians, professors, intellectuals, or what have you. They were men of common sense and of practical affairs. They were not driven by any great heroic desire to change the world. They were true experimenters, that is, men compelled to follow the implications of their own monkey business. All the evidence of their studies was pointing in one direction. Would they take the jump? They did.

Experiments in Interviewing Workers

A few tough-minded experimenters decided to go into the shops and—completely disarmed and denuded of their elaborate logical equipment and in all humility—to see if they could learn how to get the workers to talk about things that were important to them and could learn to understand what the workers were trying to tell them. This was a revolutionary idea in the year 1928, when this interviewing program started—the idea of getting a worker to talk to you and to listen sympathetically, but intelligently, to what he had to say. In that year a new era of personnel relations began. It was the first real attempt to get human data and to forge human tools to get them. In that year a novel idea was born; dimly the experimenters perceived a new method of human control. In that year the Rubicon was crossed from which there could be no return to the "good old days." Not that the experimenters ever wanted to return, because they now entered a world so exciting, so intriguing, and so full of promise that it made the "good old days" seem like the prattle and play of children.

When these experimenters decided to enter the world of "meaning," with very few tools, but with a strong sense of curiosity and a willingness to learn, they had many interesting adventures. It would be too long a story to tell all of them, or even a small part of them. They made plenty of mistakes, but they were not afraid to learn.

At first, they found it difficult to learn to give full and complete attention to what a person had to say without interrupting him before he was through. They found it difficult to learn not to give advice, not to make or imply moral judgments about the speaker, not to argue, not to be too clever, not to dominate the conversation, not to ask leading questions. They found it difficult to get the person to talk about matters which were important to him and not to the interviewer. But, most important of all, they found it difficult to learn that perhaps the thing most significant to a person was not something in his immediate work situation.

Gradually, however, they learned these things. They discovered that sooner or later a person tends to talk about what is uppermost in his mind to a sympathetic and skillful listener, and they became more proficient in interpreting what a person is saying or trying to say. Of course they protected the confidences given to them and made absolutely sure that nothing an employee said could ever be used against him. Slowly they began to forge a simple human tool—imperfect, to be sure—to get the kind of data they wanted. They called this method "interviewing." I would hesitate to say the number of manhours of labor which went into the forging of this tool. There followed from studies made through its use a gradually changing conception of the worker and his behavior.

A New Way of Viewing Employee Satisfaction and Dissatisfaction

When the experimenters started to study employee likes and dislikes, they assumed, at first, that they would find a simple and logical relation between a person's likes or dislikes and certain items and events in his immediate work situation. They expected to find a simple connection, for example, between a person's complaint and the object about which he was complaining. Hence, the solution would be easy: Correct the object of the complaint, if possible, and presto! the complaint would disappear. Unfortunately, however, the world of human behavior is not so simple as this conception of it; and it took the investigators several arduous and painful years to find this out. I will mention only a few interesting experiences they had.

Several times they changed the objects of the complaint only to find that the attitudes of the complainants remained unchanged. In these cases, correcting the object of the complaint did not remedy the complaint or the attitude of the person expressing it. A certain complaint might disappear, to be sure, only to have another one arise. Here the investigators were running into so-called "chronic kickers," people whose dissatisfactions were more deeply rooted in factors relating to their personal histories. . . .

Many times they found that people did not really want anything done about the things of which they were complaining. What they did want was an opportunity to talk about their troubles to a sympathetic listener. It was astonishing to find the number of instances in which workers complained about things which had happened many, many years ago, but which they described as vividly as if they had happened just a day before.

Here again, something was "screwy," but this time the experimenters realized that it was their assumptions which were screwy. They were assuming that the meanings which people assign to their experience are essentially logical. They were carrying in their heads the notion of the "economic man," a man primarily motivated by economic interest, whose logical capacities were being used in the service of this self-interest.

Gradually and painfully in the light of the evidence, which was overwhelming, the experimenters had been forced to abandon this conception of the worker and his behavior. Only with a new working hypothesis could they make sense of the data they had collected. The conception of the worker which they developed is actually nothing very new or startling; it is one which any effective administrator intuitively recognizes and practices in handling human beings.

First, they found that the behavior of workers could not be understood apart from their feelings or sentiments. I shall use the word "sentiment" hereafter to refer not only to such things as feelings and emotions, but also to a much wider range of phenomena which may not be expressed in violent feelings or emotions—phenomena that are referred to by such words as "loyalty," "integrity," "solidarity."

Secondly, they found that sentiments are easily disguised, and hence are difficult to recognize and to study. Manifestations of sentiment take a number of different forms. Feelings of personal integrity, for example, can be expressed by a handshake; they can also be expressed, when violated,

by a sitdown strike. Moreover, people like to rationalize their sentiments and to objectify them. We are not so likely to say "I feel bad," as to say "The world is bad." In other words, we like to endow the world with those attributes and qualities which will justify and account for the feelings and sentiments we have toward it; we tend to project our sentiments on the outside world.

Thirdly, they found that manifestations of sentiment could not be understood as things in and by themselves, but only in terms of the total situation of the person. To comprehend why a person felt the way he did, a wider range of phenomena had to be explored. The following three diagrams illustrate roughly the development of this point of view.

It will be remembered that at first the investigators assumed a simple and direct relation between certain physical changes in the worker's environment and his responses to them. This simple state of mind is illustrated in diagram I. But all the evidence of the early experiments showed that the responses of employees to changes in their immediate working environment can be understood only in terms of their attitudes—the "meaning" these changes have for them. This point of view is represented in diagram II. However, the "meaning" which these changes have for the worker is not strictly and primarily logical, for they are fraught with human feelings and values. The "meaning," therefore, which any individual worker assigns to a particular change depends upon (1) his social "conditioning," or what sentiments (values, hopes, fears, expectations, etc.) he is bringing to the work situation because of his previous family and group associations, and hence the relation of the change to these sentiments; and (2) the kind of human satisfaction he is deriving from his social participation with other workers and supervisors in the immediate work group of which he is a member, and hence the effect of the change on his customary interpersonal relations. This way of regarding the responses of workers (both verbal and overt) is represented in diagram III. It says briefly: Sentiments do not appear in a vacuum; they do not come out of the blue; they appear in a social context. They

I. Change ——————— Response

II. Change ——————— Response

Attitudes (sentiments)

III. Change ——————— Response

Attitudes (sentiments)

Personal
history

Social situation
at work

have to be considered in terms of that context, and apart from it they are likely to be misunderstood.

One further point should be made about that aspect of the worker's environment designated "Social situation at work" in diagram III. What is meant is that the worker is not an isolated, atomic individual; he is a member of a group, or of groups. Within each of these groups the individuals have feelings and sentiments toward each other, which bind them together in collaborative effort. Moreover, these collective sentiments can, and do, become attached to every item and object in the industrial environment—even to output. Material goods, output, wages, hours of work, and so on, cannot be treated as things in themselves. Instead, they must be interpreted as carriers of social value.

Output as a Form of Social Behavior

That output is a form of social behavior was well illustrated in a study made by the Hawthorne experimenters, called the Bank Wiring Observation Room. This room contained fourteen workmen representing three occupational groups—wiremen, soldermen, and inspectors. These men were on group piecework, where the more they turned out the more they earned. In such a situation one might have expected that they would have been interested in maintaining total output and that the faster workers would have put pressure on the slower workers to improve their efficiency. But this was not the case. Operating within this group were four basic sentiments, which can be expressed briefly as follows: (1) You should not turn out too much work; if you do, you are a "rate buster." (2) You should not turn out too little work; if you do, you are a "chiseler." (3) You should not say anything to a supervisor which would react to the detriment of one of your associates; if you do, you are a "squealer." (4) You should not be too officious; that is, if you are an inspector you should not act like one.

To be an accepted member of the group a man had to act in accordance with these social standards. One man in this group exceeded the group standard of what constituted a fair day's work.

Social pressure was put on him to conform, but without avail, since he enjoyed doing things the others disliked. The best-liked person in the group was the one who kept his output exactly where the group agreed it should be.

Inasmuch as the operators were agreed as to what constituted a day's work, one might have expected rate of output to be about the same for each member of the group. This was by no means the case; there were marked differences. At first the experimenters thought that the differences in individual performance were related to differences in ability, so they compared each worker's relative rank in output with his relative rank in intelligence and dexterity as measured by certain tests. The results were interesting: The lowest producer in the room ranked first in intelligence and third in dexterity; the highest producer in the room was seventh in dexterity and lowest in intelligence. Here surely was a situation in which the native capacities of the men were not finding expression. From the viewpoint of logical, economic behavior, this room did not make sense. Only in terms of powerful sentiments could these individual differences in output level be explained. Each worker's level of output reflected his position in the informal organization of the group.

What Makes the Worker Not Want to Coöperate

As a result of the Bank Wiring Observation Room, the Hawthorne researchers became more and more interested in the informal employee groups which tend to form within the formal organization of the company, and which are not likely to be represented in the organization chart. They became interested in the beliefs and creeds which have the effect of making each individual feel an integral part of the group and which make the group appear as a single unit, in the social codes and norms of behavior by means of which employees automatically work together in a group without any conscious choice as to whether they will or will not coöperate. They studied the important social functions these groups perform for their members, the histories of these informal work groups, how they spontaneously appear, how they tend to perpetuate themselves, multiply, and disappear, how they are in constant jeopardy from technical change, and hence how they tend to resist innovation. In particular, they became interested in those groups whose norms and codes of behavior are at variance with the technical and economic objectives of the company as a whole. They examined the social conditions under which it is more likely for the employee group to separate itself out in opposition to the remainder of the groups which make up the total organization. In such phenomena they felt that they had at last arrived at the heart of the problem of effective collaboration. They obtained a new enlightenment of the present industrial scene; from this point of view, many perplexing problems became more intelligible.

Some people claim, for example, that the size of the pay envelope is the major demand which the employee is making of his job. All the worker wants is to be told what to do and to get paid for doing it. If we look at him and his job in terms of sentiments, this is far from being as generally true as we would like to believe. Most of us want the satisfaction that comes from being accepted and recognized as people of worth by our friends and work associates. Money is only a small part of this social recognition. The way we are greeted by our boss, being asked to help a newcomer, being asked to keep an eye on a difficult operation, being given a job requiring special skill—all of these are acts of social recognition. They tell us how we stand in our work group. We all want tangible evidence of our social importance. We want to have a skill that is socially recognized as useful. We want the feeling of security that comes not so much from the amount of money we have in the bank as from

being an accepted member of a group. A man whose job is without social function is like a man without a country; the activity to which he has to give the major portion of his life is robbed of all human meaning and significance. . . .

In summary, therefore, the Western Electric researchers seem to me like a beginning on the road back to sanity in employee relations because (1) they offer a fruitful working hypothesis, a few simple and relatively clear ideas for the study and understanding of human situations in business; (2) they offer a simple method by means of which we can explore and deal with the complex human problems in a business organization—this method is a human method: it deals with things which are important to people; and (3) they throw a new light on the precondition for effective collaboration. Too often we think of collaboration as something which can be logically or legally contrived. The Western Electric studies indicate that it is far more a matter of sentiment than a matter of logic. Workers are not isolated, unrelated individuals; they are social animals and should be treated as such.

This statement—the worker is a social animal and should be treated as such—is simple, but the systematic and consistent practice of this point of view is not. If it were systematically practiced, it would revolutionize present-day personnel work. Our technological development in the past hundred years has been tremendous. Our methods of handling people are still archaic. If this civilization is to survive, we must obtain a new understanding of human motivation and behavior in business organizations—an understanding which can be simply but effectively practiced. The Western Electric researchers contribute a first step in this direction.

Reading 10	A Theory of Human Motivation
	Abraham H. Maslow

I. Introduction

In a previous paper (Maslow, 1943) various propositions were presented which would have to be included in any theory of human motivation that could lay claim to being definitive. These conclusions may be briefly summarized as follows:

1. The integrated wholeness of the organism must be one of the foundation stones of motivation theory.
2. The hunger drive (or any other physiological drive) was rejected as a centering point or model for a definitive theory of motivation. Any drive that is somatically based and localizable was shown to be atypical rather than typical in human motivation.
3. Such a theory should stress and center itself upon ultimate or basic goals rather than partial or superficial ones, upon ends rather than means to these ends. Such a stress would imply a more central place for unconscious than for conscious motivations.
4. There are usually available various cultural paths to the same goal. Therefore conscious, specific, local-cultural desires are not as fundamental in motivation theory as the more basic, unconscious goals.
5. Any motivated behavior, either preparatory or consummatory, must be understood to be a channel through which many basic needs may be simultaneously expressed or satisfied. Typically an act has *more* than one motivation.
6. Practically all organismic states are to be understood as motivated and as motivating.
7. Human needs arrange themselves in hierarchies of prepotency. That is to say, the appearance of one need usually rests on the prior satisfaction of another, more prepotent need. Man is a perpetually wanting animal. Also no need or drive can be treated as if it were isolated or discrete; every drive is related to the state of satisfaction or dissatisfaction of other drives.
8. *Lists* of drives will get us nowhere for various theoretical and practical reasons. Furthermore any classification of motivations must deal with the problem of levels of specificity or generalization of the motives to be classified.
9. Classifications of motivations must be based upon goals rather than upon instigating drives or motivated behavior.
10. Motivation theory should be human-centered rather than animal-centered.
11. The situation or the field in which the organism reacts must be taken into account but the field alone can rarely serve as an exclusive explanation for behavior. Furthermore the field itself must be interpreted in terms of the organism. Field theory cannot be a substitute for motivation theory.
12. Not only the integration of the organism must be taken into account, but also the possibility of isolated, specific, partial or segmental reactions.

It has since become necessary to add to these another affirmation.

13. Motivation theory is not synonymous with behavior theory. The motivations are only one class of determinants of behavior. While behavior is almost always motivated, it is also almost always biologically, culturally and situationally determined as well.

The present paper is an attempt to formulate a positive theory of motivation which will satisfy these theoretical demands and at the same time conform to the known facts, clinical and observational as well as experimental. . . . The present theory then must be considered to be a suggested program or framework for future

Source: Abraham H. Maslow, "A Theory of Human Motivation," 1943.

research and must stand or fall, not so much on facts available or evidence presented, as upon researches yet to be done, researches suggested perhaps, by the questions raised in this paper.

II. The Basic Needs

The "Physiological" Needs. The needs that are usually taken as the starting point for motivation theory are the so-called physiological drives. Two recent lines of research make it necessary to revise our customary notions about these needs, first, the development of the concept of homeostasis, and second, the finding that appetites (preferential choices among foods) are a fairly efficient indication of actual needs or lacks in the body.

Homeostasis refers to the body's automatic efforts to maintain a constant, normal state of the blood stream. Cannon (1932) has described this process for (1) the water content of the blood, (2) salt content, (3) sugar content, (4) protein content, (5) fat content, (6) calcium content, (7) oxygen content, (8) constant hydrogen-ion level (acid-base balance), and (9) constant temperature of the blood. Obviously this list can be extended to include other minerals, the hormones, vitamins, etc.

Young (1941) . . . has summarized the work on appetite in its relation to body needs. If the body lacks some chemical, the individual will tend to develop a specific appetite or partial hunger for that food element. . . .

It should be pointed out again that any of the physiological needs and the consummatory behavior involved with them serve as channels for all sorts of other needs as well. That is to say, the person who thinks he is hungry may actually be seeking more for comfort, or dependence, than for vitamins or proteins. Conversely, it is possible to satisfy the hunger need in part by other activities such as drinking water or smoking cigarettes. In other words, relatively isolable as these physiological needs are, they are not completely so.

Undoubtedly these physiological needs are the most prepotent of all needs. What this means specifically is that, in the human being who is missing everything in life in an extreme fashion, it is most likely that the major motivation would be the physiological needs rather than any others. A person who is lacking food, safety, love, and esteem would most probably hunger for food more strongly than for anything else.

If all the needs are unsatisfied, and the organism is then dominated by the physiological needs, all other needs may become simply nonexistent or be pushed into the background. . . . For the man who is extremely and dangerously hungry, no other interests exist but food. He dreams food, he remembers food, he thinks about food, he emotes only about food, he perceives only food, and he wants only food. The more subtle determinants that ordinarily fuse with the physiological drives in organizing even feeding, drinking, or sexual behavior may now be so completely overwhelmed as to allow us to speak at this time (but *only* at this time) of pure hunger drive and behavior, with the one unqualified aim of relief.

Another peculiar characteristic of the human organism when it is dominated by a certain need is that the whole philosophy of the future tends also to change. For our chronically and extremely hungry man, Utopia can be defined very simply as a place where there is plenty of food. He tends to think that, if only he is guaranteed food for the rest of his life, he will be perfectly happy and will never want anything more. Life itself tends to be defined in terms of eating. Anything else will be defined as unimportant. Freedom, love, community feeling, respect, philosophy, may all be waved aside as fripperies which are useless since they fail to fill the stomach. Such a man may fairly be said to live by bread alone.

It cannot possibly be denied that such things are true but their *generality* can be denied. Emergency conditions are, almost by definition, rare in the normally functioning peaceful society. . . .

At *once other (and "higher") needs emerge* and these, rather than physiological hungers, dominate the organism. And when these in turn are satisfied, again new (and still "higher") needs emerge and so on. This is what we mean by saying that the basic human needs are organized into a hierarchy of relative prepotency.

One main implication of this phrasing is that gratification becomes as important a concept as deprivation in motivation theory, for it releases the organism from the domination of a relatively more physiological need, permitting thereby the emergence of other more social goals. The physiological needs, along with their partial goals, when chronically gratified cease to exist as active determinants or organizers of behavior. They now exist only in a potential fashion in the sense that they may emerge again to dominate the organism if they are thwarted. But a want that is satisfied is no longer a want. The organism is dominated and its behavior organized only by unsatisfied needs. If hunger is satisfied, it becomes unimportant in the current dynamics of the individual. . . .

The Safety Needs.   If the physiological needs are relatively well gratified, there then emerges a new set of needs, which we may categorize roughly as the safety needs. . . .

Although in this paper we are interested primarily in the needs of the adult, we can approach an understanding of his safety needs perhaps more efficiently by observation of infants and children, in whom these needs are much more simple and obvious. One reason for the clearer appearance of the threat or danger reaction in infants is that they do not inhibit this reaction at all, whereas adults in our society have been taught to inhibit it at all costs. Thus even when adults do feel their safety to be threatened we may not be able to see this on the surface. Infants will react in a total fashion and as if they were endangered, if they are disturbed or dropped suddenly, startled by loud noises, flashing light, or other unusual sensory stimulation, by rough handling, by general loss of support in the mother's arms, or by inadequate support.[1]

In infants we can also see a much more direct reaction to bodily illnesses of various kinds. Sometimes these illnesses seem to be immediately and *per se* threatening and seem to make the child feel unsafe. For instance, vomiting, colic, or other sharp pains seem to make the child look at the whole world in a different way. At such a moment of pain, it may be postulated that, for the child, the appearance of the whole world suddenly changes from sunniness to darkness, so to speak, and becomes a place in which anything at all might happen, in which previously stable things have suddenly become unstable. Thus a child who because of some bad food is taken ill may, for a day or two, develop fear, nightmares, and a need for protection and reassurance never seen in him before his illness.

Another indication of the child's need for safety is his preference for some kind of undisrupted routine or rhythm. He seems to want a predictable, orderly world. For instance, injustice, unfairness, or inconsistency in the parents seems to make a child feel anxious and unsafe. This attitude may be not so much because of the injustice *per se* or any particular pains involved, but rather because this treatment threatens to make the world look unreliable, or unsafe, or unpredictable. Young children seem to thrive better under a system which has at least a skeletal outline of rigidity, in which there is a schedule of a kind, some sort of routine, something that can be counted upon, not only for the present but also far into the future. Perhaps one could express this more accurately by saying that the child needs an organized world rather than an unorganized or unstructured one. . . .

From these and similar observations, we may generalize and say that the average child in our society generally prefers a safe, orderly, predictable, organized world, which he can count on, and in which unexpected, unmanageable or other dangerous things do not happen, and in which, in any case, he has all-powerful parents who protect and shield him from harm.

That these reactions may so easily be observed in children is in a way a proof of the fact that children in our society, feel too unsafe (or, in a word, are badly brought up). Children who are reared in an unthreatening, loving family do *not* ordinarily react as we have described above (Shirley, 1942). In such children the danger reactions are apt to come mostly to objects or situations that adults too would consider dangerous.[2]

The healthy, normal, fortunate adult in our culture is largely satisfied in his safety needs. The peaceful, smoothly running, "good" society ordinarily makes its members feel safe enough from wild animals, extremes of temperature, criminals, assault and murder, tyranny, etc. Therefore, in a very real sense, he no longer has any safety needs as active motivators. Just as a sated man no longer feels hungry, a safe man no longer feels endangered. . . .

Other broader aspects of the attempt to seek safety and stability in the world are seen in the very common preference for familiar rather than unfamiliar things, or for the known rather than the unknown. The tendency to have some religion or world-philosophy that organizes the universe and the men in it into some sort of satisfactorily coherent, meaningful whole is also in part motivated by safety-seeking. Here too we may list science and philosophy in general as partially motivated by the safety needs (we shall see later that there are also other motivations to scientific, philosophical or religious endeavor).

Otherwise the need for safety is seen as an active and dominant mobilizer of the organism's resources only in emergencies, e.g., war, disease, natural catastrophes, crime waves, societal disorganization, neurosis, brain injury, chronically bad situation. . . .

The Love Needs. If both the physiological and the safety needs are fairly well gratified, then there will emerge the love and affection and belongingness needs, and the whole cycle already described will repeat itself with this new center. Now the person will feel keenly, as never before, the absence of friends, or a sweetheart, or a wife, or children. He will hunger for affectionate relations with people in general, namely, for a place in his group, and he will strive with great intensity to achieve this goal. He will want to attain such a place more than anything else in the world and may even forget that once, when he was hungry, he sneered at love. . . .

One thing that must be stressed at this point is that love is not synonymous with sex. Sex may be studied as a purely physiological need. Ordinarily sexual behavior is multi-determined, that is to say, determined not only by sexual but also by other needs, chief among which are the love and affection needs. Also not to be overlooked is the fact that the love needs involve both giving *and* receiving love.[3]

The Esteem Needs. All people in our society (with a few pathological exceptions) have a need or desire for a stable, firmly based, (usually) high evaluation of themselves, for self-respect, or self-esteem, and for the esteem of others. By firmly based self-esteem, we mean that which is soundly based upon real capacity, achievement, and respect from others. These needs may be classified into two subsidiary sets. These are, first, the desire for strength, for achievement, for adequacy, for confidence in the face of the world, and for independence and freedom.[4] Secondly, we have what we may call the desire for reputation or prestige (defining it as respect or esteem from other people), recognition, attention, importance or appreciation.[5] These needs have been relatively stressed by Alfred Adler (1938) and his followers, and have been relatively neglected by Freud (1933, 1937) and the psychoanalysts. More and more today, however, there is appearing widespread appreciation of their central importance.

Satisfaction of the self-esteem need leads to feelings of self-confidence, worth, strength, capability, and adequacy of being useful and necessary in the world. But thwarting of these needs produces feelings of inferiority, of weakness, and of helplessness. These feelings in turn give rise to either basic discouragement or else compensatory or neurotic trends. An appreciation of the necessity of basic self-confidence and an understanding of how helpless people are without it can be easily gained from a study of severe traumatic neurosis (Kardiner, 1941).[6]

The Need for Self-Actualization. Even if all these needs are satisfied, we may still often (if not always) expect that a new discontent and restlessness will soon develop, unless the individual is doing what he is fitted for. A musician must make music, an artist must paint, a poet must write, if he is to be ultimately happy. What a man *can* be, he *must* be. This need we may call self-actualization.

This term, first coined by Kurt Goldstein (1939), is being used in this paper in a much more specific and limited fashion. It refers to the desire for self-fulfillment, namely, to the tendency for him to become actualized in what he is potentially. This tendency might be phrased as the desire to become more and more what one is, to become everything that one is capable of becoming.

The specific form that these needs will take will of course vary greatly from person to person. In one individual it may take the form of the desire to be an ideal mother, in another it may be expressed athletically, and in still another it may be expressed in painting pictures or in inventions. It is not necessarily a creative urge, although in people who have any capacities for creation it will take this form.

The clear emergence of these needs rests upon prior satisfaction of the physiological, safety, love and esteem needs. We shall call people who are satisfied in these needs, basically satisfied people, and it is from these that we may expect the fullest (and healthiest) creativeness.[7] Since, in our society, basically satisfied people are the exception, we do not know much about self-actualization, either experimentally or clinically. It remains a challenging problem for research.

The Preconditions for the Basic Need Satisfactions. There are certain conditions which are immediate prerequisites for the basic need satisfactions. Danger to these is reacted to almost as if it were a direct danger to the basic needs themselves. Such conditions as freedom to speak, freedom to do what one wishes so long as no harm is done to others, freedom to express one's self, freedom to investigate and seek for information, freedom to defend one's self, justice, fairness, honesty, orderliness in the group are examples of such preconditions for basic need satisfactions. Thwarting in these freedoms will be reacted to with a threat or emergency response. These conditions are not ends in themselves but they are *almost* so since they are so closely related to the basic needs, which are apparently the only ends in themselves. . . .

We must therefore introduce another hypothesis and speak of degrees of closeness to the basic needs, for we have already pointed out that *any*

conscious desires (partial goals) are more or less important as they are more or less close to the basic needs. The same statement may be made for various behavior acts. An act is psychologically important if it contributes directly to satisfaction of basic needs. The less directly it so contributes, or the weaker this contribution is, the less important this act must be conceived to be from the point of view of dynamic psychology. A similar statement may be made for the various defense or coping mechanisms. Some are very directly related to the protection or attainment of the basic needs; others are only weakly and distantly related. Indeed if we wished, we could speak of more basic and less basic defense mechanisms, and then affirm that danger to the more basic defenses (always remembering that this is so only because of their relationship to the basic needs). . . .

III. Further Characteristics of the Basic Needs

The Degree of Fixity of the Hierarchy of Basic Needs. We have spoken so far as if this hierarchy were a fixed order, but actually it is not nearly as rigid as we may have implied. It is true that most of the people with whom we have worked have seemed to have these basic needs in about the order that has been indicated. However, there have been a number of exceptions.

1. There are some people in whom, for instance, self-esteem seems to be more important than love. This most common reversal in the hierarchy is usually due to the development of the notion that the person who is most likely to be loved is a strong or powerful person, one who inspires respect or fear, and who is self-confident or aggressive. Therefore such people who lack love and seek it may try hard to put on a front of aggressive, confident behavior. But essentially they seek high self-esteem and its behavior expressions more as a means-to-an-end than for its own sake; they seek self-assertion for the sake of love rather than for self-esteem itself.

2. There are other, apparently innately creative people in whom the drive to creativeness

seems to be more important than any other counter-determinant. Their creativeness might appear not as self-actualization released by basic satisfaction, but in spite of lack of basic satisfaction.

3. In certain people the level of aspiration may be permanently deadened or lowered. That is to say, the less prepotent goals may simply be lost, and may disappear forever, so that the person who has experienced life at a very low level, *i.e.*, chronic unemployment, may continue to be satisfied for the rest of his life if only he can get enough food.

4. The so-called "psychopathic personality" is another example of permanent loss of the love needs. These are people who, according to the best data available (Levy, 1937), have been starved for love in the earliest months of their lives and have simply lost forever the desire and the ability to give and to receive affection (as animals lose sucking or pecking reflexes that are not exercised soon enough after birth).

5. Another cause of reversal of the hierarchy is that when a need has been satisfied for a long time, this need may be underevaluated. . . .

6. Another partial explanation of *apparent* reversals is seen in the fact that we have been talking about the hierarchy of prepotency in terms of consciously felt wants or desires rather than of behavior. Looking at behavior itself may give us the wrong impression. What we have claimed is that the person will *want* the more basic of two needs when deprived in both. There is no necessary implication here that he will act upon his desires. Let us say again that there are many determinants of behavior other than the needs and desires.

7. Perhaps more important than all these exceptions are the ones that involve ideals, high social standards, high values, and the like. With such values people become martyrs; they will give up everything for the sake of a particular ideal, or value. These people may be understood, at least in part, by reference to one basic concept (or hypothesis) which may be called "increased frustration-tolerance through early gratification." People who have been satisfied in their basic needs throughout their lives, particularly in their earlier years, seem to develop exceptional power to withstand present or future thwarting of these needs simply because they have strong, healthy character structure as a result of basic satisfaction. They are the "strong" people who can easily weather disagreement or opposition, who can swim against the stream of public opinion, and who can stand up for the truth at great personal cost. It is just the ones who have loved and been well loved, and who have had many deep friendships who can hold out against hatred, rejection, or persecution.

. . . In respect to this phenomenon of increased frustration tolerance, it seems probable that the most important gratifications come in the first two years of life. That is to say, people who have been made secure and strong in the earliest years, tend to remain secure and strong thereafter in the face of whatever threatens.

Degrees of Relative Satisfaction. So far, our theoretical discussion may have given the impression that these five sets of needs are somehow in a step-wise, all-or-none relationship to each other. We have spoken in such terms as the following: "If one need is satisfied, then another emerges." This statement might give the false impression that a need must be satisfied 100 per cent before the next need emerges. In actual fact, most members of our society who are normal are partially satisfied in all their basic needs and partially unsatisfied in all their basic needs at the same time. A more realistic description of the hierarchy would be in terms of decreasing percentages of satisfaction as we go up the hierarchy of prepotency. For instance, if I may assign arbitrary figures for the sake of illustration, it is as if the average citizen is satisfied perhaps 85 per cent in his physiological needs, 70 per cent in his safety needs, 50 per cent in his love needs, 40 per cent in his self-esteem needs, and 10 per cent in his self-actualization needs.

As for the concept of emergence of a new need after satisfaction of the prepotent need, this emergence is not a sudden, saltatory phenomenon but rather a gradual emergence by slow degrees from nothingness. For instance, if prepotent need A is satisfied only 10 per cent then need B may not be visible at all. However, as this need A becomes satisfied 25 per cent, need B may emerge 5 per cent, as need A becomes satisfied 75 per cent need B may emerge 90 per cent, and so on.

Unconscious Character of Needs.   These needs are neither necessarily conscious nor unconscious. On the whole, however, in the average person, they are more often unconscious rather than conscious. . . .

Cultural Specificity and Generality of Needs.   This classification of basic needs makes some attempt to take account of the relative unity behind the superficial differences in specific desires from one culture to another. Certainly in any particular culture an individual's conscious motivational content will usually be extremely different from the conscious motivational content of an individual in another society. However, it is the common experience of anthropologists that people, even in different societies, are much more alike than we would think from our first contact with them, and that as we know them better we seem to find more and more of this commonness. . . .

Multiple Motivations of Behavior. . . .   Most behavior is multi-motivated. Within the sphere of motivational determinants, any behavior tends to be determined by several or *all* of the basic needs simultaneously rather than by only one of them. The latter would be more an exception than the former. Eating may be partially for the sake of filling the stomach, and partially for the sake of comfort and amelioration of other needs. One may make love not only for pure sexual release, but also to convince one's self of one's masculinity, or to make a conquest, to feel powerful, or to win more basic affection. . . .

Multiple Determinants of Behavior.   Not all behavior is determined by the basic needs. We might even say that not all behavior is motivated. There are

many determinants of behavior other than motives.[8] For instance, one other important class of determinants is the so-called "field" determinants. Theoretically, at least, behavior may be determined completely by the field, or even by specific isolated external stimuli, as in association of ideas, or certain conditioned reflexes. If in response to the stimulus word "table," I immediately perceive a memory image of a table, this response certainly has nothing to do with my basic needs.

Secondly, we may call attention again to the concept of "degree of closeness to the basic needs" or "degree of motivation." Some behavior is highly motivated, other behavior is only weakly motivated. Some is not motivated at all (but all behavior is determined).

Another important point[9] is that there is a basic difference between expressive behavior and coping behavior (functional striving, purposive goal seeking). An expressive behavior does not try to do anything; it is simply a reflection of the personality. A stupid man behaves stupidly, not because he wants to, or tries to, or is motivated to, but simply because he *is* what he is. . . .

We may then ask, is *all* behavior expressive or reflective of the character structure? The answer is "No." Rote, habitual, automatized, or conventional behavior may or may not be expressive. The same is true for most "stimulus-bound" behaviors.

It is finally necessary to stress that expressiveness of behavior, and goal-directedness of behavior are not mutually exclusive categories. Average behavior is usually both.

Goals as Centering Principle in Motivation Theory.
It will be observed that the basic principle in our classification has been neither the instigation nor the motivated behavior but rather the functions, effects, purposes, or goals of the behavior. It has been proven sufficiently by various people that this is the most suitable point for centering in any motivation theory.[10]

Animal- and Human-Centering.   This theory starts with the human being rather than any lower and presumably "simpler" animal. Too many of the findings that have been made in animals have been proven to be true for animals but not for the human being. There is no reason whatsoever why we should start with animals in order to study human motivation. . . .

Motivation and the Theory of Psychopathogenesis. The conscious motivational content of everyday life has, according to the foregoing, been conceived to be relatively important or unimportant accordingly as it is more or less closely related to the basic goals. A desire for an ice cream cone might actually be an indirect expression of a desire for love. If it is, then this desire for the ice cream cone becomes extremely important motivation. If however the ice cream is simply something to cool the mouth with, or a casual appetitive reaction, then the desire is relatively unimportant. Everyday conscious desires are to be regarded as symptoms, as *surface indicators of more basic needs*. If we were to take these superficial desires at their face value we would find ourselves in a state of complete confusion which could never be resolved, since we would be dealing seriously with symptoms rather than with what lay behind the symptoms.

Thwarting of unimportant desires produces no psychopathological results; thwarting of a basically important need does produce such results. Any theory of psychopathogenesis must then be based on a sound theory of motivation. A conflict or a frustration is not necessarily pathogenic. It becomes so only when it threatens or thwarts the basic needs, or partial needs that are closely related to the basic needs (Maslow, 1943).

The Role of Gratified Needs. It has been pointed out above several times that our needs usually emerge only when more prepotent needs have been gratified. Thus gratification has an important role in motivation theory. Apart from this, however, needs cease to play an active determining or organizing role as soon as they are gratified.

What this means is that, e.g., a basically satisfied person no longer has the needs for esteem, love, safety, etc. . . .

It is such considerations as these that suggest the bold postulation that a man who is thwarted in any of his basic needs may fairly be envisaged simply as a sick man. This is a fair parallel to our designation as "sick" of the man who lacks vitamins or minerals. Who is to say that a lack of love is less important than a lack of vitamins? Since we know the pathogenic effects of love starvation, who is to say that we are invoking value-questions in an unscientific or illegitimate way, any more than the physician does who diagnoses and treats pellagra or scurvy? If I were permitted this usage, I should then say simply that a healthy man is primarily motivated by his needs to develop and actualize his fullest potentialities and capacities. If a man has any other basic needs in any active, chronic sense, then he is simply an unhealthy man. He is as surely sick as if he had suddenly developed a strong salt-hunger or calcium hunger.[11]

If this statement seems unusual or paradoxical the reader may be assured that this is only one among many such paradoxes that will appear as we revise our ways of looking at man's deeper motivations. When we ask what man wants of life, we deal with his very essence.

SUMMARY

1. There are at least five sets of goals, which we may call basic needs. These are briefly physiological, safety, love, esteem, and self-actualization. In addition, we are motivated by the desire to achieve or maintain the various conditions upon which these basic satisfactions rest and by certain more intellectual desires.

2. These basic goals are related to each other, being arranged in a hierarchy of prepotency. This means that the most prepotent goal will monopolize consciousness and will tend of itself to organize the recruitment of the various capacities of the organism. The less prepotent needs are minimized, even forgotten or denied.

But when a need is fairly well satisfied, the next prepotent ("higher") need emerges, in turn to dominate the conscious life and to serve as the center of organization of behavior, since gratified needs are not active motivators.

Thus man is a perpetually wanting animal. Ordinarily the satisfaction of these wants is not altogether mutually exclusive, but only tends to be. The average member of our society is most often partially satisfied and partially unsatisfied in all of his wants. The hierarchy principle is usually empirically observed in terms of increasing percentages of non-satisfaction as we go up the hierarchy. Reversals of the average order of the hierarchy are sometimes observed. Also it has been observed that an individual may permanently lose the higher wants in the hierarchy under special conditions. There are not only ordinarily multiple motivations for usual behavior, but in addition many determinants other than motives.

3. Any thwarting or possibility of thwarting of these basic human goals, or danger to the defenses which protect them, or to the conditions upon which they rest, is considered to be a psychological threat. With a few exceptions, all psychopathology may be partially traced to such threats. A basically thwarted man may actually be defined as a "sick" man, if we wish.

4. It is such basic threats which bring about the general emergency reactions. . . .

REFERENCES

Adler, A. *Social interest.* London: Faber & Faber, 1938.

Cannon, W. B. *Wisdom of the body.* New York: Norton, 1932.

Freud, S. *New introductory lectures on psychoanalysis.* New York: Norton, 1933.

Freud, S. *The ego and the mechanisms of defense.* London: Hogarth, 1937.

Fromm, E. *Escape from freedom.* New York: Farrar and Rinehart, 1941.

Goldstein, K. *The organism.* New York: American Book, Co., 1939.

Horney, K. *The neurotic personality of our time.* New York: Norton, 1937.

Kardiner, A. *The traumatic neuroses of war.* New York: Hoeber, 1941.

Levy, D. M. Primary affect hunger. *Amer. J. Psychiat.,* 1937, 94, 643–652.

Maslow, A. H. Dominance, personality and social behavior in women. *J. Soc. Psychol.,* 1939, 10, 3–39.

Maslow, A. H. The dynamics of psychological security-insecurity. *Character & Pers.,* 1942, 10, 331–344.

Maslow, A. H. Conflict, frustration, and the theory of threat. *J. Abnorm. (soc.) Psychology.,* 1943, 38, 81–86.

Maslow, A. H. A preface to motivation theory. *Psychosomatic Med.,* 1943, 5, 85–92.

Maslow, A. H., & Mittelmann, B. *Principles of abnormal psychology.* New York: Harper & Bros., 1941.

Murray, H. A., et al. *Explorations in personality.* New York: Oxford University Press, 1938.

Plant, J. *Personality and the cultural pattern.* New York: Commonwealth Fund, 1937.

Shirley, M. Children's adjustments to a strange situation. *J. Abnorm. (soc.) Psychol.,* 1942, 37, 201–217.

Tolman, E. C. *Purposive behavior in animals and men.* New York: Century, 1932.

Wertheimer, M. Unpublished lectures at the New School for Social Research.

Young, P. T. *Motivation of behavior.* New York: John Wiley & Sons, 1936.

Young, P. T. The experimental analysis of appetite. *Psychol. Bull.,* 1941, 38, 129–164.

NOTES

1. As the child grows up, sheer knowledge and familiarity as well as better motor development make these "dangers" less and less dangerous and more and more manageable. Throughout life it may be said that one of the main cognitive functions of education is this neutralizing of apparent dangers through knowledge, e.g., I am not afraid of thunder because 1 know something about it.

2. A "test battery" for safety might be confronting the child with a small exploding firecracker, or with a bewhiskered face, having the mother leave the room, putting him upon a high ladder, a hypodermic injection, having a mouse crawl up to him, etc. Of course I cannot seriously recommend the deliberate use of such "tests" for they might very well harm the child being tested. But these and similar situations come up by the score in the child's ordinary day-to-day living and may be observed. There is no reason why these stimuli should not be used with, for example, young chimpanzees.

3. For further details see (Maslow, 1943) and (Plant, 1937, Chapter 5).

4. Whether or not this particular desire is universal we do not know. The crucial question, especially important today, is "Will men who are enslaved and dominated, inevitably feel dissatisfied and rebellious?" We may assume on the basis of commonly known clinical data that a man who has known true freedom (not paid for by giving up safety and security but rather built on the basis of adequate safety and security) will not willingly or easily allow his freedom to be taken away from him. But we do not know that this is true for the person born into slavery. The events of the next decade should give us our answer. See discussion of this problem in Fromm (1941).

5. Perhaps the desire for prestige and respect from others is subsidiary to the desire for self-esteem or confidence in oneself. Observation of children seems to indicate that this is so, but clinical data give no clear support for such a conclusion.

6. For more extensive discussion of normal self-esteem, as well as for reports of various researches, see Maslow (1939).

7. Clearly creative behavior, like painting, is like any other behavior in having multiple determinants. It may be seen in "innately creative" people whether they are satisfied or not, happy or unhappy, hungry or sated. Also it is clear that creative activity may be compensatory, ameliorative, or purely economic. It is my impression (as yet unconfirmed) that it is possible to distinguish the artistic and intellectual products of basically satisfied people from those of basically unsatisfied people by inspection alone. In any case, here too we must distinguish, in a dynamic fashion, the overt behavior itself from its various motivations or purposes.

8. I am aware that many psychologists and psycho-analysts use the terms "motivated" and "determined" synonymously, e.g., Freud. But I consider this an obfuscating usage. Sharp distinctions are necessary for clarity of thought, and precision in experimentation.

9. To be discussed fully in a subsequent publication.

10. The interested reader is referred to the very excellent discussion of this point in Murray's *Explorations in Personality* (1938).

11. If we were to use the word "sick" in this way, we should then also have to face squarely the relations of man to his society. One clear implication of our definition would be that (1) since a man is to be called sick who is basically thwarted, and (2) since such basic thwarting is made possible ultimately only by forces outside the individual, then (3) sickness in the individual must come ultimately from a sickness in the society. The "good" or healthy society would then be defined as one that permitted man's highest purposes to emerge by satisfying all his prepotent basic needs.

Reading 11	The Human Side of Enterprise

Douglas Murray McGregor

To a degree, the social sciences today are in a position like that of the physical sciences with respect to atomic energy in the thirties. We know that past conceptions of the nature of man are inadequate and, in many ways, incorrect. We are becoming quite certain that, under proper conditions, unimagined resources of creative human energy could become available within the organizational setting. . . .

Management's Task: The Conventional View

The conventional conception of management's task in harnessing human energy to organizational requirements can be stated broadly in terms of three propositions. In order to avoid the complications introduced by a label, let us call this set of propositions "Theory X":

1. Management is responsible for organizing the elements of productive enterprise—money, materials, equipment, people—in the interest of economic ends.
2. With respect to people, this is a process of directing their efforts, motivating them, controlling their actions, modifying their behavior to fit the needs of the organization.
3. Without this active intervention by management, people would be passive—even resistant—to organizational needs. They must therefore be persuaded, rewarded, punished, controlled—their activities must be directed. This is management's task. We often sum it up by saying that management consists of getting things done through other people.

Behind this conventional theory there are several additional beliefs—less explicit, but widespread:

4. The average man is by nature indolent—he works as little as possible.
5. He lacks ambition, dislikes responsibility, prefers to be led.
6. He is inherently self-centered, indifferent to organizational needs.
7. He is by nature resistant to change.
8. He is gullible, not very bright, the ready dupe of the charlatan and the demagogue.

The human side of economic enterprise today is fashioned from propositions and beliefs such as these. Conventional organization structures and managerial policies, practices, and programs reflect these assumptions.

In accomplishing its task—with these assumptions as guides—management has conceived of a range of possibilities.

At one extreme, management can be "hard" or "strong." The methods for directing behavior involve coercion and threat (usually disguised), close supervision, tight controls over behavior. At the other extreme, management can be "soft" or "weak." The methods for directing behavior involve being permissive, satisfying people's demands, achieving harmony. Then they will be tractable, accept direction.

This range has been fairly completely explored during the past half century, and management has learned some things from the exploration. There are difficulties in the "hard" approach. Force breeds counter-forces: restriction of output, antagonism, militant unionism, subtle but effective sabotage of management objectives. This "hard" approach is especially difficult during times of full employment.

Source: "The Human Side of Enterprise," Douglas Murray McGregor, from MANAGEMENT REVIEW, the American Management Assn., 1957. Reprinted by permission of the Copyright Clearance Center.

Note: This article is based on an address by Dr. McGregor before the Fifth Anniversary Convocation of the M.I.T. School of Industrial Management.

There are also difficulties in the "soft" approach. It leads frequently to the abdication of management—to harmony, perhaps, but to indifferent performance. People take advantage of the soft approach. They continually expect more, but they give less and less. . . .

Is the Conventional View Correct?

The social scientist does not deny that human behavior in industrial organization today is approximately what management perceives it to be. He has, in fact, observed it and studied it fairly extensively. But he is pretty sure that this behavior is *not* a consequence of man's inherent nature. It is a consequence rather of the nature of industrial organizations, of management philosophy, policy, and practice. The conventional approach of Theory X is based on mistaken notions of what is cause and what is effect.

Perhaps the best way to indicate why the conventional approach of management is inadequate is to consider the subject of motivation.

Physiological Needs

Man is a wanting animal—as soon as one of his needs is satisfied, another appears in its place. This process is unending. It continues from birth to death. . . .

A *satisfied need is not a motivator of behavior!* This is a fact of profound significance that is regularly ignored in the conventional approach to the management of people. Consider your own need for air: Except as you are deprived of it, it has no appreciable motivating effect upon your behavior.

Safety Needs

When the physiological needs are reasonably satisfied, needs at the next higher level begin to dominate man's behavior—to motivate him. These are called *safety needs.* They are needs for protection against danger, threat, deprivation. . . .

The fact needs little emphasis that, since every industrial employee is in a dependent relationship, safety needs may assume considerable importance. Arbitrary management actions, behavior which arouses uncertainty with respect to continued employment or which reflects favoritism or discrimination, unpredictable administration of policy—these can be powerful motivators of the safety needs in the employment relationship *at every level,* from worker to vice president.

Social Needs

When man's physiological needs are satisfied and he is no longer fearful about his physical welfare, his *social needs* become important motivators of his behavior—needs for belonging, for association, for acceptance by his fellows, for giving and receiving friendship and love.

Management knows today of the existence of these needs, but it often assumes quite wrongly that they represent a threat to the organization. . . . When man's social needs—and perhaps his safety needs, too—are thus thwarted, he behaves in ways which tend to defeat organizational objectives. He becomes resistant, antagonistic, uncooperative. But this behavior is a consequence, not a cause.

Ego Needs

Above the social needs—in the sense that they do not become motivators until lower needs are reasonably satisfied—are the needs of greatest significance to management and to man himself. They are the *egoistic needs,* and they are of two kinds:

1. Those needs that relate to one's self-esteem—needs for self-confidence, for independence, for achievement, for competence, for knowledge.
2. Those needs that relate to one's reputation—needs for status, for recognition, for appreciation, for the deserved respect of one's fellows.

. . . The typical industrial organization offers few opportunities for the satisfaction of these egoistic needs to people at lower levels in the hierarchy. The conventional methods of organizing work, particularly in mass-production industries, give little heed to these aspects of human motivation. If the practices of scientific management were deliberately calculated to thwart these needs, they could hardly accomplish this purpose better than they do.

Self-Fulfillment Needs

Finally—a capstone, as it were, on the hierarchy of man's needs—there are what we may call the *needs for self-fulfillment*. These are the needs for realizing one's own potentialities, for continued self-development, for being creative in the broadest sense of that term.

It is clear that the conditions of modern life give only limited opportunity for these relatively weak needs to obtain expression. The deprivation most people experience with respect to other lower-level needs diverts their energies into the struggle to satisfy *those* needs, and the needs for self-fulfillment remain dormant.

Management and Motivation

. . . The man whose needs for safety, association, independence, or status are thwarted is sick just as surely as the man who has rickets. And his sickness will have behavioral consequences. We will be mistaken if we attribute his resultant passivity, his hostility, his refusal to accept responsibility to his inherent "human nature." These forms of behavior are *symptoms* of illness—of deprivation of his social and egoistic needs.

The man whose lower-level needs are satisfied is not motivated to satisfy those needs any longer. For practical purposes they exist no longer. Management often asks, "Why aren't people more productive? We pay good wages, provide good working conditions, have excellent fringe benefits and steady employment. Yet people do not seem to be willing to put forth more than minimum effort."

The fact that management has provided for these physiological and safety needs has shifted the motivational emphasis to the social and perhaps to the egoistic needs. Unless there are opportunities *at*

work to satisfy these higher-level needs, people will be deprived; and their behavior will reflect this deprivation. Under such conditions, if management continues to focus its attention on physiological needs, its efforts are bound to be ineffective.

People *will* make insistent demands for more money under these conditions. It becomes more important than ever to buy the material goods and services which can provide limited satisfaction of the thwarted needs. Although money has only limited value in satisfying many higher-level needs, it can become the focus of interest if it is the *only* means available.

The Carrot-and-Stick Approach

The carrot-and-stick theory of motivation (like Newtonian physical theory) works reasonably well under certain circumstances. The *means* for satisfying man's physiological and (within limits) his safety needs can be provided or withheld by management. Employment itself is such a means, and so are wages, working conditions, and benefits. By these means the individual can be controlled so long as he is struggling for subsistence. . . .

. . . And so management finds itself in an odd position. The high standard of living created by our modern technological know-how provides quite adequately for the satisfaction of physiological and safety needs. The only significant exception is where management practices have not created confidence in a "fair break"—and thus where safety needs are thwarted. But by making possible the satisfaction of low-level needs, management has deprived itself of the ability to use as motivators the devices on which conventional theory has taught it to rely—rewards, promises, incentives, or threats and other coercive devices.

The philosophy of management by direction and control—*regardless of whether it is hard or soft*—is inadequate to motivate because the human needs on which this approach relies are today unimportant motivators of behavior. Direction and control are essentially useless in motivating people whose important needs are social and egoistic. Both the hard and the soft approaches fail today because they are simply irrelevant to the situation.

People, deprived of opportunities to satisfy at work the needs which are now important to them, behave exactly as we might predict—with indolence, passivity, resistance to change, lack of responsibility, willingness to follow the demagogue, unreasonable demands for economic benefits. It would seem that we are caught in a web of our own weaving.

A New Theory of Management

For these and many other reasons, we require a different theory of the task of managing people based on more adequate assumptions about human nature and human motivation. I am going to be so bold as to suggest the broad dimensions of such a theory. Call it "Theory Y," if you will.

1. Management is responsible for organizing the elements of productive enterprise—money, materials, equipment, people—in the interest of economic ends.
2. People are *not* by nature passive or resistant to organizational needs. They have become so as a result of experience in organizations.
3. The motivation, the potential for development, the capacity for assuming responsibility, the readiness to direct behavior toward organizational goals are all present in people. Management does not put them there. It is a responsibility of management to make it possible for people to recognize and develop these human characteristics for themselves.
4. The essential task of management is to arrange organizational conditions and methods of operation so that people can achieve their own goals *best* by directing *their own* efforts toward organizational objectives.

This is a process primarily of creating opportunities, releasing potential, removing obstacles, encouraging growth, providing guidance. It is what Peter Drucker has called "management by objectives" in contrast to "management by control." It does *not* involve the abdication of management,

the absence of leadership, the lowering of standards, or the other characteristics usually associated with the "soft" approach under Theory X.

Some Difficulties

It is no more possible to create an organization today which will be a full, effective application of this theory than it was to build an atomic power plant in 1945. There are many formidable obstacles to overcome.

The conditions imposed by conventional organization theory and by the approach of scientific management for the past half century have tied men to limited jobs which do not utilize their capabilities, have discouraged the acceptance of responsibility, have encouraged passivity, have eliminated meaning from work. Man's habits, attitudes, expectations—his whole conception of membership in an industrial organization—have been conditioned by his experience under these circumstances. . . .

Another way of saying this is that Theory X places exclusive reliance upon external control of human behavior, while Theory Y relies heavily on self-control and self-direction. It is worth noting that this difference is the difference between treating people as children and treating them as mature adults. After generations of the former, we cannot expect to shift to the latter overnight.

Steps in the Right Direction

Before we are overwhelmed by the obstacles, let us remember that the application theory is always slow. Progress is usually achieved in small steps. Some innovative ideas which are entirely consistent with Theory Y are today being applied with some success.

Decentralization and Delegation

These are ways of freeing people from the too-close control of conventional organization, giving them a degree of freedom to direct their own activities, to assume responsibility, and, importantly, to satisfy their egoistic needs. . . .

Job Enlargement

This concept, pioneered by IBM and Detroit Edison, is quite consistent with Theory Y. It encourages the acceptance of responsibility at the bottom of the organization; it provides opportunities for satisfying social and egoistic needs. In fact, the reorganization of work at the factory level offers one of the more challenging opportunities for innovation consistent with Theory Y.

Participation and Consultative Management

Under proper conditions, participation and consultative management provide encouragement to people to direct their creative energies toward organizational objectives, give them some voice in decisions that affect them, provide significant opportunities for the satisfaction of social and egoistic needs. The Scanlon Plan is the outstanding embodiment of these ideas in practice.

Performance Appraisal

Even a cursory examination of conventional programs of performance appraisal within the ranks of management will reveal how completely consistent they are with Theory X. In fact, most such programs tend to treat the individual as though he were a product under inspection on the assembly line.

A few companies—among them General Mills, Ansul Chemical, and General Electric—have been experimenting with approaches which involve the individual in setting "targets" or objectives *for himself* and in a *self*-evaluation of performance semiannually or annually. . . .

The individual is encouraged to take a greater responsibility for planning and appraising his own contribution to organizational objectives; and the accompanying effects on egoistic and self-fulfillment needs are substantial.

Applying the Ideas

The not infrequent failure of such ideas as these to work as well as expected is often attributable to the fact that management has "bought the idea" but applied it within the framework of Theory X and its assumptions.

Delegation is not an effective way of exercising management by control. Participation becomes a farce when it is applied as a sales gimmick or a device for kidding people into thinking they are important. . . .

The Human Side of Enterprise

The ingenuity and the perseverance of industrial management in the pursuit of economic ends have changed many scientific and technological dreams into commonplace realities. It is now becoming clear that the application of these same talents to the human side of enterprise will not only enhance substantially these materialistic achievements, but will bring us one step closer to "the good society."

Reading 12 | The Motivating Effect of Cognitive Dissonance
Leon Festinger

Cognitive Dissonance as a Motivating State

I should like to postulate the existence of *cognitive dissonance* as a motivating state in human beings. Since most of you probably never heard of cognitive dissonance, I assume that so far I have been no more informative than if I had said that I wish to postulate X as a motivating state. I will try, then, to provide a conceptual definition of cognitive dissonance.

Definition of Dissonance. The word "dissonance" was not chosen arbitrarily to denote this motivating state. It was chosen because its ordinary meaning in the English language is close to the technical meaning I want to give it. The synonyms which the dictionary gives for the word "dissonant" are "harsh," "jarring," "grating," "unmelodious," "inharmonious," "inconsistent," "contradictory," "disagreeing," "incongruous," "discrepant." The word, in this ordinary meaning, specifies a relation between two things. In connection with musical tones, where it is usually used, the relation between the tones is such that they sound unpleasant together. In general, one might say that a dissonant relation exists between two things which occur together, if, in some way, they do not belong together or fit together.

Cognitive dissonance refers to this kind of relation between cognitions which exist simultaneously for a person. If a person knows two things, for example, something about himself and something about the world in which he lives, which somehow do not fit together, we will speak of this as cognitive dissonance. Thus, for example, a person might know that he is a very intelligent, highly capable person. At the same time, let us imagine, he knows that he meets repeated failure. These two cognitions would be dissonant—they do not fit together. In general, two cognitions are dissonant with each other if, considering these two cognitions alone, the obverse of one follows from the other. Thus, in the example we have given, it follows from the fact that a person is highly capable that he does not continually meet with failure. . . .

How Cognitive Dissonance Resembles Other Need States. Thus far I have said nothing about the motivating aspects of cognitive dissonance. This is the next step. I wish to hypothesize that the existence of cognitive dissonance is comparable to any other need state. Just as hunger is motivating, cognitive dissonance is motivating. Cognitive dissonance will give rise to activity oriented toward reducing or eliminating the dissonance. Successful reduction of dissonance is rewarding in the same sense that eating when one is hungry is rewarding.

In other words, if two cognitions are dissonant with each other there will be some tendency for the person to attempt to change one of them so that they do fit together, thus reducing or eliminating the dissonance. . . .

Data Needed to Demonstrate the Motivating Character of Cognitive Dissonance. Before proceeding, let us consider for a moment the kinds of data one would like to have in order to document the contention that cognitive dissonance is a motivating state. One would like to have at least the following kinds of data:

1. Determination at Time 1 that a state of cognitive dissonance exists. This could be done either by measurement or by experimental manipulation.
2. Determination at Time 2 that the dissonance has been eliminated or reduced in magnitude.

Source: From Leon Festinger, "Motivating Effect of Cognitive Dissonance," ©1958 Holt, Rinehart & Winston. Used by permission of the publisher.

3. Data concerning the behavioral process whereby the person has succeeded in changing some cognition, thus reducing the dissonance.

Actually, the above three items are minimal and would probably not be sufficient to demonstrate cogently the validity of the theory concerning cognitive dissonance. . . .

The kind of data that would be more convincing concerning the motivating aspects of dissonance would be data concerning instances where the dissonance was reduced in the other direction, such as is exemplified in the old joke about the psychiatrist who had a patient who believed he was dead. After getting agreement from the patient that dead men do not bleed, and being certain that the patient understood this, the psychiatrist made a cut on the patient's arm and, as the blood poured out, leaned back in his chair, smiling. Whereupon the patient, with a look of dismay on his face, said, "Well, what do you know, dead men *do* bleed." This kind of thing, if it occurred actually, would be harder to explain in alternative ways.

In other words, one has to demonstrate the effects of dissonance in circumstances where these effects are not easily explainable on the basis of other existing theories. Indeed, if one cannot do this, then one could well ask what the usefulness was of this new notion that explained nothing that was not already understood. . . .

[An] intriguing example of the reduction of dissonance in a startling manner comes from a study I did together with Riecken and Schachter (1956) of a group of people who predicted that, on a given date, a catastrophic flood would overwhelm most of the world. This prediction of the catastrophic flood had been given to the people in direct communications from the gods and was an integral part of their religious beliefs. When the predicted date arrived and passed there was considerable dissonance established in these people. They continued to believe in their gods and in the validity of the communications from them, and at the same time they knew that the prediction of the flood had been wrong. We observed the movement

as participants for approximately two months preceding and one month after this unequivocal disproof of part of their belief. The point of the study was, of course, to observe how they would react to the dissonance. Let me give a few of the details of the disproof and how they reacted to it.

For some time it had been clear to the people in the group that those who were chosen were to be picked up by flying saucers before the cataclysm occurred. Some of the believers, these mainly college students, were advised to go home and wait individually for the flying saucer that would arrive for each of them. This was reasonable and plausible, since the data of the cataclysm happened to occur during an academic holiday. Most of the group, including the most central and most heavily committed members, gathered together in the home of the woman who received the messages from the gods to wait together for the arrival of the saucer. For these latter, disproof of the prediction, in the form of evidence that the messages were not valid, began to occur four days before the predicted event was to take place. A message informed them that a saucer would land in the back yard of the house at 4:00 P.M. to pick up the members of the group. With coat in hand they waited, but no saucer came. A later message told them there had been a delay—the saucer would arrive at midnight. Midst absolute secrecy (the neighbors and press must not know), they waited outdoors on a cold and snowy night for over an hour, but still no saucer came. Another message told them to continue waiting, but still no saucer came. At about 3:00 A.M. they gave up, interpreting the events of that night as a test, a drill, and a rehearsal for the real pickup which would still soon take place.

Tensely, they waited for the final orders to come through—for the messages which would tell them the time, place, and procedure for the actual pickup. Finally, on the day before the cataclysm was to strike, the messages came. At midnight a man would come to the door of the house and take them to the place where the flying saucer would be parked. More messages came that day, one after another, instructing them in the passwords that would be necessary in order to board the saucer, in preparatory procedures such as removal of metal from clothing, removal of personal identification, maintaining silence at certain times, and the like. The day was spent by the group in preparation and rehearsal of the necessary procedures and, when midnight came, the group sat waiting in readiness. But no knock came at the door, no one came to lead them to the flying saucer.

From midnight to five o'clock in the morning the group sat there struggling to understand what had happened, struggling to find some explanation that would enable them to recover somewhat from the shattering realization that they would not be picked up by a flying saucer and that consequently the flood itself would not occur as predicted. It is doubtful that anyone alone, without the support of the others, could have withstood the impact of this disproof of the prediction. Indeed, those members of the group who had gone to their homes to wait alone, alone in the sense that they did not have other believers with them, did not withstand it. Almost all of them became skeptics afterward. In other words, without easily obtainable social support to begin reducing the dissonance, the dissonance was sufficient to cause the belief to be discarded in spite of the commitment to it. But the members of the group that had gathered together in the home of the woman who received the messages could, and did, provide social support for one another. They kept reassuring one another of the validity of the messages and that some explanation would be found.

At fifteen minutes before five o'clock that morning an explanation was found that was at least temporarily satisfactory. A message arrived from God which, in effect, said that He had saved the world and stayed the flood because of this group and the light and strength this group had spread throughout the world that night.

The behavior of these people from that moment onwards presented a revealing contrast to their previous behavior. These people, who had been disinterested in publicity and even avoided it, became avid publicity seekers. . . .

There were almost no lengths to which these people would not go to attract publicity and potential believers in the validity of the messages. If, indeed, more and more converts could be found, more and more people who believed in the messages and the things the messages said, then the dissonance between their belief and the knowledge that the messages had not been correct could be reduced. . . .

An Experimental Investigation.   In this experiment, we created dissonance in the subjects by inducing them to say something which was at variance with their private opinion. It is clear that this kind of situation does produce dissonance between what the person believes and what he knows he has said. There are also cognitive consonances for the person. His cognitions concerning the things that induced him to make the public statement are consonant with his knowledge of having done it. The total magnitude of the dissonance between all other relevant cognitions taken together and the knowledge of what he has publicly said will, of course, be a function of the number and importance of the dissonances in relation to the number and importance of the consonances. One could, then, manipulate the total magnitude of dissonance experimentally by holding everything constant and varying the strength of the inducement for the person to state something publicly which was at variance with his private opinion. The *stronger* the inducement to do this, the *less* would be the over-all magnitude of dissonance created. . . .

Now for the details of the experiment. I will describe it as it proceeded for the subject, with occasional explanatory comments. Each subject had signed up for a two hour experiment on "measures of performance." The subjects were all students from the Introductory Psychology course at Stanford, where they are required to serve a certain number of hours as subjects in experiments. When the student arrived he was met by the experimenter and, with a minimum of explanation, was given a repetitive motor task to work on. . . .

From our point of view, the purpose of this initial part was to provide for each subject an experience which was rather dull, boring, and somewhat fatiguing. The student, however, believed this to be the whole experiment. The explanation of the experiment given to the student was that the experiment was concerned with the effect of preparatory set on performance. He was told that there were two conditions in the experiment, one of these being the condition he had experienced where the subject was told nothing ahead of time. The other condition, the experimenter explained, was one in which the subject, before working on the tasks, was led to expect that they were very enjoyable, very interesting, and lots of fun. The procedure for subjects in this other condition, the experimenter explained, proceeded in the following manner. A person working for us is introduced to the waiting subject as someone who has just finished the experiment and will tell the prospective subject a little about it. This person who works for us then tells the waiting subject that the experiment is very enjoyable, interesting, and lots of fun. In this way, the subjects in the other condition are given the set we want them to have. This concluded the false explanation of the experiment to the student and, in the control group, nothing more was done at this point.

In the experimental groups, however, the experimenter continued by telling the subject that he had a rather unusual proposal to make. It seems that the next subject is scheduled to be in that condition where he is to be convinced in advance that the experiment is enjoyable and a lot of fun. The person who works for us and usually does this, however, although very reliable, could not do it today. We thought we would take a chance and ask him (the student) to do it for us. We would like, if agreeable to him, to hire him on the same basis that the other person was hired to work for us. We would like to put him on the payroll and pay him a lump sum of money to go tell the waiting subject that the experiment is enjoyable, interesting, and fun; and he was also to be on tap for us in case this kind of emergency arises again.

There were two experimental conditions which we actually conducted. The procedure was absolutely identical in both except for the amount of money that the subjects were paid as "the lump sum." In one condition they were paid one dollar for their immediate and possible future services. In the other condition they were paid twenty dollars. When the student agreed to do this, he was actually given the money and he signed a receipt for it. He was then taken into the room where the next subject was waiting and introduced to her by the experimenter, who said that the student had just been a subject in the experiment and would tell her a bit about it. The experimenter then went out, leaving student and the waiting subject together for two and a half minutes. The waiting subject was actually a girl in our employ. Her instructions were very simple. After the student had told her that the experiment was interesting, enjoyable and lots of fun, she was to say something like, "Oh, a friend of mine who took it yesterday told me it was dull and that if I could I should get out of it." After that she was simply supposed to agree with whatever the student said. If, as almost always happened, the student reaffirmed that the experiment was fun, she was to say that she was glad to hear it. . . .

The experimenter then thanked the subject and made a brief speech in which he said that most subjects found the experimental tasks very interesting and enjoyed them, and that, when he thinks about it, he will probably agree. The purpose of this brief speech is to provide some cognitive material which the subject can use to reduce dissonance, assuming that such dissonance exists. The identical speech is, of course, made to the control subjects, too.

The only remaining problem in the experiment was to obtain a measure of what each subject honestly thought privately about the tasks on which he had worked for an hour. It seemed desirable, naturally, to obtain this measure in a situation where the subject would be inclined to be very frank in his statements. . . .

The student was told that someone from Introductory Psychology probably wanted to interview him. The experimenter confessed ignorance about what this impending interview was about but said he had been told that the subject would know about it. Usually at this point the subject nodded his head or otherwise indicated that he did, indeed, know what it was about. The experimenter then took him to an office where the interviewer was waiting, said goodbye to the subject, and left.

The interview itself was rather brief. Four questions were asked, namely, how interesting and enjoyable the experiment was, how much the subject learned from it, how important he thought it was scientifically, and how much he would like to participate in a similar experiment again. The important question, for us, is the first one concerning how interesting and enjoyable the experiment was, since this was the content area in which dissonance was established for the experimental subjects.

Let us look, then, at what the results show. . . .

In the One Dollar experimental condition there is a definite increase over the control group. Here the average rating is +1.35, definitely on the positive side of the scale and significantly different from the control group at the 1 per cent level of confidence. In other words, in the One Dollar condition the dissonance between their private opinion of the experiment and their knowledge of what they had said to the waiting subject was reduced significantly by changing their private opinion somewhat, to bring it closer to what they had overtly said.

But now let us turn our attention to the Twenty Dollar condition. Here the magnitude of dissonance experimentally created was less than in the One Dollar condition because of the greater importance of the cognition that was consonant with what they knew they had done. It seems undeniable that twenty dollars is a good deal more important then one dollar. There should hence be less pressure to reduce the dissonance, and indeed, the average rating for the Twenty Dollar condition is −.05, only slightly above the Control condition and significantly different from the One Dollar condition at the 2 per cent level of confidence.

SUMMARY AND CONCLUSION

The evidence for the validity and usefulness of conceiving cognitive dissonance as motivating is as follows:

1. Evidence that the existence of cognitive dissonance sometimes leads to behavior that appears very strange indeed when viewed only from the standpoint of commonly accepted motives. Here I have had time only to give two examples illustrating this phenomenon.

2. Evidence that the amount of reduction of dissonance is a direct function of the magnitude of dissonance which exists. I illustrated this by describing a laboratory experiment where, under controlled conditions, the magnitude of dissonance was experimentally manipulated.

REFERENCES

Festinger, Leon. *A theory of cognitive dissonance.* Evanston, Ill: Row-Peterson, 1957.

Festinger, L., Riecken, H. W., and Schachter, S. *When prophecy fails.* Minneapolis: University of Minnesota Press, 1956.

Janis, I. L., and King, B. T. The influence of role-playing on opinion change. *J. Abnorm. (soc.) Psychol.,* 1954, 49, 211–218.

King, B. T., and Janis, I. L. Comparison of the effectiveness of improvised versus nonimprovised role-playing in producing opinion changes. *Human Relations,* 1956, 9, 177–186.

Prasad, J. A comparative study of rumors and reports in earthquakes. *Brit. J. Psychol.,* 1950, 41, 129–144.

Sinha, D. Behavior in a catastrophic situation: a psychological study of reports and rumors. *Brit. J. Psychol.,* 1952, 43, 200–209.

| Reading 13 | # Work and Motivation |

Victor H. Vroom

The Nature of Motivation

There are two somewhat different kinds of questions which are typically dealt with in discussions of motivation. One of these is the question of the arousal or energizing of the organism. Why is the organism active at all? What conditions instigate action, determine its duration or persistence and finally its cessation? The phenomena to be explained include the level of activity of the organism and the vigor of amplitude of its behavior. The second question involves the direction of behavior. What determines the form that activity will take? Under what conditions will an organism choose one response or another or move in one direction or another? The problem is to explain the choices made by an organism among qualitatively different behaviors.

The latter question—concerning direction or choice—is probably the more important of the two to the psychologist. . . .

Is all behavior motivated? The answer to this question depends somewhat on the range of processes which are subsumed under the heading of motivation. We will follow the relatively common practice of viewing as motivated only the behaviors that are under central or voluntary control. . . .

To sum up, we view the central problem of motivation as the explanation of choices made by organisms among different voluntary responses. Although some behaviors, specifically those that are not under voluntary control, are defined as unmotivated, these probably constitute a rather small proportion of the total behavior of adult human beings. It is reasonable to assume that most of the behavior exhibited by individuals on their jobs as well as their behavior in the "job market" is voluntary, and consequently motivated.

An Outline of a Cognitive Model

In the remainder of this chapter, we outline a conceptual model which will guide our discussion and interpretation of research in the remainder of the book. The model to be described is similar to those developed by other investigators including Lewin (1938), Rotter (1955), Peak (1955), Davidson, Suppes, and Siegel (1957), Atkinson (1958b), and Tolman (1959). It is basically ahistorical in form. We assume that the choices made by a person among alternative courses of action are lawfully related to psychological events occurring contemporaneously with the behavior. We turn now to consider the concepts in the model and their interrelations.

The Concept of Valence. We shall begin with the simple assumption that, at any given point in time, a person has preferences among outcomes or states of nature. For any pair of outcomes, x and y, a person prefers x to y, prefers y to x, or is indifferent to whether he receives x or y. Preference, then, refers to a relationship between the strength of a person's desire for, or attraction toward, two outcomes. . . . In our system, an outcome is positively valent when the person prefers attaining it to not attaining it (i.e., he prefers x to not x). An outcome has a valence of zero when the person is indifferent to attaining or not attaining it (i.e., he is indifferent to x or not x), and it is negatively valent when he prefers not attaining it to attaining it (i.e., he prefers not x to x). It is assumed that valence can take a wide range of both positive and negative values.

We use the term motive whenever the referent is a preference for a class of outcomes. A positive (or approach) motive signifies that outcomes which are members of the class have positive

Source: Victor Vroom, "Work and Motivation," 1964. Reprinted by permission of the author.

valence, and a negative (or avoidance) motive signifies that outcomes in the class have negative valence.

It is important to distinguish between the valence of an outcome to a person and its value to that person. An individual may desire an object but derive little satisfaction from its attainment—or he may strive to avoid an object which he later finds to be quite satisfying. At any given time there may be a substantial discrepancy between the anticipated satisfaction from an outcome (i.e., its valence) and the actual satisfaction that it provides (i.e., its value).

There are many outcomes which are positively or negatively valent to persons, but are not in themselves anticipated to be satisfying or dissatisfying. The strength of a person's desire or aversion for them is based not on their intrinsic properties but on the anticipated satisfaction or dissatisfaction associated with other outcomes to which they are expected to lead. People may desire to join groups because they believe that membership will enhance their status in the community, and they may desire to perform their jobs effectively because they expect that it will lead to a promotion.

In effect, we are suggesting that means acquire valence as a consequence of their expected relationship to ends. . . . If an object is believed by a person to lead to desired consequences or to prevent undesired consequences, the person is predicted to have a positive attitude toward it. If, on the other hand, it is believed by the person to lead to undesired consequences or to prevent desired consequences, the person is predicted to have a negative attitude toward it. . . .

We do not mean to imply that all the variance in the valence of outcomes can be explained by their expected consequences. We must assume that some things are desired and abhorred "for their own sake." Desegregation may be opposed "on principle" not because it leads to other events which are disliked, and people may seek to do well on their jobs even though no externally mediated rewards are believed to be at stake.

Without pretending to have solved all of the knotty theoretical problems involved in the determinants of valence, we can specify the expected functional relationship between the valence of outcomes and their expected consequences in the following proposition.

Proposition 1. The valence of an outcome to a person is a monotonically increasing function of the algebraic sum of the products of the valences of all other outcomes and his conceptions of its instrumentality for the attainment of these other outcomes.

In equation form the same proposition reads as follows:

$$V_j = f_j \left[\sum_{k=1}^{n} (V_k I_{jk}) \right] \quad (j = 1 \ldots n)$$

$$f_j' > O; \ I_{jj} = O$$

where V_j = the valence of outcome j

I_{jk} = the cognized instrumentality $(-1 \leq I_{jk} \leq 1)$ of outcome j for the attainment of outcome k

The Concept of Expectancy. The specific outcomes attained by a person are dependent not only on the choices that he makes but also on events which are beyond his control. For example, a person who elects to buy a ticket in a lottery is not certain of winning the desired prize. Whether or not he does so is a function of many chance events. Similarly, the student who enrolls in medical school is seldom certain that he will successfully complete the program of study; the person who seeks political office is seldom certain that he will win the election; and the worker who strives for a promotion is seldom certain that he will triumph over other candidates. Most decision-making situations involve some element of risk, and theories of choice behavior must come to grips with the role of these risks in determining the choices that people do make.

Whenever an individual chooses between alternatives which involve uncertain outcomes, it seems clear that his behavior is affected not only by his preferences among these outcomes but also by the degree to which he believes these outcomes to be probable. . . .

Expectancy is an action-outcome association. It takes values ranging from zero, indicating no subjective probability that an act will be followed by an outcome, to 1, indicating certainty that the act will be followed by an outcome. Instrumentally, on the other hand, is an outcome-outcome association. It can take values ranging from -1, indicating a belief that attainment of the second outcome is certain without the first outcome and impossible with it, to $+1$, indicating that the first outcome is believed to be a necessary and sufficient condition for the attainment of the second outcome.

The Concept of Force.   It remains to be specified how valences and expectancies combine in determining choices. The directional concept in our model is the Lewinian concept of force. Behavior on the part of a person is assumed to be the result of a field of forces each of which has direction and magnitude. . . .

There are many possible ways of combining valences and expectancies mathematically to yield these hypothetical forces. On the assumption that choices made by people are subjectively rational, we would predict the strength of forces to be a monotonically increasing function of the *product* of valences and expectancies. Proposition 2 expresses this functional relationship.

Proposition 2. The force on a person to perform an act is a monotonically increasing function of the algebraic sum of the products of the valences of all outcomes and the strength of his expectancies that the act will be followed by the attainment of these outcomes.

We can express this proposition in the form of the following equation:

$$F_i = f_i \left[\sum_{j=1}^{n} (E_{ij} V_j) \right] \quad (i = n+1 \ldots m)$$

$f_i' > 0; i \cap j = \Phi, \; \Phi$ is the null set

where F_i = the force to perform act i

E_{ij} = the strength of the expectancy ($0 \le E_{ij} \le 1$) that act i will be followed by outcome j

V_j = the valence of outcome j

It is also assumed that people choose from among alternative acts the one corresponding to the strongest positive (or weakest negative) force. This formulation is similar to the notion in decision theory that people choose in a way that maximizes subjective expected utility.

Expressing force as a monotonically increasing function of the product of valence and expectancy has a number of implications which should be noted. An outcome with high positive or negative valence will have no effect on the generation of a force unless there is some expectancy (i.e., some subjective probability greater than zero) that the outcome will be attained by some act. As the strength of an expectancy that an act will lead to an outcome increases, the effect of variations in the valence of the outcome on the force to perform the act will also increase. Similarly, if the valence of an outcome is zero (i.e., the person is indifferent to the outcome), neither the absolute value nor variations in the strength of expectancies of attaining it will have any effect on forces.

Our two propositions have been stated in separate terms, but are in fact highly related to one another. Insofar as the acts and outcomes are described in different terms the separation is a useful one. We have in the first proposition a basis for predicting the valence of outcomes, and in the second proposition a basis for predicting the actions that a person will take with regard to the outcome. . . .

In practice we will find it useful to maintain the separation between the two propositions by defining sets of actions and sets of outcomes independently of one another. We will use the term action to refer to behavior which might reasonably be expected to be within the repertoire of the person, e.g., seeking entry into an occupation, while the term outcomes will be reserved for more temporally distant events which are less likely to be under complete behavioral control, e.g., attaining membership in an occupation.

Testing the Model

The model, as outlined so far, is untestable, for its concepts have not been related to observable events. In order to derive empirical hypotheses from the model, we must specify operational definitions for the formal concepts. Some further assumptions must be made which will permit the measurement or experimental manipulation of the concepts. . . .

The only concept in the model that has been directly linked with potentially observable events is the concept of force. We have assumed that the acts performed by a person reflect the relative strength of forces acting upon him. If a person performs act x rather than y the force corresponding to x is assumed to be stronger than y and vice versa.

We have, however, said nothing about observable events that would lead us to infer either that an outcome has a certain valence for a person, or that the strength of a person's expectancy that an act will lead to an outcome has a particular value. It is this kind of problem to which we now turn.

Our approach to this problem is "eclectic." Instead of proposing a single operational definition for each of the concepts, we outline a series of broad approaches to their measurement and/or experimental manipulation.

The Measurement of Valence.

What approaches can be taken to the measurement of valence? What observations of behavior need to be made in order to permit us to conclude that one outcome is positively valent and a second negatively valent, or that one is more positively valent than a second?

One approach is to use *verbal reports*. If an individual states that an event is attractive or desirable, it might be assumed to have positive valence. If he states that a second event is unattractive or undesirable, it might be assumed to have negative valence. This procedure can be extended to provide measures of the relative attractiveness or unattractiveness of a series of events or outcomes by requesting the person to make comparative judgments or by using a standard judgmental scale. . . .

The most convincing argument against the use of self-report measures is a theoretical one. If a person's reports of his desires and aversions are voluntary responses, it should be possible to explain them in terms of processes similar to those involved in other kinds of voluntary behavior. A person's statement that he prefers outcome x to outcome y should, therefore, be a more reliable indicator of the expected consequences of making this statement than of the expected consequences of attaining outcomes x and y. Investigators who use self-report measures of motivation are aware of this problem, and they try to minimize or eliminate "faking" by structuring the testing situation in such a way that the subject believes his responses are confidential or anonymous.

A second approach is found in the work of Atkinson, McClelland, and their associates (McClelland et al., 1953; Atkinson, 1958a). They assume that the motives of a person can be inferred from the *analysis of fantasy*. The thematic apperception method (Murray, 1938) is the principal device used for eliciting this fantasy. Subjects are requested to tell stories about pictures, and the content of their stories is scored according to the frequency with which different kinds of imagery appear. The achievement motive has been most frequently studied by this method, but work has also been carried out on a number of other motives including affiliation, power, and sex.

This method has both strong supporters and detractors. . . .

A third approach to the measurement of valence involves the use of outcomes to create new learning. If an outcome strengthens a response tendency, it could be assumed to be positively valent; if it weakens a response tendency, it could be assumed to be negatively valent. The measure of valence is the *amount or rate of change in response probability* when the outcome is made contingent on the response. We would expect such data to be a reliable indicator of whether an outcome is positively valent or negatively valent but not to be especially sensitive to differences in degree of positive or negative valence.

A fourth approach rests on the assumption that the valence of outcomes can be inferred from *the choices that persons make* among alternative courses of action. If a person is given a free choice between two outcomes x and y, under conditions in which his expectancies of attaining them are equal (e.g., certain), his choice between them may be assumed to reflect their relative valence. Choice of x is assumed to indicate that x is more positively valent than y, whereas choice of y is assumed to indicate that y is more positively valent than x. This approach will easily permit the ordering of a set of outcomes on an ordinal or relative scale. If we introduce differential risks into the choice situation, interval measurement becomes a possibility. Following ideas originally introduced by Von Neumann and Morgenstern (1947), Mosteller and Nogee (1951) and Davidson, Suppes, and Siegel (1957) have outlined methods for obtaining interval measurements of the utility of different amounts of money.

A fifth approach involves observation of *consummatory behavior*. It is consequently applicable primarily to those outcomes such as food, water, and sexual activity where consummation takes place. We might assume that the hungrier a person is, i.e., the greater the valence of food, the more food he will eat. Thus, measures of amount or rate of eating, drinking, or copulation could be used to indicate the extent to which the consumed outcomes were positively valent.

Finally, we might be able to use *"decision time"* as a behavioral indication of differences in valence of outcomes. If a person is given a "free choice" among two outcomes, x and y, the length of time elapsing before he makes his choice could be assumed to reflect the extent to which the outcomes differ in valence. Instantaneous choice of one over the other would indicate a substantial difference in their valence, whereas a long decision time would indicate much less difference. A theory relating decision time to differences in the strength of forces acting on the person has been advanced by Cartwright (1941). It should be noted that, at best, decision time can be used to indicate the amount of difference in valence among outcomes, not which outcome is more positively valent. However, observations of decision time and of the choice can typically be made concurrently, permitting inferences concerning both the amount and direction of difference in the valence of outcomes. . . .

The Measurement of Expectancy. How is the strength of expectancy to be measured? What behaviors can be taken as evidence that a person believes that the probability of an outcome following a response is 0, or .50, or 1.00? This problem is by no means simple. A number of different approaches are available, but each presents certain problems.

One possible approach rests on the assumption that expectancies are reflected in *verbal reports* by individuals about the probability of outcomes. Just as verbal reports may be taken as evidence for the valence of outcomes, they may also constitute the main form of evidence for expectancies. If a person states that an outcome is certain to follow an act, we assume an expectancy value of 1.00, whereas if he states that an outcome has a 50-50 chance of following that act, we assume an expectancy value of .50. This approach has not received enthusiastic support from decision theorists (Davidson, Suppes, and Siegel, 1957). The arguments against it are similar to those noted earlier in connection with self-reports of motives. . . .

Other investigators have assumed that expectancies are best inferred from *actual choices or decisions made by the person*. For example, Preston and Barrata (1948) assumed a linear relationship between psychological probabilities of attaining a given prize and the amount that the subject was willing to wager to get a chance at the prize. If a subject was willing to wager $5.00 for a possible prize of $50, his psychological probability was assumed to be .10. Psychological probabilities measured by this procedure were generally related to mathematical probabilities. However, they tended to be larger than mathematical probabilities at low values of probability, and smaller than mathematical probabilities at higher values.

The problem with this approach is to disentangle the roles of expectancies and preferences in actual decisions. . . .

REFERENCES

Atkinson, J. W. (Ed.) *Motives in fantasy, action, and society*. Princeton, NJ: Van Nostrand, 1958a.

Atkinson, J. W. Towards experimental analysis of human motivation in terms of motives, expectancies, and incentives. In Atkinson, J. W. (Ed.) *Motives in fantasy, action, and society*. Princeton: Van Nostrand, 1958b, pp. 288–305.

Cartwright, D. Decision-time in relation to the differentiation of the phenomenal field. *Psychol. Rev.*, 1941, 48, 425–442.

Davidson, D., Suppes, P., and Siegel, S. *Decision making: An experimental approach*. Stanford, CA: Stanford University Press, 1957.

Lewin, K. The conceptual representation and the measurement of psychological forces. Durham, NC: Duke University Press, 1938.

McClelland, D. C., Atkinson, J. W., Clark, R. A., and Lowell, E. L. *The achievement motive*. New York: Appleton-Century-Crofts, 1953.

Mosteller, F., and Nogee, P. An experimental measurement of utility. *J. pol. Econ.*, 1951, 59, 371–404.

Murray, H. A. *Explorations in personality*. New York: Oxford University Press, 1938.

Peak, Helen. Attitude and motivation. In Jones, M. R. (Ed.), *Nebraska symposium on motivation*. Lincoln: University of Nebraska Press, 1955, pp. 149–188.

Preston, M. G., and Baratta, P., An experimental study of the auction-value of an uncertain outcome. *Amer. J. Psychol.*, 1948, 61, 183–193.

Rotter, J. B. The role of the psychological situation in determining the direction of human behavior. In Jones, M. R. (Ed.), *Nebraska symposium on motivation*. Lincoln: University of Nebraska Press, 1955, pp. 245–268.

Tolman, E. C. Principles of purposive behavior. In Koch, S. (Ed.), *Psychology: A study of a science*. Vol. 2. New York: McGraw-Hill, 1959, pp. 92–157.

Von Neumann, J., and Morgenstern, O. *Theory of games and economic behavior*. Princeton: Princeton University Press, 1947, 2nd ed.

Reading 14

One More Time: How Do You Motivate Employees?
Not By Improving Work Conditions, Raising Salaries,
or Shuffling Tasks

Frederick Herzberg

"Motivating" with KITA

In lectures to industry on the problem, I have found that the audiences are anxious for quick and practical answers, so I will begin with a straightforward, practical formula for moving people.

What is the simplest, surest, and most direct way of getting someone to do something? Ask him? But if he responds that he does not want to do it, then that calls for a psychological consultation to determine the reason for his obstinacy. Tell him? His response shows that he does not understand you, and now an expert in communication methods has to be brought in to show you how to get through to him. Give him a monetary incentive? I do not need to remind the reader of the complexity and difficulty involved in setting up and administering an incentive system. Show him? This means a costly training program. We need a simple way.

Every audience contains the "direct action" manager who shouts, "Kick him!" And this type of manager is right. The surest and least circumlocuted way of getting someone to do something is to kick him in the pants—give him what might be called the KITA.

There are various forms of KITA, and here are some of them:

Negative Physical KITA. This is a literal application of the term and was frequently used in the past. It has, however, three major drawbacks: (1) it is inelegant; (2) it contradicts the precious image of benevolence that most organizations cherish; and (3) since it is a physical attack, it directly stimulates the autonomic nervous system, and this often results in negative feedback—the employee may just kick you in return. These factors give rise to certain taboos against negative physical KITA. . . .

Negative Psychological KITA. This has several advantages over negative physical KITA. First, the cruelty is not visible; the bleeding is internal and comes much later. Second, since it affects the higher cortical centers of the brain with its inhibitory powers, it reduces the possibility of physical backlash. Third, since the number of psychological pains that a person can feel is almost infinite, the direction and site possibility of the KITA are increased many times. Fourth, the person administering the kick can manage to be above it all and let the system accomplish the dirty work. Fifth, those who practice it receive some ego satisfaction (one-upmanship), whereas they would find drawing blood abhorrent. Finally, if the employee does complain, he can always be accused of being paranoid, since there is no tangible evidence of an actual attack.

Now, what does negative KITA accomplish? If I kick you in the rear (physically or psychologically), who is motivated? *I* am motivated; you move! Negative KITA does not lead to motivation, but to movement. So:

Positive KITA. Let us consider motivation. If I say to you, "Do this for me or the company and in return I will give you a reward, an incentive, more status, a promotion, all the quid pro quos that exist in the industrial organization," am I motivating you? The overwhelming opinion I receive from management people is "Yes, this is motivation.". . .

Why is it that managerial audiences are quick to see that negative KITA is not motivation while they are almost unanimous in their judgment that positive KITA is motivation? It is because negative KITA is rape, and positive KITA is seduction. But it is infinitely worse to be seduced than to be raped; the latter is an unfortunate

Source: One More Time: How Do You Motivate Employees? by Frederick Herzberg. Jan–Feb 1968, pp. 53–63. ©1968 by Harvard Business School Publishing. Reprinted by permission of the publisher.

occurrence, while the former signifies that you were a party to your own downfall. This is why positive KITA is so popular: it is a tradition; it is in the American way. The organization does not have to kick you; you kick yourself.

Myths About Motivation

With this in mind, we can review some positive KITA personnel practices that were developed as attempts to instill "motivation":

1. *Reducing time spent at work*—This represents a marvelous way of motivating people to work—getting them off the job! We have reduced (formally and informally) the time spent on the job over the last 50 to 60 years until we are finally on the way to the "63-day weekend." An interesting variant of this approach is the development of off-hour recreation programs. The philosophy here seems to be that those who play together, work together. The fact is that motivated people seek more hours of work, not fewer.

2. *Spiraling wages*—Have these motivated people? Yes, to seek the next wage increase. . . .

3. *Fringe benefits*—Industry has outdone the most welfare-minded of welfare states in dispensing cradle-to-the grave succor. . . .

These benefits are no longer rewards; they are rights. . . .

Unless the ante is continuously raised, the psychological reaction of employees is that the company is turning back the clock.

4. *Human relations training*—Over 30 years of teaching and, in many instances, of practicing psychological approaches to handling people have resulted in costly human relations programs and, in the end, the same question: How do you motivate workers? . . .

The failure of human relations training to produce motivation led to the conclusion that the supervisor or manager himself was not psychologically true to himself in his practice of interpersonal decency. So an advanced form of human relations KITA, sensitivity training, was unfolded.

5. *Sensitivity training*—Do you really, really understand yourself? Do you really, really, really

trust the other man? Do you really, really, really, really cooperate? The failure of sensitivity training is now being explained, by those who have become opportunistic exploiters of the technique, as a failure to really (five times) conduct proper sensitivity training courses. . . .

6. *Communications*—The professor of communications was invited to join the faculty of management training programs and help in making employees understand what management was doing for them. House organs, briefing sessions, supervisory instruction on the importance of communication, and all sorts of propaganda have proliferated until today there is even an International Council of Industrial Editors. But no motivation resulted, and the obvious thought occurred that perhaps management was not hearing what the employees were saying. That led to the next KITA.

7. *Two-way communication*—Management ordered morale surveys, suggestion plans, and group participation programs. Then both employees and management were communicating and listening to each other more than ever, but without much improvement in motivation.

The behavioral scientists began to take another look at their conceptions and their data, and they took human relations one step further. A glimmer of truth was beginning to show through in the writings of the so-called higher-order-need psychologists. People, so they said, want to actualize themselves. Unfortunately, the "actualizing" psychologists got mixed up with the human relations psychologists, and a new KITA emerged.

8. *Job participation*—Though it may not have been the theoretical intention, job participation often became a "give them the big picture" approach. For example, if a man is tightening 10,000 nuts a day on an assembly line with a torque wrench, tell him he is building a Chevrolet. Another approach had the goal of giving the employee a *feeling* that he is determining, in some measure, what he does on his job. The goal was to provide a *sense* of achievement rather than a substantive achievement in his task. Real achievement, of course, requires a task that makes it possible.

9. Employee counseling—The initial use of this form of KITA in a systematic fashion can be credited to the Hawthorne experiment of the Western Electric Company during the early 1930s. At that time, it was found that the employees harbored irrational feelings that were interfering with the rational operation of the factory. Counseling in this instance was a means of letting the employees unburden themselves by talking to someone about their problems. Although the counseling techniques were primitive, the program was large indeed. . . .

Since KITA results only in short-term movement, it is safe to predict that the cost of these programs will increase steadily and new varieties will be developed as old positive KITA reach their satiation points.

Hygiene vs. Motivators

Let me rephrase the perennial question this way: How do you install a generator in an employee? A brief review of my motivation hygiene theory of job attitudes is required before theoretical and practical suggestions can be offered. The theory was first drawn from an examination of events in the lives of engineers and accountants. At least 16 other investigations, using a wide variety of populations including some in the Communist countries have since been completed, making the original research one of the most replicated studies in the field of job attitudes.

The findings of these studies, along with corroboration from many other investigations using different procedures, suggest that the factors involved in producing job satisfaction and motivation are separate and distinct from the factors that lead to job dissatisfaction. Since separate factors need to be considered, depending on whether job satisfaction or job dissatisfaction is being examined, it follows that these two feelings are not opposites of each other. The opposite of job satisfaction is not job dissatisfaction but, rather, *no* job satisfaction; and similarly, the opposite of job dissatisfaction is not job satisfaction, but *no* job dissatisfaction. . . .

Two different needs of man are involved here. One set of needs can be thought of as stemming from his animal nature—the built-in drive to avoid pain from the environment, plus all the learned drives which become conditioned to the basic biological needs. For example, hunger, a basic biological drive, makes it necessary to earn money, and then money becomes a specific drive. The other set of needs relates to that antique human characteristic, the ability to achieve and, through achievement, to experience psychological growth. The stimuli for the growth needs are tasks that induce growth; in the industrial setting, they are the *job content*. Contrariwise, the stimuli inducing pain-avoidance behavior are found in the *job environment*.

The growth or *motivator* factors that are intrinsic to the job are: achievement, recognition for achievement, the work itself, responsibility, and growth or advancement. The dissatisfaction-avoidance or *hygiene* (KITA) factors that are extrinsic to the job include: company policy and administration, supervision, interpersonal relationships, working conditions, salary, status, and security.

A composite of the factors that are involved in causing job satisfaction and job dissatisfaction [is] drawn from samples of 1,685 employees. The results indicate that motivators were the primary cause of satisfaction, and hygiene factors the primary cause of unhappiness on the job. The employees, studied in 12 different investigations, included lower-level supervisors, professional women, agricultural administrators, men about to retire from management positions, hospital maintenance personnel, manufacturing supervisors, nurses, food handlers, military officers, engineers, scientists, housekeepers, teachers, technicians, female assemblers, accountants, Finnish foremen, and Hungarian engineers.

They were asked what job events had occurred in their work that had led to extreme satisfaction or extreme dissatisfaction on their part. Their responses are broken down in the exhibit into percentages of total "positive" job events and of total "negative" job events. . . .

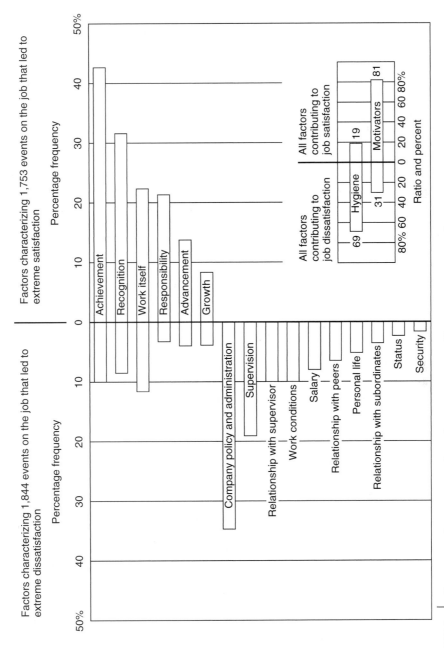

EXHIBIT I | FACTORS AFFECTING JOB ATTITUDES, AS REPORTED IN 12 INVESTIGATIONS

177

To illustrate, a typical response involving achievement that had a negative effect for the employee was, "I was unhappy because I didn't do the job successfully." A typical response in the small number of positive job events in the Company Policy and Administration grouping was, "I was happy because the company reorganized the section so that I didn't report any longer to the guy I didn't get along with."

As the lower right-hand part of *Exhibit I* shows, of all the factors contributing to job satisfaction, 81% were motivators. And of all the factors contributing to the employees' dissatisfaction over their work, 69% involved hygiene elements.

Eternal Triangle

There are three general philosophies of personnel management. The first is based on organizational theory, the second on industrial engineering, and the third on behavioral science.

The organizational theorist believes that human needs are either so irrational or so varied and adjustable to specific situations that the major function of personnel management is to be as pragmatic as the occasion demands. If jobs are organized in a proper manner, he reasons, the result will be the most efficient job structure, and the most favorable job attitudes will follow as a matter of course. The industrial engineer holds that man is mechanistically oriented and economically motivated and his needs are best met by attuning the individual to the most efficient work process. The goal of personnel management therefore should be to concoct the most appropriate incentive system and to design the specific working conditions in a way that facilitates the most efficient use of the human machine. By structuring jobs in a manner that leads to the most efficient operation, the engineer believes that he can obtain the optimal organization of work and the proper work attitudes.

The behavioral scientist focuses on group sentiments, attitudes of individual employees, and the organization's social and psychological climate. According to his persuasion, he emphasizes one or more of the various hygiene and motivator needs.

His approach to personnel management generally emphasizes some form of human relations education, in the hope of instilling healthy employee attitudes and an organizational climate which he considers to be felicitous to human values. He believes that proper attitudes will lead to efficient job and organizational structure.

The three philosophies can be depicted as a triangle, as is done in *Exhibit II,* with each persuasion claiming the apex angle. The motivation-hygiene theory claims the same angle as industrial engineering, but for opposite goals. Rather than rationalizing the work to increase efficiency, the theory suggests that work be enriched to bring about effective utilization of personnel. Such a systematic attempt to motivate employees by manipulating the motivator factors is just beginning.

The term *job enrichment* describes this embryonic movement. An older term, *job enlargement,* should be avoided because it is associated with past failures stemming from a misunderstanding of the problem. Job enrichment provides the opportunity for the employee's psychological growth, while job enlargement merely makes a job structurally bigger. Since scientific job enrichment is very new, this article only suggests the principles and practical steps that have recently emerged from several successful experiments in industry.

Job Loading

In attempting to enrich an employee's job, management often succeeds in reducing the man's personal contribution, rather than giving him an opportunity for growth in his accustomed job. Such an endeavor, which I shall call horizontal job loading (as opposed to vertical loading, or providing motivator factors), has been the problem of earlier job enlargement programs. This activity merely enlarges the meaningless of the job. Some examples of this approach, and their effect, are:

- Challenging the employee by increasing the amount of production expected of him. If he tightens 10,000 bolts a day, see if he can tighten 20,000 bolts a day. The arithmetic involved shows that multiplying zero by zero still equals zero.

EXHIBIT II
TRIANGLE OF
PHILOSOPHIES
OF PERSONNEL
MANAGEMENT

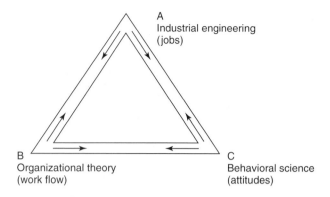

A
Industrial engineering
(jobs)

B
Organizational theory
(work flow)

C
Behavioral science
(attitudes)

EXHIBIT III | PRINCIPLES OF VERTICAL JOB LOADING

Principle	Motivators Involved
A. Removing some controls while retaining accountability	Responsibility and personal achievement
B. Increasing the accountability of individuals for own work	Responsibility and recognition
C. Giving a person a complete natural unit of work (module, division, area, and so on)	Responsibility, achievement, and recognition
D. Granting additional authority to an employee in his activity; job freedom	Responsibility, achievement, and recognition
E. Making periodic reports directly available to the worker himself rather than to the supervisor	Internal recognition
F. Introducing new and more difficult tasks not previously handled	Growth and learning
G. Assigning individuals specific or specialized tasks, enabling them to become experts	Responsibility, growth, and advancement

- Adding another meaningless task to the existing one, usually some routine clerical activity. The arithmetic here is adding zero to zero.
- Rotating the assignments of a number of jobs that need to be enriched. This means washing dishes for a while, then washing silverware. The arithmetic is substituting one zero for another zero.
- Improving the most difficult parts of the assignment in order to free the worker to accomplish more of the less challenging assignment. This traditional industrial engineering approach amounts to subtraction in the hope of accomplishing addition.

These are common forms of horizontal loading that frequently come up in preliminary brainstorming sessions on job enrichment. The principles of vertical loading have not all been worked out as yet, and they remain rather general, but I have furnished seven useful starting points for consideration in *Exhibit III.* . . .

Steps to Job Enrichment

Now that the motivator idea has been described in practice, here are the steps that managers should take in instituting the principle with their employees:

1. Select those jobs in which (a) the investment in industrial engineering does not make changes too costly, (b) attitudes are poor, (c) hygiene is becoming very costly, and (d) motivation will make no difference in performance.

2. Approach these jobs with the conviction that they can be changed. Years of tradition have led managers to believe that the content of the jobs is sacrosanct and the only scope of action that they have is in ways of stimulating people.

3. Brainstorm a list of changes that may enrich the jobs, without concern for their practicality.

4. Screen the list to eliminate suggestions that involve hygiene, rather than actual motivation.

5. Screen the list for generalities, such as "give them more responsibility," that are rarely followed in practice. This might seem obvious, but the motivator words have never left industry; the substance has just been rationalized and organized out. Words like "responsibility," "growth,"

EXHIBIT IV	ENLARGEMENT VS. ENRICHMENT OF CORRESPONDENTS' TASKS IN COMPANY EXPERIMENT

Horizontal Loading Suggestions (Rejected)	Vertical Loading Suggestions (Adopted)	Principle
Firm quotas could be set for letters to be answered each day, using a rate which would be hard to reach.	Subject matter experts were appointed within each unit for other members of the unit to consult with before seeking supervisory help. (The supervisor had been answering all specialized and difficult questions.)	G
The women could type the letters themselves as well as compose them, or take on any other clerical functions.	Correspondents signed their own names on letters. (The supervisor had been signing all letters.)	B
All difficult or complex inquiries could be channeled to a few women so that the remainder could achieve high rates of output. These jobs could be exchanged from time to time.	The work of the more experienced correspondents was proofread less frequently by supervisors and was done at the correspondents' desks, dropping verification from 100% to 10%. (Previously, all correspondents' letters had been checked by the supervisor.)	A
The women could be rotated through units handling different customers, and then sent back to their own units.	Production was discussed, but only in terms such as "full day's work is expected." As time went on, this was no longer mentioned. (Before, the group had been constantly reminded of the number of letters that needed to be answered.)	D
	Outgoing mail went directly to the mailroom without going over supervisors' desks. (The letters had always been routed through the supervisors.)	A
	Correspondents were encouraged to answer letters in a more personalized way. (Reliance on the form-letter approach had been standard practice.)	C
	Each correspondent was held personally responsible for the quality and accuracy of letters. (This responsibility had been the province of the supervisor and the verifier.)	B, E

"achievement," and "challenge," for example, have been elevated to the lyrics of the patriotic anthem for all organizations. It is the old problem typified by the pledge of allegiance to the flag being more important than contributions to the country—of following the form, rather than the substance.

6. Screen the list to eliminate any *horizontal* loading suggestions.

7. Avoid direct participation by the employees whose jobs are to be enriched. Ideas they have expressed previously certainly constitute a valuable source for recommended changes, but their direct involvement contaminates the process with human relations *hygiene* and, more specifically, gives them only a *sense* of making a contribution. The job is to be changed, and it is the content that will produce the motivation, not attitudes about being involved or the challenge inherent in setting up a job. That process will be over shortly, and it is what the employees will be doing from then on that will determine their motivation. A sense of participation will result only in short-term movement.

8. In the initial attempts at job enrichment, set up a controlled experiment. At least two equivalent groups should be chosen, one an experimental unit in which the motivators are systematically introduced over a period of time, and the other one a control group in which no changes are made. For both groups, hygiene should be allowed to follow its natural course for the duration of the experiment. Pre- and post-installation tests of performance and job attitudes are necessary to evaluate the effectiveness of the job enrichment program. The attitude test must be limited to motivator items in order to divorce the employee's view of the job he is given from all the surrounding hygiene feelings that he might have.

9. Be prepared for a drop in performance in the experimental group the first few weeks. The changeover to a new job may lead to a temporary reduction in efficiency.

Author's note: I should like to acknowledge the contribution that Robert Ford of the American Telephone and Telegraph Company has made to the ideas expressed in this paper, and in particular

10. Expect your first-line supervisors to experience some anxiety and hostility over the changes you are making. The anxiety comes from their fear that the changes will result in poorer performance for their unit. Hostility will arise when the employees start assuming what the supervisors regard as their own responsibility for performance. The supervisor without checking duties to perform may then be left with little to do.

After a successful experiment, however, the supervisor usually discovers the supervisory and managerial functions he has neglected, or which were never his because all his time was given over to checking the work of his subordinates. . . .

What has been called an employee-centered style of supervision will come about not through education of supervisors, but by changing the jobs that they do.

Concluding Note

Job enrichment will not be a one-time proposition, but a continuous management function. The initial changes, however, should last for a very long period of time. . . .

Not all jobs can be enriched, nor do all jobs need to be enriched. If only a small percentage of the time and money that is now devoted to hygiene, however, were given to job enrichment efforts, the return in human satisfaction and economic gain would be one of the largest dividends that industry and society have ever reaped through their efforts at better personnel management.

The argument for job enrichment can be summed up quite simply: If you have someone on a job, use him. If you can't use him on the job, get rid of him, either via automation or by selecting someone with lesser ability. If you can't use him and you can't get rid of him, you will have a motivation problem.

to the successful application of these ideas in improving work performance and the job satisfaction of employees.

Reading 15	The Role of Work Context in Work Motivation: A Public Sector Application of Goal and Social Cognitive Theories

Bradley E. Wright

For over two decades, public administration scholars have highlighted a need for an improved understanding of the motivational context in public sector organizations (Balk, 1974; Behn, 1995; Perry and Porter, 1982; Rainey and Steinbauer, 1999). Unfortunately, while work motivation is one of the most frequently discussed topics in psychology (Rousseau, 1997), it continues to receive only limited attention in public administration research. Admittedly, work motivation is a difficult concept to define or study (Rainey, 1993), and no single comprehensive theory of motivation currently exists. Nevertheless, theoretical advances have been made that can assist our efforts in understanding the motivational work context. In particular, there is a growing consensus that any model of work motivation should include the underlying process variables that explain how goals affect work motivation (Kanfer, 1992; Katzell and Thompson, 1990; Mitchell, 1997).

This observation regarding the importance of goals, however, is not new. Twenty years ago, Perry and Porter (1982) suggested that goal theory may be relevant to the public sector motivational setting not only because its reliance on personal significance reinforcement rather than monetary incentives but also because of the key role it plays in many motivational techniques. Although some empirical evidence has since been found to support the applicability of goal theory in public administration (Brewer and Selden, 2000; Rodgers and Hunter, 1992; Wilk and Redmon, 1990), Perry and Porter (1982) cautioned that the implementation of goal setting techniques in public organizations may be hindered by the vague and conflicting nature of government goals.

More recently, it has been suggested that an integration of goal and social cognitive theories may be particularly relevant to understanding the motivational context in public organizations specifically because of how goals and other work context variables may differ across employment sectors. If public sector organizations have conflicting or ambiguous goals and greater procedural constraints, these characteristics may have important implications for employee work motivation because of their potential influence on the job characteristics and attitudes that these theories identify as important antecedents to work motivation.

The present study contributes to our understanding of work motivation in the public sector by testing a conceptual model predicting how the work context might influence work motivation (Wright, 2001). In particular, using the framework provided by goal and social cognitive theories, this model of work motivation tests whether characteristics of the employee's work context, such as goal conflict, procedural constraints, and goal ambiguity, have a detrimental effect on work motivation through their influence on important antecedents of work motivation. The model was tested in a structural equation model using data from a self-administered survey of state employees. The resulting empirical support for this conceptual model provides a strong theoretical framework for future research on work motivation that may identify specific leverage points that can improve employee work motivation in the public sector.

Theoretical Framework

Part of goal theory's attraction to theorists is that it provides a relatively simple motivational explanation for the variation in employee performance that is not due to ability or situation: some employees perform better than others because they have different performance goals

Source: Wright, B., "The Role of Work context in Work Motivation: A Public Sector Application of Goal and Social Cognitive Theories, JOURNAL OF PUBLIC ADMINISTRATION RESEARCH AND THEORY, Vol. 14(1), 2004, pp. 59–78. Reprinted by permission of Oxford University Press, UK.

(Locke and Latham, 1990). According to social cognitive theory, however, it is not the goals themselves but rather the discrepancies created by individuals' comparing how they perform to how they want to perform that motivate behavior (Bandura, 1986). The result of this evaluation is a sense of self-approval or self-dissatisfaction that serves to motivate individuals to act in ways that produce a positive self-evaluation or reduce a negative self-evaluation. This integration of goal-setting and social cognitive theories often has been referred to as self-regulation because of the reliance on self-reaction to explain how goals regulate motivational states (Kanfer, 1990).

Although goal-performance discrepancies regulate behavior over time, a number of goal-related constructs have been identified by the literature as potentially important to understanding how goals can facilitate motivation. Seven of these goal related constructs and their relationships with work motivation are depicted in Figure 1. These influences on work motivation fall into two general types. First are the job characteristics and attitudes that have been found to have an influence on employee work motivation. Variables commonly studied under this

category include job goal specificity, job goal difficulty, self-efficacy, and feedback. The second category consists of characteristics of the work context that have important indirect influences on work motivation through their impact on these job characteristics and attitudes. In particular, this model focuses on three work context variables: procedural constraints, organizational goal specificity, and organizational goal conflict. This new model, and its potential implications for the public sector, is discussed below.

Job Characteristics and Attitudes

The majority of goal-setting research has focused on studying the importance of goal content, particularly goal difficulty and goal specificity (Kanfer, 1990). In fact, "Nearly 400 studies have shown that specific, difficult goals lead to better performance" (Locke and Latham, 1990, p. 240). Although studies rarely investigate the effects of goal difficulty and goal specificity separately, in theory there is some difference between them. In general, goal difficulty is expected to be more related to effort and arousal while goal specificity is thought to be more related to the direction of attention and effort (Locke and Latham, 1990).

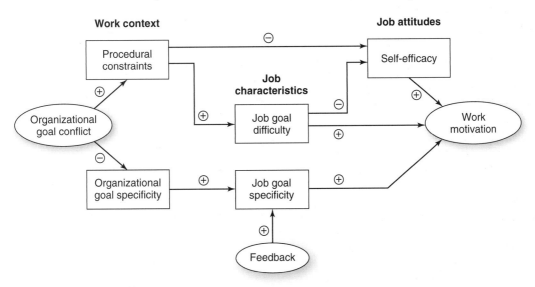

FIGURE 1 | MODEL OF WORK MOTIVATION

In their review of the research on goal specificity, Steers and Porter (1974) found that setting clear goals on an individual's job generally increases performance for two primary reasons. First, specific goals can serve to focus attention, reducing search behavior by letting the employee know precisely what he or she is expected to do. Second, setting clear goals can focus effort, making it easier for the employee to understand the relationship either between effort and resulting performance or between performance and subsequent rewards. This latter effect requires more than just job goal specificity; it also depends on the presence of performance feedback (Locke and Latham, 1990). Such summative and formative evaluations of an individual's work are instrumental to the employee's understanding the effort-performance-reward relationships, providing knowledge of results and clarification of job expectations. Consistent with these studies, two hypotheses were tested in this study:

> H_1 Job goal specificity will have a direct, positive effect on work motivation.
> H_2 Feedback will have an indirect, positive effect on work motivation through its influence on job goal specificity.

Goal difficulty, however, has two competing effects on work motivation. Job goal difficulty can enhance motivation by producing larger goal-performance discrepancies. Larger gaps between current performance and desired goals require greater effort by the individual to attain the positive self-evaluation that drives behavior (Bandura, 1986). Such performance gaps, however, will only drive behavior if employees see the performance goal as achievable and worthy of their effort. Increasing goal difficulty not only increases the goal-performance discrepancy but also affects the individual's judgment of his or her own "capabilities to organize and execute courses of action required to attain designated types of performances" (Bandura, 1986, p. 391).[1] This confidence in one's abilities, commonly referred to as self-efficacy, influences an individual's likelihood to expend the necessary effort and persist in the face of obstacles (Bandura and Cervone, 1983, 1986;

Bandura, 1988; Earley and Lituchy, 1991). Consequently, as goals become more difficult, the goal-performance discrepancy also may be less likely to drive behavior because expending any extra effort would be viewed as increasingly futile. Consistent with these studies, three additional hypotheses were tested in this study:

> H_3 Job goal difficulty will have a direct, positive effect on work motivation.
> H_4 Self-efficacy will have a direct, positive effect on work motivation.
> H_5 Job goal difficulty will have an indirect, negative effect on work motivation through its negative influence on self-efficacy.

Work Context

In addition to job characteristics and attitudes, the public administration literature has identified several aspects of the employee's work context that may influence work motivation. In particular, it is commonly suggested that public organizations are characterized by multiple, conflicting, and ambiguous goals as well as the presence of procedural constraints on employee action (Fottler, 1981; Whorton and Worthley, 1981; Rainey, 1989, 1996; Baldwin and Farley, 1991) and that these differences influence employee and organizational performance. Surprisingly little empirical research, however, has investigated the existence of these differences or their potential impact on the effective operation of public organizations (Rainey, 1989; Baldwin and Farley, 1991; Wright, 2001).

Regardless of whether sector differences do exist, it would be misleading to suggest that these are characteristics only found in public sector organizations. Important variation in work context occurs within sectors, and even private sector organizations are not devoid of procedural constraints, organizational goal conflict, and ambiguity. Consequently, although this study did not assess whether public organizations are different from their private sector counterparts, it helps to extend our understanding of the motivational context in organizations by investigating ways in which aspects of the work context might influence work motivation within the theoretical framework provided by goal and social cognitive theories. Although this model may be especially salient to public organizations if sector differences do exist, the presence and potential impact of procedural constraints or organizational goal conflict and ambiguity is important regardless of sector. To that end, each of these work context factors, and its potential role in employee work motivation, is discussed below.

Organizational Goal Specificity

One work context factor that may have an influence on employee work motivation is organizational goal specificity. In his 1987 study of federal, state, and local government employees in the Atlanta area, Baldwin found that the clarity of organizational goals had a beneficial effect on the work motivation. Although Baldwin found empirical support for this relationship, the process by which organizational goal clarity may impact work motivation was not explicitly described. Under goal theory, however, the specificity of organizational goals might be expected to affect work motivation through its influence on job-level goal specificity. In particular, if the goals of an organization are ambiguous, then the goals held at the job level are also likely to more be ambiguous. Thus the following hypothesis can be tested:

> H$_6$ Specific organizational goals will have an indirect, positive effect on work motivation through its influence on job-level goal specificity.

Procedural Constraints

In additional to organizational goal specificity, the existence of procedural constraints also may effect employee work motivation. Although Baldwin (1990) found no support for a direct relationship between organizational procedural constraints such as red tape and employee work motivation, the framework provided by goal and social cognitive theories suggests that this relationship may be indirect, moderated by job goal difficulty and self-efficacy. The level of procedural constraints employees experience in the work place, for example, may make job goals seem more difficult

to achieve by limiting the strategies, actions, or resources that may be available to the employee. As discussed above, job goal difficulty may simultaneously enhance motivation by requiring that the employee expend greater effort to avoid the dissatisfaction associated with poor performance and weaken motivation by lowering perceptions of potential goal attainment. In addition to this indirect effect on self-efficacy through job goal difficulty, there is some evidence to suggest that procedural constraints will also have a direct effect on self-efficacy. Bandura and Wood (1989) found that managers who believed that they had more control over their own performance environments displayed a stronger sense of self-efficacy and even set more challenging goals when difficult organizational standards eluded them. Employees who believe their organization environments are not easily or quickly changeable will lose faith in their capabilities, making it even more difficult to achieve any performance goals (Wood and Bandura, 1989). Thus the following hypotheses can be tested:

> H$_{7a}$ Procedural constraints will have an indirect, positive effect on work motivation through its influence on job-level goal difficulty and its direct influence on work motivation.
>
> H$_{7b}$ Procedural constraints will have an indirect, negative effect on work motivation through its influence on job-level goal difficulty and its adverse influence on self-efficacy.
>
> H$_8$ Procedural constraints will have an indirect, negative effect on work motivation through its influence on self-efficacy.

Organizational Goal Conflict

Perhaps the characteristic of the work context that has been featured most prominently in the public sector literature has been the existence of conflicting organizational goals (Rainey, 1989, 1996). The importance of goal conflict derives from its suggested causal order among the characteristics of the work context. Organizational goal conflict can make organizational performance expectations appear ambiguous, as employees may not be certain how to achieve divergent goals or even which goals to achieve. It also may be expected that organizational goal conflict may culminate in greater formal procedural constraints on employee action and compensation (Buchanan, 1975; Fottler, 1981; Baldwin, 1984; Perry and Rainey, 1988), as it is often easier to identify procedures to constrain employees from doing anything they should not do than it is to identify and guide what they should do (Whorton and Worthley, 1981; Behn, 1995). If organizational goal specificity and procedural constraints indirectly affect work motivation through their influence on job characteristics and attitudes (hypotheses 6–8), then organizational goal conflict may influence work motivation through its influence on these two work context variables. In particular, the following two hypotheses can be identified:

> H9 Organizational goal conflict will have an indirect, negative effect on work motivation through its influence on procedural constraints.
> H10 Organizational goal conflict will have an indirect, negative effect on work motivation through its influence on organizational goal specificity.

Implications for Motivating Public Employees

The research presented here not only found that just over half of the variance in work motivation among public employees can be explained by three variables—job goal specificity, job goal difficulty, and self-efficacy—but also that work context variables such as procedural constraints, organizational goal specificity, and organizational goal conflict may be relevant when attempting to understand employee work motivation. These findings have a number of important implications for how public sector organizations can motivate their workforces. In particular, public sector organizations concerned with employee motivation should pay special attention to issues of job design and assign specific tasks that challenge employees. Challenging goals require greater effort from the employee to attain a positive self-evaluation, while specific goals focus employee attention and effort toward the desired task. This finding is generally consistent with previous studies in applied psychology (Locke and Latham, 1990)

and, therefore, is not new. What is new is the salience of certain factors in the work context.

Job Goal Specificity

Two characteristics of the work context are potentially relevant to job goal specificity and its effect on work motivation. Procedural constraints and organizational goal specificity together explain 25 percent of the variance in job goal specificity and, therefore, have important indirect effects on work motivation through job goal specificity. This study suggests that the ambiguity of the organizational level goals may carry over to the job level through its relationship with feedback. The clarity of organizational goals may allow supervisors and peers to be more able to provide summative or formative evaluations an employee's performance that can help to clarify job and performance expectations. To the extent that organizational goals are ambiguous, the adverse effects of this ambiguity may be partially mitigated by programs designed to improve the quantity and quality of feedback that the employees receive from a variety of sources, including their supervisors, peers, and clients. This relationship may be particularly salient to public sector organizations if they are characterized by ambiguous goals, an assertion that has received some (Baldwin, 1987) but not complete empirical support (Rainey, 1983; Rainey, Pandey, and Bozeman, 1995). The recent focus on customer service initiatives, for example, may highlight an important source for feedback regarding job responsibilities and performance previously underutilized in the public sector.

There is considerable evidence to support high levels of perceived procedural constraints in the public sector (Rainey, 1983; Baldwin, 1990; Bozeman, Reed, and Scott, 1992; Rainey, Pandey, and Bozeman, 1995), and the results of this study indicate that procedural constraints have an indirect relationship with work motivation through their influence on job goal specificity. When the established organizational policies or procedures hinder or diverge from assigned performance objectives, employee motivation may decline as an employee becomes uncertain as to what performance is desired. These findings suggest that steps should be taken to reduce the procedural constraints found in public organizations. Fortunately, this is one of the primary goals of government reform initiatives under both the Clinton (National Performance Review) and Bush (Freedom to Manage) Administrations. Unfortunately, the proliferation of procedural constraints is often outside of the organization's control, stemming from the need to protect citizens and insure an appropriate use of the resources they provide for government action. To the extent that procedural constraints cannot or should not be reduced, the model does suggest an alternative strategy. Public sector organizations, and the managers that represent them, may be able to mitigate some of potential conflict and confusion caused by employee perceptions of procedural constraints through better communication. If public sector organizations provide employees with a better understanding of organizational goals and their relationship to their job level goals, it may reduce the appearance of organizational goal conflict and help employees recognize how the organization's rules and regulations are expected to coexist with particular performance expectations. In fact, just giving employees the opportunity to talk about the objects of their complaints may reduce the perceived existence or importance of them (Roethlisberger, 1941). While this strategy does not change existing rules or regulations, it can reduce the perception that the organization's goals conflict and that its procedures constrain employee actions.

Job Goal Difficulty

Although this study provides no evidence that aspects of the work context influence the degree of job difficulty, it does support the hypothesized relationships between job goal difficulty and work motivation. Organizations intent on improving employee performance should structure jobs in ways that challenge their employees. Together, these findings suggest an important insight regarding employee work motivation in public sector organizations. Even if sector differences exists, the aspects of the work context believed to be characteristic of public sector organizations do not seem to adversely affect the job characteristic found to have the largest effect on work motivation. Given this finding, it is remarkable that an emphasis on providing employees with challenging goals has not played more prominently in research on government performance or the reforms aimed at improving it.

Self-Efficacy

Goal-related attitudes are important for work motivation because they help establish the conditions under which the individual accepts a performance goal and is determined to reach it, even if confronted with setbacks or obstacles. Employees with higher self-efficacy will believe that the goal can be achieved and are more likely to persist in their efforts toward goal attainment. Although there are a number of individual attributes that contribute to an employee's sense of self-efficacy, this study suggests that the work context also plays a role. Both procedural constraints and organizational goal specificity have indirect effects on work motivation through job goal specificity and its influence on self-efficacy. . . . In other words, to the extent that the public sector work environment is characterized by procedural constraints and low organizational goal specificity, employee work motivation may suffer as employees perceive their performance goals as unachievable regardless of their effort. This only reinforces the recommendation that extreme care should be taken by organizations to limit the adverse effect of these contextual factors through greater communication and clarification of organizational goals. In addition to changing the environmental conditions, however, the organization can also change how the employees react to these conditions. Studies have shown that self-efficacy can remain high even as goals become more difficult and the objective probability of goal attainment decreases

(Klein et al., 1999). Organizational training and mentoring programs can improve work motivation by providing employees with the support or confidence necessary to work with the constraints placed upon them. Working with the employees to develop performance resources and strategies, for example, has been found to increase employee self-efficacy and job attendance in public sector organizations (Frayne and Latham, 1987; Latham and Frayne, 1989).

CONCLUSION

Although work motivation is just one factor influencing performance, it is a critical mediator between employee performance and ability or situation. A better understanding of work motivation, therefore, is essential to any effort to improve the efficiency and effectiveness of public organizations (Rainey and Steinbauer, 1999). Although the results of any single study should be viewed with some caution, this study advances our understanding of work motivation in the public sector by using the well-established theoretical framework provided by goal-setting and social cognitive theories to examine how the work context might influence work motivation. The findings generally lend support to this conceptual model, suggesting not only that job goals should be specific, difficult and doable, but also that organizational goal conflict, goal ambiguity, and procedural constraints may have a detrimental effect on work motivation through their influence on these antecedents of work motivation. To the extent that the purported sector differences on these work context variables exist, then this model may suggest structural problems unique to the public sector motivational context.

Just as important as the empirical support for goal-setting and social cognitive theories, however, is the potential for these theories to provide a conceptual framework to extend our understanding of other aspects of the public sector motivational context. In particular, future research should advance our understanding of work motivation in the public sector by including important variables regarding goal importance. Rainey and Steinbauer (1999) have suggested that the effectiveness and performance of government agencies may be enhanced by three interrelated levels of intrinsic rewards—task, mission, and public service—that are available through the employee's role in the organization. This assertion is consistent with the goal theory of work motivation and its expectation that employees will expend greater effort toward achieving performance goals that they believe will result in important outcomes (Locke and Latham, 1990). In fact, goal theory can provide an important theoretical framework to guide investigations of the separate but interrelated contributions of task, mission, and public service motivation. For example, similar to the concept of task significance, employees may be more likely to see their work as important if they can see how their work contributes to achieving organizational goals (Wright, 2001). This link between individual and organization goals, however, may extend beyond the boundaries of the organization in the public sector because of the congruence between the altruistic nature of public sector goals and the desire public sector employees have to do work that helps others and benefits society (Perry and Wise, 1990; Crewson, 1997). In other words, if public sector employees perceive their own work as important to accomplishing agency goals that benefit society, then they may strive harder to achieve their job level goals. Thus, future research can capitalize on the conceptual framework provided by goal and social cognitive theories to advance our understanding of the work context within organizations and how sector differences may influence employee work motivation and productivity in public organizations.

REFERENCES

Baldwin, J. Norman. 1984. Are we really lazy? *Review of Public Personnel Administration* 4 (2): 80–89.

Baldwin, J. N. 1987. Public versus private: Not that different, not that consequential. *Public Personnel Management* 16 (2): 181–93.

Baldwin, J. N. 1990. Perceptions of public versus private sector personnel and informal red tape: Their impact on motivation. *American Review of Public Administration* 20: 7–28.

Baldwin, J. Norman, and Quinton A. Farley. 1991. Comparing the public and private sectors in the United States: A review of the empirical literature. In *Handbook of Comparative and Development Public Administration,* ed. A. Farazmand, 27–39. New York: Marcel Dekker.

Balk, Walter L. 1974. Why don't public administrators take productivity more seriously? *Public Personnel Management* 3 (3): 318–24.

Bandura, Albert. 1986. *Social foundations of thought and action: A social cognitive theory.* Englewood Cliffs, NJ: Prentice-Hall.

Bandura, A. 1988. Organizational applications of social cognitive theory. *Australian Journal of Management* 13 (2): 275–302.

Bandura, Albert, and Daniel Cervone. 1983. Self-evaluation and self-efficacy mechanisms governing the motivational effects of goal systems. *Journal of Personality and Social Psychology* 45: 1017–28.

Bandura, Albert, and Daniel Cervone. 1986. Differential engagement of self-reactive influences in cognitive motivation. *Organizational Behavior and Human Decision Processes* 38: 91–113.

Bandura, Albert, and Robert Wood. 1989. Effect of perceived controllability and performance standards on self-regulation of complex decision making. *Journal of Personality and Social Psychology* 56 (5): 805–14.

Behn, Robert D. 1995. The big questions of public management. *Public Administration Review* 55 (4): 313–24.

Bollen, Kenneth A., and John S. Long. 1993. Introduction. In *Testing structural equation models,* ed. Kenneth A. Bollen and John S. Long, 1–9. Beverly Hills, CA: Sage.

Bozeman, Barry, Pamela Reed, and Patrick Scott. 1992. The presence of red tape in public and private organizations. *Administration and Society* 24: 290–322.

Brewer, Gene A., and Sally Coleman Selden. 2000. Why elephants gallop: Assessing and predicting organizational performance in federal agencies. *Journal of Public Administration Research and Theory* 10 (4): 685–712.

Buchanan, Bruce. 1975. Government managers, business executives, and organizational commitment. *Public Administration Review* 34 (4): 339–47.

Cohen, Jacob. 1988. *Statistical power analysis for the behavioral sciences.* Hillsdale, NJ: Lawrence Erlbaum.

Crewson, Philip E. 1997. Public-service motivation: Building empirical evidence of incidence and effect. *Journal of Public Administration Research and Theory* 4: 499–518.

Dillman, Don A. 1978. *Mail and telephone surveys: The total design method.* New York: Wiley.

Dillman, Don A. 1991. The design and administration of mail surveys. *Annual Review of Sociology* 17: 225–49.

Earley, P. Christopher, and Terri R. Lituchy. 1991. Delineating goal and efficacy effects: A test of three models. *Journal of Applied Psychology* 76: 81–88.

Eden, Don. 1988. Pygmalion, goal setting, and expectancy: Compatible ways to boost productivity. *Academy of Management Review* 13: 639–52.

Fottler, Myron D. 1981. Is management really generic? *Academy of Management Review* 6 (1): 1–12.

Frayne, Colette A., and Gary P. Latham. 1987. Application of social learning theory to employee self-management of attendance. *Journal of Applied Psychology* 72 (3): 387–92.

Hartline, Michael D., and O. C. Ferrell. 1996. The management of customer-contact service employees: An empirical investigation. *Journal of Marketing* 60 (4): 52–70.

Hayduk, Leslie A. 1987. *Structural equation modeling with LISREL.* Baltimore, MD: Johns Hopkins University Press.

Jaccard, James, and Choi K. Wan. 1996. *LISREL approaches to interaction effects in multiple regression.* In Sage University Papers series on Quantitative Applications in the Social Sciences, 7–114. Thousand Oaks, CA: Sage.

James, Lawrence R., and Lois A. James. 1989. Causal modeling in organizational research. In *International review of industrial and organizational psychology,* ed. Cary L. Cooper and Ivan Robertson, 371–404. Chichester, UK: Wiley.

James, Lawrence R., Stanley A. Mulaik, and Jeanne M. Brett. 1982. *Causal analysis: Assumptions, models, and data.* Beverly Hills, CA: Sage.

Jöreskog, Karl G., and Dag Sörbom. 1992. *LISREL VIII: Analysis of linear structural relations.* Mooresville, IN: Scientific Software.

Kahn, Robert L., Donald M. Wolfe, Robert P. Quinn, J. D. Snoek, and Robert A. Rosenthal. 1964.

Organizational stress: Studies in role conflict and ambiguity. New York: Wiley.

Kanfer, Ruth. 1990. Motivation theory and industrial and organizational psychology. In *Handbook of industrial and organizational psychology,* 2nd ed., vol. 1, ed. Marvin D. Dunnette and Leatta M. Hough, 75–170. Palo Alto, CA: Consulting Psychologists Press.

Kanfer, Ruth. 1992. Work motivation: New directions in theory and research. *International Review of Industrial and Organizational Psychology* 7: 1–53.

Katzell, Raymond A., and Donna E. Thompson. 1990. Work motivation: Theory and practice. *American Psychologist* 45 (2): 144–53.

Kelloway, E. Kevin. 1996. Common practices in structural equation modeling. In *International review of industrial and organizational psychology,* ed. Cary L. Cooper and Ivan Robertson, 141–80. Chichester, UK: Wiley.

Klein, Howard J. 1991. Further evidence on the relationship between goal setting and expectancy theories. *Organizational Behavior and Human Decision Processes* 49: 230–57.

Klein, Howard J., Michael J. Wesson, John R. Hollenbeck, and Bradley J. Alge. 1999. Goal commitment and the goal-setting process: Conceptual clarification and empirical synthesis. *Journal of Applied Psychology* 84 (6): 885–96.

Latham, Gary P., and Colette A. Frayne. 1989. Self-management training for increasing job attendance: A follow-up and a replication. *Journal of Applied Psychology* 74 (3): 411–16.

Lee, Cynthia L., Philip Bobko, P. Christopher Earley, P. Christopher, and Edwin A. Locke. 1991. An empirical analysis of a goal setting questionnaire. *Journal of Organizational Behavior* 12: 467–82.

Locke, Edwin A., and Gary P. Latham. 1990. *A theory of goal setting and task performance.* Englewood Cliffs, NJ: Prentice-Hall.

Meyer, Marshall W. 1982. Bureaucratic vs. profit organization. In *Research in organizational behavior,* ed. Barry M. Staw and L. L. Cummings, 89–126. Greenwich, CT: JAI Press.

Mitchell, Terrence R. 1997. Matching motivation strategies with organizational contexts. In *Research in organizational behavior,* vol. 19, ed. L. L. Cummings and Barry M. Staw, 57–149. Greenwich, CT: JAI Press.

New York State Department of Civil Service. 1999. *1999 New York State workforce management plan. Albany.*

Pandey, Sanjay K, and Patrick G. Scott. 2002. Red Tape: A review and assessment of concepts and measures. *Journal of Public Administration Research and Theory* 12 (4): 553–80.

Patchen, Martin. 1970. *Participation, achievement, and involvement on the job.* Englewood Cliffs, NJ: Prentice-Hall.

Patchen, Martin, Donald C. Pelz, and Craig W. Allen. 1965. *Some questionnaire measures of employee motivation and morale.* Ann Arbor, MI: Institute for Social Research.

Pedhazur, Elazar J. 1982. *Multiple regression in behavioral research: Explanation and prediction.* New York: Holt, Rinehart and Winston.

Perry, James L., and Lyman W. Porter. 1982. Factors affecting the context for motivation in public organizations. *Academy of Management Review* 7 (1): 89–98.

Perry, James L., and Hal G. Rainey. 1988. The public-private distinction in organizational theory: A critique and research strategy. *Academy of Management Review* 13 (2): 182–201.

Perry, James L., and Lois R. Wise. 1990. The motivational bases of public service. *Public Administration Review* 50 (3): 367–73.

Rainey, Hal G. 1983. Private agencies and private firms: Incentive structures, goals and individual roles. *Administration and Society* 15 (2): 207–42.

Rainey, Hal G. 1989. Public management: Recent research on the political context and managerial roles, structures and behaviors. *Journal of Management* 15 (2): 229–50.

Rainey, Hal G. 1993. Work motivation. In *Handbook of Organizational Behavior,* ed. Robert T. Golembiewski, 19–39. New York: Marcel Dekker.

Rainey, Hal G. 1996. *Understanding and Managing Public Organizations.* San Francisco: Jossey Bass.

Rainey, Hal G, Sanjay Pandey, and Barry Bozeman. 1995. Research note: Public and private managers' perceptions of red tape. *Public Administration Review* 55 (6): 567–74.

Rainey, Hal G., and Paula Steinbauer. 1999. Galloping elephants: Developing elements of a theory of effective government organizations. *Journal of Public Administration Research and Theory* 9 (1): 1–32.

Rodgers, Robert, and John E. Hunter. 1992. A foundation of good management practice in government: Management by objectives. *Public Administration Review* 52 (1): 27–39.

Roethlisberger, Fritz J. 1941. *Management and Morale.* Cambridge, MA: Harvard University Press.

Rousseau, Denise. M. 1997. Organizational behavior in the new organizational era. *Annual Review of Psychology* 48: 515–46.

Salancik, Gerald R. 1977. Commitment and the control of organizational behavior and belief. In *New directions in organizational behavior,* ed. Barry

M. Staw and Gerald R. Salancik, 1–54. Chicago: St. Clair Press.

Sims, Henry P., Andrew D. Szilagyi, and Dale R. McKemey. 1976. Antecedents of work related expectancies. *Academy of Management Journal* 19: 547–59.

Steers, Richard M. 1976. Factors affecting job attitudes in a goal setting environment. *Academy of Management Journal* 19: 6–19.

Steers, Richard M., and Lyman W. Porter. 1974. The role of task-goal attributes in employee performance. *Psychological Bulletin* 81 (7): 434–52.

Stone, Eugene F. 1976. The moderating effect of work-related values on the job scope-job satisfaction relationship. *Organizational Behavior and Human Performance* 15: 147–67.

Sullivan, John L., and Stanley Feldman. 1979. *Multiple indicators: An introduction.* Beverly Hills: Sage.

Warwick, Donald P. 1975. *A theory of public bureaucracy: Politics, personality, and organization in the state department.* Cambridge, MA: Harvard University Press.

Whorton, Joseph W., and John A. Worthley. 1981. A perspective on the challenge of public management: Environmental paradox and organizational culture. *Academy of Management Review* 6 (3): 357–61.

Wilk, Leslie A., and William K. Redmon. 1990. A daily-adjusted goal-setting and feedback procedure for improving productivity in a university admissions office. *Journal of Organizational Behavior Management* 11: 55–75.

Wood, Robert, and Albert Bandura. 1989. Social cognitive theory of organizational management. *Academy of Management Review* 14 (3): 361–84.

Wright, Bradley E. 2001. Public sector work motivation: Review of the current literature and a revised conceptual model. *Journal of Public Administration and Theory* 11 (4): 559–86.

NOTES

1. There is some evidence to suggest that assigning difficult goals can raise an individual's self-efficacy by signaling the confidence that others have that the individual can perform the assigned task (Bandura, 1986; Eden, 1988; Salancik, 1977). Although task assignments in laboratory settings may signal to experimental participants that a certain level of performance is expected of them, this may be less likely to occur in real life work environments because employees recognize that responsibilities are assigned more as a product of factors other than their personal competence (job descriptions, labor agreements, resource limitations, and so forth).

Reading 16

What Should We Do About Motivation Theory? Six Recommendations for the Twenty-First Century

Edwin A. Locke
Gary P. Latham

The concept of motivation refers to internal factors that impel action and to external factors that can act as inducements to action. The three aspects of action that motivation can affect are direction (choice), intensity (effort), and duration (persistence). Motivation can affect not only the acquisition of people's skills and abilities but also how and to what extent they utilize their skills and abilities.

Work motivation has been of interest to industrial/organizational (I/O) psychologists at least since the 1930s, stimulated in large part by the famous Hawthorne studies (Roethlisberger & Dickson, 1939), which focused mainly on the effects of supervision, incentives, and working conditions. However, it was not until 1964 that Vroom made the first attempt to formulate an overarching theory—namely, a hedonistic calculus called the "valence-instrumentality-expectancy model." Theory building in the field of work motivation, however, has typically been more specialized than Vroom's overarching model.

Argyris (1957), for example, focused on the congruence between the individual's needs and organizational demands. Herzberg and colleagues (Herzberg, Mausner, & Snyderman, 1959) focused primarily on sources of work satisfaction and, within that domain, mainly on ways in which the job could be designed to make the work itself enriching and challenging. Later, Hackman and Oldham (1980) extended Herzberg's work by developing a model suggesting the specific work characteristics and psychological processes that increase employee satisfaction and the motivation to excel. All these theories center on the issue of the organization's effect on the individual employee's "cognitive growth."

Other theories and approaches have focused on specific psychological processes, as does Vroom's theory. Organizational behavior (OB)

modification (Luthans & Kreitner, 1975), which is not influential today, was derived from Skinner's behavioristic philosophy that denied the importance of consciousness. This approach stresses the automatic role of rewards and feedback on work motivation; however, these effects are mediated by psychological processes such as goals and self-efficacy (Bandura, 1986; Locke, 1977). Goal-setting theory (Locke & Latham, 2002) and control theory—a mechanistic combination of cybernetics and goal theory (Lord & Hanges, 1987)—focus on the effects of conscious goals as motivators of task performance. Attribution theory's (Weiner, 1986) emphasis is on ways that the attributions one makes about one's own or others' performance affect one's subsequent choices and actions. Social-cognitive theory (Bandura, 1986) is very broad in scope—its domain is much wider than that of work motivation—but Bandura's core concept of self-efficacy has been found to have powerful motivational effects on task performance (Bandura, 1997).

Two work motivation theories have a social emphasis (although Bandura [1986] stresses the motivational effects of role modeling). Adams' (1963) theory focuses on the motivational effects of distributive justice, which is based on comparisons between the inputs and outcomes of oneself versus those of comparison others. More recently, scholars have extensively researched procedural justice (Greenberg, 2000), stressing the important effect on employee satisfaction of the methods or processes by which organizational decisions affecting employees are made.

Personality-based approaches to motivation, although in and out of fashion over the past several decades, have always had some strong supporters. McClelland and his colleagues (e.g., McClelland & Winter, 1969) stressed the effect of subconscious

Source: Advances in Motivation and Achievement, Vol. 10, 1997, pp. 375–412. Reprinted by permission of Elsevier Publications.

motivation—specifically, need for achievement—on economic growth. In recent years the study of conscious, self-reported traits has become popular, especially traits such as conscientiousness, which is fairly consistently related to effective job performance (Barrick & Mount, 2000).

Our goal in this article is not to offer yet another theory of work motivation. Rather, our focus is on metatheory—the process or processes through which we can build more valid, more complete, and more practical theories. This paper provides rationales for six categories of recommendations for advancing knowledge and understanding of employee motivation in the twenty-first century. We provide examples of specific types of studies that might be carried out relevant to each recommendation.

Six Recommendations

Recommendation 1: Use the results of existing meta-analyses to integrate valid aspects of extant theories.

When beginning to study the plethora of existing work motivation theories, one's reaction is sometimes bewilderment at the enormous variety of concepts and approaches. But, if one looks closely, it is evident that, for the most part, these theories, though flawed and/or limited in various respects (see Miner, 2002), do not so much contradict one another as focus on different aspects of the motivation process. Therefore, there is now an urgent need to tie these theories and processes together into an overall model, insofar as this is possible.

Locke (1997) made a preliminary attempt at integrating theories of motivation in the workplace. The model, shown in Figure 1, begins with an employee's needs, moves to acquired values and motives (including personality), then to goal choice, and thence to goals and self-efficacy. The latter two variables constitute a "motivation hub" in that they are often the most direct, conscious, motivational determinants of performance. Performance is followed by outcomes, and outcomes by emotional appraisals, such as employee satisfaction and involvement, that lead

to a variety of possible subsequent actions. (Job satisfaction, of course, may also affect performance; the precise causal relationship between them is not fully known [see Judge, Thoreson, Bono, & Patton, 2001].) Job characteristics are shown as affecting satisfaction. The place where a specific theory applies is shown by the dotted boxes. This is not a speculative model. Every connection but one—namely, the link from needs to values—is based on empirical research.

A useful next step would entail identifying the size or strength of the various relationships shown in Figure 1. This could be done by combining the results of all known meta-analyses relevant to each path in the model and would include calculating known mediation effects, as well as known moderator effects. It would also entail adding pathways based on theories for which there is some empirical evidence but which are not, as yet, included in the model (e.g., Kanfer & Ackerman's [1989] resource allocation theory and Weiner's [1986] attribution theory). The result could be the first motivation mega-theory in the behavioral sciences derived from combining different meta-analyses.

Using meta-analyses to build theory, which is called "mega-analysis," was originally suggested by Schmidt (1992). He and his colleagues used it on a small scale in the field of human resources management by tying together empirical studies of the relationships among job experience, ability, knowledge, and performance on work samples, as well as in the workplace (Schmidt, Hunter, & Outerbridge, 1986). However, a mega-analysis of extant work motivation theories would be on a much wider scale and would integrate an enormous amount of data into a comprehensible framework that would be useful to both theorists and practitioners. The model could be expanded, of course, as new discoveries were made.

1. Needs to values. This is the least empirically researched of the causal connections. Although motivation must start with needs, that is, the objective requirements of the organism's survival and well-being, how work values grow out of needs has not been studied. Although

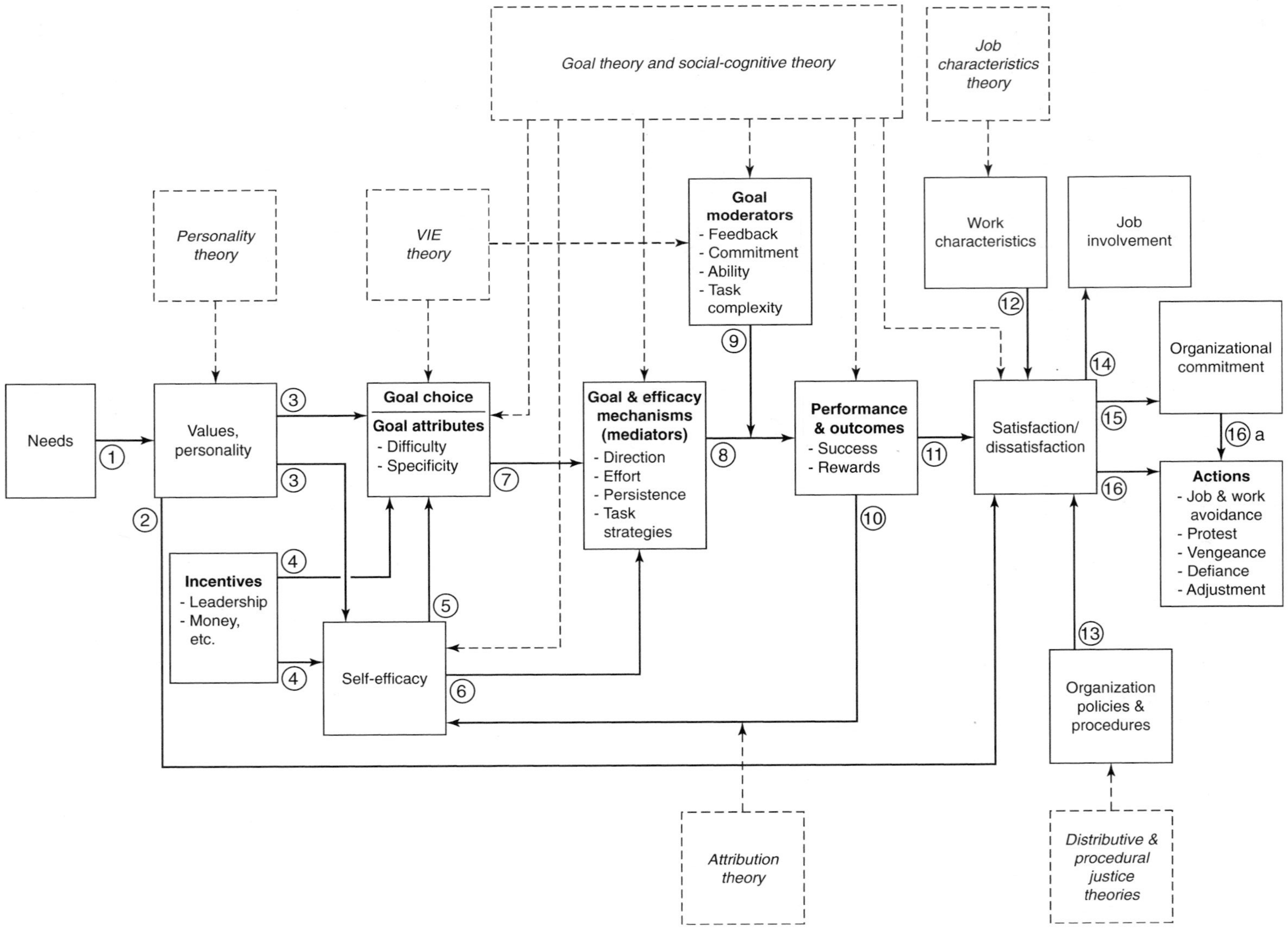

FIGURE 1

194

Maslow was partly correct in claiming that people value what they need, there are numerous exceptions to this claim. These exceptions, of course, are one of the reasons why we need both a science of mental health and a code of ethics.

2. Values and personality to satisfaction. This pertains to the relation of self-esteem and neuroticism to job perceptions and job satisfaction.

3. Values and personality to goals and self-efficacy. Values and personality affect goals and self-efficacy and their effects on performance are mediated by goals and efficacy.

4. Incentives to goals and self-efficacy. Like personality, incentives affect goals and self-efficacy which in turn mediate the effects of incentives.

5. Self-efficacy to goals. Efficacy affects goal choice and especially goal difficulty.

6. and 7. Self-efficacy and goals to mechanisms. Goals and efficacy affect performance through their effects on direction, effort, persistence, and task strategies or tactics.

8. Goals, that is, goal mechanisms, to performance. Goals, especially goal difficulty, affect performance, and performance, depending on the organization's policies, affects rewards.

9. Goal moderators. Goal effects are enhanced by feedback, commitment, ability, and (low) task complexity.

10. Performance to efficacy. Performance, including the attributions one makes for performance, affects self-efficacy.

11. Performance to satisfaction. Success and rewards produce satisfaction.

12. Work characteristics to satisfaction. Mental challenge and related job attributes enhance satisfaction.

13. Organizational policies to satisfaction. The perceived fairness of the organization's policies, procedural justice, and the perceived fairness of the results of these policies, distributive justice, affect satisfaction.

14. Satisfaction to involvement. Job satisfaction enhances job involvement.

15. Satisfaction to organizational commitment. Satisfaction enhances organizational commitment.

16. and 16a. Satisfaction and commitment to action. Satisfaction and commitment, along with other factors, affect action, especially approach and avoidance of the job or work. Several limitations of this model should be noted:

- To limit cognitive-perceptual overload some causal arrows are omitted. For example, self-efficacy affects commitment and presumably choices among action alternatives in the face of dissatisfaction. Personality and values can also affect action taken in response to job dissatisfaction. Perceived injustice undoubtedly affects goal commitment.

- The various theories, aside from goal theory, are not fully elaborated. For example, there are many complexities involved in procedural justice and a number of competing sub-theories.

- Recursive effects are not shown, except in the case of self-efficacy to performance. In the real world, almost any output can become an input over time. The model is static, not dynamic. Mone (1994) has done dynamic analyses of the goal-efficacy-performance relationship and found the basic static model to hold.

- Ability, knowledge and skill are critical to performance but, with one exception, are not shown in the motivation model. Self-efficacy, of course, reflects how people assess their skills and abilities.

- The model focuses on conscious motivation and omits the sub-conscious, except insofar as it is acknowledged as being involved in emotions.

- The model does not include theories with dubious or highly limited support. . . .

Recommendation 2: Create a boundaryless science of work motivation.

Jack Welch coined the term *boundaryless organization* when he was CEO of General Electric (GE), as a result of his frustration over knowledge that was being ignored rather than shared and embraced among the myriad divisions of GE. Similar dysfunctional behavior had been referred to within the Weyerhaeuser Company as the "not invented here" mindset—a mindset that prevented managers within one region of the company from building on the knowledge gained by managers in other regions.

This implies two things. First, work motivation theory needs to be extended into and further developed within areas other than isolated task performance settings. Second, motivation theorists should consider using concepts developed in fields outside OB and I/O psychology.

For example, motivation could be studied further in the realm of team effectiveness. There are processes affecting teams that do not arise when the focus is on the individual's motivation, such as the specific ways in which team members motivate and demotivate one another. For instance, team members might encourage one another through building efficacy by means of persuasion or the offering of useful ideas. They might undermine one another through belittlement and insults. Extending motivation research into the realm of teams would lead to the exploration of such issues as conflicts among personalities, values, and/or goals that are not yet a part of extant work motivation theories. Although team cohesion has been studied, less attention has been paid to the sources, content, and effects of team conflict and how these specifically influence team motivation (but see Weingart & Jehn, 2000, for some preliminary findings). Social loafing is another potent group motivation phenomenon that is not part of extant work motivation theories (Karau & Williams, 2001). A separate megamodel might have to be constructed to explain team motivation.

Motivation also should be studied within the realm of decision making. For example, Schneider and Lopes (1986) have argued that level of aspiration (i.e., goals) needs to be incorporated into prospect theory. Along this line, Knight, Durham, and Locke (2001) have found that goals affect the degree of risk people take when making decisions. Personality theory has implications for prospect

theory as well. For example, those high in extroversion may assess risk quite differently from those high in neuroticism.

Within the field of personality, an issue that needs to be addressed is the extent to which certain traits are stable aspects of the person versus readily manipulable motivational states. For example, Dweck and her colleagues (e.g., Dweck & Elliott, 1983) have argued that goal orientation is a relatively stable disposition. Yet there is a paucity of studies that have assessed its test-retest reliability (e.g., VandeWalle, Cron, & Slocum, 2001). Moreover, the empirical research suggests that goal orientation is readily malleable. Dweck herself has even acknowledged this in the field of educational psychology (e.g., Elliott & Dweck, 1988; Mueller & Dweck, 1998). In the OB field, Seijts, Latham, Tasa, and Latham (in press) found that when people were given do-your-best instructions, Dweck's (1986) predictions regarding the goal orientation trait were supported. But when a specific difficult learning goal was set, it masked the effect of this trait. A learning goal, as is the case with an outcome goal (Adler & Weiss, 1988), was shown to be a strong variable that mitigates the effects of this individual-difference variable (trait). Research is needed to see under what conditions situationally induced motives negate trait effects.

Motivation theory can be better incorporated into macrotheories, particularly organization theory. For example, there is little doubt that degree of centralization and decentralization has motivational consequences, as appears to be the case with span of control (Donaldson, 2000). Firms that have subsidiaries in different countries inevitably run into the issue of value differences (Erez, 2000). Hence, more knowledge is needed about how value differences actually operate. For example, are goal setting, participation in decision making, performance appraisal, and so forth differentially effective as a consequence of value differences, or are they simply used in a different form—or both?

Motivational issues are also important for strategic management. For example, strategic management frequently involves change, and the phenomenon of resistance to change is well known (Beer, 2000). When firms decide that they will employ a certain strategy (e.g., low cost), they may differ radically in how well they implement it (e.g., Wal-Mart versus K-Mart). In part, this is an issue of knowledge and skill, but it is also related to motivation. Resistance to change is discussed routinely within the field of organizational development, but the motivational issues involved are not directly included in traditional motivation theories. At best, they are addressed by implication; for example, resistance to change may imply refusal to commit to certain goals and may be motivated by low self-efficacy, low instrumentality, and/or negative valences. This issue needs to be studied explicitly. Of course, there are other aspects of strategic management that entail motivation—for example, decision choice and competitiveness—requiring further study as well.

Finally, motivation theory in the realm of work needs to draw on findings from other fields. Both the science and practice of OB have already benefited from theory in social (e.g., Bandura, 1986) and educational psychology (e.g., Dweck, 1986). In the study of motivation, findings by non-I/O scholars in clinical psychology must not be overlooked (Latham & Heslin, 2003). Two examples include research by Beck and by Seligman (and their respective colleagues).

Beck and his colleagues (Beck, 1967; Beck, Rush, Shaw, & Emery, 1979) focused on the relationship between depression and "automatic thoughts," by which they mean thoughts held in the subconscious that affect emotional responses. These researchers examined what they call "dysfunctional thinking" with respect to both content and process. Examples include overgeneralization (e.g., "If I do something bad, it means that I am a totally bad person"), (irrational) perfectionism (e.g., "If I am any good at all, I should be able to excel at everything I try"), and dependence on others (e.g., "I do things to please other people rather than please myself").

Dysfunctional thoughts lead people to evaluate information inappropriately, thus leading to negative emotional states. Beck and his colleagues developed methods of consciously correcting dysfunctional thought processes. Clients report their automatic thoughts through introspection (an issue to be dealt with at length below), and then the psychologists discuss with the clients the rationality of such beliefs. For example, a depressed client might claim, "Pat has left me; therefore, I am worthless." The psychologist might then ask, "Is that really true? What do you base that on?" Gradually, clients come to see that their implicit conclusions or "automatic thoughts" are not rational and that a different perspective is more in line with reality. By challenging dysfunctional thoughts as they arise and correcting them consciously, the clients' automatic or subconscious processing changes and, thus, their negative emotions are mitigated (Haaga, Dyck, & Ernst, 1991).

Such clinical methods have practical utility in the realm of work motivation. Millman and Latham (2001) found that they were able to train unemployed individuals to engage in functional thinking—that is, positive self-talk—and that such training significantly improved their chances of finding a new, well-paying job.

Cognitive methods could be used to teach employees the principle of reframing dysfunctional thoughts in work settings. For example, when individuals encounter difficulties during training, they can reframe a self-demeaning statement like "I can't stand always being so stupid" as "It is normal to make mistakes when I am first learning to perform a task." Reframing self-deprecating statements in constructive ways can have a positive effect on motivation and can sustain a person's self-efficacy (Bandura, 1997).

Similarly, employees might be taught to deal with stress through thought retraining. Stress is a response to the appraisal that one is being psychologically or physically threatened. But threat appraisals are not always rational, and even when they are, employees can be trained to engage in problem-focused thinking so as to develop methods that enable them to mitigate the threats they confront (Lazarus & Folkman, 1984). For example, employees faced with the possibility of layoffs could be trained to identify the exact nature of the perceived threats (e.g., financial and/or psychological) and to generate plans to cope with them.

Irrational beliefs may adversely interact with feedback provided by others. Rational beliefs can mediate the effect on performance feedback from authority figures (e.g., a supervisor). Training in ways to replace irrational with rational beliefs would also appear to be applicable to employees whose desire for inappropriate perfectionism is preventing them from completing job assignments in a timely fashion.

Managers and business leaders can engage in dysfunctional thinking, not only when the business is doing badly but also when it is doing well (e.g., "We are growing at 40 percent per year and will always grow at that rate; thus, there is no need to change our strategy"). Over-confidence leads managers to engage in poor decision making (Audia, Locke, & Smith, 2000). Training in meta-principles of how to think rationally should be beneficial to people at all organizational levels.

Based on over twenty-five years of programmatic research in the laboratory and in the clinic, Seligman (1968, 1998a, b) established a causal relationship between a person's pessimistic explanatory style and subsequent depression, on the one hand, versus an optimistic explanatory style and a person's creativity, productivity, and overall sense of well-being, on the other. Drawing on attribution theory, Seligman and his colleagues (Peterson et al., 1982) developed the Attribution Style Questionnaire (ASQ), which assesses a person's explanatory style with regard to the locus, stability, and globality of attributions. *Locus* refers to the extent to which a noncontingency between one's actions and the consequences experienced is attributed primarily to either oneself or to factors in the environment. *Stability* is the extent to which the lack of a response outcome is temporary or is likely to persist into the future. *Globality* is the extent to which noncontingent outcomes are perceived as either domain specific or likely to undermine many areas of one's life.

Learned helplessness results from setbacks that are considered long lasting (stable), undermining

the attainment of most if not all of one's goals (global), and caused by personal deficiencies (internal) rather than situational constraints. The resulting low outcome expectancy causes deficits in future learning, as well as motivational disturbances such as procrastination and depression (Seligman, 1998a).

Optimists attribute their failures to causes that are temporary rather than stable, specific to the attainment of a particular goal rather than all their goals, and see the problem as a result of the environment or setting they are in, rather than inherent in themselves. Setbacks and obstacles are seen as challenges (Seligman & Csikszent-mihalyi, 2000). Thus, optimists are usually resilient in the face of failure.

Seligman (1998b) found that optimism can be learned, using a method similar to that employed by Beck. Step 1 requires the clinician to help clients identify self-defeating beliefs they may be unaware of. Step 2 involves gathering information to evaluate and dispute the accuracy and implications of these self-defeating beliefs that are triggered by environmental events. Step 3 involves replacing maladaptive beliefs with constructive, accurate ones based on the data collected in the second step.

The ASQ may prove useful for identifying people in organizations who suffer from learned helplessness. Seligman and Schulman (1986) have provided evidence suggesting the value of ASQ for OB. They found that salespeople with an optimistic explanatory style sold 35 percent more insurance than did those whose explanatory style was pessimistic. Moreover, people with a pessimistic style were twice as likely to quit their job in the first year than those with an optimistic style. Similarly, Schulman (1999) found that those who scored high on optimism outsold those who scored as pessimists by 20 to 40 percent across a range of organizations (e.g., auto sales, tele-communications, real estate, and banking). Strutton and Lumpkin (1992) found that the mediator of the two attribution styles on employee performance is strategy. Salespeople who scored high on optimism used problem-solving techniques, whereas those who scored high on pessimism focused on ways of seeking social support.

Seligman's training technique may provide a framework for mentors, coaches, and trainers to predict, understand, and influence a person or team who has given up trying to attain goals because of repeated failures. No one as yet has shown whether the ASQ has general applications to the workforce. We also need to determine whether learned optimism is basically equivalent to trait-level self-efficacy and whether optimism effects are mediated by situationally specific self-efficacy (Bandura, 1997).

Recommendation 3: Identify how general variables such as personality get applied to and are mediated by task- and situationally-specific variables, how they are moderated by situations, and how they affect situational choice and structuring.

A problem that must be overcome in combining motivation theories is how to integrate the general with the specific. For example, a Big Five personality trait such as conscientiousness is, by definition, general. It reflects action patterns that cross tasks and situations. Typically, trait measures correlate about 0.20 with action in specific settings. This mean correlation is better than chance, but it does not answer such questions as: How do traits actually operate? How can we make better predictions?

A partial answer to these questions becomes evident when we recognize that there is no such thing as action in general; every action is task and situationally specific. Specific measures, if chosen properly, virtually always predict action better than general measures. However, general measures predict more widely than do specific ones (Judge et al., 2002).

A general value or motive must presumably be "applied," consciously or subconsciously, to each specific task and situation. It follows that situationally and task-specific knowledge, assessments, and intentions should be affected by such motives and that these assessments, in turn, should affect actions taken in the situation. A person's goals, as well as self-efficacy, have been found to partly or wholly mediate the effects of some personality traits, as well as the effects of various incentives (Locke, 2001). These traits include conscientiousness, competitiveness, Type A personality, general (trait) efficacy, need for mastery, and self-esteem. Vande Walle et al. (2001) found that goals and efficacy mediate the effects of the trait of goal orientation on performance. The mediation hypothesis is implicit in Figure 1, in that values and personality are shown to work through goals and efficacy. Nevertheless, it is possible that some trait effects are direct and, thus, not mediated at all. If so, it will be necessary to discover when and why this occurs.

The identification of personality trait mediators does not preclude the study of person-situation interactions. In "strong" or constrained situations, people may feel less free to act as they want or "really are" as compared to when they are in "weak" situations. However, this likely occurs because people appraise situations partly in terms of what they can and should do in them. Furthermore, what has yet to be studied is the other side of the strong versus weak situation coin—namely, the possibility of "strong" versus "weak" personalities. Strong personalities should be less constrained by situations than weak ones. For example, hyper-competitive people might look for ways to compete everywhere—not only in sports or business but also in social and personal relationships. Thus, they would construe every situation as an opportunity to demonstrate their superiority.

Finally, we must not overlook the fact that people are not merely the passive victims of situations. For example, employees choose the jobs they apply for and quit those they dislike. They may restructure jobs to make a better fit with their own talents and proclivities. They may also work with others to change situations they dislike. They can choose what new skills to develop and what careers to pursue. Going further afield, they can also choose (in most free countries) whom they marry, where they live, how many children they have, how they spend their money, whom they want as their friends, and what off-the-job activities they engage in. As Bandura (1986, 1997) has noted, people are not simply dropped into situations; they themselves create, choose, and change situations. We need to study how traits affect these processes.

Recommendation 4: Study subconscious as well as conscious motivation and the relationship between them.

The concept of the subconscious is not a "hypothetical construct" but a fully objective one. It refers to information that is "in consciousness" but not, at a given time, in focal awareness. Psychologists have shown that people can only hold about seven separate (disconnected) elements in focal awareness at the same time (Miller, 1956). The rest of one's knowledge, to use the usual computer analogy, is "stored in memory." We validate the concept of the subconscious by observing that we can draw knowledge out of memory without any additional learning. Typically needed information is pulled out automatically, based on our conscious purpose (e.g., when we read a book, the meanings of the words and our knowledge of spelling and grammar are automatically engaged). We can also observe that certain events and experiences (e.g., early childhood memories) are harder to recall than others.

It is undeniable that people *can* act without being aware of the motives and values underlying their behavior. This assertion does not require the positing of an unconscious that is made up of primitive instincts devoid of any access to, or contact with, the conscious mind, as Freud asserted. Nor does acknowledging the subconscious require a leap to the unwarranted conclusion that all actions are governed by unconscious forces (Wegner & Wheatley, 1999). Such a claim would clearly be arbitrary. This assertion only requires acknowledgment that the subconscious is a storehouse of knowledge and values beyond what is in focal awareness at any given point in time (Murphy, 2001) and that accessibility to this stored information differs within and between people.

McClelland, Atkinson, Clark, and Lowell (1953) claimed that the achievement motive,

which they asserted to be related to entrepreneurship, was a subconscious motive. Thus, they argued, it had to be measured with a projective test—namely, the TAT—which involves people telling stories in response to pictures. This claim may be true, but to the present authors' knowledge, no self-report measure of achievement motivation has been designed with items that match exactly the type of TAT story content that is indicative of high need for achievement. Thus, TAT-measured achievement motivation may or may not be assessing a concept different from self-reported achievement motivation measures.

Self-report measures of achievement motivation are typically uncorrelated with projective measures, even though both types of measures are significantly associated with entrepreneurial action (Collins, Hanges, & Locke, in press). Need for achievement, measured projectively, also appears to be unrelated to conscious performance goals (e.g., Tracy, Locke, & Renard, 1999). Similarly, A. Howard (personal communication) found that, in a reanalysis of her twenty-five-year AT&T study with Bray, conscious goals for promotion had no relationship with a set of projective measures that had been designed by McClelland to predict managerial progress (see Locke & Latham, 2002). McClelland (e.g., McClelland & Winter, 1969) believed that subconscious motives are differentially aroused by different situations and operate differently than conscious motivation.

Failure to specify the effect of the subconscious on action is a limitation of goal-setting theory (Locke & Latham, 2002)—not to mention other motivation theories. Yet, over a century ago, the Wurzburg school in Germany showed that goals that are assigned to people can affect their subsequent behavior, without their being aware of it. In this century, Wegge and Dibbelt (2000) have shown that high goals automatically increase the speed with which information is cognitively processed. Locke (2000b) has argued that goals may arouse task-relevant knowledge automatically, but almost nothing is known about how and when this occurs.

Studying the subconscious is difficult precisely because people, including laboratory participants and employees, cannot always directly provide the needed information stored there. Thus, indirect measures are required. Projective measures may be useful (see Lilienfeld, Wood, & Garb, 2000), but they are riddled with such difficulties as low internal reliability and the effect of choice of pictures (in the case of the TAT). In the realm of achievement motivation, a 2 (high/low projective measure) × 2 (high/low conscious self-report) factorial design might reveal whether responses to these two measurement techniques—subconscious and conscious—assuming they are actually referring to the same concept, interact or work additively. The same type of study could be conducted in relation to other traits. The Big Five, for example, might be measured projectively as well as through self-reports.

Projective tests do not have to be confined to the TAT. Other projective measures may be equally if not more useful. An example is the incomplete sentence blank (ISB), used extensively by Miner (e.g., Miner, Smith, & Bracker, 1994). Different projective methods should be compared for agreement, when the same alleged concepts or motives are measured, as well as for predictive validity.

Another way to examine subconscious effects is through "priming." Priming involves giving people information that is apparently unrelated to the task at hand but that can affect an individual's subsequent responses, without being aware of the effect. In two experiments Earley and Perry (1987) used priming to influence the task strategies that subjects used to attain goals. Priming could be used in many other types of motivation studies. Bargh, Gollwitzer, Lee-Chai, Barndollar, and Troetschel (2001) found that primed goals for performance and cooperation had significant effects on these two outcomes. Research should be conducted comparing the effect sizes of, and possible interactions between, consciously assigned versus subconsciously primed goals.

Recommendation 5: Use introspection explicitly as a method of studying and understanding motivation.

Few methodologies in the history of the behavioral sciences have been more controversial than introspection. Introspection was used extensively by Titchner, an influential psychologist in the early twentieth century, but it was subsequently rejected by his followers because they found his view of psychology to be unduly narrow. Freud and his followers also rejected introspection because they believed that motivational dynamics were in the unconscious, *not* the subconscious—or, as they called it, the "preconscious"—and, thus, inaccessible to direct awareness or observation. Drive reductionists, such as Hull and Spence, agreed with this inaccessibility argument because they believed that motivation was strictly physiological. The behaviorists, especially Watson and Skinner, rejected introspection because they believed the subject matter—consciousness—was irrelevant to understanding human behavior. Nevertheless, it is self-evident that motivational states exist in consciousness; thus, introspection *must* be used to study it. Psychological concepts (e.g., desire, self-efficacy, purpose, satisfaction, belief) could not even be formulated or grasped without introspection. Furthermore, questionnaire studies in OB have always relied on introspection by the respondents, even though all people are not equally good at it. The use of introspection, as an accepted methodology in OB, will provide at least six important benefits for advancing our understanding of employee motivation. These are as follows.

1. *Understanding traits and motives.* In the field of personality, it is often unclear whether researchers are describing behavior or an underlying motive that causes the behavior. Predicting behavior from behavior may be helpful practically, but it is psychologically trivial if the basis for the behavior is not explained. If traits are more than just behavioral regularity, they must be caused by underlying motives. We can only learn about the nature of these motives by having people with varying levels of trait scores engage in introspection. With regard to the above discussion of projective versus self-report measures of traits, such as

need for achievement, people who are highly effective versus ineffective at introspection could be studied to see if the two types of measures predict differently within each type of person. In addition, people can be trained in introspection (Schweiger, Anderson, & Locke, 1985). Research is needed to determine whether training would produce greater convergence between conscious and subconscious measures of the same concept. Motive "constructs" (i.e., concepts) in OB are often defined statistically, as a conglomeration of measures or of items. They are seldom defined experientially. This is especially true of so-called high-order constructs, which may have little or no psychological reality. For example, the Big Five personality dimensions are statistical conglomerations of a number of related subdimensions. But little is known about how people with high scores on traits such as extra-version actually experience themselves and the world. Such an understanding should enable researchers to develop better measures.

2. *Increasing accuracy.* The conditions under which self-reports of psychological states are more versus less accurate need to be identified. Ericcson and Simon (1980) have described the conditions under which introspective reports are most reliable. The evidence suggests that the more immediate and specific the information requested, the more accurately the respondent is able to introspect and, thus, to report the information accurately. It is usually difficult for respondents to formulate broad abstractions about themselves, especially personality traits or broad values. It is even harder for them to formulate accurate and comprehensive statements about the causes of their own and others' actions. A major reason Herzberg used his mentor Flanagan's (1954) critical incident technique to collect data was to avoid the problems associated with asking people to introspect in order to answer such abstract questions. Rather, he used very specific questions, such as the following: "Tell me a time when you were very satisfied with your job." "What were the events and conditions that led up to it?" What is still needed is the discovery of how to get from such specific questions to accurate, broad abstractions such as overall job satisfaction ratings.

Developing structured interviews might yield more accurate data than using questionnaires. The investigator could check with the respondents as to how they are interpreting the questions and could help them to introspect and, therefore, increase the accuracy of the answers. Studies are also needed to compare the validity of measurements conducted by well-designed interviews versus those obtained by questionnaires.

3. *Understanding the effects of attitudes.* How do people act when they like or dislike their jobs? Through introspection, we can see at once that there are many different things that we do and can do when we experience these feelings. Through introspection, we know that high or low productivity is far from a fixed response to such attitudes. This leads to asking ourselves additional questions: How do we decide what to do? How do we choose from among alternatives? Through introspection, many factors that influence choices, including internal values and organizational circumstances, can be identified. Once we have these answers as starting points, other people can be questioned to see if they give similar answers to the same questions. Such a process might have enabled us to avoid decades of torturous efforts to resolve the satisfaction-performance issue solely by means of statistical techniques. Rather than continue to look for correlations between satisfaction and productivity, we might use introspection to point to a variety of decision-making processes involved in getting from satisfaction to performance, and vice versa, that then could be studied systematically. This would enable researchers to look at the psychological processes that mediate such effects, as well as the various causal paths and the directions of causal influence. Relevant measurements of the key variables could then be developed.

4. *Learning how managers formulate and apply principles.* The first author has argued that management should be taught in terms of principles (general truths) rather than specific theories (Locke, 2002) and has asked various experts in the

field to identify core principles in OB and HR (Latham, 2000; Locke, 2000a). There is evidence that organizational leaders actually manage using principles (Locke, 2002). But we know very little about how managers formulate, adapt, apply, and orchestrate principles in a given organizational context. To study this, we need to gain knowledge about how managers actually think. In organizational settings, many decisions must be dealt with quickly, and most principles have to be adapted by managers to a specific context, since each organization is, in some way, unique. Management strategy, systems, and procedures have to be orchestrated so that they work in harmony. Introspection with highly effective and ineffective leaders might reveal (1) what principles they use, (2) how they discovered them, (3) how they orchestrate them, (4) and how they implement what they advocate—that is, "practice what they preach."

5. *Understanding self-motivation.* We know a good deal about what organizations and their leaders do to motivate people, but we know less about what people do to motivate themselves at work. Discovery of what people do to regulate their own actions may be discovered through having them introspect. Since motivation means the motivation to do something, introspection can be used to ascertain how people energize themselves to undertake and persist working at specific tasks, especially tasks in which (1) they experience various types of conflict both within themselves and between themselves and others, (2) they experience initial failure or goal frustration, and (3) there are both short- and long-term goals that require consideration. Introspection can also shed light on what people do to get themselves committed to tasks. Functional self-talk (Meichenbaum, 1977; Millman & Latham, 2001), self-induced optimism, and efficacy building may be critical factors. New discoveries about how people motivate themselves may be used by organizations, including trainers, to motivate employees, in the same way that studies in clinical psychology have been used to help people motivate themselves at work (e.g., see Frayne & Latham, 1987, and Latham & Frayne, 1989).

6. *Understanding the relationship between motivation and knowledge.* In most studies of motivation, researchers attempt to hold cognition (knowledge) constant so as not to confound their separate effects on performance. But, in reality, they always go together. Thus, we need to learn about how each affects the other. Through the use of introspection by leaders and employees, one aspect of the knowledge issue in organizations can be broken down into what motivates (1) knowledge discovery, (2) knowledge sharing, and (3) knowledge utilization when making decisions or taking action. It may be that somewhat different motivational principles govern each. To give an oversimplified example, knowledge discovery may be motivated mainly by love of discovery and personal passion for one's work (Amabile, 2000), knowledge sharing may be affected by team- or organizational-level incentives and leadership (as was done by Jack Welch at GE), and knowledge utilization may be affected by assigning goals that can best (or only) be attained by using the knowledge that is provided (Earley & Perry, 1987).

On the other side of this coin, we need to discover how knowledge affects motivation. We know that knowledge of one's personal capabilities (self-efficacy) has potent effects on task motivation (Bandura, 1997). But what about other types of knowledge? There is a long history of the study of the effects of participation in decision making—that is, consulting subordinates about their ideas—on employee motivation, but the effects have been shown not to be as powerful as was originally believed (Locke, Alavi, & Wagner, 1997). However, there are many other ways in which knowledge could have motivational effects. Answers to questions such as the following are needed: Are leaders more strongly self-motivated after they have formulated a clear vision of what their organization should be and what strategies will make it successful? Are followers more motivated when they hear such a vision explained and consider it sound? How does the discovery by employees that a leader is lacking in moral character, or the discovery that the leader is lacking in key task knowledge, affect their motivation? How does the discovery that one's company is doing badly financially affect motivation?

Recommendation 6: Acknowledge the role of volition on human action when formulating theories.

Everyone can validate by introspection that they have the power to make choices not predetermined by antecedent conditions (Binswanger, 1991). The concept of psychological determinism—the doctrine that all one's thoughts and actions are controlled solely by antecedent factors—is self-contradictory in that it makes a claim of knowledge based on a theory that makes knowledge, as distinguished from arbitrary word sounds, impossible. Free will is an axiom; it consists of the choice to think or not to think, to raise one's level of focus to the conceptual level or let it drift passively at the level of sensory perception (Binswanger, 1991).

Thus, it is important not to view the causes of action as fully determined by circumstances or by predetermined ways of processing. In his expectancy theory, Vroom (1964), for example, argued that people will multiply expectancy by instrumentality by valence (Force = E × I × V) when choosing among alternatives. This theory implies determinism, since it is argued that people are constructed to be satisfaction maximizers, yet, in fact, people are usually not maximizers of anything (Simon, 1976), nor do they have to multiply E × I × V when deciding what to do. E, I, and V are only factors that they may choose to consider, and they may choose to weight the three components in different ways, or even to ignore one or more of them. Furthermore, people may treat negative and positive outcomes differently and, thus, may consider a variety of different time spans and outcomes when considering their choices. Many people make choices every day with little or no thought—based on the emotions of the moment, for example.

Similarly, Beach's (1990) image theory states that people make decisions using a specific process (e.g., value images, trajectory images, strategic images, etc.). However, people do not have to use this process; there are many processes they can use, including mindlessly following what others say or, as noted above, following their emotions.

Descriptive studies based on introspection would doubtless uncover an enormous variety in how people make decisions about numerous issues. Normative theories should be built by first discovering what people actually do and then seeing what types of processes lead to the optimal outcomes. The optimal processes may very well be task or domain specific.

Theories of employee motivation should be contingent—namely, *if* the person chooses to follow processes a and b, *then* the outcomes will routinely be better than if the person chooses process c or d. Similarly, if people reach conclusion "a" from "b," then they are most likely to do "c," but if they reach conclusion "d," they are most likely to do "e." Consistent with this idea, goal-setting theory (Locke & Latham, 1990, 2002) states that *if* people try for specific, hard goals, *then* they will, given certain moderating conditions such as feedback, knowledge, and commitment, perform better than when they have vague and/or easy goals. Similarly contingent predictions can be found in social-cognitive theory (Bandura, 1986).

This is not to deny that people can be influenced by external factors, but the connections are not mechanical. Thus, predictions should be made conditionally. In other words, the effects of the environment depend on what people attend to and what conclusions they draw from the experiences they have and the situations they encounter (Bandura, 1986). Recall that, in the field of organization theory, it was initially hypothesized that technology determines organizational structure. Programmatic research testing this hypothesis was not very successful, however, because human choice and imagination were not taken into account (Miner, 2002).

The same caveat applies to internal factors. For example, the best known psychological predictor of quitting a job is the intention to quit, but often this intention is not carried out—the reasons for which have not been studied. People who have an intent must still choose to act on it, and for many reasons they may not do so. Similarly, people who claim to be committed to their goals may not act to achieve them. Additional studies are needed to understand the choices people make after formulating intentions or committing

themselves to a goal. Volition does not destroy the possibility of a psychological science, but it does mean that predictions must be conditional (Binswanger, 1991). The relevant conditions pertain to the individual's psychology, both conscious and subconscious.

CONCLUSION

The purpose of this article has been to argue that, in order to progress further, work motivation needs to be studied from new perspectives. Many topics have yet to be sufficiently studied, and certain methods have been underutilized. The six recommendations in this paper by no means exhaust the possibilities for new directions for research on motivation.

For example, we also need to study topics such as time perspective—how employees, managers, and leaders consider and integrate short- versus long-term considerations or outcomes—a topic not addressed in the *Academy of Management Review* (October 2001) special issue on time. The issue of time perspective is important at both the individual and organizational levels. Individuals and organizations have to survive in the short term; otherwise, there is no long term. But focusing only on "today," without regard for long-term consequences—whether these consequences are the result of failing to upgrade one's job skills or failing to fund R&D—can be disastrous. We need to know much more about how people balance short- and long-term considerations when making decisions.

A second issue, related to time perspective, is that of how people and organizational leaders prioritize their goals and values and the consequences of different types of priorities. Every decision one makes is a choice between alternatives; the decision to do x today may mean the need to postpone y until another time. We know very little about how employees and organizational leaders actually do this, and even less about what makes some people better at it, in terms of positive decision outcomes, than others.

A third issue that needs to be addressed in the field of work motivation is that of definitions. Locke (2003) has noted elsewhere that researchers tend to be careless about how—and whether—they define their terms. Even the term *motivation* is not always used clearly. For example, in the OB literature and I/O psychology literature, the term may refer to either job satisfaction or the motivation to perform, even though satisfaction versus choice, effort, and persistence are not the same phenomena, do not necessarily have the same causes or effects, and may not affect one another. At other times, key concepts are not defined at all. Whole books or chapters have been written on the subjects of emotions or justice or stress, without these terms being defined. When definitions are provided, they may be riddled with excess verbiage or nonessentials. Sometimes definitions are not justifiable, as when inanimate objects such as work equipment are claimed to possess efficacy, which is a psychological experience. The failure to define terms in a clear and valid way stifles cognitive clarity and, therefore, progress in the field of work motivation. A good project for someone would be to develop a glossary of valid definitions of motivational concepts.

The use of clinical approaches and introspection could be very useful in identifying the factors that make for effective balancing of short- and long-term considerations and effective prioritizing and in enabling investigators to formulate valid definitions. Of course, many additional topics in work motivation can be studied. There is no limit to the number of new ideas that can be explored. New discoveries are simply a matter of the researcher's creative imagination and passionate love of the work (Amabile, 2000).

REFERENCES

Adams, J. S. 1963. Toward an understanding of iniquity. *Journal of Abnormal Psychology,* 67: 422–436.

Adler, S., & Weiss, H. M. 1988. Recent developments in the study of personality and organizational behavior. In C. L. Cooper & I. T. Robertson (Eds.), *International review of industrial and organizational psychology:* 307–330. Oxford: Wiley.

Amabile, T. 2000. Stimulate creativity by fueling passion. In E. Locke (Ed.), *Handbook of principles of organizational behavior:* 331–341. Maiden, MA: Blackwell.

Argyris, C. 1957. *Personality and organization.* New York: Harper & Row.

Audia, G., Locke, E., & Smith, K. G. 2000. The paradox of success: An archival and a laboratory study of strategic persistence following a radical environmental change. *Academy of Management Journal,* 43: 837–853.

Bandura, A. 1986. *Social foundations of thought and action: A social-cognitive theory.* Englewood Cliffs, NJ: Prentice-Hall.

Bandura, A. 1997. *Self-efficacy: The exercise of control.* New York: Freeman.

Bargh, J., Gollwitzer, P., Lee-Chai, A., Barndollar, K., & Troetschel, R. 2001. The automated will: Nonconscious activation and pursuit of behavioral goals. *Journal of Personality and Social Psychology,* 81: 1014–1027.

Barrick, M., & Mount, M. 2000. Select on conscientiousness and emotional stability. In E. Locke (Ed.), *Handbook of principles of organizational behavior:* 15–28. Malden, MA: Blackwell.

Beach, L. 1990. *Image theory: Decision making in personal and organizational contexts.* Chichester, UK: Wiley.

Beck, A. 1967. *Depression: Causes and treatment.* Philadelphia: University of Pennsylvania Press.

Beck, A., Rush, A., Shaw, B., & Emery, G. 1979. *Cognitive therapy of depression.* New York: Guilford Press.

Beer, M. 2000. Lead organizational change by creating dissatisfaction and realigning the organization with new competitive realities. In E. Locke (Ed.), *Handbook of principles of organizational behavior:* 370–386. Maiden, MA: Blackwell.

Binswanger, H. 1991. Volition as cognitive self-regulation. *Organizational Behavior and Human Decision Processes,* 50: 154–178.

Collins, C., Hanges, P., & Locke, E. 2004. The relationship of need for achievement to entrepreneurial behavior: A meta-analysis. *Human Performance,* 17 (1), 95–117

Donaldson, L. 2000. Design structure to fit strategy. In E. Locke (Ed.), *Handbook of principles of organizational behavior:* 291–303. Malden, MA: Blackwell.

Dweck, C. 1986. Motivational processes affecting learning. *American Psychologist,* 41(Special Issue): 1040–1048.

Dweck, C., & Elliott, E. 1983. Achievement motivation. In P. Mussenand & E. Hetherington (Eds.), *Handbook of child psychology:* 643–691. New York: Wiley.

Earley, C., & Perry, B. 1987. Work plan availability and performance: An assessment of task strategy priming on subsequent task completion. *Organizational Behavior and Human Decision Processes,* 39: 279–302.

Elliott, E., & Dweck, C. 1988. Goals: An approach to motivation and achievement. *Journal of Personality and Social Psychology,* 54: 5–12.

Erez, M. 2000. Make management practice fit national culture. In E. Locke (Ed.), *Handbook of principles of organizational behavior:* 418–434. Malden, MA: Blackwell.

Ericcson, K., & Simon, H. 1980. Verbal reports as data. *Psychological Review,* 87: 215–251.

Flanagan, J. C. 1954. The critical incident technique. *Psychological Bulletin,* 51: 327–358.

Frayne, C., & Latham, G. 1987. The application of social learning theory to employee self-management of attendance. *Journal of Applied Psychology,* 72: 387–392.

Greenberg, J. 2000. Promote procedural justice to enhance the acceptance of work outcomes. In E. Locke (Ed.), *Handbook of principles of organizational behavior:* 181–195. Maiden, MA: Blackwell.

Haaga, D., Dyck, M., & Ernst, D. 1991. Empirical status of cognitive theory of depression. *Psychological Bulletin,* 110: 215–236.

Hackman, R., & Oldham, G. 1980. *Work redesign.* Reading, MA: Addison-Wesley.

Herzberg, F., Mausner, B., & Snyderman, B. 1959. *The motivation to work.* New York: Wiley.

Judge, T., Bono, J., Tippie, H., Erez, A., Locke, E., & Thoreson, C. 2002. The scientific merit of valid measures of general concepts: Personality research and core self-evaluation. In J. Brett & F. Drasgow (Eds.), *The psychology of work: Theoretically based empirical research:* 55–77. Mahwah, NJ: Lawrence Erlbaum Associates.

Judge, T., Thoreson, C., Bono, J., & Patton, G. 2001. The job satisfaction-job performance relationship: A qualitative and quantitative review. *Psychological Bulletin,* 127: 376–407.

Kanfer, R., & Ackerman, P. L. 1989. Motivation and cognitive abilities: An integrative/aptitude treatment interaction approach to skill acquisition. *Journal of Applied Psychology,* 74: 657–690.

Karau, S., & Williams, K. 2001. Understanding individual motivation in groups: The collective effort model. In M. Turner (Ed.), *Groups at work: Theory and research:* 113–141. Mahwah, NJ: Lawrence Erlbaum Associates.

Knight, D., Durham, C., & Locke, E. 2001. The relationship of team goals, incentives, and efficacy to strategic risk, tactical implementation, and performance. *Academy of Management Journal,* 44: 326–338.

Latham, G. 2000. Motivate employee performance through goal setting. In E. Locke (Ed.), *Handbook of principles of organizational behavior:* 107–119. Malden, MA: Oxford University Press.

Latham, G., & Frayne, C. 1989. Self-management training for increasing job attendance: A follow-up and a replication. *Journal of Applied Psychology.* 74: 411–416.

Latham, G., & Heslin, P. 2003. Lessons from clinical psychology for I/O psychology. *Canadian Psychology,* 44: 218–231.

Lazarus, R., & Folkman, S. 1984. *Stress, appraisal & coping.* New York: Springer.

Lilienfeld, S., Wood, J., & Garb, H. 2000. The scientific status of projective techniques. *Psychological Science in the Public Interest,* 1: 27–66.

Locke, E. 1977. The myths of behavior mod in organization. *Academy of Management Review,* 3: 594–601.

Locke, E. 1997. The motivation to work: What we know. In M. Maehr & P. Pintrich (Eds.), *Advances in motivation and achievement,* vol. 10: 375–412. Greenwich, CT: JAI Press.

Locke, E. 2000a. *Handbook of principles of organizational behavior.* Malden, MA: Blackwell.

Locke, E. 2000b. Motivation, cognition and action: An analysis of studies of task goals and knowledge. *Applied Psychology: An International Review,* 49: 408–429.

Locke, E. 2001. Self-set goals and self-efficacy as mediators of incentives and personality. In M. Erez, U. Kleinbeck, & H. Thierry (Eds.), *Work motivation in the context of a globalizing economy:* 13–26. Mahwah, NJ: Lawrence Erlbaum Associates.

Locke, E. 2002. The epistemological side of teaching management: Teaching through principles. *Academy of Management Learning and Education,* 2: 195–205.

Locke, E. 2003. Good definitions: The epistemological foundation of scientific progress. In J. Greenberg (Ed.), *Organizational behavior, state of the science:* 415–444. Mahwah, NJ: Lawrence Erlbaum Associates.

Locke, E., Alavi, M., & Wagner, J. 1997. Participation in decision-making: An information exchange perspective. In G. Ferris (Ed.), *Research in personal and human resources management,* vol. 15: 293–331. Greenwich, CT: JAI Press.

Locke, E., & Latham, G. 1990. *A theory of goal setting and task performance.* Englewood Cliffs, NJ: Prentice-Hall.

Locke, E., & Latham, G. 2002. Building a practically useful theory of goal setting and task motivation: A 35-year odyssey. *American Psychologist,* 57: 705–717.

Lord, R., & Hanges, P. 1987. A control system model of organizational motivation: Theoretical development and applied implications. *Behavioral Science,* 32: 161–178.

Luthans, F., & Kreitner, R. 1975. *Organizational behavior modification.* Glenview, IL: Scott, Foresman.

McClelland, D., Atkinson, R., Clark, R., & Lowell, E. 1953. *The achievement motive.* New York: Appleton-Century-Crofts.

McClelland, D., & Winter, D. 1969. *Motivating economic achievement.* New York: Free Press.

Meichenbaum, D. 1977. *Cognitive behavior modification: An integrative approach.* New York: Plenum Press.

Miller, G. A. 1956. The magical number seven, plus or minus two: Some limits on our capacity for processing information. *Psychological Review,* 63: 81–97.

Millman, Z., & Latham, G. P. 2001. Increasing reemployment through training in verbal self-guidance. In M. Erez, U. Kleinbeck, & H. K. Thierry (Eds.), *Work motivation in the context of a globalizing economy:* 87–97. Mahwah, NJ: Lawrence Erlbaum Associates.

Miner, J. 2002. *Organizational behavior theory.* New York: Oxford University Press.

Miner, J., Smith, N., & Bracker, J. 1994. Role of entrepreneurial task motivation in the growth of technologically innovative firms: Interpretations from follow-up data. *Journal of Applied Psychology,* 79: 627–630.

Mone, M. A. 1994. Comparative validity of two measures of self-efficacy in predicting academic goals and performance. *Educational and Psychological Measurement,* 54: 516–529.

Mueller, C. M., Dweck, C. S. 1998. Praise for intelligence can undermine children's motivation and performance. *Journal of Personality and Social Psychology,* 75: 33–52.

Murphy, S. T. 2001. Feeling without thinking: Affective primary and the nonconscious processing of emotion. In J. A. Bargh & D. K. Apsley (Eds.), *Unraveling the complexities of social life: A festschrift in honor of Robert B. Zajonc*: 39–53. Washington, DC: American Psychological Association.

Peterson, C., Semmel, A., von Baeyer, C., Abramson, L. Y., Metalsky, G. I., & Seligman, M. E. P. 1982. The Attributional Style Questionnaire. *Cognitive Therapy and Research*, 6: 287–299.

Roethlisberger, F., & Dickson, W. 1939. *Management and the worker*. Cambridge, MA: Harvard University Press.

Schmidt, F. 1992. What do data really mean? Research findings, meta-analysis, and cumulative knowledge in psychology. *American Psychologist*, 47: 1171–1181.

Schmidt, F., Hunter, J., & Outerbridge, A. 1986. The impact of job experience and ability on job knowledge, work sample performance, and supervisory ratings of job performance. *Journal of Applied Psychology*, 71: 432–439.

Schneider, S., & Lopes, L. 1986. Reflection in preferences under risk: Who and when may suggest why. *Journal of Experimental Psychology: Human Perception and Performance*, 12: 535–548.

Schulman, P. 1999. Applying learned optimism to increase sales productivity. *Journal of Personal Selling and Sales Management*, 19(1): 31–37.

Schweiger, D., Anderson, C., & Locke, E. 1985. Complex decision-making: A longitudinal study of process and performance. *Organizational Behavior and Human Performance*, 36: 245–272.

Seijts, G. H., Latham, G. P., Tasa, K., & Latham, B. W. 2004. In press. Goal setting and goal orientation: An integration of two different yet related literatures. *Academy of Management Journal*, 47 (2), 227–239.

Seligman, M. E. P. 1968. Chronic fear produced by unpredictable electric shock. *Journal of Comparative and Physiological Psychology*, 66: 402–411.

Seligman, M. E. P. 1998a. The prediction and prevention of depression. In D. K. Routh & R. J. DeRubeis (Eds.), *The science of clinical psychology: Accomplishments and future directions*: 201–214. Washington, DC: American Psychological Association.

Seligman, M. E. P. 1998b. *Learned optimism*. New York: Knopf.

Seligman, M. E. P., & Csikszentmihalyi, M. 2000. Positive psychology: An introduction. *American Psychologist*, 55: 5–14.

Seligman, M. E. P., & Schulman, P. 1986. Explanatory style as a predictor of productivity and quitting among life insurance sales agents. *Journal of Personality and Social Psychology*, 50: 832–838.

Simon, H. A. 1976. *Administrative behavior: A study of decision-making processes in administrative organizations*. New York: Free Press.

Strutton, D., & Lumpkin, J. 1992. Relationship between optimism and coping strategies in the work environment. *Psychological Reports*, 71: 1179–1186.

Tracy, K., Locke, E., & Renard, M. 1999. *Conscious goal setting versus subconscious motives: Longitudinal and concurrent effects on the performance of entrepreneurial firms*. Paper presented at the annual meeting of the Academy of Management, Chicago.

VandeWalle, D., Cron, W. L., & Slocum, J. W. 2001. The role of goal orientation following performance feedback. *Journal of Applied Psychology*, 86: 629–640.

Vroom, V. 1964. *Work and motivation*. New York: Wiley.

Wegge, J., & Dibbelt, S. 2000. Effects of goal setting or information processing in letter-matching tasks. *Zeitschrift fuer Experimentelle Psychologie*, 47: 89–114.

Wegner, D., & Wheatley, T. 1999. Apparent mental causation: Sources of the experience of will. *American Psychologist*, 54: 480–492.

Weiner, B. 1986. *An attributional theory of motivation and emotion*. New York: Springer-Verlag.

Weingart, L., & Jehn, K. 2000. Manage team conflict through collaboration. In E. Locke (Ed.), *Handbook of principles of organizational behavior*: 226–238. Malden, MA: Blackwell.

Individuals in Teams and Groups

Orchestras consist of individual musicians who must work together effectively in sections—a wind section, a brass section, and a string section, among others. Great musicians don't necessarily produce great orchestral music. Individuals must be molded into cohesive teams that have a common mission and an understanding and appreciation of what the conductor (formal leader) and the other musicians (individuals) and sections (groups or teams) will be doing at all moments in a performance. Orchestras need highly talented individuals who are also "team players."

This tension between individualism and organizational needs is a core issue for all work groups and teams. Membership in a group always involves a willingness to subsume some individualism for the benefit of an organization's larger purposes. In this chapter, we focus on how organizations accomplish their purposes by blending the skills and creativity of individuals into effective efforts of groups and networks of groups.

People are social beings at work as well as at play. We form and associate in groups, and groups create their own norms, values, sentiments, membership criteria, roles, and aspirations. Most work groups also develop shared beliefs and attitudes about things such as the nature of the relationship between members and their employing organization, expectations about levels of work output and pay, what it takes to get ahead, and positive and negative consequences of trusting the organization or exhibiting loyalty to it.

Deciding whether to become a member of a group usually poses an *approach-avoidance conflict* for people. Joining has positive and negative connotations. Groups help people satisfy their desire for affiliation and their need for belonging. People working with and near each other form bonds—relationships—of friendship, camaraderie, and conversation. Yet group membership always requires relinquishing some individuality—personal identity and freedom of behavior—at least temporarily. Although groups vary, most demand some degree of conforming behavior and acquiescence to claims made by other members or by the group as one price of membership and thus for satisfying affiliation wants. Thus, decisions to join groups at work often are made with tentativeness and feelings of ambiguity.

The formation of groups in the workplace is more than just a way for people to satisfy their desires for affiliation. Ever since the days of the Industrial Revolution, workplace organizations have been constructed on the foundation principles of *specialization* and *division of labor* (Smith, 1776). In our complex organizations of today, few jobs can be done from start to finish by one person. Specialization allows an organization to use people's skills and efforts more systematically and to focus their knowledge and energy on a limited number of tasks. Employee learning curves are minimized.

With division of labor, people who perform a set of specialized functions are organizationally clustered in work groups, work groups in units or branches, branches in divisions or departments, divisions in companies or agencies, and so forth. Work groups attract people with like backgrounds; for example, professional training, socialization, and experience as accountants, teachers, production managers, or human resources managers; or, perhaps, people from similar sociodemographic backgrounds, for example, from old-line New England families or particular ethnic groups. All such shared backgrounds involve the socialization of people into common value/belief/behavior systems. We learn how to think and act like doctors, teachers, accountants, or credit managers, and like Texans, New Yorkers, or Southern Californians.

Virtually all groups, and particularly purposeful, specialized, organizational groups, develop their own sets of norms (behavioral rules), values, stories, heroes, sagas, legends, myths, beliefs about their realities, and assumptions about things like the nature of their organizational environment and appropriate relations with other groups. When a group becomes institutionalized in an organization, such as a production unit or a branch office, their shared beliefs, values, and assumptions become the essence of an organizational subculture (Martin & Siehl, 1983). Most group subcultures have a resemblance to the overall organizational culture but also contain unique elements that form through the impact of events, circumstances, and personalities, including (Ott, 1989):

- The nature or type of business in which the organization is engaged.
- The *psychological script* or basic personality of the founder or other dominant early leaders.
- The general culture of the society in which the organization is located.

A specific group subculture develops from the learning members accumulate through their shared successes and failures in solving problems that threatened the survival of the group and its identity or independence (Schein, 2004).

Putting aside the question of why work groups have at least partially unique subcultures, the fact remains that they usually are distinctive. Then, considering the normal loyalties that groups demand and the affiliational needs they meet, it becomes easy to understand why *in-groups* and *out-groups* and feelings of *we* and *they* and *we* versus *they* are so characteristic of life in organizations.

Group dynamics is a subfield of organizational behavior "dedicated to achieving knowledge about the nature of groups, the laws of their development, and their interrelations with individuals, other groups, and larger institutions" (Cartwright & Zander, 1968). Kurt Lewin, perhaps the most influential social psychologist of the 20th century, is widely credited with creating and naming this field for which he was a leading contributor.

Lewin's (1943, 1947, 1951, 1952) group dynamics perspective falls under the general heading *field theory*, which holds that a person's behavior is a function of the individual and her or his immediate environment—the group and the organizational context. (Excerpts from Lewin's chapter, "Group Decision and Social Change," are reprinted in Chapter 6.) For much of the decade of the 1940s, Lewin and his associates at the Massachusetts Institute of Technology's Research Center for Group Dynamics introduced concepts like *fields*, *force fields*, and *field forces* into the study of human behavior, focusing on variables such as resistance to change and the effects of leadership on group performance. Perhaps Lewin's greatest single contribution, however, was to move the focus of behavioral theory and research from individuals to groups.

But the field of group dynamics has consisted of far more than Kurt Lewin's concepts. It has represented the first comprehensive pulling together of theories, research methods, and empirical findings from myriad social sciences. It is the acquisition of "knowledge about the ... psychological and social forces associated with groups.... It refers to a field of inquiry dedicated to achieving knowledge about the nature of groups, the laws of their development, and their interrelations with individuals, other groups, and larger institutions" (Cartwright & Zander, 1968, p. 9). Group dynamics is the accumulated contributions of many pioneering social scientists including R. F. Bales (1950), Dorwin Cartwright and Alvin Zander (1968), George Homans (1950), Jake Moreno (1934), T. M. Newcomb (1943), M. Sherif (1936), and William F. Whyte (1943, 1948).

Although definitions of a *group* vary, there is less disagreement here than there is about definitions of most other concepts of organizational behavior, such as *leader* and *motivation*. Usually, the term *group* refers to what is more technically known as a *primary group*—a group small enough to permit face-to-face interaction among its members and which remains in existence long enough for some personal relations, sentiments, and feelings of identification or belongingness to develop. Schein (1980, p. 145) uses the term *psychological*

Power structures

group: "Any number of people who [1] interact with one another, [2] are psychologically aware of one another, and [3] perceive themselves to be a group." Over the years, many labels have been used to describe different types of groups, but for understanding organizational behavior, the most important types of groups probably are these (Ivancevich & Matteson, 2002, pp. 314–316):

- *Formal groups:* Groups that are formally sanctioned, usually for the purpose of accomplishing tasks. Employees are assigned to formal groups based on their position in an organization. There are two basic types of formal groups:
  - *Command groups:* Formal groups that are specified in an organization chart—groups that include supervisors and the people who report directly to them. Groups of this type are the *building blocks* of organization structure: for example, a production work group, the staff of a small branch office, a product marketing group, or a military flight crew.
  - *Task groups:* Formally sanctioned task-oriented groups with short lives. Employees who work together to complete a particular project or task, such as solving a problem or capitalizing on a specific opportunity, and then are disbanded. Examples include task forces and committees.
- *Informal groups:* Natural groupings of people in the work situation. People who associate voluntarily, primarily to satisfy social needs. Although informal groups at work may have goals and tasks (for example, ethnic support groups, investment clubs, and luncheon bridge groups), their primary reasons for existence are friendship, affiliation, and shared interests. Although informal groups seldom are formally sanctioned, they are extremely important to the working of organizations. Their norms, values, beliefs, and expectations have significant impacts on work-related behavior and attitudes.

Groups in organizations of all types are of high importance and interest to students and practitioners of organizational behavior, both for what happens *in* them (and why) and what happens *between* them (Cohen & Fink, 2003). Thus, this chapter contains seven important readings about work groups and teams. In addition to several "classic" readings about group dynamics from the 1960s, 1970s, 1980s, and 1990s, we introduce three topics that have moved from the margin to a central place in the literature of the 1990s and 2000s: diversity, self-directed work teams, and virtual teams. We trust you will find both the older and newer readings interesting and useful.

DYNAMICS IN GROUPS

Dorwin Cartwright and Alvin Zander's contribution here is their chapter "Origins of Group Dynamics" from the landmark volume, *Group Dynamics* (1968). Cartwright and Zander define group dynamics as "a field of inquiry dedicated to advancing knowledge about the nature of groups, the laws of their development, and their interrelations with individuals, other groups, and larger institutions." The distinguishing characteristics of group dynamics— what separates group dynamics from numerous other groups of behavioral sciences that have investigated groups over the years—are these:

1. Emphasis on theoretically significant empirical research; conceptual theories and personal observations are not adequate.
2. Interest in the dynamics and interdependence of phenomena; the dynamics are more important than static elements, single-variable theories, and structural schemes.
3. Broad interdisciplinary relevance; the importance of incorporating methods and knowledge from all of the social sciences, including sociology, psychology, and cultural anthropology.
4. Potential applicability of its findings in efforts to improve the functioning of groups and their consequences on individuals and society; the results must be useful in social practice.

"Origins of Group Dynamics" provides a thorough analysis of the historical development of the field, including the positive impetus provided by advancements in other professions, most notably group psychotherapy, education, and social group work, and social research techniques such as controlled observation and sociometry. Cartwright and Zander are *the* premier chroniclers of group dynamics, and "Origins of Group Dynamics" remains the outstanding overview of this field.

INTERGROUP DYNAMICS

Robert Blake, Herb Shepard, and Jane Mouton's chapter, "Foundations and Dynamics of Intergroup Behavior" (1964, reprinted here), approaches conflict within and among groups. Blake, Shepard, and Mouton identify sets of forces that affect behavior between two or more members of an organization: formal roles and responsibilities, personal backgrounds, and the roles they feel themselves to be in as representatives of particular groups in the organization. This three-forces framework is used to distinguish between conflict in organizations caused by personal matters and conflict caused by intergroup matters. The authors offer three alternative sets of assumptions about intergroup disagreement and discuss strategies for managing disagreement under each: (1) disagreement is inevitable and permanent, (2) conflict can be avoided since interdependence between groups is unnecessary, and (3) agreement and maintaining interdependence is possible.

In "An Intergroup Perspective on Group Dynamics" (1987, included in this chapter), Clayton P. Alderfer proposes a theory of intergroup relations that incorporates individual, interpersonal, group, intergroup, and organizational relations interpretations. Alderfer argues that an intergroup perspective "can explain a broader range of phenomena than just what go on at the intersection of two or more groups." His theory relates the status of intergroup relations to the larger organizational system in which groups are embedded. It has application in a wide variety of organizational problems and opportunities, including "the development of effective work teams, the definition and management of organizational culture, the analysis and implementation of affirmative action, and the teaching of organizational behavior in management schools."

In "Why Teams: Leading to the High-Performance Organization" (reprinted here), Jon R. Katzenbach and Douglas K. Smith explain that there is far more to the "wisdom of teams" than they had expected when setting out to write their landmark 1993 book, *The Wisdom of Teams*. For example, teamwork is indeed desirable, but it needs to be seen as a means not an end. "Performance is the crux of the matter for teams," and when it is, any team "will deliver results well beyond what individuals acting alone in nonteamworking situations could achieve." The strong emphasis on individualism in the United States can destroy the potential of teams, but it shouldn't, and doesn't need to. Effective organizations use a carefully blended mix of individual and team performance approaches to enhance performance.

Katzenbach and Smith identify three widespread sources of reluctance to the use of teams in organizations: "a lack of conviction that a team or teams can work better than other alternatives; personal styles, capabilities, and preferences that make teams risky or uncomfortable; and weak organizational performance ethics that discourage the conditions in which teams flourish." They also discuss the characteristics of teams in high-performance organizations— "where the best companies are headed." They conclude with predictions that "future organization designs will seek structures simpler and more flexible than the heavily layered command-and-control hierarchies that have dominated the twentieth century.... [and] they ... emphasize teams as the key performance unit of the company."

TEAMS AND DIVERSITY

"A Diversity Framework" (1995) by Roosevelt Thomas, reprinted here, introduces a strategic diversity management framework for decision making in organizations. This framework is intended to assist individuals in organizations with managing change, and with the integration and coordination of work processes. In this article, Thomas argues that diversity is not simply an issue to be considered within the context of the workplace, but is instead something that should be clearly understood and incorporated into all aspects of our lives, and encourages the reader to focus more on diversity in thinking and behavior rather than in racial representation.

TEAMS AND TEAMWORK

Productivity in private and public sector organizations has become the overriding issue in corporate boardrooms as well as in the legislative corridors of power. Virtually all of the "new" approaches to management being advocated—the attempts to find solutions to the "productivity problem"—have blended traditional and experimental management methods with new forms of employee involvement and participative management. For the past several decades we have witnessed a never-ending series of "new" management approaches, particularly approaches that emphasize organizational flexibility through the development and empowerment of individuals and work groups.

"Japanese management," with its long-term commitment to employees and its emphasis on communications through quality circles (Ouchi, 1981; Pascale & Athos, 1981), was the first major participative/empowerment approach to emerge clearly from the post–World War II Japanese industrial experience. In the 1970s, impressive productivity gains were attributed primarily to highly goal-oriented group activity within organizations (Hyde, 1991). For the most part, quality circles—voluntary work groups that attempt to recommend solutions to organizational problems—have been merged into and given way to successively more comprehensive management approaches, including for example:

- The "search for excellence" (Peters & Waterman, 1982)
- The "M-form society" (Ouchi, 1984)
- "Total quality management" or "TQM" (Crosby, 1984; Deming, 1986, 1993; Juran, 1992)
- "Reinventing government" (Gore, 1993; Osborne & Gaebler, 1992)
- "Sociotechnical systems" or "Quality of Work Life (QWL)" (Weisbord, 1991)
- "Productivity management" (Hyde, 1991; MIT Commission on Industrial Productivity, 1989)
- "Organizational architecture" (Nadler, Gerstein, & Shaw, 1992)
- "Reengineering," "process reengineering," or "business reengineering" (Hammer & Champy, 1993)

These management approaches share many common elements but also differ in emphasis, assumptions, and specific methods—as well as in their commitment to individual and work team empowerment. For example, *reengineering* represents a radical change strategy, not an incremental "grassroots" employee involvement approach. Reengineering literally means what its name implies. "When someone asks us for a quick definition of business reengineering, we say that it means 'starting over.' It *doesn't* mean tinkering with what already exists or making incremental changes that leave basic structures intact. . . . It involves going back to the beginning and inventing a better way of doing work" (Hammer & Champy, 1993, p. 31).

In contrast to reengineering, Quality of Work Life (QWL) and Total Quality Management (TQM) had as their central themes dignity, meaning of work and life, and community in the workplace. "We hunger for community in the workplace and are a great deal more productive when we find it. To feed this hunger in ways that preserve democratic values of individual dignity, opportunity for all, and mutual support is to harness energy and productivity beyond imagining" (Weisbord, 1991, p. xiv).

"Organizational architecture," an approach that has used physical architecture as an analogy for how managers should manage, falls between process reengineering and QWL. Principles of architecture that are applicable to this new-style management of organizations include (Gerstein, 1992, pp. 14, 15):

- Architecture is a "practical art." "Ordinary people" are its consumers. Because people have to work and live in that which is created, the ultimate test of any architecture is its utility measured in human terms.
- Architecture provides a framework for the conduct of life, not a specification for what that life should be. Architecture should facilitate, guide, and provide a context; it should not provide a blueprint for conduct.
- Unlike a painting that is produced by a single artist, architecture is produced by large numbers of people working together to achieve the vision of the architect.

Organizational architecture can be seen as the art of forming organizational space to meet human needs and aspirations. "Organizational architects work in the 'behavioral space' ... creating opportunities for action, which we often call *empowerment*, and creating constraints to action which are central to the organizational architect's job" (Gerstein, 1992, p. 15). Thus, proponents of organizational architecture use principles from applied physical sciences and art with relation to the empowerment—and steering—of work teams and individuals.

Despite their differences, process reengineering, organizational architecture, QWL and TQM all share common elements, including an acknowledged need for organizations to be more flexible and innovative, recognition that people who actually do the work are the most knowledgeable about it and often have the best ideas about how to improve it, and an unwavering belief that major productivity gains cannot be achieved in bureaucracies that are top heavy with rules and administrators.

Virtually all of these flexibility- and productivity-increasing management approaches assume that groups provide individuals with opportunities for personal and professional growth and development, self-expression and creativity, and work satisfaction. They also assume that these opportunities cannot become available to workers in traditional hierarchical organizations. Also essential to the approaches, however, is the assumption that groups can and will provide structure and discipline for individuals at work. Therefore, organizations that permit empowerment do not need multiple levels and layers of supervisors and managers to coordinate, control, and monitor production and the behavior of individual workers. Work groups can and will accept responsibility for their processes and products—as well as the behavior of other group members.

In "The New Self-Directed Work Teams: Mastering the Challenge," reprinted here, Jack Orsburn and Linda Moran (2000) describe a process for creating and using self-directed work teams, and argue that such teams enhance individual commitment, responsibility, and performance, thus increasing the overall responsiveness, productivity, quality, and satisfaction in today's organizations.

VIRTUAL TEAMS

The bureaucratic–hierarchical form of organization developed in the 19th century Industrial Age of Adam Smith, when people had to work in the same physical place in order to be able to communicate and to coordinate work. In the information era of the 21st century, individuals in organizations often are not in the same location—or the same city, state, or country. In "Can Absence Make a Team Grow Stronger?" (2004), reprinted here, Ann Majchrzak, Arvind Malhotra, Jeffrey Stamps and Jessica Lipnack explore virtual teams—teams of individuals who may be dispersed around the globe and never meet face-to-face, but who work through telecommunications networks. The authors argue persuasively that high productivity and high-quality outcomes can be achieved "virtually" through careful management of team processes, dynamics, leadership, and effective use of technology. Effective virtual teams, however, require special attention and support.

REFERENCES

Alderfer, C. P. (1987). An intergroup perspective on group dynamics. In J. W. Lorsch (Ed.), *Handbook of organizational behavior* (pp. 190–222). Englewood Cliffs, NJ: Prentice-Hall.

Asch, S. E. (1951). Effects of group pressure upon the modification and distortion of judgments. In H. S. Guetzkow (Ed.), *Groups, leadership, and men* (pp. 177–190). Pittsburgh, PA: Carnegie Press.

Bales, R. F. (1950). *Interaction process analysis: A method for the study of small groups.* Reading, MA: Addison-Wesley.

Bennis, W. G. (1999). The secrets of great groups. In F. Hesselbein & P. M. Cohen (Eds.), *Leader to leader* (pp. 315–322). San Francisco: Jossey-Bass.

Blake, R. R., Shepard, H. A., & Mouton, J. S. (1964). *Managing intergroup conflict in industry.* Houston: Gulf.

Cartwright, D., & Zander, A. (Eds.). (1968). *Group dynamics: Research and theory* (3rd ed.). New York: Harper & Row.

Cobb, A. T. (2006). *Leading project teams: An introduction to the basics of project management and project team leadership.* Thousand Oaks, CA: Sage.

Cohen, A. R., & Fink. (2003). *Effective behavior in organizations* (7th ed.). New York: McGraw-Hill/Irwin.

Crosby, P. B. (1979). *Quality is free.* New York: McGraw-Hill.

Crosby, P. B. (1984). *Quality without tears.* New York: McGraw-Hill.

Davis, S. M., & Lawrence, P. R. (1977). *Matrix.* Reading, MA: Addison-Wesley.

Deming, W. E. (1986). *Out of the crisis.* Cambridge, MA: Massachusetts Institute of Technology Press.

Deming, W. E. (1993). *The new economics.* Cambridge, MA: Massachusetts Institute of Technology Press.

Fink, S. L. (1992). *High commitment workplaces.* New York: Quorum Books.

Gerstein, M. S. (1992). From machine bureaucracies to networked organizations: An architectural journey. In D. A. Nadler, M. S. Gerstein, & R. B. Shaw (Eds.), *Organizational architecture: Designs for changing organizations* (pp. 11–38). San Francisco: Jossey-Bass.

Gore, A. (1993). *The Gore report on reinventing government.* New York: Times Books.

Gouldner, A. (1960). The norm of reciprocity. *American Sociological Review, 25,* 161–178.

Hackman, J. R., & Oldham, G. R. (1980). *Work redesign.* Reading, MA: Addison-Wesley.

Hammer, M., & Champy, J. (1993). *Reengineering the corporation.* New York: HarperCollins.

Homans, G. C. (1950). *The human group.* New York: Harcourt Brace.

Hyde, A. C. (1991). Productivity management for public sector organizations. In J. S. Ott, A. C. Hyde, & J. M. Shafritz (Eds.), *Public management: The essential readings.* Chicago: Nelson-Hall.

Ivancevich, J. M., & Matteson, M. T. (2002). *Organizational behavior and management* (6th ed.). Homewood, IL: Irwin.

Janis, I. L. (1971, November). Groupthink. *Psychology Today,* 44–76.

Juran, J. M. (1992). *Juran on quality by design.* New York: The Free Press.

Juran, J. M., & Gryna, F. M. (Eds.). (1988). *Juran's quality control handbook* (4th ed.). New York: McGraw-Hill.

Kalliola, S. (2003). Self-designed teams in improving public sector performance and quality of working life. *Public Performance & Management Review, 27*(2), 110–122.

Katzenbach, J. R., & Smith, D. K. (1993). *The wisdom of teams: Creating the high-performance organization.* Boston: Harvard Business School Press.

Konopaske, R., & Ivancevich, J. M. (2004). *Global management and organizational behaviour.* New York: McGraw-Hill/Irwin.

Lawler, E. E. III, Mohrman, S. A., and Ledford, G. E., Jr. (1992). *Employee involvement and total quality management.* San Francisco: Jossey-Bass.

Lewin, K. (1943). Forces behind food habits and methods of change. *Bulletin of the National Research Council, 108,* 35–65.

Lewin, K. (1947, June). Frontiers in group dynamics: Concept, method and reality in social science; Social equilibria and social change. *Human Relations, 1*(1).

Lewin, K. (1951). *Field theory in social science.* New York: Harper & Row.

Lewin, K. (1952). Group decision and social change. In G. E. Swanson, T. N. Newcomb, & E. L. Hartley (Eds.), *Reading in social psychology* (rev. ed., pp. 207–211). New York: Holt, Rinehart & Winston.

Lindzey, G. W. (Ed.). (1954). *The handbook of social psychology.* Cambridge, MA: Addison-Wesley.

Majchrzak, A., Malhotra, A., Stamps, J., & Lipnack, J. (2004). Can absence make a team grow stronger? *Harvard Business Review, 82*(5).

Marrow, A. J. (1969). *The practical theorist: The life and work of Kurt Lewin.* New York: Basic Books.

Martin, J., & Siehl, C. (1983, Autumn). Organizational culture and counterculture: An uneasy symbiosis. *Organizational Dynamics,* 52–64.

MIT Commission on Industrial Productivity. (1989). *Made in America: Regaining the productive edge.* Cambridge, MA: Massachusetts Institute of Technology Press.

Mitroff, I. I. (1987). *Business not as usual.* San Francisco: Jossey-Bass.

Moreno, J. L. (1934). *Who shall survive? A new approach to human interrelations.* Washington, DC: Nervous and Mental Disease Publishing.

Nadler, D. A., Gerstein, M. S., & Shaw, R. B. (Eds.). (1992). *Organizational architecture: Designs for changing organizations.* San Francisco: Jossey-Bass.

Newcomb, T. M. (1943). *Personality and social change.* New York: Dryden.

Orsburn, J., & Moran, L. (2000). *The new self-directed work teams: Mastering the challenge.* New York: McGraw-Hill.

Osborne, D., & Gaebler, T. (1992). *Reinventing government.* Reading, MA: Addison-Wesley.

Ott, J. S. (1989). *The organizational culture perspective.* Belmont, CA: Wadsworth.

Ouchi, W. G. (1981). *Theory Z: How American business can meet the Japanese challenge.* Reading, MA: Addison-Wesley.

Ouchi, W. (1984, July/August). M-form: Making decisions and building consensus. *Challenge, 27*(3).

Pascale, R. T., & Athos, A. G. (1981). *The art of Japanese management.* New York: Simon & Schuster.

Peters, T. J., & Waterman, R. H., Jr. (1982). *In search of excellence.* New York: Harper & Row.

Pfeffer, J. (1981). *Power in organizations.* Boston: Pitman Publishing.

Pondy, L. R. (1967). Organizational conflict: Concepts and models. *Administrative Science Quarterly, 12,* 296–320.

Putnam, R. D. (2000). *Bowling alone: The collapse and revival of American community.* New York: Simon & Schuster.

Roy, D. F. (1960). "Banana time": Job satisfaction and informal interaction. *Human Organization, 18,* 158–168.

Schein, E. H. (1980). *Organizational psychology* (3rd ed.). Englewood Cliffs, NJ: Prentice-Hall.

Schein, E. H. (2004). *Organizational culture and leadership* (3rd ed.). San Francisco: Jossey-Bass/John Wiley.

Seashore, S. E. (1954). *Group cohesiveness in the industrial work group.* Ann Arbor: University of Michigan Press.

Shafritz, J. M., Ott, J. S., & Jang, Y. S. (Eds.). (2005). *Classics of organization theory* (6th ed.). Belmont, CA: Wadsworth-Thomson.

Sherif, M. (1936). *The psychology of social norms.* New York: Harper.

Sherif, M., Harvey, O. J., White, B. J., & Sherif, C. (1961). *Intergroup conflict and cooperation: The robbers' cave experiment.* Norman, OK: University Book Exchange.

Smith, A. (1776). *The wealth of nations.* New York: E.P. Dutton.

Strauss, G. (1962). Tactics of lateral relationship: The purchasing agent. *Administrative Science Quarterly, 7,* 161–186.

Thibaut, J., & Kelly, H. (1959). *The social psychology of groups.* New York: John Wiley.

Thomas, R. (1995). *A Diversity Framework.* In M. M. Chemmers, S. Oskamp, & M. A. Costanzo (Eds.), *Diversity in organizations: New perspectives for a changing workplace* (pp. 245–262). Thousand Oaks, CA: Sage.

Thorndike, E. L. (1935). *The psychology of wants, interests, and attitudes.* New York: Appleton-Century.

Wageman, R., & Mannix, E. A. (1998). Uses and misuses of power in task-performing teams. In R. M. Kramer & M. A. Neale (Eds.), *Power and influence in organizations* (pp. 261–285). Thousand Oaks, CA: Sage.

Walton, R. E., & Dutton, J. M. (1969, March). The management of interdepartmental conflict: A model and review. *Administrative Science Quarterly, 14*(1).

Walton, R. E., Dutton, J. M, & Fitch, H. G. (1966). A study of conflict in the process, structure, and attitudes of lateral relationships. In A. H. Rubenstein & C. J. Haberstroh (Eds.), *Some theories of organization* (rev. ed., pp. 444–465). Homewood, IL: Richard D. Irwin.

Weisbord, M. R. (1991). *Productive workplaces: Organizing and managing for dignity, meaning, and community.* San Francisco: Jossey-Bass.

Wheelan, S. A. (2005). *Creating effective teams: A guide for members and leaders* (2nd. ed.). Thousand Oaks, CA: Sage.

Whyte, W. F., Jr. (1943). *Street corner society.* Chicago: University of Chicago Press.

Whyte, W. F., Jr. (1948). *Human relations in the restaurant industry.* New York: McGraw-Hill.

Zander, A. (1982). *Making groups effective.* San Francisco: Jossey-Bass.

Zander, A. (1971). *Motives and goals in groups.* New York: Academic Press.

Reading 17	**Foundations and Dynamics of Intergroup Behavior**
	Robert R. Blake, Herbert A. Shepard, and Jane S. Mouton

Behavior at the Interpersonal Level

When a man speaks as a group representative, his behavior is to some extent dictated by the fact that he is a member of that group. In contrast, when a man speaks from the framework of his job responsibilities, he speaks only for himself. In the latter case, disagreement between the parties is a *personal* matter....

Factors Influencing the Resolution of a Dispute When Disagreement Is An Intergroup Matter

Significant differences appear when a person's interactions with another are dictated by his membership in or leadership of a group. Under these conditions, *the individual is not free* in the same sense as the person who acts independently out of job description or rank alone. Now the person's behavior is determined by many additional factors (Sheppard, 1954).

The Dynamics of Group Interplay in Resolution of Disputes

In situations where an individual is interacting with another and both are representatives of groups, additional forces, quite complex, come into play. Acting as an individual, a man is free to change his mind on the basis of new evidence. But as a group representative, if he changes his thinking or position from that of his group's and capitulates to an outside point of view, *he is likely to be perceived by them as a traitor* (Blake, 1959; Blake & Mouton, 1961b). On the other hand, if as a representative, he is able to persuade a representative of the other group to capitulate to his point of view, *his group receives him as a hero*. In other words, when a man is acting as a representative of one group in disagreement with another, the problem is no longer a personal affair. It is an *intergroup* problem. And as such, it can become

a significant factor in accounting for his actions—as we will see.

Group Responsibilities of Individual Members

Often, men are quite aware that they have responsibilities as group representatives as well as individual job responsibilities. But formal organizational practices and attitudes often prevent this awareness from being discussed or from being openly considered.

As an example, consider the situation where the Vice President of sales speaks with the Vice President of operations. Formal organizational theory commonly assumes that each man speaks for himself, out of the background of his individual job and responsibilities. In practice, however, each may be keenly aware that he is representing the goals, values and convictions of his own group, and furthermore, when he speaks for them, he also speaks for himself. When problems between sales and operations seem difficult to resolve, it is not, as a rule, a sign of rigidity, incompetence, or personality conflict (Faris, 1962). Rather, it is more likely to be a product of the complex task of seeking resolutions which will not violate the attitudes, values, and interests of the many other persons that each represents.

Incompatible Group Norms, Goals and Values

Just as formal organizational theory, as written, recognizes only that the individual speaks for himself out of his job responsibilities, similarly it may fail to recognize other facts of organizational life. Formal organization theory assumes that the goals, norms and procedures of different functional groups in the organization are, by definition, similar, complementary or identical....

There is increasing recognition, however, that neither of these circumstances accurately describes

Source: "Individuals in Teams and Groups," from FOUNDATIONS AND DYNAMICS OF INTEGROUP BEHAVIOR by Robert R. Blake, Jane S. Mouton, and Herb Sheperd, Gulf Publishing, 1964. Reprinted by permission of Grid International, Inc.

many situations in modern industrial life. This recognition has led to an acknowledgment that men, in fact, are group representatives within the framework of an organization. In turn, it has led to an awareness and appreciation of how an individual acting as a member, or as a leader, of a group, is confronted with a host of additional problems (Stogdill, 1962). These problems must be dealt with in terms of their genuine complexities if unity of organizational purpose is to be achieved.

The roots of these complex problems which group representatives face are characteristic of groups and of individuals. As will be seen, group membership is complicated further by the characteristics of intergroup relations. After looking briefly at these characteristics of groups, we will turn our attention to the dynamics of intergroup relations.

The Structure and Process of Groups-in-Isolation

5. There are a number of ways of describing the characteristics of groups-in-isolation which we should consider prior to dealing with industrial intergroup relations (Cartwright & Zander, 1960; Sherif & Sherif, 1956).

Regulation of the Interdependent Behavior of Members of Groups-in-Isolation

Fundamentally, a group consists of a number of individuals bound to each other in some stage or degree of interdependence or shared "stake." Their problem is to guarantee the survival of the group in order to attain some *purpose or goal*. Taking for granted that the group's goals are clearly understood by its members, the interdependence among individuals, then, must be regulated to insure partial or entire achievement of these goals.

The Emergence of Group Structure, Leadership and Normative Rules

The need to regulate interdependence leads to three further properties of groups. When these properties emerge in group life they become additional forces which influence individual behavior. Let us look at each of these.

1. *Group Structure.* A differentiation of individual roles often is needed to accomplish group objectives. Differentiation inevitably results in some individuals who have varying degrees of power to influence the actions of others. The result is that some group members carry greater weight than others in determining the direction of group action, it norms, values and attitudes.

2. *Leadership.* When the power system among members of an informal group is crystallized, it is common to speak of *that individual with the most power as the leader.* In some groups, he is boss, or supervisor; other members are subordinates. The leader is looked to by the members for guidance and direction. The power and influence of the leader varies according to his ability to aid the group in achieving its goals (Hamblin, Miller, & Wiggins, 1961). Where the leader is appointed by a more powerful group rather than being selected by his own group, the above generalizations must be qualified. For instance, if the goals of the subordinate group clash with those of the group by which he is appointed, he will be received not as leader, but as a representative of a different group.

3. *Normal Rules Guiding Group Behavior.* Along with the emerging set of power relations is the evolution of a normal set of "rules of the game," which specifies the conditions of interaction between group members. In other words, varying degrees of familiarity, influence, interaction, and other relationships between members are sanctioned by the group according to an individual's role and position in the group hierarchy. Deviations from the rules and procedures by a member can lead to subtle but potent pressures by his fellow members to insure that the deviant "swings back into line" (Hamblin et al., 1961). Such pressures act quite differently on each person as a function of his status and personality, but they do act.

Identification with One's Group

The preceding three characteristics of group formation and operation—goals, leadership, and norms—lead to varying degrees of identification with one's group. When feelings of identification are strong, the group is said to have high morale; it is highly cohesive (Sherif & Sherif, 1956). The opposite is true when feelings of identification with group goals are low. Under circumstances of unacceptable power distribution or inappropriate norms, for example, the result is feelings of low morale, demoralization, low cohesion, or possibly alienation. The greater the sense of identification a member has with his group, the greater are the pressures on him to follow, at times blindly, the direction and will of the group position (Cartwright & Zander, 1953; Gerard, 1954; Kelley & Volkart, 1952).

These are all common properties of organized groups. A representative of a group, whether leader or member, is compelled to acknowledge in some way these group properties as he comes in contact with members of other groups whose interests support or violate those of his own. For a representative to agree to actions which other members feel are contrary to group goals can result in his being seen to have acted in a betraying way, or in poor faith. On the other hand, acting effectively against opposition and in support of group purpose and goals, and consistent with internal norms and values, insures retention or enhancement of his status (Pryer, Flint, & Bass, 1962; Sherif & Sherif, 1956).

The Relationship of the Organization Framework to Individual and Group Relations

The internal properties of a group are only one of the significant matters involved in understanding and managing intergroup relations. When the actions of individuals and groups are viewed within the framework of a complex organization, we can identify additional determinants of behavior (Arensberg, 1951).

A Framework of Interdependent Organizational Subgroups

Consider the following circumstance in a large and complex organization: the total membership of the organization is subdivided into many smaller groups. Each subgroup has its own leadership and its own rules and regulations. Each has its own goals which may or may not be in accord with overall organizational goals (Cooper, 1961). Each operates with its own degree of cohesion which varies with feelings of failure or accomplishment (Wolman, 1960). In an organization, these groups are interdependent with one another. They may be interdependent in performing a complex task requiring coordination of effort, in geographical proximity, or in terms of the reward system of the organization. Differences among them immediately become apparent to members.

12. **Comparison Between Groups.**   Perception of differences between groups leads spontaneously to a comparison and to a "we-they" orientation (Sherif & Sherif, 1956). Attention quickly focuses on similarities and differences. Furthermore, these spontaneous comparisons are intensified by the tendency of higher levels of authority to evaluate and reward by group comparison. For example, group incentive plans, awarding of plaques or other symbols of organization success to the highest selling group, the group with the highest safety record, and so forth, all tend to highlight group differences. Thus, in a sense, "winning" and "losing" groups are held up for all to see. The organization's rationale is that a spirit of competition is a "healthy" motivating force for achieving organizational ends (Sayles, 1952; Spriegel & Lansburgh, 1955; Strauss & Sayles, 1960).

On the other hand, these comparisons sometimes lead to the discovery of common values and mutually supportive opportunities which can result in greater intergroup cohesion. When this happens, it is possible to achieve an intergroup atmosphere that can lead to effective problem-solving and cooperation. Feelings of shared responsibility may then lead to identification with overall organizational goals, and to heightened recognition of similarities with resulting reduction of differences and tensions between them (Sherif, 1958).

Pitfalls of Comparisons Across Groups. There is no assurance, however, that comparisons between groups inevitably lead to favorable outcomes. Instead, in the process of comparison, groups may discover discrepancies in treatment and privileges (Strauss, 1955), points of view, objectives, values, and so on. Then a different process unfolds. Comparisons tend to become invidious (Sherif & Sherif, 1956). Differences are spotlighted and come to the focus of attention. Distortions in perception occur which favor the in-group and deprecate the out-group (Blake & Mouton, 1961a; Cohen, 1958; Kelley, 1951; Sherif & Sherif, 1956; Thibaut, 1950). Each group finds in the other's performances an obstacle to attaining some or all of its own goals. When this situation extends beyond some critical point, each group may view the other as a threat to its own survival. At this point, disagreements are seen as permanent and inevitable, and the only possible resolution seems to lie in defeat of the other group in order to gain one's own objectives. Then all of the tools of common power struggles are brought into play.

The manner in which representatives of groups interact, then, is colored by the background and history of agreements or disagreements of the groups they represent. The forces involved are powerful. The individual group's representative does not act only in terms of his job description or his specific background or training. Nor does he act solely within the context of his position within the group. Rather, he must be governed to some extent, depending on circumstances, by pre-existing relationships between the group he represents and the opposing group or representative of it that he is addressing.

Evaluated in terms of the forces acting in intergroup life, effective management of intergroup relations is a dimension of management that requires more analysis, more theory, and more skills than has been traditional in industrial life. To gain the necessary perspective, managers must focus not only on effective methods of resolving intergroup differences, but also on dysfunctional methods which lead to undesirable and disruptive side effects. Many dysfunctional methods for resolving conflicts have become common. These common practices have become embedded in the traditions of groups and organizations and must be understood to avoid their unthoughtful repetition.

Three Basic Assumptions Toward Intergroup Disagreement

Three basic assumptions or attitudes toward intergroup disagreements and its management can be identified.

1. Disagreement Is Inevitable and Permanent

One identifiable basic assumption is that disagreement is inevitable and permanent. When A and B disagree, the assumption is that the disagreement must be resolved in favor of A or in favor of B, one way or the other. Under this assumption there seems to be no other alternative. If two points of view are seen to be mutually exclusive, and if neither party is prepared to capitulate, then any of three major mechanisms of resolution may be used:

A. *Win-lose* power struggle to the point of capitulation by one group.
B. Resolution through a *third-party* decision.
C. Agreement *not* to determine the outcome, namely, *fate* arbitration.

2. Conflict Can Be Avoided Since Interdependence Between Groups Is Unnecessary

A second orientation to intergroup relations rests on the assumption that while intergroup disagreement is not inevitable, neither is intergroup agreement possible. If these assumptions can be made, then interdependence is not necessary. Hence, when points of conflict arise between groups, they can be resolved by reducing the interdependence between parties. This reduction of interdependence may be achieved in three ways.

A. One group withdrawing from the scene of action.
B. Maintaining, or substituting *indifference* when it appears there is a conflict of interest.
C. *Isolating* the parties from each other; or the parties isolating themselves.

All of these (A, B, and C) share in common the maintenance of independence, rather than any attempt to achieve interdependence.

3. Agreement and Maintaining Interdependence Is Possible

The third orientation to intergroup disagreement is that agreement is possible and that a means of resolving it must be found. Resolving conflict in this way is achieved by smoothing over the conflict while retaining interdependence. For example, visible though trivial reference may be made to overall organizational goals to which both parties are in some degree committed. Then attention is shifted away from real issues, with surface harmony maintained. Alternatively, agreement may be achieved by bargaining, trading, or compromising. In a general sense, this is splitting the difference that separates the parties while at the same time retaining their interdependence. Finally, an effort may be made to resolve the disagreement by a genuine problem-solving approach. Here the effort is not devoted to determining who is right and who is wrong. Nor is it devoted to yielding something to gain something. Rather, a genuine effort is made to discover a creative resolution of fundamental points of difference.

As mentioned earlier, each of these three orientations is related to another dimension which determines the specific approach to be used in managing disagreement. This dimension might be pictured as extending from a *passive* attitude or low stakes to an *active* orientation involving high stakes.

Framework for Viewing Intergroup Conflict

Figure 1 pictures the possibilities within each of the three major orientations just described. These orientations (three vertical columns in Figure 1) are:

1. Conflict inevitable, agreement impossible.
2. Conflict not inevitable, yet agreement not possible.
3. Agreement possible in spite of conflict.

At the bottom of each orientation is the method of resolution likely to be used where stakes in the outcome are low. The middle shows mechanisms employed where stakes in the outcome are moderate, and the upper end shows mechanisms likely to be adopted where stakes in the outcome of the conflict are high.

All the approaches in the left-hand orientation (column) *presume a condition of win-lose between the contesting parties.* Fate strategies come into force when stakes in the outcome are low, arbitration when the stakes are moderate, and win-lose power struggles when the stakes are high.

The right-hand vertical column of the graph reflects three opposite approaches to resolving disagreement. These approaches assume that though disagreement is present, agreement can be found. The most passive orientation here is identified as "smoothing over." This approach involves such well-known cultural phenomena as efforts to achieve intergroup cohesion and co-existence without really solving problems. The assumption is that somehow or another, peaceful co-existence will arise and that people will act in accordance with it.

The more active agreement contains the element of splitting differences. This is a more positive (active) approach than smoothing over differences, but it leaves much to be desired, for it often produces only temporary resolution.

In the upper right-hand corner is the orientation of problem solving. This position identifies the circumstances under which the contesting parties search out the rationale of their agreements as well

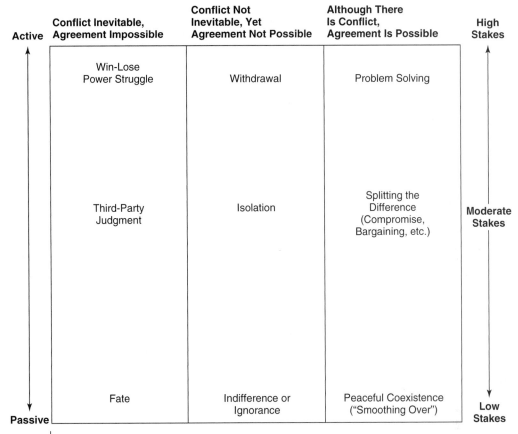

Active	Conflict Inevitable, Agreement Impossible	Conflict Not Inevitable, Yet Agreement Not Possible	Although There Is Conflict, Agreement Is Possible	High Stakes
	Win-Lose Power Struggle	Withdrawal	Problem Solving	
	Third-Party Judgment	Isolation	Splitting the Difference (Compromise, Bargaining, etc.)	Moderate Stakes
Passive	Fate	Indifference or Ignorance	Peaceful Coexistence ("Smoothing Over")	Low Stakes

FIGURE 1   THE THREE BASIC ASSUMPTIONS TOWARD INTERGROUP DISAGREEMENTS AND THEIR MANAGEMENT

as the bases of their disagreements. It also identifies the causes for reservations and doubts of both parties. Here, the parties work toward the circumstances which will eliminate reservations.

This climate affords the opportunity to actively explore means for achieving true agreement on issues without "smoothing over" or compromising differences....

SUMMARY

As a group member, whether leader or member, *an individual is a representative of his group* whenever he interacts with others in different groups, provided the groups are in some way interdependent. As a representative, a group member's opinions and attitudes are shaped by the goals, norms, and values he shares with others of his group. Normal rules of conduct and the expectations of others in his group do not allow him to act independently of his group's interests when areas of disagreement arise between his group and another.

Large organizations are composed of many small groups. Because of the size, complexity and nature of present-day organizations, group comparisons, particularly of an invidious character, are bound to occur. Under such circumstances, differences, rather than similarities and commonness of purpose, are highlighted, with conflict the inevitable result. The result is that organizational needs for interdependence and cooperation among groups are not met as well as they might have been, had managerial personnel applied greater understanding to intergroup relations.

Three basic orientations to intergroup disagreement, in combination with these different degrees of "stake in the outcome," and their accompanying approaches for achieving resolution were outlined....

REFERENCES

Arensberg, C. H. (1951). Behavior and organization: industrial studies. In J. H. Rohrer & M. Sherif (Eds.), *Social psychology at the crossroads*. New York: Harper & Bros.

Blake, R. R. (1959). Psychology and the crisis of statesmanship. *American Psychologist, 14,* 87–94.

Blake, R. R., & Mouton, J. S. (1961a). Comprehension of own and outgroup position under intergroup competition. *Journal of Conflict Resolution, 5(3),* 304–310.

Blake, R. R., & Mouton, J. S. (1961b). *Group dynamics-key to decision making.* Houston: Gulf Publishing.

Cartwright, D., & Zander, A. (1953). *Group dynamics: research and theory.* Evanston, IL: Row, Peterson.

Cartwright, D., & Zander, A. (1969). *Group dynamics: research and theory* (2nd ed.). Evanston, IL: Row, Peterson.

Cohen, A. R. (1958). Upward communication in experimentally created hierarchies. *Human Relations, 11,* 41–53.

Cooper, H. C. (1961). Perception of subgroup power and intensity of affiliation with a large organization. *American Sociology Review, 26(2),* 272–274.

Faris, R. E. L. (1962). Interaction levels and intergroup relations. In M. Sherif, (Ed.), *Intergroup relations and leadership* (pp. 24–45). New York: John Wiley and Sons.

Gerard, H. B. (1954). The Anchorage of opinion in face to face groups. *Human Relations, 7,* 313–325.

Hamblin, R. L., Miller, K., & Wiggins, J. A. (1961). Group morale and competence of the leader. *Sociometry, 24(3),* 295–311.

Kelley, H. H. (1951). Communication in experimentally created hierarchies. *Human Relations, 4,* 39–56.

Kelley, H. H., & Volkart, E. H. (1952). The resistance to change of group anchored attitudes. *American Sociology Review, 17,* 453–465.

Pryer, M. W., Flint, A. W., & Bass, B. M. (1962). Group effectiveness and consistency of leadership. *Sociometry, 25(4),* 391.

Sayles, L. R. (1952). The impact of incentives on intergroup relations: management and union problem. *Personnel, 28,* 483–490.

Sheppard, H. L. (1954). Approaches to conflict in American industrial sociology. *British Journal of Sociology, 5,* 324–341.

Sherif, M. (1958). Superordinate goals in the reduction of intergroup conflict. *American Journal of Sociology, 43,* 394–356.

Sherif, M., & Sherif, C. (1956). *Outline of social psychology* (rev.). New York: Harper & Bros.

Spriegel, W. R., & Lansburgh, R. H. (1955). *Industrial management* (5th ed.). New York: John Wiley.

Stogdill, R. M. (1962). Intragroup-intergroup theory and research. In M. Sherif (Ed.), *Intergroup relations and leadership* (pp. 48–65). New York: John Wiley and Sons.

Strauss, G. (1955). Group dynamics and intergroup relations. In W. F. White (Ed.), *Money and motivation* (pp. 90–96). New York: Harper & Bros.

Strauss, G., & Sayles, L. R. (1960). *Personnel.* Englewood Cliffs, NJ: Prentice-Hall.

Thibaut, J. W. (1950). An experimental study of the cohesiveness of under-privileged groups. *Human Relations, 3,* 251–278.

Wolman, B. B. (1960). Impact of failure on group cohesiveness. *Journal of Social Psychology, 51,* 409–418.

Reading 18	Origins of Group Dynamics
	Dorwin Cartwright and Alvin Zander

Whether one wishes to understand or to improve human behavior, it is necessary to know a great deal about the nature of groups....

What, then, is group dynamics? The phrase has gained popular familiarity since World War II but, unfortunately, with its increasing circulation its meaning has become imprecise. According to one rather frequent usage, group dynamics refers to a sort of political ideology concerning the ways in which groups should be organized and managed. This ideology emphasizes the importance of democratic leadership, the participation of members in decisions, and the gains both to society and to individuals to be obtained through cooperative activities in groups. The critics of this view have sometimes caricatured it as making "togetherness" the supreme virtue, advocating that everything be done jointly in groups that have and need no leader because everyone participates fully and equally. A second popular usage of the term group dynamics has it refer to a set of techniques, such as role playing, buzz-sessions, observation and feedback of group process, and group decision, which have been employed widely during the past decade or two in training programs designed to improve skill in human relations and in the management of conferences and committees. These techniques have been identified most closely with the National Training Laboratories whose annual training programs at Bethel, Maine, have become widely known. According to the third usage of the term group dynamics, it refers to a field of inquiry dedicated to achieving knowledge about the nature of groups, the laws of their development, and their interrelations with individuals, other groups, and larger institutions.

... [We] shall limit our usage of the term group dynamics to refer to the field of inquiry dedicated to advancing knowledge about the nature of group life.

Group dynamics, in this sense, is a branch of knowledge or an intellectual specialization. Being concerned with human behavior and social relationships, it can be located within the social sciences. And yet it cannot be identified readily as a subpart of any of the traditional academic disciplines....

In summary, then, we have proposed that group dynamics should be defined as a field of inquiry dedicated to advancing knowledge about the nature of groups, the laws of their development, and their interrelations with individuals, other groups, and larger institutions. It may be identified by four distinguishing characteristics: (a) an emphasis on theoretically significant empirical research, (b) an interest in dynamics and the interdependence among phenomena, (c) a broad relevance to all the social sciences, and (d) the potential applicability of its findings in efforts to improve the functioning of groups and their consequences on individuals and society.

Thus conceived, group dynamics need not be associated with any particular ideology concerning the ways in which groups should be organized and managed nor with the use of any particular techniques of group management. In fact, it is a basic objective of group dynamics to provide a better scientific basis for ideology and practice.

Conditions Fostering the Rise of Group Dynamics

Group dynamics began, as an identifiable field of inquiry, in the United States toward the end of the 1930s. Its origination as a distinct specialty is associated primarily with Kurt Lewin (1890–1947) who popularized the term group dynamics, made significant contributions to both research and theory in group dynamics, and in 1945

Source: Dorwin Cartwright and Alvin Zander, "Origins of Group Dynamics," 1968.

established the first organization devoted explicitly to research on group dynamics. Lewin's contribution was of great importance, but, as we shall see in detail, group dynamics was not the creation of just one person. It was, in fact, the result of many developments that occurred over a period of several years and in several different disciplines and professions. Viewed in historical perspective, group dynamics can be seen as the convergence of certain trends within the social sciences and, more broadly, as the product of the particular society in which it arose....

A Supportive Society

...In the 1930s significant resources were being allotted to the social sciences. The dramatic use of intelligence testing during World War I had stimulated research on human abilities and the application of testing procedures in school systems, industry, and government. "Scientific management," though slow to recognize the importance of social factors, was laying the groundwork for a scientific approach to the management of organizations. The belief that the solution of "social problems" could be facilitated by systematic fact-finding was gaining acceptance.... Thus, when the rapid expansion of group dynamics began after World War II, there were important segments of American society prepared to provide financial support for such research. Support came not only from academic institutions and foundations but also from business, the Federal Government, and various organizations concerned with improving human relations.

Developed Professions

...Before considering the social scientific background of group dynamics, we will describe briefly some of the developments within the professions that facilitated its rise.

By the 1930s a large number of distinct professions had come into existence in the United States, probably more than in any other country. Many of these worked directly with groups of people, and as they became concerned with improving the quality of their practice they undertook to codify procedures and to discover general principles for dealing with groups. It gradually became evident, more quickly in some professions than in others, that generalizations from experience can go only so far and that systematic research is required to produce a deeper understanding of group life. Thus, when group dynamics began to emerge as a distinct field, the leaders of some of the professions were well prepared to foster the idea that systematic research on group life could make a significant contribution to their professions. As a result, several professions helped to create a favorable atmosphere for the financing of group dynamics research, provided from their accumulated experience a broad systematic conception of group functioning from which hypotheses for research could be drawn, afforded facilities in which research could be conducted, and furnished the beginnings of a technology for creating and manipulating variables in experimentation on groups. Four professions played an especially important part in the origin and growth of group dynamics.

1. Social Group Work
2. Group Psychotherapy
3. Education
4. Administration

Developed Social Science

...A basic premise of group dynamics is that the methods of science can be employed in the study of groups. This assumption could be entertained seriously only after the more general belief had gained acceptance that man, his behavior, and his social relations can be properly subjected to scientific investigation.... Not until the last decades of the nineteenth century were there many people actually observing, measuring, or conducting experiments on human behavior. The first psychological laboratory was established only in 1879.

The Reality of Groups. An important part of the early progress in school science consisted in clarifying certain basic assumptions about the reality of social phenomena. The first extensions of the scientific method of human behavior occurred in close proximity to biology. Techniques of experimentation and measurement were first applied to investigations of the responses of organisms to stimulation of the sense organs and to modification of responses due to repeated stimulation. There was never much doubt about the "existence" of individual organisms, but when attention turned to groups of people and to social institutions, a great confusion arose. Discussion of these matters invoked terms like "group mind," "collective representations," "collective unconscious," and "culture." And people argued heatedly as to whether such terms refer to any real phenomena or whether they are mere "abstractions" or "analogies." On the whole, the disciplines concerned with institutions (anthropology, economics, political science, and sociology) have freely attributed concrete reality to supra-individual entities, whereas psychology, with its interest in the physiological bases of behavior, has been reluctant to admit existence to anything other than the behavior of organisms. But in all these disciplines there have been conflicts between "institutionalists" and "behavioral scientists."

It may appear strange that social scientists should get involved in philosophical considerations about the nature of reality. As a matter of fact, however, the social scientist's view of reality makes a great deal of difference to his scientific behavior. In the first place, it determines what things he is prepared to subject to empirical investigation. Lewin pointed out this fact succinctly in the following statement (1951, p. 190):

> Labeling something as "nonexistent" is equivalent to declaring it "out of bounds" for the scientist. Attributing "existence" to an item automatically makes it a duty of the scientist to consider this item as an object of research; it includes the necessity of considering its properties as "facts" which cannot be neglected in the total system of theories; finally, it implies that the terms with which one refers to the item are acceptable as scientific "concepts" (rather than as "mere words").

Secondly, the history of science shows a close interaction between the techniques of research which at any time are available and the prevailing assumptions about reality. Insistence on the existence of phenomena that cannot at that time be objectively observed, measured, or experimentally manipulated accomplishes little of scientific value if it does not lead to the invention of appropriate techniques of empirical research....

Development of Techniques of Research. Of extreme importance for the origin of group dynamics, then, was the shaping of research techniques that could be extended to research on groups. This process, of course, took time. It began in the last half of the nineteenth century with the rise of experimental psychology. Over the subsequent years more and more aspects of human experience and behavior were subjected to techniques of measurement and experimentation.... These advances were important, of course, not only for the rise of group dynamics but for progress in all the behavioral sciences.

Within this general development we may note three methodological gains contributing specifically to the rise of group dynamics.

1. Experiments on individual behavior in groups. As noted above, research in group dynamics is deeply indebted to experimental psychology for the invention of techniques for conducting experiments on the conditions affecting human behavior. But experimental psychology did not concern itself, at first, with social variables; it was only toward the beginning of the [20th] century that a few investigators embarked upon experimental research designed to investigate the effects of social variables upon the behavior of individuals.

2. Controlled observation of social interaction.... The first serious attempts to refine methods of observation, so that objective and

quantitative data might be obtained, occurred around 1930 in the field of child psychology. A great amount of effort went into the construction of categories of observation that would permit an observer simply to indicate the presence or absence of a particular kind of behavior or social interaction during the period of observation. Typically, reliability was heightened by restricting observation to rather overt interactions whose "meaning" could be revealed in a short span of time and whose classification required little interpretation by the observer. Methods were also developed for sampling the interactions of a large group of people over a long time so that efficient estimates of the total interaction could be made on the basis of more limited observations. By use of such procedures and by careful training of observers, quantitative data of high reliability were obtained. The principal researchers responsible for these important advances were Goodenough (1928), Jack (1934), Olson (Olson & Cunningham, 1934), Parten (1932), and Thomas (1933).

3. Sociometry.... Of the many devices for obtaining information from group members, one of the earliest and most commonly used is the sociometric test, which was invented by Moreno (1934). Although based essentially on subjective reports of individuals, the sociometric test provides quantifiable data about patterns of attractions and repulsions existing in a group. The publication by Moreno in 1934 of a major book based on experience with the test and the establishment in 1937 of a journal, *Sociometry*, ushered in a prodigious amount of research employing the sociometric test and numerous variations of it.

The significance of sociometry for group dynamics lay both in the provision of a useful technique for research on groups and in the attention it directed to such features of groups as social position, patterns of friendship, subgroup formation, and, more generally, informal structure.

Beginnings of Group Dynamics

By the mid-1930s conditions were ripe within the social sciences for a rapid advance in empirical research on groups. And, in fact, a great burst of such activity did take place in America just prior to the entry of the United States into World War II. This research, moreover, began to display quite clearly the characteristics that are now associated with work in group dynamics. Within a period of approximately five years several important research projects were undertaken, more or less independently of one another but all sharing these distinctive features. We now briefly consider four of the more influential of these.

Experimental Creation of Social Norms

In 1936 Sherif published a book containing a systematic theoretical analysis of the concept *social norm* and an ingenious experimental investigation of the origin of social norms among groups of people. Probably the most important feature of this book was its bringing together of ideas and observations from sociology and anthropology and techniques of laboratory experimentation from experimental psychology....

In formulating his research problem, Sherif drew heavily upon the findings of Gestalt psychology in the field of perception. He noted that this work had established that there need not necessarily be a fixed point-to-point correlation between the physical stimulus and the experience and behavior it arouses. The frame of reference a person brings to a situation influences in no small way how he sees that situation. Sherif proposed that psychologically a social norm functions as such a frame of reference. Thus, if two people with different norms face the same situation (for example, a Mohammedan and a Christian confront a meal of pork chops), they will see it and react to it in widely different ways. For each, however, the norm serves to give meaning and to provide a stable way of reacting to the environment.

Having thus related social norms to the psychology of perception, Sherif proceeded to ask how norms arise. It occurred to him that he might gain insight into this problem by placing people in a situation that had no clear structure and in which they would not be able to bring to bear any previously acquired frame of reference or social norm....

...Sherif's experiment consisted of placing subjects individually in the darkened room and getting judgments of the extent of apparent motion. He found that upon repeated test the subject establishes a range within which his judgments fall and that this range is peculiar to each individual. Sherif then repeated the experiment, but this time having groups of subjects observe the light and report aloud their judgments. Now he found that the individual ranges of judgment converged to a group range that was peculiar to the group. In additional variations Sherif was able to show that:

When the individual, in whom a range and a norm within that range are first developed in the individual situation, is put into a group situation, together with other individuals who also come into the situation with their own ranges and norms established in their own individual sessions, the ranges and norms tend to converge.

Moreover, "when a member of a group faces the same situation subsequently *alone,* after once the range and norm of his group have been established, he perceives the situation in terms of the range and norm that he brings from the group situation" (p. 105).

Sherif's study did much to establish the feasibility of subjecting group phenomena to experimental investigation.... And his research helped establish among psychologists the view that certain properties of groups have reality, for, as he concluded, "the fact that the norm thus established is peculiar to the group suggests that there is a factual psychological basis in the contentions of social psychologists and sociologists who maintain that new and supra-individual qualities arise in the group situations" (p. 105).

Social Anchorage of Attitudes

During the years 1935–39, Newcomb (1943) was conducting an intensive investigation of the same general kind of problem that interested Sherif, but with quite different methods. Newcomb selected a "natural" rather than a "laboratory" setting in which to study the operation of social norms and social influence processes, and he relied primarily upon techniques of attitude measurement, sociometry, and interviewing to obtain his data. Bennington College was the site of his study, the entire student body were his subjects, and attitudes toward political affairs provided the content of the social norms....

Newcomb's study showed that the attitudes of individuals are strongly rooted in the groups to which people belong, that the influence of a group upon an individual's attitudes depends upon the nature of the relationship between the individual and the group, and that groups evaluate members, partially at least, on the basis of their conformity to group norms. Although most of these points had been made in one form or another by writers in the speculative era of social science, this study was especially significant because it provided detailed, objective, and quantitative evidence. It thereby demonstrated, as Sherif's study did in a different way, the feasibility of conducting scientific research on important features of group life.

Groups in Street Corner Society

The sociological and anthropological background of group dynamics is most apparent in the third important study of this era. In 1937 W. F. Whyte moved into one of the slums of Boston to begin a three and one-half year study of social clubs, political organizations, and racketeering. His method was that of "the participant observer," which had been most highly developed in anthropological research. More specifically, he drew upon the experience of Warner and Arensberg which was derived from the "Yankee City" studies. In various ways he gained admittance to the social and political life of the community and faithfully kept notes of the various happenings that he observed or heard about. In the resulting book, Whyte (1943) reported in vivid detail on the structure, culture, and functioning of the Norton Street gang and the Italian Community Club. The importance of these social groups in the life of their members and in the political structure of the larger society was extensively documented....

The major importance of this study for subsequent work in group dynamics was three-fold: (*a*) It dramatized, and described in painstaking detail, the great significance of groups in the lives of individuals and in the functioning of larger social systems. (*b*) It gave impetus to the interpretation of group properties and processes in terms of interactions among individuals. (*c*) It generated a number of hypotheses concerning the relations among such variables as initiation of interaction, leadership, status, mutual obligations, and group cohesion. These hypotheses have served to guide much of Whyte's later work on groups as well as the research of many others.

Experimental Manipulation of Group Atmosphere

By far the most influential work in the emerging study of group dynamics was that of Lewin, Lippitt, and White (1939; Lippitt, 1940). Conducted at the Iowa Child Welfare Research Station between 1937 and 1940, these investigations of group atmosphere and styles of leadership accomplished a creative synthesis of the various trends and developments considered above....

The basic objective of this research was to study the influences upon the group as a whole and upon individual members of certain experimentally induced "group atmospheres," or "styles of leadership." Groups of ten- and eleven-year-old children were formed to meet regularly over a period of several weeks under the leadership of an adult, who induced the different group atmospheres. In creating these groups care was taken to assure their initial comparability; by utilizing the sociometric test, playground observations, and teacher interviews, the structural properties of the various groups were made as similar as possible; on the basis of school records and interviews with the children, the backgrounds and individual characteristics of the members were equated for all the groups; and the same group activities and physical setting were employed in every group.

The experimental manipulation consisted of having the adult leaders behave in a prescribed fashion in each experimental treatment, and in order to rule out the differential effects of the personalities of the leaders, each one led a group under each of the experimental conditions. Three types of leadership, or group atmosphere, were investigated: democratic, autocratic, and laissez-faire.

...Each group, moreover, developed a characteristic level of aggressiveness, and it was demonstrated that when individual members were transferred from one group to another their aggressiveness changed to approach the new group level. An interesting insight into the dynamics of aggression was provided by the rather violent emotional "explosion" which took place when some of the groups that had reacted submissively to autocratic leadership were given a new, more permissive leader....

Of major importance for subsequent research in group dynamics was the way in which Lewin formulated the essential purpose of these experiments. The problem of leadership was chosen for investigation, in part, because of its practical importance in education, social group work, administration, and political affairs. Nevertheless, in creating the different types of leadership in the laboratory the intention was not to mirror or to simulate any "pure types" that might exist in society. The purpose was rather to lay bare some of the more important ways in which leader behavior may vary and to discover how various styles of leadership influence the properties of groups and the behavior of members. As Lewin (1948) put it, the purpose "was not to duplicate any given autocracy or democracy or to study an 'ideal' autocracy or democracy, but to create set-ups which would give insight into the underlying group dynamics." This statement... appears to be the earliest use by Lewin of the phrase group dynamics.

It is important to note rather carefully how Lewin generalized the research problem. He might have viewed this research primarily as a contribution to the technology of group management in social work or education. Or he might have placed it in the context of research on leadership. Actually, however, he stated the problem in a most abstract way as one of learning about the underlying dynamics of group life. He believed that it was possible to construct a coherent body of empirical knowledge about the nature of group life that would be meaningful when specified for any particular kind of group. Thus, he envisioned a general theory of groups that could be brought to bear on such apparently diverse matters as family life, work groups, classrooms, committees, military units, and the community. Furthermore, he saw such specific problems as leadership, status, communication, social norms, group atmosphere, and intergroup relations as part of the general problem of understanding the nature of group dynamics....

SUMMARY

Group dynamics is a field of inquiry dedicated to advancing knowledge about the nature of groups, the laws of their development, and their interrelations with individuals, other groups, and larger institutions. It may be identified by its reliance upon empirical research for obtaining data of theoretical significance, its emphasis in research and theory upon the dynamic aspects of group life, its broad relevance to all the social sciences, and the potential applicability of its findings to the improvement of social practice....

By the end of the 1930s several trends converged, with the result that a new field of group dynamics began to take shape. The practical and theoretical importance of groups was by then documented empirically. The feasibility of conducting objective and quantitative research on the dynamics of group life was no longer debatable. And the reality of groups had been removed from the realm of mysticism and placed squarely within the domain of empirical social science. Group norms could be objectively measured, even created experimentally in the laboratory, and some of the processes by which they influence the behavior and attitudes of individuals had been determined. The dependence of certain emotional states of individuals upon the prevailing group atmosphere had been established. And different styles of leadership had been created experimentally and shown to produce marked consequences on the functioning of groups. After the interruption imposed by World War II, rapid advances were made in constructing a systematic, and empirically based, body of knowledge concerning the dynamics of group life.

REFERENCES

1. Allport, F. H. *Social psychology.* Boston: Houghton Mifflin, 1924.
2. Allport, G. W. The historical background of modern social psychology. In G. Lindzey (Ed.), *Handbook of social psychology.* Cambridge, Mass.: Addison-Wesley, 1954. Pp. 3–56.
3. Bach, G. R. *Intensive group psychotherapy.* New York: Ronald Press, 1954.
4. Bales, R. F. *Interaction process analysis.* Cambridge, Mass.: Addison–Wesley, 1950.
5. Barnard, C. I. *The functions of the executive.* Cambridge, Mass.: Harvard Univ. Press, 1938.
6. Bavelas, A. Morale and training of leaders. In G. Watson (Ed.), *Civilian morale.* Boston: Houghton Mifflin, 1942.

7. Bion, W. R. Experiences in groups. I–VI. *Human Relations,* 1948–1950, 1, 314–320, 487–496; 2, 13–22, 295–303; 3, 3–14, 395–402.

8. Bogardus, E. S. Measuring social distance. *Journal of Applied Sociology,* 1925, 9, 299–308.

9. Busch, H. M. *Leadership in group work.* New York: Association Press, 1934.

10. Chapple, E. D. Measuring human relations: An introduction to the study of interaction of individuals. *Generic Psychology Monographs,* 1940, 22, 3–147.

11. Coyle G. L. *Social process in organized groups.* New York: Rinehart, 1930.

12. Dashiell, J. F. Experimental studies of the influence of social situations on the behavior of individual human adults. In C. C. Murchison (Ed.), *Handbook of social psychology,* Worcester, Mass.: Clark Univ. Press, 1935. Pp. 1097–1158.

13. Follett, M. P. *The new state, group organization, the solution of popular government.* New York: Longmans, Green, 1918.

14. Follett, M. P. *Creative experience.* New York: Longmans, Green, 1924.

15. Goodenough, F. L. Measuring behavior traits by means of repeated short samples. *Journal of Juvenile Research,* 1928, 12, 230–235.

16. Gordon, K. Group judgments in the field of lifted weights. *Journal of Experimental Psychology,* 1924, 7, 398–400.

17. Haire, M. Group dynamics in the industrial situation. In A. Kornhauser, R. Dubin, & A. M. Ross (Eds.), *Industrial conflict.* New York: McGraw-Hill, 1954. Pp. 373–385.

18. Homans, G. C. *The human group.* New York: McGraw-Hill, 1954. Pp. 373–385.

19. Jack, L. M. An experimental study of ascendent behavior in preschool children. *Univ. of Iowa Studies in Child Welfare,* 1934, 9, (3).

20. Lewin, K. Forces behind food habits and methods of change. *Bulletin of the National Research Council,* 1943, 108, 35–65.

21. Lewin, K. *Resolving social conflicts.* New York: Harper, 1948.

22. Lewin, K., *Field theory in social science.* New York: Harper, 1951.

23. Lewin, K., Lippitt, R., & White, R. Patterns of aggressive behavior in experimentally created "social climates."*Journal of Social Psychology,* 1939, 10, 271–299.

24. Likert, R. A technique for the measurement of attitudes. *Archives of Psychology,* 1932, No. 140.

25. Lippitt, R. An experimental study of authoritarian and democratic group atmospheres. *Univ. of Iowa Studies in Child Welfare,* 1940, 16 (3), 43–195.

26. Marrow, A. J. *Making management human.* New York: McGraw-Hill, 1957.

27. Mayo, E. *The human problems of an industrial civilization.* New York: Macmillan, 1933.

28. Moede, W. *Experimentelle massenpsychologie.* Leipzig: S. Hirzel, 1920.

29. Moore, H. T. The comparative influence of majority and expert opinion. *American Journal of Psychology,* 1921, 32, 16–20.

30. Moreno, J. L. *Who shall survive?* Washington, D. C.: Nervous and Mental Diseases Publishing Co., 1934.

31. Myrdal, G. *An American dilemma.* New York: Harper, 1944.

32. Newcomb, T. M. *Personality and social change.* New York: Dryden, 1943.

33. Newstetter, W., Feldstein, M., &. Newcomb, T. M. *Group adjustment, a study in experimented sociology.* Cleveland: Western Reserve Univ., School of Applied Social Sciences, 1938.

34. Olson, W. C., & Cunningham, E. M. Time-sampling techniques. *Child Development,* 1934, 5, 41–58.

35. Parten, M. B. Social participation among preschool children. *Journal of Abnormal and Social Psychology,* 1932, 27, 243–269.

36. Radke, M., & Klisurich, D. Experiments in changing food habits. *Journal of American Dietetics Association,* 1947, 23, 403–409.

37. Redl, F., & Wineman, D. *Children who hate.* Glencoe, Ill.: Free Press, 1951.

38. Roethlisberger, F. J., &. Dickson, W. J. *Management and the worker.* Cambridge, Mass.: Harvard Univ. Press, 1939.

39. Scheidlinger, S. *Psychoanalysis and group behavior.* New York: Norton, 1952.

40. Shaw, C. R. *The jack roller.* Chicago: Univ. of Chicago Press, 1939.

41. Shaw, M. E. A comparison of individuals and small groups in the rational solution of complex problems. *American Journal of Psychology,* 1932, 44, 491–504.

42. Sherif, M. *The psychology of social norms.* New York: Harper, 1936.

43. Slavson, S. R. *Analytic group psychotherapy.* New York: Columbia Univ. Press. 1950.

44. Thomas, D. S. An attempt to develop precise measurement in the social behavior field. *Sociologus,* 1933, 9, 1–21.

45. Thomas, W. I., & Znaniecki, F. *The Polish peasant in Europe and America.* Boston: Badger, 1918.

46. Thrasher, F. *The gang.* Chicago: Univ. of Chicago Press, 1927.

47. Thurstone, L. L. Attitudes can be measured. *American Journal of Sociology*, 1928, 33, 529–554.
48. Thurstone, L. L., & Chave, E. J. *The measurement of attitude*. Chicago: Univ. of Chicago Press, 1929.
49. Triplett, N. The dynamogenic factors in pace-making and competition. *American Journal of Psychology*, 1897, 9, 507–533.
50. Watson, G. B. Do groups think more effectively than individuals? *Journal of Abnormal and Social Psychology*, 1928, 23, 328–336.
51. Whyte, W. F., Jr. *Street corner society*. Chicago: Univ. of Chicago Press, 1943.
52. Whyte, W. H., Jr. *The organization man*. New York: Simon and Schuster, 1956.
53. Wilson, A. T. M. Some aspects of social process. *Journal of Social Issues*, 1951 (Suppl. Series 5).
54. Wilson, G., & Ryland, G. *Social group work practice*. Boston: Houghton Mifflin, 1949.

Reading 19	An Intergroup Perspective on Group Dynamics
	Clayton P. Alderfer

Introduction

The study of intergroup relations brings to bear a variety of methods and theories from social science on a diverse set of difficult social problems (Allport, 1954; Merton, 1960; Pettigrew, 1981; Sherif & Sherif, 1969; Van Den Berge, 1972). Taken literally, intergroup relations refer to activities *between* and *among* groups. Note that the choice of preposition is significant. Whether people observe groups only two at a time or in more complex constellations has important implications for action and for understanding. Intergroup concepts can explain a broader range of phenomena than just what go on at the intersection of two or more groups. The range of concern is from how individuals think as revealed in studies of prejudice and stereotyping to how nation states deal with each other in the realm of international conflict. A central feature of virtually all intergroup analysis is the persistently problematic relationship between individual people and collective social processes. . . .

A Theory of Intergroup Relations and Organizations

In the two preceding sections I sought to establish two metatheoretical points. The first was to establish intergroup theory in general as a way of thinking about problems of human behavior; the aim was to distinguish intergroup theory from nonintergroup theory. The second was to determine dimensions on which particular versions of intergroup theory varied from one another; the objective was to differentiate among versions of intergroup theories. This section now presents a particular version of intergroup theory.

According to the dimensions of difference among intergroup theories, it has the following properties:

1. The group is the primary level of analysis.
2. Groups appear embedded in social systems.
3. The orientation toward research is clinical.
4. Concepts from the theory apply to researchers as well as to respondents. . . .

Definition of Groups in Organizations

Within the social psychology literature there is no shortage of definitions of groups, but there is also no clear consensus among those who propose definitions (Cartwright & Zander, 1968). Because much of the work leading to these definitions has been done by social psychologists studying internal properties of groups in laboratories, the resulting concepts have been comparatively limited in recognizing the external properties of groups. Looking at groups in organizations, however, produces a definition that gives more balanced attention to both functional and external properties.

> A human group is a collection of individuals (1) who have significantly interdependent relations with each other, (2) who perceive themselves as a group, reliably distinguishing members from nonmembers, (3) whose group identity is recognized by nonmembers, (4) who, as group members acting alone or in concert, have significantly interdependent relations with other groups, and (5) whose roles in the group are therefore a function of expectations from themselves, from other group members, and from non-group members. (Alderfer 1977a)

This idea of a group begins with individuals who are interdependent, moves to the sense of the group as a significant social object whose boundaries are confirmed from inside and outside,

Source: Clayton P. Alderfer, "An Intergroup Perspective on Group Dynamics," in HANDBOOK OF ORGANIZATIONAL BEHAVIOR, 1987. Reprinted by permission of Jay W. Lorsch.

recognizes that the group as a whole is an interacting unit through representatives or by collective action, and returns to the individual members whose thoughts, feelings, and actions are determined by forces within the individual and from both group members and nongroup members. This conceptualization of a group makes every individual member into a group representative wherever he or she deals with members of other groups and treats transactions among individuals as at least, in part, intergroup events (Rice, 1969; Smith, 1977).

Figure 1 shows an "intergroup transaction between individuals." This is another way of reconceptualizing what may usually be thought of as an interpersonal transaction. In the diagram, there are three classes of forces corresponding to intrapersonal, intragroup, and intergroup dynamics. The general point is that any exchange between people is subject to all three kinds of forces; most people (including behavioral scientists) tend to understand things mainly in intrapersonal or interpersonal terms. Which class of forces becomes most dominant at any time depends on how the specific dimensions at each level of analysis differentiate the individuals. Suppose I_1 is a male engineering supervisor and I_2 is a female union steward. Intrapersonally I_1 prefers abstract thinking and demonstrates persistent difficulty in expressing feelings; I_2 prefers concrete thinking and shows ease in expressing feelings. G_1 is a predominantly male professional group that communicates to I_1 that he at all times should stay in control and be rational. G_2 is a predominantly female clerical group that communicates to I_2 that she should be more assertive about the needs of the G_2s. The I–G_{1-2} relationship includes ten years of labor-management cooperation punctuated by a series of recent strike (from the labor side) and termination (from the management side) threats. The tradition in much of behavioral-science intervention is to focus on the I dynamics and to give little or no attention to G or I–G forces (Argyris, 1962; Walton, 1969).

By viewing transactions between individuals from an intergroup perspective, an observer learns to examine the condition of each participant's group, the relationship of participants to their groups, and the relationship between groups represented by participants as well as their personalities in each "interpersonal" relationship. . . .

Properties of Intergroup Relations

Research on intergroup relations has identified a number of properties characteristic of intergroup

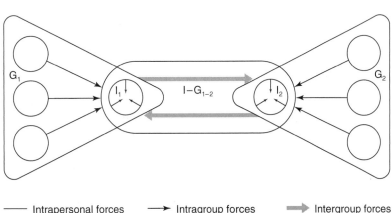

FIGURE I
INTERGROUP
TRANSACTION
BETWEEN
INDIVIDUALS

—— Intrapersonal forces   → Intragroup forces   ⟹ Intergroup forces

relations, regardless of the particular groups or the specific setting where the relationship occurs (Alderfer, 1977; Billig, 1976; Coser, 1956; Levine & Campbell, 1972; Sumner, 1906; Van Den Berge, 1972). These phenomena include

1. Group boundaries. Group boundaries, both physical and psychological, determine who is a group member and regulate transactions among groups by variations in their permeability (Alderfer, 1977b). Boundary permeability refers to the ease with which boundaries can be crossed.
2. Power differences. Groups differ in the types of resources they can obtain and use (Lasswell & Kaplan, 1950). The variety of dimensions on which there are power differences and the degree of discrepancy among groups on these dimensions influence the degree of boundary permeability among groups.
3. Affective patterns. The permeability of group boundaries varies with the polarization of feeling among the groups; that is, to the degree that group members split their feelings so that mainly positive feelings are associated with their own group and mainly negative feelings are projected onto other groups (Sumner, 1906; Coser, 1956; Levine & Campbell, 1972).
4. Cognitive formations, including "distortions." As a function of power differences and affective patterns, groups tend to develop their own language (or elements of language, including social categories), condition their members' perceptions of objective and subjective phenomena, and transmit sets of propositions—including theories and ideologies—to explain the nature of experiences encountered by members and to influence relations with other groups (Blake, Shepard, & Mouton 1964; Billig, 1976; Sherif & Sherif, 1969; Tajfel, 1970).
5. Leadership behavior. The behavior of group leaders and of members representing a group reflects the boundary permeability, power differences, affective patterns, and cognitive

formations of their group in relation to other groups. The behavior of group representatives, including formally designated leaders, is both cause and effect of the total pattern of intergroup behavior in a particular situation.

Group Relations in Organizations

Every organization consists of a large number of groups, and every organization member represents a number of these groups in dealing with other people in the organization. The full set of groups in an organization can be divided into two broad classes: identity groups and organizational groups. An identity group may be thought of as a group whose members share some common biological characteristic (such as gender), have participated in equivalent historical experiences (such as migration), currently are subjected to similar social forces (such as unemployment), and as a result have consonant world views. The coming together of world views by people who are in the same group occurs because of their having like experiences *and* developing shared meanings of these experiences through exchanges with other group members. As people enter organizations they carry with them their ongoing membership in identity groups based on variables such as their ethnicity, gender, age, and family. An organizational group may be conceived of as one whose members share (approximately) common organizational positions, participate in equivalent work experiences, and, as a consequence, have consonant organizational views. Organizations assign their members to organizational groups based on division of labor and hierarchy of authority. One critical factor in understanding intergroups in organizations is that identity-group membership and organizational-group membership are frequently highly related. Depending on the nature of the organization and the culture in which it is embedded, certain organizational groups tend to be populated by members of particular identity groups. In the United States, for example, upper-management positions tend to be held by older white males, and certain departments and ranks tend to be more accepting of females and minorities than others (Loring & Wells, 1972; Purcell & Cavanagh, 1972).

Considering the definition of a human group given above, we can observe how both identity groups and organizational groups fit the five major criteria. First, identity-group members have significant interdependencies because of their common historical experiences, and organizational groups, because of their equivalent work or organizational experiences, which result in their sharing similar fates even though members may be unaware of their relatedness or even actively deny it. Second, organization-group and identity-group members can reliably distinguish themselves as members from nonmembers on the basis of either identity factors (ethnicity, gender, etc.) or of location in the organization. However, the precision of this identification process can vary, depending on both the permeability of group boundaries and the fact that many groups overlap significantly, with individuals having multiple group memberships. A similar point applies to the third definitional characteristic, the ability of nonmembers to recognize members; this again will vary, depending on the permeability of the group's boundaries. The less permeable the boundaries, the more easily recognizable are members. The fourth and fifth aspects of the definition are highly linked when applied to identity and organizational groups. For example, members may be more or less aware of the extent to which they are acting, or being seen, as group representatives when relating to individuals from other groups. Every person has a number of identity- and organizational-group memberships. At any given moment an individual may be simultaneously a member of a large number, if not all, of these groups. However, which group will be focal at the moment will depend on who else representing which other groups is present and what identity-group and organizational-group issues are critical in the current intergroup exchanges. A white person in a predominantly black organization, for example, can rarely escape representing "white people" at some level, regardless of performance. But the same white person placed in a predominantly white organization will not be seen as representing "white people," but rather some other group, such as a particular hierarchical level. Rarely are individuals "just people" when they act in organizations. When there are no other group representatives present, individuals may experience themselves as "just people" in the context of their own group membership, but this subjective experience will quickly disappear when the individual is placed in a multiple-group setting. How group members relate to each other within their group, and to the expectations placed upon them by others, is highly dependent on the nature of both the intragroup and intergroup forces active at that time. . . .

Organizational Groups. The essential characteristic of organizational groups is that individuals belong to them as a function of negotiated exchange between the person and the organization. Often the exchange is voluntary, as when a person decides to work to earn a living or volunteers to work for a community agency. But the exchange may also be involuntary, as when children must attend school, draftees must join the military, and convicted criminals must enter a prison. Regardless of whether the exchange about entry is mainly voluntary or involuntary, becoming an organizational member assigns a person to membership in both a task group and a hierarchical group. A person who stops being an organization member, for whatever reason, also gives up membership in the task and hierarchical groups. In this way task-group and hierarchical-group memberships differ from identity-group affiliations.

Task-group membership arises because of the activities (or, in some unusual cases, such as prisons or hospitals, the inactivities) members are assigned to perform. The activities typically have a set of objectives, role relationships, and other features that shape the task-group members' experiences. As a result, people develop a perspective on their own group, other groups, and the organization as a whole, which in turn shapes their behavior and attitudes.

Membership in task groups also tends to be transferable from one organization to another because people can carry the knowledge and skills necessary to perform particular tasks with them if they leave one system and attempt to join another. As a function of developing and maintaining certain knowledge and skills, people may belong to known professional or semiprofessional organizations outside their employing (or confining) organizations. Support from these "outside interest groups" may help people achieve more power within the system where they are working, and it may make it more possible for them to leave one system and join another.

Hierarchical-group membership is assigned by those in the system with the authority to determine rank in the system. The determination of a member's hierarchical position in an organization is typically a carefully controlled, and often highly secret, process. One's place in the hierarchy determines one's legitimate authority, decision-making autonomy, scope of responsibility, and, frequently, access to benefits of membership. Group effects of the hierarchy arise from the nature of the work required of people who occupy the different levels, from the various personal attributes that the work calls for from incumbents, and from the relations that develop between people who occupy different positions in the hierarchy (Oshry, 1977; Smith, 1982)....

No one who belongs to an organization escapes the effects of hierarchy. Finer differentiations than the three offered here (e.g., upper upper, lower middle, etc.) can be made, but the same basic structure will be repeated within the microcosm of finer distinctions. The effects of hierarchy are "system" characteristics; anyone occupying a particular position in the hierarchy will tend to show the traits associated with that level.

Figure 2 provides a schematic to show the intersection of identity and organization groups. There is an inevitable tension between the two classes of groups as long as there are systematic processes that allocate people to organization

FIGURE 2
IDENTITY AND
ORGANIZATION
GROUPS

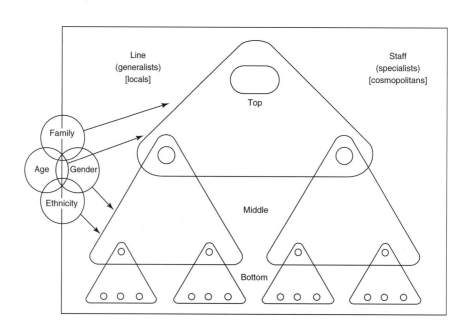

groups as a function of their identity groups. Sometimes these processes are called "institutional discrimination." (Thought question: how many 30-year-old [age group too young] Greek [ethnic group nondominant] women do you know of who are presidents of major corporations?) There is usually enough tension among organization groups to occupy the emotional energies of the top group, who have the task of managing group boundaries and transactions. Thus, unless there are special forces to strengthen the boundaries of identity groups within organizations (i.e., give them more authority), the inclination of those in senior positions will be to manage only in terms of organization groups. The manner in which an organization is embedded in its environment and the relations among identity groups in that environment will affect the degree to which management processes respond to identity *and* organization groups or just to organization groups....

Embedded-Intergroup Relations

Any intergroup relationship occurs within an environment shaped by the suprasystem in which it is embedded. In observing an intergroup relationship one has several perspectives.

1. The effects on individuals who represent the groups in relation to one another
2. The consequences for subgroups within groups as the groups deal with one another
3. The outcomes for groups as a whole when they relate to significant other groups
4. The impact of suprasystem forces on the intergroup relationship in question

Regardless of which level one observes, the phenomenon of "interpenetration" among levels will be operating. Individuals carry images of their own and other groups as they serve in representational roles (Berg, 1978; Wells, 1980). Subgroup splits within face-to-face groups reflect differing degrees of identification and involvement with the group itself, which are in turn shaped by the relationship of the group as a whole to other groups. Then the group as a whole develops a sense—which may be more or less unconscious—of how its interests are cared for or abused by the suprasystem. The concept of embedded-intergroup relations applies to both identity and task groups (Alderfer & Smith, 1982)....

Figure 3 shows how intergroup dynamics might be exhibited in the dynamics within a ten-person work group. The work group has four subgroups identified by dashed lines. Viewed exclusively from the perspective of intragroup dynamics, the work group is affected only by the individual and subgroup processes inside the group. An intergroup perspective, however, suggests that the subgroups inside the work group represent memberships in groups that exist beyond the boundaries of the work unit as indicated by the dotted lines. Suppose I_3 is a new female group leader, having recently joined the group from outside; I_1 and I_2 are men closely associated with the former male group leader; I_4, I_5, and I_6 are junior male members of the work team; and I_7, I_8, I_9, and I_{10} are junior female members of the work team. During the period of transition, and probably subsequent to it as well, embedded-intergroup theory would predict that the relationship between the new female leader and the senior men would be affected by the authority of women in the total system, and that the relationship between the junior men and junior women in the work group would be changed by the group as a whole gaining a female leader....

Application of the Intergroup Theory to Selected Problems

As a general perspective on group behavior in organizations, the intergroup theory may be used to address a variety of human problems. In this concluding section.... I selected each of the problems because it has been a subject of my attention during the last several years. The problems are,

> understanding organizational culture; responding to minorities and white women in predominantly white male organizations.

FIGURE 3
INTERGROUP
DYNAMICS
EMBEDDED
IN A SMALL
GROUP

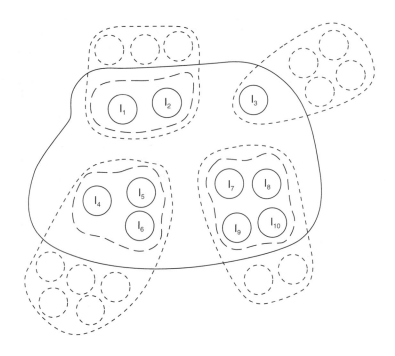

Understanding Organizational Culture

As investigators and consultants have shifted their concerns from small groups to the organization as a whole, there has been a corresponding search for concepts that offer the possibility of giving a holistic formulation to the total system. The notion of an organizational culture has, in part, emerged from this quest.[1] From the standpoint of this paper, the key question is What sort of intellectual conversation might occur between the theorist of organizational culture and the intergroup theorist?...

Martin and Siehl (1982) ... use the concept of subculture. In their case, they propose the notion of a "counterculture" formed around a charismatic figure who provides a sensitivity balanced set of assumptions and behaviors that offer an alternative to the dominant culture. Their empirical material is drawn from the activities of John DeLorean when he was a senior executive with General Motors.

The notion of subcultures, of course, suggests an intergroup perspective, but it does not explicitly propose that view. Rather the term *sub*culture implies that the diversity of cultures is really *sub*ordinate to the main culture, or perhaps, that subculture is the theorist's way of accommodating to data that are obviously present but do not quite fit a "one-group" view of cultural dynamics. What if the idea of organizational culture were viewed as a multiple-group phenomenon?

A study by McCollom (1983) provides data that were gathered and analyzed from a multiple-group perspective. Her work is especially interesting because she initially expected to find a single culture but emerged from her research to write about the cultures of the BCD School. Her own words state,

> I began this study expecting to be able to identify a culture which typified BCD. Instead, I found a number of distinct subcultures residing in the major groups in the School (students, faculty, and staff). The interaction of these cultures seemed to

produce an organizational culture that was far from homogeneous. In fact, conflict between the groups seemed to become part of the culture of the whole system (e.g., the generally held expectation that staff and faculty would disagree). My hypothesis is that the relative power of each of the groups over time in the organization is a major factor in determining the culture.

This statement exemplifies an intergroup view of organizational culture. It makes the culture of the whole system a product of the cultures of key groups in the system *in interaction with one another*. In McCollom's study the predominant pattern of interaction between at least two of these groups was conflictual. Conflict, however, need not be the major style of intergroup transaction for the organization culture to be usefully conceptualized as dynamic intergroup pattern.

An important difference between the work of McCollom and that of ... Martin and Siehl (1982) may be their own roles and group memberships in relation to the cultures they described.... Martin and Siehl were outsiders who read published materials about GM and DeLorean and who interviewed people who had been close to the scene. McCollom was a member of the organizations she studied and was committed to examining the perspectives her group memberships gave her on the system she studied. It is likely that...Martin and Siehl were prevented from fully seeing the multiple-group qualities of the organizations they studied, because they permitted themselves to become mainly associated with just one group. I suggest again that the intergroup relationships of investigators and how those relationships are managed are likely to shape the data they obtain and the concepts derived from those findings....

Responding to White Women and Minorities in Predominantly White Male Organizations

An intergroup perspective on affirmative action notably heightens the complexity of thinking and of action. Perhaps the beginning is to recognize and to accept that a white male is not only an individual but also a group condition (see Figure 1). The term *affirmative action* interpreted progressively means recognizing and changing the exclusively white-male domination of a large proportion of U.S. institutions. Acknowledging only the individual differences among white men (or any other group) and denying the group effects seriously limits what can be understood and what can be done. These limits often serve the material interests of certain groups and individuals—perhaps especially white men but also individual white women and individual members of minority groups who unconsciously or consciously have decided to cope with their group's position by using white men as models (see Davis, 1983; Davis & Watson, 1982; Joseph & Lewis, 1981).

However, once one begins to take a multiple-group perspective, the answers do not come easily nor do the actions become obvious. In fact, there is probably an increase in group-level psychic pain associated with an increase in consciousness about both the historical and contemporary relations of one's own group to other groups. For some, there may be a wish that all oppressed groups can unite in challenging the oppressor group of white males. But then new awareness develops. An historical examination of the relation between white woman and blacks reveals some periods of serious cooperation *and also* many evidences of deep-seated racism in the (white) women's movement (Davis, 1983; Joseph & Lewis, 1981). History also includes episodes when black men spoke against immediately developing voting rights for women (Davis, 1983). Contemporary research shows evidence of black women ready to capitalize on the difficulties of black men in order to advance in predominantly white male corporate cultures (Davis & Watson, 1982) and of white women in totally female interracial organizations apparently oblivious to racial dynamics unless directly confronted with the issues (Van Steenberg, 1983)....

CONCLUSION

Intergroup perspectives began to shape the understanding of human behavior from the beginning of the twentieth century. Scholars reflecting upon such diverse events as political revolution, tribal warfare, labor-management relations, and mental illness showed an awareness of group-to-group relations in their thinking and action. In the last thirty years, numerous intergroup theories have evolved and shaped methodological traditions. Currently, these theory-method combinations can be distinguished by their relative focus on group-level concepts, attention to groups in context or in isolation, acceptance of interventionist behavior by researchers, and tendency toward examining the individual and group behavior of investigators.

Intergroup theory provides interpretations for individual, interpersonal, group, intergroup, and organizational relations. The version of intergroup theory given here uses a definition of group that is concerned with both internal and external properties. It explains intergroup dynamics in terms of group boundaries, power, affect, cognition, and leadership behavior. It examines the nature of identity and organization groups. It relates the state of intergroup relations to the suprasystem in which they are embedded. It presents an understanding of the changing relations among interdependent groups and their representatives through the operation of parallel and unconscious processes.

The theory relates to a wide array of social and organizational problems, including the development of effective work teams, the definition and management of organizational culture, the analysis and implementation of affirmative action, and the teaching of organizational behavior in management schools.

The most important implication of intergroup theory may be the reorientation it offers to those who study and teach about human behavior in groups and organizations. Mannheim was among the most prominent of twentieth-century scholars who connected the sociology of knowledge with the group memberships of writers.

> Accordingly, the products of the cognitive process are already...differentiated because not every possible aspect of the world comes within the purview of the members of a group, but only those out of which difficulties and problems for the group arise. And even this common world (not shared by any outside groups in the same way) appears differently to subordinate groups within the larger group. It appears differently because the subordinate groups and strata in a functionally differentiated society have a different experiential approach. ... (Mannheim, 1936, p. 29)

Intergroup theory proposes that both organization groups (e.g., being a researcher versus being a respondent) and identity groups (e.g., being a person of particular gender, age, ethnicity, and family) affect one's intergroup relations and thereby shape one's cognitive formations. The body of data supporting this general proposition grows as changes in society broaden the range of identity groups who access to research roles (see Balmary, 1981; Eagly & Carli, 1981; Herman, 1981), and consequently the content of "well-established" empirical generalizations and conceptual frameworks are called into question. These new developments affect research and development as well as clinical methods. None of the accepted methods in their implementation escapes potential intergroup effects between researchers and respondents. Investigators who accept this idea cannot avoid questioning the part they and their groups play in the knowledge-making process. Understanding one's intergroup relationships may become a key ingredient for all who wish to study people effectively.

REFERENCES

Alderfer, C. P. 1977a. "Group and intergroup relations." In *Improving life at work,* ed. J. R. Hackman and J. L. Suttle, pp. 227–96. Santa Monica: Goodyear.

Alderfer, C. P. 1977b. "Improving organizational communication through long-term, intergroup intervention." *Journal of Applied Behavioral Science* 13:193–210.

Alderfer, C. P., and K. K. Smith. 1982. "Studying intergroup relations embedded in organizations." *Administrative Science Quarterly* 27:35–65.

Allport, G. W. 1954. *The nature of prejudice.* New York: Doubleday.

Argyris, C. 1962. *Interpersonal competence and organizational effectiveness.* Homewood, Ill.: Richard D. Irwin.

Balmary, M. 1981. *Psychoanalyzing psychoanalysis.* Baltimore: Johns Hopkins University Press.

Berg, D. N. 1978. "Intergroup relations in out patient psychiatric facility." Ann Arbor, Mich.: University of Michigan.

Billig, M. 1976. *Social psychology and intergroup relations.* London: Academic Press.

Blake, R. R., H. A. Shepard, and J. Mouton. 1964. *Managing intergroup conflict in industry.* Houston: Gulf.

Cartwright, D., and A. Zander. 1968. *Group dynamics.* 3d ed. Evanston, Ill.: Row-Peterson.

Coser, L. A. 1956. *The functions of social conflict.* Glencoe, Ill.: Free Press.

Davis, A. Y. 1983. *Women, race, and class.* New York: Vintage Books.

Davis, G., and G. Watson. 1982. *Black life in corporate America.* Garden City, N.Y.: Anchor Press/Doubleday.

Eagly, A. H., and L. L. Carli. 1981. "Sex of researchers and sex-typed communications as determinants of sex differences in influenceability: A meta-analysis of social influence studies." *Psychological Bulletin* 90:1–20.

Herman, J. L. 1981. *Father-daughter incest.* Cambridge, Mass.: Harvard University Press.

Joseph, G. I., and J. Lewis. 1981. *Common differences: Conflicts in black and white feminist perspectives.* Garden City, N.Y.: Anchor Press/Doubleday.

Lasswell, H. D., and A. Kaplan. 1950. *Power and society.* New Haven: Yale.

Levine, R. A., and D. T. Campbell. 1972. *Ethnocentrism.* New York: Wiley.

Loring, R., and T. Wells. 1972. *Breakthrough: Women into management.* New York: Van Nostrand Reinhold.

Mannheim, Karl. 1936. *Ideology and Utopia.* New York: Harcourt Brace Jovanovich.

Martin, J., and C. Siehl. 1982. "Organizational culture and counterculture: An uneasy symbiosis." Working paper, Stanford University.

McCollom, M. 1983. "Organizational culture: A cast study of the BCD school." Yale School of Organization and Management Working Paper.

Merton, R. K. 1960. "The ambivalences of Le-Bon's *The Crowd.*" In *The crowd,* ed. G. Le Bon, pp. v–xxxix. New York: Viking.

Oshry, B. 1977. *Power and position.* Boston: Power and Systems Training.

Pettigrew, T. P. 1981. "Extending the stereotype concept." In *Cognitive processes in stereotyping and intergroup behavior,* ed. D. Hamilton, pp. 303–32. Hillsdale, N.J.: Lawrence Erlbaum Associates.

Purcell, T. V., and G. F. Cavanagh. 1972. *Blacks in the industrial world.* New York: Free Press.

Rice, A. K. 1969. "Individual, group, and intergroup processes." *Human Relations* 22:565–84.

Sherif, M., and C. Sherif. 1969. *Social psychology.* New York: Harper and Row.

Singer, E. 1965. *Key Concepts in Psychotherapy.* New York: Random House.

Smith, K. K. 1977. "An intergroup perspective on individual behavior." In *Perspectives on behavior in organizations.* 2d ed., ed. J. R. Hackman, E. E. Lawler, and L. W. Porter, pp. 397–407. New York: McGraw-Hill.

Smith, K. K. 1982. *Groups in conflict: Prisons in disguise.* Dubuque, Iowa: Kendall-Hunt.

Sumner, W. J. 1906. *Folkways.* New York: Ginn.

Tajfel, H. 1970. "Experiments in intergroup discrimination." *Scientific American* 223:96–102.

Van Den Berge, P., ed. 1972. *Intergroup relations.* New York: Basic Books.

Van Steenberg, V. 1983. "Within white group differences on race relations at CTCGS." Yale School of Organization and Management Working Paper.

Walton, R. E. 1969. *Interpersonal peacemaking.* Reading, Mass.: Addison-Wesley.

Wells, L. J. 1980. "The group-as-a-whole." In *Advances in experiential social processes,* vol. 2, ed. C. P. Alderfer and C. L. Cooper, pp. 165–200. London: Wiley.

NOTE

1. The concept of organizational culture serves other functions as well, and not all organizational culture researchers are concerned with viewing organizations holistically.

Reading 20	Why Teams: Leading to the High-Performance Organization
	Jon R. Katzenbach and Douglas K. Smith

Teams have existed for hundreds of years, are the subject of countless books, and have been celebrated throughout many countries and cultures. Most people believe they know how teams work as well as the benefits teams offer. Many have had first-hand team experiences themselves, some of which were rewarding and others a waste of time. Yet, as we explored the use of teams, it became increasingly clear that the potential impact of single teams, as well as the collective impact of many teams, on the performance of large organizations is woefully underexploited—despite the rapidly growing recognition of the need for what teams have to offer. Understanding this paradox and the discipline required to deal with it are central to the basic lessons we learned about team performance.

There is much more to the wisdom of teams than we ever expected, which we highlight in the following summary of key lessons we have learned about teams and team performance.

1. Significant performance challenges energize teams regardless of where they are in an organization. No team arises without a performance challenge that is meaningful to those involved. Good personal chemistry or the desire to "become a team," for example, can foster teamwork values, but teamwork is not the same thing as a team. Rather, a common set of demanding performance goals that a group considers important to achieve will lead, most of the time, to both performance and a team. Performance, however, is the primary objective *while a team remains the means, not the end.*

Performance is the crux of the matter for teams. Its importance applies to many different groupings, including teams who recommend things, teams who make or do things, and teams who run or manage things. Each of these three types of teams do face unique challenges. Teams that make or do things often need to develop new skills for managing themselves as compared to teams elsewhere in organizations. Teams that recommend things often find their biggest challenge comes when they make the handoff to those who must implement their findings. Finally, groups who run or manage things must address hierarchical obstacles and turf issues more than groups who recommend, make, or do things. But notwithstanding such special issues, any team—if it focuses on performance regardless of where it is in an organization or what it does—will deliver results well beyond what individuals acting alone in nonteam working situations could achieve.

2. Organizational leaders can foster team performance best by building a strong performance ethic rather than by establishing a team-promoting environment alone. A performance focus is also critical to what we learned about how leaders create organizational environments that are friendly to teams. In fact, too many executives fall into the trap of appearing to promote teams for the sake of teams. They talk about entire organizations becoming a "team" and thereby equate teams with teamwork. Or they reorganize their companies around self-managing teams, and risk putting the number of officially designated teams as an objective ahead of performance. They sometimes loosely refer to their own small group at the top as a team when most people in the organization recognize they are anything but a team.

Real teams are much more likely to flourish if leaders aim their sights on performance results that balance the needs of customers, employees, and shareholders. Clarity of purpose and goals have tremendous power in our ever more change-driven world. Most people, at all organizational levels, understand that job security depends on customer satisfaction and financial performance, and are willing to be measured and rewarded accordingly. What is perhaps less well appreciated, but equally true, is how the opportunity to meet clearly stated customer and financial needs enriches jobs and leads to personal growth.

Most of us really do want to make a difference. Naturally, organization policies, designs, and processes that promote teams can accelerate team-based performance in companies already blessed with strong performance cultures. But in those organizations with weak performance ethics or cultures, leaders will provide a sounder foundation for teams by addressing and demanding performance than by embracing the latest organization design fad, including teams themselves.

3. Biases toward individualism exist but need not get in the way of team performance. Most of us grow up with a strong sense of individual responsibility. Parents, teachers, coaches, and role models of all kinds shape our values based on individual accomplishment. Rugged individualism is credited with the formation of our country and our political society. These same values carry through in our corporate families, where all advancement and reward systems are based on individual evaluations. Even when teams are part of the picture, it is seldom at the expense of individual achievement. We are taught to play fair, but "Always look out for number one!" And, most of us have taken this to heart far more deeply than sentiments such as "We're all in this together" or "If one fails, we all fail."

Self-preservation and individual accountability, however, can work two ways. Left unattended, they can preclude or destroy potential teams. But recognized and addressed for what they are, especially if done with reference to how to meet a performance challenge, individual concerns and differences become a source of collective strength. Teams are not antithetical to individual performance. Real teams always find ways for each individual to contribute and thereby gain distinction. Indeed, when harnessed to a common team purpose and goals, our need to distinguish ourselves as individuals becomes a powerful engine for team performance. Nothing we learned in looking at dozens of teams supports an argument for the wholesale abandonment of the individual in favor of teams. Nor does our book present such an either/or proposition.

4. Discipline—both within the team and across the organization—creates the conditions for team performance. Any group seeking team performance for itself, like any leader seeking to build strong performance standards across his organization, must focus sharply on performance. For organizational leaders, this entails making clear and consistent demands that reflect the needs of customers, shareholders, and employees, and then holding themselves and the organization relentlessly accountable. Out of such demands come the most fruitful conditions for teams. An analogous lesson also applies to teams. Groups become teams through *disciplined action.* They *shape* a common purpose, *agree* on performance goals, *define* a common working approach, *develop* high levels of complementary skills, and *hold* themselves mutually accountable for results. And, as with any effective discipline, they never stop doing any of these things.

The Need for Teams

We believe that teams—real teams, not just groups that management calls "teams"—should be the basic unit of performance for most organizations, regardless of size. In any situation requiring the real-time combination of multiple skills, experiences, and judgments, a team inevitably gets better results than a collection of individuals operating within confined job roles and responsibilities. Teams are more flexible than larger organizational groupings because they can be more quickly assembled, deployed, refocused, and disbanded, usually in ways that enhance rather than disrupt more permanent structures and processes. Teams are more productive than groups that have no clear performance objectives because their members are committed to deliver tangible performance results. Teams and performance are an unbeatable combination.

The record of team performance speaks for itself. Teams invariably contribute significant achievements in business, charity, schools, government, communities, and the military. Motorola, recently acclaimed for surpassing its Japanese competition in producing the world's lightest, smallest, and highest-quality cellular phones with only a few hundred parts versus over a thousand for the competition, relied heavily on teams to do it. So did Ford, which became America's most profitable car company in 1990 on the strength of its Taurus model. At 3M, teams are critical to meeting the company's well-known goal of producing half of each year's revenues from product innovations created in the prior five years. General Electric has made self-managing worker teams a centerpiece of its new organization approach.

Nonbusiness team efforts are equally numerous. The Coalition's dramatic Desert Storm victory over Iraq in the Gulf War involved many teams. A team of active duty officers and reservists, for example, lay at the heart of moving, receiving, and sustaining over 300,000 troops and 100,000 vehicles with more than 7,000,000 tons of equipment, fuel, and supplies between the late 1990 buildup through and beyond the end of hostilities in 1991. At Bronx Educational Services, a team of staff and trustees shaped the first nationally recognized adult literacy school. A team of citizens in Harlem founded and operated the first Little League there in over forty years.

We do not argue that such team achievements are a new phenomenon. But we do think there is more urgency to team performance today because of the link between teams, individual behavioral change, and high performance. A "high-performance organization" consistently outperforms its competition over an extended period of time, for example, ten years or more. It also outperforms the expectations of its key constituents: customers, shareholders, and employees. Few people today question that a new era has dawned in which such high levels of performance depend on being "customer driven," delivering "total quality," "continuously improving and innovating," "empowering the workforce," and "partnering with suppliers and customers." Yet these require specific behavioral changes in the entire organization that are difficult and unpredictable for any single person, let alone an entire company, to accomplish. By contrast, we have observed that the same team dynamics that promote performance also support learning and behavioral change, and do so more effectively than larger organizational units or individuals left to their own devices. Consequently, we believe teams will play an increasingly essential part in first creating and then sustaining high-performance organizations.

Change, of course, has always been a management challenge. But, until recently, when executives spoke of managing change, they referred to "normal" change—that is, new circumstances well within the scope of their existing management approaches. Managers deal with this kind of change every day. It is a fundamental part of their job, and includes raising prices, handling disgruntled customers, dealing with stubborn unions, replacing people, and even shifting strategic priorities. Many people, however, would agree that change today has taken on an entirely different meaning. While all managers continue to have to deal with "normal" change, more and more must also confront "major" change that requires a lot of people throughout the company—including those across the broad base of the organization—to become very good at behaviors and skills they are not very good at now. The days of viewing change as primarily concerned with strategic decisions and management reorganizations have vanished.

Several well-known phenomena explain why teams perform well. First, they bring together complementary skills and experiences that, by definition, exceed those of any individual on the team. This broader mix of skills and know-how enables teams to respond to multifaceted challenges like innovation, quality, and customer service. Second, in jointly developing clear goals and approaches, teams establish communications that support real-time problem solving and initiative. Teams are flexible and responsive to changing events and demands. As a result, teams can adjust their approach to new information and challenges with greater speed, accuracy, and effectiveness than can individuals caught in the web of larger organizational connections.

Third, teams provide a unique social dimension that enhances the economic and administrative aspects of work. Real teams do not develop until the people in them work hard to overcome barriers that stand in the way of collective performance. By surmounting such obstacles together, people on teams build trust and confidence in each other's capabilities. They also reinforce each other's intentions to pursue their team purpose above and beyond individual or functional agendas. Overcoming barriers to performance is how groups become teams. Both the meaning of work and the effort brought to bear upon it deepen, until team performance eventually becomes its own reward.

Finally, teams have more fun. This is not a trivial point, because the kind of fun they have is integral to their performance. The people on the teams we met consistently and without prompting emphasized the fun aspects of their work together. Of course this fun included parties, hoopla, and celebrations. But any group of people can throw a good party. What distinguishes the fun of teams is how it both sustains and is sustained by team performance. For example, we often see a more highly developed sense of humor on the job within the top-performing teams because it helps them deal with the pressures and intensity of high performance. And we inevitably hear that the deepest, most satisfying source of enjoyment comes from "having been part of something larger than myself."

Behavioral change also occurs more readily in the team context. Because of their collective commitment, teams are not as threatened by change as are individuals left to fend for themselves. And, because of their flexibility and willingness to enlarge their solution space, teams offer people more room for growth and change than do groups with more narrowly defined task assignments associated with hierarchical job assignments. Finally, because of their focus on performance, teams motivate, challenge, reward, and support individuals who are trying to change the way they do things.

As a result, in the kinds of broad-based change that organizations increasingly confront today, teams can help concentrate the direction and quality of top-down leadership, foster new behaviors, and facilitate cross-functional activities. When teams work, they represent the best proven way to convert embryonic visions and values into consistent action patterns because they rely on people working together. They also are the most practical way to develop a shared sense of direction among people throughout an organization. Teams can make hierarchy responsive without weakening it, energize processes across organizational boundaries, and bring multiple capabilities to bear on difficult issues.

In fact, most models of the "organization of the future" that we have heard about—"networked," "clustered," "nonhierarchical," "horizontal," and so forth—are premised on *teams surpassing individuals as the primary performance unit in the company.* According to these predictions, when management seeks faster, better ways to best match resources to customer opportunity or competitive challenge, the critical building block will be at the team, not individual, level. This does not mean that either individual performance or accountability become unimportant. Rather, the challenge for management increasingly becomes that of balancing the roles of individuals and teams versus displacing or favoring one over the other. In addition, the individual's role and performance will become more a matter for teams, instead of hierarchies of managers, to exploit; that is, in many cases teams, not managers, will figure out what the individuals on those teams should be doing and how they are performing.

Resistance to Teams

Such predictions about teams, however, induce a lot of skepticism. We believe the argument for greater focus on teams is compelling, and most people we have interviewed agree. Yet when it comes to using the team approach for themselves or those they manage, most of these same people are reluctant to rely on teams. Notwithstanding the evidence of team performance all around us, the importance of teams in managing behavioral change and high performance, and the rewards of team experiences in everyday lives, many people undervalue, forget, or openly question the team option when confronting their own performance challenges. We cannot fully explain this resistance; there probably are as many reasons and emotions as there are people. Moreover, we do not suggest that such resistance is either "bad" or "good." We do, however, think that it is powerful because it is grounded in deeply held values of individualism that neither can nor should be entirely dismissed.

Three primary sources for people's reluctance about teams stand out: a lack of conviction that a team or teams can work better than other alternatives; personal styles, capabilities, and preferences that make teams risky or uncomfortable; and weak organizational performance ethics that discourage the conditions in which teams flourish.

1. Lack of conviction. Some people do not believe that teams, except in unusual or unpredictable circumstances, really do perform better than individuals. Some think that teams cause more trouble than they are worth because the members waste time in unproductive meetings and discussions, and actually generate more complaints than constructive results. Others think that teams are probably useful from a human relations point of view, but are a hindrance when it comes to work, productivity, and decisive action. Still others believe that concepts of teamwork and empowerment applied broadly to an organization supersede the need to worry or be disciplined about the performance of specific small groups of people.

On the one hand, most people share a lot of constructive common sense about teams but fail to rigorously apply it. People know, for example, that teams rarely work without common goals; yet far too many teams casually accept goals that are neither demanding, precise, realistic, nor actually held *in common*. On the other hand, the very popularity of the word "team" courts imprecision. People rarely use "team" with much concern for its specific meaning to them in the context they face. As a consequence, most people remain unclear over what makes a real team. A team is not just any group working together. Committees, councils, and task forces are not necessarily teams. Groups do not become teams simply because someone labels them as teams. The complete workforce of any large and complex organization is never a team. Entire organizations can believe in and practice teamwork, but teamwork and teams differ.

Most executives outspokenly advocate teamwork. And they should. Teamwork represents a set of values that encourage behaviors such as listening and constructively responding to points of view expressed by others, giving others the benefit of the doubt, providing support to those who need it, and recognizing the interests and achievements of others. When practiced, such values help all of us communicate and work more effectively with one another and, therefore, are good and valuable behaviors. Obviously, teamwork values help teams perform. They also promote our performance as individuals and the performance of the entire organization. In other words, teamwork values—by themselves—are not exclusive to teams, nor are they enough to ensure team performance.

Teams are discrete units of performance, not a positive set of values. And they are a unit of performance that differs from the individual or the entire organization. A team is a small group of people (typically fewer than twenty) with complementary skills committed to a common purpose and set of specific performance goals. Its members are committed to working with each other to achieve the team's purpose and hold each other fully and jointly accountable for the team's results. Teamwork encourages and helps teams succeed; but teamwork alone never makes a team. Consequently, when senior executives call for entire organization to be a "team," they really are promoting teamwork values. However well intended, such ambiguities can cause unproductive confusion. Moreover, those who describe teams as vehicles primarily to make people feel good or get along better not only confuse teamwork with teams, but also miss the most fundamental characteristic that distinguishes real teams from nonteams—a relentless focus on performance.

Teams thrive on performance challenges; they flounder without them. Teams cannot exist for long without a performance-driven purpose to both nourish and justify the team's continuing existence. Groups established for the sake of becoming a team, job enhancement, communication, organizational effectiveness, or even excellence rarely become real teams, as demonstrated by the bad feelings left in many companies after experimenting with quality circles. While quality represents an admirable aspiration, quality circles often fail to connect specific, achievable performance objectives with the collaborative effort of those in the circle.

Ignoring performance, we suspect, also explains much of the evidence about apparent team failures. Peter Drucker, for example, has cited the difficulties GM, P&G, and Xerox, among others, have had in overshooting the mark with "team-building" efforts. Without question, teams and team efforts sometimes fail. But more often than not, such failures lie in not adhering to the discipline of what makes teams successful. In other words, unclear thinking and practice explain more about such disappointments than whether teams are appropriate units of performance to get something done. Regardless of their cause, however, such unrewarding personal experiences in groups labeled as teams weaken people's conviction about teams even further. Many of us who have observed, participated in, or watched the best intentions at team-building exercises get quickly forgotten or scorned have grown cynical, cautious, or even hostile to teams.

2. Personal discomfort and risk. Many people fear or do not like to work in teams. Some are true loners who contribute best when left to work quietly on their own. Some research scientists, university professors, and specialized consultants fit this pattern. Most people's discomfort with teams, however, is because they find the team approach too time-consuming, too uncertain, or too risky.

"My job is tough enough," goes one recurring comment, "without having to worry about meeting and getting along with a bunch of people I don't even know that well, or I do know and I'm not sure I like all that much. I just don't have that kind of time to invest." In this view, teams represent a risky extra burden that can slow down individual accomplishment and advancement. Some people are uncomfortable about speaking up, participating, or being otherwise conspicuous in group settings. Some are afraid of making commitments that they might not be able to keep. And many people just do not like the idea of having to depend on others, having to listen or agree to contrary points of view, or having to suffer the consequences of other people's mistakes. These concerns particularly afflict managers who find it difficult to be part of a team when they are not the leader.

Few people deny the benefit of teamwork values or the potentially useful performance impact of teams. But, at their core, most people have values that favor individual responsibility and performance over any form of group, whether it be a team or otherwise. Our parents, teachers, ministers, and other elders emphasize individual responsibility as paramount from our earliest days onward. We grow up under a regimen that measures (academic grades), rewards (allowances), and punishes (trips to the principal's office) individual—not collective—performance. Whenever we want to "get something done," our first thought is that of holding an individual responsible.

It is hardly surprising, then, to discover strong anxieties among individuals faced with joining a team. It is not that teams and teamwork are absent from our culture. From *The Three Musketeers* through *The Dirty Dozen* and *Star Trek,* we have read about, listened to, and watched stories of famous teams accomplishing the improbable. Most sports we follow are team sports. And our parents and other teachers have also instructed us in, and expected us to practice, teamwork values. But for most of us, these admirable notions, however potentially rewarding, forever remain secondary to our responsibilities as individuals. Individual responsibility and self-preservation remain the rule; shared responsibility based on trusting others is the exception. A reluctance to take a risk and submit one's fate to the performance of a team, therefore, is almost inbred.

3. Weak organizational performance ethics. The reluctance to commit one's own fate to a team pervades most organizations with weak performance ethics. Such companies lack compelling purposes that appeal rationally and emotionally to their people. Their leaders fail to make clear and meaningful performance demands to which they hold the organization and, most important, themselves accountable. To the organization at large, such behavior manifests more concern about internal politics or external public relations than a commitment to a clear set of goals that balances the expectations of customers, shareholders, and employees. At the worst, such environments undermine the mutual trust and openness upon which teams depend. There is a built-in expectation that any decision of consequence must be made at the top or, at a minimum, be approved by enough other layers that the implementer of that decision is well-covered. Politics displace performance as the daily focus. And, inevitably, those politics play on individual insecurities that, in turn, further erode the conviction and courage to invest in a team approach. Bad team experiences become self-fulfilling prophecies.

Modifying the strong natural emphasis on individual accountability will, of course, be necessary as teams become more important. Yet *replacing individually focused management structures and approaches with team-oriented designs will matter little, or even do damage, unless the organization has a robust performance ethic.* If it does, then shifting the organization's emphasis away from individual toward team can enrich both the number and performance of teams—particularly if management also is disciplined about how it deals with team situations. But all the team-promoting policies in the world will fall short if the teams are not convinced that performance truly matters. Some teams, of course, will always emerge—beyond all reasonable expectation. But they will remain the exception. Because of the all-important link between teams and performance, companies with weak performance ethics will always breed resistance to teams themselves.

CONCLUSION

Teams are *not* the solution to everyone's current and future organizational needs. They will not solve every problem, enhance every group's results, or help top management address every performance challenge. Moreover, when misapplied, they can be both wasteful and disruptive. Nonetheless, teams usually do outperform other groups and individuals. They represent one of the best ways to support the broad-based changes necessary for the high-performing organization. And executives who really believe that behaviorally based characteristics like quality, innovation, cost effectiveness, and customer service will help build sustainable competitive advantage will give top priority to the development of team performance.

To succeed, however, they and others must also pay a lot of attention to why most people approach teams cautiously. In large part, this resistance springs from undeniable experiences and convictions about individual responsibility and the risks involved in trusting other people. Teams, for example, do demand a merging of individual accountability with mutual accountability. Teams also do require lots of time together; indeed, it is folly to assume that teams can perform without investing time to shape and agree upon a common purpose, set of goals, and working approach. Moreover, few groups become real teams without taking risks to overcome constraints imposed by individual, functional, and hierarchical boundaries. And team members do depend on one another in pursuit of common performance.

No wonder, then, that many of us only reluctantly entrust critical issues to team resolution. We all fool ourselves if we think well-meaning aspirations to "work better as a team" will be enough to dispel the resistance to teams. Building the performance of teams throughout an organization that needs to perform better, we argue, is mandatory. But doing so also poses a far more serious challenge than any of us would like to admit.

The good news is that there is a discipline to teams that, if rigorously followed, can transform reluctance into team performance. Moreover, while some of the elements of this discipline are counterintuitive and must be learned, for example, that "becoming a team" is not the primary goal—most of it builds on common sense ideas like the importance of goal setting and mutual accountability. Furthermore, this discipline applies equally well to teams that run things, teams that recommend things, and teams that make or do things. What works at the front lines also works in the executive suite.

The bad news is that, like all disciplines, the price of success is strict adherence and practice. Very few people lose weight, quit smoking, or learn the piano or golf without constant practice and discipline. Very few small groups of people become teams without discipline as well. Extracting team performance is challenging. Long-standing habits of individualism, rampant confusion about teams and teamwork, and seemingly adverse team experiences all undercut the possibilities teams offer at the very moment that team performance has become so critical. Groups do not become teams just because we tell them to; launching hundreds of teams will not necessarily produce real teams in the right places; and building teams at the top remains among the most difficult of tests. Yet the fact remains that potential teams throughout most organizations usually can perform much better than they do. We believe this untapped potential literally begs for renewed attention, especially from the top. We also believe the key to such performance is in recognizing the wisdom of teams, having the courage to try, and then applying the discipline to learn from the experience.

Teams and the High-Performance Organization

We believe that focusing on both performance and the teams that deliver it will materially increase top management's prospects of leading their companies to become high-performance organizations. Again, we do *not* contend that teams are the only answer to this aspiration. They are, however, a very important piece of the puzzle—particularly because the dynamics that drive teams mirror the behaviors and values necessary to the high-performance organization and because teams are, simply stated, so practical.

More agreement exists today about the capabilities of high-performance organizations than about the specific organizational forms and management approaches that will support them. No one, including us, argues over the value of such company attributes as being "customer-driven," "informated," "focused on total quality," and having "empowered work forces" that "continuously improve and innovate." Behind these lie a set of six characteristics, only one of which—balanced performance results—is ever overlooked in discussions of where the best companies are headed. The six include:

1. Balanced performance results. The primary standard for the "new paradigm" organization ought to be performance itself. Companies that consistently outperform the competition over an extended period, say ten years, are high-performance organizations—regardless of how they get there. One can argue with the yardstick of a decade. Perhaps, for example, the only true high-performing organizations outperform competition in perpetuity. But we find it hard to question performance as the key criterion of a high-performance organization.

At one level, performance as a characteristic of the high-performance organization is obvious. But it often goes unstated—thereby leaving people assuming that the other characteristics of high-performance are ends rather than means to an end. One group of executives we know illustrates this point. When challenged to articulate the characteristics that would make their company qualify as a "high-performance organization," they ticked off every attribute on every list we know except one—none of them suggested a specific performance achievement.

Of equal importance is a balanced performance ethic that benefits the primary constituencies of any large business organization: customers, employees, and shareholders/owners. Proven high performers such as Levi Strauss, Procter & Gamble, Hewlett-Packard, and Goldman, Sachs are all well known for their balanced performance aspirations. They are relentless in delivering superior results to employees, customers, and shareholders. It is no accident that they attract the best people, serve enviable customer groups, and sustain the highest earnings. Equally relevant are the balanced performance goals of companies placing the highest emphasis on creating new paradigm, high-performance organizations for the future.

Recognized organizational change leaders such as General Electric, Motorola, and American Express's IDS each are explicit about achieving performance results of multidimensions.

2. Clear, challenging aspirations. Whether it goes under the name of "vision," "mission," "strategic intent," or "directional intensity," the company's purpose must reflect clear and challenging aspirations that will benefit all of its key constituencies. Too many vision statements are just that: a written attempt by top management to meet the well-accepted "vision requirement." They may be read by all, and may even be immortalized in plaques on the wall, but they have no real emotional meaning to people down the line whose behaviors and values they are supposed to influence. The purpose, meaning, and performance implications of visions must communicate, to all who matter, that they will benefit both rationally and emotionally from the company's success.

Reaching for the stars is not just an idealistic notion. Past, present, and future high performers make "meanings" as well as money. Thus, for example, "being the best" is a common phrase in high-performing organizations, although it means different things in different places. Whatever the meaning that goes beyond the money, it makes people proud to be a part of a demanding and challenging total effort.

3. Committed and focused leadership. High-performance organizations follow leaders who themselves almost evangelically pursue performance. Through their time, attention, and other symbolic behavior, such leaders express a constant focus on where the company is headed and an unrelenting dedication to the communication, involvement, measurement, and experimentation required to get there. Truly committed leaders inspire confidence throughout the organization that the pursuit of performance is the single best path to economic and personal fulfillment.

Such leadership, of course, does not require teams at the top. But the power in such teams is undeniable because of how well the members keep each other committed and focused. Moreover, when an organization confronts major change, it is hard to imagine success without the committed and focused leadership provided by a real team at the top.

4. An energized work force dedicated to productivity and learning. The "learning," "adaptive," "self-directed," and "evergreen" characteristics of high performance organizations depend on a critical mass of people who are turned on to winning as well as to the change that winning requires. Performance in a constantly changing world demands change. And change, in turn, must be understood and tested before it can be mastered. Few companies can afford a work force caught in the trap of "it's not my job" or "not invented here" attitudes. Rather, the people of the organization must share an eagerness to ask questions, to experiment with new approaches, to learn from results, and to take responsibility for making changes happen.

No major company we know is pursuing an energized, productive work force without the conscious use of teams.

Productivity and learning across the base of an organization means teams—plain and simple.

5. Skill-based sources of competitive advantage. Companies should always seek and make best use of intrinsically valuable assets like access to natural resources, control over powerful distribution channels, strong brand names, and patents and other government licenses. People generally agree, however, that most industries have entered an era in which sustainable competitive advantage will favor those who develop the core skills and core competencies that allow them to win a battle that now depends more on "movement than position." Indeed, innovation, customer-driven service, total quality, and continuous improvement are examples of the capabilities companies need for high performance.

Core skills invariably depend on team skills. To re-engineer work flows based on customer needs, for example, requires teams that integrate across functional boundaries. Whenever adding value depends on the real-time blending of multiple skills, experiences, and judgments, a team performance challenge exists. And teams provide an excellent (often unsurpassed) crucible for on-the-job skill development.

6. Open communications and knowledge management. A number of observers from academia, business, and the press believe that knowledge has become as scarce and important a factor of production as capital and labor. Few seriously doubt that information technology is critical to high performance. But that "technology"

includes more than the hardware and software behind what some people call a new industrial revolution. It also includes the shared values and behavioral norms that foster open communications and knowledge management. For example, one commentator has suggested that in "information era organizations," there are no guards, only guides. In order to "informate" company performance, the right information must get to the right people at the right time to affect performance. Moreover, those people must hold themselves accountable for their results. Otherwise, empowerment is dangerous.

We have seen how teams promote open communications and knowledge management. But, as we have noted several times, real teams *always* seek fresh facts and share information both within the team and with others beyond. Real teams communicate and learn whatever is necessary to get their job done; team "doors" are always open. Moreover, through the "extended team" influence, the communications and knowledge management of others work better.

Leading thinkers have come forth with a variety of intriguing images of what high-performance organizations with these characteristics and capabilities will actually look like. Peter Drucker pictures it as an "orchestra," Quinn Mills as "clusters," Robert Waterman as an "ad hocracy," and Ram Charan as "networked." Even one of us has a favorite entry, the "horizontal organization." Notwithstanding the range of concepts, however, these people seem to agree on three things. First, future organization designs will seek structures simpler and more flexible than the heavily layered command-and-control hierarchies that have dominated the twentieth century. Second, they strike a balance in favor of organizing work and behavior around processes instead of functions or tasks. And third, they all emphasize teams as the key performance unit of the company.

Reading 21	A Diversity Framework

R. Roosevelt Thomas, Jr.

For the past few years, much discussion has taken place around the topics of *diversity* and related subjects such as affirmative action, understanding differences, valuing differences, understanding diversity, valuing diversity, pluralism, multi-culturalism, and inclusion. All of these subjects and others are often considered under the umbrella of *diversity*. Unfortunately, because little time has been devoted to understanding diversity per se (independent of workforce issues), the ongoing discussions have positioned diversity as akin to affirmative action and have caused a substantial amount of confusion.[1]

I believe that waiting to be teased out on its own merits—rather than on the premise of being the next generation of affirmative action—is a diversity framework that can strengthen managerial and organizational approaches to a variety of issues (functional conflicts, acquisitions/mergers, multiple lines of business, managing change, teaming, work/family issues, globalism, total quality, and workforce demographic characteristics—just to name a few obvious possibilities). As such, the diversity framework most importantly will provide a way of thinking, a way of approaching and framing a set of issues.

My purpose in this brief chapter is to contribute to the evolution of this framework. Accordingly, unlike much of what I have said and written in previous settings, the focus is not on managing diversity or understanding differences or affirmative action but on *diversity* itself. What follows is only the beginning of what promises to be a long evolutionary process, given that we have just started to acknowledge and recognize something called diversity.

A Definition

Diversity refers to any mixture of items characterized by differences *and* similarities. Several thoughts flow from this definition.

1. *Diversity is not synonymous with differences but encompasses differences and similarities.* The manager addressing diversity does not have the option of dealing only with differences or similarities; instead, he or she must deal with both simultaneously.

2. *A discussion of diversity must specify the dimensions in question (race, gender, sexual orientation, product line, age, functional specialization).* A failure to specify can lead to a discussion of apples and oranges. Stated differently, in a very fundamental sense, diversity does not automatically mean "with respect to race and gender." When someone says, "I'm working on diversity issues," I do not know what he or she means unless I inquire about dimensions.

3. *Diversity refers to the collective (all-inclusive) mixture of differences and similarities along a given dimension.* The manager dealing with diversity, then, is focusing on the collective mixture. For example, the manager coping with racial diversity is not dealing with Blacks, Whites, Hispanics, or Asian Americans but with the collective mixture.

To highlight this notion of mixture, consider a jar of red jelly beans and assume that you will add some green and purple jelly beans. Many would believe that the green and purple jelly beans represent diversity. I suggest that diversity instead is represented by the resultant mixture of red, green, and purple jelly beans.

When faced with a collection of diverse jelly beans, most managers have not been addressing diversity but, instead, have been addressing how to handle the last jelly beans added to the mixture. What this means is that we have not failed to deal with diversity, but many of us are just now putting the mixture on our managerial agenda. Even today, with all the talk about

Source: R. Roosevelt Thomas, Jr., "A Diversity Framework," in DIVERSITY IN ORGANIZATIONS: New Perspectives for a Changing Workplace. ©1995, Sage Publications, pp. 245–263. Reprinted by permission.

diversity, most people are concerned with their pet aspect of a dimension. Blacks often are concerned with Black issues, senior citizens with issues of age, women with gender issues, and people with different physical abilities only with disability issues.

The true meaning of diversity suggests that if you are concerned about racism, you include all races; if you're concerned about gender, you include both genders; or if you're concerned about age issues, you include all age groups. In other words, the mixture is all inclusive.

Why Now?

Why develop and use the diversity framework now? What places it on our agenda? A prime rationale offered by many managers is the changing composition of the workforce. *Workforce 2000* (William & Packer, 1987) documented and popularized projected demographic shifts for the 1980s and the 1990s. These projections of more minorities, women, and immigrants in the workforce have moved many executives to initiate "diversity" efforts.

While I acknowledge the importance of *Workforce 2000,* I am not convinced that it is the driving force behind the reality of diversity or the increasingly urgent managerial need to address its challenges and opportunities. For me, a more fundamental causal factor has been a changing attitude toward being different. Being different historically has implied being "not as good as" or inadequate in some way. People who were different wanted to be "mainstreamed" as quickly as possible. Today, a growing number of individuals who see themselves as "different" are much more comfortable with being different. They see being different not as "less than" or as "more than" but, instead, as simply different. Some are even inclined to celebrate being different.

I offer a couple of examples of people with different attitudes about being different. Individuals with work/family parameters other than those *assumed* by corporations are now much more vocal about these differences. This is

because they are comfortable in being different. Child-care and elder-care challenges have always existed, but they were viewed as the individuals' personal problems. Accordingly, employees were to take care of these matters before or after work or make a quick monitoring telephone call at lunch. Now, individuals are comfortable in raising these issues for consideration as workplaces are modified to enhance productivity.

The second example was related by a woman of Italian ancestry. She said that when she was growing up, her father and grandfather would under no circumstances allow anything but English to be spoken in their home. The emphasis was on assimilation and minimizing differences. She indicated that she now tells her daughter: "In addition to speaking English and whatever other language, you will speak Italian as well. You will know your heritage and you will be no less an American." For her, the emphasis is on knowing who you are and how you are different while simultaneously being part of the whole as an American. As I have talked to numerous executives, managers, and employees, I have found immigrants more comfortable in being different and Americans at the same time.

Organizational participants with these new attitudes resist fitting in, or assimilating. They understand and accept the need for assimilation but want to do so only around true requirements—not preferences, conveniences, or traditions. Under these circumstances, the *mixture* of red, purple, and green jelly beans is likely to be much more unassimilated than is the case when the individual beans are uncomfortable with being different. In the past, there might have been a similar mixture of red, green, and purple beans, but they would have been much more assimilated. For example, if the dominant group were red, the green and purple beans would be inclined to act as if they were red, despite the extent to which they might differ on the surface.

The notion of "true requirement" is critical here. Most managers have not moved to differentiate requirements from traditions, preferences, and conveniences. In one accounting department, concern is surfacing about the requirement of a master's degree to secure upward mobility into the managerial ranks. Recently, the manager appointed a task force to determine why employees without a master's degree were increasingly unhappy. Their findings revealed that those without the degree believed that after they trained employees with the degree, these individuals experienced upward mobility but really did not exhibit any competencies that had not been taught by employees without graduate training. As a consequence, the nonmaster's employees were beginning to doubt that the graduate degree was a requirement.

If not a requirement, what was the degree? It was not tradition—something that had been in place through the years—as it was a recent "requirement." For some senior managers, the degree "requirement" was a preference. They preferred people with graduate training because they brought a "certain kind of thinking with them." For others in leadership, the "requirement" was an "insurance policy" that gave them the convenience of being able to assume minimum competency. With this insurance in recruiting and selecting candidates, managers benefited from the convenience of not having to screen for competency but focusing on other variables to determine the candidate's "fit" with the organization. No person—managerial or otherwise—contended that the graduate degree was essential to do department work at any level. Stated differently, no one said that the degree was a "true requirement" in the sense of being a necessary condition for competence—the job at all levels could be done without a master's, but the degree had met some managers' desires around preferences and conveniences.

The Dynamics of Diversity

How do managers respond to diversity? Essentially, there are eight basic responses.

1. *Exclude.* Here, we aim to minimize diversity by keeping diverse elements out or by expelling them once they have been included. An example would be the selection criteria used by a corporation in screening candidates for employment. While these criteria can be used to identify candidates with high potential for success, they in effect also control the amount of diversity within a corporation. Recruiting only electrical engineers produces much less diversity than simply requiring an engineering degree.

2. *Deny.* This option enables individuals to ignore diversity dimensions. They look at a green jelly bean and see only a jelly bean. Examples would be managerial aspirations to be color-blind, gender-blind, or school-blind.

It should be noted that denial is viable only if the object of your denial permits the practice. Entities that celebrate being different are reluctant to allow denial. For example, today, many Black males do not react positively toward managerial protestations of race blindness or gender blindness such as, "We assure you that we will not see you as a Black male." Twenty-five years ago, my fellow Morehouse students and I saw such a statement as an indication that our talent and performance—not race and gender—ultimately would determine our success. Students today see such statements as insults and react by saying, "I will not allow you to deny my blackness, my maleness. I will not grant you the option of denial."

3. *Suppress.* Managers here encourage entities that are different to suppress their differences. For example, holders of nonmainstream political or religious views may be encouraged not to express their philosophies for the sake of maintaining good team spirit or minimizing conflict.

Another suppression example is the treatment old-timers often give inquisitive newcomers who inquire, "Why do we do things this way?" A frequent response from old-timers is, "How long have you been here?" What they mean is, "Suppress your questions until you've been here long enough to understand how things work. At that point, if you still have questions, then you can raise them." Of interest, in some organizations, newcomers never can accumulate enough years to give them the right to question.

4. *Segregate.* Here, I am referring not only to back-of-the-bus segregation but also to other practices such as clustering members of racial or ethnic groups in certain departments (sometimes called ghettos), isolating or piloting a change in a corner of the corporation, or isolating an acquisition as a subsidiary.

I do not mean to imply that these segregational practices are wrong or should be discontinued but simply that each represents a form of segregation comparable to the prototypical back-of-the-bus racial segregation.

5. *Assimilate.* Here, managers attempt to transform the element with differences into clones of the dominant group. For example, when a corporation makes an acquisition, its managers often move to make the acquired company like the parent company, thereby minimizing differences between the two entities.

6. *Tolerate.* Here, the diverse elements adopt a "we don't bother them, they don't bother us" attitude. Each acknowledges the right of the other to exist or to be included, but takes steps to minimize interaction. Examples are the relationships between functions that are not required to interact or between subsidiaries that have little to do with each other.

7. *Build relationships.* The assumption is that a good relationship can overcome differences. While this approach has the potential to foster acceptance and understanding of differences, often it is used to minimize differences. This happens when the governing principle is as follows: "If we just can talk and learn more about each other, despite our differences, I think we'll find many similarities that can be grounds for a mutually beneficial relationship." In other words, by focusing on *similarities,* the hope is to avoid challenges associated with differences.

8. *Foster mutual adaptation.* Under this option, the parties involved accept and understand differences and diversity, recognizing full well that those realities may call for adaptation on the part of all components of the whole. As an illustration, a corporation's managers may hire people who are different while knowing and expecting that they (the managers) must explore possibilities of system and culture changes to ensure that an environment works for everyone.

Three points regarding these dynamics merit our attention. First, only one of the eight options unequivocally endorses diversity. The other seven seek to ignore, minimize, or eliminate diversity. This suggests that we have difficulty accepting the reality of diversity. Only the "foster adaptation" approach unequivocally accepts the reality of diversity and seeks to build on the mixture. In practice, the option of mutual adaptation only recently has been placed on the managerial agenda.

Second, there is no inherent positive or negative value associated with the options. Whether an option is appropriate depends on the circumstances. As an illustration, consider the case of a company buying a healthy enterprise that is substantially different. Segregation of the acquired company as a subsidiary would be appropriate, as opposed to assimilating the entity and risking compromising the success of the purchased enterprise.

Another example is provided by a White Protestant church that experienced a surge of Hispanic members. The reaction was to recruit a Hispanic minister and to encourage the new parishioners to worship at 3:00 p.m. with their newly hired leader. Obviously, this is a segregated service.

On the other hand, whether this is good or bad depends on the context. A conversation with the church's senior pastor might produce at least one of two scenarios that differ greatly. The minister might indicate, "We feel a moral responsibility to assist these people in being able to worship, but we have little desire or need to interact with them. We worship at 11:00 a.m. and leave by 2:00 p.m., while they begin arriving at 2:15 or so. We don't have to interact."

Another scenario could be: "We know we will have to change the 11:00 a.m. service eventually, but we do not know how. By allowing the new members to worship at 3:00 p.m., we are setting up a transition arrangement where their worship needs can be met until we determine how to modify the main service. In the meantime, the two groups can visit with each other in preparation for identifying the parameters of the new unified service." How one views each scenario would influence the evaluation of the segregated arrangements as good or bad.

Third, each of these response options can be used with *any* collective mixture of differences and similarities. While we are most familiar with them in the context of race and gender, they can be found where there is diversity of any kind.

The three points above collectively suggest a need to redefine *Managing Diversity*. Managing Diversity is not simply mutual adaptation but is the process of responding appropriately to diversity mixtures. In this process, the manager must (a) recognize diversity mixtures when they are present, (b) ascertain whether a response is required, and (c) select the appropriate response or blend of responses. The effective manager of diversity is capable in all aspects of the process.

In the absence of a diversity paradigm, managers have had little guidance in systematically assessing situations characterized by diversity mixtures. The framework proposed in this chapter can be used for diagnostic and action-planning purposes. It defines diversity, sets forth the notion that the amount and kind of diversity tension determine whether a response is needed, and offers an initial list of response options. As such, the framework provides a point of departure for evolving a framework to guide managers in making decisions regarding diversity mixtures of all kinds.

Determinants of Responses

How does one select the appropriate option? I believe it is a function in large part of an individual's diversity inclination. This inclination, not unlike that of a person's tendency to be left-handed, is learned or developed early in life and, accordingly, is enduring. An individual's diversity inclination can be difficult to change.

Also coming into play are the individual's mind-sets (ways of thinking about an issue), which are much more current than inclinations. My inclination, based on early learnings, teachings, and experiences, may be not to trust or respect White males, but my mind-set is that *some* White males are worthy of trust and respect, given that some of my *current* best friends are White males.

Mind-sets can reinforce inclinations or stifle them. The greater the incongruence, the greater the psychological stress for the individual. Similarly, individuals are not always able to act on their inclinations and mind-sets.

Another determinant is the individual's environment. As I indicated earlier, environmental factors have encouraged placing diversity on the managerial agenda. Similarly, environmental factors influence the manager's response to diversity. A manager's predispositions and mind-sets might argue against diversity while the environment dictates mutual adaptation. Or a manager might prefer to practice denial, but workers and peers might not allow that option.

In sum, an individual's response to diversity mixtures is shaped by his or her inclinations, mind-sets, and organizational environment. All three factors can be critical determinants. Depending on the individual and organizational parameters, in a given situation either factor can assume the dominant role.

Illustrative Applications of the Diversity Framework

As a way of demonstrating the potential of this framework, I will apply it briefly to three areas where it is not normally used: functional conflicts, acquisitions/mergers, and work/family situations.

Managers, researchers, and managerial theorists have been concerned with *functional conflicts* for decades. A major breakthrough occurred with the work of Lawrence and Lorsch (1969) in the late 1960s when they introduced the concepts of functional differentiation and functional integration.

Lawrence and Lorsch argued that a major requirement for effectiveness and efficiency is to ensure simultaneously that a corporation's functions (departments or units of specialization, such as marketing, research, engineering, and manufacturing) have appropriate amounts of differentiation and integration. Differentiation is the task of ensuring that each function's organizational parameters (for example, policies, structure, degree of formality, and reward systems) and participant behaviors are congruent with the unit's task environment. The more diverse the task environments, the more differentiated will be the organizational parameters and participant behaviors. This differentiation enhances effectiveness and efficiency. These benefits of differentiation provide the rationale for grouping similar tasks together.

A challenge materializes when it becomes necessary for differentiated units to interact. The greater the need for cross-communication, cross-cooperation, and cross-collaboration, the greater the need for integration and integrative mechanisms to bring about the required interactions. Examples of integrative mechanisms would be structural arrangements grouping units requiring integration under a common boss who would serve as the connecting link, positions such as project managers or schedulers designed to facilitate integration, policies presenting and framing the required integrative behavior, [and] reward systems that encouraged appropriate linkages.

In any event, the manager's job is that of bringing about the necessary differentiation (diversity) and integration. The driving force would be task environments, individually and collectively. Where individual task environments differed greatly (for example, the research task versus the manufacturing task), department arrangements and participant behaviors would differ greatly. And if the research and manufacturing task environments were also interdependent as well as substantially different, the successful differentiation of them would make the necessary integration more difficult. This is the prototypical Managing Diversity challenge of fostering differences while simultaneously addressing the cohesiveness and integrity of the whole.

Lawrence and Lorsch were dealing with diversity in very concrete ways. They noted the reality of functional conflicts, explored how task environments contributed, and provided a framework for coping with these challenges. The diversity framework does not contradict this approach but simply contends that the functional conflicts "tree" is part of a diversity "forest" and provides a framework for enhanced understanding and problem solving.

Incidentally, Lawrence and Lorsch were dealing with diversity because they were concerned with strengthening the effectiveness of *all* functions for the benefit of the enterprise. They were concerned about the mixture, as opposed to, for example, advocating the inclusion or greater use of a single function.

With respect to *acquisitions/mergers,* a growing awareness is evolving about the importance of diversity as a determinant of success. An executive involved in planning and implementing acquisitions and mergers recently made the following observation:

> People who actually make deals will tell you that cultural differences are the principal reasons for failures of acquisitions and mergers. A number of other factors may be cited officially for failures—declining markets, inadequate earnings, disappointing cash flow—but the real reasons are the cultural differences.

Peters and Waterman (1982), in their classic *In Search of Excellence,* recommended that companies should "stick to their knitting" when considering growth:

> Our principal finding is clear and simple, organizations that do branch out (whether by acquisition or internal diversification) but stick very close to their knitting outperform the others. The most successful of all are those diversified around a single skill—the coating and bonding technology at 3M, for example.

Because the parent organization and the acquisition or merger partner represent a mixture of similarities and differences, they are characterized by diversity. Peters and Waterman found that when corporations stray from their core, they risk compromising or diluting what has made them successful.

I concur with their findings. However, the evolving diversity paradigm and Managing Diversity suggest that managers *can* seek growth beyond their core business, *if* they have the capability to accept and manage diversity. For a corporation with a stagnant core, this possibility is most significant and further highlights diversity and Managing Diversity as managerial priorities. Without a Managing Diversity capability, corporations desiring growth have limited opportunities.

All of this means that a critical criterion for success is the ability to deal with the diversity. A company that tries *inappropriately* to minimize this diversity by *assimilating* the acquisition or merger partner threatens the viability of the partner. If the partner's business environment dictates the differences, eliminating them could reduce the partner's viability and contribute to the failure of the acquisition/merger.

On the other hand, the inappropriate fostering of differences can minimize opportunities for synergy with the acquisition/merger partner and contribute to the failure of the acquisition/merger. So, in essence, the critical task again is to determine and bring about the *required* amounts of differentiation and integration between the acquisition/merger partners. Stated differently, managers must deal effectively with diversity.

Increasingly, managers are exploring the relationship between *work/family* issues and diversity. For example, in the spring of 1994, the Women's Legal Defense Fund and Aetna Life and Casualty co-sponsored a symposium examining this relationship.

Work/family issues are now topical because men and women with different work/family parameters than those presumed by corporations have become vocal about these differences. In essence, they argued that the variety of work/family differences and similarities among

workers were much more diverse than previously thought.

Two examples deserve mention. One, men and women with different child-care and elder-care requirements have become more comfortable with bringing these issues into the workplace. These employees are more comfortable in saying "I don't fit the work/family assumptions on which this organization is grounded." This openness has transformed personal work/family issues into managerial concerns.

Two, women are becoming more comfortable in acknowledging that they are different and that being different does not imply inadequacy. This parallels what has been common throughout the diversity arena. Traditionally, given the stress on assimilation and conformity for success, people who were "different" were reluctant to admit being different. This denial helped the individual in his or her push for success and made it unnecessary for the manager to have to deal with differences.

Now that people are more comfortable in acknowledging work/family differences and women are more comfortable in admitting their differences, managers are facing a much more diverse workforce. With this increase in work/family diversity has come tension. The tension stems from realization that organizational environments are not compatible with the realities of work/family diversity and the needs of women. So managers have attempted to foster programs to meet work/family needs of men and women and also enable or empower women. Signs of this stress are the continuing debates about glass ceilings, child care, elder care, and dual-career families. Another sign is an arising backlash from single employees about the "preferential treatment" being given to those with child-care and elder-care concerns.

My point is that the diversity framework and its notions of diversity mixtures, diversity tension, and response options can help explain the rise in prominence of work/family issues on the managerial agenda.

In the discussions of functional conflicts, acquisitions/mergers, and work/family issues, I have sought to illustrate how the diversity framework can be used to examine the dynamics of differences and similarities wherever they are found, particularly in realms other than the workforce. Obviously, each of these cases could provide the basis for a much more elaborate treatment. The implications for managers dealing with diversity mixtures are threefold. First, if you wish to learn about diversity per se and Managing Diversity in general, you are not confined to the arenas of race and gender, where deliberation and analysis are compromised by emotionally charged baggage. You have the option of looking at experiences with diversity mixtures in general, gleaning lessons, and then returning to apply them to race and gender concerns. This is an important implication, given that much of the thinking and writing about diversity have been colored by experiences with race and gender in the workplace. The framework and its recognition that diversity is more than race and gender broaden the opportunity for systematic inquiry by the practitioner and the scholar.

Second, the practitioner desiring to institutionalize Managing Diversity as a process may wish to begin in an arena other than race or gender, or at least to include areas in addition to these two traditional dimensions. Often, individuals cannot come to grips with *diversity* in the context of race and gender because of their preoccupations and emotions regarding these two issues. Focusing on another dimension would enhance the possibility of more illuminating analysis and discussion.

Third, the manager who confines Managing Diversity to race and gender risks greatly underusing this process. Managing Diversity can be practical and beneficial *wherever* managers encounter diversity mixtures and diversity tensions.

Three Critical Questions

As I have discussed the diversity framework with others, they frequently have raised several questions.

Question 1: Within this diversity framework with its multiplicity of diversity dimensions, how will the manager know where to direct his or her attention? To determine where to focus, managers must assess diversity tension and direct their efforts to areas offering the greatest bottom-line gain from addressing tension. At a minimum, managers must assess the nature of the tension, its intensity, and its impact on the bottom line.

In the context of the diversity framework, the process of assessing diversity tension and determining what, if any, action is necessary requires addressing the following questions:

1. What are the requirements for the success of the enterprise?
2. What is the connection between the diversity tension noted and the organization's success factors?
3. *If* the tension is interfering with maximum realization of the key success factors, the following questions should be addressed:
   a. What response options have been used in the past around this particular diversity?
   b. What have been the strengths and weaknesses produced by the use of these options?
   c. Given the organization's mission and success factors, what is the desired state with respect to the diversity tension?
   d. Which of the options have the greatest potential to bring about the desired state?

In light of the importance of the organization's mission and key success factors as context for action, diagnosis is critical. Only through accurate and insightful diagnosis can the manager assess the potential for gain as a result of addressing a given diversity mixture and its related diversity tension.

Question 2: If we use the diversity framework with its multiple dimensions, will my preferred issue receive less attention? Under the diversity framework, it is possible that a diversity tension analysis will determine that an individual's pet issue offers a low potential for gain. If that happens, it is true that less attention will be given to this issue.

However, less attention under the diversity framework would not necessarily mean less progress for the issue involved. As attention is focused on the critical dimensions, progress will be made with understanding and using the diversity framework. A result would be spillover benefits for diversity issues that were not assessed as critical. Indeed, in the long run, for noncritical issues, I suspect that even mere spillover progress will be greater progress than would occur otherwise.

This would be true because of the transferability of the Managing Diversity capability. Regardless of the dimension or diversity mixture, where the manager hones his Managing Diversity mind-set and skills, they will be available and applicable to other diversity arenas. The critical prescription is to learn about diversity and Managing Diversity, as opposed to becoming proficient with one diversity mixture. Our challenge with the dimensions of race and gender is that they have been so emotionally charged that they have been less than excellent learning arenas. Indeed, because of this reality, managers seriously and effectively could address "workforce diversity" and "racial and gender diversity" without ever getting in touch with "diversity" per se.

Question 3: What difference does it make? Despite all the noise about diversity, aren't we talking primarily about race and gender? If so, why not just say race and gender? This is a key set of questions. What do you gain by using the diversity framework? This diversity framework highlights the reality of the diversity forest that is greater than an individual's pet diversity tree. This realization, in and of itself, suggests the opportunity to gain economies of learning through the experiences others have had with different diversity issues.

In addition to economies of learning, the diversity framework offers an opportunity to rise above the fray and to gain perspective in search of greater understanding. A frequent comment by longtime managers has been the following: "In my corporation, we're doing what was done 15 and 20 years ago. We're simply recycling as if what we are doing is new." I am seeing a growing readiness for new perspectives and freshness, not as a way of denigrating past paradigms and accomplishments, but as a way of building on them.

Another potential gain with the diversity framework is the possibility of progress with all dimensions, not just those involving the workforce. Now when the word *diversity* is used, an assumption is made that the topic is workforce diversity. This narrow focus excludes all the other arenas characterized by mixtures of differences and similarities. The diversity paradigm broadens the focus and greatly enhances the possibility of progress on many fronts.

* * *

My purpose in this brief chapter has been to contribute to the ongoing discussion and evolution regarding the nature of diversity. Before we decide what to do about diversity, I believe that we must spend more time attempting to understand the concept of diversity. Once we understand what diversity is, we can more easily evaluate affirmative action, understanding differences, managing diversity, and other action approaches.

REFERENCES

Lawrence, P. R., & Lorsch, J. W. (1969). *Organization and environment.* Homewood, IL: Irwin.

Peters, T. J., & Waterman, R. H. (1982). *In search of excellence.* New York: Harper & Row.

William, B. J., & Packer, A. H. (1987). *Workforce 2000: Work and workers for the 21st century.* Indianapolis: Hudson Institute.

NOTES

1. The following are examples of works that have explored diversity with respect to workforce issues.

Cox, T. (1994). *Cultural diversity in organizations: Theory, research, and practice.* San Francisco: Berrett-Koehler.

Cross, W. E., Foster, B. G., Hardiman, R., Jackson, B., & Jackson, G. (1988). *Workforce diversity and business.* (Available from the American Society for Training and Development, Customer Support Department, ASTD, 1640 King St., P.O. Box 1443, Alexandria, VA 22313, 703-683-8100.)

Fernandez, J. P. (1981). *Racism and sexism in corporate America.* Lexington, MA: Lexington.

Galagan, P. A. (1991, March). *Tapping the power of a diverse workforce.* (Available from the American Society for Training and Development, Customer Support Department, ASTD, 1640 King St., P.O. Box 1443, Alexandria, VA 22313, 703-683-8100.)

Jamieson, D., & O'Mara, J. (1991). *Managing workforce 2000.* San Francisco: Jossey-Bass.

Loden, M., & Rosener, J. B. (1991). *Work force America: Managing employee diversity as a vital resource.* Homewood, IL: Business One Irwin.

Madden, T. R. (1987). *Women vs. women: The uncivil business war.* New York: Amacom.

Thiedereman, S. (1991). *Bridging cultural barriers for corporate success: How to manage the multicultural work force.* Lexington, MA: Lexington.

Thomas, R. R., Jr. (1991). *Beyond race and gender: Unleashing the power of your total work force.* New York: Amacom.

The New Self-Directed Work Teams

Jack D. Orsburn and Linda Moran

According to General Electric Chief Executive Officer Jack Welch, a primary cause of stagnant productivity in this country is the oppressive weight of corporate bureaucracy—what in a 1989 *Fortune* profile he called "the cramping artifacts that pile up in the dusty attics of century-old companies: reports, meetings, rituals, approvals, and forests of paper that seem necessary until they are removed" (Sherman, 1989). Since his rise to prominence in the early 1980s, Welch has set about resolutely clearing the GE corporate attic—raising hackles as well as dust—as part of his plan to boost productivity by 5 to 6 percent every year.

A second powerful drag on U.S. productivity is employee alienation and flagging motivation in the workplace. In a national poll conducted by Daniel Yankelovich (1982) for *Psychology Today,* American workers clearly indicated that as far as they're concerned, the work ethic is alive and well. Respondents said they want to work hard, want to contribute to a satisfying group effort, and do get a sense of accomplishment from doing the best job they can. Ironically, though, many of these same people say they habitually perform only to the minimum level necessary to keep their jobs. The most commonly cited reason for half-hearted effort: long-term resentment about the way their work is structured, managed, and rewarded.

Innovation in Our Own Backyard

None of this is news to most U.S. executives. In fact, all over the country they are giving serious thought to new—even startling—ways to reduce bureaucracy, increase employee motivation, and foster continuous improvement.

One controversial tool generating intense interest is the self-directed work team. But recent cover stories aside—in *Fortune* (Dumaine, 1990), for example—self-direction is no Johnny-come-lately. During the past decade, a number of major

American companies have quietly launched and nurtured self-directed work teams, and have reaped substantial rewards with little or no fanfare. Xerox, Procter & Gamble, Tektronix, GM, Blue Cross of California, TRW, Shenandoah Life, and many others have realized the enormous power of the fully trained, fully committed team that is fully responsible for turning out a final product or service. Here are some typical results:

- Using work teams, Halliburton Energy Services dropped manufacturing cycles from 103.7 days to 28.5 days. On-time delivery improved from 64 percent to 94 percent, and spoilage as a percentage of output dropped from 1.62 percent to 0.46 percent (Teresko, online).
- At the Quaker Oats Company plant in Danville, Illinois, empowered work teams drove down manufacturing costs 37 percent, improved first-pass yields for snack products 37 percent (and now average 99.6 percent), and reduced standard order-to-shipment lead times by 30 percent (Jusko, 1998).
- Aid Association for Lutherans (AAL) raised productivity by 20 percent and cut case processing time by 75 percent (Clipp, 1990).
- Shenandoah Life processes 50 percent more applications and customer services requests using work teams, with 10 percent fewer people (Hoerr, Pollock, & Whiteside, 1986).

Results like these, common in companies willing to stick out the sometimes painful period of transition, emphasize the unique ability of self-directed work teams to shrink bureaucracy and revive employee motivation with a single competitive strategy.

What *Is* a Self-Directed Work Team?

A self-directed work team is a highly trained group of employees, from 6 to 18, on average, fully

Source: Moran, et al, "The New Self-Directed Teams: Mastering the Challenge," ©1990 McGraw-Hill Education. Reprinted by permission of McGraw-Hill Companies.

responsible for turning out a well-defined segment of finished work. The segment could be a final product, like a refrigerator or ball bearing, or a service, like a fully processed insurance claim.

Because every member of the team shares equal responsibility for this finished segment of work, self-directed teams represent the conceptual opposite of the assembly line, where each worker assumes responsibility for a narrow technical function.

Although work-team members demonstrate classic teamwork, they're much more than simply good team players. For one thing, they have more resources at their command than traditional teams do: a wider range of cross-functional skills within the team itself, much greater decision-making authority, and better access to the information they need for making sound decisions. Work teams plan, set priorities, organize, coordinate with others, measure, and take corrective action—all once considered the exclusive province of supervisors and managers. They solve problems, schedule and assign work, and in many cases handle personnel issues like absenteeism or even team member selection and evaluation. To make sure all this happens smoothly, each team member receives extensive training in the administrative, interpersonal, and technical skills required to maintain a self-managing group.

Conventional Work Groups and Self-Directed Teams

Since self-directed teams are accountable for producing a finished product or service, they differ in several "revolutionary" ways from conventional groups accountable only for performing specified tasks:

Job Categories

Companies using conventional groups divide work into narrow jobs employees can handle with minimal training and effort. But because hundreds of people may contribute to an overall process, individual employees often see little relationship between their own efforts and the finished product. This detachment plus the narrowness of their jobs add up to the apathy and alienation so many companies experience. In contrast, each member of a self-directed work team performs many activities, and managers leave the team alone, so long as the team's product or service meets or exceeds established expectations. When a conventional machine shop converts to self-direction, for example, ten or so job categories may collapse into one or two. All team members then get appropriate cross-training so they can share in the challenging, as well as the routine, activities.

Authority

Since members of a self-directed team perform many of the tasks usually handled by supervisors—communicating, planning, monitoring, scheduling, problem solving—every team needs the authority to initiate a broad range of actions. The first level of supervision over the teams usually functions at a distance to enable rather than directly control team activities. In companies where a supervisor or manager remains in close daily contact with each team, that person's title often changes to "facilitator," to reflect a new, nontraditional role. Further, because the conventional activities of some support groups (e.g., cost accounting, quality assurance, or maintenance) turn out to inhibit rather than promote team productivity, many teams absorb some of those functions as well. And even when support groups play their role more or less as before, the teams have more say about the specific services these groups provide.

Reward System

While executives and managers retain authority over strategies of "why" and "what" for the business, the teams assume substantial authority over the tactics of "how." To realize the benefits of self-directed teams, a company has to reinforce individual behaviors that promote the flexibility of the team as a whole, usually by paying team members for mastering a range of skills required

TABLE 1 | SELF-DIRECTED TEAMS: THE KEY DIFFERENCES

Issue	Conventional Group	Self-Directed Team
Job categories	Many narrow categories	One or two broad categories
Authority	Supervisor directly controls daily activities	Through group decisions, team controls daily activities
Reward system	Tied to type of job, individual performance, and seniority	Tied to team performance and individual breadth of skills

to reach team performance goals. Pay for knowledge (instead of pay for seniority and pay for a single narrow skill) promotes the flexibility teams need to respond quickly to changing conditions. Pay may increase as a team member acquires new skills, or may decrease if old skills begin to erode. Many companies also institute gain-sharing or profit-sharing programs to encourage team members to keep finding new ways to improve productivity.

Table 1 summarizes these fundamental differences between conventional work groups and self-directed teams.

Many U.S. companies, like some of their European and Japanese counterparts, have found that shifting ownership of the work processes to the employees themselves promotes employee commitment and, as a result, promotes continuous improvement of quality and productivity. "It's not all wonderful stuff," says Roger Gasaway, plant manager at GE's super-productive Salisbury plant. "But we've found that when you treat people like adults, 95 percent act like adults."

The Paranoia and the Promise

To the many people with a hip-pocket interest in the status quo, at any level, these fundamental changes in the way work gets done can look pretty threatening. Many fear that their expertise will no longer be valued, that they will no longer perform important duties, or even that they will no longer have a job. When they hear about self-

directed teams, people typically suspect that the company will use them to justify "downsizing," and indeed, some companies do reassign people and restructure to eliminate entire organizational layers. The most successful companies, however, use self-directed teams for "downloading." As the first-line teams assume responsibility for daily operations, support personnel and managers all the way up to the CEO are able to delegate, or "download," some of their duties to the level just below them. In effect, work teams release their managers to perform duties now exercised by managers at the level above, who in turn release those above them, and so on. At the top, the executives gain additional time for strategic planning, highly profitable time, because operational functions are now managed by the people who understand them best.

Once they get through the unavoidable trauma of transition, most people find themselves playing a new, vital role in the long-term health of the company. Mid-managers now have time to act on new or long-neglected opportunities.

Former supervisors, now often facilitators or team leaders, learn new skills and take pride in helping the teams achieve rising standards of quality and productivity. And front-line employees demonstrate energy and commitment all but unheard of in conventional operations. The result is improved overall performance, which typically translates as increased job security and increased opportunity for anyone who learns to contribute in new ways.

The Road to Self-Direction

The cautious Princeton economist Alan S. Blinder sees great promise in a conspicuous but widely ignored way to accelerate "our miserably slow pace of productivity improvement." At a 1989 conference that Blinder organized for the Brookings Institution (the prestigious Washington, D.C., think-tank), researchers presented five major studies and summarized 15 others on productivity in the American workplace. "To me," Blinder (1989) says in an essay in *Business Week*, "all this [research] adds up to a stronger and rather different message than I had expected.... Institutionalized participation by workers can raise productivity as well as increase the effectiveness of other productivity-enhancing measures." Blinder's judgment and a wealth of recent research confirm the practical experience of innovative companies all over the country:

> Self-directed work teams improve productivity, because deep employee involvement builds intense commitment to corporate success.

That realization, obvious as it seems, was a long time coming. Formal involvement programs caught the public eye only in the 1960s, when many American workers started demanding a bigger say over how they were managed. One early response, the "Quality of Work Life" movement, began by devising ways to make work more enjoyable: recreation facilities, spruced-up work areas, and the like. Even if these efforts begged the question of participation, they signaled the end of a frigid epoch in labor-management relations. Later decades brought more effective measures—jointly established work standards, work climate surveys, and multilevel task forces—but in this country the notion of workers as thoughtful, responsible contributors is only now coming into its own.

Many people think self-directed work teams were initially an import from Japan; in fact, they were pioneered in Britain and Sweden during the 1950s. (Volvo, for example, is now so advanced that, in their new Uddevalla plant, self-directed work teams assemble entire cars.) In the United States, Procter & Gamble and a few other forward-thinking companies implemented work teams in the early 1960s, with profitable results. Much later, the Japanese introduced their own highly successful teams, which emphasize quality, safety, and productivity. In the States, as Table 2 shows, it took a brutal decade in the global marketplace, as well as the spectacular success of Japanese teams, to build a mainstream following for self-directed teams.

These days, no U.S. company is totally unaffected by the movement toward increased involvement. Even so, very few companies are willing to grant workers the power to say yes, the power to make something happen. Certainly, more companies allow employees to say no, but being allowed to halt production to fix a problem is quite different from being empowered to improve production. Blinder is one more in a growing chorus of researchers, consultants, and

TABLE 2 | MAJOR COMPANIES USING SELF-DIRECTED WORK TEAMS

Company	Year Started	Company	Year Started
Boeing	1987	GE	1985
Caterpillar	1986	General Motors	1975
Cummins Engine	1973	Procter & Gamble	1962
Ford	1962		

From Hoerr (1989).

top executives saying more or less the same thing: To carve their niche in the world marketplace, U.S. companies must give employees the authority and resources to carry out positive actions in the technical areas they know best.

Multilevel participation is an idea whose time has come. One of the most promising tools is the self-directed work team.

The Payoffs of Self-Direction

What do companies hope to gain through self-directed work teams? The answer varies depending on strategic goals, but companies typically cite one or more of the following critical benefits:

Productivity

An article in *Fast Company* documented how in 1995 while the billion-dollar world market for hearing aids had been flat for the previous five years, Denmark's Oticon with revenues of $160 million was able to more than double in size thanks to work teams and process innovations. And while that degree of improvement is the exception, most companies moving to teams report 20 to 40 percent gains in productivity after 18 months. To cite another common occurrence, factories routinely report an 800 percent reduction in set-up and tear-down time—say, from a day-and-a-half to an hour-and-a-half—because self-directed teams find shortcuts that have absolutely no deleterious effect on productivity or the quality of finished work. Anything that brings gains like these is something that no responsible manager can dismiss out of hand.

Streamlining

Since first-line teams assume many of the functions formerly exercised by supervisors, mid-managers, and support staff, self-direction creates new options for flattening the organization—by redeveloping supervisors as facilitators or team members, or through attrition. Work teams also provide a simple way to trim other forms of redundant bureaucracy: Anything that does not support the teams is a candidate for elimination. If it's not directly useful to the teams, it's modified, eliminated, or dealt with in some other way.

Flexibility

Economists have been saying for years that to succeed in a world market, companies must be capable of producing small batches of tailored products on a tight schedule to meet growing demands in emerging markets. This practice—a creed really, among the dominant foreign competitors—calls for innovative technical procedures and workers who move easily from job to job. Because self-directed work teams have the skills, the information, and the motivation to adapt to change, the company as a whole can respond quickly to changing conditions in both the organization and the marketplace.

Quality

Self-directed work teams help drive a quality improvement effort into every fiber of the organization. When teams assume more operational responsibility, they develop a deep affinity for the technical nuances of their work. As a result, it becomes a matter of professional pride with them to seek and act on opportunities for quality improvement. Analyzing their own work processes in search of improvements is a way of life for work teams. And since team members perform both technical and administrative functions, they gain the experience they need to improve the interface between those functions.

Commitment

Company after company implementing self-directed teams has found that increased involvement breeds increased commitment to corporatewide goals. Commitment tends to remain high as well, partly because companies reward skills and contributions, not just seniority, and partly because team members take enormous satisfaction in managing their piece of the business.

Customer Satisfaction

The energy and flexibility of self-directed work teams promote customer satisfaction through quick response and improved quality. Customer satisfaction, of course, brings repeat business, which in turn brings growth, increased market share, and expanded opportunities for both employees and the community. What self-direction means to the customer is clearly illustrated by two groups of teams in a midwestern plant producing engines for heavy-duty trucks. One group of conventional teams worked assembly-line style, each installing one component of the finished engines. Another group of self-directed teams worked autonomously, each assembling entire engines from start to finish. Although the conventional teams met standards in every way, managers soon realized the work of these groups didn't match up to the higher standards achieved by the self-directed teams. When someone inadvertently shipped the conventional teams' engines to people who normally received engines produced by the self-directed teams, these formerly privileged customers besieged the plant with bitter complaints about "the sudden decline in quality."

How Employees Become Self-Directed Teams

Picture the far-too-typical U.S. organization: Executives get bogged down in tactical decisions, managers retain most of the control, supervisors make most of the operational decisions, and workers do only as much as it takes to meet externally imposed performance standards. Now picture the same organization with fully vested work teams: Executives focus on strategic decisions, and managers and team facilitators clear the way for motivated workers to exceed ambitious team standards they've set for themselves. This second is a pretty picture, but the transformation implies profound changes that many executives, managers, and supervisors find deeply unsettling.

The antidote to this quandary is foresight. If executives and other decision makers can visualize the path toward self-direction, challenging as it may seem, they're far more likely to endorse the journey. Indeed, when a company gives up and turns back, it's usually because naive guides failed to forewarn people about the predictable perils of transition.

No Train, No Gain

It takes a group of employees from two to five years to become a mature self-directed work team. During that period, teams normally experience both progress and regression as they struggle to escape the comfort and safety of their old ways. Without proper skills and understanding, virtually any team will bog down permanently in mid-process. That's why—both during and after the transition to full self-direction—an organization must provide intensive training in three critical areas:

Technical Skills. Technical cross-training, which allows team members to move from job to job within the team itself, is the foundation for the flexibility and productivity of the team as a whole. After a thorough review of all of the tasks performed by the team, individual team members receive training in the specific skills that will broaden their personal contributions to the overall effort.

Administrative Skills. Self-directed teams, as the name implies, perform many tasks formerly handled by supervisors. At first, the teams will need training in record-keeping, reporting procedures, and other aspects of working with the larger organization. Later, depending on the team's charter, they will need to learn procedures for budgeting, scheduling, monitoring, and even hiring and evaluating team members.

Interpersonal Skills. With their broader responsibilities, members of a self-directed work team must communicate more effectively than conventional workers, both one on one and in groups, with each other and with people outside the team. Conventional workers rely on the boss to ensure good communication, set priorities, and handle interpersonal conflict. The peers who make up a self-directed team must handle these critical, often explosive matters on their own, and since these skills rarely come naturally, team members will need skill-building training in several areas. Day-to-day interactions can be chaotic unless team members master the basics of listening and giving feedback. Cooperative decision making within and among teams demands the skills of group problem solving, influencing others, and resolving conflicts. In short, every team member must learn to collaborate in getting the right information, sending the right information, and using that information to increase productivity.

The Stages of Transition to Self-Directed Teams

The engine that drives the transition is ongoing training in the three skill areas—technical, administrative, and interpersonal. Not only does training give team members the operational know-how they need to turn out a finished product or service, it also helps them to cope with five predictable stages (Moran & Musselwhite, 1988) in their long-term progress toward mature self-direction.

Stage I: Start-Up

The charged atmosphere and high hopes of this honeymoon phase last a few months at most. Prior to start-up, an executive steering committee has established the feasibility of teams and developed a mission statement, and a multilevel design team has fleshed out a plan, selected the initial work-team sites, done their pre-work with mid-managers and employees, and fired the starting gun. Then, at start-up, the optimistic teams and wary supervisors begin figuring out, and acting out, what they believe to be their new roles. Even people with serious reservations, often members of support groups, either pitch in cautiously or toe the line under the watchful eyes of senior managers.

The dominant feature of start-up is intensive training for all involved. Team members learn the ABCs of communication and group dynamics,

begin using administrative procedures, and expand their repertoire of technical skills. Supervisors, who may see themselves as having the most to lose, also receive focused training and, if they've been carefully selected, generally do their best to facilitate, rather than control, the operational and decision-making efforts of the teams.

Stage 2: State of Confusion

After the initial enthusiasm, a period of confusion is predictable, normal, and perhaps necessary. Informing people of what to expect during this stage reduces the agony, but even then foot-dragging and outright obstruction can exacerbate the problems teams have in adapting to their new roles. With the supervisor fading as a clear authority figure, new teams often have difficulty reaching cooperative decisions.

Some teams fret about higher work standards or wait sullenly for hypothetical disasters. Job security is Topic A, and many speculate about the "real reasons" for the move to self-direction. Now is the time when nonteam members may openly express their opposition, and unions (if any) may predict the return of the sweat shop. Struggling managers contemplate their shrinking role in day-to-day operations and wonder if executives will delegate enough responsibilities to fill the void. More than one group secretly hopes the transition will collapse.

Stage 3: Leader-Centered Teams

If managers and facilitators continue to demonstrate their faith in the ability of teams to manage themselves, positive signs appear. Support groups begin responding more quickly and openly to requests from the teams. Confidence grows as teams master new skills, find better ways to accomplish the work, and meet ambitious goals. Lines between salaried and hourly people begin to blur. Finally, one team member steps forward as the primary source of direction and information within each team. Far from making a power play, this person usually emerges because the team wants one of their own to interface with the organization, clarify work assignments, and referee internal disputes.

The chief danger in Stage 3 is the team that becomes too reliant on its internal leader. So, to make sure everyone continues to learn and eventually exercise leadership skills, teams often rotate the leadership role or allow anyone to exercise leadership functions as needed (e.g., to deal with someone doing substandard work).

Also significant at this stage: Conflict declines between the teams and their managers; norms evolve for team meetings, assignments, and interactions with the organization; managers withdraw further from daily operations to work on external matters affecting team performance; and productivity expands dramatically.

Stage 4: Tightly Formed Teams

This next stage of the transition is deceptive because teams appear to be flying high. They manage their own scheduling, clearly express their needs, and meet challenging goals with limited resources. But at least one major kink remains: an intense team loyalty that can mask internal unrest and outright dysfunction.

Another common Stage 4 phenomenon: The teams become extremely defensive if the organization fails to meet their needs for information or resources.

These fierce loyalties often give rise to fierce competition among the teams. While friendly rivalry enhances productivity and job satisfaction, overzealous teams can withhold information and assistance in order to undermine the efforts of other teams. At this point, managers must refocus the teams on cross-team and organizationwide goals, often through councils of elected team members who review issues of mutual concern.

Stage 5: Self-Directed Teams

After the firestorm of narrow loyalties comes the period of true self-direction. Mature teams develop a powerful commitment to achieving corporate and team goals, even if those goals require reconfiguration of the teams themselves.

During Stage 5, all team members routinely acquire new skills, take on new technical tasks, seek out and respond to internal customer needs, improve support systems, handle administrative duties, and refine work processes, using detailed information about contracts, competitors, and external customers.

For the manager, mature teams are a new kind of challenge. Teams have now learned to think for themselves about strategically vital information, so they need to understand the rationale behind important management decisions. Further, to maintain the competitive advantage of multilevel involvement, managers must continuously seek new ways to foster the commitment, trust, and responsible involvement of team members. The system does not evolve into a perpetual motion machine. It must be constantly energized with training and information.

The Requirements for Success

The enormous benefits of self-direction are possible only through dramatic organizational change. The fact is, no proven shortcuts have yet been found, for unless teams get the resources and authority they need, they'll never gain the flexibility and commitment from which all benefits ultimately flow. Therefore, any organization considering self-directed teams should first make sure that all of the following elements are in place:

Top-Level Commitment

Organizations considering work teams need a dedicated and courageous champion who protects the endeavor and ensures the availability of all necessary resources. This person must be committed enough to withstand the stormy early stages of transition and clear-headed enough to earn the support of the potentially fractious groups involved.

Management-Employee Trust

Executives and managers need to trust that, given time, employees will actively support the massive changes necessary for success. Employees need to know that management is serious about wanting people to take risks and express their opinions, and not just using a new trick to get more work out of fewer people.

Willingness to Take Risks

The risks of self-direction can be very personal. Executives and managers must be willing to risk a complex and costly organizational innovation that will restructure their daily activities and probably disrupt their sleeping patterns as well. Workers and supervisors must be willing to trade their traditional jobs for less clear-cut, more demanding roles as team members, team leaders, and facilitators.

Willingness to Share Information

If teams are to make decisions that support organizational goals, they will need detailed information about overall operations, including financial information. In other words, to manage themselves, work teams need management information.

Enough Time and Resources

Work teams take time—years, really—to mature, so management needs to recognize that the rewards of self-direction depend on massive planning, intensive training and retraining, prompt access to resources, and often the physical redesigning of plants and offices.

Commitment to Training

Self-directed work teams stand or fall on the training they receive. Since people now have to put aside personal privilege and contribute to the group effort, self-direction represents a big change for anyone accustomed to blindly giving, following, or resisting orders. People therefore need intensive long-term training in the interpersonal, administrative, and technical skills that will counteract habits and attitudes left over from years of employment in a much more narrow environment.

Operations Conducive to Work Teams

Although any operation can benefit from increased employee involvement, the very deep involvement of self-directed teams requires an operation that includes a range of employee tasks, with some complex enough that improved skills and commitment can lead to improved productivity.

Union Participation

In any unionized operation, executives must take early and continued steps to make the union an active partner in the transition to teams. For its part, the union must demonstrate willingness to work for the overall health of the organization. And both union and management must find common ground in the shared understanding that a more competitive company is the best guarantor of job security.

Access to Help

Organizations going to self-directed work teams will need experienced help throughout the transition, and they must make sure at the outset that they know where to find it. This is a journey that benefits from guides who know the territory.

The Flip Side of Vision Is Caution

While the potential benefits are enormous, self-direction is no walkover. Anyone considering work teams is, therefore, strongly advised to see them as one among several proven ways to improve productivity, quality, and morale through structured employee involvement.

Teamwork once made the American way of business the economic prototype for the better part of the planet. Self-directed work teams could well make that happen all over again.

REFERENCES

Alan S. Blinder, "Want to Boost Productivity? Try Giving Workers a Say," *Business Week,* 17 April 1989, 10.

F. Paul Clipp, "Focusing Self-Managing Work Teams," *Quality Digest,* April 1990, 20–22, 24–29.

Brian Dumaine, "Who Needs a Boss?" *Fortune,* 7 May 1990, 52–55, 58, 60.

Fast Company, no. 3, 77.

John Hoerr, "The Payoff from Teamwork," *Business Week,* 10 July 1989, 58.

John Hoerr, Michael A. Pollock, David E. Whiteside, "Management Discovers the Human Side of Automation," *Business Week,* 29 September 1986, 70.

Jill Jusko, Quaker Oats Co., Danville, IL. *Industry Week:* Best Plants 1998. Available on-line http://www.industryweek.com/iwinprint/bestplants/98winners.html.

Linda Moran and Ed Musselwhite, *Self-Directed Workteams: A Lot More Than Just Teamwork* (San Jose, Calif.: Zenger-Miller, Inc., 1988), 13–18.

Stratford P. Sherman, "The Mind of Jack Welch," *Fortune,* 27 March 1989, 38–50.

John Teresko, Halliburton Energy Services, *Industry Week:* Profiles in Excellence. Available on-line.

Daniel Yankelovich, "The Work Ethic Is Under-Employed," *Psychology Today,* May 1982, 5, 6, 8.

Reading 23	# Can Absence Make a Team Grow Stronger?

Ann Majchrzak, Arvind Malhotra, Jeffrey Stamps, and Jessica Lipnack

The Cold War had been good to Rocketdyne, Boeing's propulsion and power division. Starting in 1958, when the United States launched its first orbiting satellite, all the way through the 1980s, Rocketdyne was the dominant producer of liquid-fuel rocket engines. But after the breakup of the Soviet Union, makers of communications and weather satellites started favoring the cheaper engines coming out of a newly independent Russia.

In response, Bob Carman, a program manager at Rocketdyne, envisioned an engine that was radically simpler and cheaper than anything in its catalog. But to design it, Carman needed people with a depth of expertise that didn't exist within Rocketdyne's two offices in Canoga Park, California. He needed the best simulation-software stress analysts, who knew how to test alternative designs on the computer so the company wouldn't have to build expensive prototypes, and he needed engineers who knew how to manufacture extremely precise parts in low volumes. The top simulation analysts worked at MSC Software, 100 miles away in Santa Ana, California, and the manufacturing engineers worked at Texas Instruments in Dallas. Remarkably, both groups had experience not only in modifying others' product designs for their own purposes but in originating them, a task more commonly the province of design engineers.

Going outside for expertise, specifically by forming partnerships with companies that had never produced a rocket engine, was viewed by Rocketdyne executives as "blasphemous," Carman recalls. Yet the eight-person group he assembled, about one-tenth the normal size, managed to design a reusable rocket engine, called SLICE, in only one-tenth the time span it took to develop its predecessors—and 1% of the actual number of hours. Featuring a thrust chamber and turbo pumps with only a few parts each instead of hundreds, it cost millions of dollars less to manufacture. The team was able to do

all this even though the only physical meeting held included just five of its members, and the group as a whole spent only about 15% of each work-week over ten months on the project. The very first sample unit it produced passed what is known as cold-flow testing, a simulation stage in rocket development that few designs ever reach.

How did Carman pull off this amazing feat? By using modern communications technology to fashion a virtual, far-flung team of diverse talents that no face-to-face team could match, even if its members uprooted themselves to come work together, or commuted between their home offices and the team's site, for the project's entire length. Carman then managed it so that the team's range of functions, disciplines, and temperaments didn't produce disarray.

In studying the Rocketdyne team, we noticed it had some unusual characteristics. Team members got to know one another well, though they spent absolutely no time together in person after the project began. They became remarkably attentive to one another's responses, though shifts in body language or facial expression were mostly invisible. They were working in areas outside their expertise but benefited greatly from being able to stay in familiar surroundings, continue working in their own organizations, and consult their local colleagues and extensive paper files.

We began to wonder whether other teams like SLICE existed. In 2002, we conducted a benchmarking study of successful virtual teams. Some were global, others regional. Half had members from more than one company. Half were long-term, and half had been set up just for a single project. All of them convinced us that when a project requires a diversity of competencies and perspectives and the work can be done by means of electronic documents and tools, it's better to opt for a far-flung team than for one that works face-to-face. Such teams not only have a wider variety of communication channels at their command but also are free of many of the psychological and practical obstacles to full and effective participation that hobble their traditional counterparts.

For instance, several team members mentioned that they contributed much more during virtual meetings than they would have in face-to-face settings. They said they felt compelled to articulate their views more precisely than if they had depended on visual cues. Although many did affirm the value, in theory, of meeting together in the same room, few in practice found it essential. On the contrary, they asserted, holding such traditional meetings would have harmed the teams' work processes. Decisions in a complex project have to be made continually. Postponing them until everyone assembles slows everything down—way, way down. If such a meeting is in the offing, everyone expects it to be where the real work will take place and avoids doing anything of value until the meeting occurs. Our far-flung leaders dealt with that problem by never holding one. As one team leader said, "There's nothing we don't discuss virtually."

Indeed, much of the value of virtual teams derived from members' ability to be in two places at once. Remaining tightly linked to their local organizations allowed them to keep their teammates current on developments there. Long or frequent absences would have made that difficult, in addition to diminishing team members' value to their home units.

But, clearly, far-flung virtual teams establish a sense of connectedness and immediacy differently from the way local teams do. The virtual solution: Blur the distinction between time spent at meetings and time spent away from them through the use of always open, online team rooms—and ensure that the meetings that do occur really count.

The proof of the method was in the results. One team in our study went beyond its charge and designed a manufacturing process that saved its employer millions of dollars. Another team delivered virtual training to 80% of its company's employees at one-eighth the traditional cost. Yet another group was able to merge the IT infrastructures of two billion-dollar firms without suffering a single mishap on day one.

In this article, we set out three principles that guided most of our teams. The first deals with how these teams were composed; the second with how they used technology to coordinate their efforts; and the third with how team leaders induced a collection of strangers with little in common to function as a mutually supportive group.

Rule 1: Exploit Diversity

With the assistance of his corporate partners, Bob Carman chose people for the SLICE team on the strength of their differences. They all may have spoken English, but the languages of their various disciplines were so dissimilar that, for a while, the engineers, analysts, and rocket scientists couldn't understand one another. Each subgroup also had a different style of working and a different approach to solving problems. One of the engineers from Texas Instruments, for instance, didn't believe in going to the trouble of constructing elaborate models to test how an increase in material thickness might affect ease of manufacturing. In the early stages of the design process, he was comfortable relying on his own judgment and experience. Rocketdyne's more cautious propulsion experts felt otherwise. Each team member had areas of competence that were uniquely his or her own, and, inevitably, disagreements arose over matters within one person's area of expertise that had repercussions for other team members. But the clash of perspectives produced solutions instead of acrimony. The propulsion engineers, for example, decided to thicken the edge of a casting part they had rounded to smooth the fuel's flow because the simulation engineers said the rounding diminished the part's ability to handle stress.

How were other teams able to take advantage of their diversity? Consider the example of a research and development team at Unilever Latin America that was asked to redesign a deodorant for the Colombian and Venezuelan markets. The packaging for the roll-on, stick, and cream formats were to be manufactured in Brazil; the engineer who was to develop the cream packaging was situated in Argentina. The roll-on formula itself was going to be made in Mexico and Brazil, the stick in Chile, and the cream in Colombia. But because the packaging and formula for the Colombian and Venezuelan markets differed from those the factories were already making for the rest of Latin America, the company needed the existing suppliers and manufacturing engineers, who were spread across five countries, to participate in the redesign of the new product. The kind of collaboration called for was best suited to a virtual team.

Much of the work of generating solutions happened in conference calls, which were carefully orchestrated by the team leader. "I didn't know the team members very well, didn't know how they thought and worked," the leader, who was based in Argentina, recalls, "so I couldn't always go directly to the point on an issue. Instead, I encouraged a lot of conversation, trying to reach a common view that included all of their points. We discussed different alternatives, always asking everyone, 'What do you think about this?'"

"If we had ignored even one country," the leader continues, "we would have run the risk of creating a product that could not be rolled out according to schedule. But by surfacing our differences early, we didn't ignore anyone's needs, and we rolled out the product without problems on time.'"

This level of attention paid to soliciting and discussing everyone's opinions makes for a far more detailed conversation than the sort teams have when they meet in person, where they can be led astray by excessive politeness. After all, not every nod means assent. Most of the leaders we studied worked hard to move conversations beyond tacit agreement. Typically, the teams' charters from management were broad, not prescriptive, requiring searching discussions by the entire group, not half-baked suggestions "phoned in" to the leader by people working on their own.

Leaders planned their weekly or bi-weekly conference calls as orchestrated events that team members wouldn't want to miss. To ensure that everyone communicated in the same way, some of the leaders asked those working at the same location to call in from their own desks, rather than from a conference room. Wallflowers were drawn out in the meetings and mentored between them. If they still declined to participate, they were sometimes cut.

Leaders typically started their teleconferences with an unexpected query or bit of news, then introduced a topic they knew would generate some heat. Every person was given a minute or so to respond. The call closed with what one team member called "a self-propelling ending"—that is, one that set the agenda for the next meeting.

To help overcome differences in communication styles, at the outset of a project several teams administered an online version of the Myers-Briggs Type Indicator (MBTI), the widely accepted assessment tool that places people in one of four personality "dimensions." In early teleconferences, team members agreed to remind everyone of their own MBTI styles when they spoke. "As you know, I think out loud," said one with a high extroversion score. In another team, a particularly young member often prefaced his comments with the reminder that he "hadn't been around the block yet."

These kinds of inclusive conversations proved to be indispensable for many of the teams. Although in the beginning their discussions took a lot of time, results more than made up for that. As the leader of the Unilever team says, "We got to a shared view much more quickly than any of us anticipated." Of course, teleconferencing was not the whole story.

Rule 2: Use Technology to Simulate Reality

Today, a host of technologies exist for processing and communicating information. Which of them did the teams we studied use? Our more interesting discovery was the ones they didn't.

Many in our study found e-mail a poor way for teams as a whole to collaborate. They reported what others have noticed as well: Trying to do the main work of the team through one-to-one exchanges between members can cause those not included to feel left out, diminishing trust in the group and leading ultimately to dysfunction.

To avoid this expensive mistake, some teams initially adopted the practice of copying everyone else on every e-mail exchange. They soon were drowning in messages. To cope, members resorted to deleting e-mail without reading it. Over time, it became harder to maintain control over the circulation of documents. People regularly found themselves working from different versions of the same one. They also complained about e-mail's poor documentation and storage features, which made it hard to find information quickly.

They didn't think much of videoconferencing either. Only one-third of our sample used it. The majority offered such objections as the distracting time delay of most systems and the difficulty of returning to the videoconferencing facility after normal business hours, particularly if the team members were in different hemispheres. But participating in a teleconference from home at nine or ten o'clock at night was less problematic. What's more, these teams felt that the visual cues most systems provided were too fuzzy to enhance the collaboration experience. In fact, those equipped with desktop videoconferencing found it almost impossible to watch their teammates and work collaboratively on their documents at the same time. Yet leaving the desktop and moving to a videoconferencing site was no answer either.

And while they made regular use of conference calls, team members did not report on the status of assignments during them. Instead, most (83%) relied on virtual work spaces. Here they posted their work in progress electronically and examined their colleagues' postings, well in advance of teleconferences. They tended to use the conference calls themselves to discuss disagreements, which they said were more effectively handled in conversation than in writing.

These work spaces were more than networked drives with shared files. Accessible to everyone at any time, the work space was where the group was reminded of its decisions, rationales, and commitments. A particularly good example of a team room is one that was set up at Shell Chemicals by assistant treasurer Tom Kunz, who led a project begun in February 2001 to develop a companywide, cash-focused approach to financial management. Essentially a Web site accessed on an intranet, it prominently displayed the project's mission statement on its home page, where no one could ignore it, as well as the photographs and names of team members, in a clocklike arrangement. During teleconferences, members adopted the practice of identifying themselves by their position on the clock: "This is Kate at ten o'clock," the member in Singapore would say.

The home page also had links to the other "walls," each of which was devoted to a particular aspect of the project. On the wall labeled "people," for instance, were kept not only individuals' contact information but also extensive profiles that included accomplishments, areas of expertise, and interests, as well as information about other stakeholders. On a wall labeled "purpose" was a hierarchical listing of the mission statement, the goals, and the tasks involved in meeting the goals, indicating how close each task was to completion. On the "meeting center" wall could be seen all the information needed to manage the teleconferences—notices of when they were being held, who was supposed to come, agendas, and minutes. Yet another wall displayed the team's responsibility chart, and one more contained the team's entire work product, organized into clearly numbered versions, so that people would not inadvertently work on the wrong one. Comprising seven walls in total, the team room kept information current, organized, and easily accessible.

Leaders used such online team rooms to hold virtual conversations, through threaded discussions. Organizing online conversations by topic made it easy for all those participating to follow each thread.

Team leaders tended to be the ones managing these threads, though that was not always the case. In a number of instances, a team member volunteered to serve as thread facilitator, taking responsibility for conducting the conversations the way teleconferences were run: a bit of news, a provocative question, and a self-propelling ending. To encourage participation in the online conversations, leaders posted links to documents relating to topics on the agenda of upcoming meetings and then encouraged discussion before the meetings. They also encouraged those responsible for crafting draft documents (slides, drawings, analyses, and the like) to kick off new discussion threads with requests for comments.

Members were supposed to adhere to previously agreed-upon protocols, such as how quickly to respond—typically within a week. At the end of the designated time period, there were usually enough contributions to warrant summarizing what had been said. When a topic generated a great deal of discussion, summaries would appear more frequently. The person who initiated a thread would be responsible for the summary, which highlighted areas of both agreement and disagreement. The team then took up the areas of disagreement at the next teleconference. Between teleconferences, team members continued their online threaded discussions.

Everything of substance that the team generated was always available, neatly categorized and easily retrievable, in the virtual team room. The structure of the space itself encouraged good virtual-team hygiene, since it called for similar kinds of information to be stored in corresponding spaces.

Nearly half the teams used instant messaging (IM), even when their companies barred it, which surprised us somewhat. People said that they particularly liked being able to share their "Eureka!" and "Oh, no!" moments with others logged in at the same time. Since the majority of companies had no standards for its use, most of our teams adopted IM ad hoc. In some cases, a team found itself using more than one IM program, which created IM cliques isolated by the information they alone shared. Some teams found IM sessions difficult to store and retrieve for future use. Others resented IM's power to interrupt whatever they were doing at the moment. Aware of the burgeoning of IM use and its harmful side effects, some team leaders worked with their IT organizations to develop standards and improve security.

Rule 3: Hold the Team Together

The hazards that commonly threaten to splinter face-to-face teams—mistrust, cliques, uninformed managers, and the allure of other interesting but unrelated work—can be even more pronounced on a virtual team. Ours were notably adept at wielding techniques that instead drew them together.

Team leaders rarely let a day go by when members did not communicate with one another. Frequent phone conversations between the team leader and individual members—even with those who did communicate regularly in teleconferences, in the work space, and in e-mails—were not unusual. One team leader reported being on the phone with his team for 10 to 15 hours a week.

Early in the life of a team, the leader would push it to adopt a common language—usually English, but not always. The members of the Unilever team adopted what they called "Portuñol," a hybrid of Spanish and Portuguese. Even on an unusually homogeneous team, where everyone shared a background in computer programming and spoke English, it was still necessary to compile a glossary, mostly of technical terms but also of figures of speech such as "home run" and "go for broke." A team comprising mainly Americans along with some Japanese members hit upon the idea of hiring as translators local engineering interns fluent in both Japanese and English.

Leaders also needed to create coherence when they were trying to blend the work processes of the members' home organizations. At one telecommunications company, some of the employees of a newly formed call center came from its northern operation, others from its southern. The southerners had been trained to solve customers' problems no matter how long it took or how disruptive doing so might be to the linemen's standing priorities. By contrast, the northerners were accustomed to spending a more or less standard amount of time with each customer and documenting what they'd done. After much discussion, the two sides decided that neither approach was wrong and therefore each should adopt elements of the other.

Another technique used to glue teams together was having members work in ad hoc pairs for a week or two. These subteams allowed members to get to know one another better and discouraged the formation of cliques. At one chemical products company, for instance, the leader of a strategic accounts team named subteams to flesh out the details of the account plans. The subteam members then came together to edit one another's work.

To keep the team members' home offices from trying to pull them away, team leaders negotiated in advance the extent of the team's claim on a member's time, made clear how the home office and the individual member stood to gain, and kept the home office abreast of the team's and the member's progress. Some team leaders separately negotiated a financial reward for every team member with his or her respective HR person. Needless to say, these were time-consuming commitments. While team membership was always part-time, team leadership was often more than full-time.

Even though diversity was, in some sense, a virtual team's reason for being, leaders recognized that identifying commonalities would strengthen loyalties to the group. The leader of one team, a retired military officer, started his conference calls by asking each person to spend 30 seconds describing "where the member is at."

During a conference call in 2002, when snipers were terrorizing the Washington, DC, area, a team member living there said she didn't feel so alone after she heard her fears echoed by another member in the Philippines, where insurgents were shooting people on their way to and from work.

The Power of the Small Group

If far-flung teams can be so effective, why aren't they used more? Organizational inertia rather than direct opposition often stands in the way.

There's another reason organizations have been slow to cotton to what our teams have discovered. The computer revolution missed a step. When companies went from enterprise computing to individual computing, they jumped over the small-group level, where the preponderance of work takes place. The first computers, typified by the IBM 360 behemoths of the 1960s, supported companywide operations. The generation of computers that followed supported department-level organizations, eventually morphing into today's servers. In the 1980s, personal computers boosted individuals' productivity. Then in the 1990s, the Internet and the Web connected these previously isolated individuals informally, boosting their productivity even more.

In this decade, the forgotten step, the small group, is suddenly the focus of advances in collaboration technology—shared online work spaces, on-demand teleconferencing, real-time application sharing, and instant messaging—which the massive investment in infrastructure of the late 1990s is now available to support. When small groups adopt the kinds of practices our teams have demonstrated, they can work faster, smarter, more creatively, and more flexibly than dispersed individuals or the enterprise as a whole.

EFFECTS OF THE WORK ENVIRONMENT

Individual levels of performance and creativity and even the personal satisfaction or dissatisfaction of musicians are highly influenced by the organizational environment. The imprecise term "environment" includes many factors. The orchestra's organizational structure, its financial health, communication patterns among musicians and between individual musicians and the business office, methods of coordinating among the sections, the style and temperament of the musical and business executives, the work norms, the presence or absence—and strength—of a musicians union, and the particular tastes of the orchestra's patrons all are parts of the "work environment." The work environment affects the psychological state, the attitudes, and the performance of individual musicians.

In this chapter, our analysis of organizational behavior moves away from individuals and small groups to address organizational structures, systems, culture, and behavioral norms. Although gifted individual musicians are the building blocks for any orchestra, the orchestra's organizational behavior cannot be understood without also looking beyond the individuals (the "trees") to the work environment (the "forest").

In 1959, Warren Bennis observed that such classical organizational theorists as Frederick Winslow Taylor, Henry Gantt, and Henri Fayol (see Shafritz, Ott, & Jang, 2005) were fixated on structural variables (such as the chain of command, centralization and decentralization, and span of control) to the extent that they almost seem to think about "organizations without people." In contrast, the human relations–oriented organizational behaviorists of the late 1950s and 1960s were so enamored with people and groups (with personal growth, group development, sensitivity training groups, and human relations training) that they seemed to think only about "people without organizations." Bennis's observation was equally applicable to the early industrial/organizational psychologists— to the pre-Hawthorne and pre–Theory X and Theory Y value system–based social scientists who worked with organizational behavior, but not from an organizational behavior perspective (see the Introduction to this book). However, organizational behavior reversed its field for several decades, and in the process almost forgot (or at least ignored) the substantial influences that organization systems and structures have on the people and groups in and around them.

Many things in the organizational context influence and are influenced by organizational behavior. To list only a few:

- *The type of business in which an organization is engaged.* The business of banking places different demands on and yields different rewards to employees than does making and marketing new television game shows.
- *The legal relationship between an organization and people who work for it.* Typically, there are different impacts on organizational behavior in, for example, a family-owned business, a publicly held investor-owned company, a nonprofit arts organization, and a government agency.
- *The nature of the perceived relationships between an organization and its environment at large.* The prevailing perception in some organizations seems to be that they exist in a hostile world where the media, general public, other types of organizations (such as government agencies, legislatures, or private corporations), and sometimes even clientele or customers (as well as direct competitors) all are immediate or potential enemies or threats. In contrast, the prevailing view in other organizations is more one of the organization existing in harmony with its environment.
- *The amount of direct personal contact among organization members and between organization members and nonmembers.* A large percentage of communications among organization members and between "insiders" and "outsiders" occurs electronically now. Employees, suppliers, customers, and strategic allies often are scattered around the country and the world. Thus, people do not meet face-to-face to work on problems and opportunities, resolve disagreements, or merely to socialize and build trust nearly as often as they used to.

The structure of the organization is also an important component. When someone refers to *organization structure,* usually he or she is talking about the relatively stable relationships among the positions or groups of positions (such as the units, divisions, and departments) that comprise an organization, along with the organized procedures and methods that define how things are designed for work to flow through it. *Structure* is the design of an organization, its units, and its production processes—the set of specific patterns of differentiation and integration of tasks and activities in an organization (Miles, 1980; Thompson, 1967). *Differentiation* is the (conceptual) dividing up of a total system into its component parts (units, groups, and people), which perform specialized tasks. (In essence, *differentiation* is a more sophisticated way of saying "division of labor.") *Integration* is how the divided-up parts and specialized tasks are linked together to form a coordinated whole.

A widely cited article by Lyman Porter and Edward Lawler (1965) identified the properties of organization structure that are most likely to affect individual and group attitudes and on-the-job behavior. Their list of structural properties included:

- *Organization levels* (the number of levels and in which one—or how high—one is situated)
- *Line* or *staff roles* of organization units
- *Span of control*
- *Size of units*
- *Size of the total organization*
- *Organization shape* (flat or tall)
- *Centralized* or *decentralized authority* and responsibility

The structure—an organization's shape, size, procedures, production technology, position descriptions, reporting arrangements, and coordinating relationships—affects the feelings and emotions, and therefore the behavior, of the people and groups inside them (Mastracci & Thompson, 2005). There are incongruities between the needs of a mature personality and of formal organization—between the growth trends of healthy people and the requirements of organizations (Argyris, 1957b). The impacts of structure on behavior partially result from the unique functions structure performs. In each organization, structure defines the unique ways labor is divided, how specialized roles and functions are to be coordinated (related to each other and to other organizational levels and functions), how information is to flow among people and groups who are near each other or connected over a distance electronically (Majchrzak, Malhotra, Stamps, & Lipnack, 2004) or are from different backgrounds (Hagberg, 2003; Kanter, 1979; Thomas, 1995), and how the system of controls (how tasks are measured, evaluated, and altered) is to work (Organ & Bateman, 1986; Orsburn & Moran, 2000). Structure establishes how *roles, expectations,* and *resource allocations* are defined for people and groups in any given organization. Structure is a primary reason organizational behavior differs from individual behavior, and thus why organizational behavior developed as a separate field of study within the applied behavioral sciences.

Structure, however, is only one of several forces that affect the behavior of people in organizations. Attitudes and behaviors also are shaped by *peer group pressure* (Asch, 1951; Harvey 1974; Janis, 1971; Porter, Lawler, & Hackman, 1975); *group norms*—the standards that develop are shared and enforced by the members of groups (Cohen & Fink, 2003; Feldman, 1984; Roy, 1960); the particular blending of social and technical aspects of work tasks—the *sociotechnical systems* (Thorsrud, 1968; Trist, 1960; Trist & Bamforth, 1951); and the *organizational culture* (Greiner, 1998; Ott, 1989; Schein, 1992; Senge, 1990; Whyte, 1956).

To an extent, all formal and informal groups require and expect people to conform to norms—prescriptions for behavior (see Chapter 3). Norms are behavioral blueprints that provide organizations with coherence. Acceptance of and adherence to group norms permit people to know what to expect from each other and to predict what other members will do in different circumstances. Norms cause people to behave in patterned and predictable ways; "because their behaviors are guided by common expectations, attitudes and understandings . . . norms are strong stabilizers of organizational behavior" (Schmuck, 1971, pp. 215–216). Norms establish some conformity, stability, and predictability—states that are both necessary and desirable.

On the other hand, too much adherence to norms causes overconformance and can hurt or destroy individualism (Merton, 1957; Porter, Lawler, & Hackman, 1975; Whyte, 1956). Potential damage, though, is not limited to individuals who work in organizations. Excessive conformity also can result in organizational rigidity. Organizations must be open to divergent information, viewpoints, realities, and value systems. Indeed, organizations must seek diversity and reward individuals and groups who succeed in injecting diversity into strategic decision processes (Cox, 1993; Thomas, 1995).

The readings in this chapter examine ways in which structure, group norms and pressures to conform, and organizational culture influence the behavior of individuals and groups in organizations. The focus is on how norms, expectations (Schein, 1980), structures of relationships, group pressures, and organizational culture combine to shape organizational behavior. Two of the selections also examine ways in which the forces that lead to conformity potentially damage individuals (Asch, 1951; Merton, 1957).

The first reading describes research in the problematic area of group effects on individuals' decisions. In "Effects of Group Pressure Upon the Modification and Distortion of Judgments," Solomon Asch (1951) describes his famous investigations into ways individuals cope when a group's majority opinion is directly contrary to the facts of a situation. Asch put lone experimental subjects (college students) in rooms with people who had been instructed to give blatantly wrong answers to factual questions. Only the experimental subjects did not know what was going on. Although a slim majority of experimental subjects retained their independence and reported the facts accurately, a sizable minority of subjects *altered their judgment to match that of the majority.* When faced with a group opinion that was obviously wrong, they were not willing to report their observations as they saw them. They changed their judgments. Asch attributes people's decisions to retain independence of judgment or to yield to the majority to several factors. The two most important factors are these:

- The size of the majority and the extent of unanimity among members of the majority
- Identifiable, enduring differences among individuals, particularly character differences involving social relations

Asch's experiments provide dramatic evidence of group impacts on people in organizations. From a managerial perspective, they show why it is extremely important to focus attention on the group's beliefs, values, composition, and activities. Nevertheless, for the most part, informal groups are outside the formal organization's direct sphere of influence.

In "Bureaucratic Structure and Personality," Robert Merton (1940, 1957) analyzes how one form of organization structure—*bureaucracy*—impinges on the personalities of people who work inside them. Merton uses *bureaucracy* to mean the pervasive form of organization that Max Weber (1922) described in *Wirtschat und Gesellschaft*. In this use, *bureaucracy* is not an epithet per se, nor is it limited in applicability to government agencies. According to Merton, bureaucracy exerts constant pressures on people to be methodical and disciplined, to conform to patterns of obligations. These pressures eventually cause people to adhere to rules as an end rather than a means—as a matter of blind conformance. Bureaucratic structure also stresses depersonalized relations and power and authority gained by virtue of organizational position rather than by thought or action. Without question, Merton sees bureaucratic structure as more than *affecting* organizational behavior and thinking: it also *determines and controls it*. As a form of organization, bureaucracy has its advantages: order, predictability, stability, professionalism, and consistency (Shafritz, Ott, & Jang, 2005). Nevertheless, the behavioral consequences of bureaucratic structure are mostly negative, including reduced organizational flexibility and efficiency and, adapting a phrase coined by Merton, eventually "bureaupathological personalities" of members.

Twenty years after Solomon Asch's experiments, Irving Janis (1971) published the equally well-known study, "Groupthink," which is reprinted in this chapter. Like Asch, Janis explores pressures for conformance—the reasons social conformity is encountered frequently in groups. But unlike Asch's experimental use of college students, Janis looked at high-level decision makers in times of real major fiascos: the 1962 Bay of Pigs, the 1950 decision to send General MacArthur to the Yalu River, and the 1941 failure to prepare for the attack on Pearl Harbor. *Groupthink* is "the mode of thinking that persons engage in when *concurrence seeking* becomes so dominant in a cohesive in-group that it tends to override realistic appraisal of alternative courses of action . . . the desperate drive for consensus at any cost that suppresses dissent among the mighty in the corridors of power." Janis identifies eight symptoms of groupthink that are relatively easy to observe:

- An illusion of invulnerability
- Collective construction of rationalizations that permit group members to ignore warnings or other forms of negative feedback
- Unquestioning belief in the morality of the in-group
- Strong, negative, stereotyped views about the leaders of enemy groups
- Rapid application of pressure against group members who express even momentary doubts about virtually any illusions the group shares
- Careful, conscious, personal avoidance of deviation from what appears to be a group consensus

- Shared illusions of unanimity of opinion
- Establishment of *mindguards*—people who "protect the leader and fellow members from adverse information that might break the complacency they shared about the effectiveness and morality of past decisions"

Janis concludes with an assessment of the negative influence of groupthink on executive decision making (including overestimation of the group's capability and self-imposed isolation from new or opposing information and points of view) and some preventive and remedial steps for groupthink.

Jerry B. Harvey examines a group phenomenon that differs from Janis's *groupthink* but also shares many similarities, in "The Abilene Paradox: The Management of Agreement" (1974), which is reprinted here. The Abilene Paradox is: "Organizations frequently take actions in contradiction to what they really want to do and therefore defeat the very purposes they are trying to achieve." The paradox's major corollary is: "The inability to manage agreement is a major source of organization dysfunction." Harvey uses a simple parable to illustrate a major symptom of organizational dysfunction—the management of agreement as opposed to the management of disagreement or conflict—and how we do or do not engage in deep inquiry and in self-disclosure when attempting to come to agreement with others. "The Abilene Paradox" describes the symptoms exhibited by organizations caught in the paradox, describes how the symptoms occur, discusses the underlying causal dynamics and the implications for individuals and organizations, and recommends ways for individuals and groups to cope with the Abilene Paradox.

Harvey also uses testimony from the Senate Watergate cover-up hearings to illustrate how the Abilene Paradox can strike in any type of organizations and at all levels. "It is possible that because of the inability of White House staff members to cope with the fact that they agreed, the organization took a trip to Abilene." "The Abilene Paradox" concludes on an existential note: Both agreement and disagreement are organizational realities, "however, the decision to confront the possibility of organization agreement is all too difficult and rare, and its opposite, the decision to accept the evils of the present, is all too common."

Porter, Lawler, and Hackman's chapter, "Social Influences on Work Effectiveness" (reprinted in this chapter), from their 1975 book *Behavior in Organizations,* analyzes how groups and members of a person's reference group exert influence on individuals in organizations, and how these social influences affect work effectiveness. This piece focuses particularly on the "notion that the nature and degree of such social influences depend crucially on the type of work being performed and thus on the demands that the work makes on the person." The chapter specifically examines dysfunctional aspects of eliminating deviance from group norms, why high group cohesiveness can be dysfunctional, and ways that groups influence individual work effectiveness. "The point is that the people who surround an individual at work can facilitate as well as hinder . . . performance effectiveness—and that any serious attempt to diagnose the social environment in the interest of improving work performance should explicitly address unrealized possibilities for enhancing performance as well as issues for which remedial action may be required."

The readings in Chapter 4 conclude with Edgar H. Schein's "The Psychological Contract and Motivation in Perspective" (1980)—an examination of one specific type of influence on the motivation and behavior of individuals: when people believe an organization is living up to its commitments to them or, on the other hand, has violated its commitments to them. "The notion of a psychological contract implies that there is an unwritten set of expectations operating at all times between every member of an organization and the various managers and others in that organization." Because the needs of individuals and organizations change over time, expectations also change. Thus, the psychological contract which is "a powerful determiner of behavior in organizations" requires periodic renegotiation.

Whether individuals accept or reject an organization's *pivotal norms* and *peripheral norms* determines whether they will respond to power and authority with conformity, subversive rebellion, creative individualism, or open revolution. "Ultimately the relationship between the individual and the organization is interactive, unfolding through mutual influence and mutual bargaining to establish and reestablish a workable psychological contract."

REFERENCES

Argyris, C. (1957a). *Personality and organization.* New York: Harper.

Argyris, C. (1957b). The individual and organization: Some problems of mutual adjustment. *Administrative Science Quarterly, 2,* 1–24.

Asch, S. E. (1951). Effects of group pressure upon the modification and distortion of judgments. In H. S. Guetzkow (Ed.), *Groups, leadership, and men* (pp. 177–190). Pittsburgh, PA: Carnegie Press.

Barsky, N. P. (1999). *Organizational determinants of budgetary influence and involvement.* New York: Garland.

Bolman, L. G., & Deal, T. E. (2003). People and organizations. In L. G. Bolman & T. E. Deal, *Reframing organizations: Artistry, choice, and leadership* (3rd ed., pp. 113–132). San Francisco: Jossey-Bass/John Wiley.

Clemmons, S. Y. (2006). *Resource planning system influence on job design and organizational culture.* Ann Arbor, MI: ProQuest Information and Learning.

Cohen, A. R., & Bradford, D. L. (2005). *Influence without authority.* New York: John Wiley.

Cohen, A. R., & Fink, S. L. (2003). *Effective behavior in organizations* (7th ed.). New York: McGraw-Hill/Irwin.

Cox, T. H., Jr. (1993). *Cultural diversity in organizations: Theory, research & practice.* San Francisco: Berrett-Koehler.

Feldman, D. C. (1984, January). The development and enforcement of group norms. *Academy of Management Review,* 47–53.

Gabbert, J. A. (2006). *The relationship between organizational values and management behaviors and their influence on organizational effectiveness in an army project management organization.* Ann Arbor, MI: ProQuest Information and Learning.

Greiner, L. E. (1998, May/June). Revolution as organizations grow. *Harvard Business Review,* 55–67.

Haass, R. N. (1999). *The bureaucratic entrepreneur.* Washington, DC: Brookings Institution.

Hagberg, J. O. (2003). *Real power: The stages of personal power in organizations* (3rd ed.). Salem, WI: Sheffield.

Harvey, J. B. (1974, Summer). The Abilene paradox: The management of agreement. *Organizational Dynamics,* 63–80.

Harvey, J. B. (1988). *The Abilene paradox and other meditations on management.* Lexington, MA: Lexington.

Janis, I. L. (1971). Groupthink. *Psychology Today, 5,* 44–76.

Jaques, E. (1950). Collaborative group methods in a wage negotiation situation (The Glacier Project—I). *Human Relations, 3*(3).

Kahn, W. A. (1990). Psychological conditions of personal engagement and disengagement at work. *Academy of Management Journal, 33*(4), 692–724.

Kanter, R. M. (1979, July/August). Power failure in management circuits. *Harvard Business Review, 57,* 65–75.

Katz, D., & Kahn, R. L. (1966). *The social psychology of organizations.* New York: John Wiley.

Majchrzak, A., Malhotra, A., Stamps, J., & Lipnack, J. (2004, May). Can absence make a team grow stronger? *Harvard Business Review,* 131–137.

Mastracci, S. H., & Thompson, J. R. (2005). Nonstandard work arrangements in the public sector: Trends and issues. *Review of Public Personnel Administration, 25*(4), 299–324.

Merton, R. K. (1957). Bureaucratic structure and personality. In R. K. Merton, *Social theory and social structure* (rev. & enl. ed.). New York: The Free Press. (A revised version of an article of the same title that appeared in *Social Forces, 18* [1940].)

Miles, R. H. (1980). *Macro organizational behavior.* Santa Monica, CA: Goodyear.

Mills, T. (1976, October). Altering the social structure in coal mining: A case study. *Monthly Labor Review,* 3–10.

Organ, D. W., & Bateman, T. (1986). *Organizational behavior: An applied psychological approach* (3rd ed.). Plano, TX: Business Publications.

Orsburn, J. D., & Moran, L. (2000). *The new self directed work teams: Mastering the challenge.* New York: McGraw-Hill.

Ott, J. S. (1989). *The organizational culture perspective.* Belmont, CA: Wadsworth.

Pfeffer, J. (1991). Organization theory and structural perspectives on management. *Journal of Management, 17*(4), 789–803.

Porter, L. W., & Lawler, E. E. III (1964). The effects of tall vs. flat organization structures on managerial job satisfaction. *Personnel Psychology, 17,* 135–148.

Porter, L. W., & Lawler, E. E. III (1965). Properties of organization structure in relation to job attitudes and job behavior. *Psychological Bulletin, 64*(1), 23–51.

Porter, L. W., Lawler, E. E. III, & Hackman, J. R. (1975). Social influences on work effectiveness. In L. W. Porter, E. E. Lawler III, & J. R. Hackman (Eds.), *Behavior in organizations* (pp. 403–422). New York: McGraw-Hill.

Rice, A. K. (1953). Productivity and social organization in an Indian weaving shed: An examination of some aspects of the sociotechnical system of an experimental automatic loom shed. *Human Relations, 6,* 297–329.

Rice, A. K., Hill, J. M. M., & Trist, E. L. (1950). The representation of labour turnover as a social process (The Glacier Project—II). *Human Relations, 3*(4).

Rousseau, D. M. (1995). *Psychological contracts in organizations: Understanding written and unwritten agreements.* Thousand Oaks, CA: Sage.

Roy, D. F. (1960). "Banana time": Job satisfaction and informal interaction. *Human Organization, 18,* 158–168.

Schein, E. H. (1980). *Organizational psychology* (3rd ed.). Englewood Cliffs, NJ: Prentice-Hall.

Schein, E. H. (1992). *Leadership and organizational culture* (2nd ed.). San Francisco: Jossey-Bass.

Schmuck, R. A. (1971). Developing teams of organizational specialists. In R. A. Schmuck & M. B. Miles (Eds.), *Organization development in schools* (pp. 213–230). Palo Alto, CA: National Press Books.

Senge, P. M. (1990). *The fifth discipline: The art and practice of the learning organization.* New York: Doubleday Currency.

Shafritz, J. M., Ott, J. S., & Jang, Y. S. (2005). *Classics of organization theory* (5th ed.). Belmont, CA: Thomson-Wadsworth.

Thomas, R. (1995). A diversity framework. In M. M. Chemers, S. Oskamp, & M. A. Costanzo (Eds.), *Diversity in organizations: New perspectives for a changing workplace* (pp. 245–263). Thousand Oaks, CA: Sage.

Thompson, J. D. (1967). *Organizations in action.* New York: McGraw-Hill.

Thorsrud, D. E. (1968). Sociotechnical approach to job design and organization development. *Management International Review, 8,* 120–131.

Tocqueville, A. de (1847). *Democracy in America.* New York: Walker.

Trist, E. L. (1960). *Socio-technical systems.* London: Tavistock Institute of Human Relations.

Trist, E. L., & Bamforth, K. (1951). Some social and psychological consequences of the longwall method of coal-getting. *Human Relations, 4,* 3–38.

Trist, E. L., Higgin, G. W., Murray, H., & Pollock, A. B. (1965). *Organizational choice.* London: Tavistock Institute of Human Relations.

Trist, E., & Murray, H. (Eds.). *The social engagement of social science: The socio-psychological perspective.* London: Free Association Books.

Tsai, M.-T., & Shih, C.-M. (2005). The influences of organizational and personal ethics on role conflict among marketing managers: An empirical investigation. *International Journal of Management, 22*(1), 54–61.

Walton, R. E. (1975). From Hawthorne to Topeka and Kalmar. In E. L. Cass & F. G. Zimmer (Eds.), *Man and work in society* (pp. 116–129). New York: Western Electric.

Weber, M. (1922). Bureaucracy. In H. Gerth & C. W. Mills (Eds.), *Max Weber: Essays in sociology.* Oxford, UK: Oxford University Press.

Whyte, W. F. (1961). *Men at work.* Homewood, IL: Dorsey.

Whyte, W. H., Jr. (1956). *The organization man.* New York: Simon & Schuster.

Reading 24	**Effects of Group Pressure Upon the Modification and Distortion of Judgments**

Solomon E. Asch

. . . Our immediate objective was to study the social and personal conditions that induce individuals to resist or to yield to group pressures when the latter are perceived to be *contrary to fact*. The issues which this problem raises are of obvious consequence for society; it can be of decisive importance whether or not a group will, under certain conditions, submit to existing pressures. Equally direct are the consequences for individuals and our understanding of them, since it is a decisive fact about a person whether he possesses the freedom to act independently, or whether he characteristically submits to group pressures. . . .

Basic to the current approach has been the axiom that group pressures characteristically induce psychological changes *arbitrarily*, in far-reaching disregard of the material properties of the given conditions. This mode of thinking has almost exclusively stressed the slavish submission of individuals to group forces, has neglected to inquire into their possibilities for independence and for productive relations with human environment, and has virtually denied the capacity of men under certain conditions to rise above group passion and prejudice. It was our aim to contribute to a clarification of these questions, important both for theory and for their human implications, by means of direct observation of the effects of groups upon the decisions and evaluations of individuals.

The Experiment and First Results

To this end we developed an experimental technique which has served as the basis for the present series of studies. We employed the procedure of placing an individual in a relation of radical conflict with all the other members of a group, of measuring its effect upon him in quantitative terms, and of describing its psychological consequences.

A group of eight individuals was instructed to judge a series of simple, clearly structured perceptual relations—to match the length of a given line with one of three unequal lines. Each member of the group announced his judgments publicly. In the midst of this monotonous "test" one individual found himself suddenly contradicted by the entire group, and this contradiction was repeated again and again in the course of the experiment. The group in question had, with the exception of one member, previously met with the experimenter and received instructions to respond at certain points with wrong—and unanimous—judgments. The errors of the majority were large (ranging between ½″ and 1 ¾″) and of an order not encountered under control conditions. The outstanding person—the critical subject—whom we had placed in the position of a *minority of one* in the midst of a *unanimous majority*—was the object of investigation. He faced, possibly for the first time in his life, a situation in which a group unanimously contradicted the evidence of his senses.

This procedure was the starting point of the investigation and the point of departure for the study of further problems. Its main features were the following: (1) The critical subject was submitted to two contradictory and irreconcilable forces—the evidence of his own experience of an utterly clear perceptual fact and the unanimous evidence of a group of equals. (2) Both forces were part of the immediate situation; the majority was concretely present, surrounding the subject physically. (3) The critical subject, who was requested together with all others to state his judgments publicly, was obliged to declare himself and to take a definite stand vis-à-vis the group. (4) The situation possessed a self-contained character. The critical

Source: Solomon Asch, "Effects of Group Pressure Upon the Modification and Distortion of Judgments," GROUPS, LEADERSHIP, AND MEN, H. Guetzkow. © 1951 Carnegie Mellon University. Reprinted by permission of the publisher.

subject could not avoid or evade the dilemma by reference to conditions external to the experimental situation. (It may be mentioned at this point that the forces generated by the given conditions acted so quickly upon the critical subjects that instances of suspicion were rare.)

The technique employed permitted a simple quantitative measure of the "majority effect" in terms of the frequency of errors in the direction of the distorted estimates of the majority. At the same time we were concerned from the start to obtain evidence of the ways in which the subjects perceived the group, to establish whether they became doubtful, whether they were tempted to join the majority. Most important, it was our object to establish the grounds of the subject's independence or yielding—whether, for example, the yielding subject was aware of the effect of the majority upon him, whether he abandoned his judgment deliberately or compulsively. To this end we constructed a comprehensive set of questions which served as the basis of an individual interview immediately following the experimental period. Toward the conclusion of the interview each subject was informed fully of the purpose of the experiment, of his role and of that of the majority. The reactions to the disclosure of the purpose of the experiment became in fact an integral part of the procedure. We may state here that the information derived from the interview became an indispensable source of evidence and insight into the psychological structure of the experimental situation, and in particular, of the nature of the individual differences. Also, it is not justified or advisable to allow the subject to leave without giving him a full explanation of the experimental conditions. The experimenter has a responsibility to the subject to clarify his doubts and to state the reasons for placing him in the experimental situation. When this is done most subjects react with interest and many express gratification at having lived through a striking situation which has some bearing on wider human issues.

Both the members of the majority and the critical subjects were male college students. We shall report the results for a total of fifty critical subjects in this experiment. In Table 1 we summarize the successive comparison trials and the majority estimates. The quantitative results are clear and unambiguous.

1. There was a marked movement toward the majority. One-third of all the estimates in the critical group were errors identical with or in the direction of the distorted estimates of the majority.

   The significance of this finding becomes clear in the light of the virtual absence of errors in control groups the members of which recorded their estimates in writing. . . .

2. At the same time the effect of the majority was far from complete. The preponderance of estimates in the critical group (68 per cent) was correct despite the pressure of the majority.

3. We found evidence of extreme individual differences. There were those in the critical group subjects who remained independent without exception, and there were those who went nearly all the time with the majority. (The maximum possible number of errors was 12, while the actual range of errors was 0–11.) One-fourth of the critical subjects was completely independent; at the other extreme, one-third of the group displaced the estimates toward the majority in one-half or more of the trials.

The differences between the critical subjects in their reactions to the given conditions were equally striking. There were subjects who remained completely confident throughout. At the other extreme were those who became disoriented, doubt-ridden, and experienced a powerful impulse not to appear different from the majority. . . .

A First Analysis of Individual Differences

On the basis of the interview data described earlier, we undertook to differentiate and describe the major forms of reaction to the experimental situation, which we shall now briefly summarize.

TABLE I | LENGTHS OF STANDARD AND COMPARISON LINES

Trials	Length of Standard Line (in inches)	Comparison Lines (in inches)			Correct Response	Group Response	Majority Error (in inches)
		1	2	3			
1	10	8¾	10	8	2	2	—
2	2	2	1	1½	1	1	—
3	3	3¾	4¼	3	3	1*	+¾
4	5	5	4	6½	1	2*	−1.0
5	4	3	5	4	3	3	—
6	3	3¾	4¼	3	3	2*	+1¼
7	8	6¼	8	6¾	2	3*	−1¼
8	5	5	4	6½	1	3*	+1½
9	8	6¼	8	6¾	2	1*	−1¾
10	10	8¾	10	8	2	2	—
11	2	2	1	1½	1	1	—
12	3	3¾	4¼	3	3	1*	+¾
13	5	5	4	6½	1	2*	−1.0
14	4	3	5	4	3	3	—
15	3	3¾	4¼	3	3	2*	+1¼
16	8	6¼	8	6¾	2	3*	−1¼
17	5	5	4	6½	1	3*	+1½
18	8	6¼	8	6¾	2	1*	−1¾

*Starred figures designate the erroneous estimates by the majority.

Among the *independent* subjects we distinguished the following main categories:

1. Independence based on *confidence* in one's perception and experience. The most striking characteristic of these subjects is the vigor with which they withstand the group opposition. Though they are sensitive to the group, they show a resilience in coping with it, which is expressed in their continuing reliance on their perception and the effectiveness with which they shake off the oppressive group opposition.

2. Quite different are those subjects who are independent and *withdrawn*. These do not react in a spontaneously emotional way, but rather on the basis of explicit principles concerning the necessity of being an individual.

3. A third group of independent subjects manifest considerable tension and *doubt,* but

adhere to their judgments on the basis of a felt necessity to deal adequately with the task.

The following were the main categories of reaction among the *yielding* subjects, or those who went with the majority during one-half or more of the trials.

1. *Distortion of perception* under the stress of group pressure. In this category belong a very few subjects who yield completely, but are not aware that their estimates have been displaced or distorted by the majority. These subjects report that they came to perceive the majority estimates as correct.
2. *Distortion of judgment.* Most submitting subjects belong to this category. The factor of greatest importance in this group is a decision the subjects reach that their perceptions are inaccurate, and that those of the majority are correct. These subjects suffer from primary doubt and lack of confidence; on this basis they feel a strong tendency to join the majority.
3. *Distortion of action.* The subjects in this group do not suffer a modification of perception nor do they conclude that they are wrong. They yield because of an overmastering need not to appear different from or inferior to others, because of an inability to tolerate the appearance of defectiveness in the eyes of the group. These subjects suppress their observations and voice the majority position with awareness of what they are doing.

The results are sufficient to establish that independence and yielding are not psychologically homogeneous, that submission to group pressure (and freedom from pressure) can be the result of different psychological conditions. It should also be noted that the categories described above, being based exclusively on the subjects' reactions to the experimental conditions, are descriptive, not presuming to explain why a given individual responded in one way rather than another. The further exploration of the basis for the individual differences is a separate task upon which we are now at work.

Experimental Variations

The results described are clearly a joint function of two broadly different sets of conditions. They are determined first by the specific external conditions, by the particular character of the relation between social evidence and one's own experience. Second, the presence of pronounced individual difference points to the important role of personal factors, of factors connected with the individual's character structure. We reasoned that there are group conditions which would produce independence in all subjects, and that there probably are group conditions which would induce intensified yielding in many, though not in all. Accordingly we followed the procedure of *experimental variation*, systematically altering the quality of social evidence by means of systematic variation of group conditions. . . .

The Effect of Nonunanimous Majorities

Evidence obtained from the basic experiment suggested that the condition of being exposed *alone* to the opposition of a "compact majority" may have played a decisive role in determining the course and strength of the effects observed. Accordingly we undertook to investigate in a series of successive variations the effects of *nonunanimous* majorities. The technical problem of altering the uniformity of a majority is, in terms of our procedure, relatively simple. In most instances, we merely directed one or more members of the instructed group to deviate from the majority in prescribed ways. It is obvious that we cannot hope to compare the performance of the same individual in two situations on the assumption that they remain independent of one another. At best we can investigate the effect of an earlier upon a later experimental condition. . . . The following were some of the variations we studied:

1. *The presence of a "true partner."* (a) In the midst of the majority were *two* naive, critical subjects. The subjects were separated, spatially, being seated in the fourth and eighth positions, respectively. Each therefore heard

his judgment confirmed by one other person (provided the other person remained independent), one prior to, the other subsequently to announcing his own judgment. In addition, each experienced a break in the unanimity of the majority. There were six pairs of critical subjects.

(b) In a further variation the "partner" to the critical subject was a member of the group who had been instructed to respond correctly throughout. This procedure permits the exact control of the partner's responses. The partner was always seated in the fourth position; he therefore announced his estimates in each case before the critical subject.

The results clearly demonstrate that a disturbance of the unanimity of the majority markedly increased the independence of the critical subjects. The frequency of pro-majority errors dropped to 10.4 per cent of the total number of estimates in variation (a), and to 5.5 per cent in variation (b). These results are to be compared with the frequency of yielding to the unanimous majorities in the basic experiment, which was 32 per cent of the total number of estimates. It is clear that the presence in the field of *one other* individual who responded correctly was sufficient to deplete the power of the majority, and in some cases to destroy it. This finding is all the more striking in the light of other variations which demonstrate the effect of even small minorities provided they are unanimous. Indeed, we have been able to show that a unanimous majority of three is, under the given conditions, far more effective than a majority of eight containing one dissenter. That critical subjects will under these conditions free themselves of a majority of seven and join forces with one other person in the minority is, we believe, a result significant for theory. It points to a fundamental psychological difference between the condition of being alone and having a minimum of human support. It further demonstrates that the effects obtained are not the result of a summation of influences proceeding from each member of the group; it

is necessary to conceive the results as being relationally determined.

2. *Withdrawal of a "true partner."* What will be the effect of providing the critical subject with a partner who responds correctly and then withdrawing him? The critical subject started with a partner who responded correctly. The partner was a member of the majority who had been instructed to respond correctly and to "desert" to the majority in the middle of the experiment. This procedure permits the observation of the same subject in the course of transition from one condition to another. The withdrawal of the partner produced a powerful and unexpected result. We had assumed that the critical subject, having gone through the experience of opposing the majority with a minimum of support, would maintain his independence when alone. Contrary to this expectation, we found that the experience of having had and then lost a partner restored the majority effect to its full force, the proportion of errors rising to 28.5 per cent of all judgments, in contrast to the preceding level of 5.5 per cent. Further experimentation is needed to establish whether the critical subjects were responding to the sheer fact of being alone, or to the fact that the partner abandoned them.

3. *Late arrival of a "true partner."* The critical subject started as a minority of one in the midst of a unanimous majority. Toward the conclusion of the experiment one member of the majority "broke" away and began announcing correct estimates. This procedure, which reverses the order of conditions of the preceding experiment, permits the observation of the transition from being alone to being a member of a pair against a majority. It is obvious that those critical subjects who were independent when alone would continue to be so when joined by another partner. The variation is therefore of significance primarily for those subjects who yielded during the first phase of the experiment. The appearance of the late partner exerts a freeing effect, reducing the level to 8.7 per cent. Those who had previously

yielded also became markedly more independent, but not completely so, continuing to yield more than previously independent subjects. The reports of the subjects do not cast much light on the factors responsible for the result. It is our impression that having once committed himself to yielding, the individual finds it difficult and painful to change his direction. To do so is tantamount to a public admission that he has not acted rightly. He therefore follows the precarious course he has already chosen in order to maintain an outward semblance of consistency and conviction.

4. *The presence of a "compromise partner."* The majority was consistently extremist, always matching the standard with the most unequal line. One instructed subject (who, as in the other variations, preceded the critical subject) also responded incorrectly, but his estimates were always intermediate between the truth and the majority position. The critical subject therefore faced an extremist majority whose unanimity was broken by one more moderately erring person. Under these conditions the frequency of errors was reduced, but not significantly. However, the lack of unanimity determined in a strikingly consistent way the *direction* of the errors. The preponderance of the errors, 75.7 per cent of the total, was moderate, whereas, in a parallel experiment in which the majority was unanimously extremist (*i.e.,* with the "compromise" partner excluded), the incidence of moderate errors was reduced to 42 per cent of the total. As might be expected, in a unanimously moderate majority, the errors of the critical subjects were without exception moderate.

The Role of Majority Size

To gain further understanding of the majority effect, we varied the size of the majority in several different variations. The majorities, which were in each case unanimous, consisted of 16, 8, 4, 3, and 2 persons, respectively. In addition, we studied the limited case in which the critical subject was opposed by one instructed subject. . . .

With the opposition reduced to one, the majority effect all but disappeared. When the opposition proceeded from a group of two, it produced a measurable though small distortion, the errors being 12.8 per cent of the total number of estimates. The effect appeared in full force with a majority of three. Larger majorities of four, eight, and sixteen did not produce effects greater than a majority of three.

The effect of a majority is often silent, revealing little of its operation to the subject, and often hiding it from the experimenter. To examine the range of effects it is capable of inducing, decisive variations of conditions are necessary. An indication of one effect is furnished by the following variation in which the conditions of the basic experiment were simply reversed. Here the majority, consisting of a group of sixteen, was naive; in the midst of it we placed a single individual who responded wrongly according to instructions. Under these conditions the members of the naive majority reacted to the lone dissenter with amusement and disdain. Contagious laughter spread through the group at the droll minority of one. Of significance is the fact that the members lack awareness that they draw their strength from the majority, and that their reactions would change radically if they faced the dissenter individually. In fact, the attitude of derision in the majority turns to seriousness and increased respect as soon as the minority is increased to three. These observations demonstrate the role of social support as a source of power and stability, in contrast to the preceding investigations which stressed the effect of withdrawal of social support, or to be more exact, the effects of social opposition. Both aspects must be explicitly considered in a unified formulation of the effects of group conditions on the formation and change of judgments.

The Role of the Stimulus-Situation

It is obviously not possible to divorce the quality and course of the group forces which act upon the individual from the specific stimulus-conditions. Of necessity the structure of the situation molds the group forces and determines their direction as well as their strength. Indeed, this was the reason that we took pains in the investigations described above to center the issue between the individual and the group around an elementary and fundamental matter of fact. And there can be no doubt that the resulting reactions were directly a function of the contradiction between the objectively grasped relations and the majority position. . . .

We have also varied systematically the structural clarity of the task, including in separate variations judgments based on mental standards. In agreement with other investigators, we find that the majority effect grows stronger as the situation diminishes in clarity. Concurrently, however, the disturbance of the subjects and the conflict-quality of the situation decrease markedly. We consider it of significance that the majority achieves its most pronounced effect when it acts most painlessly.

SUMMARY

We have investigated the effects upon individuals of majority opinions when the latter were seen to be in a direction contrary to fact. By means of a simple technique, we produced a radical divergence between a majority and a minority, and observed the ways in which individuals coped with the resulting difficulty. Despite the stress of the given conditions, a substantial proportion of individuals retained their independence throughout. At the same time, a substantial minority yielded, modifying their judgments in accordance with the majority. Independence and yielding are a joint function of the following major factors: (1) The character of the stimulus situation. Variations in structural clarity have a decisive effect: With diminishing clarity of the stimulus-conditions the majority effect increases. (2) The character of the group forces. Individuals are highly sensitive to the structural qualities of group opposition. In particular, we demonstrated the great importance of the factor of unanimity. Also, the majority effect is a function of the size of group opposition. (3) The character of the individual. There were wide, and indeed, striking differences among individuals within the same experimental situation. The hypothesis was proposed that these are functionally dependent on relatively enduring character differences, in particular those pertaining to the person's social relations.

REFERENCES

1. Asch, S. E. Studies in the principles of judgments and attitudes: II. Determination of judgments by group and by ego-standards. *J. soc. Psychol.,* 1940, *12,* 433–465.

2. ———. The doctrine of suggestion, prestige and imitation in social psychology. *Psychol. Rev.,* 1948, *55,* 250–276.

3. Asch, S. E., Block, H., and Hertzman, M. Studies in the principles of judgments and attitudes. 1. Two Basic principles of judgment. *J. Psychol.,* 1938, *5,* 219–251.

4. Coffin, E. E. Some conditions of suggestion and suggestibility: A study of certain attitudinal and situational factors influencing the process of suggestion. *Psychol. Monogr.* 1941, *53,* No. 4.

5. Lewis, H. B. Studies in the principles of judgments and attitudes: IV. The operation of prestige suggestion. *J. soc. Psychol.,* 1941, *14,* 229–256.

6. Lorge, I. Prestige, suggestion, and attitudes. *J. soc. Psychol.,* 1936, *7,* 386–402.

7. Miller, N. E. and Dollard, J. *Social learning and imitation.* New Haven: Yale University Press, 1941.

8. Moore, H. T. The comparative influence of majority and expert opinion. *Amer. J. Psychol.,* 1921, *32,* 16–20.

9. Sherif, M. A study of some social factors in perception. *Arch. Psychol.,* N. Y. 1935, No. 187.

10. Thorndike, E. L. *The Psychology of wants, interests, and attitudes.* New York: D. Appleton-Century Company, Inc., 1935.

Reading 25	Bureaucratic Structure and Personality
	Robert K. Merton

The Structure of Bureaucracy

The ideal type of ... formal organization is bureaucracy and, in many respects, the classical analysis of bureaucracy is that by Max Weber.[1] As Weber indicates, bureaucracy involves a clear-cut division of integrated activities which are regarded as duties inherent in the office. A system of differentiated controls and sanctions is stated in the regulations. The assignment of roles occurs on the basis of technical qualifications which are ascertained through formalized, impersonal procedures (*e.g.*, examinations). Within the structure of hierarchically arranged authority, the activities of "trained and salaried experts" are governed by general, abstract, and clearly defined rules which preclude the necessity for the issuance of specific instructions for each specific case. The generality of the rules requires the constant use of *categorization*, whereby individual problems and cases are classified on the basis of designated criteria and are treated accordingly. The pure type of bureaucratic official is appointed, either by a superior or through the exercise of impersonal competition; he is not elected. A measure of flexibility in the bureaucracy is attained by electing higher functionaries who presumably express the will of the electorate (*e.g.*, a body of citizens or a board of directors). The election of higher officials is designed to affect the purposes of the organization, but the technical procedures for attaining these ends are carried out by continuing bureaucratic personnel.[2]

Most bureaucratic offices involve the expectation of life-long tenure, in the absence of disturbing factors which may decrease the size of the organization. Bureaucracy maximizes vocational security.[3] The function of security of tenure, pensions, incremental salaries, and regularized procedures for promotion is to ensure the devoted performance of official duties, without regard for extraneous pressures.[4] The chief merit of bureaucracy is its technical efficiency, with a premium placed on precision, speed, expert control, continuity, discretion, and optimal returns on input. The structure is one which approaches the complete elimination of personalized relationships and nonrational considerations (hostility, anxiety, affectual involvements, etc.).

With increasing bureaucratization, it becomes plain to all who would see that man is to a very important degree controlled by his social relations to the instruments of production. This can no longer seem only a tenet of Marxism, but a stubborn fact to be acknowledged by all, quite apart from their ideological persuasion. Bureaucratization makes readily visible what was previously dim and obscure. More and more people discover that to work, they must be employed. For to work, one must have tools and equipment. And the tools and equipment are increasingly available only in bureaucracies, private or public. Consequently, one must be employed by the bureaucracies in order to have access to tools in order to work and in order to live. It is in this sense that bureaucratization entails separation of individuals from the instruments of production, as in modern capitalistic enterprise or in state communistic enterprise (of the midcentury variety), just as in the postfeudal army, bureaucratization entailed complete separation from the instruments of destruction. Typically, the worker no longer owns his tools, nor the soldier his weapons. And in this special sense, more and more people become workers, either blue collar or white collar or stiff shirt. So develops, for example, the new type of scientific worker, as the scientist is "separated" from his technical equipment—after all, the physicist does not ordinarily own his cyclotron.

To work at his research, he must be employed by a bureaucracy with laboratory resources.

Bureaucracy is administration which almost completely avoids public discussion of its techniques, although there may occur public discussion of its policies.[5] This secrecy is confirmed neither to the public nor to private bureaucracies. It is held to be necessary to keep valuable information from private economic competitors or from foreign and potentially hostile political groups. . . .

The Dysfunctions of Bureaucracy

The transition to a study of the negative aspects of bureaucracy is afforded by the application of Veblen's concept of "trained incapacity," Dewey's notion of "occupational psychosis," or Warnotte's view of "professional deformation." Trained incapacity refers to that state of affairs in which one's abilities function as inadequacies or blind spots. Actions based upon training and skills which have been successfully applied in the past may result in inappropriate responses *under changed conditions*. An inadequate flexibility in the application of skills, will, in a changing milieu, result in more or less serious maladjustments.[6] . . .

Dewey's concept of occupational psychosis rests upon much the same observations. As a result of their day to day routines, people develop special preferences, antipathies, discriminations and emphases.[7] (The term psychosis is used by Dewey to denote a "pronounced character of the mind.") These psychoses develop through demands put upon the individual by the particular organization or his occupational role. . . .

For reasons which we have already noted, the bureaucratic structure exerts a constant pressure upon the official to be "methodical, prudent, disciplined." If the bureaucracy is to operate successfully, it must attain a high degree of reliability of behavior, an unusual degree of action. Hence, the fundamental importance of discipline which may be as highly developed in a religious or economic bureaucracy as in the army. Discipline can be effective only if the ideal patterns are buttressed by strong sentiments which entail devotion to one's duties, a keen sense of the limitation of one's authority and competence, and methodical performance of routine activities. The efficacy of social structure depends ultimately upon infusing group participants with appropriate attitudes and sentiments. As we shall see, there are definite arrangements in the bureaucracy for inculcating and reinforcing these sentiments.

At the moment, it suffices to observe that in order to ensure discipline (the necessary reliability of response), these sentiments are often more intense than is technically necessary. There is a margin of safety, so to speak, in the pressure exerted by these sentiments upon the bureaucrat to conform to his patterned obligations, in much the same sense that added allowances (precautionary over-estimations) are made by the engineer in designing the supports for a bridge. But this very emphasis leads to a transference of the sentiments from the *aims* of the organization onto the particular details of behavior required by the rules. Adherence to the rules, originally conceived as a means, becomes transformed into an end-in-itself; there occurs the familiar process of *displacement of goals* whereby "an instrumental value becomes a terminal value."[8] Discipline, readily interpreted as conformance with regulations, whatever the situation, is seen not as a measure designed for specific purposes but becomes an immediate value in the life-organization of the bureaucrat. This emphasis, resulting from the displacement of the original goals, develops into rigidities and an inability to adjust readily. Formalism, even ritualism, ensues with an unchallenged insistence upon punctilious adherence to formalized procedures.[9] This may be exaggerated to the point where primary concern with conformity to the rules interferes with the achievement of the purposes of organization, in which case we have the familiar phenomenon of the technicism or red tape of the official. An extreme product of this process of displacement of goals is the bureaucratic virtuoso, who never forgets a single rule binding his action and hence is unable to assist many of his clients.[10] . . .

Structural Sources of Overconformity

Thus far, we have treated the ingrained sentiments making for rigorous discipline simply as data, as given. However, definite features of the bureaucratic structure may be seen to conduce to these sentiments. The bureaucrat's official life is planned for him in terms of a graded career, through the organizational devices of promotion by seniority, pensions, incremental salaries, etc., all of which are designed to provide incentives for disciplined action and conformity to the official regulations.[11] The official is tacitly expected to and largely does adapt his thoughts, feelings and actions to the prospect of this career. But *these very devices* which increase the probability of conformance also lead to an over-concern with strict adherence to regulations which induces timidity, conservatism, and technicism. Displacement of sentiments from goals onto means is fostered by the tremendous symbolic significance of the means (rules).

Another feature of the bureaucratic structure tends to produce much the same result. Functionaries have the sense of a common destiny for all those who work together. They share the same interests, especially since there is relatively little competition in so far as promotion is in terms of seniority. In-group aggression is thus minimized and this arrangement is therefore conceived to be positively functional for the bureaucracy. However, the *esprit de corps* and informal social organization which typically develop in such situations often lead the personnel to defend their entrenched interests rather than to assist their clientele and elected higher officials. . . .

In a stimulating paper, Hughes has applied the concepts of "secular" and "sacred" to various types of division of labor; "the sacredness" of caste and *Stände* prerogatives contrasts sharply, with the increasing secularism of occupational differentiation in our society.[12] However, as our discussion suggests, there may ensue, in particular vocations and in particular types of organization, the *process of sanctification* (viewed as the counterpart of the process of secularization). This is to say that through sentiment-formation, emotional dependence upon bureaucratic symbols and status, and affective involvement in spheres of competence and authority, there develop prerogatives involving attitudes of moral legitimacy which are established as values in their own right, and are no longer viewed as merely technical means for expediting administration. One may note a tendency for certain bureaucratic norms, originally introduced for technical reasons, to become rigidified and sacred, although, as Durkheim would say, they are *laïque en apparence*.[13] Durkheim has touched on this general process in his description of the attitudes and values which persist in the organic solidarity of a highly differentiated society.

Primary versus Secondary Relations

Another feature of the bureaucratic structure, the stress on depersonalization of relationships, also plays its part in the bureaucrat's trained incapacity. The personality pattern of the bureaucrat is nucleated about this norm of impersonality. Both this and the categorizing tendency, which develops from the dominant role of general, abstract rules, tend to produce conflict in the bureaucrat's contacts with the public or clientele. Since functionaries minimize personal relations and resort to categorization, the peculiarities of individual cases are often ignored. But the client who, quite understandably, is convinced of the special features of *his* own problem often objects to such categorical treatment. Stereotyped behavior is not adapted to the exigencies of individual problems. The impersonal treatment of affairs which are at times of great personal significance to the client gives rise to the charge of "arrogance" and "haughtiness" of the bureaucrat. . . .

Still another source of conflict with the public derives from the bureaucratic structure. The bureaucrat, in part irrespective of his position wit*hin* the hierarchy, acts as a representative of the power and prestige of the entire structure. In his official role he is vested with definite authority. This often leads to an actually or apparently domineering attitude, which may only be exaggerated by a discrepancy between his position within the hierarchy and his position with reference to the public.[14] Protest and recourse to other officials on the part of the client are often ineffective or largely precluded by the previously mentioned *esprit de corps* which joins the officials into a more or less solidary in-group. This source of conflict *may* be minimized in private enterprise since the client can register an effective protest by transferring his trade to another organization within the competitive system. But with the monopolistic nature of the public organization, no such alternative is possible. Moreover, in this case, tension is increased because of a discrepancy between ideology and fact: the governmental personnel are held to be "servants of the people," but in fact they are often superordinate, and release of tension can seldom be afforded by turning to other agencies for the necessary service.[15] This tension is in part attributable to the confusion of the status of bureaucrat and client; the client may consider himself socially superior to the official who is at the moment dominant.[16]

... The conflict may be viewed, then, as deriving from the introduction of inappropriate attitudes and relationships. Conflict with*in* the bureaucratic structure arises from the converse situation, namely, when personalized relationships are substituted for the structurally required impersonal relationships. This type of conflict may be characterized as follows.

The bureaucracy, as we have seen, is organized as a secondary, formal group. The normal responses involved in this organized network of social expectations are supported by affective attitudes of members of the group. Since the group is oriented toward secondary norms of impersonality, any failure to conform to these norms will arouse antagonism from those who have identified themselves with the legitimacy of these rules. Hence, the substitution of personal for impersonal treatment within the structure is met with widespread disapproval and is characterized by such epithets as graft, favoritism, nepotism, apple-polishing, etc. These epithets are clearly manifestations of injured

sentiments.[17] The function of such virtually automatic resentment can be clearly seen in terms of the requirements of bureaucratic structure.

Bureaucracy is a secondary group structure designed to carry on certain activities which cannot be satisfactorily performed on the basis of primary group criteria.[18] Hence behavior which runs counter to these formalized norms becomes the object of emotionalized disapproval. This constitutes a functionally significant defence set up against tendencies which jeopardize the performance of socially necessary activities. . . .

Problems for Research

A large number of specific questions invite our attention. To what extent are particular personality types selected and modified by the various bureaucracies (private enterprise, public service, the quasi-legal political machine, religious orders)? Inasmuch as ascendancy and submission are held to be traits of personality, despite their variability in different stimulus-situations, do bureaucracies select personalities of particularly submissive or ascendant tendencies? And since various studies have shown that these traits can be modified, does participation in bureaucratic office tend to increase ascendant tendencies? Do various systems of recruitment (*e.g.*, patronage, open competition involving specialized knowledge or general mental capacity, practical experience) select different personality types?[19] Does promotion through seniority lessen competitive anxieties and enhance administrative efficiency? A detailed examination of mechanisms for imbuing the bureaucratic codes with affect would be instructive both sociologically and psychologically. Does the general anonymity of civil service decisions tend to restrict the area of prestige-symbols to a narrowly defined inner circle? Is there a tendency for differential association to be especially marked among bureaucrats?

The range of theoretically significant and practically important questions would seem to be limited only by the accessibility of the concrete data. . . .

NOTES

1. Max Weber, *Wirtschaft und Gesellschaft* (Tübingen: J. C. B. Mohr, 1922), Pt. III, chap. 6; 650–678. For a brief summary of Weber's discussion, see Talcott Parsons, *The Structure of Social Action*, esp. 506 ff. For a description, which is not a caricature, of the bureaucrat as a personality type, see C. Rabany, "Les types sociaux: le fonctionnaire," *Revue générale d'administration* 88 (1907), 5–28.

2. Karl Mannheim, *Ideology and Utopia* (New York: Harcourt Brace Jovanovich, 1936), 18n., 105 ff. See also Ramsay Muir, *Peers and Bureaucrats* (London: Constable, 1910), 12–13.

3. E. G. Cahen-Salvador suggests that the personnel of bureaucracies is largely constituted by those who value security above all else. See his "La situation matérielle et morale des fonctionnaires," *Revue politique et parlementaire* (1926), 319.

4. H. J. Laski, "Bureaucracy," *Encyclopedia of the Social Sciences*. This article is written primarily from the standpoint of the political scientist rather than that of the sociologist.

5. Weber, *op. cit.,* 671.

6. For a stimulating discussion and application of these concepts, see Kenneth Burke, *Permanence and Change* (New York: New Republic, 1935), pp. 50 ff.; Daniel Warnotte, "Bureaucratie et Fonctionnarisme," *Revue de l'Institut de Sociologie* 17, (1937), 245.

7. *Ibid.,* 58–59.

8. This process has often been observed in various connections. Wundt's *heterogony of ends* is a case in point; Max Weber's *Paradoxie der Folgen* is another. See also MacIver's observations on the transformation of civilization into culture and Lasswell's remark that "the human animal distinguishes himself by his infinite capacity for making ends of his means." See Merton, "The unanticipated consequences of purposive social action," *American Sociological Review* 1 (1936), 894–904. In terms of the psychological mechanisms involved, this process has been analyzed most fully by Gordon W. Allport, in his discussion of what he calls "the functional autonomy of motives." Allport emends the earlier formulations of Woodworth, Tolman, and William Stern, and arrives at a statement of the process from the standpoint of individual motivation. He does not

consider those phases of the social structure which conduce toward the "transformation of motives." The formulation adopted in this paper is thus complementary to Allport's analysis; the one stressing the psychological mechanisms involved, the other considering the constraints of the social structure. The convergence of psychology and sociology toward this central concept suggests that it may well constitute one of the conceptual bridges between the two disciplines. See Gordon W. Allport, *Personality* (New York: Henry Holt & Co., 1937), chap. 7.

9. See E. C. Hughes, "Institutional office and the person," *American Journal of Sociology*, 43, (1937), 404–413; E. T. Hiller, "Social structure in relation to the person," *Social Forces* 16 (1937), 34–44.

10. Mannheim, *Ideology and Utopia,* 106.

11. Mannheim, *Mensch and Gesellshaft,* 32–33. Mannheim stresses the importance of the "Lebensplan" and the "Amtskarriere." See the comments by Hughes, *op. cit.,* 413.

12. E. C. Hughes, "Personality types and the division of labor," *American Journal of Sociology* 33, (1928), 754–768. Much the same distinction is drawn by Leopold von Wiese and Howard Becker, *Systematic Sociology* (New York: John Wiley & Sons, 1932), 22–25 *et passim.*

13. Hughes recognizes one phase of this process of sanctification when he writes that professional training "carries with it as a by-product assimilation of the candidate to a set of professional attitudes and controls, *a professional conscience and solidarity. The profession claims and aims to become a moral unit.*" Hughes, *op. cit.,* 762, (italics inserted). In this same connection, Sumner's concept of *pathos,* as the halo of sentiment which protects a social value from criticism, is particularly relevant, inasmuch as it affords a clue to the mechanism involved in the process of sanctification. See his *Folkways,* 180–181.

14. In this connection, note the relevance of Koffka's comments on certain features of the pecking-order of birds. "If one compares the behavior of the bird at the top of the pecking list, the despot, with that of one very far down, the second or third from the last, then one finds the latter much more cruel to the few others over whom he lords it than the

former in this treatment of all members. As soon as one removes from the group all members above the penultimate, his behavior becomes milder and may even become very friendly. . . . It is not difficult to find analogies to this in human societies, and therefore one side of such behavior must be primarily the effects of the social groupings, and not of individual characteristics." K. Koffka, *Principles of Gestalt Psychology* (New York: Harcourt Brace Jovanovich, 1935), 668–669.

15. At this point the political machine often becomes functionally significant. As Steffens and others have shown, highly personalized relations and the abrogation of formal rules (red tape) by the machine often satisfy the needs of individual "clients" more fully than the formalized mechanism of governmental bureaucracy.

16. As one of the unemployed men remarked about the clerks at the Greenwich Employment Exchange: "And the bloody blokes wouldn't have their jobs if it wasn't for us men out of a job either. That's what gets me about their holding their noses up." Bakke, *op. cit.*, 80. See also H. D. Lasswell and G. Almond, "Aggressive behavior by clients towards public relief administrators," *American Political Science Review* 28 (1934), 643–655.

17. The diagnostic significance of such linguistic indices as epithets has scarcely been explored by the sociologist. Sumner properly observes that epithets produce "summary criticisms" and definitions of social situations. Dollard also notes that "epithets frequently define the central issues in a society," and Sapir has rightly emphasized the importance of context of situations in appraising the significance of epithets. Of equal relevance is Linton's observation that "in case histories the way in which the community felt about a particular episode is, if anything, more important to our study than the actual behavior. . . ." A sociological study of "vocabularies of encomium and opprobrium" should lead to valuable findings.

18. *Cf.* Ellsworth Faris, *The Nature of Human Nature* (New York: McGraw-Hill, 1937), 41 ff.

19. Among recent studies of recruitment to bureaucracy are: Reinhard Bendix, *Higher Civil Servants in American Society* (Boulder: University of Colorado Press, 1949); Dwaine Marwick, *Career Perspectives in a Bureaucratic Setting* (Ann Arbor: University of Michigan Press, 1945); R. K. Kelsall, *Higher Civil Servants in Britain* (London: Routledge & Kegan Paul, 1955); W. L. Warner and J. C. Abegglen, *Occupational Mobility in American Business and Industry* (Minneapolis: University of Minnesota Press, 1955).

Reading 26	Groupthink: The Desperate Drive for Consensus at Any Cost
	Irving L. Janis

"How could we have been so stupid!" President John F. Kennedy asked after he and a close group of advisers had blundered into the Bay of Pigs invasion. For the last two years I have been studying that question, as it applies not only to the Bay of Pigs decision-makers but also to those who led the United States into such other major fiascos as the failure to be prepared for the attack on Pearl Harbor, the Korean War stalemate, and the escalation of the Vietnam War.

Stupidity certainly is not the explanation. The men who participated in making the Bay of Pigs decision, for instance, comprised one of the greatest arrays of intellectual talent in the history of American Government—Dean Rusk, Robert McNamara, Douglas Dillon, Robert Kennedy, McGeorge Bundy, Arthur Schlesinger Jr., Allen Dulles and others.

It also seemed to me that explanations were incomplete if they concentrated only on disturbances in the behavior of each individual within a decision-making body: temporary emotional states of elation, fear, or anger that reduce a man's mental efficiency, for example, or chronic blind spots arising from a man's social prejudices or idiosyncratic biases.

I preferred to broaden the picture by looking at the fiascos from the standpoint of group dynamics as it has been explored over the past three decades, first by the great social psychologist Kurt Lewin and later in many experimental situations by myself and other behavioral scientists. My conclusion after poring over hundreds of relevant documents—historical reports about formal group meetings and informal conversations among the members—is that the groups that committed the fiascos were victims of what I call "groupthink."

"Groupy." In each case study, I was surprised to discover the extent to which each group displayed the typical phenomena of social conformity that are regularly encountered in studies of group dynamics among ordinary citizens. For example, some of the phenomena appear to be completely in line with findings from social-psychological experiments showing that powerful social pressures are brought to bear by the members of a cohesive group whenever a dissident begins to voice his objections to a group consensus. Other phenomena are reminiscent of the shared illusions observed in encounter groups and friendship cliques when the members simultaneously reach a peak of "groupy" feelings.

Above all, there are numerous indications pointing to the development of group norms that bolster morale at the expense of critical thinking. One of the most common norms appears to be that of remaining loyal to the group by sticking with the policies to which the group has already committed itself, even when those policies are obviously working out badly and have unintended consequences that disturb the conscience of each member. This is one of the key characteristics of groupthink.

1984. I use the term groupthink as a quick and easy way to refer to the mode of thinking that persons engage in when *concurrence-seeking* becomes so dominant in a cohesive in-group that it tends to override realistic appraisal of alternative courses of action. Groupthink is a term of the same order as the words in the newspeak vocabulary George Orwell used in his dismaying world of *1984*. In that context, groupthink takes on an invidious connotation. Exactly such a connotation is intended, since the term refers to a deterioration in mental efficiency, reality testing, and moral judgments as a result of group pressures.

The symptoms of groupthink arise when the members of decision-making groups become

Source: Irving L. Janis, "Groupthink," November 1971, PSYCHOLOGY TODAY. Reprinted by permission of Sussex Publishers, Inc.

motivated to avoid being too harsh in their judgments of their leaders' or their colleagues' ideas. They adopt a soft line of criticism, even in their own thinking. At their meetings, all the members are amiable and seek complete concurrence on every important issue, with no bickering or conflict to spoil the cozy, "we-feeling" atmosphere.

Kill.   Paradoxically, soft-headed groups are often hard-hearted when it comes to dealing with outgroups or enemies. They find it relatively easy to resort to dehumanizing solutions—they will readily authorize bombing attacks that kill large numbers of civilians in the name of the noble cause of persuading an unfriendly government to negotiate at the peace table. They are unlikely to pursue the more difficult and controversial issues that arise when alternatives to a harsh military solution come up for discussion. Nor are they inclined to raise ethical issues that carry the implication that *this fine group of ours, with its humanitarianism and its high-minded principles, might be capable of adopting a course of action that is inhumane and immoral.*

Norms.   There is evidence from a number of social-psychological studies that as the members of a group feel more accepted by the others, which is a central feature of increased group cohesiveness, they display less overt conformity to group norms. Thus we would expect that the more cohesive a group becomes, the less the members will feel constrained to censor what they say out of fear of being socially punished for antagonizing the leader or any of their fellow members.

In contrast, the groupthink type of conformity tends to increase as group cohesiveness increases. Groupthink involves nondeliberate suppression of critical thoughts as a result of internalization of the group's norms, which is quite different from deliberate suppression on the basis of external threats of social punishment. The more cohesive the group, the greater the inner compulsion on the part of each member to avoid creating disunity, which inclines him to believe in the soundness of whatever proposals are promoted by the leader or by a majority of the group's members.

In a cohesive group, the danger is not so much that each individual will fail to reveal his objections to what the others propose, but that he will think the proposal is a good one, without attempting to carry out a careful, crucial scrutiny of the pros and cons of the alternatives. When groupthink becomes dominant, there also is considerable suppression of deviant thoughts, but it takes the form of each person's deciding that his misgivings are not relevant and should be set aside, that the benefit of the doubt regarding any lingering uncertainties should be given to the group consensus.

Stress.   I do not mean to imply that all cohesive groups necessarily suffer from groupthink. All ingroups may have a mild tendency toward groupthink, displaying one or another of the symptoms from time to time, but it need not be so dominant as to influence the quality of the group's final decision. Neither do I mean to imply that there is anything necessarily inefficient or harmful about group decisions in general. On the contrary, a group whose members have properly defined roles, with traditions concerning the procedures to follow in pursuing a critical inquiry, probably is capable of making better decisions than any individual group member working alone.

The problem is that the advantages of having decisions made by groups are often lost because of powerful psychological pressures that arise when the members work closely together, share the same set of values and, above all, face a crisis situation that puts everyone under intense stress.

The main principle of groupthink, which I offer in the spirit of Parkinson's Law, is this: *The more amiability and esprit de corps there is among the members of a policy-making in-group, the greater the danger that independent critical thinking will be replaced by groupthink, which is likely to result in irrational and dehumanizing actions directed against out-groups.*

Symptoms.   In my studies of high-level governmental decision-makers, both civilian and military, I have found eight main symptoms of groupthink.

1. INVULNERABILITY. Most or all of the members of the in-group share an illusion of invulnerability that provides for them some degree of reassurance about obvious dangers and leads them to become over-optimistic and willing to take extraordinary risks. It also causes them to fail to respond to clear warnings of danger.

The Kennedy in-group, which uncritically accepted the Central Intelligence Agency's disastrous Bay of Pigs plan, operated on the false assumption that they could keep secret the fact that the United States was responsible for the invasion of Cuba. Even after news of the plan began to leak out, their belief remained unshaken. They failed even to consider the danger that awaited them: a worldwide revulsion against the U.S. . . .

2. RATIONALE. As we see, victims of groupthink ignore warnings; they also collectively construct rationalizations in order to discount warnings and other forms of negative feedback that, taken seriously, might lead the group members to reconsider their assumptions each time they recommit themselves to past decisions. Why did the Johnson in-group avoid reconsidering its escalation policy when time and again the expectations on which they based their decisions turned out to be wrong? James C. Thompson Jr., a Harvard historian who spent five years as an observing participant in both the State Department and the White House, tells us that the policymakers avoided critical discussion of their prior decisions and continually invented new rationalizations so that they could sincerely recommit themselves to defeating the North Vietnamese.

In the fall of 1964, before the bombing of North Vietnam began, some of the policymakers predicted that six weeks of air strikes would induce the North Vietnamese to seek peace talks. When someone asked, "What if they don't?" the answer was that another four weeks certainly would do the trick. . . .

3. MORALITY. Victims of groupthink believe unquestioningly in the inherent morality of their in-group; this belief inclines the members to ignore the ethical or moral consequences of their decisions.

Evidence that this symptom is at work usually is of a negative kind—the things that are left unsaid in group meetings. At least two influential persons had doubts about the morality of the Bay of Pigs adventure. One of them, Arthur Schlesinger Jr., presented his strong objections in a memorandum to President Kennedy and Secretary of State Rusk but suppressed them when he attended meetings of the Kennedy team. The other, Senator J. William Fulbright, was not a member of the group, but the President invited him to express his misgivings in a speech to the policymakers. However, when Fulbright finished speaking the President moved on to other agenda items without asking for reactions of the group.

David Kraslow and Stuart H. Loory, in *The Secret Search for Peace in Vietnam*, report that during 1966 President Johnson's in-group was concerned primarily with selecting bomb targets in North Vietnam. They based their selections on four factors—the military advantage, the risk to American aircraft and pilots, the danger of forcing other countries into the fighting, and the danger of heavy civilian casualties. At their regular Tuesday luncheons, they weighed these factors the way school teachers grade examination papers, averaging them out. Though evidence on this point is scant, I suspect that the group's ritualistic adherence to a standardized procedure induced the members to feel morally justified in their destructive way of dealing with the Vietnamese people—after all, the danger of heavy civilian casualties from U.S. air strikes was taken into account on their checklists.

4. STEREOTYPES. Victims of groupthink hold stereotyped views of the leaders of enemy groups: they are so evil that genuine attempts at negotiating differences with them are unwarranted, or they are too weak or too stupid to deal effectively with whatever attempts the in-group makes to defeat their purposes, no matter how risky the attempts are.

Kennedy's groupthinkers believed that Premier Fidel Castro's air force was so ineffectual that obsolete B-26s could knock it out completely in a surprise attack before the invasion began. They also believed that Castro's army was so weak that a small Cuban-exile brigade could establish a well-protected beach-head at the Bay of Pigs. In addition, they believed that Castro was not smart enough to put down any possible internal uprisings in support of the exiles. They were wrong on all three assumptions. Though much of the blame was attributable to faulty intelligence, the point is that none of Kennedy's advisers even questioned the CIA planners about these assumptions. . . .

5. PRESSURE. Victims of groupthink apply direct pressure to any individual who momentarily expresses doubts about any of the group's shared illusions or who questions the validity of the arguments supporting a policy alternative favored by the majority. This gambit reinforces the concurrence-seeking norm that loyal members are expected to maintain.

President Kennedy probably was more active than anyone else in raising skeptical questions during the Bay of Pigs meetings, and yet he seems to have encouraged the group's docile, uncritical acceptance of defective arguments in favor of the CIA's plan. At every meeting, he allowed the CIA representatives to dominate the discussion. He permitted them to give their immediate refutations in response to each tentative doubt that one of the others expressed, instead of asking whether anyone shared the doubt or wanted to pursue the implications of the new worrisome issue that had just been raised. And at the most crucial meeting, when he was calling on each member to give his vote for or against the plan, he did not call on Arthur Schlesinger, the one man there who was known by the President to have serious misgivings.

Historian Thomson informs us that whenever a member of Johnson's in-group began to express doubts, the group used subtle social pressures to "domesticate" him. To start with, the dissenter was made to feel at home provided that he lived up to two restrictions: (1) that he did not voice his doubts to outsiders, which would play into the hands of the opposition; and (2) that he kept his criticisms within the bounds of

acceptable deviation, which meant not challenging any of the fundamental assumptions that went into the group's prior commitments. One such "domesticated dissenter" was Bill Moyers. When Moyers arrived at a meeting, Thomson tells us, the President greeted him with, "Well, here comes Mr. Stop-the-Bombing."

6. SELF-CENSORSHIP. Victims of groupthink avoid deviating from what appears to be group consensus; they keep silent about their misgivings and even minimize to themselves the importance of their doubts.

As we have seen, Schlesinger was not at all hesitant about presenting his strong objections to the Bay of Pigs plan in a memorandum to the President and the Secretary of State. But he became keenly aware of his tendency to suppress objections at the White House meetings. "In the months after the Bay of Pigs, I bitterly reproached myself for having kept so silent during those crucial discussions in the cabinet room," Schlesinger writes in *A Thousand Days*, "I can only explain my failure to do more than raise a few timid questions by reporting that one's impulse to blow the whistle on this nonsense was simply undone by the circumstances of the discussion."

7. UNANIMITY. Victims of groupthink share an illusion of unanimity within the group concerning almost all judgments expressed by members who speak in favor of the majority view. This symptom results partly from the preceding one, whose effects are augmented by the false assumption that any individual who remains silent during any part of the discussion is in full accord with what the others are saying.

When a group of persons who respect each other's opinions arrives at a unanimous view, each member is likely to feel that the belief must be true. This reliance on consensual validation within the group tends to replace individual critical thinking and reality testing, unless there are clear-cut disagreements among the members. In contemplating a course of action such as the invasion of Cuba, it is painful for the members to confront disagreements within their group, particularly if it becomes apparent that there are widely divergent views about whether the preferred course of action is too risky to undertake at all. Such disagreements are likely to arouse anxieties about making a serious error. Once the sense of unanimity is shattered, the members no longer can feel complacently confident about the decision they are inclined to make. Each man must then face the annoying realization that there are troublesome uncertainties and he must diligently seek out the best information he can get in order to decide for himself exactly how serious the risks might be. This is one of the unpleasant consequences of being in a group of hardheaded, critical thinkers.

To avoid such an unpleasant state, the members often become inclined, without quite realizing it, to prevent latent disagreements from surfacing when they are about to initiate a risky course of action. The group leader and the members support each other in playing up the areas of convergence in their thinking, at the expense of fully exploring divergencies that might reveal unsettled issues. . . .

8. MINDGUARDS. Victims of groupthink sometimes appoint themselves as mindguards to protect the leader and fellow members from adverse information that might break the complacency they shared about the effectiveness and morality of past decisions. At a large birthday party for his wife, Attorney General Robert F. Kennedy, who had been constantly informed about the Cuban invasion plan, took Schlesinger aside and asked him why he was opposed. Kennedy listened coldly and said, "You may be right or you may be wrong, but the President has made his mind up. Don't push it any further. Now is the time for everyone to help him all they can. . . ."

Products.   When a group of executives frequently displays most or all of these interrelated symptoms, a detailed study of their deliberations is likely to reveal a number of immediate consequences. These consequences are, in effect, products of poor decision-making practices because they lead to inadequate solutions to the problems under discussion.

First, the group limits its discussions to a few alternative courses of action (often only two) without an initial survey of all the alternatives that might be worthy of consideration.

Second, the group fails to reexamine the course of action initially preferred by the majority after they learn of risks and drawbacks they had not considered originally.

Third, the members spend little or no time discussing whether there are non-obvious gains they may have overlooked or ways of reducing the seemingly prohibitive costs that made rejected alternatives appear undesirable to them.

Fourth, members make little or no attempt to obtain information from experts within their own organizations who might be able to supply more precise estimates of potential losses and gains.

Fifth, members show positive interest in facts and opinions that support their preferred policy, they tend to ignore facts and opinions that do not.

Sixth, members spend little time deliberating about how the chosen policy might be hindered by bureaucratic inertia, sabotaged by political opponents, or temporarily derailed by common accidents. Consequently, they fail to work out contingency plans to cope with foreseeable setbacks that could endanger the overall success of their chosen course.

Support.   The search for an explanation of why groupthink occurs has led me through a quagmire of complicated theoretical issues in a murky area of human motivation. My belief, based on recent social psychological research, is that we can best understand the various symptoms of groupthink as a mutual effort among the group members to maintain self-esteem and emotional equanimity by providing social support to each other, especially at times when they share responsibility for making vital decisions.

Even when no important decision is pending, the typical administrator will begin to doubt the wisdom and morality of his past decisions each time he receives information about setbacks, particularly if the information is accompanied by negative feedback from prominent men who originally had been his supporters. It should not be surprising, therefore, to find that individual members strive to develop unanimity and esprit de corps that will help bolster each other's morale, to create an optimistic outlook about the success of pending decisions, and to reaffirm the positive value of past policies to which all of them are committed.

Pride.   Shared illusions of invulnerability, for example, can reduce anxiety about taking risks. Rationalizations help members believe that the risks are really not so bad after all. The assumption of inherent morality helps the members to avoid feelings of shame or guilt. Negative stereotypes function as stress-reducing devices to enhance a sense of moral righteousness as well as pride in a lofty mission.

The mutual enhancement of self-esteem and morale may have functional value in enabling the members to maintain their capacity to take action, but it has maladaptive consequences insofar as concurrence-seeking tendencies interfere with critical, rational capacities and lead to serious errors of judgment. . . .

Remedies.   To counterpoint my case studies of the major fiascos, I have also investigated two highly successful group enterprises, the formulation of the Marshall Plan in the Truman Administration and the handling of the Cuban missile crisis by President Kennedy and his advisers. I have found it instructive to examine the steps Kennedy took to change his group's decision-making processes. These changes ensured that the mistakes made by his Bay of Pigs in-group were not repeated by the missile-crisis in-group, even though the membership of both groups was essentially the same.

The following recommendations for preventing groupthink incorporate many of the good practices I discovered to be characteristic of the Marshall Plan and missile crisis groups:

1. The leader of a policy-forming group should assign the role of critical evaluator to each member, encouraging the group to give high priority to open airing of objections and doubts. This practice needs to be reinforced by the leader's acceptance of criticism of his own judgments in order to discourage members from soft-pedaling their disagreements and from allowing their striving for concurrence to inhibit critical thinking.

2. When the key members of a hierarchy assign a policy-planning mission to any group within their organization, they should adopt an impartial stance instead of stating preferences and expectations at the beginning. This will encourage open inquiry and impartial probing of a wide range of policy alternatives.

3. The organization routinely should set up several outside policy-planning and evaluation groups to work on the same policy question, each deliberating under a different leader. This can prevent the insulation of an in-group.

4. At intervals before the group reaches a final consensus, the leader should require each member to discuss the group's deliberations with associates in his own unit of the organization—assuming that those associates can be trusted to adhere to the same security regulations that govern the policy-makers—and then to report back their reactions to the group.

5. The group should invite one or more outside experts to each meeting on a staggered basis and encourage the experts to challenge the views of the core members.

6. At every general meeting of the group, whenever the agenda calls for an evaluation of policy alternatives, at least one member should play devil's advocate, functioning as a good lawyer in challenging the testimony of those who advocate the majority position.

7. Whenever the policy issue involves relations with a rival nation or organization, the group should devote a sizable block of time, perhaps an entire session, to a survey of all warning signals from the rivals and should write alternative scenarios on the rivals' intentions.

8. When the group is surveying policy alternatives for feasibility and effectiveness, it should from time to time divide into two or more subgroups to meet separately under different

chairmen, and then come back together to hammer out differences.

9. After reaching a preliminary consensus about what seems to be the best policy, the group should hold a "second-chance" meeting at which every member expresses as vividly as he can all his residual doubts, and rethinks the entire issue before making a definitive choice.

How. These recommendations have their disadvantages. To encourage the open airing of objections, for instance, might lead to prolonged and costly debates when a rapidly growing crisis requires immediate solution. It also could cause rejection, depression, and anger. A leader's failure to set a norm might create cleavage between leader and members that could develop into a disruptive power struggle if the leader looks on the emerging consensus as anathema. Setting up outside evaluation groups might increase the risk of security leakage. Still, inventive executives who know their way around the organizational maze probably can figure out how to apply one or another of the prescriptions successfully, without harmful side effects. . . .

In this era of atomic warheads, urban disorganization and ecocatastrophes, it seems to me that policymakers should collaborate with behavioral scientists and give top priority to preventing groupthink and its attendant fiascos.

Reading 27	The Abilene Paradox: The Management of Agreement
	Jerry B. Harvey

The July afternoon in Coleman, Texas (population 5,607) was particularly hot—104 degrees as measured by the Walgreen's Rexall Ex-Lax temperature gauge. In addition, the wind was blowing fine-grained West Texas topsoil through the house. But the afternoon was still tolerable—even potentially enjoyable. There was a fan going on the back porch; there was cold lemonade; and finally, there was entertainment. Dominoes. Perfect for the conditions. The game required little more physical exertion than an occasional mumbled comment, "Shuffle 'em," and an unhurried movement of the arm to place the spots in the appropriate perspective on the table. All in all, it had the makings of an agreeable Sunday afternoon in Coleman—that is, it was, until my father-in-law suddenly said, "Let's get in the car and go to Abilene and have dinner at the cafeteria."

I thought, "What, go to Abilene? Fifty-three miles? In this dust storm and heat? And in an unairconditioned 1958 Buick?"

But my wife chimed in with, "Sounds like a great idea. I'd like to go. How about you, Jerry?" Since my own preferences were obviously out of step with the rest I replied, "Sounds good to me," and added, "I just hope your mother wants to go."

"Of course I want to go," said my mother-in-law. "I haven't been to Abilene in a long time."

So into the car and off to Abilene we went. My predictions were fulfilled. The heat was brutal. We were coated with a fine layer of dust that was cemented with perspiration by the time we arrived. The food at the cafeteria provided first-rate testimonial material for antacid commercials.

Some four hours and 106 miles later we returned to Coleman, hot and exhausted. We sat in front of the fan for a long time in silence. Then, both to be sociable and to break the silence, I said, "It was a great trip, wasn't it?"

No one spoke.

Finally my mother-in-law said, with some irritation, "Well, to tell the truth, I really didn't enjoy it much and would rather have stayed here. I just went along because the three of you were so enthusiastic about going. I wouldn't have gone if you all hadn't pressured me into it."

I couldn't believe it. "What do you mean 'you all'?" I said. "Don't put me in the 'you all' group. I was delighted to be doing what we were doing. I didn't want to go. I only went to satisfy the rest of you. You're the culprits."

My wife looked shocked. "Don't call me a culprit. You and Daddy and Mama were the ones who wanted to go. I just went along to be sociable and to keep you happy. I would have had to be crazy to want to go out in heat like that."

Her father entered the conversation abruptly. "Hell!" he said.

He proceeded to expand on what was already absolutely clear. "Listen, I never wanted to go to Abilene. I just thought you might be bored. You visit so seldom I wanted to be sure you enjoyed it. I would have preferred to play another game of dominoes and eat the leftovers in the icebox."

After the outburst of recrimination we all sat back in silence. Here we were, four reasonably sensible people who, of our own volition, had just taken a 106-mile trip across a godforsaken desert in a furnace-like temperature through a cloud-like dust storm to eat unpalatable food at a hole-in-the-wall cafeteria in Abilene, when none of us had really wanted to go. In fact, to be more accurate, we'd done just the opposite of what we wanted to do. The whole situation simply didn't make sense.

At least it didn't make sense at the time. But since that day in Coleman, I have observed, consulted with, and been a part of more than one organization that has been caught in the same situation. As a result, they have either taken a

Source: Harvey, "The Abilene Paradox," ORGANIZATIONAL DYNAMICS, Vol. 3, No. 1, 1974, pp. 63–80. Reprinted with permission from Elsevier Science.

side-trip, or, occasionally, a terminal journey to Abilene, when Dallas or Houston or Tokyo was where they really wanted to go. And for most of those organizations, the negative consequences of such trips, measured in terms of both human misery and economic loss, have been much greater than for our little Abilene group.

This article is concerned with that paradox—the Abilene Paradox. Stated simply, it is as follows: Organizations frequently take actions in contradiction to what they really want to do and therefore defeat the very purposes they are trying to achieve. It also deals with a major corollary of the paradox, which is that *the inability to manage agreement is a major source of organization dysfunction.* Last, the article is designed to help members of organizations cope more effectively with the paradox's pernicious influence.

As a means of accomplishing the above, I shall: (1) describe the symptoms exhibited by organizations caught in the paradox; (2) describe, in summarized case-study examples, how they occur in a variety of organizations; (3) discuss the underlying causal dynamics; (4) indicate some of the implications of accepting this model for describing organizational behavior; (5) make recommendations for coping with the paradox; and, in conclusion, (6) relate the paradox to a broader existential issue.

Symptoms of the Paradox

The inability to manage agreement, not the inability to manage conflict, is the essential symptom that defines organizations caught in the web of the Abilene Paradox. That inability effectively to manage agreement is expressed by six specific subsymptoms, all of which were present in our family Abilene group.

1. Organization members agree privately, as individuals, as to the nature of the situation or problem facing the organization. For example, members of the Abilene group agreed that they were enjoying themselves sitting in front of the fan, sipping lemonade, and playing dominoes.

2. Organization members agree privately, as individuals, as to the steps that would be required to cope with the situation or problem they face. For members of the Abilene group "more of the same" was a solution that would have adequately satisfied their individual and collective desires.

3. Organization members fail to accurately communicate their desires and/or beliefs to one another. In fact, they do just the opposite and thereby lead one another into misperceiving the collective reality. Each member of the Abilene group, for example, communicated inaccurate data to other members of the organization. The data, in effect, said, "Yeah, it's a great idea. Let's go to Abilene," when in reality members of the organization individually and collectively preferred to stay in Coleman.

4. With such invalid and inaccurate information, organization members make collective decisions that lead them to take actions contrary to what they want to do, and thereby arrive at results that are counterproductive to the organization's intent and purposes. Thus, the Abilene group went to Abilene when it preferred to do something else.

5. As a result of taking actions that are counterproductive, organization members experience frustration, anger, irritation, and dissatisfaction with their organization. Consequently, they form subgroups with trusted acquaintances and blame other subgroups for the organization's dilemma. Frequently, they also blame authority figures and one another. Such phenomena were illustrated in the Abilene group by the "culprit" argument that occurred when we had returned to the comfort of the fan.

6. Finally, if organization members do not deal with the generic issue—the inability to manage agreement—the cycle repeats itself with greater intensity. The Abilene group, for a variety of reasons, the most important of which was that it became conscious of the process, did not reach that point.

To repeat, the Abilene Paradox reflects a failure to manage agreement. In fact, it is my contention that the inability to cope with (manage) agreement, rather than the inability to cope with (manage) conflict is the single most pressing issue of modern organization.

Other Trips to Abilene

The Abilene Paradox is no respecter of individuals, organizations, or institutions.

Case: The Watergate.

Apart from the grave question of who did what, Watergate presents America with the profound puzzle of why. What is it that led such a wide assortment of men, many of them high public officials, possibly including the President himself, either to instigate or to go along with and later try to hide a pattern of behavior that by now appears not only reprehensible, but stupid? (*The Washington Star and Daily News,* editorial, May 27, 1973.)

One possible answer to the editorial writer's question can be found by probing into the dynamics of the Abilene paradox. I shall let the reader reach his own conclusions, though, on the basis of the following excerpts from testimony before the Senate investigating committee on "The Watergate Affair."

In one exchange, Senator Howard Baker asked Herbert Porter, then a member of the White House staff, why he (Porter) found himself "in charge of or deeply involved in a dirty tricks operation of the campaign." In response, Porter indicated that he had had qualms about what he was doing, but that he ". . . was not one to stand up in a meeting and say that this should be stopped. . . . I kind of drifted along."

And when asked by Baker why he had "drifted along," Porter replied, "In all honesty, because of the fear of the group pressure that would ensue, of not being a team player," and ". . . I felt a deep sense of loyalty to him [the President] or was appealed to on that basis." (*The Washington Post,* June 8, 1973, p. 20.)

Jeb Magruder gave a similar response to a question posed by committee counsel Dash. Specifically, when asked about his, Mr. Dean's, and Mr. Mitchell's reactions to Mr. Liddy's proposal, which included bugging the Watergate, Mr. Magruder replied, "I think all three of us were appalled. The scope and size of the project were something that at least in my mind were not envisioned. I do not think it was in Mr. Mitchell's mind or Mr. Dean's, although I can't comment on their states of mind at that time."

Mr. Mitchell, in an understated way, which was his way of dealing with difficult problems like this, indicated that this was not an "acceptable project." (*The Washington Past,* June 15, 1973, p. A14.)

Later in his testimony Mr. Magruder said, ". . . I think I can honestly say that no one was particularly overwhelmed with the project. But I think we felt that this information could be useful, and Mr. Mitchell agreed to approve the project, and I then notified the parties of Mr. Mitchell's approval." (*The Washington Post,* June 15, 1973, p. A14.)

Although I obviously was not privy to the private conversations of the principal characters, the data seem to reflect the essential elements of the Abilene Paradox. First, they indicate agreement. Evidently, Mitchell, Porter, Dean, and Magruder agreed that the plan was inappropriate. ("I think I can honestly say that no one was particularly overwhelmed with the project.") Second, the data indicate that the principal figures then proceeded to implement the plan in contradiction to their shared agreement. Third, the data surrounding the case clearly indicate that the plan multiplied the organization's problems rather than solved them. And finally, the organization broke into subgroups with the various principals, such as the President, Mitchell, Porter, Dean, and Magruder, blaming one another for the dilemma in which they found themselves, and internecine warfare ensued.

In summary, it is possible that because of the inability of White House staff members to cope with the fact that they agreed, the organization took a trip to Abilene.

Analyzing the Paradox

The Abilene Paradox can be stated succinctly as follows: Organizations frequently take actions in contradiction to the data they have for dealing with problems and, as a result, compound their problems rather than solve them. Like all paradoxes, the Abilene Paradox deals with absurdity. On the surface, it makes little sense for organizations, whether they are couples or companies, bureaucracies or governments, to take actions that are diametrically opposed to the data they possess for solving crucial organizational problems. Such actions are particularly absurd since they tend to compound the very problems they are designed to solve and thereby defeat the purposes the organization is trying to achieve. However, as Robert Rapaport and others have so cogently expressed it, paradoxes are generally paradoxes only because they are based on a logic or rationale different from what we understand or expect.

Discovering that different logic not only destroys the paradoxical quality but also offers alternative ways for coping with similar situations. Therefore, part of the dilemma facing an Abilene-bound organization may be the lack of a map—a theory or model—that provides rationality to the paradox. The purpose of the following discussion is to provide such a map.

The map will be developed by examining the underlying psychological themes of the profit-making organization and the bureaucracy and it will include the following landmarks: (1) Action Anxiety; (2) Negative Fantasies; (3) Real Risk; (4) Separation Anxiety; and (5) the Psychological Reversal of Risk and Certainty. I hope that the discussion of such landmarks will provide harried organization travelers with a new map that will assist them in arriving at where they really want to go and, in addition, will help them in assessing the risks that are an inevitable part of the journey.

Action Anxiety

Action anxiety provides the first landmark for locating roadways that bypass Abilene. The concept of action anxiety says that the reason organization members take actions in contradiction to their understanding of the organization's problems lies in the intense anxiety that is created as they think about acting in accordance with what they believe needs to be done. As a result, they opt to endure the professional and economic degradation of pursuing an unworkable research project or the consequences of participating in an illegal activity rather than act in a manner congruent with their beliefs. It is not that organization members do not know what needs to be done—they do know. Why does action anxiety occur?

Negative Fantasies

Part of the answer to that question may be found in the negative fantasies organization members have about acting in congruence with what they believe should be done.

Hamlet experienced such fantasies. Specifically, Hamlet's fantasies of the alternatives to current evils were more evils, and he didn't entertain the possibility that any action he might take could lead to an improvement in the situation. Hamlet's was not an unusual case. All of the organization protagonists had negative fantasies about what would happen if they acted in accordance with what they believed needed to be done.

Members of the White House staff feared being made scapegoats, branded as disloyal, or ostracized as non–team players if they acted in accordance with their understanding of reality.

To sum up, action anxiety is supported by the negative fantasies that organization members have about what will happen as a consequence of their acting in accordance with their understanding of what is sensible. The negative fantasies, in turn, serve an important function for the persons who have them. Specifically, they provide the individual with an excuse that releases him psychologically, both in his own eyes and frequently in the eyes of others, from the responsibility of having to act to solve organization problems.

What is the source of the negative fantasies? Why do they occur?

Real Risk

Risk is a reality of life, a condition of existence. John Kennedy articulated it in another way when he said at a news conference, "Life is unfair." By that I believe he meant we do not know, nor can we predict or control with certainty, either the events that impinge upon us or the outcomes of actions we undertake in response to those events.

Consequently, Mr. Porter's saying that an illegal plan of surveillance should not be carried out could have caused his ostracism as a non–team player. There are too many cases when confrontation of this sort has resulted in such consequences. The real question, though, is not, Are such fantasized consequences possible? but, Are such fantasized consequences likely?

Thus, real risk is an existential condition, and all actions do have consequences that, to paraphrase Hamlet, may be worse than the evils of the present. As a result of their unwillingness to accept existential risk as one of life's givens, however, people may opt to take their organizations to Abilene rather than run the risk, no matter how small, of ending up somewhere worse.

Again, though, one must ask, What is the real risk that underlies the decision to opt for Abilene? What is at the core of the paradox?

Fear of Separation

One is tempted to say that the core of the paradox lies in the individual's fear of the unknown. Actually, we do not fear what is unknown, but we are afraid of things we do know about. What do we know about that frightens us into such apparently inexplicable organizational behavior?

Separation, alienation, and loneliness are things we do know about—and fear. Both research and experience indicate that ostracism is one of the most powerful punishments that can be devised. Solitary confinement does not draw its coercive strength from physical deprivation. The evidence is overwhelming that we have a fundamental need to be connected, engaged, and related and a reciprocal need not to be separated or alone. Everyone of us, though, has experienced aloneness. From the time the umbilical cord was cut, we have experienced the real anguish of separation—broken friendships, divorces, deaths, and exclusions.

That fear of taking risks that may result in our separation from others is at the core of the paradox. It finds expression in ways of which we may be unaware, and it is ultimately the cause of the self-defeating, collective deception that leads to self-destructive decisions within organizations.

The Psychological Reversal of Risk and Certainty

One piece of the map is still missing. It relates to the peculiar reversal that occurs in our thought processes as we try to cope with the Abilene Paradox. For example, we frequently fail to take action in an organizational setting because we fear that the actions we take may result in our separation from others, or, in the language of Mr. Porter, we are afraid of being tabbed as "disloyal" or are afraid of being ostracized as "non–team players." But therein lies a paradox within a paradox, because our very unwillingness to take such risks virtually ensures the separation and aloneness we so fear. In effect, we reverse "real existential risk" and "fantasied risk" and by doing so transform what is a probability statement into what, for all practical purposes, becomes a certainty.

[In the] Watergate situation the principals evidently feared being ostracized as disloyal non–team players. When the illegality of the act surfaced, however, it was nearly inevitable that blaming, self-protective actions, and scapegoating would result in the very emotional separation from both the President and one another that the principals feared. Thus, by reversing real and fantasied risk, they had taken effective action to ensure the outcome they least desired.

One final question remains: Why do we make this peculiar reversal? I support the general thesis of Alvin Toffler and Philip Slater, who contend that our cultural emphasis on technology, competition, individualism, temporariness, and mobility has resulted in a population that has frequently experienced the terror of loneliness and seldom the satisfaction of engagement.

A Possible Abilene Bypass

Existential risk is inherent in living, so it is impossible to provide a map that meets the no-risk criterion, but it may be possible to describe the route in terms that make the landmarks understandable and that will clarify the risks involved. In order to do that, however, some commonly used terms such as victim, victimizer, collusion, responsibility, conflict, conformity, courage, confrontation, reality, and knowledge have to be redefined. In addition, we need to explore the relevance of the redefined concepts for bypassing or getting out of Abilene.

- *Victim and victimizer.* Blaming and fault-finding behavior is one of the basic symptoms of organizations that have found their way to Abilene, and the target of blame generally doesn't include the one who criticizes. Stated in different terms, executives begin to assign one another to roles of victims and victimizers. Ironic as it may seem, however, this assignment of roles is both irrelevant and dysfunctional, because once a business or a government fails to manage its agreement and arrives in Abilene, all its members are victims. Thus, arguments and accusations that identify victims and victimizers at best become symptoms of the paradox, and, at worst, drain energy from the problem-solving efforts required to redirect the organization along the route it really wants to take.
- *Collusion.* A basic implication of the Abilene Paradox is that human problems of organization are reciprocal in nature. As Robert Tannenbaum has pointed out, you can't have an autocratic boss unless subordinates are willing to collude with his autocracy, and you can't have obsequious subordinates unless the boss is willing to collude with their obsequiousness.

Thus, in plain terms, each person in a self-defeating, Abilene-bound organization *colludes* with others, including peers, superiors, and subordinates, sometimes consciously and sometimes subconsciously, to create the dilemma in which the organization finds itself. It neither helps the organization handle its dilemma of unrecognized agreement nor does it provide psychological relief for the individual, because focusing on conflict when agreement is the issue is devoid of reality. In fact, it does just the opposite, for it causes the organization to focus on managing conflict when it should be focusing on managing agreement.

- *Responsibility for problem-solving action.* A second question is, Who is responsible for getting us out of this place? To that question is frequently appended a third one, generally rhetorical in nature, with "should" overtones, such as, Isn't it the boss (or the ranking government official) who is responsible for doing something about the situation?

The answer to that question is no.

The key to understanding the functionality of the *no* answer is the knowledge that, when the dynamics of the paradox are in operation, the authority figure—and others—are in unknowing agreement with one another concerning the organization's problems and the steps necessary to solve them. Consequently, the power to destroy the paradox's pernicious influence comes from confronting and speaking to the underlying reality of the situation, and not from one's hierarchical position within the organization. Therefore, any organization member who chooses to risk confronting that reality possesses the necessary leverage to release the organization from the paradox's grip.

It may be Jeb Magruder's response to this question of Senator Baker:

If you were concerned because the action was known to you to be illegal, because you thought it improper or unethical, you thought the prospects for success were very meager, and you doubted the reliability of Mr. Liddy, what on earth would it have taken to decide against the plan?

Magruder's reply was brief and to the point:

Not very much, sir. I am sure that if I had fought vigorously against it, I think any of us could have had the plan cancelled. (*Time*, June 25, 1973, p. 12.)

- *Reality, knowledge, confrontation.* Accepting the paradox as a model describing certain kinds of organizational dilemmas also requires rethinking the nature of reality and knowledge, as they are generally described in organizations. In brief, the underlying dynamics of the paradox clearly indicate that organization members generally know more about issues confronting the organization than they don't know.

Given this concept of reality and its relationship to knowledge, confrontation becomes the process of facing issues squarely, openly, and directly in an effort to discover whether the nature of the underlying collective reality is agreement or conflict. Accepting such a definition of confrontation has an important implication for change agents interested in making organizations more effective. That is, organization change and effectiveness may be facilitated as much by confronting the organization with what it knows and agrees upon as by confronting it with what it doesn't know or disagrees about.

Real Conflict and Phony Conflict

Conflict is a part of any organization. Couples, R&D divisions, and White House staffs all engage in it. However, analysis of the Abilene Paradox opens up the possibility of two kinds of conflict— real and phony. On the surface, they look alike, but, like headaches, have different causes and therefore require different treatment.

Real conflict occurs when people have real differences. ("I suggest we 'bug' the Watergate." "I'm not in favor of it.")

Phony conflict, on the other hand, occurs when people agree on the actions they want to take, and then do the opposite. The resulting anger, frustration, and blaming behavior generally termed "conflict" are not based on real differences. Rather, they stem from the protective reactions that occur when a decision that no one believed in or was committed to in the first place goes sour. In fact, as a paradox within a paradox, such conflict is symptomatic of agreement!

Group Tyranny and Conformity

Understanding the dynamics of the Abilene Paradox also requires a "reorientation" in thinking about concepts such as "group tyranny"—the loss of the individual's distinctiveness in a group, and the impact of conformity pressures on individual behavior in organizations.

Group tyranny and its result, individual conformity, generally refer to the coercive effect of group pressures on individual behavior. Sometimes referred to as Groupthink, it has been damned as the cause for everything from the lack of creativity in organizations ("A camel is a horse designed by a committee") to antisocial behavior in juveniles ("My Johnny is a good boy. He was just pressured into shoplifting by the kids he runs around with").

However, analysis of the dynamics underlying the Abilene Paradox opens up the possibility that individuals frequently perceive and feel as if they are experiencing the coercive organization conformity pressures when, in actuality, they are responding to the dynamics of mismanaged agreement. Conceptualizing, experiencing, and responding to such experiences as reflecting the tyrannical pressures of a group again serves an important psychological use for the individual: As was previously said, it releases him from the responsibility of taking action and thus becomes a defense against action. Thus, much behavior within an organization that heretofore has been conceptualized as reflecting the tyranny of conformity pressures is really an expression of collective anxiety and therefore must be reconceptualized as a defense against acting.

A well-known example of such faulty conceptualization comes to mind. It involves the heroic sheriff in the classic Western movies who stands alone in the jailhouse door and single-handedly protects a suspected (and usually innocent) horse thief or murderer from the irrational, tyrannical forces of group behavior—that is, an armed lynch mob. Few ever take the challenge, and the reason is not the sheriff's six-shooter. The gun in fact serves as a face-saving measure for people who don't wish to participate in a hanging anyway. ("We had to back off. The sheriff threatened to blow our heads off.")

The situation is one involving agreement management, for a careful investigator canvassing the crowd under conditions in which the anonymity of the interviewees' responses could be guaranteed would probably find: (1) that few of the individuals in the crowd really wanted to take part in the hanging; (2) that each person's participation came about because he perceived, falsely, that others wanted to do so; and (3) that each person was afraid that others in the crowd would ostracize or in some other way punish him if he did not go along.

Diagnosing the Paradox

Unfortunately, the underlying reality of the paradox makes it impossible to provide either no-risk solutions or action technologies divorced from existential attitudes and realities. I do, however, have two sets of suggestions for dealing with these situations. One set of suggestions relates to diagnosing the situation, the other to confronting it.

When faced with the possibility that the paradox is operating, one must first make a diagnosis of the situation, and the key to diagnosis is an answer to the question, Is the organization involved in a conflict-management or an agreement-management situation? As an organization member, I have found it relatively easy to make a preliminary diagnosis as to whether an organization is on the way to Abilene or is involved in legitimate, substantive conflict by responding to the Diagnostic Survey shown in the accompanying figure.

In brief, for reasons that should be apparent from the theory discussed here, the more times "characteristic" is checked, the more likely the organization is on its way to Abilene. In practical terms, a process for managing agreement is called for. And finally, if the answer to the first question falls into the "characteristic" category and most of the other answers fall into the category "not characteristic," one may be relatively sure the organization is in a real conflict situation and some sort of conflict management intervention is in order.

Coping with the Paradox

Assuming a preliminary diagnosis leads one to believe he and/or his organization is on the way to Abilene, the individual may choose to actively confront the situation to determine directly whether the underlying reality is one of agreement or conflict. Although there are, perhaps, a number of ways to do it, I have found one way in particular to be effective—confrontation in a group setting. The basic approach involves gathering organization members who are key figures in the problem and its solution into a group setting. Working within the context of a group is important, because the dynamics of the Abilene Paradox involve collusion among group members; therefore, to try to solve the dilemma by working with individuals and small subgroups would involve further collusion with the dynamics leading up to the paradox.

The first step in the meeting is for the individual who "calls" it (that is, the confronter) to own up to his position first and be open to the feedback he gets. The owning up process lets the others know that he is concerned lest the organization may be making a decision contrary to the desires of any of its members.

FIGURE 1 | ORGANIZATION DIAGNOSTIC SURVEY

Instructions: For each of the following statements please indicate whether it IS or IS NOT characteristic of your organization.

1. There is conflict in the organization.
2. Organization members felt frustrated, impotent, and unhappy when trying to deal with it. Many are looking for ways to escape. They may avoid meetings at which the conflict is discussed, they may be looking for other jobs, or they may spend as much time away from the office as possible by taking unneeded trips or vacation or sick leave.
3. Organization members place much of the blame for the dilemma on the boss or other groups. In "back room" conversations among friends the boss is termed incompetent, ineffective, "out of touch," or a candidate for early retirement. To his face, nothing is said, or at best, only oblique references are made concerning his role in the organization's problems. If the boss isn't blamed, some other group, division, or unit is seen as the cause of the trouble: "We would do fine if it were not for the damn fools in Division X."
4. Small subgroups of trusted friends and associates meet informally over coffee, lunch, and so on to discuss organizational problems. There is a lot of agreement among the members of these subgroups as to the cause of the troubles and the solutions that would be effective in solving them. Such conversations are frequently punctuated with statements beginning with, "We should do. . . ."
5. In meetings where those same people meet with members from other subgroups to discuss the problem they "soften their positions," state them in ambiguous language, or even reverse them to suit the apparent positions taken by others.
6. After such meetings, members complain to trusted associates that they really didn't say what they wanted to say, but also provide a list of convincing reasons why the comments, suggestions, and reactions they wanted to make would have been impossible. Trusted associates commiserate and say the same was true for them.
7. Attempts to solve the problem do not seem to work. In fact, such attempts seem to add to the problem or make it worse.
8. Outside the organization individuals seem to get along better, be happier, and operate more effectively than they do within it.

What kinds of results can one expect if he decides to undertake the process of confrontation?

- *The technical level.* If one is correct in diagnosing the presence of the paradox, I have found the solution to the technical problem may be almost absurdly quick and simple, nearly on the order of this:

  "Do you mean that you and I and the rest of us have been dragging along with a research project that one of us has thought would work? It's crazy. I can't believe we would do it, but we did. Let's figure out how we can cancel it and get to doing something productive." In fact, the simplicity and quickness of the solution frequently don't seem possible to most of us, since we have been trained to believe that the solution to conflict requires a long, arduous process of debilitating problem solving.

Also, since existential risk is always present, it is possible that one's diagnosis is incorrect, and the process of confrontation lifts to the level of public examination real, substantive conflict, which may result in heated debate about technology, personalities, and/or administrative approaches. There is evidence that such debates, properly managed, can be the basis for creativity in organizational problem solving. There is also the possibility, however, that such debates cannot be managed, and, substantiating the concept of existential risk, the person who initiates the risk may get fired or ostracized. But that again leads to the necessity of evaluating the results of such confrontation at the existential level.

- *Existential results.* Evaluating the outcome of confrontation from an existential framework is quite different from evaluating it from a set of technical criteria. How do I reach this conclusion? Simply from interviewing a variety of people who have chosen to confront the paradox and listening to their responses. In short, for them, psychological success and failure apparently are divorced from what is traditionally accepted in organizations as criteria for success and failure.

Most important, the act of confrontation apparently provides intrinsic psychological satisfaction, regardless of the technological outcomes for those who attempt it. The real meaning of that existential experience, and its relevance to a wide variety of organizations, may lie, therefore, not in the scientific analysis of decision making but in the plight of Sisyphus. That is something the reader will have to decide for himself.

In essence, this paper proposes that there is an underlying organizational reality that includes both agreement and disagreement, cooperation and conflict. However, the decision to confront the possibility of organization agreement is all too difficult and rare, and its opposite, the decision to accept the evils of the present, is all too common. Yet those two decisions may reflect the essence of both our human potential and our human imperfectability. Consequently, the choice to confront reality in the family, the church, the business, or the bureaucracy, though made only occasionally, may reflect those "peak experiences" that provide meaning to the valleys.

Selected Bibliography

Chris Argyris in *Intervention Theory and Method: A Behavioral Science View* (Addison-Wesley, 1970) gives an excellent description of the process of "owning up" and being "open," both of which are major skills required if one is to assist his organization in avoiding or leaving Abilene.

Albert Camus in *The Myth of Sisyphus and Other Essays* (Vintage Books, Random House, 1955) provides an existential viewpoint for coping with absurdity, of which the Abilene Paradox is a clear example.

Jerry B. Harvey and R. Albertson in "Neurotic Organizations: Symptoms, Causes and Treatment," Parts I and II, *Personnel Journal* (September and October 1971) provide a detailed example of a third-party intervention into an organization caught in a variety of agreement-management dilemmas.

Irving Janis in *Victims of Groupthink* (Houghton Mifflin Co., 1972) offers an alternative viewpoint for understanding and dealing with many of the dilemmas described in "The Abilene Paradox." Specifically, many of the events that Janis describes as examples of conformity pressures (that is, group tyranny) I would conceptualize as mismanaged agreement.

In his *The Pursuit of Loneliness* (Beacon Press, 1970), Philip Slater contributes an in-depth description of the impact of the role of alienation, separation, and loneliness (a major contribution to the Abilene Paradox) in our culture.

Richard Walton in *Interpersonal Peacemaking: Confrontation and Third Party Consultation* (Addison-Wesley, 1969) describes a variety of approaches for dealing with conflict when it is real, rather than phony.

Reading 28 | Social Influences on Work Effectiveness

Lyman W. Porter, Edward E. Lawler III, and J. Richard Hackman

Conditions within Groups That Moderate Their Impact on Work Effectiveness

Before proceeding to consider (in the next section) the ways that groups can influence the work effectiveness of individuals, we should first take into account certain conditions within groups that can affect how much and what kind of impact they will have. Uppermost among these are a group's characteristic reactions to deviance and the degree of cohesiveness that exists within the group.

Deviance and Group Effectiveness

The experimental work on how groups react to members who engage in behaviors which are inconsistent with group norms . . . reveals a fairly primitive type of group process. Caricatured a bit, the process operates as follows: Uniformity, conformity to norms, and adherence to one's role is the rule. When someone steps out of line, other members provide him with potent doses of discretionary stimuli designed to persuade or coerce him back to "normal." This pressure continues until the would-be deviant (1) gives in and ceases expressing his deviant thoughts or exhibiting his deviant behavior; (2) is psychologically or bodily rejected by the group or becomes institutionalized by the group as the "house deviant"; or (3) finally convinces the other group members of the rightness of his thoughts or the appropriateness of his behavior.

The more the group has control of discretionary stimuli which are important to group members, the more it can effectively eliminate most appearances of deviance on the part of its members. The members, in such circumstances, may faithfully behave in accord with their roles in the group, refrain from violating group norms, and express their endorsement of

the "right" attitudes and beliefs. And from all visible indicators, at least in the short term, everything seems well with the group.

Dysfunctional Aspects of Eliminating Deviance from Group Norms

It can be argued, however, that this pattern of dealing with deviance is highly dysfunctional for the long-term effectiveness of a group, for at least two reasons (Hackman, 1975). First, if members comply primarily because of the application of pressure from the group (or the expected application of that pressure), the result may be public compliance *at the expense of* private acceptance and personal commitment to what is being done (cf. Kelman, 1961; Kiesler, 1969). And when a group is heavily populated by individuals who are saying and doing one thing but thinking and feeling another, high effectiveness in the long haul is unlikely.

Second, to the extent that a group uses its control of discretionary stimuli to swiftly extinguish any signs of deviance, it loses the opportunity to explore the usefulness and ultimate validity of the very attitudes, beliefs, norms and roles it is enforcing. For example, if compliance to a given norm about work behavior is enforced so effectively that deviance from that norm virtually never occurs, the group will be unable to discover whether that norm is actually helpful or detrimental to the achievement of the goals of the group. In essence, it may be that an unexamined norm is not worth enforcing—at least if high group effectiveness is aspired to in the long run.

Despite these and other dysfunctions of excessive pressures against deviance, the research literature suggests that groups have a strong tendency to stamp out (or at least sweep under the rug) behaviors which are not congruent with

Source: Lyman W. Porter, Edward E. Lawler III, and J. Richard Hackman, "Social Influences on Work Effectiveness." Pages 404–422 in Porter, Lawler, and Hackman, *Behavior in Organizations* (McGraw-Hill, 1975). Reprinted by permission of the publisher.

traditional standards of acceptability in the group. Apparently groups rarely attempt to work through the more basic problems of why people deviate from the group, what the consequences of such deviance for the group are, and how deviance can be most effectively dealt with for the good of both individual members and the group as a whole. . . .

It is emotionally quite stressful and difficult for group members to deal openly with core questions of conformity, deviation, and interpersonal relationships in a group. Indeed, research (Argyris, 1969; Bion, 1959) suggests that it may be impossible for a group to break out of a traditional pattern of interpersonal behavior without outside professional assistance. Even with such assistance, it may take a great deal of time and effort before a group can overcome the basic assumptions which guided its early behavior and develop into an effective and truly independent work group (Bion, 1959). When a group becomes able to make more open and conscious choices about the use of those discretionary stimuli under its control to deal with issues of conformity and deviance, the long-term effectiveness of the group should be greatly enhanced.

Why High Group Cohesiveness Can Be Dysfunctional

In general, as the cohesiveness of a work group increases, the overall level of member conformity to the norms of the group would also be expected to increase—for two different but mutually reinforcing reasons: First, . . . there tend to be stronger group-generated pressures toward uniformity and conformity in groups which are highly cohesive than in groups which are not (cf. Festinger, Schachter, & Black, 1950). And second, group members are likely to value especially strongly the interpersonal rewards which are available in highly cohesive groups—precisely because of the strong positive feelings members have for one another in such groups. Therefore, group members are unlikely to risk losing those rewards by ignoring or defying pressures to conform to group norms. And, in fact, research evidence confirms that conformity is especially high in cohesive groups (cf. Hackman, 1975; Lott & Lott, 1965; Tajfel, 1969).

The problem is that conformity to group norms which occurs in highly cohesive groups may *not* be functional for group or individual productivity. Indeed, cohesiveness may be strongly dysfunctional for effectiveness in some situations for several reasons, which are discussed below.

Deviance Is Dealt With Ineffectively. As noted previously, groups tend in general to stamp out deviant behavior on the part of individual group members—rather than use such deviance to increase either the learning of individual group members or the capability of the group as a whole to respond effectively to a changing or turbulent state of affairs. Since pressures toward uniformity are highest in highly cohesive groups, the risk of quick and ill-considered elimination of all appearances of deviance in the group also are likely to be highest in cohesive groups—even though exploration of such deviant behaviors might actually be helpful to the group in the long run.

Norms Are Strong, but Their Direction May Be Negative. While it is generally true that cohesive groups are able to effectively control members such that their behavior closely approximates that specified by the group norm, the *direction* of the group norm itself (i.e., toward high versus low performance) has been found to be unrelated to the level of cohesiveness (Berkowitz, 1954; Darley, Gross, & Martin, 1952; Schachter, 1951; Seashore, 1954).

For example, in several studies (e.g., Schachter, 1951; Berkowitz, 1954) conditions of high versus low cohesiveness and high- versus low-productivity norms were created by experimental manipulation. It was found that member productivity was indeed closer to the group norm in the high- than in the low-cohesiveness groups—for both the high- *and* the low-production norms. There have been similar findings in industrial situations using survey techniques (Seashore, 1954). In this study of over 200 work groups in a machinery factory, no correlation was found between cohesiveness and productivity—but, as would be expected, when cohesiveness was high, the amount of *variation* in the productivity of group members was low, and vice versa.

Groupthink May Develop. One of the seeming advantages of having a great deal of uniformity or conformity in a group is that members do not have to deal with the thorny interpersonal problems which can arise when members behave in non-uniform ways—e.g., when each member of a work group is allowed to select his own level of production and the levels selected turn out to vary a good deal from member to member. This "group-maintenance" function of uniformity may be especially important to members of highly cohesive groups, since members of such groups typically value strongly the rewards controlled by their fellows—and would be particularly upset to receive negative interpersonal reactions from them.

It has been suggested, however, that as a group becomes excessively close-knit and develops a strong feeling of "we-ness," it becomes susceptible to a pattern of behavior known as "groupthink" (Janis, 1972). Among the several symptoms of groupthink are an excessive concern with maintaining uniformity among members, a marked decrease in the openness of the group to discrepant or unsettling information (from sources either inside or outside the group), and a simultaneous unwillingness to examine seriously and process such negative information if it ever is brought to the attention of the group.

These social processes may often serve immediate group-maintenance functions and help perpetuate the warm and cohesive feelings which characterize the group. In addition, however, they result in an increased likelihood that the group, in a spirit of goodwill and shared confidence, will develop and implement a course of action which is grossly inappropriate and ineffective. It has been shown (Janis, 1972), for example, how the groupthink phenomenon may have contributed substantially to a number of historical fiascoes planned and executed by groups of government officials (e.g., the Bay of Pigs invasion and Britain's appeasement policy toward Hitler prior to World War II).

Should Cohesiveness Be Avoided?

It might appear from the above discussion that high cohesiveness of groups in organizations is something that should be avoided—to minimize the possibility of enforced low-production norms in work settings or the likelihood that groupthink-like phenomena will develop among decision makers. Such a conclusion would be a very pessimistic one: low cohesiveness among members of work groups or decision-making groups would indeed lower the possibility of obtaining the negative outcomes mentioned but also would require that the positive potential of cohesive groups be forgone as well—such as the increased capability of such groups to regulate behavior so as to *increase* the attainment of group and organizational goals.

The question, then, becomes how the norms of highly cohesive groups can be changed such that they encourage careful examination of the task environment (including negative or unsettling information which may be present), exploration of interpersonal issues, which may be impairing group performance, and high rather than low levels of group and member productivity. Although presently little is known about what factors affect the kinds of norms developed by work groups in organizations (cf. Vroom, 1969), two general approaches to the problem are discussed briefly below.

Fostering Intergroup Competition. One frequently espoused tactic for developing simultaneously high work-group cohesiveness and commitment to organizational goals can be referred to as the "best damn group in the whole damn organization" ploy. Many managers realize that if they can get their subordinates, as a group, to experience themselves in competition with other groups in the organization, a kind of team spirit often develops which results in high group cohesiveness and great member commitment to be the "best" in whatever it is that defines the competition. And, in fact, there is considerable research evidence that when groups enter into competitive relationships with other groups, internal cohesiveness and high individual task commitment do increase—often dramatically (cf. Blake & Mouton, 1964; Sherif, 1965).

The problem is that such intergroup competitiveness often actually works against the best interests of the total organization in the long run. For example, in the interest of "winning," information which really should be shared among groups for optimal organizational functioning often is withheld—and at times even misinformation is communicated up and down the line in a way intended to make sure that "our group looks best." The pervasive line-staff and interdepartment (e.g., sales versus production) conflicts in contemporary organizations often reflect exactly this type of intergroup competition.

One common means of attempting to overcome such problems of dysfunctional intergroup competition within organizations (while maintaining high commitment within groups) is to introduce or make especially salient a superordinate goal which all groups share. Research evidence does support the idea that a superordinate goal can reduce or eliminate hostilities between groups (Sherif, 1965). And, in fact, many business organizations use the idea of the superordinate goal in their attempts to get employees in diverse groups to pull together for the good of the organization as a whole—for example, by prominently posting the number of trinkets sold this month by one's own company versus the number sold by the chief competitor. The problem, of course, is that it is not likely that a lower-level employee who hates his job and feels he is grossly and unfairly underpaid is going to *care* very much about whether or not his own organization is ahead in the trunketselling competition—regardless of the attempts of the company employee-relations department to make that competition an organizing theme of the company.

Basing Cohesiveness on Task Rather Than Social Rewards. It may be that one of the major reasons for the failure of many cohesive groups to work as effectively as they might toward group and organizational goals has to do with the basis of the cohesiveness itself—i.e., the reasons why the group members have a strong desire to stick together.

In virtually all the research which has been discussed here, cohesiveness was based upon the *interpersonal rewards* present or potentially present in the group. The "stake" of most group members in such situations, then, would be to refrain from behaviors that might disrupt the interpersonal satisfactions which are obtained from group membership. The control of the group over its members in such cases rests largely upon its capability to provide or withhold such valued social satisfactions. In the groupthink situation, for example, such control results in interpersonal strategies characterized by lessened vigilance for new and potentially disruptive information, acceptance of the views of "high-status others" as the doctrine of the group, and suppression of any interpersonal unpleasantries—all of which can severely impair the work effectiveness of the group.

If the basis for the cohesiveness were a shared commitment to the *task* of the group (instead of a commitment to maintaining the interpersonal rewards received in the group), the picture might change considerably. The criterion for when to accept information and direction from others in the group, for example, might change from something like "Will questioning what is being said by the leader risk my being rejected or ridiculed by the group?" to "Will such questioning contribute to our succeeding in the task?" Conformity, then, should remain high in such groups, but the norms to which conformity is enforced would focus on facilitating the group's task performance activities rather than on maintaining interpersonal comfortableness. This change in orientation also would bear on the question of the *direction* of norms for individual production in work groups: if one of the major reasons for the cohesiveness of the group were a shared commitment to succeeding in the task, then that commitment should in most cases lead to group norms oriented toward high rather than low task effectiveness. . . .

The problem in attempting to develop task-based cohesiveness in real-world work groups is twofold. First, many tasks (and perhaps most production tasks) in organizations are not such as to generate genuine group commitment. Instead, the reverse may often be true: the task may be so uninteresting that the group accepts as an alternative a task of "getting" management or of avoiding hard work. In such cases, the power resident in the group cohesiveness may be exceptionally dysfunctional for organizational goals. Second, it is quite difficult, even for objectively important tasks, for group members to overcome their orientation to interpersonal rewards and rejections. The group of Kennedy advisors during the Bay of Pigs crisis, for example, certainly had an important task; but the heavy investment of each member toward remaining a member of the high-status, high-prestige group apparently was so strong that "not rocking the interpersonal boat" overwhelmed "doing the task well" as a behavioral criterion for most group members.

Thus, while there appears to be much to be said for the development of tasks which can provide a strong positive basis for group cohesiveness, few guidelines for designing such tasks currently exist. The crux of the problem, it seems, is to create conditions such that the rewards from genuinely shared task activities become as salient and as attractive to group members as are the more skin-surface interpersonal satisfactions, which, unfortunately, currently typify relationships within most "cohesive" groups in organizations.

Ways Groups Influence Individual Work Effectiveness

Now we are in a position to turn to the question of *how* groups can in fact have an impact on how hard and how well their members work. . . . The major direct determinants of the work behavior of organization members can be summarized in terms of four major classes of variables:

1. The job-relevant knowledge and skills of the individual
2. The level of psychological arousal the individual experiences while working

3. The performance strategies the individual uses doing his work
4. The level of effort the individual exerts in doing his work

Which (or which combination) of the four classes of variables can contribute substantially to increased individual work *effectiveness,* of course, very much depends upon the nature of the task or job being performed. On a routine and simple clerical job, for example, where the sole performance criterion is quantity of acceptable output, only effort is likely to be of real importance in influencing measured work effectiveness. On a more complex job, where there are many ways to go about performing it (e.g., most managerial jobs), the performance *strategies* used may critically influence effectiveness. For yet other jobs, arousal and/or the job-relevant skills of the individual may be critical.[1] . . .

Group Influences by Affecting Member Knowledge and Skills

Performance on many tasks and jobs in organizations is strongly affected by the job-relevant knowledge and skills of the individuals who do the work. Thus, even if an employee has both high commitment toward accomplishing a particular piece of work and a well-formed strategy about how to go about doing it, the implementation of that plan can be constrained or terminated if he does not know how to carry it out, or if he knows how but is incapable of doing so. While ability is relevant to the performance of jobs at all levels in an organization, its impact probably is somewhat reduced for lower-level jobs. The reason is that such jobs often are not demanding of high skill levels. Further, to the extent that organizational selection, placement, and promotion practices are adequate, *all* jobs should tend to be occupied by individuals who possess the skills requisite for adequate performance.

. . . The impact of groups on member performance effectiveness by improving member knowledge and skill probably is one of the lesser influences groups can have—both because employees on many jobs tend already to have many or all of the skills needed to perform them effectively and because there are other sources for improving skills which may be more useful and more potent than the work group, such as formal job training programs and self-study programs.

Group Influences by Affecting Member Arousal Level

...[A] group can substantially influence the level of psychological arousal experienced by a member—through the mere presence of the other group members and by those others sending the individual messages which are directly arousal-enhancing or arousal-depressing. The conditions under which such group-promoted changes in arousal level will lead to increased performance effectiveness, however, very much depend upon the type of task being worked on (Zajonc, 1965).

In this case, the critical characteristics of the job have to do with whether the initially *dominant task responses* of the individual are likely to be correct or incorrect. Since the individual's output of such responses is facilitated when he is in an aroused state, arousal should improve performance effectiveness on well-learned tasks (so-called performance tasks) in which the dominant response is correct and needs merely to be executed by the performer. By the same token, arousal should impair effectiveness for new or unfamiliar tasks (learning tasks) in which the dominant response is likely to be incorrect. . . .

Groups can, of course, increase member arousal in ways other than taking an evaluative stance toward the individual. Strongly positive, encouraging statements also should increase arousal in some performance situations—for example, by helping the individual become personally highly committed to the group goal, and making sure he realizes that he is a very important part of the team responsible for reaching that goal. What must be kept in mind, however, is that such devices represent a double-edged sword: while they may facilitate effective performance for well-learned tasks, they may have the opposite effect for new and unfamiliar tasks.

What, then, can be said about the effects on performance of group members when their presence (and interaction) serves to *decrease* the level of arousal of the group member—as, for example, when individuals coalesce into groups under conditions of high stress? When the other members of the group are a source of support, comfort, or acceptance to the individual (and serve to decrease his arousal level), it would be predicted that performance effectiveness would follow a pattern exactly opposite to that described above: the group would impair effectiveness for familiar or well-learned performance tasks (because arousal helps on these tasks, and arousal is being lowered) and facilitate effectiveness for unfamiliar or complicated learning tasks (because in this case arousal is harmful, and it is being lowered).

...As the group becomes increasingly threatening, evaluative, or strongly encouraging, effectiveness should increase for performance tasks and decrease for learning tasks. When the group is experienced as increasingly supportive, comforting, or unconditionally accepting, effectiveness should decrease for performance tasks and increase for learning tasks. And when no meaningful relationship at all is experienced by the individual between himself and the group, performance should not be affected. While some of these predictions have been tested and confirmed in small group experimental settings, others await research. . . .

It is well known that overly routine jobs can decrease a worker's level of arousal to such an extent that his performance effectiveness is impaired. It seems quite possible, therefore, that the social environment of workers on such jobs can be designed so as to compensate partially for the deadening effects of the job itself and thereby lead to an increment in performance on well-learned tasks.

Finally, . . . the supervisor probably has a more powerful effect on the level of arousal of a worker than any other single individual in his immediate social environment. By close supervision (which usually results in the worker's feeling more or less constantly evaluated), supervisors can and do increase the level of arousal experienced by workers. While this may, for *routine* jobs, have some potential for improving performance effectiveness, it also is quite likely that the worker's negative reactions to being closely supervised ultimately will result in his attention being diverted from the job itself and focused instead on ways he can either get out from "under the gun" of the supervisor or somehow get back at the supervisor to punish him for his unwanted close supervision.

Group Influences by Affecting Level of Member Effort and Member Performance Strategies

The level of effort a person exerts in doing his work and the performance strategies he follows are treated together here because both variables are largely under the performer's *voluntary* control.

Direct Versus Indirect Influences on Effort and Strategy. Throughout this book we have used a general "expectancy theory" approach to analyze those aspects of a person's behavior in organizations which are under his voluntary control. From this perspective, a person's choices about his effort and work strategy can be viewed as hinging largely upon (1) his *expectations* regarding the likely consequences of his choices and (2) the degree to which he *values* those expected consequences. Following this approach, it becomes clear that the group can have both a direct and an indirect effect on the level of effort a group member exerts at his job and his choices about performance strategy.

The *direct* impact of the group on effort and strategy, of course, is simply the enforcement by the group of its own norms regarding what is an "appropriate" level of effort to expend on the job and what is the "proper" performance strategy. We previously discussed in some detail how groups use their control of discretionary stimuli to enforce group norms, and thereby affect such voluntary behaviors. Thus, if the group has established a norm about the level of member effort or the strategies members should use in going about their work, the group can control

individual behavior merely by making sure that individual members realize that their receipt of valued group-controlled rewards is contingent upon their behaving in accord with the norm.

The *indirect* impact of the group on the effort and performance strategies of the individual involves the group's control of information regarding the state of the organizational environment outside the boundaries of the group. Regardless of any norms the group itself may have about effort or strategy, it also can communicate to the group member "what leads to what" in the broader organization, and thereby affect the individual's *own* choices about his behavior. . . .

Moreover . . . groups can affect the *personal preferences and values* of individual members—although such influences tend to occur relatively slowly and over a long period of time. When such changes do occur, the level of desire (or the valence) individuals have for various outcomes available in the organizational setting will change as well. And as the kinds of outcomes valued by the individual change, his behavior also will change to increase the degree to which the newly valued outcomes are obtained at work. The long-term result can be substantial revision of the choices made by the individual about the work he will expend and the performance strategies he will use at work.

It should be noted, however, that such indirect influences on member effort and performance strategy will be most potent early in the individual's tenure in the organization when he has not yet had a chance to develop through experience his own personal "map" of the organization. When the individual becomes less dependent upon the group for data about "what leads to what" and "what's good" in the organization, the group may have to revert to direct norm enforcement to maintain control of the work behavior of individual members.

In summary, the group can and does have a strong impact on both the level of effort exerted by its members and the strategies members use in carrying out their work. This impact is realized both directly (i.e., by enforcement of group norms) and indirectly (i.e., by affecting the beliefs and values of the members). When the direct and indirect influences of a group are congruent—which is often the case—the potency of the group's effects on its members can be quite strong. For example, if at the same time that a group is enforcing its *own* norm of, say, moderately low production, it also is providing a group member with data regarding the presumably *objective* negative consequences of hard work in the particular organization, the group member will experience two partially independent and mutually reinforcing influences aimed at keeping his rate of production down.

Effort, Strategy, and Performance Effectiveness. What, then, are the circumstances under which groups can improve the work *effectiveness* of their members through influences on individual choices about level of effort and about strategy? Again, the answer depends upon the nature of the job. Unless a job is structured so that effort level or performance strategy actually can make a real difference in work effectiveness, group influences on effort or strategy will be irrelevant to how well individual members perform.

Strategy: In general, groups should be able to facilitate member work effectiveness by influencing strategy choices more for complex jobs than for simple, straightforward, or routine ones. The reason is that on simple jobs, strategy choices usually cannot make much of a difference in effectiveness; instead, how well one does is determined almost entirely by how hard one works. On jobs characterized by high variety and autonomy, on the other hand, the work strategy used by the individual usually is of considerable importance in determining work effectiveness. By helping an individual develop and implement an appropriate work strategy—of where and how to put in his effort—the group should be able to substantially facilitate his effectiveness.

Effort: In the great majority of organizational settings, most jobs are structured such that the harder one works, the more effective his performance is likely to be. Thus, group influences on the effort expended by members on their jobs are both very pervasive and very potent determiners of individual work effectiveness. There are, nevertheless, some exceptions to this generalization: the success of a complicated brain operation, for example, is less likely to depend upon effort expended than it is upon the strategies used and the job-relevant knowledge and skills of the surgeon.

When either effort or strategy or both are in fact important in determining performance effectiveness, the individual has substantial personal control over how well he does in his work. In such cases, the degree to which the group facilitates (rather than hinders) individual effectiveness will depend jointly upon (1) the degree to which the group has accurate information regarding the task and organizational contingencies which are operative in that situation and makes such information available to the individual and (2) the degree to which the norms of the group are congruent with those contingencies and reinforce them.

Participation. One management practice which in theory should contribute positively to meeting both of the above conditions is the use of group participation in making decisions about work practices. Participation has been widely advocated as a management technique, both on ideological grounds and as a direct means of increasing work effectiveness. And, in fact, some studies have shown that participation can lead to higher work effectiveness (e.g., Coch & French, 1948; Lawler & Hackman, 1969). In the present framework, participation should contribute to increased work effectiveness in two different ways.

1. Participation can increase the amount and the accuracy of information workers have about work practices and the environmental contingencies associated with them. . . .
2. Participation can increase the degree to which group members feel they "own" their work practices—and therefore the likelihood that the group will develop a norm of support for those practices. In the participative groups in the study cited above, for example, the nature of the work-related

communication among members changed from initial "shared warnings" about management and "things management proposes" to helping members (especially new members) come to understand and believe in "our plan." In other words, as group members come to experience the work or work practices *as under their own control or ownership,* it becomes more likely that informal group norms supportive of effective behavior vis-à-vis those practices will develop. Such norms provide a striking contrast to the "group protective" norms which often emerge when control is perceived to be exclusively and unilaterally under management control.

We can see, then, that group participative techniques can be quite facilitative of individual work effectiveness—but only under certain conditions:

1. The topic of participation must be relevant to the work itself. There is no reason to believe that participation involving task-irrelevant issues (e.g., preparing for the Red Cross Bloodmobile visit to the plant) will have facilitative effects on work productivity. While such participation may indeed help increase the cohesiveness of the work group, it clearly will not help group members gain information or develop norms which are facilitative of high work effectiveness. Indeed, such task-irrelevant participation may serve to direct the attention and motivation of group members *away from* work issues and thereby even lower productivity (cf. French, Israel, & As, 1960).

2. The objective task and environmental contingencies in the work setting must actually be supportive of more effective performance. That is, if through participation group members learn more about what leads to what in the organization, then it is increasingly important that there be real and meaningful positive outcomes which result from effective performance. If, for example, group members gain a quite complete and accurate impression through participation that "hard

work around here pays off only in backaches," then increased effort as a consequence of participation is most unlikely. If, on the other hand, participation results in a new and better understanding that hard work can lead to increased pay, enhanced opportunities for advancement, and the chance to feel a sense of personal and group accomplishment, then increased effort should be the result.

3. Finally, the work must be such that increased effort (or a different and better work strategy) objectively can lead to higher work effectiveness. If it is true—as argued here—that the main benefits of group participation are (1) increased understanding of work practices and the organizational environment and (2) increased experienced "ownership" by the group of the work and work practices, then participation should increase productivity only when the *objective determinants of productivity are under the voluntary control of the worker.* There is little reason to expect, therefore, that participation should have a substantial facilitative effect on productivity when work outcomes are mainly determined by the level of skill of the worker and/or by his arousal level (rather than effort expended or work strategy used) or when outcomes are controlled by objective factors in the environment over which the worker can have little or no control (e.g., the rate or amount of work which is arriving at the employee's station).

Implications for Diagnosis and Change

This section has focused on ways that the group can influence the performance effectiveness of individual group members. While it has been maintained throughout that the group has a substantial impact on such performance effectiveness, it has been emphasized that the nature and extent of this impact centrally depends upon the characteristics of the work being done.

To diagnose and change the direction or extent of social influences on individual performance in an organization, then, the following three steps might be taken.

1. An analysis of the task or job would be made to determine which of the four classes of variables (i.e., skills, arousal, strategies, effort) objectively affect measured performance effectiveness. This might be done by posing this analytical question: "If skills (or arousal, or effort, or strategies) were brought to bear on the work differently than is presently the case, would a corresponding difference in work effectiveness be likely to be observed as a consequence?" By scrutinizing each of the four classes of variables in this way, it usually is possible to identify which specific variables are objectively important to consider for the job. In many cases, of course, more than one class of variables will turn out to be of importance.

2. After one or more "target" classes of variables have been identified, the work group itself would be examined to unearth any ways in which the group was blocking effective individual performance. It might be determined, for example, that certain group norms were impeding the expression and use of various skills which individuals potentially could bring to bear on their work. Or it might turn out that the social environment of the worker created conditions which were excessively (or insufficiently) arousing for optimal performance on the task at hand. For effort and strategy, which are under the voluntary control of the worker, there are two major possibilities to examine: (a) that norms are enforced in the group which coerce individuals to behave in ineffective ways or (b) that the group provides information to the individual members about task and environmental contingencies in an insufficient or distorted fashion, resulting in their making choices about their work behavior which interfere with task effectiveness. . . .

3. Finally, it would be useful to assess the group and the broader social environment to determine if there are ways that the "people resources" in the situation could be more fully utilized in the interest of increased work effectiveness. That is, rather than focusing solely on ways the group may be blocking or impeding performance effectiveness, attention should be given as well to any unrealized *potential* which resides in the group. It could turn out, for example, that some group members would be of great help to others in increasing the level of individual task-relevant skills, but these individuals have never been asked for help. Alternatively, it might be that the group could be assisted in finding new and better ways of ensuring that each group member has available accurate and current information about those tasks and environmental contingencies which determine the outcomes of various work behaviors.

The point is that the people who surround an individual at work can facilitate as well as hinder his performance effectiveness—and that any serious attempt to diagnose the social environment in the interest of improving work performance should explicitly address unrealized possibilities for enhancing performance as well as issues for which remedial action may be required.

What particular organizational changes will be called for on the basis of such a diagnosis—or what techniques should be used to realize these changes—will, of course, largely depend upon the particular characteristics of the organization and of the resources which are available there. The major emphasis of this section has been that there is *not* any single universally useful type of change or means of change—and that, instead, intervention should always be based on a thorough diagnosis of the existing social, organizational, and task environment. Perhaps especially intriguing in this regard is the prospect of developing techniques of social intervention which will help groups see the need for (and develop the capability of) making such interventions *on their own* in the interest of increasing the work effectiveness of the group as a whole. . . .

REFERENCES

Argyris, C. The incompleteness of social psychological theory: Examples from small group, cognitive consistency and attribution research. *American Psychologist*, 1969, **24**, 893–908.

Berkowitz, L. Group standards, cohesiveness and productivity. *Human Relations*, 1954, **7**, 509–519.

Bion, W. R. *Experiences in groups.* New York: Basic Books, 1959.

Blake, R. R., & Mouton, J. S. *The managerial grid.* Houston: Gulf, 1964.

Coch, L., & French, J. R. P., Jr. Overcoming resistance to change. *Human Relations*, 1948, **1**, 512–532.

Darley, J., Gross, N., & Martin, W. Studies of group behavior: Factors associated with the productivity of groups. *Journal of Applied Psychology*, 1952, **36**, 396–403.

Festinger, L. Informal social communication. *Psychological Review*, 1950, **57**, 271–282.

Festinger, L., Schachter, S., & Black, K. *Social pressures in informal groups.* Stanford: Stanford University Press, 1950.

French, J. R. P., Jr. Israel, J., & Ås, D. An experiment on participation in a Norwegian factory. *Human Relations*, 1960, **13**, 3–19.

Hackman, J. R. Group influences on individuals in organizations. In M. D. Dunnette (Ed.), *Handbook of industrial and organizational psychology.* Chicago: Rand-McNally, 1975.

Janis, I. L. *Victims of groupthink: A psychological study of foreign-policy decisions and fiascos.* Boston: Houghton Mifflin, 1972.

Kelman, H. C. Processes of opinion change. *Public Opinion Quarterly*, 1961, **25**, 57–58.

Kiesler, C. A. Group pressure and conformity. In J. Mills (Ed.), *Experimental social psychology.* New York: Macmillan, 1969.

Lawler, E. E., & Hackman, J. R. The impact of employee participation in the development of pay incentive plans: A field experiment. *Journal of Applied Psychology*, 1969, **53**, 467–471.

Lott, A. J., & Lott, B. E. Group cohesiveness as interpersonal attraction: A review of relationships with antecedent and consequent variables. *Psychological Bulletin*, 1965, **64**, 259–309.

Schachter, S. Deviation, rejection and communication. *Journal of Abnormal and Social Psychology,* 1951, **46**, 190–207.

Seashore, S. *Group cohesiveness in the industrial work group.* Ann Arbor: Institute for Social Research, University of Michigan, 1954.

Sherif, M. Formation of social norms: The experimental paradigm. In H. Proshansky & B. Seidenberg (Eds.), *Basic studies in social psychology.* New York: Holt, Rinehart & Winston, 1965.

Tajfel, H. Social and cultural factors in perception. In G. Lindzey & E. Aronson (Eds.), *The handbook of social psychology* (2nd ed.). Reading, Mass.: Addison-Wesley, 1969.

Vroom, V. H. Industrial social psychology. In G. Lindzey & E. Aronson (Eds.), *The handbook of social psychology* (2nd ed.). Reading, Mass.: Addison-Wesley, 1969.

Zajonc, R. B. Social facilitation. *Science*, 1965, **149**, 269–274.

NOTE

1. The characteristics of tasks or jobs which identify which classes of variables are of most importance in determining work effectiveness have been termed "critical task contingencies," i.e., those contingencies which specify what behaviors are critical to effective or successful performance for the job in question. Depending upon what the critical task contingencies are for a given task or job, it is possible to determine on an a priori basis which variables must be dealt with in any attempt to improve performance effectiveness on that job. This notion is developed more completely by Hackman (1975).

Reading 29	The Psychological Contract and Motivation in Perspective

Edgar H. Schein

Once people have been recruited, selected, trained, and allocated to jobs, the organization must focus on creating conditions that will facilitate a high level of performance over a long period of time, and also permit individual employees to meet some of their own most important needs through membership and work in the organization. Traditionally, this problem has been attacked by searching out and cataloging the motives and needs of workers, and relating these to the incentives and rewards offered by the organization. As studies have accumulated, it has become apparent that the problem is complex and can better be conceptualized in terms of a "psychological contract" entered into by both the individual and the organization.

The notion of a psychological contract implies that there is an unwritten set of expectations operating at all times between every member of an organization and the various managers and others in that organization.[1] This idea is implicit in the concept of organizational role, in that every role is basically a set of behavioral expectations (Kahn, Wolfe, Quinn, Snoek, & Rosenthal, 1964). The psychological contract implies further that each role player, that is, employee, also has expectations about such things as salary or pay rate, working hours, benefits and privileges that go with a job, guarantees not to be fired unexpectedly, and so on. Many of these expectations are implicit and involve the person's sense of dignity and worth. We expect organizations to treat us as human beings, to provide work and facilities which are need-fulfilling rather than demeaning, to provide opportunities for growth and further learning, to provide feedback on how we are doing, and so on. Some of the strongest feelings leading to labor unrest, strikes, and employee turnover have to do with violations of these aspects of the psychological contract, even though the *public* negotiations are

often over the more explicit issues of pay, working hours, job security, and so on.

The organization also has more implicit, subtle expectations—that the employee will enhance the image of the organization, will be loyal, will keep organizational secrets, and will do his or her best on behalf of the organization (that is, will always be highly motivated and willing to make sacrifices for the organization). Some of the greatest disappointments of managers arise when a valued employee seems to have become less motivated or "unwilling to put out for the company."

The psychological contract changes over time as the organization's needs and the employee's needs change. What the employee is looking for in a job at age 25 may be completely different from what that same employee is looking for at age 50 (Hall, 1976; Schein, 1978a). Similarly, what the organization expects of a person during a period of rapid growth may be completely different from what that same organization expects when it has leveled off or is experiencing economic decline.

For example, at the beginning of the career, people's needs and expectations revolve very much around "self-tests." They need to learn whether they can, in fact, contribute to an organization, whether they have the skill and strength to do certain kinds of work, whether they can make a contribution (Schein, 1964). They, therefore, expect the organization to provide them with challenges to try out their skills and are most disappointed if they are kept too long in meaningless training assignments or at tasks they regard as menial. If this happens, neither they nor the organization can learn what their talents really are.

At a later career stage, needs and expectations shift to identifying an area in which the person can experience a sense of contribution and also develop this area of specialization; in turn, the individual expects the organization to recognize

Source: Schein, Edgar H., ORGANIZATIONAL PSYCHOLOGY 3/e © 1980, pp. 22–25, 98–101. Adapted by permission of Pearson Education, Inc. Upper Saddle River NJ.

his or her contribution in various ways (Dalton, Thompson, & Price, 1977). In mid-career when we are most productive we also expect the most in terms of recognition and rewards. At a later career stage, as we level off and begin to contribute less visibly, our needs for reassurance and for security may rise, and the expectations implicit in the psychological contract may shift toward being "taken care of," not being "put out to pasture" or thrown out the door. Retired people often complain that their psychological contract was violated dramatically because they had many good years of contribution left, their company was their whole life, they had really devoted themselves to it for decades, and felt that in return the company "owed" them something more than being put out of work at an age when they felt they could still contribute.

For its part, the organization needs and expects higher levels of motivation and effort when it is a young, struggling concern or in a severe competitive battle with other organizations. It expects more loyalty when it is under attack or in trouble and more "steady performance" in stable times when it feels it is offering a long-range sense of security to its employees.

Both individual employee and manager forge their expectations from their inner needs, what they have learned from others, traditions and norms which may be operating, their own past experience, and a host of other sources. As needs and external forces change, so do these expectations, making the psychological contract a *dynamic* one which must be constantly *renegotiated*. Though it remains unwritten, the psychological contract is a powerful determiner of behavior in organizations.

Power and Authority

One key element of the psychological contract is the organization's expectation that a new member will accept the authority system of that organization. Deciding to join implies acceptance of the basic rules that constitute the organization's authority system. Within defined areas the person must be willing to accept the dictates of some other person or some written rules, to accept limitations on his or her own behavior, and to curb personal inclinations if they go against rules or orders (Schein & Ott, 1962).

Authority is not the same thing as power. Pure power implies the ability to actually control others through the exercise of naked strength, the manipulation of rewards or punishments which are meaningful to others, or the manipulation of information. Power implies that others really have no choice because they are not strong enough to be self-determining or do not have access to the resources they need. It is what sociologists would call "nonlegitimate authority." Legitimate authority, on the other hand, implies the willingness on the part of subordinates to obey rules, laws, or orders because they consent to the system by which the rules, laws, or rank were arrived at—that is, they grant the person in authority the *right* to dictate to them. Authority is legitimate when there is consensus among the members of an organization or a society about (1) the basis on which a rule or law is to be derived, and/or (2) the system by which a person is to be put into a position of authority. In other words, a law will be obeyed only if there is consensus on the method by which laws are made, and a foreman will be obeyed by workers only if there is consensus among the workers that the promotional system by which one gets to be a foreman is fair. It is consent to the total system which permits subordinates to tolerate and take orders even from an occasional bad boss.

The organization can enforce its side of the psychological contract through the exercise of power and the use of authority. How can the employee enforce his or her side of the contract? Depending upon the total circumstances, the employee has a range of options: quitting the organization, reducing involvement in the work, going on strike, sabotage, and/or attempts to influence the situation on his or her own behalf. For employees to feel comfortable as members of the organization, they must be able to believe that they have some power to influence their own situation, to enforce their side of the contract, to ensure that if the organization does not meet their expectations in some crucial area that they have, at least, the power to be listened to, and, at most, the power to leave without severe penalty.

The actual mode of influence—whether as a free agent introducing innovations or as a member of a union—is not as important as the fundamental belief on the part of employees that they have some power to influence the situation if their side of the psychological contract is not met. The pattern of authority and influence that develops in a given society or organization will depend upon the actual basis on which the consent of the members rests. Let us turn now to an analysis of several different bases of consent.

By way of conclusion, I would like to underline the importance of the *psychological contract* as a major variable of analysis. It is my central hypothesis that whether people work effectively, whether they generate commitment, loyalty, and enthusiasm for the organization and its goals, and whether they obtain satisfaction from their work depends to a large measure on two conditions:

1. The degree to which their own *expectations* of what the organization will provide to them and what they owe the organization in return matches what the organization's expectations are of what it will give and get in return.
2. The nature of *what is actually to be exchanged* (assuming there is some agreement)—money in exchange for time at work; social need satisfaction and security in exchange for hard work and loyalty; opportunities for self-actualization and challenging work in exchange for high productivity, high quality work, and creative effort in the service of organizational goals; or various combinations of these and other things.

Ultimately the relationship between the individual and the organization is interactive, unfolding through mutual influence and mutual bargaining to establish and reestablish a workable psychological contract. We cannot understand the psychological dynamics if we look only to the individual's motivations or only to organizational conditions and practices. The two

interact in a complex fashion that demands a systems approach capable of handling interdependent phenomena.

Furthermore, our concepts must reflect the fact that the psychological contract is constantly renegotiated throughout the organizational career. Both the individual's and the organization's needs change over time, requiring repeated episodes of *organizational socialization* as organizational norms change (Schein, 1968, 1971). Some of these norms can be thought of as *pivotal,* in the sense that adherence to them is a requirement of continued membership in the organization. For example, American managers are socialized to believe in the validity of the free enterprise system; professors must accept the canons of research and scholarship; engineers must believe in product safety. Other organizational norms are *peripheral,* in the sense that it is desirable but not essential for members to adhere to them. For example, it may be desirable from the point of view of the organization that managers be men, have certain political views, wear the right kind of clothes, buy only company brands, and so on. For professors, it may be desirable that they like to teach, be willing to help in the administration of the university, spend most of their time on campus rather than on consulting trips, and so on. Violation of these norms does not cause loss of membership, however, if the pivotal norms continue to be adhered to.

The adjustment of the individual to the organization can then be conceived of in terms of acceptance or rejection of pivotal and/or peripheral norms, as shown in Table 1. Acceptance of both pivotal and peripheral norms can be thought of as "conformity," the tendency to try to fit in completely and to take a custodial orientation toward how things have been done in the past—becoming the loyal but uncreative "organization man." Acceptance of peripheral norms combined with rejection of pivotal ones is "subversive rebellion" in that, by rejecting the organization's basic premises but adhering to its peripheral norms, the person is concealing his or her rebellion. In contrast, rejecting both sets of norms is open rebellion or

TABLE 1 INDIVIDUAL ADJUSTMENT TO THE ORGANIZATION		*Accept*	*Reject*
	Pivotal Norms		
Accept		Conformity	Subversive Rebellion
	Peripheral Norms		
Reject		Creative Individualism	Open Revolution

revolutionary behavior, usually leading to voluntary or involuntary loss of membership.

If an organization is concerned about its own capacity to grow and innovate in the face of a complex and changing environment, the ideal individual response might be what I have termed "creative individualism," which is based on accepting pivotal norms but rejecting peripheral ones. The creative individualist is strongly concerned both about basic organizational goals and about retaining his or her sense of identity, and is willing to exercise creativity to help the organization achieve its basic goals.

Creativity on behalf of the organization can be thought of in two ways. One can focus one's energies on creating new products or services, the kind of creativity traditionally identified in most organizations as research and development. Or creativity can be conceived of as "role innovation," the development of new ways of doing a job or fulfilling a role to make the organization more effective, efficient, or adaptable (Schein, 1970b; Van Maanen & Schein, 1979). A manager can invent a new product (content innovation) or can focus his or her creative energies on new ways of integrating the efforts of two departments, new ways of establishing effective financial controls, new ways of supervising people to maximize their productivity, and so on (role innovation). A professor can derive a new scientific law or publish a new theory (content innovation), or can invent new ways of teaching more effectively, making better use of others' skills, or involving them in social causes (role innovation).

One might hypothesize that people's needs to be conformist, rebellious, or innovative are tied in complex ways to their underlying motive system, and also that such needs change over the course of their career. For example, at the beginning of their career, as apprentices, people are probably most conformist. Upon obtaining organizational "tenure" and reasonable security, they embark on a period of maximum creativity, sometimes involving rebellion. Later stages of the career probably produce more of a tendency to become either role innovative or conformist depending upon the degree to which the individual remains work involved. How the organization manages people's transitions from one organizational segment to another across functional, hierarchical, or inclusionary boundaries probably strongly affects whether the person will become more custodial and conformist or more innovative (Van Maanen & Schein, 1979).

For individuals, for organization managers, and for members of social institutions who are concerned about social policy, the most important conclusion to be drawn from this entire discussion is that human motivation and career development are highly complex and not yet fully understood. Therefore, a continued spirit of inquiry and a commitment to diagnosing situations before leaping into action appears to be the only safe course. It is not clear whether the "best" kind of psychological contract is one that maximizes creative individualism, for it is easy to imagine conditions under which both the individual and the organization would be happier with a conformist response. However, one must diagnose the potential consequences of whatever course one embarks on, using whatever analytical tools are available. And one must be aware that personal assumptions and biases can operate as powerful filters to make the world look simpler than it actually is.

REFERENCES

Argyris, C. (1960). *Understanding organizational behavior*. Homewood, IL: Dorsey.

Dalton, G. W., Thompson. P. H., & Price, R. (1977). Career stages: A model of professional careers in organizations. *Organizational Dynamics, 6,* 19–42.

Hall, D. T. (1976). *Careers in organizations*. Pacific Palisades, CA: Goodyear.

Homans, G. (1961). *Social behavior: Its elementary forms*. New York: Harcourt, Brace.

Kahn, R. L., Wolfe, D. M., Quinn, R. P., Snoek, J. D., & Rosenthal, R. A. (1964). *Organizational stress: Studies in role conflict and ambiguity*. New York: Wiley.

Kotter, J. P. (1973). The psychological contract. *California Management Review, 15,* 91–99.

Levinson H. (1962). *Men, management, and mental health*. Cambridge, MA: Harvard University Press.

March, J. G., & Simon, H. A. (1958). *Organizations*. New York: Wiley.

Schein, E. H. (1964, November–December). How to break in the college graduate. *Harvard Business Review*, pp. 68–76.

Schein, E. H. (1968). Organizational socialization and the profession of management. *Industrial Management Review, 9,* 1–15.

Schein, E. H. (1970a). The reluctant professor: Implications for university management. *Sloan Management Review, 12* (1), 35–49.

Schein, E. H. (1970b). The role innovator and his education. *Technology Review, 72,* 33–37.

Schein, E. H. (1971). The individual, the organization, and the career: A conceptual scheme. *Journal of Applied Behavioral Science, 7,* 401–426.

Schein, E. H. (1978a). *Career dynamics*. Reading, MA: Addison-Wesley.

Schein, E. H. (1978b, February). The role of the consultant: Content expert or process facilitator? *Personnel and Guidance Journal*, pp. 339–343.

Schein, E. H., & Bennis, W. G. (1965). *Personal and organizational change through group methods*. New York: Wiley.

Schein, E. H., & Ott, J. S. (1962). The legitimacy of organizational influence. *American Journal of Sociology, 67,* 682–689.

Van Maanen, J., & Schein, E. H. (1979). Toward a theory of organizational socialization. In B. Staw (Ed.), *Research in organizational behavior* (vol. I). Greenwich, CT: JAI Press.

NOTE

1. The concept of psychological contract is an extension of all that has been written by social philosophers about social contracts. In the organizational sphere it was first discussed in detail by Argyris (1960) and by Levinson (1962). The same idea is implicit in March and Simon's (1958) "inducement-contribution" model and has been worked out in some detail by Homans (1961) in his social exchange theory of elementary social forms. Kotter (1973) has tested the idea by measuring both the employees' and supervisors' expectations and developed workshops to permit resolutions of possible mismatches in those expectations.

5 CHAPTER | POWER AND INFLUENCE

Power and influence are key aspects of behavior in all organizations. The members must recognize and understand this fact of organizational life if they hope to be effective contributors to the orchestra's success. Acceptance of the conductor's authority, interpersonal influence, coalition building and dynamics within and between the sections, and action (or inaction) all affect the orchestra's ability to perform positively or negatively.

Imagine a situation in which members of the string section deliberately slow their tempo in an attempt to influence the actions of the other musicians. Whatever their purpose may be, and like it or not, the strings are using their political skills and group cohesiveness to enhance their own power—perhaps to the detriment of others. The musicians in the other sections and the conductor must decide whether to resist or to go along with the string section. They must assess the purpose and strategy behind the maneuver and decide on their course of action. An orchestra, like any other type of organization, is not immune from issues of power and influence—nor should it be.

Power is the latent ability to influence others' actions, thoughts, or emotions. It is the potential to get people to do things the way you want them done—a social energy waiting to be used, to be transformed into influence or, as in the words of R. G. H. Siu, to be transformed from *potential power* into *kinetic power*. Power is influence over the beliefs, emotions, and behaviors of people and, according to Siu, "potential power is the capacity to do so, but kinetic power is the act of doing so.... One person exerts power over another to the degree that he is able to exact compliance as desired" (1979, p. 31).

As we have seen throughout this book, almost everything necessary for understanding organizational behavior is related to everything else, and *power* is no exception. The subject of power in organizations is inseparable from the topics and issues that have been the focus of essentially all other chapters in this volume.

As a concept of organizational behavior, *power* is associated with several other organizational subjects that many people find distasteful. First, for most of us, power suggests an ability to use force to overcome resistance (Wageman & Mannix, 1998). This "black side" of power is behind Rosabeth Moss Kanter's (1979) observation: "Power is America's last dirty word. It is easier to talk about money—and much easier to talk about sex—than it is to talk about power. People who have it deny it; people who want it do not want to appear hungry for it; and people who engage in its machinations do so secretly" (reprinted in this chapter). Second, power owes much of its existence to feelings of dependence. Power exists only when there is an unequal relationship between two people and thus one possesses less power than the other—where one of the two is dependent upon the other (Bies & Tripp, 1998; Emerson, 1962) or has been devalued, for example, because of discrimination (Cox, 1993; Hagberg, 2003; Kanter, 1979; Thomas, 1995).

THE ORGANIZATIONAL CONTEXT AND POWER

Power starts with structural issues. Although individual skill determines the effectiveness of the use of power, power is not fundamentally an issue of person or personality. "Power is first and foremost a structural phenomenon, and should be understood as such" (Pfeffer, 1981, p. x). *Specialization* and *division of labor,* two related subjects that were discussed rather extensively in the Introduction to this book, are the fundamental causes of dependence among individuals and organizational units. With division of labor, people in organizations are dependent upon others for all sorts of things they need to accomplish their tasks: they depend on timely completion of prior tasks, accurate information, materials and supplies, competent people, and political support (Wageman & Mannix, 1998).

In this chapter we assert that structure establishes how *roles, expectations,* and *resource allocations* are defined for people and groups in any given organization. Thus, the structural forces caused by specialization and division of labor are extended (by the vital importance of these three functions of structure) to the people and groups in organizations. The functions of structure in the establishment of organizational roles, expectations, and resource allocations make it very clear why power is first and foremost a structural phenomenon, and why effective use of power in organizations is crucial for success. Jeffrey Pfeffer emphasizes this point in his Preface to *Power in Organizations* (1981): "Those persons and those units that have the responsibility for performing the more critical tasks in the organization have a natural advantage in developing and exercising power in the organization" (p. x). Resource allocation decisions have enormous impacts on a person's (or group's) ability to do its job, to "shine" or "excel." Structure affects resource allocations. A primary reason for using power is to affect resource allocations, and resource allocations affect the balance of power in organizations; these variables are inseparable. Power cannot be understood independently of the structural context, and vice versa.

INTERGROUP DYNAMICS AND POWER

Organizations are complex systems that often can be visualized most clearly as grids or spiderwebs of overlapping, interwoven, and competing *coalitions* of individuals, formal groups, and informal groups, each having its own interests, beliefs, values, preferences, perspectives, and perceptions. The coalitions compete with each other continuously for scarce organizational resources. Conflict is inevitable. Influence—and the power and political activities through which influence is acquired and maintained—is the primary "weapon" for use in competition and conflicts. Thus, power, politics, and influence are critically important and permanent facts of organizational life.

Power relations are permanent features of organizations primarily because specialization and the division of labor result in many interdependent organizational units with varying degrees of importance. The units compete with each other—as well as with the transitory coalitions—for scarce resources. As James D. Thompson points out in *Organizations in Action* (1967), lack of balance in the interdependence among units sets the stage for the use of power relations.

LEADERSHIP AND POWER

Leadership involves "an interpersonal process through which one individual influences the attitudes, beliefs, and especially the behavior of one or more other people" (see Chapter 1). The parallels and overlaps among issues of *leadership* and of *power in organizations* are obvious, and this chapter emphasizes the parallels and explains how they overlap.

Historically, power in organizations and authority were viewed as being essentially synonymous. "Classical era" students of organization such as Max Weber (1922) and Henri Fayol (1949 [1916]) simply *assumed* that power and formal rules (promulgated and enforced by those in authority) flow downward in hierarchical organizations through people who occupy offices to successively lower levels. Even today, proponents of the "modern structural perspective of organization theory" (see Shafritz, Ott, & Jang, 2005) tend to see authority as the source of power in organizations (or, at least the primary source). From this perspective, *leader, supervisor,* and *manager* mean the same thing: people who possess power by virtue of the authority inherent in the organizational position they occupy. Power is legitimized by virtue of a person being in such a position. In fact, the aptly descriptive phrases *legitimate power* and *legitimate authority* gained common usage and still are seen and heard occasionally in today's management literature.

In contrast, most organizational behavioralists see power in a very different light. For example, Broom (2002) argues that when power is used positively, it advances organizational ends. Kotter (1985) explains that the gap has increased between the power one needs to get the job done and the power that automatically comes with the job (authority). Hagberg (2003) asserts that for women to be able to use power effectively they must differentiate between the types or levels of power that are available to them. Most organizational behavioralists view authority as only one of many available sources of organizational power, and power is aimed in *all* directions in the hierarchy—not just down. For example, Porter, Allen, and Angle divide their 2003 book of readings on *Organizational Influence Processes* into three major parts: downward influence (authority), lateral influence, and upward influence.

Authority-based power is far from being the only form of power in organizations. In fact, other forms of power and influence often prevail over authority-based power. Several of this chapter's selections identify different sources of power in organizations (particularly the first reading, "The Bases of Social Power," by John R. P. French and Bertram Raven), so only a few are listed here as examples:

- *Control over scarce resources:* for example, office space, discretionary funds, current and accurate information, and time and skill to work on projects.
- *Easy access to others who are perceived as having power:* important customers or clients, members of the board of directors, or someone else with formal authority or who controls scarce resources.
- *A central place in a potent coalition.*
- *Ability to "work the organizational rules":* such as knowing how to get things done or to prevent others from getting things done.
- *Credibility:* for example, that one's word can be trusted.

The more that leadership issues in organizations are separated or differentiated from management issues, the more closely they become aligned with power issues—issues that extend beyond authority issues.

SELECTIONS IN THIS CHAPTER

The readings on power that comprise this chapter span almost 35 years and address a spectrum of issues associated with power and behavior in organizations. The first, "The Bases of Social Power," by John R. P. French and Bertram Raven (1959), starts from the premise that power and influence always involve relations between at least two agents and theorize that the reaction of the *recipient agent* is the more useful focus for explaining the phenomena of social influence and power. The core of French and Raven's piece, however, is their identification of five bases or sources of social power: reward power, the perception of coercive power, legitimate power (organizational authority), referent power (through association with others who possess power), and expert power (power of knowledge or ability).

French and Raven examine the effects of power derived from the five bases on *attraction* (the recipient's sentiment toward the agent who uses power) and *resistance* to the use of power. Their investigations show that the use of power from the different bases has different consequences. For example, coercive power typically decreases attraction and causes high resistance, whereas reward power increases attraction and creates minimal levels of resistance. In what amounts to one of the earliest looks at ethical limits on the use of power, they conclude that "the more legitimate the coercion (is perceived to be) the less it will produce resistance and decreased attraction."

David Mechanic's influential 1962 *Administrative Science Quarterly* article, "Sources of Power of Lower Participants in Complex Organizations" (reprinted here), examines sources of influence and power that can be aimed at targets who possess more formal authority than that possessed by the potential "influencer." As John Kotter (1977) explains, power requires feelings of dependence, and lower-level organization members have an array of tools with which to make others dependent on them. These tools include expertise, effort and interest, attractiveness (or charisma), location and position in the organization, membership in intraorganizational and interorganizational coalitions, and knowledge of rules. All of this is a more formal way of saying something that we all know—some people are treated like prima donnas or "get away with murder" in organizations because they have some special skills that give them power in the context of their organizations. "Hawkeye" and "Trapper," from the *MASH* movie and television series, are ready examples. If they had not been badly needed surgeons at the battlefront, they would have been court-martialed years before.

Amitai Etzioni's *A Comparative Analysis of Complex Organizations: On Power, Involvement, and Their Correlates* (1975 [1965]) is truly a landmark book—an enduring classic in the literature of organization theory. Etzioni's subchapter, "Three Kinds of Power: A Comparative Dimension," contains important implications for organizational behavior from a power perspective. "Power is an actor's ability to induce or influence another actor to carry out his directives or any other norms he supports." The "power means" an actor uses to induce or influence another to carry out directives fall into three categories: *coercive power,* the application or threat of application of physical sanctions; *remunerative power,* the allocation of material resources and rewards; and *normative power* (alternatively referred to as *persuasive power* or *manipulative power*), which rests on the use of symbolic manipulations, rewards, and deprivations. All three types of power are used in most organizations, "but the degree to which they rely on each [type of power] differs from organization to organization." Most organizations tend to specialize in the application of only one type of power, because when two types are used at the same time, they often neutralize each other.

Gerald Salancik and Jeffrey Pfeffer's 1977 analysis, "Who Gets Power—And How They Hold on to It: A Strategic-Contingency Model of Power" reflects the tremendous advances between the 1950s and the 1970s made by the field of organizational behavior in accepting power as a legitimate subject for serious investigation. Salancik and Pfeffer view power as one of the few mechanisms available for aligning an organization with the realities of its environment. Their assertion rests on the premise that power is derived from being essential to an organization's functional needs. According to Salancik and Pfeffer's notion (which they label *strategic-contingency theory*), power accrues to individuals and subunits that handle an organization's most critical problems. Effective use of power allows the subunits that are engaged in critical activities to "place allies in key positions," "control scarce critical resources," and thereby enhance the probability of their survival and expansion. Subunits engaged in critical functions prosper, those engaged in noncritical functions wither, and the organization realigns itself. Because the most critical contingencies organizations face involve the environmental context, this power-allocating process explains how organizations constantly readjust themselves with the needs of their external worlds.

Salancik and Pfeffer believe power is shared in organizations "out of necessity more than out of concern for principles of organizational development or participatory democracy." It is shared out of structural–functional need. To repeat an earlier quotation: "Power is first and foremost a structural phenomenon, and should be understood as such."

Strategic-contingency theory has far-reaching consequences. If the use of power by subunits helps organizations align themselves with their critical needs, then suppression of the use of power—for example, to reduce unwanted *politics* and *conflicts*—reduces organizational adaptability. Thus, in the current literature of organizational behavior, one seldom sees the phrase "conflict resolution." It has been almost totally replaced with the concept of "conflict management"—using conflict (and power struggles) constructively for the organization's benefit.

"Who Gets Power—And How They Hold on to It" contains a second very important contribution to the understanding of power in organizations. Salancik and Pfeffer identify three contextual conditions under which the use of power by members of subunits can be expected to determine how important decisions are decided. (For Salancik and Pfeffer, "important decisions" usually are resource-allocation decisions.) These contextual decisions are identified as follows:

- The degree of resource scarcity
- The criticalness of the resources to the core activities of subunits
- The level of uncertainty existing about what an organization should do and how it should be done

When these conditions are linked with Salancik and Pfeffer's identification of subunits that are most likely to get and hold on to power, it is possible to predict an organization's decision processes (under certain circumstances) by using a power perspective of organizational behavior. When clear-cut criteria do not exist, the use of power to control resource-allocation decisions is likely to be most effective.

In her 1979 *Harvard Business Review* article, "Power Failure in Management Circuits," which is reprinted here, Rosabeth Moss Kanter explains that executive and managerial power is a necessary ingredient for moving organizations toward their goals. "Power can mean efficacy and capacity" for organizations. The ability of managers to lead effectively cannot be predicted by studying their styles or traits. It requires, instead, knowledge of a leader's real power sources. Kanter carefully distinguishes between *power* and *dominance, control,* and *oppression.* Her primary concern is at higher organizational levels, at which the power exists to "punish, to prevent, to sell off, to reduce, to fire, all without appropriate concern for consequences," but the power needed for positive accomplishments does not.

Managers who views themselves as being powerless and who think their subordinates are discounting them tend to use more dominating or punishing forms of influence. Therefore in large organizations, powerlessness—or perceived powerlessness—can be a more substantive problem than the possession of power. By empowering others, however, leaders and managers can acquire more "productive power"—the power needed to accomplish organizational goals. "Power Failure in Management Circuits" contains an embedded sub-article on the particular problems that power poses for women managers.

"Two Faces of the Powerless: Coping with Tyranny in Organizations," by Robert J. Bies and Thomas M. Tripp, which is reprinted in this chapter, reports on a study of tyranny in the workplace. The authors emphasize tyranny as manifested in the "abusive boss"—the boss "whose primary objective is control of others, and such control is achieved through methods that create fear and intimidation." Their study identified specific behaviors that comprise tyranny: "acts as a 'micromanager,' provides inexplicit direction with decisive delivery, exhibits 'mercurial' mood swings, demonstrates an obsession with loyalty and obedience, derogates the status of employees, is capricious, exercises raw power for personal gain, obsesses on gathering personal information about employees, and at times uses coercion to corrupt employees." When employees were subjected to tyrannical behavior, their typical patterns of response included: "thoughts and feelings of betrayal, distrust, resentment, frustration, and mental exhaustion." Some also reported strong physiological reactions. "Control was achieved through creating fear and intimidation and creating confusion and disorientation. Several respondents reported feeling "paranoid," and a few "terror-stricken" and "paralyzed."

Bies and Tripp propose a typology of ranges of responses to tyranny. Individuals use a variety of coping strategies to protect themselves, often forms of *disguise.* "Respondents reported that through their acts of disguise they led the tyrant bosses to believe that they have a more supportive and submissive group of employees than was actually true.... Duplicity was central to managing conflict."

Janet O. Hagberg examines an array of gender-related power issues in "Women and Power," a chapter from her 2003 book, *Real Power: The Stages of Personal Power in Organizations.* "Power is a women's issue, whether we like it or not." Because relations between women and organizations are in a period of transition, it is necessary to understand the six stages of personal power and how each influences leadership. Masculinity and femininity each have positive and negative aspects, and thus, men and women should develop the ability to use both masculine and feminine behavior.

Hagberg assess the sources, uses, approaches to, and limits on the use of power that are available to women who are at different stages in her "power model": Stage One—powerlessness; Stage Two—power by association; Stage Three—power by achievement; Stage Four—power by reflection; Stage Five—power by purpose; and Stage Six—power by wisdom. Hagberg concludes: "The future of leadership in America is being formed through the values and behaviors that are being learned right now; if women are the hope for a different kind of leadership, they must begin to develop further now."

CONCLUSION

Power and influence are integral aspects of organizational behavior. Their contributions to understanding the behavior of people in organizations can be understood only in relation to leadership, group and intergroup dynamics, the organizational context, and motivational structures. In 1959, Dorwin Cartwright wrote about power as a neglected variable in social psychology. In 1979, Rosabeth Moss Kanter identified power as "America's last dirty word," a word and a concept that people in organizations (and elsewhere) try to avoid. In 2003, Hagberg was urging women to become more adept at using power.

Power cannot and should not be avoided by anyone who seeks to understand the theory or practice of organizational behavior. The importance of power will become even more evident in Chapter 6, *Organizational Change.*

REFERENCES

Alvesson, M. (1996). *Communication, power and organization.* Berlin: Walter de Gruyter.

Bies, R. J., & Tripp, T. M. (1998). Two faces of the powerless: Coping with tyranny in organizations. In R. M. Kramer & M. A. Neale (Eds.), *Power and influence in organizations* (pp. 203–219). Thousand Oaks, CA: Sage.

Broom, M. F. (2002). *The infinite organization: Celebrating the positive use of power in organizations.* Palo Alto, CA: Davies-Black.

Cartwright, D. (1959). Power: A neglected variable in social psychology. In D. Cartwright (Ed.), *Studies in social power* (pp. 1–14). Ann Arbor: University of Michigan Institute for Social Research.

Cox, T. H., Jr. (1993). *Cultural diversity in organizations: Theory, research & practice.* San Francisco: Berrett-Koehler.

Emerson, R. M. (1962). Power-dependence relations. *American Sociological Review, 27,* 31–40.

Etzioni, A. (1975). *A comparative analysis of complex organizations: On power, involvement, and their correlates* (Rev. and enlarged ed.). New York: Free Press.

Fayol, H. (1949). *General and industrial management* (C. Storrs, Trans.). London: Pitman Publishing. (Original work published 1916.)

French, J. R. P., & Raven, B. (1959). The bases of social power. In D. Cartwright & A. Zander (Eds.), *Studies in social power* (pp. 150–167). Ann Arbor: University of Michigan Institute for Social Research.

Hagberg, J. O. (2003). Women and power. In J. O. Hagberg, *Real power: The stages of personal power in organizations* (3rd ed., pp. 237–254). Salem, WI: Sheffield.

Haire, M. (1962). The concept of power and the concept of man. In G. B. Strother (Ed.), *Social science approaches to business behavior* (pp. 163–183). Homewood, IL: Richard D. Irwin.

Hobbes, T. (1651). *Leviathan*. Reprinted in 1904, Cambridge, UK: University Press.

Kanter, R. M. (1979, July/August). Power failure in management circuits. *Harvard Business Review, 57,* 65–75.

Kanter, R. M. (1983). *The change masters*. New York: Simon & Schuster.

Kipnis, D. (1976). *The powerholders*. Chicago: University of Chicago Press.

Korda, M. (1975). *Power*. New York: Ballantine Books.

Kotter, J. P. (1977, July/August). Power, dependence, and effective management. *Organizational Dynamics,* 125–136.

Kotter, J. P. (1985). *Power and influence*. New York: Free Press.

Kramer, R. M., & Neale, M. A. (Eds.). (1998). *Power and influence in organizations*. Thousand Oaks, CA: Sage.

March, J. G. (1962). The business firm as a political coalition. *Journal of Politics, 24,* 662–678.

Mayes, B. T., & Allen, R. W. (1977). Toward a definition of organizational politics. *Academy of Management Review, 2,* 672–678.

McClelland, D., & Burnham, D. (1976, March/April). Power is the great motivator. *Harvard Business Review,* 100–110.

Mechanic, D. (1962, December). Sources of power of lower participants in complex organizations. *Administrative Science Quarterly, 7*(3), 349–364.

Mintzberg, H. (1983). *Power in and around organizations*. Englewood Cliffs, NJ: Prentice-Hall.

Mumby, D. K. (1988). *Communication and power in organizations: Discourse, ideology and domination*. Norwood, NJ: Ablex.

Nicolson, P. (1996). *Gender, power and organisation: A psychological perspective*. London: Routledge.

Nietzsche, F. (1912). *Der Wille zur Macht*. Book 3, sec. 702. In F. Nietzsche, *Werke* (vol. 16). Leipzig: Alfred Kroner.

Perrow, C. (1970). Departmental power and perspectives in industrial firms. In M. N. Zald (Ed.), *Power in organizations* (pp. 59–89). Nashville, TN: Vanderbilt University Press.

Pfeffer, J. (1981). *Power in organizations*. Marshfield, MA: Pitman Publishing.

Pfeffer, J. (1992). *Managing with power: Politics and influence in organizations*. Boston: Harvard Business School Press.

Porter, L. W., Allen, R. W., & Angle, H. L. (1981). The politics of upward influence in organizations. In L. L. Cummings & B. M. Staw (Eds.), *Research in organizational behavior* (vol. 3, pp. 408–422). Greenwich, CT: JAI Press.

Porter, L. W., Angle, H. L., & Allen, R. W. (Eds.). (2003). *Organizational influence processes* (2nd ed.). Armonk, NY: M. E. Sharpe.

Salancik, G. R., & Pfeffer, J. (1977). Who gets power—and how they hold on to it: A strategic-contingency model of power. *Organizational Dynamics, 5,* 2–21.

Shafritz, J. M., Ott, J. S., & Jang, Y. S. (2005). *Classics of organization theory* (6th ed.). Belmont, CA: Thomson-Wadsworth.

Siu, R. G. H. (1979). *The craft of power*. New York: John Wiley.

Thomas, R. (1995). A diversity framework. In M. M. Chemers, S. Oskamp, & M. A. Costanzo (Eds.), *Diversity in organizations: New perspectives for a changing workplace* (pp. 245–263). Thousand Oaks, CA: Sage.

Thompson, J. D. (1967). *Organizations in action.* New York: McGraw-Hill.

Tushman, M. L. (1977, April). A political approach to organizations: A review and rationale. *Academy of Management Review, 2,* 206–216.

Wageman, R., & Mannix, E. A. (1998). Uses and misuses of power in task-performing teams. In R. M. Kramer & M. A. Neale (Eds.), *Power and influence in organizations* (pp. 261–285). Thousand Oaks, CA: Sage.

Weber, M. (1922). Bureaucracy. In H. Gerth & C. W. Mills (Eds.), *Max Weber: Essays in sociology.* Oxford, UK: Oxford University Press.

Yates, D., Jr. (1985). *The politics of management.* San Francisco: Jossey-Bass.

Zald, M. N. (Ed.). (1970). *Power in organizations.* Nashville: Vanderbilt University Press.

Reading 30	# The Bases of Social Power
	### John R. P. French, Jr., and Bertram Raven

The processes of power are pervasive, complex, and often disguised in our society. Accordingly one finds in political science, in sociology, and in social psychology a variety of distinctions among different types of social power or among qualitatively different processes of social influence (Asch, 1952; Festinger, 1953; Goldhammer & Shils, 1939; Jahoda, 1956; Kelman, 1956; Linton, 1945; Lippitt, Polansky, Redl, & Rosen, 1952; Russell, 1938; Torrance & Mason, 1956). Our main purpose is to identify the major types of power and to define them systematically so that we may compare them according to the changes which they produce and the other effects which accompany the use of power. The phenomena of power and influence involve a dyadic relation between two agents which may be viewed from two points of view: (a) What determines the behavior of the agent who exerts power? (b) What determines the reactions of the recipient of this behavior? We take this second point of view and formulate our theory in terms of the life space of P, the person upon whom the power is exerted. In this way we hope to define basic concepts of power which will be adequate to explain many of the phenomena of social influence, including some which have been described in other less genotypic terms....

Power, Influence, and Change

Psychological Change

Since we shall define power in terms of influence, and influence in terms of psychological change, we begin with a discussion of change. We want to define change at a level of generality which includes changes in behavior, opinions, attitudes, goals, needs, values, and all other aspects of the person's psychological field. We shall use the word "system" to refer to any such part of the life space.[1] Following Lewin (1951) the state of a system at time 1 will be noted $s_1(a)$.

Psychological change is defined as any alteration of the state of some system a over time. The amount of change is measured by the size of the difference between the states of the system a at time 1 and at time 2: $ch(a) = s_2(a) - s_1(a)$.

Change in any psychological system may be conceptualized in terms of psychological forces. But it is important to note that the change must be coordinated to the resultant force of all the forces operating at the moment. Change in an opinion, for example, may be determined jointly by a driving force induced by another person, a restraining force corresponding to anchorage in a group opinion, and an own force stemming from the person's needs.

Social Influence

Our theory of social influence and power is limited to influence on the person, P, produced by a social agent, O, where O can be either another person, a role, a norm, a group, or a part of a group. We do not consider social influence exerted on a group.

The influence of O on system a in the life space of P is defined as the resultant force on system a which has its source in an act of O. This resultant force induced by O consists of two components: a force to change the system in the direction induced by O and an opposing resistance set up by the same act of O.

By this definition the influence of O does not include P's own forces nor the forces induced by other social agents. Accordingly the "influence" of O must be clearly distinguished from O's "control" of P. O may be able to induce strong forces on P to carry out an activity (i.e., O exerts strong influence on P); but if the opposing forces induced by another person or by P's own

Source: "The Bases of Social Power," by French & Raven, 1959. Used by permission of the Institute for Social Research.

needs are stronger, then P will locomote in an opposite direction (i.e., O does not have control over P). Thus psychological change in P can be taken as an operational definition of the social influence of O on P only when the effects of other forces have been eliminated. . . .

Commonly social influence takes place through an intentional act on the part of O. However, we do not want to limit our definition of "act" to such conscious behavior. Indeed, influence might result from the passive presence of O, with no evidence of speech, or overt movement. A policeman's standing on a corner may be considered an act of an agent for the speeding motorist. Such acts of the inducing agent will vary in strength, for O may not always utilize all of his power. The policeman, for example, may merely stand and watch or act more strongly by blowing his whistle at the motorist.

The influence exerted by an act need not be in the direction intended by O. The direction of the resultant force on P will depend on the relative magnitude of the induced force set up by the act of O and the resisting force in the opposite direction which is generated by that same act. In cases where O intends to influence P in a given direction, a resultant force in the same direction may be termed positive influence whereas a resultant force in the opposite direction may be termed negative influence. . . .

Social Power

The strength of power of O/P in some system *a* is defined as the maximum potential ability of O to influence P in *a*.

By this definition influence is kinetic power, just as power is potential influence. It is assumed that O is capable of various acts which, because of some more or less enduring relation to P, are able to exert influence on P.[2] O's power is measured by his maximum possible influence, though he may often choose to exert less than his full power.

An equivalent definition of power may be stated in terms of the resultant of two forces set up by the act of O: one in the direction of O's influence attempt and another resisting force in the opposite direction. Power is the maximum resultant of these two forces:

$$\text{Power of O/P(a)} = (f_{a,x} - f_{a,x})^{\max}$$

where the source of both forces is an act of O.

Thus the power of O with respect to system *a* of P is equal to the maximum resultant force of two forces set up by any possible act of O: (a) the force which O can set up on the system *a* to change in the direction x, (b) the resisting force,[3] in the opposite direction. Whenever the first component force is greater than the second, positive power exists; but if the second component force is greater than the first, then O has negative power over P. . . .

For certain purposes it is convenient to define the range of power as the set of all systems within which O has power of strength greater than zero. A husband may have a broad range of power over his wife, but a narrow range of power over his employer. We shall use the term "magnitude of power" to denote the summation of O's power over P in all systems of his range.

The Dependence of s(a) on O

We assume that any change in the state of a system is produced by a change in some factor upon which it is functionally dependent. The state of an opinion, for example, may change because of a change either in some internal factor such as a need or in some external factor such as the arguments of O. Likewise, the maintenance of the same state of a system is produced by the stability or lack of change in the internal and external factors. In general, then, psychological change and stability can be conceptualized in terms of dynamic dependence. Our interest is focused on the special case of dependence on an external agent, O (March, 1955).

In many cases the initial state of the system has the character of a quasistationary equilibrium with a central force field around $s_1(a)$ (Lewin, 1951). In such cases we may derive a tendency toward retrogression to the original state as soon as the force induced by O is removed.[4]

Consider the example of three separated employees who have been working at the same steady level of production despite normal, small fluctuations in the work environment. The supervisor orders each to increase his production, and the level of each goes up from 100 to 115 pieces per day. After a week of producing at the new rate of 115 pieces per day, the supervisor is removed for a week. The production of employee A immediately returns to 100 but B and C return to only 110 pieces per day. Other things being equal, we can infer that A's new rate was completely dependent on his supervisor whereas the new rate of B and C was dependent on the supervisor only to the extent of 5 pieces. Let us further assume that when the supervisor returned, the production of B and of C returned to 115 without further orders from the supervisor. Now another month goes by during which B and C maintain a steady 115 pieces per day. However, there is a difference between them: B's level of production still depends on O to the extent of 5 pieces whereas C has come to rely on his own sense of obligation to obey the order of his legitimate supervisor rather than on the supervisor's external pressure for the maintenance of his 115 pieces per day. Accordingly, the next time the supervisor departs, B's production again drops to 110 but C's remains at 115 pieces per day. In cases like employee B, the degree of dependence is contingent on the perceived probability that O will observe the state of the system and note P's conformity (Dittes & Kelley, 1956; Festinger, 1953; French, Morrison, & Levinger, 1960; French & Raven, in preparation; Kelman 1956). The level of observability will in turn depend on both the nature of the system (e.g., the difference between a covert opinion and overt behavior) and on the environmental barriers to observation (e.g., O is too far away from P). . . .

The Bases of Power

By the basis of power we mean the relationship between O and P which is the source of that power. It is rare that we can say with certainty that a given empirical case of power is limited to one source. Normally, the relation between O and P will be characterized by several qualitatively different variables which are bases of power (Lippitt et al., 1952). Although there are undoubtedly many possible bases of power which may be distinguished, we shall here define five which seem especially common and important. These five bases of O's power are: (1) reward power, based on P's perception that O has the ability to mediate rewards for him; (2) coercive power, based on P's perception that O has the ability to mediate punishments for him; (3) legitimate power, based on the perception by P that O has a legitimate right to prescribe behavior for him; (4) referent power, based on P's identification with O; (5) expert power, based on the perception that O has some special knowledge or expertness. . . .

Reward Power

Reward power is defined as power whose basis is the ability to reward. The strength of the reward power of O/P increases with the magnitude of the rewards which P perceives that O can mediate for him. Reward power depends on O's ability to administer positive valences and to remove or decrease negative valences. The strength of reward power also depends upon the probability that O can mediate the reward, as perceived by P. A common example of reward power is the addition of a piecework rate in the factory as an incentive to increase production.

The new state of the system induced by a promise of reward (for example, the factory worker's increased level of production) will be highly dependent on O. Since O mediates the reward, he controls the probability that P will receive it. Thus P's new rate of production will be dependent on his subjective probability that O will reward him for conformity minus his subjective probability that O will reward him even if he returns to his old level. Both probabilities will be greatly affected by the level of observability of P's behavior. . . .

The utilization of actual rewards (instead of promises) by O will tend over time to increase the attraction of P toward O and therefore the referent power of O over P. As we shall note later, such referent power will permit O to induce changes which are relatively independent. Neither rewards nor promises will arouse resistance in P, provided P considers it legitimate for O to offer rewards.

The range of reward power is specific to those regions within which O can reward P for conforming. The use of rewards to change systems within the range of reward power tends to increase reward power by increasing the probability attached to future promises. However, unsuccessful attempts to exert reward power outside the range of power would tend to decrease the power; for example if O offers to reward P for performing an impossible act, this will reduce for P the probability of receiving future rewards promised by O.

Coercive Power

Coercive power is similar to reward power in that it also involves O's ability to manipulate the attainment of valences. Coercive power of O/P stems from the expectation on the part of P that he will be punished by O if he fails to conform to the influence attempt. Thus negative valences will exist in given regions of P's life space, corresponding to the threatened punishment by O. The strength of coercive power depends on the magnitude of the negative valence of the threatened punishment multiplied by the perceived probability that P can avoid the punishment by conformity, i.e., the probability of punishment for nonconformity minus the probability of punishment for conformity (French et al., in preparation). Just as an offer of a piece-rate bonus in a factory can serve as a basis for reward power, so the ability to fire a worker if he falls below a given level of production will result in coercive power.

Coercive power leads to dependent change also; and the degree of dependence varies with the level of observability of P's conformity. An excellent illustration of coercive power leading to dependent change is provided by a clothes presser in a factory observed by Coch and French (1948). As her efficiency rating climbed above average for the group, the other workers began to "scapegoat" her. That the resulting plateau in her production was not independent of the group was evident once she was removed from the presence of the other workers. Her production immediately climbed to new heights.[5] . . .

The distinction between these two types of power is important because the dynamics are different. The concept of "sanctions" sometimes lumps the two together despite their opposite effects. While reward power may eventually result in an independent system, the effects of coercive power will continue to be dependent. Reward power will tend to increase the attraction of P toward O; coercive power will decrease this attraction (French & Raven, in preparation; French et al., in preparation). The valence of the region of behavior will become more negative, acquiring some negative valence from the threatened punishment. The negative valence of punishment would also spread to other regions of the life space. Lewin (1935) has pointed out this distinction between the effects of rewards and punishment. In the case of threatened punishment, there will be a resultant force on P to leave the field entirely. Thus, to achieve conformity, O must not only place a strong negative valence in certain regions through threat of punishment, but O must also introduce restraining forces, or other strong valences, so as to prevent P from withdrawing completely from O's range of coercive power. Otherwise, the probability of receiving the punishment, if P does not conform, will be too low to be effective.

Legitimate Power

There has been considerable investigation and speculation about socially prescribed behavior, particularly that which is specific to a given role or position. Linton (1945) distinguishes group norms according to whether they are universals for everyone in the culture, alternatives (the individual having a choice as to whether or not to accept them), or specialties (specific to given positions). Whether we speak of internalized norms, role prescriptions and expectations (Newcomb, 1950), or internalized pressures (Herbst, 1953), the fact remains that each individual sees certain regions toward which he should locomote, some regions toward which he should not locomote, and some regions toward which he may locomote if they are generally attractive for him. This applies to specific behaviors in which he may, should, or should not engage; it applies to certain attitudes or beliefs which he may, should, or should not hold. The feeling of "oughtness" may be an internalization from his parents, from his teachers, from his religion, or may have been logically developed from some idiosyncratic system of ethics. He will speak of such behaviors with expressions like "should," "ought to," or "has a right to." In many cases, the original source of the requirement is not recalled.

Though we have oversimplified such evaluations of behavior with a positive-neutral-negative trichotomy, the evaluation of behaviors by the person is really more one of degree. This dimension of evaluation, we shall call "legitimacy." Conceptually, we may think of legitimacy as a valence in a region which is induced by some internalized norm or value. This value has the same conceptual property as power, namely an ability to induce force fields (Lewin, 1951). . . .

Legitimate power of O/P is here defined as that power which stems from internalized values in P which dictate that O has a legitimate right to influence P and that P has an obligation to accept this influence. We note that legitimate power is very similar to the notion of legitimacy of authority which has long been explored by sociologists, particularly by Weber (1947), and more recently by Goldhammer and Shils (1939). However, legitimate power is not always a role relation: P may accept an induction from O simply because he had previously promised to help O and he values his word too much to break the promise. In all cases, the notion of legitimacy involves some sort of code or standard, accepted by the individual, by virtue of which the external agent can assert his power. We shall attempt to describe a few of these values here.

Bases for Legitimate Power. Cultural values constitute one common basis for the legitimate power of one individual over another. O has characteristics which are specified by the culture as giving him the right to prescribe behavior for P, who may not have these characteristics. These bases, which Weber (1947) has called the authority of the "eternal yesterday," include such things as age, intelligence, caste, and physical characteristics. In some cultures, the aged are granted the right to prescribe behavior for others in practically all behavior areas. In most cultures, there are certain areas of behavior in which a person of one sex is granted the right to prescribe behavior for the other sex.

Acceptance of the social structure is another basis for legitimate power. If P accepts as right the social structure of his group, organization, or society, especially the social structure involving a hierarchy of authority, P will accept the legitimate authority of O, who occupies a superior office in the hierarchy. Thus legitimate power in a formal organization is largely a relationship between offices rather than between persons. And the acceptance of an office as *right* is a basis for legitimate power—a judge has a right to levy fines, a foreman should assign work, a priest is justified in prescribing religious beliefs, and it is the management's prerogative to make certain decisions (French, Israel, & Ås, 1957). However, legitimate power also involves the perceived right of the person to hold the office.

Designation by a legitimizing agent is a third basis for legitimate power. An influencer O may be seen as legitimate in prescribing behavior for P because he has been granted such power by a legitimizing agent whom P accepts. Thus a department head may accept the authority of his vice-president in a certain area because that authority has been specifically delegated by the president. An election is perhaps the most common example of a group's serving to legitimize the authority of one individual or office for other individuals in the group. The success of such legitimizing depends upon the acceptance of the legitimizing agent and procedure. In this case it depends ultimately on certain democratic values concerning election procedures. The election process is one of legitimizing a person's right to an office which already has a legitimate range of power associated with it.

Range of Legitimate Power of O/P. The areas in which legitimate power may be exercised are generally specified along with the designation of that power. A job description, for example, usually specifies supervisory activities and also designates the person to whom the jobholder is responsible for the duties described. Some bases for legitimate authority carry with them a very broad range. Culturally derived bases for legitimate power are often especially broad. It is not uncommon to find cultures in which a member of a given caste can legitimately prescribe behavior for all members of lower castes in practically all regions. More common, however, are instances of legitimate power where the range is specifically and narrowly prescribed. A sergeant in the army is given a specific set of regions within which he can legitimately prescribe behavior for his men.

The attempted use of legitimate power which is outside of the range of legitimate power will decrease the legitimate power of the authority figure. Such use of power which is not legitimate will also decrease the attractiveness of O (French & Raven, in preparation; French et al., in preparation; Raven & French, 1958).

Legitimate Power and Influence. The new state of the system which results from legitimate power usually has high dependence on O though it may become independent. Here, however, the degree of dependence is not related to the level of observability. Since legitimate power is based on P's values, the source of the forces induced by O include both these internal values and O. O's induction serves to activate the values and to relate them to the system which is influenced, but thereafter the new state of the system may become directly dependent on the values with no mediation by O. Accordingly this new state will be relatively stable and consistent across varying environmental situations since P's values are more stable than his psychological environment. . . .

Referent Power

The referent power of O/P has its basis in the identification of P with O. By identification, we mean a feeling of oneness of P with O, or a desire for such an identity. If O is a person toward whom P is highly attracted, P will have a feeling of membership or a desire to join. If P is already closely associated with O he will want to maintain this relationship (Stotland, Zander, Burnstein, Wolfe, & Natsoulas, in preparation; Torrance & Mason, 1956). P's identification with O can be established or maintained if P behaves, believes, and perceives as O does. Accordingly, O has the ability to influence P, even though P may be unaware of this referent power. A verbalization of such power by P might be, "I am like O, and therefore I shall behave or believe as O does," or "I want to be like O, and I will be more like O if I behave or believe as O does." The stronger the identification of P with O the greater the referent power of O/P. . . .

We must try to distinguish between referent power and other types of power which might be operative at the same time. If a member is attracted to a group and he conforms to its norms only because he fears ridicule or expulsion from the group for nonconformity, we would call this coercive power. On the other hand if he conforms in order to obtain praise for conformity, it is a case of reward power. . . . Conformity with majority opinion is sometimes based on a respect for the collective wisdom of the group, in which case it is expert power. It is important to distinguish these phenomena, all grouped together elsewhere as "pressures toward uniformity," since the type of change which occurs will be different for different bases of power.

The concepts of "reference group" (Swanson, Newcomb, & Hartley, 1952) and "prestige suggestion" may be treated as instances of referent power. In this case, O, the prestigeful person or group, is valued by P; because P desires to be associated or identified with O, he will assume attitudes or beliefs held by O. Similarly a negative reference group which O dislikes and evaluates negatively may exert negative influence on P as a result of negative referent power.

It has been demonstrated that the power which we designate as referent power is especially great when P is attracted to O (Back, 1951; Festinger, 1950; Festinger, Gerard, Hymovitch, Kelley, & Raven, 1952; Festinger, Schachter, & Back, 1953; Gerard, 1954; Kelman, 1956; Lippitt et al., 1952). In our terms, this would mean that the greater the attraction, the greater the identification, and consequently the greater the referent power. In some cases, attraction or prestige may have a specific basis, and the range of referent power will be limited accordingly: a group of campers may have great referent power over a member regarding campcraft, but considerably less effect on other regions (Lippitt et al., 1952). However, we hypothesize that the greater the attraction of P toward O, the broader the range of referent power of O/P. . . .

Expert Power

The strength of the expert power of O/P varies with the extent of the knowledge or perception which P attributes to O within a given area. Probably P evaluates O's expertness in relation to his own knowledge as well as against an absolute standard. In any case, expert power results in primary social influence on P's cognitive structure and probably not on other types of systems. Of course, changes in the cognitive structure can change the direction of forces and hence of locomotion, but such a change of behavior is secondary social influence. Expert power has been demonstrated experimentally (Festinger et al., 1952; Moore, 1921). Accepting an attorney's advice in legal matters is a common example of expert influence; but there are many instances based on much less knowledge, such as the acceptance by a stranger of directions given by a native villager.

Expert power, where O need not be a member of P's group, is called "informational power" by Deutsch and Gerard (1955). This type of expert power must be distinguished from influence based on the content of communication as described by Hovland et al. (Hovland, Lumsdaine, & Sheffield, 1949; Hovland & Weiss, 1951; Kelman, 1956; Kelman & Hovland, 1953). The influence of the content of a communication upon an opinion is presumably a secondary influence produced after the *primary* influence (i.e., the acceptance of the information). Since power is here defined in terms of the primary changes, the influence of the content on a related opinion is not a case of expert power as we have defined it, but the initial acceptance of the validity of the content does seem to be based on expert power or referent power. . . .

The range of expert power, we assume, is more delimited than that of referent power. Not only is it restricted to cognitive systems, but the expert is seen as having superior knowledge or ability in very specific areas, and his power will be limited to these areas, though some "halo effect" might occur. Recently, some of our renowned physical scientists have found quite painfully that their expert power in physical sciences does not extend to regions involving international politics. Indeed, there is some evidence that the attempted exertion of expert power outside of the range of expert power will reduce that expert power. An undermining of confidence seems to take place.

SUMMARY

We have distinguished five types of power: referent power, expert power, reward power, coercive power, and legitimate power. These distinctions led to the following hypotheses.

1. For all five types, the stronger the basis of power the greater the power.

2. For any type of power the size of the range may vary greatly, but in general referent power will have the broadest range.

3. Any attempt to utilize power outside the range of power will tend to reduce the power.

4. A new state of a system produced by reward power or coercive power will be highly dependent on O, and the more observable P's conformity the more dependent the state. For the other three types of power, the new state is usually dependent, at least in the beginning, but in any case the level of observability has no effect on the degree of dependence.

5. Coercion results in decreased attraction of P toward O and high resistance; reward power results in increased attraction and low resistance.

6. The more legitimate the coercion the less it will produce resistance and decreased attraction.

REFERENCES

1. Asch, S. E. *Social psychology*. New York: Prentice-Hall, 1952.
2. Back, K. W. Influence through social communication. *J. abnorm. soc. Psychol.*, 1951, 46, 9–23.
3. Coch, L., & French, J. R. P., Jr. Overcoming resistance to change. *Hum. Relat.*, 1948, 1, 512–532.
4. Deutsch, M., & Gerard, H. B. A study of normative and informational influences upon individual judgment. *J. abnorm. soc. Psychol.*, 1955, 51, 629–636.
5. Dittes, J. E., & Kelley, H. H. Effects of different conditions of acceptance upon conformity to group norms. *J. abnorm. soc. Psychol.*, 1956, 53, 100–107.
6. Festinger, L. Informal social communication. *Psychol. Rev.*, 1950, 57, 271–282.
7. Festinger, L. An analysis of compliant behavior. In Sherif, M., & Wilson, M. O., (Eds.), *Group relations at the crossroads*. New York: Harper, 1953, 232–256.
8. Festinger, L., Gerard, H. B., Hymovitch, B., Kelley, H. H., & Raven, B. H. The influence process in the presence of extreme deviates. *Hum. Relat.*, 1952, 5, 327–346.
9. Festinger, L., Schachter, S., & Back, K. The operation of group standards. In Cartwright, D., & Zander, A. *Group dynamics: research and theory*. Evanston: Row, Peterson, 1953, 204–223.
10. French, J. R. P., Jr., Israel, Joachim, & Ås, Dagfinn. "Arbeidernes medvirkning i industribedriften. En eksperimentell undersøkelse." Institute for Social Research, Oslo, Norway, 1957.
11. French, J. R. P., Jr., Levinger, G., & Morrison, H. W. The legitimacy of coercive power. In preparation.
12. French, J. R. P., Jr., & Raven, B. H. An experiment in legitimate and coercive power. In preparation.
13. Gerard, H. B. The anchorage of opinions in face-to-face groups. *Hum. Relat.*, 1954, 7, 313–325.
14. Goldhammer, H., & Shils, E. A. Types of power and status. *Amer. J. Sociol.*, 1939, 45, 171–178.
15. Herbst, P. G. Analysis and measurement of a situation. *Hum. Relat.*, 1953, 2, 113–140.
16. Hochbaum, G. M. Self-confidence and reactions to group pressures. *Amer. soc. Rev.*, 1954, 19, 678–687.
17. Hovland, C. I., Lumsdaine, A. A., & Sheffield, F. D. *Experiments on mass communication*. Princeton: Princeton Univer. Press, 1949.
18. Hovland, C. I., & Weiss, W. The influence of source credibility on communication effectiveness. *Publ. Opin. Quart.*, 1951, 15, 635–650.
19. Jackson, J. M., & Salzstein, H. D. The effect of person-group relationships on conformity processes. *J. abnorm. soc. Psychol.*, 1958, 57, 17–24.

20. Jahoda, M. Psychological issues in civil liberties. *Amer. Psychologist,* 1956, **11**, 234–240.
21. Katz, D., & Schank, R. L. *Social psychology.* New York: Wiley, 1938.
22. Kelley, H. H., & Volkart, E. H. The resistance to change of group-anchored attitudes. *Amer. soc. Rev.,* 1952, **17**, 453–465.
23. Kelman, H. Three processes of acceptance of social influence: compliance, identification and internalization. Paper read at the meetings of the American Psychological Association, August 1956.
24. Kelman, H., & Hovland, C. I. "Reinstatement" of the communicator in delayed measurement of opinion change. *J. abnorm. soc. Psychol.,* 1953, **48**, 327–335.
25. Lasswell, H. D., & Kaplan, A. *Power and society: A framework for political inquiry.* New Haven: Yale Univer. Press, 1950.
26. Lewin, K. *Dynamic theory of personality.* New York: McGraw-Hill, 1935, 114–170.
27. Lewin, K. *Field theory in social science.* New York: Harper, 1951.
28. Lewin, K., Lippitt, R., & White, R. K. Patterns of aggressive behavior in experimentally created social climates. *J. soc. Psychol.,* 1939, **10**, 271–301.
29. Linton, R. *The cultural background of personality.* New York: Appleton-Century-Crofts, 1945.
30. Lippitt, R., Polansky, N., Redl, F., & Rosen, S. The dynamics of power. *Hum. Relat.,* 1952, **5**, 37–64.
31. March, J. G. An introduction to the theory and measurement of influence. *Amer. polit. Sci. Rev.,* 1955, **49**, 431–451.
32. Miller, J. G. Toward a general theory for the behavioral sciences. *Amer. Psychologist,* 1955, **10**, 513–531.
33. Moore, H. T. The comparative influence of majority and expert opinion. *Amer. J. Psychol.* 1921, **32**, 16–20.
34. Newcomb, T. M. *Social psychology.* New York: Dryden, 1950.
35. Raven, B. H. The effect of group pressures on opinion, perception, and communication. Unpublished doctoral dissertation, University of Michigan, 1953.
36. Raven, B. H., & French, J. R. P., Jr. Group support, legitimate power, and social influence. *J. Person.,* 1958, **26**, 400–409.
37. Rommetveit, R. *Social norms and roles.* Minneapolis: Univer. Minnesota Press, 1953.
38. Russell, B. *Power: A new social analysis.* New York: Norton, 1938.
39. Stotland, E., Zander, A., Burnstein, E., Wolfe, D., & Natsoulas, T. Studies on the effects of identification. University of Michigan, Institute for Social Research. Forthcoming.
40. Swanson, G. E., Newcomb, T. M., & Hartley, E. L. *Readings in social psychology.* New York: Henry Holt, 1952.
41. Torrance, E. P., & Mason, R. Instructor effort to influence: an experimental evaluation of six approaches. Paper presented at USAF-NRC Symposium on Personnel, Training, and Human Engineering. Washington, D.C., 1956.
42. Weber, M. *The theory of social and economic organization.* Oxford: Oxford Univer. Press, 1947.

NOTES

1. The word "system" is here used to refer to a whole or to a part of the whole.
2. The concept of power has the conceptual property of *potentiality;* but it seems useful to restrict this potential influence to more or less enduring power relations between O and P by excluding from the definition of power those cases where the potential influence is so momentary or so changing that it cannot be predicted from the existing relationship. Power is a useful concept for describing social structure only if it has a certain stability over time; it is useless if every momentary social stimulus is viewed as actualizing social power.
3. We define resistance to an attempted induction as a force in the opposite direction which is set up by the same act of O. It must be distinguished from opposition, which is defined as existing opposing forces which do not have their source in the same act of O. For example, a boy might resist his mother's order to eat spinach because of the manner of the induction attempt, and at the same time he might oppose it because he [doesn't] like spinach.
4. Miller (33) assumes that all living systems have this character. However, it may be that some systems in the life space do not have this elasticity.
5. Though the primary influence of coercive power is dependent, it often produces secondary changes which are independent. Brainwashing, for example, utilizes coercive power to produce many primary changes in the life space of the prisoner, but these dependent changes can lead to identification with the aggressor and hence to secondary changes in ideology which are independent.

Reading 31 | Sources of Power of Lower Participants in Complex Organizations
David Mechanic

It is not unusual for lower participants[1] in complex organizations to assume and wield considerable power and influence not associated with their formally defined positions within these organizations. In sociological terms they have considerable personal power but no authority. Such personal power is often attained, for example, by executive secretaries and accountants in business firms, by attendants in mental hospitals, and even by inmates in prisons. The personal power achieved by these lower participants does not necessarily result from unique personal characteristics, although these may be relevant, but results rather from particular aspects of their location within their organizations.

Informal versus Formal Power

Clarification of Definitions

The purpose of this paper is to present some hypotheses explaining why lower participants in organizations can often assume and wield considerable power which is not associated with their positions as formally defined within these organizations. For the purposes of this analysis the concepts "influence," "power," and "control" will be used synonymously. Moreover, we shall not be concerned with type of power, that is, whether the power is based on reward, punishment, identification, power to veto, or whatever.[2] Power will be defined as *any force that results in behavior that would not have occurred if the force had not been present.* We have defined power as a force rather than a relationship because it appears that much of what we mean by power is encompassed by the normative framework of an organization, and thus any analysis of power must take into consideration the power of norms as well as persons.

I shall also argue, following Thibaut and Kelley,[3] that power is closely related to dependence. To the extent that a person is dependent on another, he is potentially subject to the other person's power. Within organizations one makes others dependent upon him by controlling access to information, persons, and instrumentalities, which I shall define as follows:

a. *Information* includes knowledge of the organization, knowledge about persons, knowledge of the norms, procedures, techniques, and so forth.

b. *Persons* include anyone within the organization or anyone outside the organization upon whom the organization is in some way dependent.

c. *Instrumentalities* include any aspect of the physical plant of the organization or its resources (equipment, machines, money, and so on).

Power is a function not only of the extent to which a person controls information, persons, and instrumentalities, but also of the importance of the various attributes he controls.[4] . . .

A Classic Example

Like many other aspects of organizational theory, one can find a classic statement of our problem in Weber's discussion of the political bureaucracy. Weber indicated the extent to which bureaucrats may have considerable power over political incumbents, as a result, in part, of their permanence within the political bureaucracy, as contrasted to public officials, who are replaced rather frequently.[5] Weber noted how the low-ranking bureaucrat becomes familiar with the organization—its rules and operations, the work flow, and so on—which gives him considerable power over the new political

Source: David Mechanic, "Sources of Power of Lower Participants in Complex Organizations," in ADMINISTRATIVE SCIENCE QUARTERLY, Vol. 7, No. 4, Dec. 1962. Used by permission of the publisher.

incumbent, who might have higher rank but is not as familiar with the organization. While Weber does not directly state the point, his analysis suggests that bureaucratic permanence has some relationship to increased access to persons, information, and instrumentalities. To state the hypothesis suggested somewhat more formally:

H1 Other factors remaining constant, organizational power is related to access to persons, information, and instrumentalities.

H2 Other factors remaining constant, as a participant's length of time in an organization increases, he has increased access to persons, information, and instrumentalities. . . .

Implications of Role Theory for the Study of Power

Role theorists approach the question of influence and power in terms of the behavioral regularities which result from established identities within specific social contexts like families, hospitals, and business firms. The underlying premise of most role theorists is that a large proportion of all behavior is brought about through socialization within specific organizations, and much behavior is routine and established through learning the traditional modes of adaptation in dealing with specific tasks. Thus the positions persons occupy in an organization account for much of their behavior. Norms and roles serve as mediating forces in influence processes.

While role theorists have argued much about vocabulary, the basic premises underlying their thought have been rather consistent. The argument is essentially that knowledge of one's identity or social position is a powerful index of the expectations such a person is likely to face in various social situations. Since behavior tends to be highly correlated with expectations, prediction of behavior is therefore possible. The approach of role theorists to the study of behavior within organizations is of particular merit in that it provides a consistent set of concepts which is useful analytically in describing recruitment, socialization, interaction, and personality, as well as the formal structure of organizations. Thus the

concept of role is one of the few concepts clearly linking social structure, social process, and social character. . . .

It should be clear that lower participants will be more likely to circumvent higher authority, other factors remaining constant, when the mandates of those in power, if not the authority itself, are regarded as illegitimate. Thus, as Etzioni points out, when lower participants become alienated from the organization, coercive power is likely to be required if its formal mandates are to be fulfilled.[6]

Moreover, all organizations must maintain control over lower participants. To the extent that lower participants fail to recognize the legitimacy of power, or believe that sanctions cannot or will not be exercised when violations occur, the organization loses, to some extent, its ability to control their behavior. Moreover, in-so-far as higher participants can create the impression that they can or will exert sanctions above their actual willingness to use such sanctions, control over lower participants will increase. It is usually to the advantage of an organization to externalize and impersonalize controls, however, and if possible to develop positive sentiments toward its rules.

In other words, an effective organization can control its participants in such a way as to make it hardly perceivable that it exercises the control that it does. It seeks commitment from lower participants, and when commitment is obtained, surveillance can be relaxed. On the other hand, when the power of lower participants in organizations is considered, it often appears to be clearly divorced from the traditions, norms, and goals and sentiments of the organization as a whole. Lower participants do not usually achieve control by using the role structure of the organization, but rather by circumventing, sabotaging, and manipulating it.

Sources of Power of Lower Participants

The most effective way for lower participants to achieve power is to obtain, maintain, and control access to persons, information, and instrumentalities. To the extent that this can be accomplished, lower participants make higher-ranking participants dependent upon them. Thus dependence together with the manipulation of the dependency relationship is the key to the power of lower participants.

A number of examples can be cited which illustrate the preceding point. Scheff, for example, reports on the failure of a state mental hospital to bring about intended reform because of the opposition of hospital attendants.[7] He noted that the power of hospital attendants was largely a result of the dependence of ward physicians on attendants. This dependence resulted from the physician's short tenure, his lack of interest in administration, and the large amount of administrative responsibility he had to assume. An implicit trading agreement developed between physicians and attendants, whereby attendants would take on some of the responsibilities and obligations of the ward physician in return for increased power in decision-making processes concerning patients. Failure of the ward physician to honor his part of the agreement resulted in information being withheld, disobedience, lack of co-operation, and unwillingness of the attendants to serve as a barrier between the physician and a ward full of patients demanding attention and recognition. When the attendant withheld co-operation, the physician had difficulty in making a graceful entrance and departure from the ward, in handling necessary paperwork (officially his responsibility), and in obtaining information needed to deal adequately with daily treatment and behavior problems. When attendants opposed change, they could wield influence by refusing to assume responsibilities officially assigned to the physician.

Similarly, Sykes describes the dependence of prison guards on inmates and the power obtained by inmates over guards.[8] He suggests that although guards could report inmates for disobedience, frequent reports would give prison officials the impression that the guard was unable to command obedience. The guard, therefore, had some stake in ensuring the good behavior of prisoners without use of formal sanctions against them. The result was a trading agreement whereby the guard allowed violations of certain rules in return for cooperation. A similar situation is found in respect to officers in the Armed Services or foremen in industry. To the extent that they require formal sanctions to bring about co-operation, they are usually perceived by their superiors as less valuable to the organization. For a good leader is expected to command obedience, at least, if not commitment.

Factors Affecting Power

Expertise

Increasing specialization and organizational growth has made the expert or staff person important. The expert maintains power because high-ranking persons in the organization are dependent upon him for his special skills and access to certain kinds of information. One possible reason for lawyers obtaining many high governmental offices is that they are likely to have access to rather specialized but highly important means to organizational goals.[9]

We can state these ideas in hypotheses, as follows:

H3   Other factors remaining constant, to the extent that a low-ranking participant has important expert knowledge not available to high-ranking participants, he is likely to have power over them. Power stemming from expertise, however, is likely to be limited unless it is difficult to replace the expert. This leads to two further hypotheses:

H4   Other factors remaining constant, a person difficult to replace will have greater power than a person easily replaceable.

H5   Other factors remaining constant, experts will be more difficult to replace than nonexperts. . . .

The application of our hypothesis about expertise is clearly relevant if we look at certain organizational issues. For example, the merits of medical versus lay hospital administrators are often debated. It should be clear, however, that all other factors remaining unchanged, the medical administrator has clear advantage over the lay administrator. Where lay administrators receive preference, there is an implicit assumption that the lay person is better at administrative duties. This may be empirically valid but is not necessarily so. The special expert knowledge of the medical administrator stems from his ability legitimately to oppose a physician who contests an administrative decision on the basis of medical necessity. Usually hospitals are viewed primarily as universalistic in orientation both by the general public and most of their participants. Thus medical necessity usually takes precedence over management policies, a factor contributing to the poor financial position of most hospitals. The lay administrator is not in a position to contest such claims independently, since he usually lacks the basis for evaluation of the medical problems involved and also lacks official recognition of his competence to make such decisions. If the lay administrator is to evaluate these claims adequately on the basis of professional necessity, he must have a group of medical consultants or a committee of medical [personnel] to serve as a buffer between medical staff and the lay administration.

As a result of growing specialization, expertise is increasingly important in organizations. As the complexity of organizational tasks increases, and as organizations grow in size, there is a limit to responsibility that can be efficiently exercised by one person. Delegation of responsibility occurs, experts and specialists are brought in to provide information and research, and the higher participants become dependent upon them. Experts have tremendous potentialities for power by withholding information, providing incorrect information, and so on, and to the extent that experts are dissatisfied, the probability of organizational sabotage increases.

Effort and Interest

The extent to which lower participants may exercise power depends in part on their willingness to exert effort in areas where higher-ranking participants are often reluctant to participate. Effort exerted is directly related to the degree of interest one has in an area.

H6   Other factors remaining constant, there is a direct relationship between the amount of effort a person is willing to exert in an area and the power he can command.

For example, secretarial staffs in universities often have power to make decisions about the purchase and allocation of supplies, the allocation of their services, the scheduling of classes, and, at times, the disposition of student complaints. Such control may in some instances lead to sanctions against a professor by polite reluctance to furnish supplies, ignoring his preferences for the scheduling of classes, and giving others preference in the allocation of services. While the power to make such decisions may easily be removed from the jurisdiction of the lower participant, it can only be accomplished at a cost—the willingness to allocate time and effort to the decisions dealing with these matters. To the extent that responsibilities are delegated to lower participants, a certain degree of power is likely to accompany the responsibility. Also, should the lower participant see his perceived rights in jeopardy, he may sabotage the system in various ways. . . .

When an organization gives discretion to lower participants, it is usually trading the power of discretion for needed flexibility. The cost of constant surveillance is too high, and the effort required too great; it is very often much easier for all concerned to allow the secretary discretion in return for cooperation and not too great an abuse of power.

H7   Other factors remaining constant, the less effort and interest high-ranking participants are willing to devote to a task, the more likely are lower participants to obtain power relevant to this task.

Attractiveness

Another personal attribute associated with the power of low-ranking persons in an organization is attractiveness or what some call "personality."

People who are viewed as attractive are more likely to obtain access to persons, and, once such access is gained, they may be more likely to succeed in promoting a cause. But once again dependence is the key to the power of attractiveness, for whether a person is dependent upon another for a service he provides, or for approval or affection, what is most relevant is the relational bond which is highly valued.

H8 Other factors remaining constant, the more attractive a person, the more likely he is to obtain access to persons and control over these persons.

Location and Position

In any organization the person's location in physical space and position in social space are important factors influencing access to persons, information, and instrumentalities.[10] Propinquity affects the opportunities for interaction, as well as one's position within a communication network. Although these are somewhat separate factors, we shall refer to their combined effect as centrality[11] within the organization.

H9 Other factors remaining constant, the more central a person is in an organization, the greater is his access to persons, information, and instrumentalities.

Some low participants may have great centrality within an organization. An executive's or university president's secretary not only has access, but often controls access in making appointments and scheduling events. Although she may have no great formal authority, she may have considerable power.

Coalitions

It should be clear that the variables we are considering are at different levels of analysis; some of them define attributes of persons, while others define attributes of communication and organization. Power processes within organizations are particularly interesting in that there are many channels of power and ways of achieving it.

In complex organizations different occupational groups attend to different functions, each group often maintaining its own power structure within the organization. Thus hospitals have administrators, medical personnel, nursing personnel, attendants, maintenance personnel, laboratory personnel, and so on. Universities, similarly, have teaching personnel, research personnel, administrative personnel, maintenance personnel, and so on. Each of these functional tasks within organizations often becomes the sphere of a particular group that controls activities relating to the task. While these tasks usually are coordinated at the highest levels of the organization, they often are not coordinated at intermediate and lower levels. It is not unusual, however, for coalitions to form among lower participants in these multiple structures. A secretary may know the man who manages the supply of stores, or the person assigning parking stickers. Such acquaintances may give her the ability to handle informally certain needs that would be more time-consuming and difficult to handle formally. Her ability to provide services informally makes higher-ranking participants in some degree dependent upon her, thereby giving her power, which increases her ability to bargain on issues important to her.

Rules

In organizations with complex power structures, lower participants can use their knowledge of the norms of the organization to thwart attempted change. In discussing the various functions of bureaucratic rules, Gouldner maintains that such rules serve as excellent substitutes for surveillance, since surveillance, in addition to being expensive in time and effort, arouses considerable hostility and antagonism.[12] Moreover, he argues, rules are a functional equivalent for direct, personally given orders, since they specify the obligations of workers to do things in specific ways. Standardized rules, in addition, allow simple screening of violations, facilitate remote control, and to some extent legitimize punishment when the rule is violated. The worker who violates a bureaucratic rule has little recourse to the excuse that he did not know what was expected, as he might claim for a direct order. Finally, Gouldner argues that rules are "the 'chips' to which the company staked the supervisors and which they could use to play the game"[13]; that is, rules established a punishment which could be withheld, and this facilitated the supervisors' bargaining power with lower participants.

While Gouldner emphasizes the functional characteristics of rules within an organization, it should be clear that full compliance to all the rules at all times will probably be dysfunctional for the organization. Complete and apathetic compliance may do everything but facilitate achievement of organizational goals. Lower participants who are familiar with an organization and its rules can often find rules to support their contention that they not do what they have been asked to do, and rules are also often a rationalization for inaction on their part. The following of rules becomes especially complex when associations and unions become involved, for there are then two sets of rules to which the participant can appeal.

What is suggested is that rules may be chips for everyone concerned in the game. Rules become the "chips" through which the bargaining process is maintained. Scheff, as noted earlier, observed that attendants in mental hospitals often took on responsibilities assigned legally to the ward physician, and when attendants refused to share these responsibilities the physician's position became extremely difficult.[14]...

Given the time-consuming formal chores of the physician, and his many other duties, he usually worked out an arrangement with the ward personnel, particularly the charge (supervisory attendant), to handle these duties. On several wards, the charge called specific problems to the doctor's attention, and the two of them, in effect, would have a consultation. The charge actually made most of the decisions concerning dosage change in the back wards. Since the doctor delegated portions of his formal responsibilities to the charge, he was dependent on her good will toward him. If she withheld her cooperation, the physician had absolutely no recourse but to do all the work himself.[15]...

There are occasions, of course, when rules are regarded as illegitimate by lower participants, and they may disregard them. Gouldner observed that, in the mine, men felt they could resist authority in a situation involving danger to themselves.[16] They did not feel that they could legitimately be ordered to do anything that would endanger their lives. It is probably significant that in extremely dangerous situations organizations are more likely to rely on commitment to work than on authority. Even within nonvoluntary groups dangerous tasks are regarded usually as requiring task commitment, and it is likely that commitment is a much more powerful organizational force than coercive authority....

NOTES

1. The term "lower participants" comes from Amitai Etzioni in his 1961 book, *A comparative analysis of complex organizations,* and is used by him to designate persons in positions of lower rank: employees, rank-and-file, members, clients, customers, and inmates. We shall use the term in this paper in a relative sense, denoting position vis-à-vis a higher-ranking participant.
2. One might observe, for example, that the power of lower participants is based primarily on the ability to "veto" or punish. For a discussion of bases of power, see John R. P. French, Jr., and Bertram Raven, "The bases of social power," in D. Cartwright and A. Zander, eds., *Group dynamics* (Evanston, Ill., 1960), pp. 607–623.
3. John Thibaut and Harold H. Kelley, *The social psychology of groups* (New York, 1959). For a similar emphasis on dependence, see Richard M. Emerson, Power-dependence relationships, *American Sociological Review,* 28(1962), 31–41.
4. Although this paper will not attempt to explain how access may be measured, the author feels confident that the hypotheses concerned with access are clearly testable.

5. Max Weber, "The essentials of bureaucratic organization: an ideal-type construction," in Robert Merton et al., *Reader in bureaucracy* (Glencoe, Ill., 1952), pp. 18–27.

6. Etzioni, *op. cit.*

7. Thomas J. Scheff, Control over policy by attendants in a mental hospital, *Journal of Health and Human Behavior, 2* (1961), 93–105.

8. Gresham M. Sykes, "The corruption of authority and rehabilitation," in A. Etzioni, ed., *Complex organizations* (New York, 1961), pp. 191–197.

9. As an example, it appears that 6 members of the cabinet, 30 important subcabinet officials, 63 senators, and 230 congressmen are lawyers (*New Yorker,* April 14, 1962, p. 62). Although one can cite many reasons for lawyers holding political posts, an important one appears to be their legal expertise.

10. There is considerable data showing the powerful effect of propinquity on communication. For summary, see Thibaut and Kelley, *op. cit.,* pp. 39–42.

11. The concept of centrality is generally used in a more technical sense in the work of Bavelas, Shaw, Gilchrist, and others. For example, Bavelas defines the central region of a structure as the class of all cells with the smallest distance between one cell and any other cell in the structure, with distance measured in link units. Thus the most central position in a pattern is the position closest to all others. Cf. Harold Leavitt, "Some effects of certain communication patterns on group performance," in E. Maccoby, T. N. Newcomb, and E. L. Hartley, eds., *Reading in social psychology* (New York, 1958), p. 559.

12. Alvin W. Gouldner, *Patterns of industrial bureaucracy* (Glencoe, Ill., 1954).

13. *Ibid.,* p. 173.

14. Scheff, *op. cit.*

15. *Ibid.,* p. 97.

16. Gouldner, *op. cit.*

| ## Three Kinds of Power: A Comparative Dimension
Amitai Etzioni

A Classification of Power

Power is an actor's ability to induce or influence another actor to carry out his directives or any other norms he supports.[1] Goldhamer and Shils (1939) state that "a person may be said to have power to the extent that he influences the behavior of others in accordance with his own intentions" (p. 171). Of course, "his own intentions" might be to influence a person to follow others' "intentions" or those of a collectivity. In organizations, enforcing the collectivity norms is likely to be a condition determining the power-holder's access to the means of power.

Power positions are positions whose incumbents regularly have access to means of power. Statements about power positions imply a particular group (or groups) who are subject to this power. For instance, to state that prison guards have a power position implies the subordination of inmates. We refer to those in power positions, who are higher in rank, as *elites* or as organizational *representatives*. We refer to those in subject positions, who are lower in rank, as *lower participants*.

Power differs according to the *means* employed to make the subjects comply. These means may be physical, material, or symbolic.[2]

Coercive power rests on the application, or the threat of application, of physical sanctions such as infliction of pain, deformity, or death; generation of frustration through restriction of movement; or controlling through force the satisfaction of needs such as those for food, sex, comfort, and the like.

Remunerative power is based on control over material resources and rewards through allocation of salaries and wages, commissions and contributions, "fringe benefits," services, and commodities.

Normative power rests on the allocation and manipulation of symbolic rewards and deprivations through employment of leaders, manipulation of mass media, allocation of esteem and prestige symbols, administration of ritual, and influence over the distribution of "acceptance" and "positive response." (A more eloquent name for this power would be persuasive, or manipulative, or suggestive power. But all these terms have negative value connotations which we wish to avoid.)

There are two kinds of normative power. One is based on the manipulation of esteem, prestige, and ritualistic symbols (such as a flag or a benediction); the other, on allocation and manipulation of acceptance and positive response (Parsons, 1951). Although both powers are found both in vertical and in horizontal relationships, the first is more frequent in vertical relations, between actors who have different ranks, while the second is more common in horizontal relations, among actors equal in rank—in particular, in the power of an "informal" or primary group over its members. Lacking better terms, we refer to the first kind as *pure normative power*, and to the second as *social power*.[3] Social power could be treated as a distinct kind of power. But since powers are here classed according to the means of control employed, and since both social and pure normative powers rest on the same set of means—manipulation of symbolic rewards—we treat these two powers as belonging to the same category.

From the viewpoint of the organization, pure normative power is more useful, since it can be exercised directly down the hierarchy. Social power becomes organizational power only when the organization can influence the group's powers, as when a teacher uses the class climate to control a deviant child, or a union steward agitates the members to use their informal power to bring a deviant into line.

Organizations can be ordered according to their power structure, taking into account which power is predominant, how strongly it is stressed

Source: From A COMPARATIVE ANALYSIS OF COMPLEX ORGANIZATIONS, 2/e.

compared with other organizations in which the same power is predominant, and which power constitutes the secondary source of control.

Neutralization of Power

Most organizations employ all three kinds of power, but the degree to which they rely on each differs from organization to organization. Most organizations tend to emphasize only one means of power, relying less on the other two.[4] The major reason for power specialization seems to be that when two kinds of power are emphasized at the same time, over the same subject group, they tend to neutralize each other.

Applying force, for instance, usually creates such a high degree of alienation that it becomes impossible to apply normative power successfully. This is one of the reasons why rehabilitation is rarely achieved in traditional prisons, why custodial measures are considered as blocking therapy in mental hospitals, and why teachers in progressive schools tend to oppose corporal punishment.

Similarly, the application of remunerative powers makes appeal to "idealistic" (pure normative) motives less fruitful. In a study of the motives which lead to purchase of war bonds, Merton pointed out that in one particularly effective drive (the campaign of Kate Smith), all "secular" topics were omitted and the appeal was centered on patriotic, "sacred" themes. Merton asked a sample of 978 people: "Do you think that it is a good idea to give things to people who buy bonds?"

> Fifty per cent were definitely opposed in principle to premiums, bonuses and other such inducements, and many of the remainder thought it a good idea only for "other people" who might not buy otherwise. (p. 47)

> By omitting this [secular] argument, the authors of her scripts were able to avoid the strain and incompatibility between the two main lines of motivation: unselfish, sacrificing love of country and economic motives of sound investment. (p. 45)

It is possible to make an argument for the opposite position. It might be claimed that the larger the number of personal needs whose satisfaction the organization controls, the more power it has over the participants. For example, labor unions that cater to and have control over the social as well as the economic needs of their members have more power over those members than do unions that focus only on economic needs. There may be some tension between the two modes of control, some ambivalence and uneasy feeling among members about the combination, but undoubtedly the total control is larger. Similarly, it is obvious that the church has more power over the priest than over the average parishioner. The parishioner is exposed to normative power, whereas the priest is controlled by both normative and remunerative powers.

The issue is complicated by the fact that the *amount* of each kind of power applied must be taken into account. If a labor union with social powers has economic power which is much greater than that of another union, this fact may explain why the first union has greater power in sum, despite some "waste" due to neutralization. A further complication follows from the fact that neutralization may also occur through application of the "wrong" power in terms of the cultural definition of what is appropriate to the particular organization and activity. For example, application of economic power in religious organizations may be less effective than in industries, not because two kinds of power are mixed, but because it is considered illegitimate to use economic pressures to attain religious goals. Finally, some organizations manage to apply two kinds of power abundantly and without much waste through neutralization, because they segregate the application of one power from that of the other....

We have discussed some of the factors related to the tendency of organizations to specialize their power application. In conclusion, it seems that although there can be little doubt that such a tendency exists, its scope and a satisfactory explanation for it have yet to be established.

REFERENCES

Barton, A. H. The concept of property space in social research. In Lazarsfeld, P.F., & Rosenberg, M. (Eds.). *The language of social research: A reader in the methodology of social research* (pp. 40–53). Glencoe, Ill.: The Free Press.

Boulding, K. E. *The organizational revolution.* New York: Harper, 1953.

Cartwright, D. A field theoretical conception of power. In Cartwright, D., & Zander, A. (Eds.). *Group dynamics: Research and theory* (pp. 183–220). New York: Row, Peterson, 1959.

Coleman, J. S. Multidimensional scale analysis. *Am. J. Soc,* 1957, 63: 253–263.

Commons, J. R. *Legal foundations of capitalism.* Madison: University of Wisconsin, 1957.

Dahl, R. A. The concept of power. *Behav. Sci.,* 1957, 2: 201–215.

Deutsch, K. W. *Nationalism and social communication.* New York: Wiley, 1953.

Easton, D. *The political system.* New York: Knopf, 1952.

Goldhamer, H. & Shils, E. A. Types of power and status. *Am. J. Soc,* 1939, 45: 171–182.

Janowitz, M. *The professional soldier.* Glencoe, Ill.: The Free Press, 1960.

Lasswell, H. D. & Kaplan, A. *Power and society.* New Haven: Yale University Press, 1950.

Merton, R. K. *Mass persuasion: The social psychology of a war bond drive.* New York: Harper, 1946.

Neuman, F. L. Approaches to the study of political power. *Poli. Sci. Q.,* 1950, 65: 161–180.

Parsons, T. *The social system.* Glencoe, Ill.: The Free Press, 1951.

Parsons, T. The distribution of power in American society. *World Politics,* 1957, 10: 123–143.

Parsons, T., Bales, R. F. & Shils, E. A. *Working papers in the theory of action.* Glencoe, Ill.: The Free Press, 1953.

NOTES

1. See Parsons (1951, p. 121). See also Lasswell and Kaplan (1950, pp. 74–102); Easton (1952, p. 116); Dahl (1957); and Cartwright (1959).

2. We suggest that this typology is exhaustive, although the only way we can demonstrate this is by pointing out that every type of power we have encountered so far can be classified as belonging to one of the categories or a combination of them.

3. This distinction draws on the difference between social and normative integration, referred to by Parsons, Bales, and Shils (1953, p. 182) as the distinction between the "integrative" and the "latent pattern maintenance" phases. In a volume in progress, Shils distinguishes between social and ideological primary groups (private communication). Coleman (1957, p. 255) has pointed to the difference between group-oriented and idea-oriented attachments.

4. In more technical language, one can say that the three continua of power constitute a three-dimensional property space. If we collapse each dimension into high, medium, and low segments, there are 27 possible combinations or cells. Our hypothesis reads that most organizations fall into cells which are high on one dimension and low or medium on the others; this excludes 18 cells (not counting three types of dual structures discussed below). On multi-dimensional property space, see Barton (1955, pp. 40–52).

Reading 33

Who Gets Power—And How They Hold on to It: A Strategic-Contingency Model of Power

Gerald R. Salancik and Jeffrey Pfeffer

Power is held by many people to be a dirty word or, as Warren Bennis has said, "It is the organization's last dirty secret."

This article will argue that traditional "political" power, far from being a dirty business, is, in its most naked form, one of the few mechanisms available for aligning an organization with its own reality. However, institutionalized forms of power—what we prefer to call the cleaner forms of power: authority, legitimization, centralized control, regulations, and the more modern "management information systems"—tend to buffer the organization from reality and obscure the demands of its environment. Most great states and institutions declined, not because they played politics, but because they failed to accommodate to the political realities they faced. Political processes, rather than being mechanisms for unfair and unjust allocations and appointments, tend toward the realistic resolution of conflicts among interests. And power, while it eludes definition, is easy enough to recognize by its consequences—the ability of those who possess power to bring about the outcomes they desire.

The model of power we advance is an elaboration of what has been called strategic-contingency theory, a view that sees power as something that accrues to organizational subunits (individuals, departments) that cope with critical organizational problems. Power is used by subunits, indeed, used by all who have it, to enhance their own survival through control of scarce critical resources, through the placement of allies in key positions, and through the definition of organizational problems and policies. Because of the processes by which power develops and is used, organizations become both more aligned and more misaligned with their environments. This contradiction is the most interesting aspect of organizational

power, and one that makes administration one of the most precarious of occupations.

What Is Organizational Power?

You can walk into most organizations and ask without fear of being misunderstood, "Which are the powerful groups or people in this organization?" Although many organizational informants may be *unwilling* to tell you, it is unlikely they will be *unable* to tell you. Most people do not require explicit definitions to know what power is.

Power is simply the ability to get things done the way one wants them to be done. For a manager who wants an increased budget to launch a project that he thinks is important, his power is measured by his ability to get that budget. For an executive vice-president who wants to be chairman, his power is evidenced by his advancement toward his goal.

People in organizations not only know what you are talking about when you ask who is influential but they are likely to agree with one another to an amazing extent....

Where Does Organizational Power Come From?

Earlier we stated that power helps organizations become aligned with their realities. This hopeful prospect follows from what we have dubbed the strategic-contingencies theory of organizational power. Briefly, those subunits most able to cope with the organization's critical problems and uncertainties acquire power. In its simplest form, the strategic-contingencies theory implies that when an organization faces a number of lawsuits that threaten its existence, the legal department will gain power and influence over organizational

Source: Salancik and Pfeffer, "Who Gets Power—And How They Hold On To It," ORGANIZATIONAL DYNAMICS, Winter, 1977. Reprinted with permission from Elsevier Science.

decisions. Somehow other organizational interest groups will recognize its critical importance and confer upon it a status and power never before enjoyed. This influence may extend beyond handling legal matters and into decisions about product design, advertising production, and so on. Such extensions undoubtedly would be accompanied by appropriate, or acceptable, verbal justifications. In time, the head of the legal department may become the head of the corporation, just as in times past the vice-president for marketing had become the president when market shares were a worrisome problem and, before him, the chief engineer, who had made the production line run as smooth as silk.

Stated in this way, the strategic-contingencies theory of power paints an appealing picture of power. To the extent that power is determined by the critical uncertainties and problems facing the organization and, in turn, influences decisions in the organization, the organization is aligned with the realities it faces. In short, power facilitates the organization's adaptation to its environment—or its problems. . . .

Ignoring Critical Consequences

When organizational members are not aware of the critical contingencies they face, and do not share influence accordingly, the failure to do so can create havoc. In one case, an insurance company's regional office was having problems with the performance of one of its departments, the coding department. From the outside, the department looked like a disaster area. The clerks who worked in it were somewhat dissatisfied; their supervisor paid little attention to them, and they resented the hard work. Several other departments were critical of this manager, claiming that she was inconsistent in meeting deadlines. The person most critical was the claims manager. He resented having to wait for work that was handled by her department, claiming that it held up his claims adjusters. Having heard the rumors about dissatisfaction among her subordinates, he attributed the situation to poor supervision. He was second

in command in the office, and therefore took up the issue with her immediate boss, the head of administrative services. They consulted with the personnel manager and the three of them concluded that the manager needed leadership training to improve her relations with her subordinates. The coding manager objected, saying it was a waste of time, but agreed to go along with the training and also agreed to give more priority to the claims department's work. Within a week after the training, the results showed that her workers were happier but that the performance of her department had decreased, save for the people serving the claims department.

About this time, we began, quite independently, a study of influence in this organization. We asked the administrative services director to draw up flow charts of how the work of one department moved on to the next department. In the course of the interview, we noticed that the coding department began or interceded in the work flow of most of the other departments and casually mentioned to him, "The coding manager must be very influential." He said "No, not really. Why would you think so?" Before we could reply he recounted the story of her leadership training and the fact that things were worse. We then told him that it seemed obvious that the coding department would be influential from the fact that all the other departments depended on it. It was also clear why productivity had fallen. The coding manager took the training seriously and began spending more time raising her workers' spirits than she did worrying about the problems of all the departments that depended on her. Giving priority to the claims area only exaggerated the problem, for their work was getting done at the expense of the work of the other departments. Eventually the company hired a few more clerks to relieve the pressure in the coding department and performance returned to a more satisfactory level.

Originally we got involved with this insurance company to examine how the influence of each manager evolved from his or her department's handling of critical organizational contingencies.

We reasoned that one of the most important contingencies faced by all profit-making organizations was that of generating income. Thus we expected managers would be influential to the extent to which they contributed to this function. Such was the case. The underwriting managers, who wrote the policies that committed the premiums, were the most influential; the claims managers, who kept a lid on the funds flowing out, were a close second. Least influential were the managers of functions unrelated to revenue, such as mailroom and payroll managers. And contrary to what the administrative services manager believed, the third most powerful department head (out of 21) was the woman in charge of the coding function, which consisted of rating, recording, and keeping track of the codes of all policy applications and contracts. Her peers attributed more influence to her than could have been inferred from her place on the organization chart. And it was not surprising, since they all depended on her department. The coding department's records, their accuracy and the speed with which they could be retrieved, affected virtually every other operating department in the insurance office. The underwriters depended on them in getting the contracts straight; the typing department depended on them in preparing the formal contract document; the claims department depended on them in adjusting claims; and accounting depended on them for billing. Unfortunately, the "bosses" were not aware of these dependences, . . . while the coding manager, who was a hard-working but quiet person, did little to announce her importance.

The cases of this plant and office illustrate nicely a basic point about the source of power in organizations. The basis for power in an organization derives from the ability of a person or subunit to take or not take actions that are desired by others. . . . Whether power is used to influence anything is a separate issue. We should not confuse this issue with the fact that power derives from a social situation in which one person has a capacity to do something and another person does not, but wants it done.

Power Sharing in Organizations

Power is shared in organizations, and it is shared out of necessity more than out of concern for principles of organizational development or participatory democracy. Power is shared because no one person controls all the desired activities in the organization. While the factory owner may hire people to operate his noisy machines, once hired they have some control over the use of the machinery. And thus they have power over him in the same way he has power over them. Who has more power over whom is a mooter point than that of recognizing the inherent nature of organizing as a sharing of power. . . .

Because power derives from activities rather than individuals, an individual's or subgroup's power is never absolute and derives ultimately from the context of the situation. The amount of power an individual has at any one time depends not only on the activities he or she controls, but also on the existence of other persons or means by which the activities can be achieved and on those who determine what ends are desired and, hence, on what activities are desired and critical for the organization. One's own power always depends on other people for these two reasons. Other people, or groups or organizations, can determine the definition of what is a critical contingency for the organization and can also undercut the uniqueness of the individual's personal contribution to the critical contingencies of the organization.

Perhaps one can best appreciate how situationally dependent power is by examining how it is distributed. In most societies, power organizes around scarce and critical resources. Rarely does power organize around abundant resources. In the United States, a person doesn't become powerful because he or she can drive a car. There are simply too many others who can drive with equal facility. In certain villages in Mexico, on the other hand, a person with a car is accredited with enormous social status and plays a key role in the community. In addition to scarcity, power is also limited by the need for one's capacities in a social system.

While a racer's ability to drive a car around a 90° turn at 80 mph may be sparsely distributed in a society, it is not likely to lend the driver much power in the society. The ability simply does not play a central role in the activities of the society.

The fact that power revolves around scarce and critical activities, of course, makes the control and organization of those activities a major battleground in struggles for power. Even relatively abundant or trivial resources can become the bases for power if one can organize and control their allocation and the definition of what is critical. Many occupational and professional groups attempt to do just this in modern economies. Lawyers organize themselves into associations, regulate the entrance requirements for novitiates, and then get laws passed specifying situations that require the services of an attorney. Workers had little power in the conduct of industrial affairs until they organized themselves into closed and controlled systems. In recent years, women and blacks have tried to define themselves as important and critical to the social system, using law to reify their status....

The power to define what is critical in an organization is no small power. Moreover, it is the key to understanding why organizations are either aligned with their environments or misaligned. If an organization defines certain activities as critical when in fact they are not critical, given the flow of resources coming into the organization, it is not likely to survive, at least in its present form.

Most organizations manage to evolve a distribution of power and influence that is aligned with the critical realities they face in the environment. The environment, in turn, includes both the internal environment, the shifting situational contexts in which particular decisions get made, and the external environment that it can hope to influence but is unlikely to control.

The Critical Contingencies

The critical contingencies facing most organizations derive from the environmental context within which they operate. This determines the available needed resources and thus determines the problems to be dealt with. That power organizes around handling these problems suggests an important mechanism by which organizations keep in tune with their external environments. The strategic-contingencies model implies that subunits that contribute to the critical resources of the organization will gain influence in the organization. Their influence presumably is then used to bend the organization's activities to the contingencies that determine its resources. This idea may strike one as obvious. But its obviousness in no way diminishes its importance. Indeed, despite its obviousness, it escapes the notice of many organizational analysts and managers, who all too frequently think of the organization in terms of a descending pyramid, in which all the departments in one tier hold equal power and status. This presumption denies the reality that departments differ in the contributions they are believed to make to the overall organization's resources, as well as to the fact that some are more equal than others.

Because of the importance of this idea to organizational effectiveness, we decided to examine it carefully in a large midwestern university. A university offers an excellent site for studying power. It is composed of departments with nominally equal power and is administered by a central executive structure much like other bureaucracies. However, at the same time it is a situation in which the departments have clearly defined identities and face diverse external environments. Each department has its own bodies of knowledge, its own institutions, its own sources of prestige and resources. Because the departments operate in different external environments, they are likely to contribute differentially to the resources of the overall organization. Thus a physics department with close ties to NASA may contribute substantially to the funds of the university; and a history department with a renowned historian in residence may contribute to the intellectual credibility or prestige of the whole university. Such variations permit one to examine how these various contributions lead to obtaining power within the university.

We analyzed the influence of 29 university departments throughout an 18-month period in their history. Our chief interest was to determine whether departments that brought more critical resources to the university would be more powerful than departments that contributed fewer or less critical resources.

To identify the critical resources each department contributed, the heads of all departments were interviewed about the importance of seven different resources to the university's success. The seven included undergraduate students (the factor determining size of the state allocations by the university), national prestige, administrative expertise, and so on. The most critical resource was found to be contract and grant monies received by a department's faculty for research or consulting services. At this university, contract and grants contributed somewhat less than 50 percent of the overall budget, with the remainder primarily coming from state appropriations. The importance attributed to contract and grant monies, and the rather minor importance of undergraduate students, was not surprising for this particular university. The university was a major center for graduate education; many of its departments ranked in the top ten of their respective fields. Grant and contract monies were the primary source of discretionary funding available for maintaining these programs of graduate education, and hence for maintaining the university's prestige. The prestige of the university itself was critical both in recruiting able students and attracting top-notch faculty.

From university records it was determined what relative contributions each of the 29 departments made to the various needs of the university (national prestige, outside grants, teaching). Thus, for instance, one department may have contributed to the university by teaching 7 percent of the instructional units, bringing in 2 percent of the outside contracts and grants, and having a national ranking of 20. Another department, on the other hand, may have taught one percent of the instructional units, contributed 12 percent to the grants, and be ranked the third best department in its field within the country.

The question was: Do these different contributions determine the relative power of the departments within the university? Power was measured in several ways; but regardless of how measured, the answer was "yes." Those three resources together accounted for about 70 percent of the variance in subunit power in the university.

But the most important predictor of departmental power was the department's contribution to the contracts and grants of the university. Sixty percent of the variance in power was due to this one factor, suggesting that the power of departments derived primarily from the dollars they provided for graduate education, the activity believed to be the most important for the organization.

The Impact of Organizational Power on Decision Making

While it is perhaps not absolutely valid, we can generally gauge the relative importance of a department of an organization by the size of the budget allocated to it relative to other departments. Clearly it is of importance to the administrators of those departments whether they get squeezed in a budget crunch or are given more funds to strike out after new opportunities. And it should also be clear that when those decisions are made and one department can go ahead and try new approaches while another must cut back on the old, then the deployment of the resources of the organization in meeting its problems is most directly affected.

Thus our study of the university led us to ask the following question: Does power lead to influence in the organization? To answer this question, we found it useful first to ask another one, namely: Why should department heads try to influence organizational decisions to favor their own departments to the exclusion of other departments? While this second question may seem a bit naive to anyone who has witnessed the political realities of organizations, we posed it in a context of research on organizations that sees power as an illegitimate threat to the neater rational authority of modern bureaucracies. In this context, decisions are not believed to be made because of the dirty business of politics but because of the overall goals and purposes of the organization. In a university, one reasonable basis for decision making is the teaching workload of departments and the demands that follow from that workload. We would expect, therefore, that departments with heavy student demands for courses would be able to obtain funds for teaching. Another reasonable basis for decision making is quality. We would expect, for that reason, that departments with esteemed reputations would be able to obtain funds both because their quality suggests they might use such funds effectively and because such funds would allow them to maintain their quality. A rational model of bureaucracy intimates, then, that the organizational decisions taken would favor those who perform the stated purposes of the organization—teaching undergraduates and training professional and scientific talent—well.

The problem with rational models of decision making, however, is that what is rational to one person may strike another as irrational. For most departments, resources are a question of survival.... Thus goals, rather than being clearly defined and universally agreed upon, are blurred and contested throughout the organization. If such is the case, then the decisions made on behalf of the organization as a whole are likely to reflect the goals of those who prevail in political contests, namely, those with power in the organization....

We have examined three conditions that are likely to affect the use of power in organizations: scarcity, criticality, and uncertainty. The first suggests that sub-units will try to exert influence when the resources of the organization are scarce. If there is an abundance of resources, then a particular department or a particular individual has little need to attempt influence. With little effort, he can get all he wants anyway.

The second condition, criticality, suggests that a subunit will attempt to influence decisions to obtain resources that are critical to its own survival and activities. Criticality implies that one would not waste effort, or risk being labeled obstinate, by fighting over trivial decisions affecting one's operations....

The third condition that we believe affects the use of power is uncertainty: When individuals do not agree about what the organization should do or how to do it, power and other social processes will affect decisions. The reason for this is simply that, if there are no clear-cut criteria available for resolving conflicts of interest, then the only means for resolution is some form of social process, including power, status, social ties, or some arbitrary process like flipping a coin or drawing straws. Under conditions of uncertainty, the powerful manager can argue his case on any grounds and usually win it. Since there is no real consensus, other contestants are not likely to develop counter arguments or amass sufficient opposition. Moreover, because of his power and their need for access to the resources he controls, they are more likely to defer to his arguments.

Although the evidence is slight, we have found that power will influence the allocations of scarce and critical resources. In the analysis of power in the university, for instance, one of the most critical resources needed by departments is the general budget. First granted by the state legislature, the general budget is later allocated to individual departments by the university administration in response to requests from the department heads. Our analysis of the factors that contribute to a department getting more or less of this budget indicated that subunit power was the major predictor, overriding such factors as student demand for courses, national reputations of departments, or even the size of a department's faculty. Moreover, other research has shown that when the general budget has been cut back or held below previous uninflated levels, leading to monies becoming more scarce, budget allocations mirror departmental powers even more closely.

Student enrollment and faculty size, of course, do themselves relate to budget allocations, as we would expect since they determine a department's need for resources, or at least offer visible testimony of needs. But departments are not always able to get what they need by the mere fact of needing them. In one analysis it was found that high-power departments were able to obtain budget without regard to their teaching loads and, in some cases, actually in inverse relation to their teaching loads. In contrast, low-power departments could get increases in budget only when they could justify the increases by a recent growth in teaching load, and then only when it was far in excess of norms for other departments. . . .

When the four resources were arrayed from the most to the least critical and scarce, we found that departmental power best predicted the allocations of the most critical and scarce resources. In other words, the analysis of how power influences organizational allocations leads to this conclusion: Those subunits most likely to survive in times of strife are those that are more critical to the organization. Their importance to the organization gives them power to influence resource allocations that enhance their own survival.

How External Environment Impacts Executive Selection

Power not only influences the survival of key groups in an organization, it also influences the selection of individuals to key leadership positions, and by such a process further aligns the organization with its environmental context. . . .

As with the selection of administrators, the context of organizations has also been found to affect the removal of executives. The environment, as a source of organizational problems, can make it more or less difficult for executives to demonstrate their value to the organization. In the hospitals we studied, long-term administrators came from hospitals with few problems. They enjoyed amicable and stable relations with their local business and social communities and suffered little competition for funding and staff. The small-city hospital director who attended civic and Elks meetings while running the only hospital within a 100-mile radius, for example, had little

difficulty holding on to his job. Turnover was highest in hospitals with the most problems, a phenomenon similar to that observed in a study of industrial organizations, in which turnover was highest among executives in industries with competitive environments and unstable market conditions. The interesting thing is that instability characterized the industries rather than the individual firms in them. The troublesome conditions in the individual firms were attributed, or rather misattributed, to the executives themselves.

It takes more than problems, however, to terminate a manager's leadership. . . . For those hospitals dependent upon private donations, the length of an administrator's term depended not at all on the status of the operating budget but was fairly predictable from the hospital's relations with the business community. On the other hand, in hospitals dependent on the operating budget for capital financing, the greater the deficit the shorter was the tenure of the hospital's principal administrators.

Changing Contingencies and Eroding Power Bases

The critical contingencies facing the organization may change. When they do, it is reasonable to expect that the power of individuals and subgroups will change in turn. . . .

One implication of the idea that power shifts with changes in organizational environments is that the dominant coalition will tend to be that group that is most appropriate for the organization's environment, as also will the leaders of an organization. . . .

The Nonadaptive Consequences of Adaptation

From what we have said thus far about power aligning the organization with its own realities, an intelligent person might react with a resounding ho-hum, for it all seems too obvious: Those with the ability to get the job done are given the job to do.

However, there are two aspects of power that make it more useful for understanding organizations and their effectiveness. First, the "job" to be done has a way of expanding itself until it becomes less and less clear what the job is. Napoleon began by doing a job for France in the war with Austria and ended up Emperor, convincing many that only he could keep the peace. Hitler began by promising an end to Germany's troubling postwar depression and ended up convincing more people than is comfortable to remember that he was destined to be the savior of the world. In short, power is a capacity for influence that extends far beyond the original bases that created it. Second, power tends to take on institutionalized forms that enable it to endure well beyond its usefulness to an organization.

There is an important contradiction in what we have observed about organizational power. On the one hand we have said that power derives from the contingencies facing an organization and that when those contingencies change so do the bases for power. On the other hand we have asserted that subunits will tend to use their power to influence organizational decisions in their own favor, particularly when their own survival is threatened by the scarcity of critical resources. The first statement implies that an organization will tend to be aligned with its environment since power will tend to bring to key positions those with capabilities relevant to the context. The second implies that those in power will not give up their positions so easily; they will pursue policies that guarantee their continued domination. In short, change and stability operate through the same mechanism, and, as a result, the organization will never be completely in phase with its environment or its needs. . . .

Mistaking Critical Contingencies

One thing that allows subunits to retain their power is their ability to name their functions as critical to the organization when they may not be. Consider again our discussion of power in the university. One might wonder why the most critical tasks were defined as graduate education and scholarly research, the effect of which was to

lend power to those who brought in grants and contracts. Why not something else? The reason is that the more powerful departments argued for those criteria and won their case, partly because they were more powerful.

In another analysis of this university, we found that all departments advocate self-serving criteria for budget allocation. Thus a department with large undergraduate enrollments argued that enrollments should determine budget allocations, a department with a strong national reputation saw prestige as the most reasonable basis for distributing funds, and so on. We further found that advocating such self-serving criteria actually benefited a department's budget allotments but, also, it paid off more for departments that were already powerful.

Organizational needs are consistent with a current distribution of power also because of a human tendency to categorize problems in familiar ways. An accountant sees problems with organizational performance as cost accountancy problems or inventory flow problems. A sales manager sees them as problems with markets, promotional strategies, or just unaggressive salespeople. But what is the truth? Since it does not automatically announce itself, it is likely that those with prior credibility, or those with power, will be favored as the enlightened. This bias, while not intentionally self-serving, further concentrates power among those who already possess it, independent of changes in the organization's context.

Institutionalizing Power

A third reason for expecting organizational contingencies to be defined in familiar ways is that the current holders of power can structure the organization in ways that institutionalize themselves. By institutionalization we mean the establishment of relatively permanent structures and policies that favor the influence of a particular subunit. While in power, a dominant coalition has the ability to institute constitutions, rules, procedures, and information systems that limit the potential power of others while continuing their own.

The key to institutionalizing power always is to create a device that legitimates one's own authority and diminishes the legitimacy of others. When the "Divine Right of Kings" was envisioned centuries ago, it was to provide an unquestionable foundation for the supremacy of royal authority. There is generally a need to root the exercise of authority in some higher power. Modern leaders are no less affected by this need. Richard Nixon, with the aid of John Dean, reified the concept of executive privilege, which meant in effect that what the President wished not to be discussed need not be discussed.

In its simpler form, institutionalization is achieved by designating positions or roles for organizational activities. The creation of a new post legitimizes a function and forces organization members to orient to it. By designating how this new post relates to older, more established posts, moreover, one can structure an organization to enhance the importance of the function in the organization....

The structures created by dominant powers sooner or later become fixed and unquestioned features of the organization. Eventually, this can be devastating. It is said that the battle of Jena in 1806 was lost by Frederick the Great, who died in 1786. Though the great Prussian leader had no direct hand in the disaster, his imprint on the army was so thorough, so embedded in its skeletal underpinnings, that the organization was inappropriate for others to lead in different times.

Another important source of institutionalized power lies in the ability to structure information systems. Setting up committees to investigate particular organizational issues and having them report only to particular individuals or groups, facilitates the awareness of problems by members of those groups while limiting the awareness of problems by the members of other groups. Obviously, those who have information are in a better position to interpret the problems of an organization, regardless of how realistically they may, in fact, do so.

Still another way to institutionalize power is to distribute rewards and resources. The dominant group may quiet competing interest groups with small favors and rewards. The credit for this artful form of cooperation belongs to Louis XIV. To avoid usurpation of his power by the nobles of France and the Fronde that had so troubled his father's reign, he built the palace at Versailles to occupy them with hunting and gossip. Awed, the courtiers basked in the reflected glories of the "Sun King" and the overwhelming setting he had created for his court.

At this point, we have not systematically studied the institutionalization of power. But we suspect it is an important condition that mediates between the environment of the organization and the capabilities of the organization for dealing with that environment. The more institutionalized power is within an organization, the more likely an organization will be out of phase with the realities it faces. President Richard Nixon's structuring of his White House is one of the better documented illustrations....

One of the more interesting implications of institutionalized power is that executive turnover among the executives who have structured the organization is likely to be a rare event that occurs only under the most pressing crisis. If a dominant coalition is able to structure the organization and interpret the meaning of ambiguous events like declining sales and profits or lawsuits, then the "real" problems to emerge will easily be incorporated into traditional molds of thinking and acting. If opposition is designed out of the organization, the interpretations will go unquestioned. Conditions will remain stable until a crisis develops, so overwhelming and visible that even the most adroit rhetorician would be silenced.

Implications for the Management of Power in Organizations

Instead of ending with homilies, we will end with a reversal of where we began. Power, rather than being the dirty business it is often made out to be, is probably one of the few mechanisms for reality testing in organizations. And the cleaner forms of power, the institutional forms, rather than having the virtues they are often credited with, can lead the organization to become out of touch. The real trick to managing power in organizations is to ensure somehow that leaders cannot be unaware of the realities of their environments and cannot avoid changing to deal with those realities. That, however, would be like designing the "self-liquidating organization," an unlikely event since anyone capable of designing such an instrument would be obviously in control of the liquidations. . . .

One conclusion you can, and probably should, derive from our discussion is that power—because of the way it develops and the way it is used—will always result in the organization suboptimizing its performance. However, to this grim absolute, we add a comforting caveat: If any criteria other than power were the basis for determining an organization's decisions, the results would be even worse.

Reading 34	Power Failure in Management Circuits
	Rosabeth Moss Kanter

Power is America's last dirty word. It is easier to talk about money—and much easier to talk about sex—than it is to talk about power. People who have it deny it; people who want it do not want to appear to hunger for it; and people who engage in its machinations do so secretly.

Yet, because it turns out to be a critical element in effective managerial behavior, power should come out from undercover. Having searched for years for those styles or skills that would identify capable organization leaders, many analysts, like myself, are rejecting individual traits or situational appropriateness as key and finding the sources of a leader's real power.

Access to resources and information and the ability to act quickly make it possible to accomplish more and to pass on more resources and information to subordinates. For this reason, people tend to prefer bosses with "clout." When employees perceive their manager as influential upward and outward, their status is enhanced by association and they generally have high morale and feel less critical of or resistant to their boss.[1] More powerful leaders are also more likely to delegate (they are too busy to do it all themselves), to reward talent, and to build a team that places subordinates in significant positions.

Powerlessness, in contrast, tends to breed bossiness rather than true leadership. In large organizations, at least, it is powerlessness that often creates ineffective, desultory management and petty, dictatorial, rules-minded managerial styles. Accountability without power—responsibility for results without the resources to get them—creates frustration and failure. People who see themselves as weak and powerless and find their subordinates resisting or discounting them tend to use more punishing forms of influence. If organizational power can "ennoble," then, recent research shows, organizational powerlessness can (with apologies to Lord Acton) "corrupt."[2]

So perhaps power, in the organization at least, does not deserve such a bad reputation. Rather than connoting only dominance, control, and oppression, *power* can mean efficacy and capacity—something managers and executives need to move the organization toward its goals. Power in organizations is analogous in simple terms to physical power: it is the ability to mobilize resources (human and material) to get things done. The true sign of power, then, is accomplishment—not fear, terror, or tyranny. Where power is "on," the system can be productive; where the power is "off," the system bogs down. . . .

Where Does Power Come From?

The effectiveness that power brings evolves from two kinds of capacities: first, access to resources, information, and support necessary to carry out a task; and, second, ability to get cooperation in doing what is necessary. (Table 1 identifies some symbols of an individual manager's power.). . .

We can regard the uniquely organizational sources of power as consisting of three "lines":

1. *Lines of Supply.* Influence outward, over the environment, means that managers have the capacity to bring in the things that their own organizational domain needs—materials, money, resources to distribute as rewards, and perhaps even prestige.
2. *Lines of Information.* To be effective, managers need to be "in the know" in both the formal and the informal sense.
3. *Lines of Support.* In a formal framework, a manager's job parameters need to allow for nonordinary action, for a show of discretion or exercise of judgment. Thus managers need

Source: Power Failure in Management Circuits by Rosabeth Moss Kanter, July–Aug 1979, pp. 65–75. © 1979 by Harvard Business School Publishing. Reprinted by permission of the publisher.

TABLE 1	To What Extent a Manager Can—
SOME COMMON SYMBOLS OF A MANAGER'S ORGANIZATIONAL POWER (INFLUENCE UPWARD AND OUTWARD)	Intercede favorably on behalf of someone in trouble with the organization.
	Get a desirable placement for a talented subordinate.
	Get approval for expenditures beyond the budget.
	Get above-average salary increases for subordinates.
	Get items on the agenda at policy meetings.
	Get fast access to top decision makers.
	Get regular, frequent access to top decision makers.
	Get early information about decisions and policy shifts.

to know that they can assume innovative, risk-taking activities without having to go through the stifling multi-layered approval process. And, informally, managers need the backing of other important figures in the organization whose tacit approval becomes another resource they bring to their own work unit as well as a sign of the manager's being "in."

Note that productive power has to do with *connections* with other parts of a system. Such systemic aspects of power derive from two sources—job activities and political alliances:

1. Power is most easily accumulated when one has a job that is designed and located to allow discretion (nonroutinized action permitting flexible, adaptive, and creative contributions), recognition (visibility and notice), and relevance (being central to pressing organizational problems).
2. Power also comes when one has relatively close contact with sponsors (higher-level people who confer approval, prestige, or backing), peer networks (circles of acquaintanceship that provide reputation and information, the grapevine often being faster than formal communication channels), and subordinates (who can be developed to relieve managers of some of their burdens and to represent the manager's point of view).

When managers are in powerful situations, it is easier for them to accomplish more. Because the tools are there, they are likely to be highly motivated and, in turn, to be able to motivate subordinates. Their activities are more likely to be on target and to net them successes. They can flexibly interpret or shape policy to meet the needs of particular areas, emergent situations, or sudden environmental shifts. They gain the respect and cooperation that attributed power brings. Subordinates' talents are resources rather than threats. And, because powerful managers have so many lines of connection and thus are oriented outward, they tend to let go of control downward, developing more independently functioning lieutenants. The powerless live in a different world. Lacking the supplies, information, or support to make things happen easily, they may turn instead to the ultimate weapon of those who lack productive power—oppressive power: holding others back and punishing with whatever threats they can muster. Table 2 summarizes some of the major ways in which variables in the organization and in job design contribute to either power or powerlessness.

Positions of Powerlessness

Understanding what it takes to have power and recognizing the classic behavior of the powerless can immediately help managers make sense out of a number of familiar organizational problems that are usually attributed to inadequate people:

The ineffectiveness of first-line supervisors.

TABLE 2 WAYS ORGANIZA- TIONAL FACTORS CONTRIBUTE TO POWER OR POWERLESSNESS	Factors	Generates Power When Factor Is	Generates Powerlessness When Factor Is
	Rules inherent in the job	Few	Many
	Predecessors in the job	Few	Many
	Established routines	Few	Many
	Task variety	High	Low
	Rewards for reliability/predictability	Few	Many
	Rewards for unusual performance/innovation	Many	Few
	Flexibility around use of people	High	Low
	Approvals needed for nonroutine decisions	Few	Many
	Physical location	Central	Distant
	Publicity about job activities	High	Low
	Relation of tasks to current problem areas	Central	Peripheral
	Focus of tasks	Outside work unit	Inside work unit
	Interpersonal contact in the job	High	Low
	Contact with senior officials	High	Low
	Participation in programs, conferences, meetings	High	Low
	Participation in problem-solving task forces	High	Low
	Advancement prospects of subordinates	High	Low

The petty interest protection and conservatism of staff professionals.

The crises of leadership at the top.

Instead of blaming the individuals involved in organizational problems, let us look at the positions people occupy....

First-Line Supervisors

Because an employee's most important work relationship is with his or her supervisor, when many of them talk about "the company," they mean their immediate boss. Thus a supervisor's behavior is an important determinant of the average employee's relationship to work and is in itself a critical link in the production chain.

Yet I know of no U.S. corporate management entirely satisfied with the performance of its supervisors. Most see them as supervising too closely and not training their people. In one manufacturing company where direct laborers were asked on a survey how they learned their job, on a list of seven possibilities "from my supervisor" ranked next to last. (Only company training programs ranked worse.) Also, it is said that supervisors do not translate company policies into practice—for instance, that they do not carry out the right of every employee to frequent performance reviews or to career counseling.

In court cases charging race or sex discrimination, first-line supervisors are frequently cited as the "discriminating official."[3] And, in studies of innovative work redesign and quality of work life projects, they often appear as the implied villains; they are the ones who are said to undermine the program or interfere with its effectiveness. In short, they are often seen as "not sufficiently managerial."...

A large part of the problem lies in the position itself—one that almost universally creates powerlessness.

First-line supervisors are "people in the middle," and that has been seen as the source of many of their problems.[4] But by recognizing that first-line supervisors are caught between higher management and workers, we only begin to skim the surface of the problem. There is practically no other organizational category as subject to powerlessness.

First, these supervisors may be at a virtual dead end in their careers. Even in companies where the job used to be a stepping stone to higher-level management jobs, it is now common practice to bring in MBAs from the outside for those positions. Thus moving from the ranks of direct labor into supervision may mean, essentially, getting "stuck" rather than moving upward. Because employees do not perceive supervisors as eventually joining the leadership circles of the organization, they may see them as lacking the high-level contacts needed to have clout. Indeed, sometimes turnover among supervisors is so high that workers feel they can outwait—and outwit—any boss.

Second, although they lack clout, with little in the way of support from above, supervisors are forced to administer programs or explain policies that they have no hand in shaping. In one company, as part of a new personnel program supervisors were required to conduct counseling interviews with employees. But supervisors were not trained to do this and were given no incentives to get involved. Counseling was just another obligation. Then managers suddenly encouraged the workers to bypass their supervisors or to put pressure on them. The personnel staff brought them together and told them to demand such interviews as a basic right. If supervisors had not felt powerless before, they did after that squeeze from below, engineered from above.

The people they supervise can also make life hard for them in numerous ways. This often happens when a supervisor has himself or herself risen up from the ranks. Peers that have not made it are resentful or derisive of their former colleague, whom they now see as trying to lord it over them. Often it is easy for workers to break the rules and let a lot of things slip.

Yet first-line supervisors are frequently judged according to rules and regulations while being limited by other regulations in what disciplinary actions they can take. They often lack the resources to influence or reward people; after all, workers are guaranteed their pay and benefits by someone other than their supervisors. Supervisors cannot easily control events; rather, they must react to them....

It is not surprising, then, that supervisors frequently manifest symptoms of powerlessness: overly close supervision, rules-mindedness, and a tendency to do the job themselves rather than to train their people (since job skills may be one of the few remaining things they feel good about). Perhaps this is why they sometimes stand as roadblocks between their subordinates and the higher reaches of the company.

Staff Professionals

Also working under conditions that can lead to organizational powerlessness are the staff specialists. As advisers behind the scenes, staff people must sell their programs and bargain for resources, but unless they get themselves entrenched in organizational power networks, they have little in the way of favors to exchange. They are seen as useful adjuncts to the primary tasks of the organization but inessential in a day-to-day operating sense. This disenfranchisement occurs particularly when staff jobs consist of easily routinized administrative functions which are out of the mainstream of the currently relevant areas and involve little innovative decision making.

Box 1   WOMEN MANAGERS EXPERIENCE SPECIAL POWER FAILURES

The traditional problems of women in management are illustrative of how formal and informal practices can combine to engender powerlessness. Historically, women in management have found their opportunities in more routine, low-profile jobs. In staff positions, where they serve in support capacities to line managers but have no line responsibilities of their own, or in supervisory jobs managing "stuck" subordinates, they are not in a position either to take the kinds of risks that build credibility or to develop their own team by pushing bright subordinates.

Such jobs, which have few favors to trade, tend to keep women out of the mainstream of the organization. This lack of clout, coupled with the greater difficulty anyone who is "different" has in getting into the information and support networks, has meant that merely by organizational situation women in management have been more likely than men to be rendered structurally powerless. This is one reason those women who have achieved power have often had family connections that put them in the mainstream of the organization's social circles.

A disproportionate number of women managers are found among first-line supervisors or staff professionals; and they, like men in those circumstances, are likely to be organizationally powerless. But the behavior of other managers can contribute to the powerlessness of women in management in a number of less obvious ways.

One way other managers can make a woman powerless is by patronizingly overprotecting her: putting her in "a safe job," not giving her enough to do to prove herself, and not suggesting her for high-risk, visible assignments. This protectiveness is sometimes born of "good" intentions to give her every chance to succeed (why stack the deck against her?). Out of managerial concerns, out of awareness that a woman may be up against situations that men simply do not have to face, some very well-meaning managers protect their female managers ("It's a jungle, so why send her into it?").

Overprotectiveness can also mask a manager's fear of association with a woman should she fail. One senior bank official at a level below vice president told me about his concerns with respect to a high-performing, financially experienced woman reporting to him. Despite *his* overwhelmingly positive work experiences with her, he was still afraid to recommend her for other assignments because he felt it was a personal risk. "What if other managers are not as accepting of women as I am?" he asked. "I know I'd be sticking my neck out; they would take her more because of my endorsement than her qualifications. And what if she doesn't make it? My judgment will be on the line."

Overprotection is relatively benign compared with rendering a person powerless by providing obvious signs of lack of managerial support. For example, allowing someone supposedly in authority to be bypassed easily means that no one else has to take him or her seriously. If a woman's immediate supervisor or other managers listen willingly to criticism of her and show they are concerned every time a negative comment comes up and that they assume she must be at fault, then they are helping to undercut her. If managers let other people know that they have concerns about this person or that they are testing her to see how she does, then they are inviting other people to look for signs of inadequacy or failure.

Furthermore, people assume they can afford to bypass women because they "must be uninformed" or "don't know the ropes." Even though women may be respected for their competence or expertise, they are not necessarily seen as being informed beyond the technical requirements of the job. There may be a grain of historical truth in this. Many women come to senior management positions as "outsiders" rather than up through the usual channels.

Also, because until very recently men have not felt comfortable seeing women as business-people (business clubs have traditionally excluded women), they have tended to seek each other out for informal socializing. Anyone, male or female, seen as organizationally naive and lacking sources of "inside dope" will find his or her own lines of information limited.

Finally, even when women are able to achieve some power on their own, they have not necessarily been able to translate such personal credibility into an organizational power base. To create a network of supporters out of individual clout requires that a person pass on and share power, that subordinates and peers be empowered by virtue of their connection with that person. Traditionally, neither men nor women have seen women as capable of sponsoring others, even though they may be capable of achieving and succeeding on their own. Women have been viewed as the *recipients of sponsorship rather than as the sponsors themselves*. . . .

Continued

| Box 1 | WOMEN MANAGERS EXPERIENCE SPECIAL POWER FAILURES (*CONTINUED*)

Viewing managers in terms of power and powerlessness helps explain two familiar stereo-types about women and leadership in organizations: that no one wants a woman boss (although studies show that anyone who has ever had a woman boss is likely to have had a positive experience), and that the reason no one wants a woman boss is that women are "too controlling, rules-minded, and petty."

The first stereotype simply makes clear that power is important to leadership. Underneath the preference for men is the assumption that, given the current distribution of people in organizational leadership positions, men are more likely than women to be in positions to achieve power and, therefore, to share their power with others. Similarly, the "bossy woman boss" stereotype is a perfect picture of powerlessness. All of those traits are just as characteristic of men who are powerless, but women are slightly more likely, because of circumstances I have mentioned, to find themselves powerless than are men. Women with power in the organization are just as effective—and preferred—as men.

Recent interviews conducted with about 600 bank managers show that, when a woman exhibits the petty traits of powerlessness, people assume that she does so "because she is a woman." A striking difference is that, when a man engages in the same behavior, people assume the behavior is a matter of his own individual style and characteristics and do not conclude that it reflects on the suitability of men for management.

Furthermore, in some organizations, unless they have had previous line experience, staff people tend to be limited in the number of jobs into which they can move. Specialists' ladders are often very short, and professionals are just as likely to get "stuck" in such jobs as people are in less prestigious clerical or factory positions.

Staff people, unlike those who are being groomed for important line positions, may be hired because of a special expertise or particular background. But management rarely pays any attention to developing them into more general organizational resources. Lacking growth prospects themselves and working alone or in very small teams, they are not in a position to develop others or pass on power to them. They miss out on an important way that power can be accumulated....

Staff people tend to act out their powerlessness by becoming turf-minded. They create islands within the organization. They set themselves up as the only ones who can control professional standards and judge their own work. They create sometimes false distinctions between themselves as experts (no one else could possibly do what they do) and lay people, and this continues to keep them out of the mainstream.

One form such distinctions take is a combination of disdain when line managers attempt to act in areas the professionals think are their preserve and of subtle refusal to support the managers' efforts. Or staff groups battle with each other for control of new "problem areas," with the result that no one really handles the issue at all. To cope with their essential powerlessness, staff groups may try to evaluate their own status and draw boundaries between themselves and others.

When staff jobs are treated as final resting places for people who have reached their level of competence in the organization—a good shelf on which to dump managers who are too old to go anywhere but too young to retire—then staff groups can also become pockets of conservatism, resistant to change. Their own exclusion from the risk-taking action may make them resist *anyone's* innovative proposals. In the past, personnel departments, for example, have sometimes been the last in their organization to know about innovations in human resource development or to be interested in applying them.

Top Executives

Despite the great resources and responsibilities concentrated at the top of an organization, leaders can be powerless for reasons that are not very different from those that affect staff and supervisors: lack of supplies, information, and support.

We have faith in leaders because of their ability to make things happen in the larger world, to create possibilities for everyone else, and to attract resources to the organization. These are their supplies. But influence outward—the source of much credibility downward—can diminish as environments change, setting terms and conditions out of the control of the leaders. Regardless of top management's grand plans for the organization, the environment presses. At the very least, things going on outside the organization can deflect a leader's attention and drain energy. And more detrimental, decisions made elsewhere can have severe consequences for the organization and affect top management's sense of power and thus its operating style inside....

As powerlessness in lower levels of organizations can manifest itself in overly routinized jobs where performance measures are oriented to rules and absence of change, so it can at upper levels as well. Routine work often drives out nonroutine work. Accomplishment becomes a question of nailing down details. Short-term results provide immediate gratifications and satisfy stockholders or other constituencies with limited interests.

It takes a powerful leader to be willing to risk short-term deprivations in order to bring about desired long-term outcomes. Much as first-line supervisors are tempted to focus on daily adherence to rules, leaders are tempted to focus on short-term fluctuations and lose sight of long-term objectives. The dynamics of such a situation are self-reinforcing. The more the long-term goals go unattended, the more a leader feels powerless and the greater the scramble to prove that he or she is in control of daily events at least. The more he is involved in the organization as a short-term Mr. Fix-it, the more out of control of long-term objectives he is, and the more ultimately powerless he is likely to be.

Credibility for the top executives often comes from doing the extraordinary: exercising discretion, creating, inventing, planning, and acting in nonroutine ways. But since routine problems look easier and more manageable, require less change and consent on the part of anyone else, and lend themselves to instant solutions that can make any leader look good temporarily, leaders may avoid the risk by taking over what their subordinates should be doing. Ultimately, a leader may succeed in getting all the trivial problems dumped on his or her desk. This can establish expectations even for leaders attempting more challenging tasks. When Warren Bennis was president of the University of Cincinnati, a professor called him when the heat was down in a classroom. In writing about this incident, Bennis commented, "I suppose he expected me to grab a wrench and fix it."[5]

People at the top need to insulate themselves from the routine operations of the organization in order to develop and exercise power. But this very insulation can lead to another source of powerlessness—lack of information. In one multinational corporation, top executives who are sealed off in a large, distant office, flattered and virtually babied by aides, are frustrated by their distance from the real action.[6]

At the top, the concern for secrecy and privacy is mixed with real loneliness. In one bank, organization members were so accustomed to never seeing the top leaders that when a new senior vice president went to the branch offices to look around, they had suspicion, even fear, about his intentions.

Thus leaders who are cut out of an organization's information networks understand neither what is really going on at lower levels nor that their isolation may be having negative effects. All too often top executives design "beneficial" new employee programs or declare a new humanitarian policy (e.g., "Participatory management is now our style") only to find the policy ignored or mistrusted because it is perceived as coming from uncaring bosses.

The information gap has more serious consequences when executives are so insulated from the rest of the organization or from other decision makers that, as Nixon so dramatically did, they fail to see their own impending downfall. Such insulation is partly a matter of organizational position and, in some cases, of executive style.

For example, leaders may create closed inner circles consisting of "doppelgangers," people just like themselves, who are their principal sources of organizational information and tell them only what they want to know. The reasons for the distortions are varied: key aides want to relieve the leader of burdens, they think just like the leader, they want to protect their own positions of power, or the familiar "kill the messenger" syndrome makes people close to top executives reluctant to be the bearers of bad news.

Finally, just as supervisors and lower-level managers need their supporters in order to be and feel powerful, so do top executives. But for them sponsorship may not be so much a matter of individual endorsement as an issue of support by larger sources of legitimacy in the society. For top executives the problem is not to fit in among peers; rather, the question is whether the public at large and other organization members perceive a common interest which they see the executives as promoting....

When common purpose is lost, the system's own politics may reduce the capacity of those at the top to act. Just as managing decline seems to create a much more passive and reactive stance than managing growth, so does mediating among conflicting interests. When what is happening outside and inside their organizations is out of control, many people at the top turn into decline managers and dispute mediators. Neither is a particularly empowering role.

Thus when top executives lose their own lines of supply, lines of information, and lines of support, they too suffer from a kind of powerlessness. The temptation for them then is to pull in every shred of power they can and to decrease the power available to other people to act. Innovation loses out in favor of control. Limits rather than targets are set. Financial goals are met by reducing "overhead" (people) rather than by giving people the tools and discretion to increase their own productive capacity. Dictatorial statements come down from the top, spreading the mentality of powerlessness farther until the whole organization becomes sluggish and people concentrate on protecting what they can....

To Expand Power, Share It

In no case am I saying that people in the three hierarchical levels described are always powerless, but they are susceptible to common conditions that can contribute to powerlessness. Table 3 summarizes the most common symptoms of powerlessness for each level and some typical sources of that behavior....

The absence of ways to prevent individual and social harm causes the polity to feel it must surround people in power with constraints, regulations, and laws that limit the arbitrary use of their authority. But if oppressive power corrupts, then so does the absence of productive power. In large organizations, powerlessness can be a bigger problem than power....

Organizational power can grow, in part, by being shared. We do not yet know enough about new organizational forms to say whether productive power is infinitely expandable or where we reach the point of diminishing returns. But we do know that sharing power is different from giving or throwing it away. Delegation does not mean abdication.

Some basic lessons could be translated from the field of economics to the realm of organizations and management. Capital investment in plants and equipment is not the only key to productivity. The productive capacity of nations, like organizations, grows if the skill base is upgraded. People with the tools, information, and support to make more informed decisions and act more quickly can often accomplish more. By empowering others, a leader does not decrease his power; instead he may increase it—especially if the whole organization performs better....

Also, if the powerless bosses could be encouraged to share some of the power they do have, their power would grow. Yet, of course, only those leaders who feel secure about their own power outward—their lines of supply, information, and support—can see empowering subordinates as a gain rather than as a loss. The two sides of power (getting it and giving it) are closely connected.

TABLE 3 | COMMON SYMPTOMS AND SOURCES OF POWERLESSNESS FOR THREE KEY ORGANIZATIONAL POSITIONS

Position	Symptoms	Sources
First-line supervisors	Close, rules-minded supervision	Routine, rules-minded jobs with little control over lines of supply
	Tendency to do things oneself, blocking of subordinates' development and information	Limited lines of information
	Resistant, underproducing subordinates	Limited advancement or involvement prospects for oneself/subordinates
Staff professionals	Turf protection, information control	Routine tasks seen as peripheral to "real tasks" of line organization
		Retreat into professionalism
		Block careers
	Conservative resistance to change	Easy replacement by outside experts
Top executives	Focus on internal cutting, short-term results, "punishing"	Uncontrollable lines of supply because of environmental changes
	Dictatorial top-down communications	Limited or blocked lines of information about lower levels of organization
	Retreat to comfort of like-minded lieutenants	Diminished lines of support because of challenges to legitimacy (e.g., from the public or special interest groups)

There are important lessons here for both subordinates and those who want to change organizations, whether executives or change agents. Instead of resisting or criticizing a powerless boss, which only increases the boss's feeling of powerlessness and need to control, subordinates instead might concentrate on helping the boss become more powerful. Managers might make pockets of ineffectiveness in the organization more productive not by training or replacing individuals but by structural solutions such as opening supply and support lines.

Similarly, organizational change agents who make a new program or policy to succeed should make sure that the change itself does not render any other level of the organization powerless. In making changes, it is wise to make sure that the key people in the level or two directly above and in neighboring functions are sufficiently involved, informed, and taken into account, so that the program can be used to build their own sense of power also. If such involvement is impossible, then it is better to move these people out of the territory altogether than to leave behind a group from whom some power has been removed and who might resist and undercut the program.

In part, of course, spreading power means educating people to this new definition of it. But words alone will not make the difference; managers will need the real experience of a new way of managing....

Naturally, people need to have power before they can learn to share it. Exhorting managers to change their leadership styles is rarely useful by itself. In one large plant of a major electronics company, first-line production supervisors were the source of numerous complaints from managers who saw them as major roadblocks to overall plant productivity and as insufficiently skilled supervisors. So the plant personnel staff undertook two pilot programs to increase the supervisor's effectiveness. The first program was based on a traditional competency and training model aimed at teaching the specific skills of successful supervisors. The second program, in contrast, was designed to empower the supervisors by directly affecting their flexibility, access to resources, connections with higher-level officials, and control over working conditions....

One might wonder why more organizations do not adopt such empowering strategies. There are standard answers: that giving up control is threatening to people who have fought for every shred of it; that people do not want to share power with those they look down on; that managers fear losing their own place and special privileges in the system; that "predictability" often rates higher than "flexibility" as an organizational value; and so forth.

But I would also put skepticism about employee abilities high on the list. Many modern bureaucratic systems are designed to minimize dependence on individual intelligence by making routine as many decisions as possible. So it often comes as a genuine surprise to top executives that people doing the more routine jobs could, indeed, make sophisticated decisions or use resources entrusted to them in intelligent ways....

NOTES

1. Donald C. Pelz, "Influence: A Key to Effective Leadership in the First-Line Supervisor," *Personnel*, November 1952, p. 209.
2. See my book, *Men and Women of the Corporation* (New York: Basic Books, 1977), pp. 164–205; and David Kipnis, *The Powerholders* (Chicago: University of Chicago Press, 1976).
3. William E. Fulmer, "Supervisory Selection: The Acid Test of Affirmative Action," *Personnel*, November–December 1976, p. 40.
4. See my chapter (coauthor, Barry A. Stein), "Life in the Middle: Getting In, Getting Up, and Getting Along," in *Life in Organizations,* eds. Rosabeth M. Kanter and Barry A. Stein (New York: Basic Books, 1979).
5. Warren Bennis, *The Unconscious Conspiracy: Why Leaders Can't Lead* (New York: AMACOM, 1976).
6. See my chapter, "How the Top Is Different," in *Life in Organizations*.

Reading 35	## Two Faces of the Powerless: *Coping with Tyranny in Organizations*

Robert J. Bies and Thomas M. Tripp

I dread each day coming to work. Once inside the door, I feel "chained" to my desk like a prisoner. My boss is the "prison warden" who delights in "torturing" me with a daily barrage of public criticism and ridicule. I feel so powerless, like a "pawn" being played in one of his power games. My friends ask me why I just don't quit?... Why do I stay and take that abuse? I don't know why... I guess I hope things will change, even though they don't. So I stay... hating him, and hating myself.

—Manager, global telecommunication company

The words persecution, oppression, and tyranny conjure up terrifying images of evil dictators, such as Hitler and Stalin, who employed brutal and ruthless methods to dominate nations and people. Indeed, these words bring to mind the frightening vision of a totalitarian world in which those in power are obsessed with controlling the hearts and minds of people through fear and intimidation (Orwell, 1949).

Although political scientists and sociologists study the dynamics of tyranny (Gilliom, 1997; Scott, 1990), there is little, if any, mention of tyranny in the dominant models of leadership and power (Pfeffer, 1992). As the introductory quotation to this chapter suggests, however, people can and do describe their work experiences in those exact terms (see Shorris, 1981, for additional examples). Moreover, the popular press has provided ample anecdotal evidence of tyranny in organizations in articles on the "intolerable boss" (Lombardo & McCall, 1984), the "unbearable boss" (Goleman, 1986), and the "psycho boss from hell" (Dumaine, 1993). Ironically, these types of bosses, which are celebrated on business magazine covers, are deeply resented and scorned by their employees, who nickname them "Captain Bligh" (Nordhoff & Hall, 1932) and "Captain Queeg" (Wouk, 1951)—names that have become synonymous with tyranny in the workplace.

Although contemporary academics have been silent on tyranny by leaders and those in power, the most important and influential organizational theorist, Max Weber, was not. Weber (1946) worried about the potential for tyranny when he wrote about the concentration of power in the hands of a few masters in bureaucracy, which would imprison humanity in an "iron cage"[1] (p. 228).

In acknowledging the existence of tyranny in the workplace, the important theoretical (and practical) question is raised as to how people cope with tyranny (Bies, 2001). History is filled with inspiring examples of people under the oppression of tyranny who, through creativity and the sheer will to live, have invented coping strategies to maintain their dignity (Scott, 1990) and sustain them in their pursuit of freedom (Havel, 1985).

The purpose of this chapter is threefold. First, we present the results of an empirical study of tyranny in the workplace, thus adding to a much needed empirical foundation for analyzing this phenomenon. In our study, we chose to focus on tyranny as manifested in the "abusive boss." The abusive boss is one whose primary objective is the control of others, and such control is achieved through methods that create fear and intimidation (Hornstein, 1996).

Second, we present data on how people cope with the tyranny of an abusive boss in the workplace. Our study finds evidence of a variety of coping responses, ranging from resignation to resistance. Finally, we explore implications of our findings and conclude with reflections on the academic silence—if not suppression—with respect to the study of tyranny in organizations.

Source: From Power and Influence in Organizations, pp. 203–219. Reprinted by permission of Sage Publications, Inc.

The Abusive Boss: Profiles in Tyranny

In this study, we surveyed working managers about their experiences with the tyranny of abusive bosses. The respondents were participants in an Executive MBA program, a group that included 30 men and 17 women that had an average of 12 years of work experience. In the survey, we asked respondents to think of a specific boss for whom they had worked whom they would label as an abusive boss or a boss from hell. They were asked to describe the boss in as much detail as possible and then to identify how they coped with that boss.

The unit of analysis was the profile or description of the particular boss for whom the respondent had once worked. Respondents described the behaviors and characteristics of the abusive boss and how they coped with the abuse. To ensure accuracy and reliability of the coding process, the same data were coded independently by two raters.

The data suggest that the abusive boss engages in specific behaviors that comprise tyranny.[2] Specifically, the abusive boss displays one or more of the following behaviors: acts as a "micromanager," provides inexplicit direction with decisive delivery, exhibits "mercurial" mood swings, demonstrates an obsession with loyalty and obedience, derogates the status of employees, is capricious, exercises raw power for personal gain, obsesses on gathering personal information about employees, and at times uses coercion to corrupt employees.

Micromanager

In describing the abusive boss as a micromanager, respondents agreed on two key characteristics of a micromanager: an obsession with details and an obsession with perfection.

Obsession with Details. One of the signature features of abusive bosses is that they must have "their hands in everything." One respondent described her boss as follows: "He had to attend every meeting, and then he had to review and sign off on *every* piece of paper produced by the group." Indeed, as another respondent reported,

"No detail was too small for his [boss's] concern or inspection." The obsession with details also causes abusive bosses to want to know every movement and action of employees. For example, one respondent described his boss as "demanding knowledge of everybody's calendars 2 months in advance." Another respondent described her boss as "wanting to know my whereabouts *to the minute*, even when I was in the bathroom."

Obsession with Perfection. In almost "Queeg-like" fashion, our respondents reported the abusive boss has an obsession with perfection. This obsession manifests itself in the setting of unreasonably high performance expectations and, at the same time, being impatient with, and unforgiving of, any mistakes. Also, not surprisingly, it was never the boss's fault for performance failures; blame was always assigned to the subordinates. As one respondent described her boss, "No excuses was his motto." The obsession with perfection was also manifest in the "second-guessing" of employees' actions and decisions. One respondent reported, "No matter what I did, he second-guessed me. He was so pathological that he was even 'second-guessing' his second guesses!"

Inexplicit Direction with Decisive Delivery

The abusive boss created a "double bind" for many respondents because, although they were asked to provide high-quality performance, the abusive boss would never define what "quality" meant. One respondent described his boss as one who demanded quality "with precision in his commands, but precisely what he meant by quality was never clear. What it meant, ultimately, was what we did not do to his satisfaction." In a similar fashion, abusive bosses usually articulate no priorities because "everything is a priority," as one respondent described her boss's motto. As a result, many respondents felt they received "inexplicit direction with decisive delivery."

What further heightened the vagueness of directions was when the boss would send conflicting signals and messages. One method of sending conflicting signals was playing a question "cat-and-mouse" game. In this game, one respondent described her difficulty in reading "my boss's mind and anticipating his every need" because she typically had no clue about the boss's intentions.

Mercurial Mood Swings

Several respondents reported that the abusive boss exhibited volatile mood swings, which were mercurial in nature and often for no apparent reason. One manager reported that his boss had a "Dr. Jekyll and Mr. Hyde" personality. This meant that in one moment the boss could be very calm, peaceful, and satisfied; then, without any warning, the boss would erupt into a loud, angry, temper tantrum, a public tirade directed at one or all employees. Moreover, the intensity of the mood swings did not vary as a function of the seriousness of the triggering event—that is, the tirades were always loud and emotional.

Tirades were not limited to emotional outbursts. Respondents reported tirades that included the destruction of physical property (e.g., throwing telephones at the wall) or threatening, and occasionally even using, physical violence (e.g., shoving an employee). One respondent stated that when "he [the boss] went ballistic, we went for cover."

Obsession with Loyalty and Obedience

Much like a dictator, the abusive boss exhibits an obsession with loyalty and obedience. This obsession manifests itself in punishing those employees who dissented with the boss's viewpoint or position. For example, one manager, who challenged her boss's decision on technical and ethical grounds, received a strong negative performance appraisal, even though her record heretofore had been exemplary.

In another form of punishment, the abusive boss would often stigmatize any dissenter with pejorative labels (e.g., "traitor" and "troublemaker"). As loyal "subjects," employees were expected to humbly submit to and endure the public tirades and other punishments meted out by the boss.

Finally, abusive bosses may also test the loyalty of employees in an almost *1984*-like (Orwell, 1949) fashion by demanding that employees bring gossip and rumors about other employees. Respondents reported of bosses who would use their secretaries as "spies" to ferret out the "disloyal."

Status Derogation

Another signature feature of the abusive boss was the boss's willingness and ability to derogate employees in public. An example, shared by several respondents, is the boss who publicly criticizes the performance and character of an employee, even to the point of ridiculing him or her. Also, on more than one occasion, such actions would "bring men and women to tears," reported one respondent. Another respondent described his boss as the "master of sarcasm" who delighted in "putting people down" in public.

Capricious Actions

The abusive boss is also noted for arbitrariness and hypocrisy. For example, one respondent described how, when the sales group was just about to reach their target for the year (a record level), the boss raised the sales target, without any justification, causing the group to lose their bonus. Indeed, making arbitrary decisions, with no justification, was a common behavior of abusive bosses.

Hypocrisy took the form of employing double standards in dealing with employees. One example of hypocrisy was the boss "who left work early to run personal errands, but chastised me for attempting to do the same," as reported by one respondent. When she brought the hypocrisy to the boss's attention, she was told by the boss to "do as I say not as I do."

Exercises Raw Power for Personal Gain

For several respondents, it was in the use of "raw power" that defined the essence of tyranny. One example of raw power was the boss who "held up my approved job transfer because he wanted me to stay to serve his interests," reported one respondent. Another respondent reported an example of the boss who kept employees waiting for 3 hours into the early morning after their job was completed satisfactorily just because the boss had not finished his job. Raw power also took the form of blatantly stealing credit for a subordinate's idea.

In some cases, raw power took the form of coercion. Two stories illustrate this coercion. First, an employee was told that he had to fire one of his own subordinates, even though that subordinate was a good performer. The boss, however, did not personally like that subordinate and implied that if the employee did not fire his subordinate, it may reflect adversely on his managerial capabilities and limit his future at this company. This employee, being young and recently married with a newborn, submitted and terminated the employee, even though he knew it was wrong.

Second, one boss forced an employee to add a fourth vendor to a competitive bidding process, even though the vendor had failed to meet the requirements. Then, after one of the original three vendors technically won the competition, the employee was told to give it to the fourth vendor, with whom the boss had connections.

The Social Toxins of Tyranny: Poisoning the Mind, Body, and Spirit

In describing abusive bosses, respondents provided us with some insight on how they "experienced" the effects of tyranny. Specifically, they outlined some effects of tyranny in cognitive, affective, and physiological terms. Often, these effects were lingering and interrelated. Furthermore, the effects went beyond mere issues of dissatisfaction and lower productivity; indeed, tyranny was viewed by many of our respondents as a "social toxin," poisoning their professional and personal lives.

Common responses to tyranny were the thoughts and feelings of betrayal, distrust, resentment, frustration, and mental exhaustion. In addition, several respondents reported a variety of physiological reactions to tyranny, including uncontrollable crying, "knots in the stomach," and physical exhaustion.

According to the respondents in our study, the bosses' actions were oriented toward one primary goal—control. Control was achieved through creating fear and intimidation and creating confusion and disorientation. Indeed, several respondents reported feeling "paranoid," and a few reported feeling "terror-stricken" and, at times, "paralyzed." One person reported that "I would stay at my desk and not even go to the bathroom, for the fear, if I was away from my desk, my boss would 'hammer' me in public." Not surprisingly, such people reported feeling vulnerable and powerless because the boss's tyranny had "broken the spirit and willingness to fight back," as described by one respondent.

Responses to Tyranny: Coping Strategies

Our analysis of the data suggests that responses to tyranny can be fruitfully explored in a framework that has two dimensions. The first dimension is the persona or face that we project to the public. The second dimension is the persona or face that we keep private or hidden to ourselves—one that reflects our true beliefs and attitudes.

With respect to the tyrant boss, people can present two faces—one that consents to or agrees with the boss and the other that dissents from or disagrees with the boss. In this framework, then, the public persona may or may not be consistent with the private face, resulting in a two-by-two framework for analysis. Table 1 presents this

TABLE 1 RESPONSES TO TYRANNY	Public Face	
Private Face	Consent	Dissent
Consent	Surrender	Disguise
Dissent	Disguise	Confrontation

framework, and in the following sections we describe the more specific coping strategies as reflected in this framework.

Public Consent, Private Consent: Surrender

For some of our respondents, coping with their tyrant bosses was made "easy" by changing their own private beliefs to be consistent with those of the boss. A few respondents coped by realigning their private beliefs with their boss's beliefs and policies. Such realignment, they reported, resolved the conflict they had with their bosses. In other words, they "surrendered" and "gave up" completely.

Similarly, other respondents reported coping by loyally following orders or by simply accepting the tyranny as social reality. By accepting their "fate," it made the tyranny less oppressive. One respondent described her position as follows: "Once I gave in, and stopped trying to fight it, it became easier."

Public Consent, Private Dissent: Disguise

Several respondents reported that they coped with their tyrannical bosses by only appearing to change their own private beliefs. That is, respondents would publicly espouse their bosses' beliefs and support the bosses' policies but privately vehemently disagree with their bosses' beliefs and policies. In other words, our respondents reported disguising their true feelings by presenting a public face that was quite different than their private beliefs.

The acts of disguise can take a variety of forms, according to our respondents. One common form of disguise is in how people "manage" their bosses. For many respondents, efforts to better manage their bosses included keeping their bosses informed of all details, better preparing for meetings with their bosses, and better determining their bosses' needs and goals. Respondents also reported that they mirrored their bosses' working styles to avoid criticisms of their own work styles.

Managing the boss also included the strategic use of information. For example, one respondent reported how he "told the boss just enough information to avoid trouble, and reported successes, not failures." Most respondents noted that they managed their relationships with their bosses not because they liked their bosses but because they viewed it as "a personally effective survival strategy," as one respondent reported. They did not believe it was in their own best interests to make their bosses aware of the depth of their disaffection, so they hid their true feelings and tried to work with their bosses.

A second form of disguise involved keeping a "low profile." This meant "offering no challenges or criticisms," in the words of one respondent. Other respondents kept a low profile by minimizing contact with their bosses—an "evade and avoid" strategy. While keeping a low profile, respondents also secretly documented their bosses mistakes and transgressions, predicting that such documentation might become beneficial in the future.

A third form of disguise occurred in one's head. For example, many respondents highlighted the value of "revenge fantasies" in which they dreamed of getting even with their bosses, but they projected the public face of "getting along" with the bosses. Relying on revenge fantasies was viewed by one respondent as a "mental survival" strategy. Another respondent described his perspective as follows: "While he plays his mind games with me, I play my own mind games."

As another enactment of disguise, some respondents acted out their revenge fantasies, but in ways that could not be recognized as getting even or as any kind of challenge. For example, some respondents reported withholding support from their bosses at critical times, resulting in failures for the bosses. Others reported following all orders, no matter how stupid some orders might be. Also, with those bosses who were obsessed with details and information, some respondents would deliberately feed their bosses so much information as to overload them while appearing as "dutiful subordinates keeping the boss informed," as one respondent stated.

A fifth form of disguise was "carnival" techniques. By carnival, respondents meant a festive gathering held at the boss's expense but without the boss knowing. For example, in small private gatherings, employees would demonize their bosses—that is, vent their frustrations, assign blame, call the bosses names (e.g., "Beelzebub"), and generally bad-mouth their bosses. In one case, subordinates used humor to ridicule their boss by holding an initiation ceremony for a new employee who had just had his first abusive encounter with the boss.

Finally, some respondents reported creating "refuges" from the boss for other subordinates. These people acted as buffers between the boss and the other subordinates. The buffer worked in two directions: It shielded the subordinates from the boss's tantrums and confusing edicts and shielded the boss from the subordinates' dissent.

Public Dissent, Private Dissent: Confrontation

More than a few respondents reported engaging in confrontation in which they openly challenged their bosses. Some would directly confront their bosses, challenging them on their decisions in an open, public forum. Others would take the public challenge even further by openly ridiculing the boss. In a few cases, public challenges involved acts of insubordination, such as making decisions without the boss's knowledge or approval.

Confrontation also took the form of going around the boss to deal with the boss. Examples of such an "end-runs" around the boss included talking to the boss's boss, involving a third party such as a representative from human resources or legal departments, and consulting a lawyer. As part of these strategies, any private documentation of the boss's actions was brought to public light.

A final act of confrontation involved exiting the situation. Exit took the form of quitting or leaving the organization but with "a little panache" in the words of one respondent. For example, one respondent stated that her exit was done with a "blaze of glory, distributing e-mail and hard copy documentation with a list of her boss's crimes."

Public Dissent, Private Consent: Disguise

Our data did not reveal any direct evidence of this form of disguised behavior. Indirect evidence, however, was provided by a few respondents in their examples of secretaries and other employees acting as spies for the boss. In this role of the "mole" for the boss, secretaries would express their public disaffection with the boss as a means of disarming other employees to become more forthcoming about their true negative feelings about the boss. This intelligence gathered by the spies was then fed back to the boss.

Beyond the Data: Impressions and Implications

In interpreting these data, some interesting, albeit preliminary, conclusions emerge. First, even though our sample is small, leading us to be reasonably tentative, the findings are strikingly similar to descriptions made by other researchers, such as Hornstein (1996) and Ashforth (1994). They identified dimensions to describe tyranny in organizations similar to those found in our study (e.g., micromanagers, obsession with protection, and exercise of raw power). This convergence with the findings of other researchers suggests that we are capturing the essence and dynamics of tyranny in organizations, particularly in the form of the abusive boss.

Second, our data shed additional light on the dark side of power and politics in organizations. Abuse does not take its toll in only economic terms; it also has a toxic effect and impact on the human lives of people who work in organizations. Any complete analysis of power can not only focus on its functional rationality in achieving organizational goals and objectives but also must account for the dysfunctional and irrational consequences of its use.

What distinguishes our research from the work of Hornstein (1996) and Ashforth (1994) is the identification of a broader range of coping strategies. The most intriguing finding to us was people's rather extensive use of disguise and, in particular, the use of carnival techniques.

Although this "two-faced" approach can be difficult because employees are "living within a lie" (Havel, 1985), our respondents reported that the use of disguise can, in fact, be a rational and functional coping strategy. It is functional because it protects them to some extent from the unbridled wrath of a tyrant bent on harming those who disagree or dislike the tyrant. In addition, it is functional because it provides the employee with some measure of control and efficacy with respect to his or her environment (Bies & Tripp, 1996, 1998; Tripp & Bies, 1997).

In particular, two aspects of the use of disguise proved especially interesting to us. First, respondents reported that through their acts of disguise they led the tyrant bosses to believe that they have a more supportive and submissive group of employees than was actually true. In other words, bosses, based on their observations of the employees' loyal and obedient behavior, made inferences that led to a false consciousness and a false consensus as to the level of affection or disaffection with their leadership (Nord & Doherty, 1994). In that sense, duplicity was central to managing conflict.

Indeed, in our data, there is clear evidence of a rich "underground" in organizations. In this underground world, people share common experiences and provide social support in a rich, liturgical fashion. They often engage in party-like social gatherings with initiation rites and storytelling. The evidence of this underground is strikingly similar to that found in research on how citizens cope with repressive political regimes (Scott, 1990) and quite consistent with evidence of the "everyday resistance" by those under the scrutiny of surveillance and regulation (Gilliom, 1997).

Beyond the Sounds of Silence: The Study of Tyranny in Organizations

An emerging body of research on tyranny and its consequences leads us to ask the following question: Why are our organization and management theories so silent on the abuse of power by leaders?

A likely answer to the question is found in the prevailing ideological assumptions of organization and management theory—the organizational imperative (Scott & Hart, 1979). The organizational imperative is based on a primary and absolute proposition, "Whatever is good for the individual can only come from the modern organization" (p. 43), and the related secondary proposition, "Therefore, *all behavior must enhance the health of such organizations* (italics added)" (p. 43). The ideology of the organizational imperative has resulted in "blinding" people from "seeing" tyranny and its consequences (Bies & Tripp, 1998; Treviño & Bies, 1997). As the empirical evidence continues to grow, however, ignoring or failing to see tyranny will become harder to do. Thus, the "defenders" of the ideology will be faced with the task of inventing new responses to legitimate the ideology.

One likely response will be "reframing" the methods and consequences of tyranny. That is, while acknowledging tyranny, it will be argued that although such methods may be harsh or even cruel, they are absolutely necessary and essential for creating high-performance organizations. In other words, the survival of the organization demands tyranny!

A second possible response will be to shift the focus away from the tyrant and the agents of tyranny and to highlight—and "condemn"—the actions of those who fight back against oppression in the workplace.

This move to "blaming the victim" also results in a biased punctuation of the research problem because the focus will not be on the situational events or organizational practices that can precipitate, or even justify, a victim's response to harm and wrongdoing (Bies & Tripp, 1996, 1998; McLean Parks, 1997; Tripp & Bies, 1997). This biased punctuation of the problem should not be surprising because it follows from the ideology of the organizational imperative that any response to tyranny that attacks the interest of the organization—as articulated by its leaders—is by definition "wrong," "bad," and "deviant" (Robinson & Bennett, 1995).

For those theorists and researchers who have the courage to study tyranny—let alone speak out against it—your role will be that of a social critic: on the margin, not in the mainstream, motivated by what Beaney (1966) calls "a never-ending quest to increase the respect of all ... for the essential values of human life" (p. 271). The choice to join this quest is yours. It always has been.

REFERENCES

Alinsky, S. D. (1971). *Rules for radicals: A pragmatic primer for realistic radicals*. New York: Random House.

Ashforth, B. (1994). Petty tyranny in organizations. *Human Relations, 47,* 755–778.

Barley, S. R., & Kunda, G. (1992). Design and devotion: Surges of rational and normative ideologies of control in managerial discourse. *Administrative Science Quarterly, 37,* 363–399.

Beaney, W. M. (1966). The right to privacy and American law. *Law and Contemporary Problems, 31,* 253–271.

Bies, R. J. (2001). Interactional (in)justice: The sacred and the profane. In J. Greenberg & R. Cropanzano (Eds.), *Advances in organizational justice*. Stanford, Calif.: Stanford University Press.

Bies, R. J., & Tripp, T. M. (1995). The use and abuse of power: Justice as social control. In R. Cropanzano & M. Kacmar (Eds.), *Organizational politics, justice, and support: Managing social climate at work* (pp. 131–145). New York: Quorum.

Bies, R. J., & Tripp, T. M. (1996). Beyond distrust: "Getting even" and the need for revenge. In R. M. Kramer & T. Tyler (Eds.), *Trust in organizations* (pp. 246–260). Thousand Oaks, CA: Sage.

Bies, R. J., & Tripp, T. M. (1998). Revenge in organizations: The good, the bad, and the ugly. In R. W. Griffin, A. O'Leary Kelly, & J. Collins (Eds.), *Dysfunctional behavior in organizations, Vol. 1: Violent behaviors in organizations*. Greenwich, CT: JAI.

Dumaine, B. (1993, October 18). America's toughest bosses. *Fortune,* 39–50.

Gilliom, J. (1997). Everyday surveillance, everyday resistance: Computer monitoring in the lives of the Appalachian poor. In A. Sarat & S. S. Silbey (Eds.), *Studies in law, politics, and society* (Vol. 16, pp. 275–297). Greenwich, CT: JAI.

Glaser, B. G., & Strauss, A. L. (1967). *The discovery of grounded theory: Strategies for qualitative research*. New York: Aldine.

Goleman, D. (1986, December 28). When the boss is unbearable. *New York Times,* Section 3, pp. 1, 29.

Handler, J. F. (1992). Postmodernism, protest, and the new social movements. *Law and Society Review, 26,* 697–732.

Hatch, M. J. (1997). *Organization theory: Modern, symbolic, and postmodern perspectives*. Oxford, UK: Oxford University Press.

Havel, V. (1985). The power of the power less. In J. Keane (Ed.), *The power of the power less: Citizens against the state in central-eastern Europe*. Armonk, NY: M. E. Sharpe.

Hornstein, H. A. (1996). *Brutal bosses and their prey*. New York: Riverhead Books.

Lombardo, M. M., & McCall, M. W., Jr. (1984, January). The intolerable boss. *Psychology Today,* pp. 44–48.

McLean Parks, J. (1997). The fourth arm of justice: The art and science of revenge. In R. J. Lewicki, R. J. Bies, & B. H. Sheppard (Eds.), *Research on negotiation in organizations* (Vol. 6, pp. 113–144). Greenwich, CT: JAI.

Miller, D. E., Weiland, M. W., & Couch, C. J. (1978). Tyranny. In N. Denzin (Ed.), *Studies in symbolic interaction* (Vol. 1, pp. 267–288). Greenwich, CT: JAI.

Nord, W. R., & Doherty, E. M. (1994). Toward an improved framework for conceptualizing the conflict process. In R. J. Lewicki, B. H. Sheppard, & R. J. Bies (Eds.), *Research on negotiation in organizations* (pp. 173–240). Greenwich, CT: JAI.

Nordhoff, C., & Hall, J. N. (1932). *Mutiny on the bounty*. Boston: Little, Brown.

Orwell, G. (1949). *1984*. New York: Harcourt Brace.

Pfeffer, J. (1992). *Managing with power*. Cambridge, MA: Harvard Business School Press.

Robinson, S. L., & Bennett, R. J. (1995). A typology of deviant work place behaviors: A multidimensional scaling study. *Academy of Management Journal, 38,* 555–572.

Scott, J. C. (1990). *Domination and the arts of resistance*. New Haven, CT: Yale University Press.

Scott, W. G., & Hart, D. K. (1971). The moral nature of man in organizations: A comparative analysis. *Academy of Management Journal, 14,* 255.

Scott, W. G., & Hart, D. K. (1979). *Organizational America: Can individual freedom survive within the security it promises?* Boston: Houghton Mifflin.

Shorris, E. (1981). *The oppressed middle: Politics of middle management (scenes from corporate life).* Garden City, NY: Anchor/Doubleday.

Treviño, L. K., & Bies, R. J. (1997). Through the looking glass: A normative manifest of organizational behavior. In C. L. Cooper & S. E. Jackson (Eds.), *Creating tomorrow's organizations: A handbook for future research in organizational behavior* (pp. 439–452). London: Wiley.

Tripp, T. M., & Bies, R. J. (1997). What's good about revenge? The avenger's perspective. In R. J. Lewicki, R. J. Bies, & B. H. Sheppard (Eds.), *Research on negotiation in organizations* (Vol. 6, pp. 145–160). Greenwich, CT: JAI.

Weber, M. (1946). *From Max Weber: Essays in sociology* (H. H. Gerth & C. W. Mills, Eds.). New York: Oxford University Press.

Wouk, H. (1951). *The Caine mutiny.* Garden City, New York: Doubleday.

NOTES

1. We thank Mayer Zald for this reference.
2. We do not suggest that abusive bosses do not possess other qualities that assist them in accomplishing tasks. Just because an abusive boss may be "effective" on some performance indicators, however, it does not follow that his or her behavior is any less abusive, nor does the boss's success mitigate judgments about his or her abusive behavior.

Women and Power

Janet O. Hagberg

Power is a women's issue, whether we like it or not. We are in transition and therefore confused as to what we will become. Women are the poorest of the poor in our country and, at the same time, are increasingly taking their places in the ranks of the wealthy and ruling classes. And there are thousands in between. Women have awakened and now are stretching.

Traditionally, women often experience a new burst of energy, a second life in their forties or fifties, generally after children are launched. A forty-year-old former homemaker and community activist, now an association executive, told me that she feels like she's twenty-five in terms of her work, just launching into her second career. Full-time career women may feel that their lives are a strange concoction, including some characteristics of women's traditional patterns and some characteristics of men's patterns, as described in Levinson's (1979) classic study, *Seasons of a Man's Life*. He describes much more predictable stages in men's lives based on longitudinal studies of many men.

My own observation has shown that for working women, age thirty-five (plus or minus two) is an important decision-making time or a turning point. At thirty-five, women feel more compelled to pursue marriage or let it go, to decide whether to have more or any children. Careers have been or can still be launched and the commitment to career becomes more conscious. What was just a job is now a career. When women decide what they want out of life, they then begin to take themselves more seriously and to invest in themselves. They realize that there is a wider variety of possibilities for them. That is the point at which the personal power model takes on the most significance. And that's where the frustration and potential excitement begin.

The Paradox for Women

In a provocative and timeless book entitled *Reinventing Womanhood*, Carolyn Heilbrun (1973) writes that women's movements have failed to maintain momentum in their achievements because of three factors:

1. The failure of women to bond.
2. The failure of women to imagine themselves as autonomous.
3. The failure of achieving women to resist... entering the male mainstream, thus becoming honorary men.

I interpret Heilbrun to mean by "bonding" that women don't stick together as closely as men do. There is an analogy that may fit here, derived from an old tradition on the east coast. It seems that crab pails do not have to be covered to prevent the crabs from escaping because when one of the crabs reaches the top of the pail, the others pull it back down in their attempts to escape too. This analogy fits some women. Another reason may be that women see the resources as limited (money, jobs, manager's time) and want to get their share, like children wanting attention from mother but knowing it has to be divided among others. It may also be related to some of our messages that the only people worth bonding with are men. Men, we were told, will help us out if we are coy and seductive. Women can be closer, more intimate friends with each other than most men can be, but we were led to believe that true intimacy is sexual, and that is reserved generally for men. Sexual intimacy as a bonding force has not held up very well, so there is even more confusion about whom we can trust. Women need to feel good about being women. They need to see other women as allies and partners. We need all the help we can get and we must not be divided against each other if we are to make continuing progress.

Heilbrun's second point, of women not being able to see themselves as autonomous, seems like a paradox. We cannot bond together and we cannot stand alone. We have been taught that we need to rely on, even live through, a man. If we stand alone we are either seen as so self-sufficient that we could not find anyone, or we are undesirable.

Women need to learn how to be autonomous, to practice the art of being alone and self-sufficient within a community of friends, family, and coworkers. This could include making financial decisions, traveling alone, having a private room of one's own, living alone, running a business, leading an organization, or having one's own name. It means keeping part of you as an individual identity, no matter what your life circumstances are, yet doing so in a context of community. Once a woman has learned to be autonomous, both her work relationships and her intimate relationships are usually healthier.

Thirdly, Heilbrun says achieving women cannot resist becoming honorary men by entering the male mainstream. She sees these women as dependent on men professionally, not supportive of other women, seeking social status through men, being feminine but giving up womanhood. We call them Queen Bees. I see a new breed of achieving women—those who have perhaps gone one step further. They have risen in organizations with all the right degrees and moves, and they think that the way to get ahead is to play the games and compete just like the "boys" do. They sacrifice their feminine side and act like men, especially in language and behavior with colleagues. It may, in fact, work for a while and bring the same rewards that men seem to be getting—money, status, success, position, control. But sooner or later the word gets out. The behavior she thought would buy acceptance is now labeled aggressive. She's called a tigress, a "tough broad," and, worst of all, a bitch or a castrating female. The pendulum has swung too far, and she is losing out because she is understandably out of her element and not being herself.

The catch-22 here is that she is once again dependent on men—their style, their dress, their games, their acceptance—to provide her with the self-esteem that she can get only from being herself. And the result is anger at herself, anger at others, and anger at men for deceiving her into thinking it would work. I am not suggesting that women not take on their masculine side. On the

contrary. It is wonderful, even exhilarating, to be strong and to have a mature ego. It is inspiring to be considered knowledgeable and competent. We've been waiting for this for a long time. We are treated more equally than ever before. But we must not let the pendulum swing too far for too long. Women can be strong, self-sufficient, analytic, decisive, and still be women who love, care, nurture, and feel. A woman gubernatorial candidate stated that women can be loving and tough, can wield power and have a gentle touch. Women can be good wives, mothers, and sisters and still ask for positions on boards and ballots without a contradiction.

Women need to move to the position of being themselves, at once masculine and feminine and individual. They need to ask the broader and deeper questions like "What are my real spiritual longings? What would make me whole? What do I really want out of life and work? How can I be respected and competent and still be true to myself?" It involves finding out who you are rather than who you thought you should be in order to get ahead or prove yourself. It is more authentic and successful in the long run.

Masculine-Feminine

I've been alluding to masculine-feminine dichotomies in this chapter. It's time to discuss more fully what I mean by this language, since it is useful as well as irritating at times. Women (including myself) can easily slip into the male versus female debate, asking which system is better. Some suggest that if the predominant system were only female, things would be better for everyone. I think that is much too simple and perhaps even naive. Organizations are less than effective whenever any one system dominates, because the whole picture is not represented.

We get into difficulty when we categorize all men like "this" and all women like "that," because all men and women are not like all other men and women. Both masculinity and femininity have negative as well as positive aspects. So how do we work this out and find ways to work together amidst all this confusion?

One answer to the confusion is for both men and women to develop the ability to use either masculine or feminine behavior depending on what is the most appropriate for the situation. This concept of behavior flexibility is described by the term "androgyny." Androgyny is the harmonious coexistence of masculinity and femininity within the same individual (June Singer, Jungian analyst). Men and women always have been and always will be different. I applaud that. What I will call flexibility means that men can be masculine, and at appropriate times can draw upon their feminine behavior; it also means women can be feminine, and at appropriate times draw upon their masculine behavior. This is obviously ideal behavior I am suggesting, for none of us would ever be totally balanced. But it gives greater ranges of behavior for those who want that. In organizations and families, flexible (androgynous) people use all their emotions; they can nurture others, make tough decisions, use their intuition, disagree openly, do kind things for others, and be strong. The key is that they know what the appropriate behavior is for the given situation and they use it. It means men can cry and women can shout. And it means crying may not necessarily be seen as reflecting weakness but as evincing feeling and wisdom. And shouting may not be seen as evidence of aggressiveness but as rising to the occasion.

I am concerned that the management and leadership potential in women will be stifled if they are not able to achieve this balance and if men do not appreciate it in themselves. Effective management theory can support a flexible way of relating without sacrificing the bottom line. Some people feel that women in organizations have a greater capacity for interdependence than men do. It is threatening for men to exchange dependencies because it goes against the culture, threatens sex role differences, is seen as a sexual come-on or an invitation to take care of women. Women's most important contribution may be to role model the forms of interdependence that some men need to learn. Research shows that having people of color and women in organizations makes for better-managed companies.

I firmly believe that women will be a key factor in helping to move organizational leadership to Stage Five (Power by Purpose). But in order to do that, women will have to stay in the system without becoming honorary men and they will need support from men to do that. Men will have to be willing to learn from, as well as teach, women. They will both have to help the management and organizational norms change slowly from within to bring about flexibility, a use of both masculine and feminine, without losing either.

Betty Friedan (1981) summed up our challenge forcefully in an excerpt from her classic book *Second Stage*. It holds true equally well today as it did over two decades ago. "We have to break through our own feminist mystique now and move into the second stage—no longer against, but with men.... We have to free ourselves from male power traps, understand the limits of women's power as a separate interest group and grasp the possibility of generating a new kind of power, which was the real promise for the women's movement."

Emerging Women

Three groups of women are rapidly emerging in our society, who I think will be very involved in different ways in the leadership and power issues of the next decade.

Ambitious Career Women: Dropping Out

The first group consists of those ambitious career women who were born in the period from the mid-thirties to the mid-sixties, who are between the old and the new worlds of women in organizations and who are not living the traditional homemaker lifestyle. A friend of mine described them as being "on the seam" between the old and the new. They have had more options than their mothers in education and opportunity and they grew up as the forerunners of today's opportunities. They were the "front line" in a lot of ways. They were super achievers and are quite successful in their careers—sometimes even more successful (position, salary) than their husbands. They are strong, independent, educated, goal-directed, determined, self-confident, and career-oriented. Many of these women are single or married with no children. They simply do not have strong domestic ties. Now many of these women are once again forging new territory as senior activists.

Another part of this group has decided to work and raise children—and achieve superwoman status all the way around. This puts enormous pressures on them both at home and work, and they feel they can opt out of neither. If this were ten years hence, they might hire live-in help, but being on the seam means they want the old and new at once and at the same level. They don't want to give up their career success and they don't want to change their view of what a good wife and mother should be—so they have more guilt to deal with. None of us has the energy or stamina to carry both roles at a super level and surely not the amount these women need in order to once again lead the way by creating options that will relieve the pressure on them. This may be the time for men to do more than ponder their role as parent, to take action in a more concrete way (as many have), to really share the childrearing and homemaking. Lack of action on the part of men may lead to burned out women.

A somewhat alarming option for many professional women who have had children in their mid or late thirties is to leave their organizations altogether. I understand why this occurs, because several women have told me that some organizations will not bend an inch to accommodate family responsibilities and neither will some spouses. It is sad that these women feel this is their only option at this point and it would not be their choice. Thousands of other professional women are voluntarily dropping out or dropping back for reasons unrelated to children. And it is not totally related to the glass ceiling either, at least not for the women to whom I have spoken. It has more to do with an inner gnawing that

comes at odd times asking the question "Is this all there is?" These are highly successful women who leave or somehow even sabotage themselves so they can get time to sort out their lives, find more balance, and live out their deeper values.

It's yet unclear exactly when or where they will reemerge—but believe me, they will. Many of them are taking the descending journey into their own shadows and finding their strength at the bottom of the well. They are developing themselves as more profound leaders. They are connecting with women in poverty and women on the fringe to forge new communities. They are developing courage. And as a result, they will transform glass ceilings into blue sky, releasing themselves and their leadership from the constraints they knew.

These women will be the leaders who become the wisdom figures of our era. They will help us rethink what success is and how to live it out. They will revive our hope for the future. They will lead us in this new millennium in a peaceful and healing way.

Young Pacesetters

The second group of women emerging these days consists of the young pacesetters in their twenties and thirties, who have all the qualities of the older pacesetters except that they are not on the seam. They have not had to fight for what they want (yet), nor do they feel much discrimination. They simply do not have the history of their older female colleagues. All education and graduate programs are open to them, and their male peers are more like brothers than potential spouses. They make a better starting salary than many women who have been working ten years. They have almost no conception of what it's like to be poor or displaced or dependent or rebuffed by society. They are starting out, in fact, more even with men for the first time in history—capable, intelligent, educated, determined, motivated, and knowing no bounds.

But do they identify with other women? And what will happen to them in the next decade as they watch their older female colleagues achieve, have children later, and drop out? Will they become more balanced, more flexible, and more feminine? Or will they take the male world on and become honorary men? I think the saving grace for these women will be that which is inherent in most, if not all, women: the need for balance and for loving, caring relationships. Many of these women will face, sooner or later, the idea that life is too short to be successful if it means being lonely. Another saving grace is this: these women are motivated more by self-actualization and income than by traditional forms of power. So people at higher stages should be able to influence them by modeling androgynous behavior.

Women in Poverty

The third group consists of the growing number of women in our society who are in poverty. In fact, some writers now call poverty a female issue. These women in poverty are usually single heads of households, uneducated, and unskilled. They are discontented and lack self-esteem, feeling trapped by the system in which they once believed. They are in a vicious circle, not knowing how to break out. At the same time, they shrink back from responsibility even when given it, perhaps because they don't believe anything will change. The concern I have is that the first two groups are moving far out of touch with the third group. In the past more women could identify with "women's issues." Now it seems there are distinctly different issues for different groups of women; there is some danger that women leaders may increasingly become the enemy.

Unless high-achieving women stay connected to women on the fringes they will lose the essence of what it means to be women and leaders. They will lose touch with the poverty within themselves and grow calloused. We as women need to experience a new idea of community for women—a community without walls—in which women on the fringes are our mentors. Only then can we say no to poverty and victimization, in ourselves and in the culture.

Critical Issues

In summary, the critical issues I see for women in this new era are:

1. Staying true to their inner selves, no matter what their age.
2. Finding the courage to face their inner secrets and demons.
3. Finding and claiming the strengths of female community across artificial boundaries.
4. Developing leadership.
5. Saying no to victimization and poverty, in themselves and in the culture.

Women and the Power Model in Organizations

In an over-simplified summary, the power model operates in the following manner for women:

Stage One—Powerlessness

Women at this stage are powerless and dependent on others (some women, but mostly men) for almost everything, even though many of them live alone or with children. Men are our bosses, our teachers, our partners, even our knights in shining armor. We can feel secure as a result but we can also feel like children. Some of us, in fact, don't like ourselves and may even allow ourselves to be used, physically, emotionally, or intellectually, in order to obtain love or attention. To move to the next stage, we need to learn who we are, what we can do, what our worth is, and get support for ourselves, preferably from other women. This may be the hardest stage for women to break out of because of the cultural pressures on us to depend on and wait for others.

Stage Two—Power by Association

We learn that we are individuals and that we have skills and abilities. We look to role models or mentors (bosses or others) whom we can work for or emulate. We get to know the culture of the organization that sometimes frightens us and at other times gives us energy and exhilaration. We are striving for the credentials that will make us acceptable to others. We make mistakes. But we need to learn, especially from our mistakes.

To move to the next stage, we need to take more responsibility for ourselves, volunteer for assignments, go out on a limb, push ourselves, get degrees or credentials, set goals, take risks. At the end of this stage, we need to take on the masculine side of ourselves, those behaviors that may not come naturally and that may make us uncomfortable. This is a major turning point for women and difficult to do. Movement out of Stage Two doesn't have to entail a promotion in the organization. Much development can occur inside of us as a result of our involvement in the community or in professional associations.

Stage Three—Power by Achievement

This is our most uncomfortable stage but it can be highly rewarding. Our egos are developing and we can stand on our own, make good and tough decisions, and be independent. We enter the masculine side of ourselves, requiring us to be more responsible, competitive, and energetic. The rewards are alluring—money, success, prestige, and moving up. If we buy in totally, we lose our womanhood. If we don't buy in at all, we're not accepted or respected. We can become bitter and discouraged and drop out, or we can recognize and understand Stage Three as potentially fun but certainly temporary and ultimately a necessary experience in order to move to the future stages. We need to be in Stage Three but not of Stage Three. We can get support from others who understand, avoid getting trapped in games, ask a lot of good questions, take our bumps in stride, not resort to tantrums, and be straight and clear about our feelings. To move we need to become more reflective about who we are and what it is we truly want. Can we be more our real selves now within the organization?

We need to learn more about the scope of the organization and be clear about our strengths and limitations, fitting into that scope, not trying to do everything and burning ourselves out in our prime. Third, we need to stay closely connected to supportive women and men at all levels, those who are below us in the organization, those who are our peers, and those who are our role models and mentors. It is important to maintain contact with other women, because at this stage we can too easily believe we can do it alone or that we do not need the feminine. We need to gain visibility, but within our own areas of strength. One way to do this is to get involved more widely in the organization on committees or projects, always doing a very competent job.

Stage Four—Power by Reflection

At this stage we can increasingly take on our own personal style because we have proven that we understand but do not necessarily always play the game. We can take more risks and broaden our activities in the organization and in the community because we have a base of support. We're trusted, perhaps because we trust ourselves. And we trust others, delegating much to them or sharing with them. We are finding our sense of integrity, what we truly stand for as opposed to what others want us to be. We should avoid becoming haughty, self-sufficient people who think we've made it. This could be a hollow victory if abrupt changes occur in the management of the organization. Collaboration is even more important to develop now so we don't get caught in tricky Stage Three games. Our confidence should be much broader in the organization now as well because we have wider spheres of influence. Most important, we need to remember that our energy no longer goes toward our own personal gain, but toward helping others to gain what they need. Our focus must shift, or we will get stuck in reflection at Stage Four.

To move we need to reaffirm the feminine in us, our true nature as women, no matter where we are in the organization—manager, secretary, supervisor, director, clerk, engineer, president, or chair of the board. We are beginning to take on the other form of power, power for others. We need to be reflective, to assess our deepest values, to look at larger visions, to take a deep breath, to experience the Wall, and possibly observe a whole new world for ourselves. We need to let go. . . .

The Wall

The Wall is a profound place for women. They must go deep inside and let the pain and healing occur in order for the Wall experience to be a growing experience for them. Sometimes the Wall is triggered by deep disappointment at work, but more often it is triggered by a loss of relationship, by a loss of connection, or the loss of a dream. It feels like a rupture in one's soul. Women do well to get a mentor, counselor, or spiritual guide while struggling in the Wall, since the true nature of who women are in the world is forged in this dark place.

In the Wall we find out what we are really afraid of, what we ignore, and what we regret. It is not an easy path but one that is necessary to our future vitality and our compassion for others. And courage is often the result of a Wall experience that connects women not only with their pain but with their deepest heart's desire.

Great leadership is forged in the Wall.

Stage Five—Power by Purpose

Stage Five women are in the most comfortable stage of all for them, although it is decidedly less secure than Stage One. We are able to channel energy to others in the organization, give things away, delegate more, be role models for men, but only as we fully accept ourselves and the struggles we face in organizations that reward Twos, Threes, and Fours. We will feel at home and free ourselves but out of sync with many other people. They may misread our motivations. We know our life calling, our inner aims and goals. And these things go beyond us, our egos, our reputations, and the organization. But particularly, our thinking goes beyond our egos. We draw our strength from a source beyond ourselves. Stage Five women do not calculate where a decision will get them but how it will affect others and whether it is the best for all in the long run. In fact, they involve a lot of others in their decisions,

teaching and learning as they go. We trust our judgment, and we are not aroused by promises of money, titles, or power plays; or threats of losing these things. We are part of a much larger life plan in which our work efforts now take their proper part. We involve ourselves in the larger world, in visions for the organization or professional groups. We mentor men, we nurture others, without knowing where it will lead, and without having to. We may have gotten pretty far in the organizational sense, or we may not have, but we like ourselves and accept ourselves. And we enjoy respect from others for our competence and integrity. To move we need to relax.

Stage Six—Power by Wisdom

Stage Six is a wonder to behold in women. We are personally purposeful, but in a quiet sort of way, integrated and calm because life is best when we try the least. We have internal calm and external respect based on the painful and joyous experiences of life that have formed us. We see paradox and we love it because we know too much to believe otherwise. We have nothing to prove, no one to impress, and our community is the world. We care not for titles or even for glory. We're victorious because we're human and can fully admit it. Our behavior is truly our own and the masculine-feminine dichotomies seem to have slipped away somewhere a long way back. We say what we think, and it is usually wise because we are not trying to be wise anymore. We are at peace with ourselves. We may believe strongly in causes or questions or ideas and work valiantly for them but our identity is not tied up in the ends, only the means. No one fights us for control because we have voluntarily given up control to others and our need for self-control long ago. Now we just are. To move, we need to enter into another level of reality.

Women and Leadership

Many women are natural leaders. We just don't think we are because we don't tend to lead in the traditional Stage Three ways that are so accepted.

So we lack confidence in our ability to guide others, particularly men. Women can learn much from men about leadership at Stage Three but, to go beyond it to true leadership, they must learn from each other, from themselves, and from the few role models, both male and female, who are at those higher stages. The worst thing women could do is to accept a lesser model of leadership that is evident in many people today. Women, being less constricted by roles and expectations at this point in time, have the potential to go beyond the familiar territory, to be models for others of the way true leaders (Stage Four and beyond) behave. It will be challenging but also frustrating.

Women in organizations are beginning to come together to discuss among themselves what power and leadership mean in their organizations. This is a wonderful first step in breaking down the barriers that separate women from each other and encourage competition.

I strongly encourage women to meet together, preferably with some higher stage women present, to discuss their own feelings about leadership honestly and sincerely and to discourage women from getting stuck as honorary men in organizations. The future leadership of America is being formed through the values and behaviors that are being learned right now; if women are the hope for a different kind of leadership, they must begin to develop further now.

REFERENCES

Friedan, Betty. *Second stage*. New York: Summit Books, 1981.

Heilbrun, Carolyn. *Toward a recognition of androgyny*. New York: Harper & Row, 1973.

Heilbrun, Carolyn. *Reinventing womanhood*. New York: W. W. Norton Co., 1979.

Levinson, Daniel, et al. *Seasons of a man's life*. New York: Ballantine, 1979.

Singer, June. *Androgyny*. Garden City, NY: Anchor Books, 1977.

6 CHAPTER | ORGANIZATIONAL CHANGE

For the audience, the orchestra experience during the past few performances has been "average at best." Many members of the orchestra would say the same. Attendance is above average, and everyone is just going along with the status quo. But in this community, there are many competing options for people interested in the arts. Within the leadership group, there is a sense that "change" is necessary. The board of trustees has been talking about funding, the future, and new strategic directions. There is a vague sense of unease—that things may not remain stable for long.

As rumors about a new agenda for the orchestra emerge, rumbles of resistance arise from every corner. Many believe strongly that the orchestra should hold the course. No change is needed! Why fix something that isn't broken? The signs and signals come in gradually at first—lower attendance and fewer contributions. Orchestra members start to fuss and fume among themselves. There are meetings to discuss "who is to blame" and "what should be done." The conductor sees peers across the country and internationally doing new things and orchestras going in exciting new directions. The momentum for change increases. But what direction to take? How do we know? Experts are gathered; studies are conducted. Market research is recommended, and consultants are employed and deployed. Politics intensify as competing interests emerge. Ethics are questioned. Finances are reviewed. Orchestra members gather and bond with a sense of impending disaster. The conductor updates her resume.

Leadership emerges within the board of trustees, and a common mission and purpose are defined. The conductor takes another job, and a new conductor is hired. Positive momentum takes hold; a new agenda is crafted. The new conductor is introduced to the community with a gala kick-off. Attendance swells. Everyone senses that the orchestra is on the right track. Maybe leadership has learned a thing or two.

The board recognizes that it cannot wait as long the next time around. When success is at a high point, board members should be planning for the next changes. The unpredictable and somewhat fickle marketplace requires constant attention. Change is the norm, not the exception. Paying attention and constantly learning are requisites. Leadership matters: the more alert the leaders are, the better the organization functions. Intelligence, leadership, learning, change, and organizational excellence are all interrelated.

To confront organizational change in theory or in practice, one must tie together and use knowledge about human motivation, leadership, group and intergroup behavior, the relationship between people and their organizational contexts, and power and influence—all from the organizational behavior perspective. In examining the historical foundations and current practice of organizational change, we must become familiar with pivotal ideas such as:

- The Hawthorne experiments, as described by Fritz Roethlisberger (included in Chapter 2, "Motivation")
- Transformative leadership, as explained in the 1984 article by Noel Tichy and David Ulrich (reprinted in Chapter 1, "Leadership")
- Groupthink, as explained by Irving Janis in Chapter 4, "Effects of the Work Environment"
- Survey research and feedback techniques that draw extensively from work done by Kurt Lewin and his associates
- The development of sensitivity training (or T-groups), a phenomenon that incorporates theory, research, and practice on leadership, group development and behavior, intergroup behavior, motivation, power and influence, and individual-organizational context impacts

ORGANIZATIONAL CHANGE FROM THE ORGANIZATIONAL BEHAVIOR PERSPECTIVE

The subject of organizational change has received wide attention in the literature on organizational behavior and organizational theory. Like the Hugo Münsterberg (1913) and Henry Gantt (1908) works on behavior in organizations that preceded the development of the organizational behavior perspective, much of the new writing about change in organizations is not based on familiar humanistic-type assumptions. Change has perhaps been the most visible and heated battleground between proponents of the organizational behavior perspective (and its assumptions, values, and methods) and the advocates of change through manipulation of power and/or perceptions. (For more on this subject, see Shafritz, Ott, & Jang, 2005.) So, organizational change provides a fitting, integrative subject with which to close this collection of classic readings in organizational behavior.

For more than 45 years (since about 1960), the organizational behavior perspective's interest in change has been riveted on *planned change*. The organizational behavior/planned change perspective assumptions have constituted the mainstream of organizational behavior literature and practice for so long that it sometimes is hard to think about any other. Thus, it is instructive to first take a brief glance at one of the more recent viewpoints on organizational change. A comparison between the 1960s-style "planned change" and "transformational change" makes it easy to understand and appreciate the uniqueness of the planned organizational change assumptions.

FOR COMPARISON: A DIFFERENT VIEW OF ORGANIZATIONAL CHANGE—TRANSFORMATION

The 1984 article by Noel Tichy and David Ulrich, "The Leadership Challenge—A Call for the Transformational Leader" (reprinted in Chapter 1), provides an excellent example of the transformational view of organizational change. Tichy and Ulrich call for leaders who are able to manage *planned revolutionary organizational change* ("organizational transformations"). Transformational leaders (or as some authors call them, transformative leaders [Bennis, 1984; Bennis & Nanus, 1985]) are expected to accomplish different magnitudes of organizational change (qualitative and quantitative) using strategies and methods that are not compatible with the mores of the human relations/planned change perspective. Transformative leaders use *transformative power* (Bennis, 1984) or *transforming leadership* (Adams, 1986) literally to transform organizations and their cultures—to alter organizational norms, realities, beliefs, values, and assumptions (Allaire & Firsirotu, 1985; Gemmill & Smith, 1985; Kilmann & Covin, 1988). In essence, transformative change is accomplished by violating organizational norms: by creating a new vision of the organization, often through conscious manipulation of symbols, and then "selling" the new vision to important stakeholders.

As we move into the second half of the first decade of the 21st century, transformational views of organizational change continue to evolve. A few examples include:

- Garvin and Roberto (2005) review research into successful organizational transformations in settings as diverse as multinational corporations, government agencies, nonprofit organizations, and high-performing teams such as mountaineering expeditions and firefighting crews. They propose a model supportive of transformative change called *a persuasion campaign*.
- Lawrence, Mauws, Dyck, and Kleysen (2005) argue that power and politics provide the social energy that transforms the insights of individuals and groups into the institutions of an organization. Different forms and uses of power are related to specific learning processes that are necessary for organizational change.

- Richardson and Vandenberg (2005) report on the importance of integrating managerial perceptions and transformational leadership with employee involvement at work-unit levels. Organization change efforts are often critically dependent on supervisory processes within the immediate work unit.
- Durand and Calori (2006) have enriched the organizational change literature by integrating organizational ethics literature into a model for valuing and using both differences and similarities in transformative organizational change initiatives.

ASSUMPTIONS ABOUT CHANGE FROM THE ORGANIZATIONAL BEHAVIOR/PLANNED CHANGE PERSPECTIVE

Before transformational leadership and radical change started to attract national and international attention, the literature and practice of people-oriented organizational change had been dominated by the assumptions, beliefs, and tactics of the organizational behavior perspective. These assumptions, which provided the technological and normative direction for two decades of change-oriented organizational behavior theory and practice, were articulated most clearly by Chris Argyris in the first chapter of his seminal 1970 book, *Intervention Theory and Methods*. Although Argyris's words are descriptive, his tone and his message are very prescriptive:

> Valid information, free choice, and internal commitment are considered integral parts of any intervention activity, no matter what the substantive objectives are (for a change). These three processes are called the primary intervention tasks. (p. 17)

As Argyris lists his three primary intervention tasks, his normative assumptions become unmistakably evident:

1. Without valid, usable information (including knowledge of the consequences of alternatives), there can be no free informed choice.
2. Without free informed choice, there can be no personal responsibility for decisions.
3. Without personal responsibility for decisions, there can be no internalized commitment to the success of a decision (no *psychological ownership*).

The organizational behavior perspective also embraces strong beliefs about what constitutes organizational effectiveness. These beliefs have further steered the pursuit of organizational improvement away from the manipulation of extrinsic variables such as systems of rewards and punishments. Under this line of reasoning, organizational effectiveness is not defined as *outcomes* but rather as *ongoing process states*. Warren Bennis uses the analogy of *health* or *healthy organization* to communicate his widely accepted concept of organizational process effectiveness. Bennis has four criteria for assessing organizational health, or effectiveness (as cited in Schein, 1980, p. 232):

1. *Adaptability:* The ability to solve problems and to react with flexibility to changing environmental demands.
2. *A sense of identity:* Knowledge and insight on the part of the organization of what it is, what its goals are, and what it is to do....
3. *Capacity to test reality:* The ability to search out, accurately perceive, and correctly interpret the real properties of the environment, particularly those that have relevance for the functioning of the organization.
4. *Integration:* A fourth, often-cited criterion that in effect underlies the others is a state of "integration" among the subparts of the total organization, such that the parts are not working at cross-purposes.

In a philosophically consistent vein, Schein (1980) identifies the organizational coping processes that are necessary conditions for maintaining or increasing organizational effectiveness (health):

1. The ability to take in and communicate information reliably and validly.
2. ... internal flexibility and creativity to make changes which are demanded by the information obtained.
3. ... integration of and commitment to the multiple goals of the organization, from which comes the willingness to change when necessary.
4. ... an internal climate of support and freedom from threat, since being threatened undermines good communications, reduces flexibility, and stimulates self-protection rather than concern for the total system.
5. ... the ability to continuously redesign the organization's structure to be congruent with its goal and tasks. (p. 249)

By comparing Bennis's and Schein's necessary conditions for organizational health/effectiveness with those of Hugo Münsterberg (1913) or Frederick Winslow Taylor (1911) (they are summarized in the Introduction), the vastness of the differences between these organizational perspectives becomes very evident. The organizational behavior perspective defines organizational effectiveness as a process state—not as it has been defined traditionally in terms of organizational outcomes such as market penetration, profitability, or quantity and/or quality levels of output.

ORGANIZATION DEVELOPMENT

One of the most dynamic and energetic manifestations of organizational behavior-based change has been the subfield of *organization development,* or simply OD. OD is a particular form of planned organizational changes (or development) that embodies the full set of premises, assumptions, values, and strategies of the organizational behavior perspective. Although authors' definitions of organization development may vary in emphasis, most are quite consistent in substance. For example:

Organization development is an effort (1) *planned* (2) *organization-wide,* and (3) *managed* from the *top,* to (4) *increase organization effectiveness* and *health* through

(5) *planned intervention* in the organization's "process," using *behavioral-science* knowledge. (Emphasis in original) (Beckhard, 1969)

and

Organization development is a long-range effort to improve an organization's problem-solving and renewal processes, particularly through a more effective and collaborative management of organizational culture...with the assistance of a change agent, or catalyst, and the use of the theory and technology of applied behavioral science, including action research. (French & Bell, 1984)

Organization development is about planned organizational change as a process or strategy. OD is as concerned about *how* planned change is implemented as it is about specifically *where* change will lead an organization. Typically, the product or result of OD activities is an ongoing set of processes for organizational renewal that are *in and of themselves defined as criteria of organizational effectiveness.* OD assumes that change is purposeful and dynamic, is accomplished through application of behavioral science knowledge, and is accomplished according to carefully prescribed ground rules derived from the assumptions of the organizational behavior perspective. Thus, for example, revolutionary and evolutionary change generally are not considered to be within the purview of OD.

OD is concerned with deep, long-lasting, organization-wide change or improvement—not in superficial changes in isolated organizational pockets. This concern for the broad based and long term led OD practitioners to an interest in the concept of organizational culture long before it became a fashionable management topic in the 1980s.

OD practitioners have developed numerous strategies and techniques for improving organizations. Most of them use interventions facilitated by outsiders (often called *change agents*). Some of the most common strategies include organizational diagnosis, process consultation, team building (in many forms), action research, data feedback, job enlargement, job enrichment, and conflict management. But each author has his or her own preferred tactics. For example, in one of the best-known such lists, Schmuck and Miles (1971) included training and education, process consultation or coaching, confrontation meetings, data feedback, problem solving, goal setting, OD task force establishment, and techno-structural activity. Thus, organization development represents a very notable effort to apply to ongoing organizational improvement an impressive array of research-based social science knowledge within a prescriptive value framework.

The origins of organization development can be traced to several events and movements that started in the 1930s and 1940s:

1. The *Hawthorne studies.*
2. The *sensitivity training* (or "T-group") *movement,* which originated in the late 1940s at the National Training Laboratories, under the leadership of such luminaries as Leland Bradford.

3. *Developments in survey research and feedback techniques,* particularly through the work of Kurt Lewin (1952a, b), which presaged creation of the basic *action research* model of organizational change.
4. *The sociotechnical "school" of research and analysis,* pioneered at the Tavistock Institute by Eric Trist and Kenneth Bamforth (1951), A. K. Rice (1953), and Elliott Jaques (1951).

The *Hawthorne studies* and their importance to understanding organizational behavior-oriented change processes are discussed extensively in the Introduction and in Chapter 1, "Leadership." So, other than referring the reader to Fritz Roethlisberger's "The Hawthorne Experiments" (reprinted in Chapter 2), we will move on to the remaining three historical trends and events that opened the way for organization development.

The *sensitivity training* (or "T-group") *movement* had its start in 1946 when Kurt Lewin, Leland Bradford, Ronald Lippitt, and Kenneth Benne collaboratively conducted a training workshop to help improve race relations and community leadership in New Britain, Connecticut (Bradford, Gibb, & Benne, 1964). During their evening staff meetings, they discussed the behavior of workshop participants and the dynamics of events. Several workshop participants asked to join the night discussions, and the results of the process eventually led to the initiation and institutionalization of *T-group technology.* Although the early T-groups focused primarily on individual growth and development, they quickly were adapted for organizational application. T-groups became the method by which organizational members learned how to communicate honestly and directly about facts and feelings (Argyris, 1962). (From the human relations perspective, *feelings are facts.*) Thus, T-groups became a keystone strategy for increasing organizational effectiveness by improving interpersonal communications (e.g., feedback), reducing defensiveness (and thus rigidity), and otherwise helping organizations achieve Bennis's criteria for organizational effectiveness—adaptability, sense of identity, capacity to test reality, and integration—through the development of coping processes that are necessary conditions for maintaining or increasing organizational effectiveness:

1. The ability to take in and communicate information reliably and validly.
2. The internal flexibility and creativity to make changes demanded by the information obtained.
3. The integration of and commitment to the multiple goals of the organization, from which comes the willingness to change when necessary.
4. An internal climate of support and freedom from threat.
5. The ability to continuously redesign the organization's structure to be congruent with its goal and tasks. (Schein, 1980, p. 249)

Survey research and feedback techniques particularly characterized the work initiated by Kurt Lewin and his associates at the Research Center for Group Dynamics first at M.I.T. and, after his death, at the University of Michigan. Survey research methods, when combined with feedback/communication techniques, and applied to planned organizational change, resulted in the development of the *action research* model of organizational change—another mainstay of OD practitioners and theorists. The action research model is a pre-scribed process for identifying needs for organizational improvement and cre-ating improvement strategies that uses external consultation but creates psychological ownership of problems and solutions by organizational members. Briefly, action research involves the following:

- Collecting organizational diagnostic-type data, usually either by ques-tionnaire or through consultant interviews
- Systematically feeding back information to groups of people (organization members) who provided input
- Discussing what the information means to members and its implications for the organization in order to be certain the "diagnosis" is accurate and to generate psychological ownership of the need for improvement actions
- Jointly developing action-improvement plans, using the knowledge and skills of the consultant and the insider perspective of members, and generating psychological ownership of the improvement action plan

The action research model is diagrammed in Figure 1.

The *sociotechnical approach to research and analysis* made its appearance in the late 1940s and early 1950s through a group of organizational researchers at the Tavistock Institute in London, who identified a tight link between human and technological factors in the workplace. They concluded that neither people nor work/technology takes precedence over the other. Once again, as was true with the Hawthorne studies, the sociotechnical group does not assume that the task is to increase productivity by fitting people to the work. Eric Trist and Kenneth Bamforth (1951) found that changing the coal-mining technology from small group production to a physically spaced *longwall* method disrupts the social structure of the miners and in turn production. By modifying the work (technical) system to allow the social structure to reform, workers returned to helping each other, productivity and morale increased, and accidents and absenteeism decreased.

Organizational development and change as areas of research and practice continue to excite leaders, administrators, and managers. The field is diverse, complex, and interesting. Fernandez and Rainey (2006) help to dispel the stereotype that large organizations, especially government bureaucracies, are resistant to change. They report evidence that organizational change can—and does—succeed frequently in the public sector, that career civil servants often lead change efforts, and that they often succeed. In another important study of organizational change, Buckingham (2005) identifies what excellent managers do as they perform their magic in organizational change—they discover, develop, and celebrate what is different about each person who works for them. Tsoukas (2005) reports on important research that explains why language matters in the analysis of organizational change. Tsoukas reviews, compares, and contrasts two traditional perspectives on organizational change (behav-iorist and cognitivist) with the newly emerging linguistic view. He argues that a discourse-analytic approach offers great potential for understanding the nature and complexity of organizational change.

FIGURE 1
THE
ORGANIZATION
DEVELOPMENT
ACTION
RESEARCH
MODEL

Initial Diagnostic and Planning Phase

Preliminary conceptualization of organizational problems by management and consultant

Consultant gathers diagnostic data through, for example, questionnaires, interviews, and observations

Consultant prepares the data for feedback to organization members

Consultant feeds back diagnostic data to organization members

Joint interpretation of the meaning and implications of the data by organization members and the consultant

Joint action planning by organization members and consultant

Implementation Phase I

Organization members implement action plans with assistance from consultant as desired or needed

Consultant collects data on progress and effectiveness of action plan implementation

Consultant feeds back data to organization members

Joint interpretation of the meaning and implications of the data by organization members and the consultant

Joint action planning by organization members and consultant

Implementation Phase n

Organization members implement new action plans with assistance from consultant as desired or needed

Repeat steps in Implementation Phase I

INTRODUCTION TO THE ARTICLES IN THIS CHAPTER

This chapter's first selection is one of the best known and most frequently quoted experiments on the introduction of organizational change, Lester Coch and John R. P. French's 1948 *Human Relations* article, "Overcoming Resistance to Change." Coch and French studied the relationship between worker participation in design decisions leading to the introduction of changes in work process, and their resistance to changes. The authors used a research design complete with experimental and control groups of pajama folders, pressers, and examiners at the Harwood Manufacturing Corporation in Marion, Virginia. Using Kurt Lewin's concepts of quasi-stationary equilibriums and change force fields, Coch and French concluded that group participation in planning reduces workers' resistance to changes, decreases turnover during and after changes, and accelerates worker relearning curves (the rapidity with which workers return to full-speed production following process changes).

Whenever organizational change is discussed, Kurt Lewin heads everyone's list of people who have made invaluable and lasting contributions to our understanding of change processes and dynamics. His 1952 article reprinted here, "Group Decision and Social Change," is a condensed restatement of ideas Lewin articulated in one of his best-known works, "Frontiers in Group Dynamics: Concept, Method and Reality in Social Science; Social Equilibria and Social Change" (1947). Lewin describes social organizations as resting in a state of stable quasi-stationary equilibrium. To effect social change, one must begin with an "analysis of the conditions for 'no change,' that is, for the state of equilibrium." Quite obviously, the now-familiar technique of *force field analysis* evolved from this concept, in which there are but two basic approaches for accomplishing change: "Adding forces in the desired direction, or by diminishing opposing forces." Lewin argued that the former approach is preferable because it tends to be accompanied by a "high state of tension," which in turn causes anger, aggressiveness, and a lower propensity to be constructive. In this piece, Lewin articulates his well-known assertion that social change must be viewed as a three-step process of unfreezing, change, and refreezing. If one focuses only on the change process per se, change will be short-lived at best.

Chris Argyris's 1970 book, *Intervention Theory and Methods,* is a comprehensive, widely cited, and enduring work on organizational consulting for change written from an organizational behavior/organization development perspective (a portion of the first chapter is reprinted here). This book has remained central to the field because Argyris unambiguously lays out the fundamental tenets that undergird the organizational behavior perspective of change. (Argyris calls the tenets "the three primary intervention tasks.") These tenets define fundamentals such as the nature of the change-agent/client relationship, the necessity for valid and usable information, and necessary preconditions for organization members to internalize change.

For Peter Senge, change is learning, and learning is change—for people and organizations. Thus, it is possible for organizations to learn to change because "deep down, we are all learners." In Chapter One from *The Fifth Discipline: The Art and Practice of the Learning Organization* (1990, reprinted in this chapter), Senge proposes that five new "component technologies" are gradually converging that will collectively permit the emergence of learning organizations. He labels these component technologies the "five disciplines": *systems thinking*—"systems" of the variety described by Wheatley (2000); *personal mastery*—people approaching life and work "as an artist would approach a work of art"; *mental models*—deeply ingrained assumptions or mental images "that influence how we understand the world and how we take action"; *building shared vision*—"when there is a genuine vision . . . people excel and learn, not because they are told to, but because they want to"; and *team learning*—team members engaging in true dialogue with their assumptions suspended.

A learning organization uses the five disciplines in a never-ending quest to expand its capacity to create its future. As Senge explains, "systems thinking" is the fifth discipline—the integrative discipline that fuses the others into a coherent body of theory and practice. Learning organizations are organizations that are able to move past mere survival learning to engage in generative learning—"learning that enhances our capacity to create."

In his best-selling book, *Leading Change* (1996, a chapter is reprinted here), John P. Kotter writes about the major challenges inherent in the process of organizations remaking themselves. Most major transformation efforts are unsuccessful or fail entirely. Failure to adhere to reasonable sequencing of process elements is a primary cause. Change usually should follow a logical series of steps or phases requiring planning and an extended period of time. Errors in process steps can be highly disruptive or, at worst, can negate gains. Kotter lists eight steps for transforming an organization, describes how to avoid pitfalls, and explains how to leverage the driving forces for change within the model.

Larry E. Greiner, in his classic piece included in this chapter, develops a model of the processes of evolution and revolution as organizations grow and change. He focuses on how organizations involved in change, growth, and development move through five clearly distinguishable phases of development. Each of the five phases contains unique combinations of relative calm and then crisis, and each phase is influenced by the previous phase. Greiner provides a prescription for appropriate managerial action steps in each phase and describes how to leverage each for optimal success in the change processes.

David Cooperrider and Diana Whitney, in "Appreciative Inquiry," which is their unique approach to change, claim that AI always begins an adventure. Their approach (included in a reading in this chapter) represents a conceptual reconfiguration of action research based on a "socio-rationalist" view of science. In lieu of the traditional "identification of a problem," we should shift to an "appreciation and valuing" or an understanding of "what is." Instead of analyzing causes or problems, managers should focus on what might be. Through our assumptions and choice of method we largely create the world we later discover. Thus, when organizational members engage in dialogue about what could and should be, the result is often positive change. Thus, AI is an interesting approach to organizational change and an important, viable complement to conventional forms of action research.

Warren Bennis is a classic writer and a long-time contributor to the evolving fields of leadership and organizational change. In a chapter from his book *Managing the Dream: Reflections on Leadership and Change* (2000), reprinted in this chapter, Bennis notes that "change is the metaphysics of our age." He discusses avenues of change, the nature of innovators and leaders, and how to avoid disaster during the change. Bennis's wisdom continues to enliven and enrich our concepts and practices in this important organizational arena.

Organizational change is a fitting topic on which to end this book of classic readings in organizational behavior or, alternatively, it is a place to begin. Each of us in our own way want to leave the world (or our organization) a better place because we were here. Organizational change is the process of people making relatively permanent alterations in their behavior as a function of their experiences and learning over time. With learning, change becomes possible. With change and experience, the quality of organizational lives can improve.

Organizational learning and change are anchored in the knowledge and application of the central topics of this book—leadership, motivation, teamwork, creating exciting and supportive work environments, and the effective use of power and influence. Let the adventure begin!

REFERENCES

Adams, J. D. (Ed.). (1986). *Transforming leadership: From vision to results.* Alexandria, VA: Miles River Press.

Allaire, Y., & Firsirotu, M. (1985, Spring). How to implement radical strategies in large organizations. *Sloan Management Review, 26*(3), 19–34.

Argyris, C. (1962). *Interpersonal competence and organizational effectiveness.* Homewood, IL: The Dorsey Press and Richard D. Irwin.

Argyris, C. (1970). *Intervention theory and methods.* Reading, MA: Addison-Wesley.

Argyris, C. (1993). *Knowledge for action: A guide to overcoming barriers to organizational change.* San Francisco: Jossey-Bass.

Beckhard, R. (1969). *Organization development: Strategies and models.* Reading, MA: Addison-Wesley.

Beckhard, R., & Harris, R. T. (1977). *Organizational transitions: Managing complex change.* Reading, MA: Addison-Wesley.

Beckhard, R., & Pritchard, W. (1992). *Changing the essence: The art of creating and leading fundamental change in organizations.* San Francisco: Jossey-Bass.

Bennis, W. G. (1966). Applying behavioral sciences to planned organizational change. In W. G. Bennis, *Changing organizations* (pp. 81–94). New York: McGraw-Hill.

Bennis, W. G. (1969). *Organization development: Its nature, origins and prospects.* Reading, MA: Addison-Wesley.

Bennis, W. G. (1984). Transformative power and leadership. In T. J. Sergiovanni & J. E. Corbally (Eds.), *Leadership and organizational culture* (pp. 64–71). Urbana: University of Illinois Press.

Bennis, W. G. (2000). Change: The new metaphysics. In W. G. Bennis, *Managing the dream: Reflections on leadership and change* (pp. 31–38). Cambridge, MA: Perseus.

Bennis, W. G., Benne, K. D., & Chin, R. (1961). *The planning of change.* New York: Holt, Rinehart & Winston.

Bennis, W. G., & Nanus, B. (1985). *Leaders.* New York: Harper & Row.

Bradford, L., Gibb, J. R., & Benne, K. D. (Eds.). (1964). *T-group theory and laboratory method; innovation in re-education.* New York: Wiley.

Brown, L. M., & Posner, B. Z. (2001). Exploring the relationship between learning and leadership. *Leadership and Organization Development Journal, 122*(5–6), 274–280.

Buckingham, M. (2005, March). What great managers do. *Harvard Business Review,* 1–12.

Coch, L., & French, J. R. P., Jr. (1948, August). Overcoming resistance to change. *Human Relations,* 512–532.

Cooperrider, D. L., & Whitney, D. (1999). *Appreciative inquiry.* San Francisco: Berrett-Koehler.

Durand, R., & Calori, R. (2006). Sameness, otherness? Enriching organizational change theories with philosophical considerations on the same and the other. *Academy of Management Review, 31*(1), 93–114.

Fernandez, S., & Rainey, H. G. (2006, March/April). Managing successful organizational change in the public sector: An agenda for research and practice. *Public Administration Review, 66*(2), 1–25.

French, W. L., & Bell, C. H., Jr. (1984). *Organization development* (3rd ed.). Englewood Cliffs, NJ: Prentice-Hall.

French, W. L., Bell, C. H., Jr., & Zawacki, R. A. (Eds.). (1983). *Organization development: Theory, practice, and research* (rev. ed.). Plano, TX: Business Publications.

Gantt, H. L. (1908). Training workmen in habits of industry and cooperation. Paper presented to the American Society of Mechanical Engineers.

Garvin, D. A., & Roberto, M. A. (2005, February). Change through persuasion. *Harvard Business Review,* 1–9.

Gemmill, G., & Smith, C. (1985). A dissipative structure model of organization transformation. *Human Relations, 38,* 751–766.

Gersick, C. (1991, January). Revolutionary change theories: A multilevel exploration of the punctuated equilibrium paradigm. *Academy of Management Review,* 10–36.

Greiner, L. E. (1998, May/June). Revolution and evolution as organizations grow. *Harvard Business Review,* 55–66.

Huber, G. P., & Glick, W. H. (1993). *Organizational change and redesign: Ideas and insights for improving performance.* New York: Oxford University Press.

Iacocca, L. (1984). *Iacocca, an autobiography.* Toronto: Bantam Books.

Jaques, E. (1951). *The changing culture of a factory.* London, UK: Tavistock Publications.

Kelman, H. C., & Warwick, D. (1978). The ethics of social intervention: Goals, means, and consequences. In H. C. Bermant, H. C. Kelman, & D. P. Warwick (Eds.), *The ethics of social intervention* (pp. 3–27). New York: Hemisphere.

Kilmann, R. H., & Colvin, T. J. (Eds.). (1988). *Corporate transformation.* San Francisco: Jossey-Bass.

Kotter, J. (1996). Transforming organizations: Why firms fail. In J. Kotter, *Leading Change* (pp. 3–17). Boston: Harvard Business School Press.

Kozmetsky, G. (1985). *Transformational management.* Cambridge, MA: Ballinger.

Lawrence, T. B., Mauws, M. K., Dyck, B., & Kleysen, R. F. (2005). The politics of organizational learning: Integrating power into the 4I framework. *Academy of Management Review, 30*(1), 180–191.

Leavitt, H. J. (1965). Applied organizational change in industry: Structural, technological, and humanistic approaches. In J. G. March (Ed.), *Handbook of organizations* (pp. 1144–1170). Chicago: Rand McNally.

Lewin, K. (1947, June). Frontiers in group dynamics: Concept, method and reality in social science; Social equilibria and social change. *Human Relations, 1*(1).

Lewin, K. (1952a). Group decision and social change. In G. E. Swanson, T. N. Newcomb, & E. L. Hartley (Eds.), *Readings in social psychology* (rev. ed., pp. 459–473). New York: Holt, Rinehart & Winston.

Lewin, K. (1952b). Quasi-stationary social equilibria and the problem of permanent change. In G. E. Swanson, T. N. Newcomb, & E. L. Hartley (Eds.), *Readings in social psychology* (rev. ed., pp. 207–211). New York: Holt, Rinehart & Winston.

McWhinney, W. (1992). *Paths of change: Strategic choices for organizations and society.* Newbury Park, CA: Sage.

Münsterberg, H. (1913). *Psychology and industrial efficiency.* Boston: Houghton Mifflin.

Ott, J. S. (1989). *The organizational culture perspective.* Belmont, CA: Wadsworth.

Pascale, R. T. (2001). Laws of the jungle and the new laws of business. *Leader to Leader, 20,* 21–35.

Rice, A. K. (1953). Productivity and social organization in an Indian weaving shed: An examination of some aspects of the socio-technical system of an experimental automatic loom shed. *Human Relations, 6,* 297–329.

Richardson, H. A., & Vandenberg, R. J. (2005, June). Integrating managerial perceptions and transformational leadership into a work-unit level model of employee involvement. *Journal of Organizational Behavior, 26*(5), 561–589.

Schein, E. H. (1980). *Organizational psychology* (3rd ed.). Englewood Cliffs, NJ: Prentice-Hall.

Schein, E. H. (1988). *Process consultation: Its role in organization development* (2nd ed.). Reading, MA: Addison-Wesley.

Schmuck, R. A., & Miles, M. B. (Eds.). (1971). *Organization development in schools.* Palo Alto, CA: National Press Books.

Senge, P. M. (1990). *The fifth discipline: The art and practice of the learning organization.* New York: Doubleday Currency.

Shafritz, J. M., Ott, J. S., & Jang, Y. S. (Eds.) (2005). *Classics of organization theory* (6th ed.). Belmont, CA: Wadsworth.

Taylor, F. W. (1911). *The principles of scientific management.* New York: W. W. Norton.

Tichy, N. M., & Ulrich, D. O. (1984, Fall). The leadership challenge—A call for the transformational leader. *Sloan Management Review, 26*(1), 59–68.

Trist, E., & Bamforth, K. W. (1951). Some social and psychological consequences of the longwall method of coal-getting. *Human Relations, 4,* 3–38.

Tsoukas, H. (2005). Afterword: Why language matters in the analysis of organizational change. *Journal of Organizational Change Management, 18*(1), 96–104.

Wheatley, M. J. (2000). *Leadership and the new science.* San Francisco: Jossey-Bass.

Reading 37	Overcoming Resistance to Change[1]
	Lester Coch and John R. P. French, Jr.

Introduction

It has always been characteristic of American industry to change products and methods of doing jobs as often as competitive conditions or engineering progress dictates. This makes frequent changes in an individual's work necessary. In addition, the markedly greater turnover and absenteeism of recent years result in unbalanced production lines which again makes for frequent shifting of individuals from one job to another. One of the most serious production problems faced at the Harwood Manufacturing Corporation has been the resistance of production workers to the necessary changes in methods and jobs. This resistance expressed itself in several ways, such as grievances about the piece rates that went with the new methods, high turnover, very low efficiency, restriction of output, and marked aggression against management. Despite these undesirable effects, it was necessary that changes in methods and jobs continue....

Background

The main plant of the Harwood Manufacturing Corporation, where the present research was done, is located in the small town of Marion, Virginia. The plant produces pajamas and, like most sewing plants, employs mostly women. The plant's population is about 500 women and 100 men. The workers are recruited from the rural, mountainous areas surrounding the town, and are usually employed without previous industrial experience. The average age of the workers is 23; the average education is eight years of grammar school.

The policies of the company in regard to labor relations are liberal and progressive. A high value has been placed on fair and open dealing with the employees, and they are encouraged to take up any problems or grievances with the management at any time. Every effort is made to help foremen find effective solutions to their problems in human relations, using conferences and role-playing methods. Carefully planned orientation, designed to help overcome the discouragement and frustrations attending entrance upon the new and unfamiliar situation, is used. Plant-wide votes are conducted, where possible, to resolve problems affecting the whole working population. The company has invested both time and money in employee services such as industrial music, health services, lunchroom, and recreation programs. In the same spirit, the management has been conscious of the importance of public relations in the local community; they have supported both financially and otherwise any activity which would build up good will for the company. As a result of these policies, the company has enjoyed good labor relations since the day it commenced operations.

Harwood employees work on an individual incentive system. Piece rates are set by time study and are expressed in terms of units. One unit is equal to one minute of standard work: 60 units per hour equal the standard efficiency rating. Thus, if on a particular operation the piece rate for one dozen is 10 units, the operator would have to produce 6 dozen per hour to achieve the standard efficiency rating of 60 units per hour. The skill required to reach 60 units per hour is great. On some jobs, an average trainee may take 34 weeks to reach the skill level necessary to perform at 60 units per hour. Her first few weeks of work may be on an efficiency level of 5 to 20 units per hour....

When it is necessary to change an operator from one type of work to another, a transfer

Source: Lester Coch and John R. P. French, Jr., "Overcoming Resistance to Change," 1948, pp. 512–532, HUMAN RELATIONS. Reprinted by permission of Sage Publications.

FIGURE I
A COMPARISON
OF THE
LEARNING
CURVE FOR
NEW,
INEXPERIENCED
EMPLOYEES
WITH THE
RELEARNING
CURVE FOR
ONLY THOSE
TRANSFERS
(38 PER CENT)
WHO EVEN-
TUALLY
RECOVER TO
STANDARD
PRODUCTION

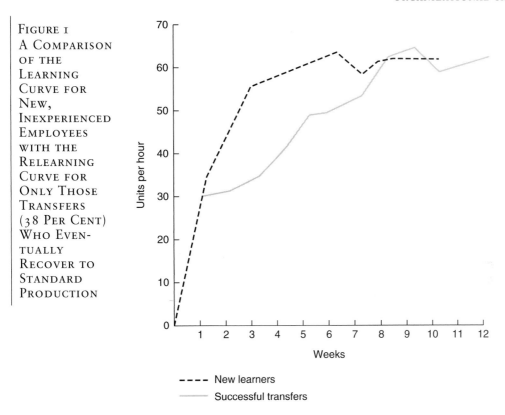

- - - - New learners
———— Successful transfers

bonus is given. This bonus is so designed that the changed operator who relearns at an average rate will suffer no loss in earnings after change. Despite this allowance, the general attitudes toward job changes in the factory are markedly negative. Such expressions as, "When you make your units (standard production), they change your job," are all too frequent. Many operators refuse to change, preferring to quit.

The Transfer Learning Curve

An analysis of the after-change relearning curve of several hundred experienced operators rating standard or better prior to change showed that 38 per cent of the changed operators recovered to the standard unit rating of 60 units per hour. The other 62 per cent either became chronically sub-standard operators or quit during the relearning period.

The average relearning curve for those who recover to standard production on the simplest type job in the plant (Figure 1) is eight weeks long, and, when smoothed, provides the basis for the transfer bonus. The bonus is the percent difference between this expected efficiency rating and the standard of 60 units per hour. Progress is slow for the first two or three weeks, as the relearning curve shows, and then accelerates markedly to about 50 units per hour, with an increase of 15 units in two weeks. . . .

It is interesting to note in Figure 1 that the relearning period for an experienced operator is longer than the learning period for a new operator. . . .

Figure 2, which presents the relearning curves for 41 experienced operators who were changed to very difficult jobs, gives a comparison between the recovery rates for operators making standard

FIGURE 2
THE DROP IN
PRODUCTION
AND THE RATE
OF RECOVERY
AFTER
TRANSFER
FOR SKILLFUL
AND FOR
SUBSTANDARD
OPERATORS

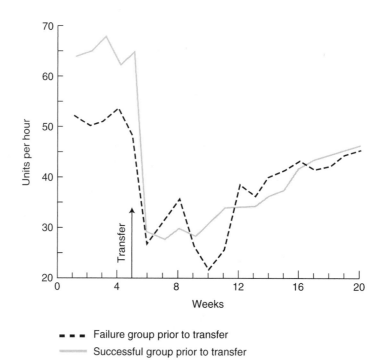

- - - Failure group prior to transfer
——— Successful group prior to transfer

or better prior to change, and those below standard prior to change. Both classes of operators dropped to a little below 30 units per hour and recovered at a very slow but similar rate. These curves show a general (though by no means universal) phenomenon; that the efficiency rating prior to change does not indicate a faster or slower recovery rate after change.

A Preliminary Theory of Resistance to Change

The fact that relearning after transfer to a new job is so often slower than initial learning on first entering the factory would indicate, on the face of it, that the resistance to change and the slow relearning is primarily a motivational problem. The similar recovery rates of the skilled and unskilled operators shown in Figure 2 tend to confirm the hypothesis that skill is a minor factor and motivation is the major determinant of the rate of recovery. Earlier experiments at Harwood by Alex Bavelas demonstrated this point conclusively. He found that

the use of group decision techniques on operators who had just been transferred resulted in very marked increases in the rate of relearning, even though no skill training was given and there were no other changes in working conditions (Lewin, 1947).

Interviews with operators who have been transferred to a new job reveal a common pattern of feelings and attitudes which are distinctly different from those of successful nontransfers. In addition to resentment against the management for transferring them, the employees typically show feelings of frustration, loss of hope of ever regaining their former level of production and status in the factory, feelings of failure, and a very low level of aspiration. In this respect these transferred operators are similar to the chronically slow workers studied previously.

Earlier unpublished research at Harwood has shown that the nontransferred employees generally have an explicit goal of reaching and maintaining an efficiency rating of 60 units per hour. A questionnaire administered to several groups of operators indicated that a large majority of them accept as their goal the management's quota of 60 units per hour. This standard of production is the level of aspiration according to which the operators measure their own success or failure; and those who fall below standard lose status in the eyes of their fellow employees. Relatively few operators set a goal appreciably above 60 units per hour.

The actual production records confirm the effectiveness of this goal of standard production. The distribution of the total population of operators in accordance with their production levels is by no means a normal curve. Instead there is a very large number of operators who rate 60 to 63 units per hour and relatively few operators who rate just above or just below this range. Thus we may conclude that:

• Hypothesis (1): There is a force acting on the operator in the direction of achieving a production level of 60 units per hour or more. It is assumed that the strength of this driving force (acting on an operator below standard) increases as she gets nearer the goal—a typical goal gradient (see Figure 1).

On the other hand restraining forces operate to hinder or prevent her from reaching this goal. These restraining forces consist among other things of the difficulty of the job in relation to the operator's level of skill. Other things being equal, the faster an operator is sewing the more difficult it is to increase her speed by a given amount. Thus we may conclude that:

• Hypothesis (2): The strength of the restraining force hindering higher production increases with increasing level of production.

In line with previous studies, it is assumed that the conflict of these two opposing forces— the driving force corresponding to the goal of reaching 60 and the restraining force of the difficulty of the job—produces frustration. In such a conflict situation, the strength of frustration will depend on the strength of these forces. If the restraining force against increasing

production is weak, then the frustration will be weak. But if the driving force toward higher production (i.e., the motivation) is weak, then the frustration will also be weak. Probably both of the conflicting forces must be above a certain minimum strength before any frustration is produced; for all goal-directed activity involves some degree of conflict of this type, yet a person is not usually frustrated so long as he is making satisfactory progress toward his goal. Consequently we assume that:

• Hypothesis (3): The strength of frustration is a function of the weaker of these two opposing forces, provided that the weaker force is stronger than a certain minimum necessary to produce frustration (Hypothesis [1]).

An analysis of the effects of such frustration in the factory showed that it resulted, among other things, in high turnover and absenteeism. The rate of turnover for successful operators with efficiency ratings above standard was much lower than for unsuccessful operators. Likewise, operators on the more difficult jobs quit more frequently than those on the easier jobs. Presumably the effect of being transferred is a severe frustration which should result in similar attempts to escape from the field.

In line with this theory of frustration, and the finding that job turnover is one resultant of frustration, an analysis was made of the turnover rate of transferred operators as compared with the rate among operators who had not been transferred recently....

The results are given in Figure 3. Both the levels of turnover and the form of the curves are strikingly different for the two groups. Among operators who have not been transferred recently the average turnover per month is about 4½ per cent; among recent transfers the monthly turnover is nearly 12 per cent. Consistent with the previous studies, both groups show a very marked drop in the turnover curve after an operator becomes a success by reaching 60 units per hour, or standard production. However, the form of the curves at lower unit ratings is

FIGURE 3
THE RATE OF
TURNOVER AT
VARIOUS
LEVELS OF
PRODUCTION
FOR TRANSFERS
AS COMPARED
WITH NON-
TRANSFERS

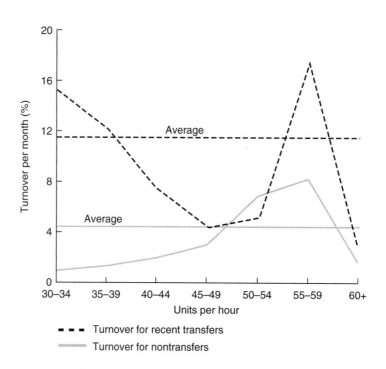

markedly different for the two groups. The non-transferred operators show a gradually increasing rate of turnover up to a rating of 55 to 59 units per hour. The transferred operators, on the other hand, show a high peak at the lowest unit rating of 30 to 34 units per hour, decreasing sharply to a low point at 45 to 49 units per hour. Since most changed operators drop to a unit rating of around 30 units per hour when changed and then drop no further, it is obvious that the rate of turnover was highest for these operators just after they were changed and again much later just before they reached standard. Why?

It is assumed that the strength of frustration for an operator who has *not* been transferred gradually increases because both the driving force towards the goal of reaching 60 and the restraining force of the difficulty of the job increase with increasing unit rating. This is in line with hypotheses (1), (2), and (3). For the transferred operator on the other hand the frustration is greatest immediately after transfer, when the contrast of her present status with her former status is most evident. At this point the strength of the restraining forces is at a maximum because the difficulty is unusually great due to proactive inhibition. Then as she overcomes the interference effects between the two jobs and learns the new job, the difficulty and the frustration gradually decrease and the rate of turnover declines until the operator reaches 45–49 units per hour. Then at higher levels of production the difficulty starts to increase again, and the transferred operator shows the same peak in frustration and turnover at 55–59 units per hour....

Another factor which seems to affect recovery rates of changed operators is the amount of we-feeling. Observations seem to indicate that a strong psychological sub-group with negative attitudes toward management will display the strongest resistance to change. On the other hand, changed groups with high we-feeling and positive cooperative attitudes are the best relearners. Collections of individuals with little or no we-feeling display some resistance to change but not so strongly as the groups with high we-feeling and negative attitudes toward management. However, turnover for the individual transfers is much higher than in the latter groups. This phenomenon of the relationship between we-feeling and resistance to change is so overt that for years the general policy of the management of the plant was never to change a group as a group but rather to scatter the individuals in different areas throughout the factory.

An analysis of turnover records for changed operators with high we-feeling showed a 4 per cent turnover rate per month at 30 to 34 units per hour, not significantly higher than in unchanged operators but significantly lower than in changed operators with little or no we-feeling. However, the acts of aggression are far more numerous among operators with high we-feeling than among operators with little we-feeling. Since both types of operators experience the same frustration as individuals but react to it so differently, it is assumed that the effect of the in-group feeling is to set up a restraining force against leaving the group and perhaps even to set up driving forces toward staying in the group. In these circumstances, one would expect some alternative reaction to frustration rather than escape from the field. This alternative is aggression. Strong we-feeling provides strength so that members dare to express aggression which would otherwise be suppressed.

One common result in a sub-group with strong we-feeling is the setting of a group standard concerning production. Where the attitudes toward management are antagonistic, this group standard may take the form of a definite restriction of production to a given level. This phenomenon of restriction is particularly likely to happen in a group that has been transferred to a job where a new piece rate has been set; for they have some hope that if production never approaches the standard, the management may change the piece rate in their favor.

A group standard can exert extremely strong forces on an individual member of a small sub-group....

The Experiment

On the basis of the preliminary theory that resistance to change is a combination of an individual reaction to frustration with strong group-induced forces it seemed that the most appropriate methods for overcoming the resistance to change would be group methods. Consequently an experiment was designed employing two variations of democratic procedure in handling groups to be transferred. The first variation involved participation through representation of the workers in designing the changes to be made in the jobs. The second variation consisted of total participation by all members of the group in designing the changes. A third control group was also used. Two experimental groups received the total participation treatment. The three experimental groups and the control group were roughly matched with respect to: (a) the efficiency ratings of the groups before transfer; (b) the degree of change involved in the transfer; (c) the amount of we-feeling observed in the groups....

The control group of hand pressers went through the usual factory routine when they were changed. The production department modified the job, and a new piece rate was set. A group meeting was then held in which the control group was told that the change was necessary because of competitive conditions, and that a new piece rate had been set. The new piece rate was thoroughly explained by the time study man, questions were answered, and the meeting was dismissed.

Experimental group 1 was changed in a different manner. Before any changes took place, a group meeting was held with all the operators to be changed. The need for the change was presented as dramatically as possible, showing two identical garments produced in the factory; one was produced in 1946 and had sold for 100 per cent more than its fellow in 1947. The group was asked to identify the cheaper one and could not do it. This demonstration effectively shared with the group the entire problem of the necessity of cost reduction. A general agreement was reached that a savings could be effected by removing the "frills" and "fancy" work from the garment without affecting the folders' opportunity to achieve a high efficiency rating. Management then presented a plan to set the new job and piece rate:

1. Make a check study of the job as it was being done.
2. Eliminate all unnecessary work.
3. Train several operators in the correct methods.
4. Set the piece rate by time studies on these specially trained operators.
5. Explain the new job rate to all the operators.
6. Train all operators in the new method so they can reach a high rate of production within a short time.

The group approved this plan (though no formal group decision was reached), and chose the operators to be specially trained. A sub-meeting with the "special" operators was held immediately following the meeting with the entire group. They displayed a cooperative and interested attitude and immediately presented many good suggestions. This attitude carried over into the working out of the details of the new job; and when the new job and piece rates were set, the "special" operators referred to the resultants as "our job," "our rate," etc. The new job and piece rates were presented at a second group meeting to all the operators involved. The "special" operators served to train the other operators on the new job.

Experimental groups 2 and 3 went through much the same kind of change meetings. The groups were smaller than experimental group 1, and a more intimate atmosphere was established. The need for a change was once again made dramatically clear; the same general plan was presented by management. However, since the groups were small, all operators were chosen as "special" operators; that is, all operators were to participate directly in the designing of the new jobs, and all operators would be studied by the time study man. It is interesting to note that in the

meetings with these two groups, suggestions were immediately made in such quantity that the stenographer had great difficulty in recording them. The group approved of the plans, but again no formal group decision was reached.

Results

... The control group improved little beyond their early efficiency ratings. Resistance developed almost immediately after the change occurred. Marked expressions of aggression against management occurred, such as conflict with the methods engineer, expression of hostility against the supervisor, deliberate restriction of production, and lack of cooperation with the supervisor. There were 17 per cent quits in the first forty days. Grievances were filed about the piece rate, but when the rate was checked, it was found to be a little "loose."

Experimental group 1 showed an unusually good relearning curve. At the end of fourteen days, the group averaged 61 units per hour. During the fourteen days, the attitude was cooperative and permissive. They worked well with the methods engineer, the training staff, and the supervisor. (The supervisor was the same person in the cases of the control group and experimental group 1.) There were no quits in this group in the first forty days. This group might have presented a better learning record if work had not been scarce during the first seven days. There was one act of aggression against the supervisor recorded in the first forty days. It is interesting to note that the three special representative operators in experimental group 1 recovered at about the same rate as the rest of their group.

Experimental groups 2 and 3 recovered faster than experimental group 1. After a slight drop on the first day of change, the efficiency ratings returned to a pre-change level and showed sustained progress thereafter to a level about 14 per cent higher than the pre-change level. No additional training was provided them after the second day. They worked well with their supervisors, and no indications of aggression were observed from these groups. There were no quits in either of these groups in the first forty days.

A fourth experimental group, composed of only two sewing operators, was transferred by the total participation technique. Their new job was one of the most difficult jobs in the factory, in contrast to the easy jobs for the control group and the other three experimental groups. As expected, the total participation technique again resulted in an unusually fast recovery rate and a final level of production well above the level before transfer. Because of the difficulty of the new job, however, the rate of recovery was slower than for experimental groups 2 and 3, but faster than for experimental group 1.

In the first experiment, the control group made no progress after transfer for a period of 32 days. At the end of this period the group was broken up and the individuals were reassigned to new jobs scattered throughout the factory. Two and a half months after their dispersal, the thirteen remaining members of the original control group were again brought together as a group for a second experiment.

This second experiment consisted of transferring the control group to a new job, using the total participation technique in meetings which were similar to those held with experimental groups 2 and 3. The new job was a pressing job of comparable difficulty to the new job in the first experiment. On the average it involved about the same degree of change. In the meetings no reference was made to the previous behavior of the group on being transferred.

The results of the second experiment were in sharp contrast to the first. With the total participation technique, the same control group now recovered rapidly to their previous efficiency rating, and, like the other groups under this treatment, continued on beyond it to a new high level of production. There was no aggression or turnover in the group for 19 days after change, a marked modification of their previous behavior after transfer. Some anxiety concerning their seniority status was expressed, but this

was resolved in a meeting of their elected delegate, the union business agent, and a management representative. It should be noted that the pre-change level on the second experiment is just above 60 units per hour; thus the individual transfers had progressed to just above standard during the two and a half months between the two experiments.

Interpretation

... The first experiment showed that the rate of recovery is directly proportional to the amount of participation, and that the rates of turnover and aggression are inversely proportional to the amount of participation. The second experiment demonstrated more conclusively that the results obtained depended on the experimental treatment rather than on personality factors like skill or aggressiveness, for identical individuals yielded markedly different results in the control treatment as contrasted with the total participation treatment.

Apparently total participation has the same type of effect as participation through representation, but the former has a stronger influence. In regard to recovery rates, this difference is not unequivocal because the experiment was unfortunately confounded. Right after transfer, experimental group number 1 had insufficient material to work on for a period of seven days. Hence their slower recovery during this period is at least in part due to insufficient work. In succeeding days, however, there was an adequate supply of work and the differential recovery rate still persisted. Therefore we are inclined to believe that participation through representation results in slower recovery than does total participation....

Where we are dealing with a quasi-stationary equilibrium, the resultant forces upward and the forces downward are opposite in direction and equal in strength at the equilibrium level. Of course either resultant forces may fluctuate over a short period of time, so that the forces may not be equally balanced at a given moment. However, over a longer period of time and on the average

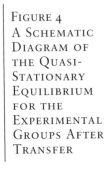

FIGURE 4
A SCHEMATIC
DIAGRAM OF
THE QUASI-
STATIONARY
EQUILIBRIUM
FOR THE
EXPERIMENTAL
GROUPS AFTER
TRANSFER

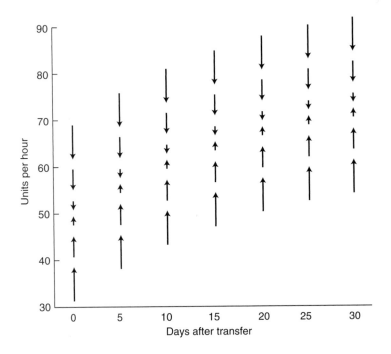

the forces balance out. Fluctuations from the average occur but there is a tendency to return to the average level.

Just before being transferred, all of the groups in both experiments had reached a stable equilibrium level at just above the standard production of 60 units per hour. This level was equal to the average efficiency rating for the entire factory during the period of the experiments. Since this production level remained constant, neither increasing nor decreasing, we may be sure that the strength of the resultant force upward was equal to the strength of the resultant force downward. This equilibrium of forces was maintained over the period of time when production was stationary at this level. But the forces changed markedly after transfer, and these new constellations of forces were distinctly different for the control and the experimental groups.

For the control group the period after transfer is a quasi-stationary equilibrium at a lower level, and the forces do not change during the period of thirty days. The resultant force upward remains

equal to the resultant force downward and the level of production remains constant. . . .

The situation for the experimental groups after transfer can be viewed as a quasi-stationary equilibrium of a different type. Figure 4 gives a schematic diagram of the resultant forces for the experimental groups. At any given level of production, such as 50 units per hour or 60 units per hour, both the resultant forces upward and the resultant forces downward change over the period of thirty days. During this time the point of equilibrium, which starts at 50 units per hour, gradually rises until it reaches a level of over 70 units per hour after thirty days. Yet here again the equilibrium level has the character of a "central force field," where at any point in the total field the resultant of the upward and the downward forces is in the direction of the equilibrium level. . . .

There are three main component forces influencing production in a downward direction: (1) the difficulty of the job; (2) a force corresponding to avoidance of strain; (3) a force corresponding to a group standard to restrict production to a given level. The resultant force upward in the direction of greater production is composed of three additional component forces; (4) the force corresponding to the goal of standard production; (5) a force corresponding to pressures induced by the management through supervision; (6) a force corresponding to a group standard of competition. Let us examine each of these six component forces.

1. *Job Difficulty.* For all operators the difficulty of the job is one of the forces downward on production. The difficulty of the job, of course, is relative to the skill of the operator. The given job may be very difficult for an unskilled operator but relatively easy for a highly skilled one. In the case of a transfer a new element of difficulty enters. For some time the new job is much more difficult, for the operator is unskilled at that particular job. In addition to the difficulty experienced by any learner, the transfer often encounters the added difficulty of proactive inhibition. Where the new job is similar to the old job there will be a period of interference between the two similar but different skills required. . . .

2. *Strain Avoidance.* The force toward lower production corresponding to the difficulty of the job (or the lack of skill of the person) has the character of a restraining force—that is, it acts to prevent locomotion rather than as a driving force causing locomotion. However, in all production there is a closely related driving force towards lower production, namely "strain avoidance." We assume that working too hard and working too fast is an unpleasant strain; and corresponding to this negative valence there is a driving force in the opposite direction, namely towards taking it easy or working slower. The higher the level of production the greater will be the strain and, other things being equal, the stronger will be the downward force of strain avoidance. Likewise, the greater the difficulty of the job the stronger will be the force corresponding to strain avoidance. But the greater the operator's skill the smaller will be the strain and the strength of the force of strain avoidance. Therefore:

• Hypothesis (4): The strength of the force of strain avoidance =

$$\frac{job\ difficulty \times production\ level}{skill\ of\ operator}$$

The differential recovery rates of the control group in both experiments and the three experimental groups in Experiment I cannot be explained by strain avoidance because job difficulty, production level, and operator skill were matched at the time immediately following transfer. . . .

3. *The Goal of Standard Production.* In considering the negative attitudes toward transfer and the resistance to being transferred, there are several important aspects of the complex goal of reaching and maintaining a level of 60 units per hour. For an operator producing below standard, this goal is attractive because it means success, high status in the eyes of her fellow employees, better pay, and job security. On the other hand, there is a strong force against remaining below standard because this lower level means failure, low status, low pay, and the danger of being fired. Thus it is clear that the upward force corresponding to the goal of standard production will indeed be strong for the transfer who has dropped below standard.

It is equally clear why any operator, who accepts the stereotype about transfer, shows such strong resistance to being changed. She sees herself as becoming a failure and losing status, pay, and perhaps the job itself. The result is a lowered level of aspiration and a weakened force toward the goal of standard production.

Just such a weakening of the force toward 60 units per hour seems to have occurred in the control group in Experiment I. The participation treatments, on the other hand, seem to have involved the operators in designing the new job and setting the new piece rates in such a way that they did not lose hope of regaining the goal of standard production. Thus the participation resulted in a stronger force toward higher production.

However, this force alone can hardly account for the large differences in recovery rate between the control group and the experimental groups; certainly it does not explain why the latter increased to a level so high above standard.

4. *Management Pressure.* On all operators below standard the management exerts a pressure for higher production. This pressure is not harsh and autocratic treatment involving threats. Rather it takes the form of persuasion and encouragement by the supervisors. They attempt to induce the low rating operator to improve her performance and to attain standard production....

The reaction of a person to an effective induced force will vary depending, among other things, on the person's relation to the inducing agent. A force induced by a friend may be accepted in such a way that it acts more like an own force. An effective force induced by an enemy may be resisted and rejected so that the person complies unwillingly and shows signs of conflict and tension. Thus in addition to what might be called a "neutral" induced force, we also distinguish an *accepted* induced force and a *rejected* induced force. Naturally the acceptance and the rejection of an induced force can vary in degree from zero (i.e., a neutral induced force) to very strong acceptance or rejection. To account for the difference in character between the acceptance and the rejection of an induced force, we make the following assumptions:

• Hypothesis (5): The acceptance of an induced force sets up additional own forces in the same direction.

• Hypothesis (6): The rejection of an induced force sets up additional own forces in the opposite direction.

The grievances, aggression, and tension in the control group in Experiment I indicate that they rejected the force toward higher production induced by the management. The group accepted the stereotype that transfer is a calamity, but the control procedure did not convince them that the change was necessary and they viewed the new job and the new piece rates set by management as arbitrary and unreasonable.

The experimental groups, on the contrary, participated in designing the changes and setting the piece rates so that they spoke of the new job as "our job" and the new piece rates as "our rates." Thus they accepted the new situation and accepted the management induced force toward higher production....

5. *Group Standards.* Probably the most important force affecting the recovery under the control procedure was a group standard, set by the group, restricting the level of production to 50 units per hour. Evidently this explicit agreement to restrict production is related to the group's rejection of the change and of the new job as arbitrary and unreasonable. Perhaps they had faint hopes of demonstrating that standard production could not be attained and thereby obtain a more favorable rate. In any case there was a definite group phenomenon which affected all the members of the group. We have already noted the striking example of the presser whose production was restricted in the group situation to about half the level she attained as an individual. In the control group, too, we would expect the group to induce strong forces on the members. The more a member deviates above the standard the stronger would be the group-induced force to conform to the standard, for such deviations both negate any possibility of management's increasing the piece rate and at the same time expose the other members to increased pressure from management. Thus individual differences in levels of production should be sharply curtailed in the control group after transfer.

An analysis was made for all groups of the individual differences within the group in levels of production. In Experiment I the 40 days before change were compared with the 30 days after change; in Experiment II the 10 days before change were compared to the 17 days after change. As a measure of variability, the standard deviation was calculated each day for each group.

The average daily standard deviations *before* and *after* change were as follows:

Group	Variability	
	Before Change	After Change
Experiment I		
Control group	9.8	1.9
Experimental 1	9.7 ...	3.8
Experimental 2	10.3 ...	2.7
Experimental 3	9.9 ...	2.4
Experiment II		
Control group	12.7 ...	2.9

There is indeed a marked decrease in individual differences within the control group after their first transfer. In fact the restriction of production resulted in a lower variability than in any other group....

The table of variability also shows that the experimental treatments markedly reduced variability in the other four groups after transfer. In experimental group 1 (participation by representation) this smallest reduction of variability was produced by a group standard of individual competition. Competition among members of the group was reported by the supervisor soon after transfer. This competition was a force toward higher production which resulted in good recovery to standard and continued progress beyond standard.

Experimental groups 2 and 3 showed a greater reduction in variability following transfer. These two groups under total participation were transferred on the same day. Group competition developed between the two groups. This group competition, which evidently resulted in stronger forces on the members than did the individual competition, was an effective group standard. The standard gradually moved to higher and higher levels of production, with the result that the groups not only reached but far exceeded their previous levels of production.

Turnover and Aggression

Returning now to our preliminary theory of frustration, we can see several revisions. The difficulty of the job and its relation to skill and strain avoidance has been clarified in hypothesis (4). It is now clear that the driving force toward 60 is a complex affair; it is partly a negative driving force corresponding to the negative valence of low pay, low status, failure, and job insecurity. Turnover results not only from the frustration produced by the conflict of these two forces, but also as a direct attempt to escape from the region of these negative valences. For the members of the control group, the group standard to restrict production prevented escape by increasing production, so that quitting their jobs was the only remaining escape. In the participation groups, on the contrary, both the group standards and the additional own forces resulting from the acceptance of management-induced forces combined to make increasing production the distinguished path of escape from this region of negative valence....

The control procedure had the effect for the members of setting up management as a hostile power field. They rejected the forces induced by this hostile power field, and group standards to restrict production developed within the group in opposition to management. In this conflict between the power field of management and the power field of the group, the control group attempted to reduce the strength of the hostile power field relative to the strength of their own power field. This change was accomplished in three ways: (a) the group increased its own power by developing a more cohesive and well-disciplined group, (b) they secured "allies" by getting the backing of the union in filing a formal grievance about the new piece rate, (c) they attacked the hostile power field directly in the form of aggression against the supervisor, the time study engineer, and the higher management. Thus the aggression was derived not only from individual frustration but also from the conflict between two groups. Furthermore, this situation of group conflict both helped to define management as the frustrating agent and gave the members strength to express any aggressive impulses produced by frustration.

CONCLUSIONS

It is possible for management to modify greatly or to remove completely group resistance to changes in methods of work and the ensuing piece rates. This change can be accomplished by the use of group meetings in which management effectively communicates the need for change and stimulates group participation in planning the changes.

For Harwood's management, and presumably for managements of other industries using an incentive system, this experiment has important implications in the field of labor relations. A majority of all grievances presented at Harwood have always stemmed from a change situation. By preventing or greatly modifying group resistance to change, this concomitant to change may well be greatly reduced. The reduction of such costly phenomena as turnover and slow relearning rates presents another distinct advantage.

REFERENCES

1. French, John R. P., Jr. The Behaviour of Organized and Unorganized Groups under Conditions of Frustration and Fear, Studies in Topological and Vector Psychology, III, *University of Iowa Studies in Child Welfare,* 1944, Vol. XX, pp. 229–308.
2. Lewin, Kurt. Frontiers in Group Dynamics, *Human Relations,* Vol. I, No. 1, 1947, pp. 5–41.

NOTE

1. Grateful acknowledgements are made by the authors to Dr. Alfred J. Marrow, president of the Harwood Manufacturing Corporation, and to the entire Harwood staff for their valuable aid and suggestions in this study. The authors have drawn repeatedly from the works and concepts of Kurt Lewin for both the action and theoretical phases of this study. Many of the leadership techniques used in the experimental group meetings were techniques developed at the first National Training Laboratory for Group Development held at Bethel, Maine, in the summer of 1947. Both authors attended this laboratory.

Reading 38 | # Group Decision and Social Change
Kurt Lewin

Quasi-Stationary Social Equilibria and the Problem of Permanent Change

1. *The Objective of Change.* The objective of social change might concern the nutritional standard of consumption, the economic standard of living, the type of group relation, the output of a factory, the productivity of an educational team. It is important that a social standard to be changed does not have the nature of a "thing" but of a "process." A certain standard of consumption, for instance, means that a certain action—such as making certain decisions, buying, preparing, and canning certain food in a family—occurs with a certain frequency within a given period. Similarly, a certain type of group relations means that within a given period certain friendly and hostile actions and reactions of a certain degree of severity occur between the members of two groups. Changing group relations or changing consumption means changing the level at which these multitude of events proceed. In other words, the "level" of consumption, of friendliness, or of productivity is to be characterized as the aspect of an ongoing social process.

Any planned social change will have to consider a multitude of factors characteristic for the particular case. The change may require a more or less unique combination of educational and organizational measures; it may depend upon quite different treatments or ideology, expectation, and organization. Still, certain general formal principles always have to be considered.

2. *The Conditions of a Stable Quasi-stationary Equilibrium.* The study of the conditions for change begins appropriately with an analysis of the conditions for "no change," that is, for the state of equilibrium.

From what has been just discussed, it is clear that by a state of "no social change" we do not refer to a stationary but to a quasi-stationary equilibrium; that is, to a state comparable to that of a river which flows with a given velocity in a given direction during a certain time interval. A social change is comparable to a change in the velocity or direction of that river.

A number of statements can be made in regard to the conditions of quasi-stationary equilibrium. (These conditions are treated more elaborately elsewhere.[1])

A. The strength of forces which tend to lower that standard of social life should be equal and opposite to the strength of forces which tend to raise its level. The resultant of forces on the line of equilibrium should therefore be zero.

B. Since we have to assume that the strength of social forces always shows variations, a quasi-stationary equilibrium presupposes that the forces against raising the standard increase with the amount of raising and that the forces against lowering increase (or remain constant) with the amount of lowering. This type of gradient which is characteristic for a "positive central force field"[2] has to hold at least in the neighborhood of the present level (Fig. 1).

C. It is possible to change the strength of the opposing forces without changing the level of social conduct. In this case the tension (degree of conflict) increases.

3. *Two Basic Methods of Changing Levels of Conduct.* For any type of social management, it is of great practical importance that levels of quasi-stationary equilibria can be changed in either of two ways: by adding forces in the desired

Source: Kurt Lewin, "Group Decision and Social Change," 1952.

FIGURE I
GRADIENTS
OF RESULTANT
FORCES (f*)

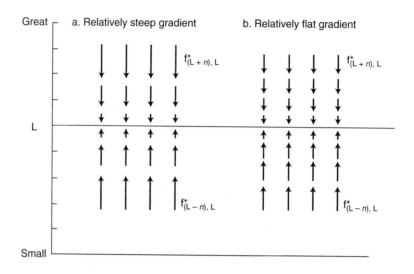

direction or by diminishing opposing forces. If a change from the level L_1 to L_2 is brought about by increasing the forces toward L_2, the secondary effects should be different from the case where the same change of level is brought about by diminishing the opposing forces.

In both cases the equilibrium might change to the same new level. The secondary effect should, however, be quite different. In the first case, the process on the new level would be accompanied by a state of relatively high tension; in the second case, by a state of relatively low tension. Since increase of tension above a certain degree is likely to be paralleled by higher aggressiveness, higher emotionality, and lower constructiveness, it is clear that as a rule the second method will be preferable to the high pressure method.

The group decision procedure which is used here attempts to avoid high pressure methods and is sensitive to resistance to change. In the experiment by Bavelas on changing production in factory work (as noted below), for instance, no attempt was made to set the new production goal by majority vote because a majority vote forces some group members to produce more than they consider appropriate. These individuals are likely to have some inner resistance. Instead a procedure

was followed by which a goal was chosen on which everyone could agree fully.

It is possible that the success of group decision and particularly the permanency of the effect is, in part, due to the attempt to bring about a favorable decision by removing counterforces within the individuals rather than by applying outside pressure.

The surprising increase from the second to the fourth week in the number of mothers giving cod liver oil and orange juice to the baby can probably be explained by such a decrease of counterforces. Mothers are likely to handle their first baby during the first weeks of life somewhat cautiously and become more ready for action as the child grows stronger.

4. *Social Habits and Group Standards.* Viewing a social stationary process as the result of a quasi-stationary equilibrium, one may expect that any added force will change the level of the process. The idea of "social habit" seems to imply that, in spite of the application of a force, the level of the social process will not change because of some type of "inner resistance" to change. To overcome this inner resistance, an additional force seems to be required, a force sufficient to "break the habit," to "unfreeze" the custom.

Many social habits are anchored in the relation between the individuals and certain group standards. An individual P may differ in his personal level of conduct (L_p) from the level which represents group standards (L_{Gr}) by a certain amount. If the individual should try to diverge "too much" from group standards, he would find himself in increasing difficulties. He would be ridiculed, treated severely, and finally ousted from the group. Most individuals, therefore, stay pretty close to the standard of the groups they belong to or wish to belong to. In other words, the group level itself acquires value. It becomes a positive valence corresponding to a central force field with the force $f_{P,L}$ keeping the individual in line with the standards of the group.

5. Individual Procedures and Group Procedures of Changing Social Conduct. If the resistance to change depends partly on the value which the group standard has for the individual, the resistance to change should diminish if one diminishes the strength of the value of the group standard or changes the level perceived by the individual as having social value.

This second point is one of the reasons for the effectiveness of "group carried" changes[3] resulting from procedures which approach the individuals as part of face-to-face groups. Perhaps one might expect single individuals to be more pliable than groups of like-minded individuals. However, experience in leadership training, in changing of food habits, work production, criminality, alcoholism, prejudices, all indicate that it is usually easier to change individuals formed into a group than to change any one of them separately.[4] As long as group standards are unchanged, the individual will resist changes more strongly the farther he is to depart from group standards. If the group standard itself is changed, the resistance which is due to the relation between individual and group standard is eliminated.

6. Changing as a Three-step Procedure: Unfreezing, Moving, and Freezing of a Level. A change toward a higher level of group performance is frequently short lived: after a "shot in the arm," group life soon returns to the previous level.

This indicates that it does not suffice to define the objective of a planned change in group performance as the reaching of a different level. Permanency of the new level, or permanency for a desired period, should be included in the objective. A successful change includes therefore three aspects: unfreezing (if necessary) the present level L_1 moving to the new level L_2, and freezing group life on the new level. Since any level is determined by a force field, permanency implies that the new force field is made relatively secure against change.

The "unfreezing" of the present level may involve quite different problems in different cases. Allport[5] has described the "catharsis" which seems to be necessary before prejudices can be removed. To break open the shell of complacency and self-righteousness, it is sometimes necessary to bring about deliberately an emotional stir-up.

Figure 2 presents an example of the effect of three group decisions of a team in a factory reported by Maier[6] which illustrates an unusually good case of permanency of change measured over nine months.

The experiments on group decision reported here cover but a few of the necessary variations. Although in some cases the procedure is relatively easily executed, in others it requires skill and presupposes certain general conditions. Managers rushing into a factory to raise production by group decisions are likely to encounter failure. In social management as in medicine there are no patent medicines, and each case demands careful diagnosis.

One reason why group decision facilitates change is illustrated by Lewin.[7] Figure 3 shows the degree of eagerness to have the members of a students' eating cooperative change from the consumption of white bread to whole wheat. When the change was simply requested the degree of eagerness varied greatly with the degree of personal preference for whole wheat. In case of group decision the eagerness seems to be relatively independent of personal preference; the individual seems to act mainly as a "group member."

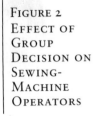

FIGURE 2
EFFECT OF
GROUP
DECISION ON
SEWING-
MACHINE
OPERATORS

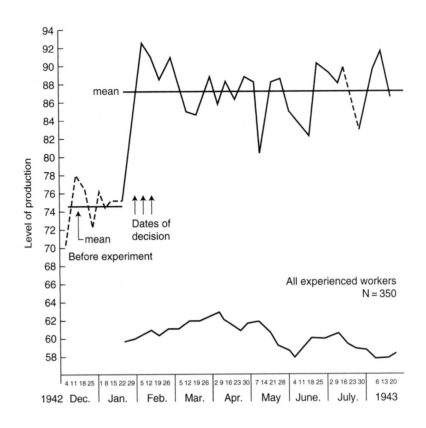

FIGURE 3
RELATION
BETWEEN OWN
FOOD
PREFERENCES
AND EAGERNESS
TO SUCCEED

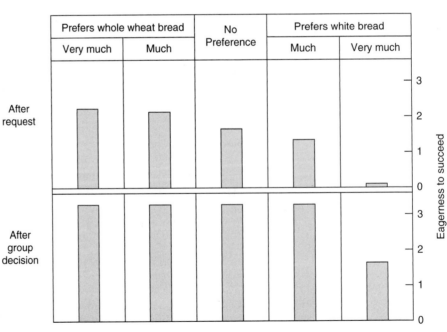

SUMMARY

Group decision is a process of social management or self management of groups. It is related to social channels, gates and gatekeepers; to the problem of social perception and planning; and to the relation between motivation and action, and between the individual and the group.

Experiments are reported in which certain methods of group decision prove to be superior to lecturing and individual treatment as means of changing social conduct.

The effect of group decision can probably be best understood by relating it to a theory of quasi-stationary social equilibria, to social habits and resistance to change, and to the various problems of unfreezing, changing and freezing social levels.

NOTES

1. K. Lewin, "Frontiers in Group Dynamics: Concept, Method and Reality in Social Science; Social Equilibria and Social Change," *Human Relations,* I, 1, June, 1947, pp. 5–42.
2. *Ibid.*
3. N. R. F. Maier, *Psychology in Industry* (Boston: Houghton Mifflin Co., 1946).
4. K. Lewin and P. Grabbe (eds.) *op. cit.*
5. G. W. Allport, "Catharsis and the Reduction of Prejudice" in K. Lewin and P. Grabbe (eds.), *op. cit.,* 3–10.
6. N. R. F. Maier, *op. cit.*
7. K. Lewin "Forces behind Food Habits...," *op. cit.*

Reading 39

Intervention Theory and Methods
Chris Argyris

A Definition of Intervention

To intervene is to enter into an ongoing system of relationship, to come between or among persons, groups, or objects for the purpose of helping them. There is an important implicit assumption in the definition that should be made explicit: the system exists independently of the intervenor. There are many reasons one might wish to intervene. These reasons may range from helping the clients make their own decisions about the kind of help they need to coercing the clients to do what the intervenor wishes them to do. Examples of the latter are modern black militants who intervene to demand that the city be changed in accordance with their wishes and choices (or white racists who prefer the same); executives who invite interventionists into their system to manipulate subordinates for them; trade union leaders who for years have resisted systematic research in their own bureaucratic functioning at the highest levels because they fear that valid information might lead to entrenched interests—especially at the top—being unfrozen.

The more one conceives of the intervenor in this sense, the more one implies that the client system should have little autonomy from the intervenor; that its boundaries are indistinguishable from those of the intervenor; that its health or effectiveness are best controlled by the intervenor.

In contrast, our view acknowledges interdependencies between the intervenor and the client system but focuses on how to maintain, or increase, the client system's autonomy; how to differentiate even more clearly the boundaries between the client system and the intervenor; and how to conceptualize and define the client system's health independently of the intervenor's. This view values the client system as an ongoing, self-responsible unity that has the obligation to be in control over its own destiny. An intervenor, in this view, assists a system to become more effective in problem solving, decision making, and decision implementation in such a way that the system can continue to be increasingly effective in these activites and have a decreasing need for the intervenor.

Another critical question the intervenor must ask is, how is he helping—management or employees, black militants or Negro moderates, white racists or white moderates?... At this point, it is suggested that the intervenor must be concerned with the system as a whole even though his initial contact may be made with only a few people. He therefore focuses on those intervention activities that eventually (not necessarily immediately) will provide *all* the members' opportunities to enhance their competence and effectiveness. If any individual or subsystem wishes help to prevent other individuals or subsystems from having these opportunities, then the intervenor may well have to question seriously his involvement in the project.[1]

Basic Requirements for Intervention Activity

Are there any basic or necessary processes that must be fulfilled regardless of the substantive issues involved, if intervention activity is to be helpful with any level of client (individual, group, or organizational)? One condition that seems so basic as to be defined axiomatic is the generation of *valid information*. Without valid information, it would be difficult for the client to learn and for the interventionist to help.

A second condition almost as basic flows from our assumption that intervention activity, no matter what its substantive interests and objectives, should be so designed and executed that

Source: Chris Argyris, INTERVENTION THEORY AND METHODS, 1970. Reprinted by permission of the author.

the client system maintains its discreteness and autonomy. Thus *free, informed choice* is also a necessary process in effective intervention activity.

Finally, if the client system is assumed to be ongoing (that is, existing over time), the clients require strengthening to maintain their autonomy not only vis-à-vis the interventionist but also vis-à-vis other systems. This means that their commitment to learning and change has to be more than temporary. It has to be so strong that it can be transferred to relationships other than those with the interventionist and can do so (eventually) without the help of the interventionist. The third basic process for any intervention activity is therefore the client's *internal commitment* to the choices made.

In summary, valid information, free choice, and internal commitment are considered integral parts of any intervention activity, no matter what the substantive objectives are (for example, developing a management performance evaluation scheme, reducing intergroup rivalries, increasing the degree of trust among individuals, redesigning budgetary systems, or redesigning work). These three processes are called the primary intervention tasks.

Primary Tasks of an Interventionist

Why is it necessary to hypothesize that in order for an interventionist to behave effectively and in order that the integrity of the client system be maintained, the interventionist has to focus on three primary tasks, regardless of the substantive problems that the client system may be experiencing?

Valid and Useful Information

First, it has been accepted as axiomatic that valid and useful information is the foundation for effective intervention. Valid information is that which describes the factors, plus their interrelationships, that create the problem for the client system. There are several tests for checking the validity of the information. In increasing

degrees of power they are public verifiability, valid prediction, and control over the phenomena. The first is having several independent diagnoses suggest the same picture. Second is generating predictions from the diagnosis that are subsequently confirmed (they occurred under the conditions that were specified). Third is altering the factors systematically and predicting the effects upon the system as a whole. All these tests, if they are to be valid, must be carried out in such a way that the participants cannot, at will, make them come true. This would be a self-fulfilling prophecy and not a confirmation of a prediction. The difficulty with a self-fulfilling prophecy is its indication of more about the degree of power an individual (or subset of individuals) can muster to alter the system than about the nature of the system when the participants are behaving without knowledge of the diagnosis. For example, if an executive learns that the interventionist predicts his subordinates will behave (a) if he behaves (b), he might alter (b) in order not to lead to (a). Such an alteration indicates the executive's power but does not test the validity of the diagnosis that if (a), then (b).

The tests for valid information have important implications for effective intervention activity. First, the interventionist's diagnoses must strive to represent the total client system and not the point of view of any subgroup or individual. Otherwise, the interventionist could not be seen only as being under the control of a particular individual or subgroup, but also his predictions would be based upon inaccurate information and thus might not be confirmed.

This does not mean that an interventionist may not begin with, or may not limit his relationship to, a subpart of the total system. It is totally possible, for example, for the interventionist to help management, blacks, trade union leaders, etc. With whatever subgroup he works he simply should not agree to limit his diagnosis to its wishes.

It is conceivable that a client system may be helped even though valid information is not generated. Sometimes changes occur in a positive direction without the interventionist having played any important role. These changes, although helpful in that specific instance, lack the attribute of helping the organization to learn and to gain control over its problem-solving capability.

The importance of information that the clients can use to control their destiny points up the requirement that the information must not only be valid, it must be useful. Valid information that cannot be used by the clients to alter their system is equivalent to valid information about cancer that cannot be used to cure cancer eventually. An interventionist's diagnosis should include variables that are manipulable by the clients and are complete enough so that if they are manipulated effective changes will follow.

Free Choice

In order to have free choice, the client has to have a cognitive map of what he wishes to do. The objectives of his action are known at the moment of decision. Free choice implies voluntary as opposed to automatic; proactive rather than reactive. The act of selection is rarely accomplished by maximizing or optimizing. Free and informed choice entails what Simon has called "satisficing," that is, selecting the alternative with the highest probability of succeeding, given some specified cost constraints. Free choice places the locus of decision making in the client system. Free choice makes it possible for the clients to remain responsible for their destiny. Through free choice the clients can maintain the autonomy of their system.

It may be possible that clients prefer to give up their responsibility and their autonomy, especially if they are feeling a sense of failure. They may prefer, as we shall see in several examples, to turn over their free choice to the interventionist. They may insist that he make recommendations and tell them what to do. The interventionist resists these pressures, because if he does not, the clients will lose their free choice and he will lose his own free choice also. He will be controlled by the anxieties of the clients.

The requirement of free choice is especially important for those helping activities where the processes of help are as important as the actual help. For example, a medical doctor does not require that a patient with a bullet wound participate in the process by defining the kind of help he needs. However, the same doctor may have to pay much more attention to the processes he uses to help patients when he is attempting to diagnose blood pressure or cure a high cholesterol. If the doctor behaves in ways that upset the patient, the latter's blood pressure may well be distorted. Or, the patient can develop a dependent relationship if the doctor cuts down his cholesterol—increasing habits only under constant pressure from the doctor—and the moment the relationship is broken off, the count goes up.

Effective intervention in the human and social spheres requires that the processes of help be congruent with the outcome desired. Free choice is important because there are so many unknowns, and the interventionist wants the client to have as much willingness and motivation as possible to work on the problem. With high client motivation and commitment, several different methods for change can succeed.

A choice is free to the extent the members can make their selection for a course of action with minimal internal defensiveness; can define the path (or paths) by which the intended consequence is to be achieved; can relate the choice to their central needs; and can build into their choices a realistic and challenging level of aspiration. Free choice therefore implies that the members are able to explore as many alternatives as they consider significant and select those that are central to their needs.

Why must the choice be related to the central needs and why must the level of aspiration be realistic and challenging? May people not choose freely unrealistic or unchallenging objectives? Yes, they may do so in the short run, but not for long if they still want to have free and informed choice. A freely chosen course of action means that the action must be based on an accurate analysis of the situation and not on the biases or defenses of the decision makers. We know, from the level of aspiration studies, that choices which are too high or too low, which are too difficult or not difficult enough will tend to lead to psychological failure. Psychological failure will lead to increased defensiveness, increased failure, and decreased self-acceptance on the part of the members experiencing the failure. These conditions, in turn, will tend to lead to distorted perceptions by the members making the choices. Moreover, the defensive members may unintentionally create a climate where the members of surrounding and interrelated systems will tend to provide carefully censored information. Choices made under these conditions are neither informed nor free.

Turning to the question of centrality of needs, a similar logic applies. The degree of commitment to the processes of generating valid information, scanning, and choosing may significantly vary according to the centrality of the choice to the needs of the clients. The more central the choice, the more the system will strive to do its best in developing valid information and making free and informed choices. If the research from perceptual psychology is valid, the very perception of the clients is altered by the needs involved. Individuals tend to scan more, ask for more information, and be more careful in their choices when they are making decisions that are central to them. High involvement may produce perceptual distortions, as does low involvement. The interventionist, however, may have a greater probability of helping the clients explore possible distortion when the choice they are making is a critical one.

Internal Commitment

Internal commitment means the course of action or choice that has been internalized by each member so that he experiences a high degree of ownership and has a feeling of responsibility about the choice and its implications. Internal commitment means that the individual has reached the point where he is acting on the choice because it fulfills his own needs and sense of responsibility, as well as those of the system.

The individual who is internally committed is acting primarily under the influence of his own forces and not induced forces. The individual (or any unity) feels a minimal degree of dependence upon others for the action. It implies that he has obtained and processed valid information and that he has made an informed and free choice. Under these conditions there is a high probability that the individual's commitment will remain strong over time (even with reduction of external rewards) or under stress, or when the course of action is challenged by others. It also implies that the individual is continually open to reexamination of his position because he believes in taking action based upon valid information.

NOTE

1. There is an important function within the scope of responsibility of the interventionist that will not be discussed systematically in this volume. It is the public health function. There are many individuals who do not ask for help because they do not know they need help or that help could be available to them. The societal strategy for developing effective intervention activity must therefore include a function by which potential clients are educated about organizational health and illness as well as the present state of the art in effecting change. The writer hopes that this volume plays a role in facilitating this function.

Reading 40	The Fifth Discipline: The Art and Practice of the Learning Organization
	Peter M. Senge

From a very early age, we are taught to break apart problems, to fragment the world. This apparently makes complex tasks and subjects more manageable, but we pay a hidden, enormous price. We can no longer see the consequences of our actions; we lose our intrinsic sense of connection to a larger whole. When we then try to "see the big picture," we try to reassemble the fragments in our minds, to list and organize all the pieces. But, as physicist David Bohm says, the task is futile—similar to trying to reassemble the fragments of a broken mirror to see a true reflection. Thus, after a while we give up trying to see the whole altogether.

... When we give up this illusion—we can then build "learning organizations," organizations where people continually expand their capacity to create the results they truly desire, where new and expansive patterns of thinking are nurtured, where collective aspiration is set free, and where people are continually learning how to learn together.

As *Fortune* magazine recently said, "Forget your tired old ideas about leadership. The most successful corporation of the 1990s will be something called a learning organization." "The ability to learn faster than your competitors," said Arie De Geus, head of planning for Royal Dutch/Shell, "may be the only sustainable competitive advantage." As the world becomes more interconnected and business becomes more complex and dynamic, work must become more "learningful." It is no longer sufficient to have one person learning for the organization, a Ford or a Sloan or a Watson. It's just not possible any longer to "figure it out" from the top, and have everyone else following the orders of the "grand strategist." The organizations that will truly excel in the future will be the organizations that discover how to tap people's commitment and capacity to learn at *all* levels in an organization.

Learning organizations are possible because, deep down, we are all learners. No one has to teach an infant to learn. In fact, no one has to teach infants anything. They are intrinsically inquisitive, masterful learners who learn to walk, speak, and pretty much run their households all on their own. Learning organizations are possible because not only is it our nature to learn but we love to learn. Most of us at one time or another have been part of a great "team," a group of people who functioned together in an extraordinary way—who trusted one another, who complemented each others' strengths and compensated for each others' limitations, who had common goals that were larger than individual goals, and who produced extraordinary results. I have met many people who have experienced this sort of profound teamwork—in sports, or in the performing arts, or in business. Many say that they have spent much of their life looking for that experience again. What they experienced was a learning organization. The team that became great didn't start off great—it *learned* how to produce extraordinary results....

There is also another, in some ways deeper, movement toward learning organizations, part of the evolution of industrial society. Material affluence for the majority has gradually shifted people's orientation toward work—from what Daniel Yankelovich called an "instrumental" view of work, where work was a means to an end, to a more "sacred" view, where people seek the "intrinsic" benefits of work (Yankelovich, 1981). Our grandfathers worked six days a week to earn what most of us now earn by Tuesday afternoon," says Bill O'Brien, CEO of Hanover Insurance. "The ferment in management will continue until we build organizations that are more consistent with man's higher aspirations beyond food, shelter and belonging."

Moreover, many who share these values are now in leadership positions. I find a growing number of organizational leaders who, while still a minority, feel they are part of a profound evolution in the nature of work as a social institution. "Why can't we do good works at work?" asked Edward Simon, president of Herman Miller, recently. "Business is the only institution that has a chance, as far as I can see, to fundamentally improve the injustice that exists in the world. But first, we will have to move through the barriers that are keeping us from being truly vision-led and capable of learning."

Perhaps the most salient reason for building learning organizations is that we are only now starting to understand the capabilities such organizations must possess. For a long time, efforts to build learning organizations were like groping in the dark until the skills, areas of knowledge, and paths for development of such organizations became known. What fundamentally will distinguish learning organizations from traditional authoritarian "controlling organizations" will be the mastery of certain basic disciplines. That is why the "disciplines of the learning organization" are vital.

Disciplines of the Learning Organization

On a cold, clear morning in December 1903, at Kitty Hawk, North Carolina, the fragile aircraft of Wilbur and Orville Wright proved that powered flight was possible. Thus was the airplane invented; but it would take more than thirty years before commercial aviation could serve the general public.

Engineers say that a new idea has been "invented" when it is proven to work in the laboratory. The idea becomes an "innovation" only when it can be replicated reliably on a meaningful scale at practical costs. If the idea is sufficiently important, such as the telephone, the digital computer, or commercial aircraft, it is called a "basic innovation," and it creates a new industry or transforms an existing industry. In these terms, learning organizations have been invented, but they have not yet been innovated. . . .

Today, I believe, five new "component technologies" are gradually converging to innovate learning organizations. Though developed separately, each will, I believe, prove critical to the others' success, just as occurs with any ensemble. Each provides a vital dimension in building organizations that can truly "learn," that can continually enhance their capacity to realize their highest aspirations:

Systems Thinking

A cloud masses, the sky darkens, leaves twist upward, and we know that it will rain. We also know that after the storm, the runoff will feed into groundwater miles away, and the sky will grow clear by tomorrow. All these events are distant in time and space, and yet they are all connected within the same pattern. Each has an influence on the rest, an influence that is usually hidden from view. You can only understand the system of a rainstorm by contemplating the whole, not any individual part of the pattern.

Business and other human endeavors are also systems. They, too, are bound by invisible fabrics of interrelated actions, which often take years to fully play out their effects on each other. Since we are part of that lacework ourselves, it's doubly hard to see the whole pattern of change. Instead, we tend to focus on snapshots of isolated parts of the system, and wonder why our deepest problems never seem to get solved. Systems thinking is a conceptual framework, a body of knowledge and tools that has been developed over the past fifty years, to make the full patterns clearer, and to help us see how to change them effectively.

Though the tools are new, the underlying worldview is extremely intuitive; experiments with young children show that they learn systems thinking very quickly.

Personal Mastery

Mastery might suggest gaining dominance over people or things. But mastery can also mean a special level of proficiency. A master craftsman doesn't dominate pottery or weaving. People with a high level of personal mastery are able to consistently realize the results that matter most deeply to them—in effect, they approach their life as an artist would approach a work of art. They do that by becoming committed to their own lifelong learning.

Personal mastery is the discipline of continually clarifying and deepening our personal vision, of focusing our energies, or developing patience, and of seeing reality objectively. As such, it is an essential cornerstone of the learning organization—the learning organization's spiritual foundation. An organization's commitment to and capacity for learning can be no greater than that of its members. The roots of this discipline lie in both Eastern and Western spiritual traditions, and in secular traditions as well.

But surprisingly few organizations encourage the growth of their people in this manner. This results in vast untapped resources: "People enter business as bright, well-educated, high-energy people, full of energy and desire to make a difference," says Hanover's O'Brien. "By the time they are 30, a few are on the "fast track" and the rest 'put in their time' to do what matters to them on the weekend. They lose the commitment, the sense of mission, and the excitement with which they started their careers. We get damn little of their energy and almost none of their spirit."

And surprisingly few adults work to rigorously develop their own personal mastery. When you ask most adults what they want from their lives, they often talk first about what they'd like to get rid of: "I'd like my mother-in-law to move out," they say, or "I'd like my back problems to clear up." The discipline of personal mastery, by contrast, starts with clarifying the things that really matter to us, of living our lives in the service of our highest aspirations.

Here, I am most interested in the connections between personal learning and organizational learning, in the reciprocal commitments between individual and organization, and in the special spirit of an enterprise made up of learners.

Mental Model

"Mental models" are deeply ingrained assumptions, generalizations, or even pictures or images that influence how we understand the world and how we take action. Very often, we are not consciously aware of our mental models or the effects they have on our behavior. For example, we may notice that a co-worker dresses elegantly, and say to ourselves, "She's a country club person." About someone who dresses shabbily, we may feel, "He doesn't care about what others think." Mental models of what can or cannot be done in different management settings are no less deeply entrenched. Many insights into new markets or outmoded organizational practices fail to get put into practice because they conflict with powerful, tacit mental models.

Royal Dutch/Shell, one of the first large organizations to understand the advantages of accelerating organizational learning, came to this realization when they discovered how pervasive was the influence of hidden mental models, especially those that become widely shared. Shell's extraordinary success in managing through the dramatic changes and unpredictability of the world oil business in the 1970s and 1980s came in large measure from learning how to surface and challenge managers' mental models. (In the early 1970s Shell was the weakest of the big seven oil companies; by the late 1980s it was the strongest.) Arie de Geus (1988), Shell's recently retired Coordinator of Group Planning, says that continuous adaptation and growth in a changing business environment depends on "institutional learning, which is the process whereby management teams change their shared mental models of the company, their markets, and their competitors. For this reason, we think of planning as learning and of corporate planning as institutional learning."

The discipline of working with mental models starts with turning the mirror inward; learning to unearth our internal pictures of the world, to bring them to the surface and hold them rigorously to scrutiny. It also includes the ability to carry on "learningful" conversations that balance inquiry and advocacy, where people expose their own thinking effectively and make that thinking open to the influence of others.

Building Shared Vision

If any one idea about leadership has inspired organizations for thousands of years, it's the capacity to hold a shared picture of the future we seek to create. One is hard pressed to think of any organization that has sustained some measure of greatness in the absence of goals, values, and missions that become deeply shared throughout the organization. IBM had "service," Polaroid had instant photography, Ford had public transportation for the masses, and Apple had computing power for the masses. Though radically different in content and kind, all these organizations managed to bind people together around a common identity and sense of destiny.

When there is a genuine vision (as opposed to the all-too-familiar "vision statement"), people excel and learn, not because they are told to, but because they want to. But many leaders have personal visions that never get translated into shared visions that galvanize an organization. All too often, a company's shared vision has revolved around the charisma of a leader, or around a crisis that galvanizes everyone temporarily. But, given a choice, most people opt for pursuing a lofty goal, not only in times of crisis but at all times. What has been lacking is a discipline for translating individual vision into shared vision— not a "cookbook" but a set of principles and guiding practices.

The practice of shared vision involves the skills of unearthing shared "pictures of the future" that foster genuine commitment and enrollment rather than compliance. In mastering this discipline, leaders learn the counterproductiveness of trying to dictate a vision, no matter how heartfelt.

Team Learning

How can a team of committed managers with individual IQs above 120 have a collective IQ of 63? The discipline of team learning confronts this paradox. We know that teams can learn; in sports, in the performing arts, in science, and even, occasionally, in business, there are striking examples where the intelligence of the team exceeds the intelligence of the individuals in the team, and where teams develop extraordinary capacities for coordinated action. When teams are truly learning, not only are they producing extraordinary results but the individual members are growing more rapidly than could have occurred otherwise.

The discipline of team learning starts with "dialogue," the capacity of members of a team to suspend assumptions and enter into a genuine "thinking together." To the Greeks *dia-logos* meant a free-flowing of meaning through a group, allowing the group to discover insights not attainable individually. Interestingly, the practice of dialogue has been preserved in many "primitive" cultures, such as that of the American Indian, but it has been almost completely lost to modern society. Today, the principles and practices of dialogue are being rediscovered and put into a contemporary context. (Dialogue differs from the more common "discussion," which has its roots with "percussion" and "concussion," literally a heaving of ideas back and forth in a winner-takes-all competition.)

The discipline of dialogue also involves learning how to recognize the patterns of interaction in teams that undermine learning. The patterns of defensiveness are often deeply engrained in how a team operates. If unrecognized, they undermine learning. If recognized and surfaced creatively, they can actually accelerate learning.

Team learning is vital because teams, not individuals, are the fundamental learning unit in modern organizations. This is where "the rubber meets the road"; unless teams can learn, the organization cannot learn.

If a learning organization were an engineering innovation, such as the airplane or the personal computer, the components would be called "technologies." For an innovation in human behavior, the components need to be seen as *disciplines*. By "discipline," I do not mean an "enforced order" or "means of punishment," but a body of theory and technique that must be studied and mastered to be put into practice. A discipline is a developmental path for acquiring certain skills or competencies. As with any discipline, from playing the piano to electrical engineering, some people have an innate "gift," but anyone can develop proficiency through practice.

To practice a discipline is to be a lifelong learner. You "never arrive"; you spend your life mastering disciplines. You can never say, "We are a learning organization," any more than you can say, "I am an enlightened person." The more you learn, the more acutely aware you become of your ignorance. Thus, a corporation cannot be "excellent" in the sense of having arrived at a permanent excellence; it is always in the state of practicing the disciplines of learning, of becoming better or worse.

That organizations can benefit from disciplines is not a totally new idea. After all, management disciplines such as accounting have been around for a long time. But the five learning disciplines differ from more familiar management disciplines in that they are "personal" disciplines. Each has to do with how we think, what we truly want, and how we interact and learn with one another. In this sense, they are more like artistic disciplines than traditional management disciplines. Moreover, while accounting is good for "keeping score," we have never approached the subtler tasks of building organizations, of enhancing their capabilities for innovation and creativity, of crafting strategy and designing policy and structure through assimilating new disciplines. Perhaps this is why, all too often, great organizations are fleeting, enjoying their moment in the sun, then passing quietly back to the ranks of the mediocre.

Practicing a discipline is different from emulating "a model." All too often, new management innovations are described in terms of the "best practices" of so-called leading firms. While interesting, I believe such descriptions can often do more harm than good, leading to piecemeal copying and playing catch-up. I do not believe great organizations have ever been built by trying to emulate another, any more than individual greatness is achieved by trying to copy another "great person."

When the five component technologies converged to create the DC-3 the commercial airline industry began. But the DC-3 was not the end of the process. Rather, it was the precursor of a new industry. Similarly, as the five component learning disciplines converge they will not create *the* learning organization but rather a new wave of experimentation and advancement.

The Fifth Discipline

It is vital that the five disciplines develop as an ensemble. This is challenging because it is much harder to integrate new tools than simply apply them separately. But the payoffs are immense.

This is why systems thinking is the fifth discipline. It is the discipline that integrates the disciplines, fusing them into a coherent body of theory and practice. It keeps them from being separate gimmicks or the latest organization change fads. Without a systemic orientation, there is no motivation to look at how the disciplines interrelate. By enhancing each of the other disciplines, it continually reminds us that the whole can exceed the sum of its parts.

For example, vision without systems thinking ends up painting lovely pictures of the future with no deep understanding of the forces that must be mastered to move from here to there. This is one of the reasons why many firms that have jumped on the "vision bandwagon" in recent years have found that lofty vision alone fails to turn around a firm's fortunes. Without systems thinking, the seed of vision falls on harsh soil. If non-systemic thinking predominates, the first condition for nurturing vision is not met: a genuine belief that we can make our vision real in the future. We may say "We can achieve our vision" (most American managers are conditioned to this belief), but our tacit view of current reality as a set of conditions created by somebody else betrays us.

But systems thinking also needs the disciplines of building shared vision, mental models, team learning, and personal mastery to realize its potential. Building shared vision fosters a commitment to the long term. Mental models focus on the openness needed to unearth shortcomings in our present ways of seeing the world. Team learning develops the skills of groups of people to look for the larger picture that lies beyond individual perspectives. And personal mastery fosters the personal motivation to continually learn how our actions affect our world. Without personal mastery, people are so steeped in the reactive mindset ("someone/something else is creating my problems") that they are deeply threatened by the systems perspective.

Lastly, systems thinking makes understandable the subtlest aspect of the learning organization—the new way individuals perceive themselves and their world. At the heart of a learning organization is a shift of mind—from seeing ourselves as separate from the world to connected to the world, from seeing problems as caused by someone or something "out there" to seeing how our own actions create the problems we experience. A learning organization is a place where people are continually discovering how they create their reality. And how they can change it. As Archimedes has said, "Give me a lever long enough ... and single-handed I can move the world."

Metanoia—A Shift of Mind

When you ask people about what it is like being part of a great team, what is most striking is the meaningfulness of the experience. People talk about being part of something larger than themselves, of being connected, of being generative. It becomes quite clear that, for many, their experiences as part of truly great teams stand out as singular periods of life lived to the fullest. Some spend the rest of their lives looking for ways to recapture that spirit.

The most accurate word in Western culture to describe what happens in a learning organization is one that hasn't had much currency for the past several hundred years. It is a word we have used in our work with organizations for some ten years, but we always caution them, and ourselves, to use it sparingly in public. The word is "metanoia" and it means a shift of mind. The word has a rich history. For the Greeks, it meant a fundamental shift or change, or more literally transcendence ("meta"—above or beyond, as in "metaphysics") of mind ("noia," from the root "nous," of mind). In the early (Gnostic) Christian tradition, it took on a special meaning of awakening shared intuition and direct knowing of the highest, of God. "Metanoia" was probably the key term of such early Christians as John the Baptist. In the Catholic corpus the word metanoia was eventually translated as "repent."

To grasp the meaning of "metanoia" is to grasp the deeper meaning of "learning," for learning also involves a fundamental shift or movement of mind. The problem with talking about "learning organizations" is that the "learning" has lost its central meaning in contemporary usage. Most people's eyes glaze over if you talk to them about "learning" or "learning organizations." Little wonder—for, in everyday use, learning has come to be synonymous with "taking in information." "Yes, I learned all about that at the course yesterday." Yet, taking in information is only distantly related to real learning. It would be nonsensical to say, "I just read a great book about bicycle riding—I've now learned that."

Real learning gets to the heart of what it means to be human. Through learning we re-create ourselves. Through learning we become able to do something we never were able to do. Through learning we reperceive the world and our relationship to it. Through learning we extend our capacity to create, to be part of the generative process of life. There is within each of us a deep hunger for this type of learning. It is, as Bill O'Brien of Hanover Insurance says, "as fundamental to human beings as the sex drive."

This, then, is the basic meaning of a "learning organization"—an organization that is continually expanding its capacity to create its future. For such an organization, it is not enough merely to survive. "Survival learning" or what is more often termed "adaptive learning" is important—indeed it is necessary. But for a learning organization, "adaptive learning" must be joined by "generative learning," learning that enhances our capacity to create.

A few brave organizational pioneers are pointing the way, but the territory of building learning organizations is still largely unexplored. It is my fondest hope that this book can accelerate that exploration. . . .

REFERENCES

Arie de Geus, "Planning as Learning," *Harvard Business Review* (March/April 1988): 70–74.

Daniel Yankelovich, *New Rules: Searching for Self-fulfillment in a World Turned Upside Down* (New York: Random House), 1981.

Reading 41	Transforming Organizations: Why Firms Fail

John P. Kotter

By any objective measure, the amount of significant, often traumatic, change in organizations has grown tremendously over the past two decades. Although some people predict that most of the reengineering, restrategizing, mergers, downsizing, quality efforts, and cultural renewal projects will soon disappear, I think that is highly unlikely. Powerful macroeconomic forces are at work here, and these forces may grow even stronger over the next few decades. As a result, more and more organizations will be pushed to reduce costs, improve the quality of products and services, locate new opportunities for growth, and increase productivity.

To date, major change efforts have helped some organizations adapt significantly to shifting conditions, have improved the competitive standing of others, and have positioned a few for a far better future. But in too many situations the improvements have been disappointing and the carnage has been appalling, with wasted resources and burned-out, scared, or frustrated employees.

To some degree, the downside of change is inevitable. Whenever human communities are forced to adjust to shifting conditions, pain is ever present. But a significant amount of the waste and anguish we've witnessed in the past decade *is* avoidable. We've made a lot of errors, the most common of which are these.

Error #1: Allowing Too Much Complacency

By far the biggest mistake people make when trying to change organizations is to plunge ahead without establishing a high enough sense of urgency in fellow managers and employees. This error is fatal because transformations always fail to achieve their objectives when complacency levels are high.

When Adrien was named head of the specialty chemicals division of a large corporation, he saw lurking on the horizon many problems and opportunities, most of which were the product of the globalization of his industry. As a seasoned and self-confident executive, he worked day and night to launch a dozen new initiatives to build business and margins in an increasingly competitive marketplace. He realized that few others in his organization saw the dangers and possibilities as clearly as he did, but he felt this was not an insurmountable problem. They could be induced, pushed, or replaced.

Two years after his promotion, Adrien watched initiative after initiative sink in a sea of complacency. Regardless of his inducements and threats, the first phase of his new product strategy required so much time to implement that competitor counter-moves offset any important benefit. He couldn't secure sufficient corporate funding for his big reengineering project. A reorganization was talked to death by skilled filibusters on his staff. In frustration, Adrien gave up on his own people and acquired a much smaller firm that was already successfully implementing many of his ideas. Then, in a subtle battle played out over another two years, he watched with amazement and horror as people in his division with little sense of urgency not only ignored all the powerful lessons in the acquisition's recent history but actually stifled the new unit's ability to continue to do what it had been doing so well.

Smart individuals like Adrien fail to create sufficient urgency at the beginning of a business transformation for many different but interrelated reasons. They overestimate how much they can force big changes on an organization. They underestimate how hard it is to drive people out of their comfort zones. They don't recognize how their own actions can inadvertently reinforce the status quo. They lack patience: "Enough with the preliminaries, let's get on with it." They become paralyzed by the downside possibilities associated with reducing complacency: people becoming

Source: Leading Change, by John P. Kotter. © 1996 by Harvard Business School Publishing. Reprinted by permission of the publisher.

defensive, morale and short-term results slipping. *Or,* even worse, they confuse urgency with anxiety, and by driving up the latter they push people even deeper into their foxholes and create even more resistance to change.

If complacency were low in most organizations today, this problem would have limited importance. But just the opposite is true. Too much past success, a lack of visible crises, low performance standards, insufficient feedback from external constituencies, and more all add up to: "Yes, we have our problems, but they aren't that terrible and I'm doing my job just fine," or "Sure we have big problems, and they are all over there." Without a sense of urgency, people won't give that extra effort that is often essential. They won't make needed sacrifices. Instead they cling to the status quo and resist initiatives from above. As a result, reengineering bogs down, new strategies fail to be implemented well, acquisitions aren't assimilated properly, downsizings never get at those least necessary expenses, and quality programs become more surface bureaucratic talk than real business substance.

Error #2: Failing to Create a Sufficiently Powerful Guiding Coalition

Major change is often said to be impossible unless the head of the organization is an active supporter. What I am talking about here goes far beyond that. In successful transformations, the president, division general manager, or department head plus another five, fifteen, or fifty people with a commitment to improved performance pull together as a team. This group rarely includes all of the most senior people because some of them just won't buy in, at least at first. But in the most successful cases, the coalition is always powerful—in terms of formal titles, information and expertise, reputations and relationships, and the capacity for leadership. Individuals alone, no matter how competent or charismatic, never have all the assets needed to overcome tradition and inertia except in very small organizations. Weak committees are usually even less effective.

Efforts that lack a sufficiently powerful guiding coalition can make apparent progress for a while. The organizational structure might be changed, or a reengineering effort might be launched. But sooner or later, countervailing forces undermine the initiatives. In the behind-the-scenes struggle between a single executive or a weak committee and tradition, short-term self-interest, and the like, the latter almost always win. They prevent structural change from producing needed behavior change. They kill reengineering in the form of passive resistance from employees and managers. They turn quality programs into sources of more bureaucracy instead of customer satisfaction.

As director of human resources for a large U.S.-based bank, Claire was well aware that her authority was limited and that she was not in a good position to head initiatives outside the personnel function. Nevertheless, with growing frustration at her firm's inability to respond to new competitive pressures except through layoffs, she accepted an assignment to chair a "quality improvement" task force. The next two years would be the least satisfying in her entire career.

The task force did not include even one of the three key line managers in the firm. After having a hard time scheduling the first meeting—a few committee members complained of being exceptionally busy—she knew she was in trouble. And nothing improved much after that. The task force became a caricature of all bad committees: slow, political, aggravating. Most of the work was done by a small and dedicated subgroup. But other committee members and key line managers developed little interest in or understanding of this group's efforts, and next to none of the recommendations was implemented. The task force limped along for eighteen months and then faded into oblivion.

Failure here is usually associated with underestimating the difficulties in producing change and thus the importance of a strong guiding coalition. Even when complacency is relatively low, firms with little history of transformation or teamwork often undervalue the need for such a team or assume that it can be led by a staff executive from human resources, quality, or strategic planning instead of a key line manager. No matter how capable or dedicated the staff head, guiding coalitions without strong line leadership never seem to achieve the power that is required to overcome what are often massive sources of inertia.

Error #3: Underestimating the Power of Vision

Urgency and a strong guiding team are necessary but insufficient conditions for major change. Of the remaining elements that are always found in successful transformations, none is more important than a sensible vision.

Vision plays a key role in producing useful change by helping to direct, align, and inspire actions on the part of large numbers of people. Without an appropriate vision, a transformation effort can easily dissolve into a list of confusing, incompatible, and time-consuming projects that go in the wrong direction or nowhere at all. Without a sound vision, the reengineering project in the accounting department, the new 360-degree performance appraisal from human resources, the plant's quality program, and the cultural change effort in the sales force either won't add up in a meaningful way or won't stir up the kind of energy needed to properly implement any of these initiatives.

Sensing the difficulty in producing change, some people try to manipulate events quietly behind the scenes and purposefully avoid any public discussion of future direction. But without a vision to guide decision making, each and every choice employees face can dissolve into an interminable debate. The smallest of decisions can generate heated conflict that saps energy and destroys morale. Insignificant tactical choices can dominate discussions and waste hours of precious time.

In many failed transformations, you find plans and programs trying to play the role of vision. As the so-called quality czar for a communications company, Conrad spent much time and money producing four-inch-thick notebooks that described his change effort in mind-numbing detail. The books spelled out procedures, goals, methods, and deadlines. But nowhere was there a clear and compelling statement of where all this was leading. Not surprisingly, when he passed out hundreds of these notebooks, most of his employees reacted with either confusion or alienation. The big thick books neither rallied them together nor inspired change. In fact, they may have had just the opposite effect.

In unsuccessful transformation efforts, management sometimes does have a sense of direction, but it is too complicated or blurry to be useful. Recently I asked an executive in a midsize British manufacturing firm to describe his vision and received in return a barely comprehensible thirty-minute lecture. He talked about the acquisitions he was hoping to make, a new marketing strategy for one of the products, his definition of "customer first," plans to bring in a new senior-level executive from the outside, reasons for shutting down the office in Dallas, and much more. Buried in all this were the basic elements of a sound direction for the future. But they were buried, deeply.

A useful rule of thumb: Whenever you cannot describe the vision driving a change initiative in five minutes or less and get a reaction that signifies both understanding and interest, you are in for trouble.

Error #4: Undercommunicating the Vision by a Factor of 10 (or 100 or Even 1,000)

Major change is usually impossible unless most employees are willing to help, often to the point of making short-term sacrifices. But people will not make sacrifices, even if they are unhappy with the status quo, unless they think the potential benefits of change are attractive and unless they really believe that a transformation is possible. Without credible communication, and a lot of it, employees' hearts and minds are never captured.

Three patterns of ineffective communication are common, all driven by habits developed in more stable times. In the first, a group actually develops a pretty good transformation vision and then proceeds to sell it by holding only a few meetings or sending out only a few memos. Its members, thus having used only the smallest fraction of the yearly intracompany communication, react with astonishment when people don't seem to understand the new approach. In the second pattern, the head of the organization spends a considerable amount of time making speeches to employee groups, but most of her managers are virtually silent. Here vision captures more of the total yearly communication than in the first case, but the volume is still woefully inadequate. In the third pattern, much more effort goes into newsletters and speeches, but some highly visible individuals still behave in ways that are antithetical to the vision, and the net result is that cynicism among the troops goes up while belief in the new message goes down.

One of the finest CEOs I know admits to failing here in the early 1980s. "At the time," he tells me, "it seemed like we were spending a great deal of effort trying to communicate our ideas. But a few years later, we could see that the distance we went fell short by miles. Worse yet, we would occasionally make decisions that others saw as inconsistent with our communication. I'm sure that some employees thought we were a bunch of hypocritical jerks."

Communication comes in both words and deeds. The latter is generally the most powerful form. Nothing undermines change more than behavior by important individuals that is inconsistent with the verbal communication. And yet this happens all the time, even in some well-regarded companies.

Error #5: Permitting Obstacles to Block the New Vision

The implementation of any kind of major change requires action from a large number of people. New initiatives fail far too often when employees, even though they embrace a new vision, feel disempowered by huge obstacles in their paths.

Occasionally, the roadblocks are only in people's heads and the challenge is to convince them that no external barriers exist. But in many cases, the blockers are very real.

Sometimes the obstacle is the organizational structure. Narrow job categories can undermine efforts to increase productivity or improve customer service. Compensation or performance-appraisal systems can force people to choose between the new vision and their self-interests. Perhaps worst of all are supervisors who refuse to adapt to new circumstances and who make demands that are inconsistent with the transformation.

One well-placed blocker can stop an entire change effort. Ralph did. His employees at a major financial services company called him "The Rock," a nickname he chose to interpret in a favorable light. Ralph paid lip service to his firm's major change efforts but failed to alter his behavior or to encourage his managers to change. He didn't reward the ideas called for in the change vision. He allowed human resource systems to remain intact even when they were clearly inconsistent with the new ideals. With these actions, Ralph would have been disruptive in any management job. But he wasn't in just any management job. He was the number three executive at his firm.

Ralph acted as he did because he didn't believe his organization needed major change and because he was concerned that he couldn't produce both change and the expected operating results. He got away with this behavior because the company had no history of confronting personnel problems among executives, because some people were afraid of him, and because his CEO was concerned about losing a talented contributor. The net result was disastrous. Lower-level managers concluded that senior management had misled them about their commitment to transformation, cynicism grew, and the whole effort slowed to a crawl.

Whenever smart and well-intentioned people avoid confronting obstacles, they disempower employees and undermine change.

Error #6: Failing to Create Short-Term Wins

Real transformation takes time. Complex efforts to change strategies or restructure businesses risk losing momentum if there are no short-term goals to meet and celebrate. Most people won't go on the long march unless they see compelling evidence within six to eighteen months that the journey is producing expected results. Without short-term wins, too many employees give up or actively join the resistance.

Creating short-term wins is different from hoping for short-term wins. The latter is passive, the former active. In a successful transformation, managers actively look for ways to obtain clear performance improvements, establish goals in the yearly planning system, achieve these objectives, and reward the people involved with recognition, promotions, or money. In change initiatives that fail, systematic effort to guarantee unambiguous wins within six to eighteen months is much less common. Managers either just assume that good things will happen or become so caught up with a grand vision that they don't worry much about the short term.

Nelson was by nature a "big ideas" person. With assistance from two colleagues, he developed a conception for how his inventory control (IC) group could use new technology to radically reduce inventory costs without risking increased stock outages. The three managers plugged away at implementing their vision for a year, then two. By their own standards, they accomplished a great deal: new IC models were developed, new hardware was purchased, new software was written. By the standards of skeptics, especially the divisional controller, who wanted to see a big dip in inventories or some other financial benefit to offset the costs, the managers had produced nothing. When questioned, they explained that big changes require time. The controller accepted that argument for two years and then pulled the plug on the project.

People often complain about being forced to produce short-term wins, but under the right circumstances that kind of pressure can be a useful element in a change process. When it becomes clear that quality programs or cultural change efforts will take a long time, urgency levels usually drop. Commitments to produce short-term wins can help keep complacency down and encourage the detailed analytical thinking that can usefully clarify or revise transformational visions.

In Nelson's case, that pressure could have forced a few money-saving course corrections and speeded up partial implementation of the new inventory control methods. And with a couple of short-term wins, that very useful project would probably have survived and helped the company.

Error #7: Declaring Victory Too Soon

After a few years of hard work, people can be tempted to declare victory in a major change effort with the first major performance improvement. While celebrating a win is fine, any suggestion that the job is mostly done is generally a terrible mistake. Until changes sink down deeply into the culture, which for an entire company can take three to ten years, new approaches are fragile and subject to regression.

In the recent past, I have watched a dozen change efforts operate under the reengineering theme. In all but two cases, victory was declared and the expensive consultants were paid and thanked when the first major project was completed, despite little, if any, evidence that the original goals were accomplished or that the new approaches were being accepted by employees. Within a few years, the useful changes that had been introduced began slowly to disappear. In two of the ten cases, it's hard to find any trace of the reengineering work today.

I recently asked the head of a reengineering-based consulting firm if these instances were unusual. She said: "Not at all, unfortunately. For us, it is enormously frustrating to work for a few years, accomplish something, and then have the effort cut off prematurely. Yet it happens far too often. The time frame in many corporations is too short to finish this kind of work and make it stick."

Over the past few decades, I've seen the same sort of thing happen to quality projects, organization development efforts, and more. Typically, the problems start early in the process: the urgency level is not intense enough, the guiding coalition is not powerful enough, the vision is not clear enough. But the premature victory celebration stops all momentum. And then powerful forces associated with tradition take over.

Ironically, a combination of idealistic change initiators and self-serving change resisters often creates this problem. In their enthusiasm over a clear sign of progress, the initiators go overboard. They are then joined by resisters, who are quick to spot an opportunity to undermine the effort. After the celebration, the resisters point to the victory as a sign that the war is over and the troops should be sent home. Weary troops let themselves be convinced that they won. Once home, foot soldiers are reluctant to return to the front. Soon thereafter, change comes to a halt and irrelevant traditions creep back in.

Declaring victory too soon is like stumbling into a sinkhole on the road to meaningful change. And for a variety of reasons, even smart people don't just stumble into that hole. Sometimes they jump in with both feet.

Error #8: Neglecting to Anchor Changes Firmly in the Corporate Culture

In the final analysis, change sticks only when it becomes "the way we do things around here," when it seeps into the very bloodstream of the work unit or corporate body. Until new behaviors are rooted in social norms and shared values, they are always subject to degradation as soon as the pressures associated with a change effort are removed.

Two factors are particularly important in anchoring new approaches in an organization's culture. The first is a conscious attempt to show people how specific behaviors and attitudes have helped improve performance. When people are left on their own to make the connections, as is often the case, they can easily create inaccurate

links. Because change occurred during charismatic Coleen's time as department head, many employees linked performance improvements with her flamboyant style instead of the new "customer first" strategy that had in fact made the difference. As a result, the lesson imbedded in the culture was "Value Extroverted Managers" instead of "Love Thy Customer."

Anchoring change also requires that sufficient time be taken to ensure that the next generation of management really does personify the new approach. If promotion criteria are not reshaped, another common error, transformations rarely last. One bad succession decision at the top of an organization can undermine a decade of hard work.

Poor succession decisions at the top of companies are likely when boards of directors are not an integral part of the effort. In three instances I have recently seen, the champions for change were retiring CEOs. Although their successors were not resisters, they were not change leaders either. Because the boards simply did not understand the transformations in any detail, they could not see the problem with their choice of successors. The retiring executive in one case tried unsuccessfully to talk his board into a less seasoned candidate who better personified the company's new ways of working. In the other instances, the executives did not resist the board choices because they felt their transformations could not be undone. But they were wrong. Within just a few years, signs of new and stronger organizations began to disappear at all three companies.

Smart people miss the mark here when they are insensitive to cultural issues. Economically oriented finance people and analytically oriented engineers can find the topic of social norms and values too soft for their tastes. So they ignore culture—at their peril.

The Eight Mistakes

None of these change errors would be that costly in a slower-moving and less competitive world. Handling new initiatives quickly is not an essential component of success in relatively stable or

EXHIBIT I   EIGHT ERRORS COMMON TO ORGANIZATIONAL CHANGE EFFORTS
AND THEIR CONSEQUENCES

COMMON ERRORS

- Allowing too much complacency
- Failing to create a sufficiently powerful guiding coalition
- Underestimating the power of vision
- Undercommunicating the vision by a factor of 10 (or 100 or even 1,000)
- Permitting obstacles to block the new vision
- Failing to create short-term wins
- Declaring victory too soon
- Neglecting to anchor changes firmly in the corporate culture

CONSEQUENCES

- New strategies aren't implemented well
- Acquisitions don't achieve expected synergies
- Reengineering takes too long and costs too much
- Downsizing doesn't get costs under control
- Quality programs don't deliver hoped-for results

These errors are not inevitable. With awareness and skill, they can be avoided or at least greatly mitigated. The key lies in understanding why organizations resist needed change, what exactly is the multistage process that can overcome destructive inertia, and, most of all, how the leadership that is required to drive that process in a socially healthy way means more than good management.

cartel-like environments. The problem for us today is that stability is no longer the norm. And most experts agree that over the next few decades the business environment will become only more volatile.

Making any of the eight errors common to transformation efforts can have serious consequences (see Exhibit 1...). In slowing down the new initiatives, creating unnecessary resistance, frustrating employees endlessly, and sometimes completely stifling needed change, any of these errors could cause an organization to fail to offer the products or services people want at prices they can afford. Budgets are then squeezed, people are laid off, and those who remain are put under great stress. The impact on families and communities can be devastating. As I write this, the fear factor generated by this disturbing activity is even finding its way into presidential politics.

Reading 42	Evolution and Revolution as Organizations Grow
	Larry E. Greiner

Key executives of a retail store chain hold on to an organizational structure long after it has served its purpose because the structure is the source of their power. The company eventually goes into bankruptcy.

A large bank disciplines a "rebellious" manager who is blamed for current control problems, when the underlying causes are centralized procedures that are holding back expansion into new markets. Many young managers subsequently leave the bank, competition moves in, and profits decline.

The problems at these companies are rooted more in past decisions than in present events or market dynamics. Yet management, in its haste to grow, often overlooks such critical developmental questions as, Where has our organization been? Where is it now? and What do the answers to these questions mean for where it is going? Instead, management fixes its gaze outward on the environment and toward the future, as if more precise market projections will provide the organization with a new identity.

In stressing the force of history on an organization, I have drawn from the legacies of European psychologists who argue that the behavior of individuals is determined primarily by past events and experiences, rather than by what lies ahead. Extending that thesis to problems of organizational development, we can identify a series of developmental phases through which companies tend to pass as they grow. Each phase begins with a period of evolution, with steady growth and stability, and ends with a revolutionary period of substantial organizational turmoil and change—for instance, when centralized practices eventually lead to demands for decentralization. The resolution of each revolutionary period determines whether or not a company will move forward into its next stage of evolutionary growth.

A Model of How Organizations Develop

To date, research on organizational development has been largely empirical, and scholars have not attempted to create a model of the overall process. When we analyze the research, however, five key dimensions emerge: an organization's age and size, its stages of evolution and revolution, and the growth rate of its industry.

Age of the Organization

The most obvious and essential dimension for any model of development is the life span of an organization. History shows that the same organizational practices are not maintained throughout a long life span. This demonstrates a most basic point: management problems and principles are rooted in time. The concept of decentralization, for example, can describe corporate practices at one period but can lose its descriptive power at another.

The passage of time also contributes to the institutionalization of managerial attitudes. As these attitudes become rigid and eventually outdated, the behavior of employees becomes not only more predictable but also more difficult to change.

Size of the Organization

A company's problems and solutions tend to change markedly as the number of its employees and its sales volume increase. Problems of coordination and communication magnify, new functions emerge, levels in the management hierarchy multiply, and jobs become more interrelated. Thus, time is not the only determinant of structure; in fact, organizations that do not become larger can retain many of the same management issues and practices over long periods.

Stages of Evolution

As organizations age and grow, another phenomenon emerges: prolonged growth that we can term the *evolutionary period*. Most growing organizations do not expand for two years and then contract for one; rather, those that survive a crisis usually enjoy four to eight years of continuous growth without a major economic setback or severe internal disruption. The term *evolution* seems appropriate for describing these quiet periods because only modest adjustments appear to be necessary for maintaining growth under the same overall pattern of management.

Stages of Revolution

Smooth evolution is not inevitable or indefinitely sustainable; it cannot be assumed that organizational growth is linear. *Fortune*'s "500" list, for example, has had considerable turnover during the past 50 years. In fact, evidence from numerous case histories reveals periods of substantial turbulence interspersed between smoother periods of evolution.

We can term the turbulent times *periods of revolution* because they typically exhibit a serious upheaval of management practices. Traditional management practices that were appropriate for a smaller size and earlier time no longer work and are brought under scrutiny by frustrated top-level managers and disillusioned lower-level managers. During such periods of crisis, a number of companies fall short. Those that are unable to abandon past practices and effect major organizational changes are likely either to fold or to level off in their growth rates.

The critical task for management in each revolutionary period is to find a new set of organizational practices that will become the basis for managing the next period of evolutionary growth. Interestingly enough, those new practices eventually sow the seeds of their own decay and lead to another period of revolution. Managers therefore experience the irony of seeing a major solution in one period become a major problem in a later period.

Growth Rate of the Industry

The speed at which an organization experiences phases of evolution and revolution is closely related to the market environment of its industry. For example, a company in a rapidly expanding market will have to add employees quickly; hence, the need for new organizational structures to accommodate large staff increases is accelerated. Whereas evolutionary periods tend to be relatively short in fast-growing industries, much longer evolutionary periods occur in mature or slow-growing industries. Evolution can also be prolonged, and revolutions delayed, when profits come easily. For instance, companies that make grievous errors in a prosperous industry can still look good on their profit-and-loss statements; thus, they can buy time before a crisis forces changes in management practices. The aerospace industry in its highly profitable infancy is an example. Yet revolutionary periods still occur, as one did in aerospace when profit opportunities began to dry up. By contrast, when the market environment is poor, revolutions seem to be much more severe and difficult to resolve.

Phases of Growth

With the foregoing framework in mind, we can now examine in depth the five specific phases of evolution and revolution. As shown in the graph "The Five Phases of Growth," each evolutionary period is characterized by the dominant management style used to achieve growth; each revolutionary period is characterized by the dominant management problem that must be solved before growth can continue. The pattern presented in the chart seems to be typical for companies in industries with moderate growth over a long period; companies in faster-growing industries tend to experience all five phases more rapidly, whereas those in slower-growing industries encounter only two or three phases over many years.

It is important to note that each phase is at once a result of the previous phase and a cause for the next phase. For example, the evolutionary management style in Phase 3 is delegation, which

THE FIVE PHASES OF GROWTH

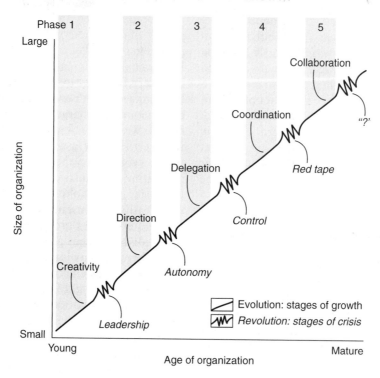

grows out of and becomes the solution to demands for greater autonomy in the preceding Phase 2 revolution. The style of delegation used in Phase 3, however, eventually provokes a revolutionary crisis that is characterized by attempts to regain control over the diversity created through increased delegation.

For each phase, managers are limited in what they can do if growth is to occur. For example, a company experiencing an autonomy crisis in Phase 2 cannot return to directive management for a solution; it must adopt a new style—delegation—in order to move forward.

Phase 1: Creativity

In the birth stage of an organization, the emphasis is on creating both a product and a market. The following are the characteristics of the period of creative evolution:

- The founders of the company are usually technically or entrepreneurially oriented, and they generally disdain management activities; their physical and mental energies are absorbed entirely by making and selling a new product.

- Communication among employees is frequent and informal.

- Long hours of work are rewarded by modest salaries and the promise of ownership benefits.

- Decisions and motivation are highly sensitive to marketplace feedback; management acts as customers react.

All the foregoing individualistic and creative activities are essential for a company to get off the ground. But as the company grows, those very activities become the problem. Larger production runs require knowledge about the efficiencies of manufacturing. Increased numbers of employees cannot be managed exclusively through informal communication, and new employees are not motivated by an intense dedication to the product or organization. Additional capital must be secured, and new accounting procedures are needed for financial control. The company's founders find themselves burdened with unwanted management responsibilities. They long for the "good old days" and try to act as they did in the past. Conflicts among harried leaders emerge and grow more intense.

At this point, a *crisis of leadership* occurs, which is the onset of the first revolution. Who will lead the company out of confusion and solve the managerial problems confronting it? Obviously, a strong manager is needed—one who has the necessary knowledge and skills to introduce new business techniques. But finding that manager is easier said than done. The founders often resist stepping aside, even though they are probably temperamentally unsuited to the job. So here is the first critical choice in an organization's development: to locate and install a strong business manager who is acceptable to the founders and who can pull the organization together.

Phase 2: Direction

Those companies that survive the first phase by installing a capable business manager usually embark on a period of sustained growth under able, directive leadership. Here are the characteristics of this evolutionary period:

- A functional organizational structure is introduced to separate manufacturing from marketing activities, and job assignments become increasingly specialized.
- Accounting systems for inventory and purchasing are introduced.
- Incentives, budgets, and work standards are adopted.
- Communication becomes more formal and impersonal as a hierarchy of titles and positions grows.

- The new manager and his or her key supervisors assume most of the responsibility for instituting direction; lower-level supervisors are treated more as functional specialists than as autonomous decision-making managers.

Although the new directive techniques channel employees' energy more efficiently into growth, they eventually become inappropriate for controlling a more diverse and complex organization. Lower-level employees find themselves restricted by a cumbersome and centralized hierarchy. They have come to possess more direct knowledge about markets and machinery than do their leaders at the top; consequently, they feel torn between following procedures and taking initiative on their own.

Thus, the second revolution emerges from a *crisis of autonomy*. The solution adopted by most companies is to move toward more delegation. Yet it is difficult for top-level managers who previously were successful at being directive to give up responsibility to lower-level managers. Moreover, the lower-level managers are not accustomed to making decisions for themselves. As a result, numerous companies founder during this revolutionary period by adhering to centralized methods, while lower-level employees become disenchanted and leave the organization.

Phase 3: Delegation

The next era of growth evolves from the successful application of a decentralized organizational structure. It exhibits these characteristics:

- Much greater responsibility is given to the managers of plants and market territories.
- Profit centers and bonuses are used to motivate employees.
- Top-level executives at headquarters limit themselves to managing by exception based on periodic reports from the field.
- Management often concentrates on acquiring outside enterprises that can be lined up with other decentralized units.
- Communication from the top is infrequent and usually occurs by correspondence, telephone, or brief visits to field locations.

The delegation phase allows companies to expand by means of the heightened motivation of managers at lower levels. Managers in decentralized organizations, who have greater authority and incentives, are able to penetrate larger markets, respond faster to customers, and develop new products.

A serious problem eventually emerges, however, as top-level executives sense that they are losing control over a highly diversified field operation. Autonomous field managers prefer to run their own shows without coordinating plans, money, technology, and personnel with the rest of the organization. Freedom breeds a parochial attitude.

Soon, the organization falls into a *crisis of control*. The Phase 3 revolution is under way when top management seeks to regain control over the company as a whole. Some top-management teams attempt a return to centralized management, which usually fails because of the organization's newly vast scope of operations. Those companies that move ahead find a new solution in the use of special coordination techniques.

Phase 4: Coordination

The evolutionary period of the coordination phase is characterized by the use of formal systems for achieving greater coordination and by top-level executives taking responsibility for the initiation and administration of these new systems. For example:

- Decentralized units are merged into product groups.
- Formal planning procedures are established and intensively reviewed.
- Numerous staff members are hired and located at headquarters to initiate companywide programs of control and review for line managers.
- Capital expenditures are carefully weighed and parceled out across the organization.
- Each product group is treated as an investment center where return on invested capital is an important criterion used in allocating funds.

- Certain technical functions, such as data processing, are centralized at headquarters, while daily operating decisions remain decentralized.
- Stock options and companywide profit sharing are used to encourage employees to identify with the organization as a whole.

All these new coordination systems prove useful for achieving growth through the more efficient allocation of a company's limited resources. The systems prompt field managers to look beyond the needs of their local units. Although these managers still have a great deal of decision-making responsibility, they learn to justify their actions more carefully to a watchdog audience at headquarters.

A lack of confidence, however, gradually builds between line and staff, and between headquarters and the field. The many systems and programs introduced begin to exceed their usefulness. A *red-tape crisis* is in full swing. Line managers, for example, increasingly resent direction from those who are not familiar with local conditions. And staff people, for their part, complain about uncooperative and uninformed line managers. Together, both groups criticize the bureaucratic system that has evolved. Procedures take precedence over problem solving, and innovation dims. In short, the organization has become too large and complex to be managed through formal programs and rigid systems. The Phase 4 revolution is under way.

Phase 5: Collaboration

The last observable phase emphasizes strong interpersonal collaboration in an attempt to overcome the red-tape crisis. Where Phase 4 was managed through formal systems and procedures, Phase 5 emphasizes spontaneity in management action through teams and the skillful confrontation of interpersonal differences. Social control and self-discipline replace formal control. This transition is especially difficult for the experts who created the coordination systems as well as for the line managers who relied on formal methods for answers.

The Phase 5 evolution, then, builds around a more flexible and behavioral approach to management. Here are its characteristics:

- The focus is on solving problems quickly through team action.
- Teams are combined across functions to handle specific tasks.
- Staff experts at headquarters are reduced in number, reassigned, and combined into interdisciplinary teams that consult with, not direct, field units.
- A matrix-type structure is frequently used to assemble the right teams for the appropriate problems.
- Formal control systems are simplified and combined into single multipurpose systems.
- Conferences of key managers are held frequently to focus on major problems.
- Educational programs are used to train managers in behavioral skills for achieving better teamwork and conflict resolution.
- Real-time information systems are integrated into daily decision-making processes.
- Economic rewards are geared more to team performance than to individual achievement.
- Experimenting with new practices is encouraged throughout the organization.

What will be the revolution in response to this stage of evolution? Many large U.S. companies are now in the Phase 5 evolutionary stage, so the answer is critical. Although there is little clear evidence regarding the outcome, I imagine that the revolution arising from the *"?" crisis* will center around the psychological saturation of employees who grow emotionally and physically exhausted from the intensity of teamwork and the heavy pressure for innovative solutions.

My hunch is that the Phase 5 revolution will be solved through new structures and programs that allow employees to periodically rest, reflect, and revitalize themselves. We may even see companies with dual organizational structures: a *habit structure* for getting the daily work done and a *reflective structure* for stimulating new perspective and personal enrichment.

Employees could move back and forth between the two structures as their energies dissipate and are refueled.

One European organization has implemented just such a structure. Five reflective groups have been established outside the company's usual structure for the purpose of continuously evaluating five task activities basic to the organization. The groups report directly to the managing director, although their findings are made public throughout the organization. Membership in each group includes all levels and functions in the company, and employees are rotated through the groups every six months.

Other concrete examples now in practice include providing sabbaticals for employees, moving managers in and out of hot-spot jobs, establishing a four-day workweek, ensuring job security, building physical facilities for relaxation during the workday, making jobs more interchangeable, creating an extra team on the assembly line so that one team is always off for reeducation, and switching to longer vacations and more flexible work hours.

The Chinese practice of requiring executives to spend time periodically on lower-level jobs may also be worth a nonideological evaluation. For too long, U.S. management has assumed that career progress should be equated with an upward path toward title, salary, and power. Could it be that some vice presidents of marketing might just long for, and even benefit from, temporary duty in field sales?

Implications of History

Let me now summarize some important implications for practicing managers. The main features of this discussion are depicted in the table "Organizational Practices in the Five Phases of Growth," which shows the specific management actions that characterize each growth phase. These actions are also the solutions that ended each preceding revolutionary period.

In one sense, I hope that many readers will react to my model by seeing it as obvious and

ORGANIZATIONAL PRACTICES IN THE FIVE PHASES OF GROWTH

Category	Phase 1	Phase 2	Phase 3	Phase 4	Phase 5
Management Focus	Make and sell	Efficiency of operations	Expansion of market	Consolidation of organization	Problem solving and innovation
Organizational Structure	Informal	Centralized and functional	Decentralized and geographical	Line staff and product groups	Matrix of teams
Top-Management Style	Individualistic and entrepreneurial	Directive	Delegative	Watchdog	Participative
Control System	Market results	Standards and cost centers	Reports and profit centers	Plans and investment centers	Mutual goal setting
Management Reward Emphasis	Ownership	Salary and merit increases	Individual bonus	Profit sharing and stock options	Team bonus

natural for depicting the growth of an organization. To me, this type of reaction is a useful test of the model's validity.

But at a more reflective level, I imagine some of these reactions come more from hindsight than from foresight. Experienced managers who have been through a developmental sequence can identify that sequence now, but how did they react when in the midst of a stage of evolution or revolution? They can probably recall the limits of their own developmental understanding at that time. Perhaps they resisted desirable changes or were even swept emotionally into a revolution without being able to propose constructive solutions. So let me offer some explicit guidelines for managers of growing organizations to keep in mind.

Know Where You Are in the Developmental Sequence

Every organization and its component parts are at different stages of development. The task of top management is to be aware of the stages; otherwise, it may not recognize when the time for change has come, or it may act to impose the wrong solution.

Leaders at the top should be ready to work with the flow of the tide rather than against it; yet they should be cautious because it is tempting to skip phases out of impatience. Each phase produces certain strengths and learning experiences in the organization that will be essential for success in subsequent phases. A child prodigy, for example, may be able to read like a teenager, but he cannot behave like one until he matures through a sequence of experiences.

I also doubt that managers can or should act to avoid revolutions. Rather, these periods of tension provide the pressure, ideas, and awareness that afford a platform for change and the introduction of new practices.

Recognize the Limited Range of Solutions

In each revolutionary stage, it becomes evident that the stage can come to a close only by means of certain specific solutions; moreover, these solutions are different from those that were applied to the problems of the preceding revolution. Too often, it is tempting to choose solutions that were tried before but that actually make it impossible for the new phase of growth to evolve.

Management must be prepared to dismantle current structures before the revolutionary stage becomes too turbulent. Top-level managers, realizing that their own managerial styles are no longer appropriate, may even have to take themselves out of leadership positions. A good Phase 2 manager facing Phase 3 might be wise to find a position at another Phase 2 organization that better fits his or her talents, either outside the company or with one of its newer subsidiaries.

Finally, evolution is not an automatic affair; it is a contest for survival. To move ahead, companies must consciously introduce planned structures that not only solve a current crisis but also fit the next phase of growth. That requires considerable self-awareness on the part of top management as well as great interpersonal skills in persuading other managers that change is needed.

Realize that Solutions Breed New Problems

Managers often fail to recognize that organizational solutions create problems for the future, such as when a decision to delegate eventually causes a problem of control. Actions in the past determine much of what will happen to a company in the future.

An awareness of this effect should help managers evaluate company problems with a historical understanding instead of pinning the blame on a current development. Better yet, it should place managers in a position to predict problems and thereby to prepare solutions and coping strategies before a revolution gets out of hand.

Top management that is aware of the problems ahead could well decide not to expand the organization. Managers may, for instance, prefer to retain the informal practices of a small company, knowing that this way of life is inherent in the organization's limited size, not in their congenial personalities. If they choose to grow, they may actually grow themselves out of a job and a way of life they enjoy.

And what about very large organizations? Can they find new solutions for continued evolution? Or are they reaching a stage when the government will act to break them up because they are too large?

Clearly, there is still much to learn about processes of development in organizations. The phases outlined here are merely five in number and are still only approximations. Researchers are just beginning to study the specific developmental problems of structure, control, rewards, and management style in different industries and in a variety of cultures.

One should not, however, wait for conclusive evidence before educating managers to think and act from a developmental perspective. The critical dimension of time has been missing for too long from our management theories and practices. The intriguing paradox is that by learning more about history, we may do a better job in the future.

Revolution Is Still Inevitable

I wrote the first draft of this article while I was felled by a bad leg during a ski vacation in Switzerland. At the time, the business world was buzzing with numerous faddish techniques. Perhaps it was the size and height of the mountains that made me feel that there were deeper and more powerful forces at work in organizations.

Four basic points still seem valid about the model. First, we continue to observe major phases of development in the life of growing companies, lasting anywhere from 3 to 15 years each. Although scholars debate the precise length and nature of these phases, everyone agrees that each phase contains its own unique structure, systems, and leadership. The growth rate of the industry seems to determine the phases' length.

Second, transitions between developmental phases still do not occur naturally or smoothly, regardless of the strength of top management. All organizations appear to experience revolutionary difficulty and upheaval, and many of these organizations falter, plateau, fail, or get acquired rather than grow further. IBM before Lou

Gerstner and General Electric before Jack Welch both suffered badly at the end of the fourth phase of coordination, when sophisticated management systems evolved into rigid bureaucracies.

Third, the logic of paradox underlying the model continues to ring true, although it often haunts and confuses the managerial psyche. Managers have difficulty in understanding that an organizational solution introduced by them personally in one phase eventually sows the seeds of revolution.

Fourth, the greatest resistance to change appears at the top because revolution often means that units under each senior executive will be eliminated or transformed. That is why we so often see new chief executives recruited from the outside and why senior managers frequently leave companies. Executives depart not because they are "bad" managers but because they just don't fit with where the company needs to go.

As for the differences that I have observed since the article's original publication, there is obviously much more "death" in the life of organizations today. Few organizations make it through all the phases of growth. If they don't fail, as most do in the initial phase of creativity and entrepreneurship, they often get acquired by companies that are in a later phase.

The phases are not as cleanly marked off as I depicted them. The vestiges of one phase remain as new approaches are introduced. Such overlaps are most notable in the case of the first-phase entrepreneur hanging on when professional management is added in the second phase of direction.

There are also miniphases within each evolutionary stage. The delegation phase, for example, does not typically begin with the complete decentralization of the entire organization into multiple product units, as the article implies. Usually one product group is launched, and then others are added over time. Also, as delegation—or *decentralization,* as I now prefer to call this phase—advances, senior managers at the corporate office are not as hands-off as I depicted them. The addition of multiple product or geographic units over time requires a sophisticated level of involvement by senior management to review strategies, evaluate results, and communicate the organization's values—but not to micro-manage the units under them.

I would change some of the things I said about the fifth phase of collaboration. My original description of this phase suggests that the entire organization is turned into a matrix of teams, I now see the matrix as confined largely to senior management, where the heads of geographic areas, product lines, and functional disciplines collaborate as a team in order to ensure that their decisions are coordinated and implemented across global markets. The most significant change in this phase occurs when the previously bureaucratic Phase 4 control-oriented staff and systems are replaced by a smaller number of consulting staff experts who help facilitate, rather than control, decisions.

My speculation that "psychological saturation" is the crisis ending Phase 5 now seems wrong. Instead, I think the crisis is one of realizing that there is no internal solution, such as new products, for stimulating further growth. Rather, the organization begins to look outside for partners or for opportunities to sell itself to a bigger company.

A sixth phase may be evolving in which growth depends on the design of extra-organizational solutions, such as creating a holding company or a network organization composed of alliances and cross-ownership. GE may have developed a similar model in which a periphery of companies is built around a core "money" company or bank (GE Capital) that attracts capital, earns high returns, and feeds the growth of other units.

I doubt that the advancement of information technology has made much of a difference in the basic aspects of the model. Information technology appears useful as a tool that evolves in different forms to fit each phase. For example, the Phase 2 functional organizational structure requires data that reflect revenue and cost centers, whereas Phase 3 decentralization needs data that measure profit center performance.

I wrote the article mainly about industrial and consumer goods companies, not about knowledge organizations or service businesses, which had yet to come into prominence. After recently studying a number of consulting, law, and investment firms, our research team found that those organizations also experience evolution and revolution as they grow.

In the first, entrepreneurial, phase the professional, service firm pursues and tests a variety of market paths. The phase ends with the partners arguing about whether or not to stay together to concentrate on one partner's vision for the future. In the second phase, the firm focuses on one major service and eventually finds itself with a debate among the partners about whether to continue focusing on the current practice or to open another office or add additional services. A third phase of geographic or service expansion typically ends with a struggle over ownership: how much equity are the original partners willing to share with the younger partners who led the expansion and brought in new clients? The fourth phase involves institutionalizing the firm's name, reputation, and its standard way of operating, and ends in a crisis of cultural conformity in the face of which the firm must restore innovation and flexibility.

Finally, as a strong caveat, I always remind myself and others that the "ev and rev" model depicted in this article provides only a simple outline of the broad challenges facing a management concerned with growth. It is not a cookie-cutter solution or panacea. The rate of growth, the effective resolution of revolutions, and the performance of the company within phases still depend on the fundamentals of good management: skillful leadership, a winning strategy, the heightened motivation of employees, and a deep concern for customers.

| # Appreciative Inquiry
David L. Cooperrider and Diana Whitney

"Appreciative inquiry (AI) begins an adventure. Even in the first steps, one senses an exciting direction in our language and theories of change—an invitation, as some have declared, to 'a positive revolution.'" The words just quoted *are* strong and, unfortunately, not ours. The more we replay the high-wire moments of our work at GTE, the more we ask the same question the people of GTE asked their senior executives: "Are you really ready for the momentum being generated? This is igniting a grass roots movement ... it *is* creating an organization in full voice, a center stage for positive revolutionaries!"

Tom White, president of what was then called GTE Telops (making up 80 percent of GTE's 67,000 employees) replied with no hesitation: "Yes, and what I see in this meeting are zealots, people with a mission and passion for creating the new GTE. Count me in, I'm your number one recruit, number one zealot." People cheered.

Fourteen months later—based on significant and measurable changes in stock prices, morale survey measures, quality/customer relations, union-management relations, and so on—GTE's whole-system change initiative won the 1997 ASTD (American Society for Training and Development) award for best organization-change program in the country. Appreciative Inquiry was cited as the "backbone."

How Did GTE Do It?

Tom White interprets AI in executive language:

> Appreciative Inquiry gets much better results than seeking out and solving problems. That's an interesting concept for me—and I imagine most of you—because telephone companies are among the world's best problem solvers. We concentrate enormous resources on correcting problems ... when used continually over a long time, this approach leads to a negative culture. If you combine a negative culture with the challenges we face today, we could easily convince ourselves that we

have too many problems to overcome—to slip into a paralyzing sense of hopelessness.... Don't get me wrong. I'm not advocating mindless happy talk. Appreciative Inquiry is a complex science designed to make things better. We can't ignore problems— we just need to approach them from the other side.[1]

What Tom White called "the other side" we describe as the *positive change core*. AI is a tool for connecting to the transformational power of this core by opening every strength, innovation, achievement, imaginative story, hope, positive tradition, passion, and dream to systematic inquiry. It involves asking appreciative questions, such as the following:

1. Describe a high-point experience in your organization, a time when you have been most alive and engaged.
2. Without being modest, tell me what is it that you most value about yourself, your work, your organization.
3. What are the core factors that give life to your organization, without which the organization would not be the same?
4. What three wishes do you have to enhance the health and vitality of your organization?

AI then uses the stories generated to create new, more compelling images of the organization and its future.

To achieve this stunning shift in the GTE culture, we asked, "How can we engage the positive potential of all employees toward transforming the company?" We wanted whatever we did to recognize and invite frontline employee self-sovereignty. We set a goal of creating a narrative-rich culture with a ratio of five positive stories to every negative one.

In the ten years since the AI theory and vision were published,[2] hundreds of people have cocreated AI practices, bringing AI's spirit and methodology into organizations all over the world. While the outcomes and illustrations we

Source: From Appreciative Inquiry by Cooperrider and Whitney. Reprinted by permission of Barrett-Koehler Publishers, Inc.

have selected are often dramatic, we emphasize that AI is in its infancy.

What Is Appreciative Inquiry?

AI has been described in a myriad of ways: a radically affirmative approach to change that completely lets go of problem-based management,[3] the most important advance in action research in the past decade,[4] and organization development's philosopher's stone.[5] Summing up AI is difficult—a philosophy of knowing, a methodology for managing change, an approach to leadership and human development. Here is a practice-oriented definition:

> Appreciative Inquiry is the cooperative search for the best in people, their organizations, and the world around them. It involves systematic discovery of what gives a system "life" when it is most effective and capable in economic, ecological, and human terms. AI involves the art and practice of asking questions that strengthen a system's capacity to heighten positive potential. It mobilizes inquiry through crafting an "unconditional positive question" often involving hundreds or sometimes thousands of people. In AI, intervention gives way to imagination and innovation; instead of negation, criticism, and spiraling diagnosis there is discovery, dream, and design. AI assumes that every living system has untapped, rich, and inspiring accounts of the positive. Link this "positive change core" directly to any change agenda, and changes never thought possible are suddenly and democratically mobilized.

The positive change core is one of the greatest and largely unrecognized resources in change management today. The most important insight we have learned with AI to date is that *human systems grow toward what they persistently ask questions about.* The single most important action a group can take to liberate the human spirit and consciously construct a better future is *to make the positive change core the common and explicit property of all.*

Getting Started

The Appreciative Inquiry 4-D Cycle

The AI cycle can be as rapid and informal as a conversation with a friend or colleague, or as formal as an organization-wide process involving every stakeholder. While there is no formula for Appreciative Inquiry, most organization-change efforts flow through the 4-D Cycle (see Figure 1). Each AI process is homegrown—designed to meet the unique challenges of the organization and industry involved.

At AI's heart is the *appreciative interview.* The uniqueness and power of an AI interview stem from its fundamentally affirmative focus. Appreciative interviews uncover what gives life to an organization, department, or community when at its best. They discover personal and organizational high points, what people value, and what they hope and wish for to enhance their organization's social, economic, and environmental vitality.

The First "D"—Discovery. The core Discovery Phase task is disclosing positive capacity. AI ignites this "spirit of inquiry" through the interviewing process. When asked how many people should be interviewed or who should do the interviews, we increasingly say "everyone" because in the process, people reclaim their ability to admire, to be surprised, to be inspired. What distinguishes AI at this phase is that every question is positive. As people throughout a system connect to study qualities, examples, and analysis of the positive core—each appreciating and everyone being appreciated—hope grows and community expands.

From Discovery to Dream. An artist's imagination is kindled not by searching for "what is wrong with this picture" but by being inspired by those things worth valuing. Appreciation draws our eye toward life, stirs our feelings, sets in motion our curiosity, and inspires the envisioning mind. The Dream Phase uses interview stories and insights discovered through the interviews. People listen together to moments when the organization was "alive," and the future becomes visible though ideals interwoven with actual experiences.

Design. Once the strategic focus or dream is articulated (a vision of a better world, a powerful purpose, and a compelling statement of strategic

FIGURE I
THE
APPRECIATIVE
INQUIRY 4-D
CYCLE

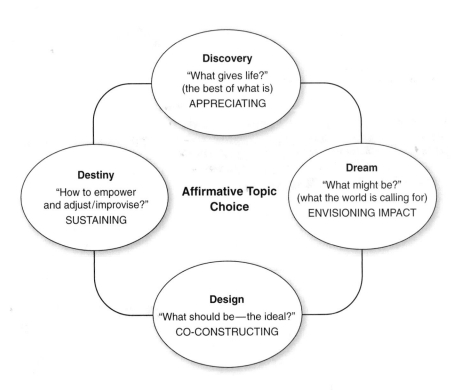

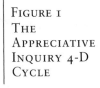

intent), attention turns to creating the ideal organization, a design of the system in relation to its world. One aspect differentiating Appreciative Inquiry from other planning methodologies is that future images emerge through grounded examples from an organization's positive past. Good news stories are used to craft possibility propositions that bridge the best of "what is" with collective aspiration of "what might be." People challenge the status quo as well as common assumptions underlying the organization's design. They explore: "What would our organization look like if it were designed to maximize the positive core and accelerate realizing our dreams?" When inspired by a great dream we have yet to find an organization that did not feel compelled to design something very new and very necessary.

We recently worked with Dee Hock, a truly visionary CEO. Dee founded VISA, a breakthrough organization with over 20,000 offices. The VISA system in over two hundred countries would not be manageable using centralized, command-and-control design principles of the traditional organization. If General Motors defined the old model, perhaps Dee's "chaordic organization"—combining chaos and order (like nature's designs)—foreshadows an emerging prototype. From Dee, we learned how to move pragmatically and substantively from appreciative Discovery and Dream to a postbureaucratic Design that distributes power and liberates human energy in a way we have never seen.

Destiny. We used to call the fourth "D" Delivery. We emphasized planning and dealing with conventional implementation challenges. Then we discovered that momentum for change and long-term sustainability increased the more we abandoned "delivery" ideas of action planning, monitoring progress, and building implementation strategies. Instead, we focused on giving AI to everyone and stepped back. The GTE story, still

Table 1 | AI 4-D Cycle and the AI Summit

Day—Cycle		Focus Participants ...
1—Discovery	Mobilize a systemic or systemwide inquiry into the positive change core	• Engage in appreciative interviews • Reflect on interview highlights
2—Dream	Envision the organization's greatest potential for positive influence and impact in the world	• Share dreams collected during the interviews • Create and present dramatic enactments
3—Design	Craft an organization in which the positive change core is boldly alive in all strategies, processes, systems, decisions, and collaborations	• Identify high-impact design elements and create an organization design • Draft provocative propositions (design statements) incorporating the positive change core
4—Destiny	Invite action inspired by the days of discovery, dream, and design	• Publicly declare intended actions and ask for support • Self-selected groups plan next steps

unfolding but attracting national recognition, is suggestive. This story says organizational change needs to look more like an inspired movement than a neatly packaged or engineered product. Dan Young, head of OD at GTE, and his colleagues call it "organizing for change from the grassroots to the frontline." Call it the path of positive protest or a strategy for positive subversion—it is virtually unstoppable once up and running.

Applying the 4-D Cycle

Two totally different approaches to applying the 4-D cycle AI are emerging. One says get the whole system into the same room. We have called this the AI Organization Summit (like climbing to the peak of the Himalayas). The other says let the whole thing out of the room—make the later phases more web-like, more self-organizing, more like a social movement. It is an autopoietic[6] network-structure within a bureaucracy. The first, the summit, is a modality that often results in "home runs" and strong relational ties. The second appears to be built on "the strength of weak ties" and "small wins." Both have led to huge momentum.

The Appreciative Inquiry Organization Summit

The AI Summit is among the most exciting Appreciative Inquiry applications. It is a large-scale meeting process that focuses on discovering and developing the organization's positive change core and designing it into strategic business processes such as marketing, customer service, human resource development, and new product development. Participation is diverse by design and includes all the organization's stakeholders. It is generally four days long and involves 50 to 2,000 participants or more.

While each Summit is a unique design, there are some common aspects of successful AI Summits. The four days flow through the AI 4-D Cycle (Table 1).

GTE: The 4-D Cycle Self-Organizes

The "GTE Together" article described a grassroots movement to build the new GTE. Initiated as a pilot to see what would happen if appreciative inquiry was given to frontline employees, things took off. All of a sudden, without any permission, frontline employees were launching interview studies into positive topics like innovation,

TABLE 2 | AI ROLES AND RESPONSIBILITIES

	Before	During	After
Consultants	• Introduce AI to the organization • Focus on the "business case" for AI	• Train groups in AI • Support the Core Team • Facilitate the Summit	• Assist the organization to integrate AI into daily practices
Sponsors	• Become knowledgeable in AI • Plant the AI seed	• Champion AI in the organization • Participate—as an equal, essential voice	• Ask, How might we take an AI approach to this? • Lead by affirmation
Core Team	• Become knowledgeable in AI	• Select affirmative topics • Create interview protocol • Determine interview strategy • Communicate "best" stories	• Use AI as a daily practice
Interviewers	• Become knowledgeable in AI	• Conduct interviews • Summarize "best" stories	• Use AI as a daily practice
Summit Participants	• Conduct interviews or be interviewed • Review interview report	• Engage in discovery and dialogue • Dare to dream • Design the ideal organizational	• Sustain AI organization processes and practices • Create new systems and structures using AI • Share success stories

inspired leadership, revolutionary customer responsiveness, labor-management partnerships, and "fun." Fresh from an AI training, one employee did two hundred interviews about the positive core of a major call center. Who is going to say no to a request like "Please help me. . . . I'm trying to learn about the best innovations. I see you as someone with insight into creating settings where innovation happens. . . . It is part of my leadership development. I will share my learnings with you!" Soon the topics were finding their way into meetings, corridor conversations, and senior planning sessions. The questions, enthusiastically received, were changing corporate attention, language, agendas, and learnings. Many started brainstorming AI applications. Ever done focus groups with customers who are 100 percent satisfied? How about changing call center measures? What

if we replaced deficit measures with equally powerful measures of the positive? How about a gathering with senior executives celebrating our learnings, sharing how seeing the positive has changed our work and family lives, and recruiting them to join us?

The pilot created an avalanche of requests for participation—confirming the large numbers at GTE ready for the task of positive change. Ten-region training sessions, linked by satellite conferencing were held. Quite suddenly the power of a 1,000-person network caught people's attention. Changes happened not by organized confrontation, diagnosis, burning platforms, or piecemeal reform but through irresistibly vibrant and real visions. And when everyone's awareness grows at the same time, it is easier to believe that fundamental change is possible.

Then the unions raised questions. There were serious concerns, including the fact that they were not consulted earlier. We were told the initiative was over. A meeting of the unions and GTE would put the whole thing to rest. At the meeting, IBEW and CWA leaders said they saw something fresh and unique about AI. They agreed to bring two hundred union leaders together for an "AI evaluation . . . to see if it had any place in GTE's future." Picture the session: tables of eight evaluating the ideas and casting a vote of either "yes, move forward with AI" or "no, withhold endorsement." For thirty minutes thirty groups deliberated. And when asked "Table one, how do you vote?" the response was "We vote 100 percent for moving forward with AI and feel this is an historic opportunity for the whole system." Then the next table said, "We vote 100 percent with a caveat— that every person at GTE have the opportunity for AI training, and all new projects be done in partnership with the unions and the company." On and on the vote went. All thirty tables voted to move forward. Eight months later, a new era of partnership is announced. The historic Statement of Partnership: "The company and the Unions realize that traditional adversarial labor-management relations must change to adapt to the new global telecommunications marketplace . . . the company and the Unions have agreed to move in a new direction emphasizing partnership."

AI accelerates organization breakthroughs by uncovering positive traditions and strengths, creating network-like structures that liberate an organization's positive core and enabling people to empower one another—to connect, cooperate, and cocreate. Changes never thought possible are suddenly and democratically mobilized when people constructively appropriate the power of the positive core and—*let go* of accounts of the negative.

Roles, Responsibilities, and Relationships

The role of an organization's leadership is that of *Positive Change Catalyst*—to plant the AI seed and to let it grow in its own way, in its own time. Leaders are invited to participate equally as one of the many essential voices at the table. Given the opportunity to listen to and hear the creative ideas, hopes, and dreams of their colleagues and organization stakeholders, leaders recognize that their greatest job is to get out of the way. Once the positive revolution begins, what it needs most is affirmation and a clear pathway for experimentation and innovation. AI is a high-participation process that once begun continues in remarkable ways, with remarkable results.

The consultant's role in AI is that of *Agent of Inquiry*.[7] It includes four aspects:

- To view organizations as living spiritual-social systems, mysteries of creation to be nurtured and affirmed, not as mechanistic or scientific operations with problems to be solved;
- To work in the affirmative, continually seeking to discover what gives life to the organization and its members;
- To be facilitators of possibilities, hope, and inspired action;
- To continually seek ways to give the process away, to support organization members in making it their own.

The primary role of an Appreciative Inquiry participant is that of *Student of Organization Life*. AI engages all levels and stakeholders in a cooperative learning and cocreation process. To be a Student of Organization Life emphasizes curiosity and learning in the most pragmatic ways possible. The best of what has been and what is possible can be linked to inspired action. Future dreams are grounded in reality and hence believable.

Stewardship of an organization-wide Appreciative Inquiry generally rests with a *Core Team* selected for diverse backgrounds, functional experience, and organizational responsibility. The Core Team oversees the process, monitoring its overall impact.

Appreciative Inquiry and Power in Organizations

We could have called this section "Eulogy for Problem Solving." In our view the problem-solving paradigm, while once perhaps quite effective, is out of sync with the realities of today's virtual worlds.[8] Problem-solving approaches to change are painfully slow (always asking people to look backward to yesterday's causes). They rarely result in new vision (a problem, implicitly, assumes an ideal, so we are not searching for new knowledge but are searching for how to close gaps). Finally, problem approaches generate defensiveness and separation among people (it is not my problem but yours).

Our real concern is with power, control, and ways in which the problem-solving paradigm limits human potential. In particular, our concern is with more consciously linking the use of language to human potential and change. Words do create worlds—even in unintended ways.

> It was an unforgettable moment in a conference on AI for inner city change agents, mostly community mobilizers from the Saul Alinsky school of thought (*Rules for Radicals*). After two days a participant challenged: This is naïve ... have you ever worked in the depths of the inner city, like the Cabrini Green public housing projects? You're asking me to "appreciate" it ... just yesterday the impoverished children were playing soccer, not with a ball—no money for that, but with a dead rat. Tell me about appreciative inquiry in the housing projects!

A powerful question. It made us go deeper. First we argued that problem-diagnosis approaches, including Alinsky's confrontation methods, work, but at half AI's speed. As we explored the cultural consequences of deficit language (e.g., he's "manic-depressive"; she's "antisocial"), we saw a disconcerting relationship between the society-wide escalation of deficit-based change methods and the erosion of people power. From a constructionist perspective, words do not mirror the world out there; they coordinate our actions. Professional languages function like tools. When I gave my son a hammer, inevitably everything became a nail. What happens when the "scientific" human-deficit vocabularies become everyone's tool kit? In particular, scholars have documented that deficit-based change approaches reinforce hierarchy, erode community, and instill a sense of self-enfeeblement.[9]

Back at the inner city conference:

> After tracing human-deficit vocabularies to the mental health professions, the rise of bureaucracy, skeptical science, original sin, and the cynical media, the Alinsky-trained activist gasped: "In the name of entertainment my people are fed negative views of human violence—surrounded by endless descriptions of their 'problem lives.' The result? People asleep in front of their TVs, unable to move. They have a voice in the housing project assessments. But it is a ... visionless voice. They get to confirm the deficit analysis.... What hits me now is how radical the AI message is. Marx could have said it better: human deficit vocabularies are the opiates of the masses. People have voice but are not mobilized by it anymore. Visionless voice is worse than no voice."

It is not problem-solving methodologies per se that are of concern, but that we have taken the tools a step further. Somewhere this shift happened: it is not that organizations *have* problems, but that they *are* problems (see Figure 2). Once accepted as fundamental truth, change management becomes infused with a deficit consciousness. For example, "Action-research is both an approach to problem solving, a model or paradigm, and a problem-solving process."[10]

Tough questions remain about power and deficit discourse. Our hypothesis is that when AI is conducted as a whole systems approach moving through the 4-D Cycle, the positive core becomes the explicit and common property of all. In every case there is movement toward greater equality and less hierarchy. Inevitably, post-bureaucratic organization designs that distribute power and liberate human energy emerge.

Conditions for Success

Appreciative Inquiry best serves when there is a high level of *process integrity*, where the means and the ends are the same. If an organization wants greater cooperation across functional lines, greater employee commitment and responsibility, and faster cycle time, the process must engage people in interviews across functional lines,

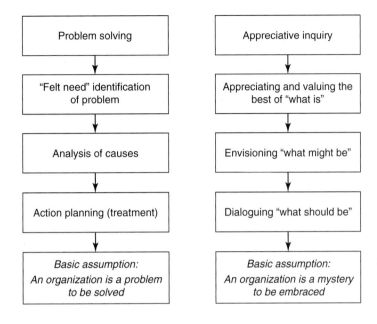

FIGURE 2
PROBLEM
SOLVING AND
APPRECIATIVE
INQUIRY

involve employees in making decisions and determining the process, and do it faster than usual.

Human change integrity also contributes to AI's success. This is the capacity for system members to be, in Gandhi's words, "the change they want to see." AI impacts personal, relational, and organizational performance profoundly and simultaneously. As individuals are interviewed, they experience unfamiliar validation and support. Telling their stories and being witnessed by other people is an exceptionally transforming experience. At the relational level, the interview taps a human longing to experience and recognize meaningful connections. Once discovered, the stories, the shared experience, and the connections become part of the individuals' and the organization's identities. With AI, the organization, its members, and stakeholders transform simultaneously in relation to one another.

Perseverance in change is another success criterion. Change is life itself, not an event. At its best, AI leaves greater organizational capacity to change through inquiry, sharing stories, relationship-enhancing communication, and cooperative

innovation. We do not leave organizations in a final state called effectiveness or excellence. We persist in being open to learning, discovering new possibilities for understanding and performance, and sharing our best with others to raise the collective standard of living within our organizations and on the planet.

Creating *narrative-rich communication* ensures a fertile field for success. In contrast to memos, plans, and policies, Appreciative Inquiry works into the organization's communication through storytelling, testimonials, and large-group forums. AI taps into the organization's inner dialogue— the stories that members tell about themselves and their organization. In effect, sharing best practices, magic moments, and life-giving experiences is how organizing occurs. Through narrative-rich communication, best practices are disseminated and enhance enthusiasm and the sense of well-being. When appreciative stories "have wings" and fly around, the capacity for change and high performance expands.

Inquiry and dialogue create rich *anticipatory images*. AI is based on the principle that our future images guide our present performance. Where the images are hopeful and expansive, organization performance and personal motivation are generally high. Where the images are depressed or deficient, morale tends to be low and turnover high. By fostering the discovery and sharing of success stories—past and imagined— AI invites affirmation and expansion.

Theoretical Basis

AI accelerates organization breakthroughs. Changes never thought possible are suddenly and democratically mobilized when people constructively adopt the power of the positive core and simply *let go* of negative accounts.

But then the question is always voiced, "What do we do with the *real* problems?"

Basic Appreciative Inquiry Principles

To address this question in anything other than Pollyannaish terms, we need to comment on the work that inspired AI. Five principles central to AI's theory base are discussed below:

The Constructionist Principle. Human knowledge and organizational destiny are interwoven. To be effective, we must understand organizations as living, human constructions.

We are constantly involved in working to understand the world around us—doing strategic planning, environmental scans, audits, surveys, and so on. Constructionism replaces the *individual* with the *relationship* as the locus of knowledge by valuing the power of language to create our sense of reality.

Inquiry is inseparable from action. Its purpose is to create "generative theory." Rather than explaining yesterday's world, it articulates tomorrow's possibilities.

The Principle of Simultaneity. Inquiry and change are not separate moments but are simultaneous. Inquiry is intervention. The seeds of change—the things people think and talk about, the things people discover and learn, and the things that

inform dialogue and inspire images of the future—are implicit in the first questions we ask. They set the stage for what we "find." What we "discover" (the data) becomes the stories out of which the future is conceived. Therefore, one of the most impactful actions a change agent takes is to articulate questions.

One great myth is that first we analyze, and then we decide on change. Not so, says the constructionist view. Even the most innocent question evokes change—even if reactions are simply changes in awareness, dialogue, feelings of boredom, or laughter. When we consider that inquiry and change are a simultaneous moment, it is no longer, "Is my question leading to right or wrong answers?" but rather, "How does my question impact our lives together. Is it generating conversations about the good, the better, the possible?"

The Poetic Principle. Human organizations are like open books. An organization's story is constantly being coauthored. Pasts, presents, and futures are endless sources of learning, inspiration, and interpretation—like the endless interpretive possibilities in a good poem. The implication is that we can study any topic related to human experience. We can inquire into the nature of alienation or joy, enthusiasm or low morale, efficiency or excess, in any human organization.

Constructionism reminds us that the "world out there" doesn't dictate our inquiries; rather, the topics are products of social processes (cultural habits, rhetoric, power relations). AI makes sure we are not just reproducing the same worlds over and over again through simple and boring repetition of our questions (not one more morale survey). AI also says, with excitement, that there are great gains in linking the means and ends of inquiry. For example, in talks with great leaders in nongovernmental organizations (Save the Children, World Vision) we have begun to appreciate the profound joy that CEOs feel as "servant leaders." This positive orientation plays a profound role in creating healthy organizations. Does this mean that joy has something to do with good leadership? Why aren't we including this topic in our change efforts? What might happen if we did?

The Anticipatory Principle. Our positive images of the future lead our positive actions—this is the increasingly energizing basis and presupposition of Appreciative Inquiry.

The infinite human resource we have for generating constructive organizational change is our collective imagination and discourse about the future. The image of the future guides any organization's current behavior. Much like a movie projector to a screen, human systems are forever projecting expectations ahead of themselves. The talk in hallways, the metaphors and language, bring the future powerfully into the present as a mobilizing agent. Inquiring in ways that redefine anticipatory reality[11]—creating positive images together—may be the most important aspect of any inquiry.

In studies of positive imagery from athletics, research into relationships between optimism and health, placebo studies in medicine, and studies of the Pygmalion dynamic in the classroom, the conclusions are converging on something Aristotle said long ago: "A vivid imagination compels the whole body to obey it."

The Positive Principle. Our experience is that building and sustaining momentum for change requires large amounts of positive outlook and social bonding—things like hope, excitement, inspiration, caring, camaraderie, sense of urgent purpose, and sheer joy in creating something meaningful together. We find that the more positive the question we ask, the more long-lasting and successful the change effort.

Sustaining the Results

Results generated through Appreciative Inquiry are immediate, often surprisingly dramatic and broad in scope, touching personal as well as whole-system transformation and enhancing organization performance, productivity, and profitability.

The key to sustaining high participation, enthusiasm and morale, inspired action, and organizational agility and innovation lies in an organization-wide commitment to becoming an Appreciative Inquiry Organization (AIO). Sustainability depends on consciously and strategically reconstructing the organization's core processes—human resources, management, planning, and measurement—in alignment with the AI principles and methodologies.

As AI's principles and methodologies become embedded in daily practices, the organizational capacity to sustain high levels of participation and enthusiasm increases. For example, at one AIO, all meetings begin with a brief inquiry into "magic moments"—times of extraordinary success among members. Other organizational enactments of AI include annual strategic planning summits, appreciative interviewing as an employee-orientation process, appreciative feedback, and affirmatively focused measurement systems.

CONCLUSION

To be sure, Appreciative Inquiry begins an adventure.

We are infants in understanding appreciative processes of knowing and social construction. Yet we are increasingly clear that the world is ready to leap beyond deficit-based change methodologies and enter a life-centric domain. Organizations, says AI theory, are centers of human relatedness, first and foremost, and relationships thrive where there is an appreciative eye—when people see the best in one another, when they share their dreams and ultimate concerns in affirming ways, and when they are connected in full voice to create not just new worlds but better worlds. The velocity and largely informal spread of the appreciative learnings suggests a growing disenchantment with exhausted change theories, especially those wedded to human-deficit vocabularies, and a corresponding urge to work with people, groups, and organizations in more constructive, positive, life-affirming, even spiritual ways. AI, we hope it is being said, is more than a simple 4-D Cycle of discovery, dream, design, and destiny; what is being introduced is something deeper at the core.

Perhaps our inquiry must become the positive revolution we want to see in the world. Albert Einstein's words clearly compel: "There are only two ways to live your life. One is as though nothing is a miracle. The other is as though everything is a miracle."

NOTES

1. White, T. W. "Working in Interesting Times." In *Vital Speeches of the Day,* vol. LXII, no. 15 (1996), pp. 472–474.

2. Cooperrider, D. L., and S. Srivastva. "Appreciative Inquiry in Organizational Life." In *Research in Organization Change and Development,* vol. 1, edited by W. Pasmore and R. Woodman, pp. 129–169. Greenwich, Conn.: JAI Press, 1987.

3. White, T. W. "Working in Interesting Times." In *Vital Speeches of the Day,* vol. LXII, no. 15 (1996), pp. 472–474.

4. Bushe, G. R., and T Pitman. "Appreciative Process: A Method for Transformational Change." In *OD Practitioner,* vol. 23, no. 3 (1991), pp. 1–4.

5. Sorenson, P. F., Jr. "About This Issue." In *OD Practitioner,* vol. 28, nos. 1 & 2 (1996), pp. 3–4.

6. The term *autopoiesis* was coined by two neuroscientists, Humberto Maturana and Francisco Varela. *Auto* means "self" and refers to the autonomy of self-organizing systems; *poiesis* means "making"; so *autopoiesis* means "self-making." Autopoiesis is the process whereby an organization produces itself. An autopoietic organization is an autonomous and self-maintaining entity that contains component-producing processes. In this way, the entire network continually "makes itself." See Maturana, H., and Varela, F., "Autopoiesis and Cognition: The Realization of the Living." In *Boston Studies in the Philosophy of Science.* Cohen, R. S., and M. W. Wartofsky (eds.) *42.* Dordecht, Holland: D. Reidel Publishing Co., 1980.

7. Cooperrider, D. L. "The 'Child' as Agent of Inquiry." In *OD Practitioner,* vol. 28, nos. 1 & 2 (1996), pp. 5–11.

8. Cooperrider, D. L. "Resources for Getting Appreciative Inquiry Started: An Example OD Proposal." In *OD Practitioner,* vol. 28, nos. 1 & 2 (1996), pp. 23–33.

9. Gergen, K. *Saturated Self: Dilemmas of Identity in Contemporary Life.* New York: Basic Books, 1992.

10. French, W. L., and C. H. Bell, Jr. *Organization Development: Behavioral Science Interventions for Organizational Improvement.* 5th ed. Englewood Cliffs, N.J.: Prentice-Hall, 1994.

11. Cooperrider, D. L. "Positive Image Positive Action: The Affirmative Basis of Organizing." In *Appreciative Management and Leadership,* Rev. ed., edited by S. Srivastva and D. L. Cooperrider, pp. 91–125. Cleveland, Ohio: Williams Publishing Co., 1999.

Reading 44	**Change: The New Metaphysics**
	Warren G. Bennis

Change is the metaphysics of our age. Everything is in motion. Everything mechanical has evolved, become better, more efficient, more sophisticated. In this century, automobiles have advanced from the Model T to the BMW, Mercedes, and Rolls Royce. Meanwhile, everything organic—from ourselves to tomatoes—has devolved. We have gone from such giants as Teddy Roosevelt, D. W. Griffith, Eugene Debs, Frank Lloyd Wright, Thomas Edison, and Albert Michelson to Yuppies. Like the new tomatoes, we lack flavor and juice and taste. Manufactured goods are far more impressive than the people who make them. We are less good, less efficient, and less sophisticated with each passing decade.

People in charge have imposed change rather than inspiring it. We have had far more bosses than leaders, and so, finally, everyone has decided to be his or her own boss. This has led to the primitive, litigious, adversarial society we now live in. As the newscaster in the movie *Network* said, "I'm mad as hell, and I'm not going to take it anymore."

What's going on is a middle-class revolution. The poor in America have neither the time nor the energy to revolt. They're just trying to survive in an increasingly hostile world. By the same token, the rich literally reside above the fray—in New York penthouses, Concordes, and sublime ignorance of the world below. The middle class aspires to that same sublime ignorance.

A successful dentist once told me that people become dentists to make a lot of money fast and then go into the restaurant business or real estate, where they will really make money. Young writers and painters are not content to practice their craft and perfect it. Now they want to see and be seen, wheel and deal, and they are as obsessed with the bottom line as are IBM executives. The deal for the publication of a book is far more significant than the book itself, and the cover of *People* magazine is more coveted than a good review in the *New York Times*. The only unions making any noise now are middle-class unions. Professors who once professed an interest in teaching are now far more interested in deals—for the book, the TV appearance, the consulting job, the conference in Paris—leaving teaching to assistants.

When everyone is his or her own boss, no one is in charge, and chaos takes over. Leaders are needed to restore order, by which I mean not obedience but progress. It is time for us to control events rather than be controlled by them.

Avenues of Change

Change occurs in several ways.

• *Dissent and conflict.* We have tried dissent and conflict and have merely become combative. In corporations, change can be mandated by the powers that be. But this leads inevitably to the escalation of rancor. We are perpetually angry now, all walking around with chips on our shoulders.

• *Trust and truth.* Positive change requires trust, clarity, and participation. Only people with virtue and vision can lead us out of this bog and back to the high ground, doing three things: (1) gaining our trust; (2) expressing their vision clearly so that we all not only understand but concur; and (3) persuading us to participate.

• *Cliques and cabals.* The cliques have the power, the money and the resources. The cabals, usually younger and always ambitious, have drive and energy. Unless the cliques can co-opt the cabals, revolution is inevitable. This avenue, too, is messy. It can lead to either a stalemate or an ultimate victory for the cabals, if for no other reason than they have staying power.

• *External events*. Forces of society can impose themselves on the organization. For example, the auto industry was forced to change its ways and its products, both by government regulation and by foreign competition. In the same way, student activists forced many universities to rewrite their curricula and add black studies and women's studies programs. Academicians are still debating both the sense and the efficacy of such programs, as they have altered not only what students learn but how they learn it.

• *Culture or paradigm shift*. The most important avenue of change is culture or paradigm. In *The Structure of Scientific Revolution*, Thomas Kuhn notes that the paradigm in science is akin to a Zeitgeist or climate of opinion that governs choices. He defines it as "the constellation of values and beliefs shared by the members of a scientific community that determines the choice, problems which are regarded as significant, and the approaches to be adopted in attempting to solve them." The people who have revolutionized science have always been those who have changed the paradigm.

Innovators and Leaders

People who change not merely the content of a particular discipline but its practice and focus are not only innovators but leaders. Ralph Nader, who refocused the legal profession to address consumer problems, was such a person. Betty Friedan, in truthfully defining how women lived, inspired them to live in different ways.

It's not the articulation of a profession's or organization's goals that creates new practices but rather the imagery that creates the understanding, the compelling moral necessity for the new way. The clarity of the metaphor and the energy and courage its maker brings to it are vital to its acceptance. For example, when Branch Rickey, general manager of the Brooklyn Dodgers, decided to bring black players into professional baseball, he chose Jackie Robinson, a paragon among players and among men.

How do we identify and develop such innovators? How do we spot new information in institutions, organizations and professions? Innovators, like all creative people, see things differently, think in fresh and original ways. They have useful contacts in other areas; they are seldom seen as good organization men or women and often viewed as mischievous troublemakers. The true leader not only is an innovator but makes every effort to locate and use other innovators in the organization. He or she creates a climate in which conventional wisdom can be challenged and one in which errors are embraced rather than shunned in favor of safe, low-risk goals.

In organizations, people have norms, values, shared beliefs and paradigms of what is right and what is wrong, what is legitimate and what is not, and how things are done. One gains status and power through agreement, concurrence, and conformity with these paradigms. Therefore, both dissent and innovation are discouraged. Every social system contains these forces for conservatism, for maintaining the status quo at any cost, but it must also contain means for movement, or it will eventually become paralyzed.

Basic changes take place slowly because those with power typically have no knowledge, and those with knowledge have no power. Anyone with real knowledge of history and the world as it is today could redesign society, develop a new paradigm in an afternoon, but turning theory into fact could take a lifetime.

Still, we have to try because too many of our organizations and citizens are locked into roles and practices that simply do not work. True leaders work to gain the trust of their constituents, communicate their vision lucidly, and thus involve everyone in the process of change. They then try to use the inevitable dissent and conflict creatively and positively, and out of all that, sometimes, a new paradigm emerges.

A Harris poll showed that over 90 percent of the people polled would change their lives dramatically if they could, and they ranked such intangibles as self-respect, affection, and acceptance higher than status, money, and power.

They don't like the way they live now, but they don't know how to change. The poll is evidence of our need for real leaders and should serve as impetus and inspiration to potential leaders and innovators. If such people have the will to live up to their potential—and the rest of us have the gumption to follow them—we might finally find our way out of this bog we're in.

Avoiding Disaster During Change

Constant as change has been and vital as it is now, it is still hard to effect, because the sociology of institutions is fundamentally antichange. Here, then, are 10 ways to avoid disaster during periods of change—any time, all the time—except in those organizations that are dying or dead.

1. *Recruit with scrupulous honesty.* Enthusiasm or plain need often inspires recruiters to transmogrify visible and real drawbacks and make them reappear as exhilarating challenges. Recruiting is, after all, a kind of courtship ritual. The suitor displays his or her assets and masks his or her defects. The recruit, flattered by the attention and the promises, does not examine the proposal thoughtfully. He or she looks forward to opportunities to be truly creative and imaginative and to support from the top.

Inadvertently, the recruiter has cooked up the classic recipe for revolution as suggested by Aaron Wildavsky: "Promise a lot; deliver a little. Teach people to believe they will be much better off, but let there be no dramatic improvement. Try a variety of small programs but marginal in impact and severely underfinanced. Avoid any attempted solution remotely comparable in size to the dimensions of the problem you're trying to solve."

2. *Guard against the crazies.* Innovation is seductive. It attracts interesting people. It also attracts people who will distort your ideas into something monstrous. You will then be identified with the monster and be forced to spend precious energy combating it. Change-oriented managers should be sure that the people they recruit are change agents but not agitators. It is difficult sometimes to tell the difference between the innovators and the crazies. Eccentricities and idiosyncrasies in change agents are often useful and valuable. Neurosis isn't.

3. *Build support among like-minded people,* whether or not you recruited them. Change-oriented administrators are particularly prone to act as though the organization came into being the day they arrived. This is a delusion, a fantasy of omnipotence. There are no clean slates in established organizations. A new CEO can't play Noah and build the world anew with a hand-picked crew of his or her own. Rhetoric about new starts is frightening to those who sense that this new beginning is the end of their careers. There can be no change without history and continuity. A clean sweep, then, is often a waste of resources.

4. *Plan for change from a solid conceptual base.* Have a clear understanding of how to change as well as what to change. Planning changes is always easier than implementing them. If change is to be permanent, it must be gradual. Incremental reform can be successful by drawing on a rotating nucleus of people who continually read the data provided by the organization and the society in which it operates for clues that it's time to adapt. Without such critical nuclei, organizations cannot be assured of continued self-renewal. Such people must not be faddists but must be hypersensitive to ideas whose hour has come. They also know when ideas are antithetical to the organization's purposes and values and when they will strengthen the organization.

5. *Don't settle for rhetorical change.* Significant change cannot be decreed. Any organization has two structures: one on paper and another that consists of a complex set of intramural relationships. A good administrator understands the relationships and creates a good fit between them and any planned alterations. One who gets caught up in his or her own rhetoric almost inevitably neglects the demanding task of maintaining established constituencies and building new ones.

6. Don't *allow those who are opposed to change to appropriate basic issues.* Successful change agents make sure that respectable people are not afraid of what is to come and that the old guard isn't frightened at the prospect of change. The moment such people get scared is the moment they begin to fight dirty. They not only have some built-in clout, they have tradition on their side.

7. *Know the territory.* Learn everything there is to know about the organization and about its locale, which often means mastering the politics of local chauvinism, along with an intelligent public relations program. In Southern California, big developers are constantly being blind-sided by neighborhood groups because they have not bothered to acquaint the groups with their plans. Neighborhood groups often triumph, forcing big changes or cancellations. They know their rights and they know the law, and the developers haven't made the effort to know them.

8. *Appreciate environmental factors.* No matter how laudable or profitable or imaginative, a change that increases discomfort in the organization is probably doomed. Adding a sophisticated new computer system is probably a good thing, but it can instantly be seen as a bad thing if it results in overcrowded offices.

9. *Avoid future shock.* When an executive becomes too involved in planning, he or she frequently forgets the past and neglects the present. As a result, before the plan goes into effect, employees are probably already opposed to it.

They, after all, have to function in the here and now, and if their boss's eye is always on tomorrow, he or she is not giving them the attention and support they need.

10. *Remember that change is most successful when those who are affected are involved in the planning.* This is a platitude of planning theory, but it is as true as it is trite. Nothing makes people resist new ideas or approaches more adamantly than their belief that change is being imposed on them.

The problems connected with innovation and change are common to every modern bureaucracy. University, government and corporation all respond similarly to challenge and to crisis, with much the same explicit or implicit codes, punctilios and mystiques.

Means must be found to stimulate the pursuit of truth—that is, the true nature of the organization's problems—in an open and democratic way. This calls for classic means: an examined life, a spirit of inquiry and genuine experimentation, a life based on discovering new realities, taking risks, suffering occasional defeats, and not fearing the surprises of the future. The model for truly innovative organizations in an era of constant change is the scientific model. As scientists seek and discover truths, so organizations must seek and discover their own truths—carefully, thoroughly, honestly, imaginatively, and courageously.